A Radical Green Political Theory

This volume is the first systematic, comprehensive and cogent environmental political philosophy. It exposes the relationships between the ever-worsening environmental crises, the nature of prevailing economic structures and the role of the modern state, and concludes that the combination of these factors is driving humanity towards destruction.

After analysing authoritarian, reformist, Marxist and anarchist approaches to the environmental problem, the author argues strongly that only the most radical of political practices can prevent an ecological catastrophe. This is explored through a detailed and original analysis of social relationships, power, the state, anarchism and Third World development.

Innovative, provocative and cutting-edge, *A Radical Green Political Theory* will be of enormous value to all those with an interest in the environment, political theory and moral and political philosophy.

Alan Carter is Chair of the Department of Philosophy at Heythrop College, University of London and Visiting Professor at the University of Colorado at Boulder. He was formerly a lecturer in Political Theory at University College, Dublin and an elected director of Friends of the Earth. His previous publications include *Marx: A Radical Critique* (1988) and *The Philosophical Foundations of Property Rights* (1989).

Routledge Innovations in Political Theory

1 **A Radical Green Political Theory**
Alan Carter

2 **Rational Woman**
A feminist critique of dualism
Raia Prokhovnik

3 **Rethinking State Theory**
Mark J. Smith

A Radical Green Political Theory

Alan Carter

London and New York

First published 1999
by Routledge
11 New Fetter Lane, London EC4P 4EE

Simultaneously published in the USA and Canada
by Routledge
29 West 35th Street, New York, NY 10001

Routledge is an imprint of the Taylor & Francis Group

Typeset in Galliard by RefineCatch Limited, Bungay, Suffolk
Printed and bound in Great Britain by
MPG Books Ltd, Bodmin

British Library Cataloguing in Publication Data
A catalogue record for this book is available from the British Library

Library of Congress Cataloging in Publication Data
Carter, Alan B.
A Radical Green Political Theory / Alan Carter.
p. cm.
Includes bibliographical references and index.
1. Political ecology. 2. Green movement. I. Title.
JA75.8.C37 1999
304.2′01 – dc21 98–41317
CIP

ISBN 0–415–20309–0

Contents

Figures and tables

Figures

Tables

Preface

We are standing at a cross-roads. All roads but one lead to oblivion, and it is certain that our one escape route does not lie straight ahead.

This, at least, is what the radical green political theory offered here suggests. For over two and a half decades those working within what is now referred to as 'the green movement' have been issuing warnings of the impending cataclysmic consequences of current human behaviour. And their conclusion is, not surprisingly, that such behaviour must change if an environmental catastrophe of unimaginable extent is to be avoided. Such a conclusion, of course, raises a host of political questions. Thus, as Charlene Spretnak and Fritjof Capra note:

> The starting point of Green politics is the recognition that we find ourselves in a multifaceted, global crisis that touches every aspect of our lives: our health and livelihood, the quality of our environment and our social relationships, our economy, technology, our politics – our very survival on this planet. The nations of the world have stockpiled more than 50,000 nuclear warheads, enough to destroy the entire world several times over, and the arms race continues at undiminished speed. While world-wide military spending is more than one billion dollars a day, more than fifteen million people die of starvation annually – thirty-two every minute, most of them children. Developing countries spend more than three times as much on armaments as on health care. Thirty-five per cent of humanity lack safe drinking water, while nearly half of its scientists and engineers are engaged in the technology of making weapons. Economists are obsessed with building economies based on unlimited growth, while our finite resources are rapidly dwindling; industrial corporations dump toxic wastes somewhere else, rather than neutralizing them, without caring that in an ecosystem there is no 'somewhere else'. Modern medicine often endangers our health, and the Defence Department itself has become a threat to our national security.[1]

Such aspects of the modern world are clearly irrational. But is there any

1 Charlene Spretnak and Fritjof Capra, *Green Politics* (London: Paladin, 1985), p. xv.

explanation for them, or are they merely random problems? Is there anything that links them systematically?

To demonstrate that there is a systematic link between the major problems that we face today is a fundamental task of this book. For if one can show that there is a systematic connection between the problems that ecologically-minded social critics address, then one might also be in a position to reveal some coherence within green political thought – which is a second task of this book. A third task is to ascertain the extent of the changes that are necessary in order to avoid an ecological catastrophe.[2] The argument presented in this book suggests that the changes would need to be very extensive indeed – in fact, so extensive that *any green political practice would have to be radical in the extreme for it to be genuinely green at all.* And this is because it is difficult to see how a practice which is unable to meet the environmental challenge effectively can be accepted as *genuinely* green.

Now, the three tasks that I have just mentioned all involve theoretical issues. Theories rely on models, and models abstract from the seemingly limitless phenomena before us those apparently salient features that cry out for explanation. A good theory presents an account of the connection between those salient features that helps us to understand them and to predict their behaviour. Bad theories obscure important connections, confuse us and lead us to rely on erroneous predictions. If we are to understand the links between the major problems that confront us today, if we are to think coherently about those problems, and if we are to ascertain which political practices will solve them, we require a political theory appropriate to those tasks. And as the really major problems of today would appear to be environmental ones, then it is surely a *green* political theory that we now require.

Unfortunately, there has been, until relatively recently, a noticeable lack of any cogent, never mind comprehensive, green political theory. Much of the thinking produced within the green movement over the past quarter of a century and more has lacked academic rigour, while a great deal of the recent academic work on green issues, coming from outside the green movement, often shows insufficient familiarity with the full range of green thinking and with the full extent of environmental activism that greens have involved themselves in over the past twenty-five years. Such academic work on green thinking is, thus, the converse of that produced by many greens: it is theoretically sophisticated at times, but

2 In the words of John Passmore: 'As a direct consequence of our agricultural and industrial technology, we are rapidly causing to degenerate our sole habitation, that narrow strip of soil, air and water – the biosphere – in which we live and move and have our being. So much must be granted: the evidence in its favour is daily made more apparent to our nose, our ears, our palate, our eyes, and is reinforced by scientific investigation. That action must be taken, that if Western civilization is to survive, it must, in important respects, change its ways, is also sufficiently obvious.' And as he adds: 'The only point at issue is just how fundamental these changes will need to be.' John Passmore, *Man's Responsibility for Nature: Ecological Problems and Western Traditions* (London: Duckworth, 1980), p. 3.

frequently rests on a limited acquaintance with the vast amount of literature, thought and, in particular, activity which the green movement as a whole has generated.

But is a green political *theory* actually necessary? Many anarchists within the green movement (and there are quite a number of them) are highly anti-theoretical. The reason usually offered is that theories are complications which are inaccessible to many and are, therefore, deemed to be essentially elitist. Hence, the injunction that we are often given is that we should just do what we all know intuitively to be right and simply get on with environmental campaigning. The problem with this is that we don't just know intuitively what is right. Such anarchists, for example, will tell us that we can't use the state to create a better society. Instead, we have to eliminate the state. They will also tell us that we can't use a vanguard party, either. It will just recreate after the revolution the problems we currently face.

These claims may well be true – in fact, I think that they probably *are* true. But they certainly aren't intuitively obvious. Why can't we employ the state or a vanguard party? The most likely answers have to do with power. For example, either human nature is such that those in power will abuse it, or power corrupts, or (if one wants a slightly more sophisticated response) hierarchical organizations are such that one can only rise in their ranks by highly competitive behaviour, and this means that the most competitive, most ruthless and least caring will end up in control – hence, those who would most abuse power will inevitably be the ones who gain it.[3] But any such answer is *theoretical*. It involves a theory of human nature or a theory of the consequences of holding power or a theory of its acquisition. No such answer is intuitively obvious. In fact, most, if not all, of the claims we make are theoretically laden. The problem with thinking that they are just intuitively obvious is that the theory they rely on is left unexamined.[4] And if a theory is left unexamined, then we don't know how good it is, nor what its limitations are. For example, it might be a good theory within certain limits. But if one does not subject the theory to critical appraisal – if the theory remains

3 For example, Bernard Williams sets out 'a list of four propositions which some would regard as all true, and which, if they were all true, would make the hope of finding politicians of honourable character, except in minor roles and in favourable circumstances, very slim.' These four propositions are: '(i) There are violent acts which the state is justified in doing which no private citizen as such would be justified in doing. (ii) Anything the state is justified in doing, some official such as, often, a politician is justified in ordering to be done. (iii) You are not morally justified in ordering to be done anything which you would not be prepared to do yourself. (iv) Official violence is enough like unofficial violence for the preparedness referred to in (iii) to amount to a criminal tendency.' Bernard Williams, 'Politics and moral character' in *Moral Luck* (Cambridge: Cambridge University Press, 1981), p. 69. Williams notes that anarchists are likely to deny (i).

4 And as Murray Bookchin writes: 'Indeed, the myth that "doing" is more important than "thinking", that "constructive action" is more important than rational critique – these are actually mystified forms of theory, critique, and rationalism.' Murray Bookchin, *Toward an Ecological Society* (Montreal: Black Rose, 1980), p. 20.

hidden in the background – then one will not know when the theory is applicable and when its use is highly problematic.

Furthermore, different people regard different things as intuitively obvious. The possibility of agreement is seriously impaired if those in disagreement refuse to expose their respective underlying theories to the light of criticism. And adherents of one theory are unlikely to adopt another's theory unless they perceive the need for abandoning their own. That means, if we are to persuade others to change their underlying theory, we have to subject their theory to criticisms formulated at its own level of sophistication, otherwise they would reject our criticisms as simplistic. Hence, sometimes it *is* necessary, no matter how unfortunate or undesirable it may be, to engage in fairly complicated theoretical discussions because of the complicated nature of alternative theories. One's own theoretical position will be needlessly disempowered if it is prevented from an effective engagement with competing theories because of some political fiat that rules out any complexity.

For these reasons, certain anarchists, I would argue, are profoundly mistaken if they insist on remaining anti-theoretical.[5] They are right in opposing needlessly complicated theories. To complicate unnecessarily is to restrict access needlessly, and that *is* elitist. Hence, if one is at all egalitarian, one ought to try to make one's theory as simple as possible. But when one's opponents offer complex arguments, one must be prepared to reply in as complex a way as an effective response requires. Consequently, in developing a green political theory, I have not avoided complicated arguments when they appear to be a necessary response to an opposing theory or to sophisticated objections. But I have also endeavoured to keep the theory presented here as simple and accessible as possible.

This said, it might be helpful if I provide in advance a map of the argument that follows. There are a host of interconnected problems that we fail to take

5 I would also argue that anarchists are profoundly mistaken if they assume that anarchist theory can be equated with 'anything goes'. One example is Adrian Atkinson, who wishes to replace 'rationalistic modes of social and cultural interpretation with relativistic ones'. Adrian Atkinson, *Principles of Political Ecology* (London: Belhaven, 1991), p. 62. The political corollary of such epistemological libertarianism, he assumes, is mutualistic libertarianism. Atkinson sees these as being connected because, in his view, 'Green Utopianism' requires 'an anarchist political philosophy' which 'is essentially informed by a relativistic epistemology' (ibid., p. 63). But cultural relativism, which he values alongside epistemological relativism, could easily mean that some localities thought purely instrumentally and some took authoritarian forms, both of which Atkinson opposes. If anarchist political theory is right, then it is because it has correctly analyzed the problematic nature of centralized authoritarian societies. Epistemological relativism would make that analysis no better than its contrary. Atkinson seems, in general, to fall into the standard relativist confusion of saying everything is relative and then preferring one kind of culture, knowledge, etc., but obviously having to do so from a standpoint that could not be relative but absolute. For example, 'in accordance with anarchist theory, "anything goes"' (ibid., p. 215) hardly entails that '[e]cological culture, if it comes to pass, will comprise a confederation of locally self-reliant regions based upon mutualist and necessarily egalitarian, relations in which the guiding spirit is an aesthetic self-consciousness that knits together local ecology with social metabolism' (ibid., p. 216).

sufficiently seriously – or so many environmentalists insist. In Chapter 1, I attempt to provide a manageable entry into the maze of ecological considerations by focusing upon just one such problem: namely, our continued ability to feed ourselves. The implication is that if environmentalists are correct in their claims, then the future which lies in store for humanity is likely to be extremely bleak.

However, if we do face such environmental problems, then the reason is not simply the result of some natural catastrophe. Social, economic and political factors are clearly the cause of whatever major environmental problems we happen to face. The sheer weight of evidence provided by environmentalists, if not in itself conclusive, at least makes it clear that it is incumbent upon us to take their warnings seriously – so much so that there would appear to be a pressing need to develop an environmental political philosophy: a green political theory.

Such a theory would have to explain how it is that we might well have created such problems for ourselves. And it would have to provide some indication, at least, of how we are to respond to them. But a precondition for addressing these questions is some familiarity with the principles of ecology. Chapter 1 concludes by outlining some of the simpler principles of ecology which, environmentalists argue, we ignore at our peril.

But do we really need a new political theory in order to answer the political questions which the risk of environmental catastrophe raises? With the relevant principles of ecology having already been outlined in Chapter 1, Chapter 2 assesses three common political approaches to see if they are likely to provide an adequate grounding for a green political theory.

Authoritarian responses to environmental problems are often radical, but they are unlikely to be immune to standard criticisms levelled against authoritarian approaches in general. Reformist responses, on the other hand, attempt solutions by starting from (and often remaining within) the present political and economic arrangement. But, or so I argue, there are core features of capitalist societies which seem likely to exacerbate environmental problems. Given the problems which market economies are likely to be unable to address effectively, it might seem that the solution is the one most famously proposed by Marx: namely, production according to a common plan.

Unfortunately, an analysis of traditional Marxist theory and practice suggests that it, too, fails to provide the requisite foundations for a green political theory. However, a recent development in Marxist theory – analytical Marxism – seems to provide a solution to the problems in Marxist theory which have been identified by analytical philosophers. This notwithstanding, after examining the defence of Marx's theory of history offered by the leading analytical Marxist, G. A. Cohen, I argue that, upon assuming state power, the practice of certain revolutionaries who described themselves as Marxists actually contradicts key theoretical claims made by analytical Marxism. But this does not make the work of analytical Marxists redundant, for, or so I argue, the device of functional explanation which some of them have employed to defend Marx actually provides a possible basis for an alternative theory of history – one suitable for providing a grounding for a radical green political theory. Moreover, the weaknesses in eco-authoritarian, eco-reformist and eco-Marxist responses to the environmental threat suggest that, in a sense, we do need to return to basics if we are to construct a compelling green political theory.

If, as Chapters 1 and 2 imply, we face an environmental crisis of alarming proportions, and yet we do not have a political theory capable of understanding the causes of those problems and able to provide a solution to them, then an obvious question to ask is: What kind of theory is most compatible with the insights of ecology? In Chapter 3, I argue that both individualist and collectivist social theories are deeply flawed and incompatible with a genuinely ecological perspective. However, by identifying the inadequacies in individualism and collectivism, a third theoretical approach is made possible – an approach I term 'interrelationism'. And it is an interrelationist approach which seems to be most homologous with ecological theory.

I then argue that there are approaches to freedom and power which are associated with individualism and collectivism, respectively. An interrelationist perspective, on the other hand, is compatible with different, and less problematic, conceptions of both freedom and power: in particular, with a triadic conception of freedom and a four-dimensional view of power. And from the standpoint of these alternative conceptions, the flaws in eco-authoritarianism, eco-reformism and eco-Marxism become more apparent. Thus, the remainder of the book develops an interrelationist environmental political philosophy.

The inadequate conceptions of power associated with individualism and collectivism have led to inadequate theorizations of the state. An alternative theory of the state is proposed in Chapter 4. This alternative theory employs the conceptual tools developed by analytical Marxism, but deploys them in a novel way. This alternative theory is then argued to be able to deal with central problems in Marxist theory, such as the core, and seemingly intractable, problem of how the fettering of the productive forces is to be construed.

However, the behaviour of transnational corporations within the Third World would seem, at first glance, to refute the alternative theory. In Chapter 5, the two dominant theoretical approaches to Third World politics – Huntington's and underdevelopment theory – are argued to be inadequate. Then I argue that the alternative theory in fact provides a superior explanation of economic and political developments within the Third World. In addition, Third World debt, rather than posing a problem for the theory, as might be assumed, seems to provide it with further corroboration.

Having defended the alternative theory from possible objections, it is then used in Chapter 6 to pull together the core threads of a comprehensive green political theory. The alternative theory can be argued to expose an environmentally hazardous dynamic which is likely to drive us towards species suicide. Unfortunately, the dynamic appears to be so self-reinforcing that only the most radical of political responses would be able to inhibit it. But such a radical response, and only such a response, would seem to allow us to live within an alternative environmentally benign interrelationship. The chapter proceeds to discuss several objections to the egalitarian, decentralist and pacifist political programme proposed, and then shows that the core features of green political thought are rendered coherent by the alternative theory.

But why, it might be asked, should one be motivated to work towards an egalitarian, decentralist and pacifist society? Chapter 7 concludes the argument by defending the claim that we have important obligations to future generations; and those obligations are then argued to demonstrate that we are morally obliged to work towards the kind of egalitarian, decentralist and pacifist society advocated. Moreover, the duty to future generations which the argument defends helps show precisely why it is that other attempts at an environmental political philosophy – eco-authoritarian, eco-reformist or eco-Marxist – ultimately fail.

After I have first paid the customary homage to those who have aided me in this project, let us proceed to consider how it can be argued that the time has come for political theory to choose a green direction or, alternatively, face obsolescence.

Acknowledgements

Drafts of papers that eventually became sections of this book have been read by Robin Attfield, Brian Barry, Andrew Brennan, Andrew Chitty, Noam Chomsky, Steven R. L. Clark, Mark Cowling, Tom Deidun, Teddy Goldsmith, David Goodway, Gerry Hughes, Carl Levy, David Lloyd-Thomas, Steven Lukes, David Miller, John O'Neill, Tim O'Riordan, Jonathon Porritt, Andrew Pyle, Shahid Qadir, John Quail, Michael Rosen, Neil Stammers, Laura Summers, Richard Sylvan and Geoffrey Thomas. I am indebted to them all for their criticisms, suggestions or encouragement. I would also like to thank my fellow participants at the workshop on green political theory at the European Consortium for Political Research, Joint Sessions, at Essex University in March 1991 – in particular, Wouter Achterberg, Ted Benton, Andrew Dobson, Bob Goodin, Paul Lucardie and Michael Saward for their comments on a paper which was the first presentation of a core argument contained in this book. I am also grateful to those who participated in the Green Political Theory Workshop at Malvern, Worcestershire in December 1989, especially Tom Cahill, Mary Mellor and Adrian Wright.

Jo Wolff read the first draft of this book and made numerous astute criticisms. Victoria Harrison was kind enough to read a later draft, saving me from committing several solecisms and prompting me to expand some of my more laconic remarks. For that, she has done the general reader a considerable service. A later version was read by John Barry, who offered some insightful criticisms. I also received comments on it from Robyn Eckersley, Keekok Lee, David Pepper and Mathew Humphrey. Sections of an earlier draft were read by Jerry Cohen, who made a number of invaluable suggestions for improvements, as always. I am indebted to them all. And of course, it goes without saying that all remaining errors, 'deviations' and eccentricities are mine and mine alone.

Thanks are also due to several of my former teachers who affected my way of thinking. Of those not already mentioned I would like to single out Tom Bottomore, April Carter, Krishan Kumar, David McLellan, Gillian Rose and, especially, Tony Skillen. I am indebted to David Bull for persuading me nearly a quarter of a century ago that anarchism can be far from incoherent. And I have benefited from many conversations with academics and activists alike, but, in particular, from discussions with John Baker, Ron Bailey, Uta Bellion, Murray Bookchin, Alan Carling, Paula Casal, John Charvet, Keith Graham, Andrew Lees,

Peter Marshall, Charles Secrett, Mike Seifert, Michael Smith and Andrew Williams.

I would also like to express my gratitude to the following journals for permission to include parts of articles which have developed into sections of this book. Thanks are due to: *The Journal of Applied Philosophy*, with respect to 'In defence of radical disobedience', from Vol. 15, No. 1 (1998): 29–47, and 'Game theory and decentralization', forthcoming (© Society for Applied Philosophy/Blackwell Publishers Ltd); *Cogito*, with respect to 'Creating cooperative autonomy', from Vol. 7, No. 3 (Winter 1993): 194–200, 'Revolution, Lenin and the party', from Vol. 8. No. 1 (Spring 1994): 66–73, 'The environmental crises and political theory', from Vol. 10, No. 1 (Spring 1996): 40–49, 'Eco-authoritarianism, eco-reformism or eco-Marxism?', from Vol. 10, No. 2 (Summer 1996): 115–23, and 'A radical environmentalist political theory', from Vol. 10, No. 3 (Winter 1996): 209–19 (all © The Cogito Society); *The Heythrop Journal*, with respect to 'On individualism, collectivism and interrelationism', from Vol. 31, No. 1 (January 1990): 23–38, 'A "counterfactualist", four-dimensional theory of power', from Vol. 33, No. 2 (April 1992): 192–203, 'Deep Ecology or Social Ecology?', from Vol. 36, No. 3 (July 1995): 328–50, 'State-Primacy and Third World debt', from Vol. 38, No. 3 (July 1997): 300–14, and 'Fettering, development and revolution', from Vol. 39, No. 2 (April 1998): 170–88 (all © The Editor/Blackwell Publishers Ltd); *Anarchist Studies*, with respect to 'Some notes on anarchism', from Vol. 1, No. 2 (Autumn 1993): 141–5 (© The White Horse Press); *Studies in Marxism*, with respect to 'Marxism/Leninism: the science of the proletariat?', from Vol. 1 (Winter 1994): 125–41; and *Third World Quarterly*, with respect to 'The nation-state and underdevelopment', from Vol. 16, No. 4 (December 1995): 595–618 (© Third World Quarterly).

I would also like to thank Routledge for permission to include part of 'Outline of an anarchist theory of history', from David Goodway (ed.), *For Anarchism: History, Theory, and Practice* (London, 1989); and 'Towards a green political theory', from Andrew Dobson and Paul Lucardie (eds), *The Politics of Nature: Explorations in Green Political Theory* (London, 1993). I am also grateful to Avebury Press for permission to include part of 'Functional explanation and the state', from Paul Wetherly (ed.), *Marx's Theory of History: The Contemporary Debate* (Aldershot, 1992).

My greatest debt, however, is to Lynne Dyer, my late partner, for more than seventeen years of shared campaigning, travelling, discussions and love, and without whom my life and thought would have been greatly impoverished. It is to her memory that I dedicate this book.

Hymn to the New Age

Bringing in the New Age, do we feel it with a passion?
A total transformation, or is it just a fashion?
Cocooned in our flotariums, no dying whales or apes,
Still a sweat-shop made the hi-fi where we play our New Age tapes.

When we're balancing our chakras in a life of chants and prayer,
We can meditate on crystals to heal the ozone layer,
We can grow our giant cabbages and circle dance like elves,
But there's more to healing planets than just healing ourselves.

We're favourable to solar, wind, wave and even tidal,
But the energies we're mad about won't even take a bridle,
A guru or a charlatan? A mystic or a fake?
The dawning of Aquarius with no one left to wake.

Still we're balancing our chakras in a life of chants and prayer,
And we can meditate on crystals to heal the ozone layer,
We can grow our giant cabbages and circle dance like elves,
But there's more to healing planets than just healing ourselves.

And who obtains the benefit at thirty pounds a session?
Once it was skill-sharing, now a middle-class profession,
And how can we be centred when disaster looms apace,
'Cos selfish generations have lost the human race?

While we're balancing our chakras in a life of chants and prayer,
We can meditate on crystals to heal the ozone layer,
We can grow our giant cabbages and circle dance like elves,
But there's more to healing planets than just healing ourselves.

And even if there is a God, and hence a point in praying,
It's up to us to save the world, yet still we keep on saying:
'An environmental crisis! That's for others to avert.'
It's simpler not to listen since we learned how to assert.

So, we're balancing our chakras in a life of chants and prayer,
And we can meditate on crystals to heal the ozone layer,
We can grow our giant cabbages and circle dance like elves,
But there's more to healing planets than just healing ourselves.

An angel up at Findhorn, or a sprite by the Fountain,
It's easy doing nothing when we're thinking like a mountain,
From Skyros to Iona, then to Glastonbury Tor,
While the locals think: 'Oh, God! Not another New Age bore.'

While we're balancing our chakras in a life of chants and prayer,
We can meditate on crystals to heal the ozone layer,
We can grow our giant cabbages and circle dance like elves,
But there's more to healing planets than just healing ourselves.

Now, please don't get me wrong, I'm not all that irate,
I'm partial to a sweat-lodge and that mud-bath was just great,
I'm into aromatherapy and acupuncture, too,
But the Bhagwan's Rolls-Royces, when others can't make do?

There's more than balancing our chakras in a life of chants and prayer,
And meditating on crystals to heal the ozone layer,
And growing giant cabbages and dancing like the elves,
'Cos there's more to healing planets, yes, more to healing planets,
Far more to healing planets, than just feeling ourselves.

1 The need for a green political theory

We are now entering the most momentous period in the whole of human history – if, that is, environmentalists are right. But do we have a political theory capable of guiding us through such times? Although human beings have frequently acted so as to ensure the extinction of other species, never before have we had to face the very real possibility of our own collective extinction.[1] And yet, according to many environmentalists, that is precisely the situation we must now confront. In their view, we have so damaged the environment upon which we are completely dependent for our own continued survival as a species that we must now face squarely the choice of radically altering how we live on this finite planet or stampeding like lemmings into oblivion.[2]

But isn't this all rather too dramatic? Surely the situation can't be *that* bad? And even if it is, surely it is better to keep quiet about it, for as Robert C. Paehlke muses: 'Tales of global doom . . . are not necessarily a sound means of inducing long-term social change. . . . If the situation is hopeless, why not enjoy the moment? Why not burn the last few gallons of oil in a barbecue of endangered species?'[3] Of course, if the situation were hopeless, then it would be irrational to try to do anything about it. But, it might be argued, it is not the case that there is no hope; rather, our only hope is to acknowledge the full extent of the threat we collectively pose to our own survival so that we can understand the magnitude of the changes we must effect if the situation is not very soon to become hopeless. And, the argument would continue, we will simply not face up to the task ahead if we pretend that things are not as worrying as they actually are.

1 'As far as we know, [ours] is the first species to face the responsibility of deciding whether to become extinct.' Robert C. Burton, 'A philosopher looks at the population bomb' in W. T. Blackstone (ed.), *Philosophy and Environmental Crisis* (Georgia: University of Georgia Press, 1974), p. 110.

2 For example, the United Nations Environment Programme stated in 1997 that present resource use and profligate consumption are 'driving us towards an environmental precipice'. Quoted in Duncan McLaren, Simon Bullock and Nusrat Yousuf, *Tomorrow's World: Britain's Share in a Sustainable Future* (London: Friends of the Earth/Earthscan, 1998), p. xii.

3 Robert C. Paehlke, *Environmentalism and the Future of Progressive Politics* (New Haven: Yale University Press, 1989), p. 54.

But even if we cannot establish conclusively that the environmental threat is as portentous as some say, wouldn't it be prudent in any case to take their concern seriously and alter whatever, plausibly, is driving us towards disaster? Yet, sadly, most modern political theory is quite oblivious of any environmental threat looming before us. Its conception of the 'end of history', for example, could thus be argued to be utterly divorced from ecological reality – a reality that, in the opinion of many, threatens the end of history quite literally. Whereas 'pure' philosophy has often divorced its concerns from the 'real world', political philosophy cannot afford to do so.[4] Certainly, political philosophers can usefully make abstractions. But they cannot so abstract from empirical considerations that their conclusions exist in a vacuum. The work of political philosophers usually involves enquiries into normative considerations and often implies recommendations regarding which political goals to pursue. But unless we survive as a species, we can have no goals whatsoever to pursue. Hence, it is essential that both empirical political theorists and normative political philosophers acquire an awareness of the magnitude of the challenge that, in the view of environmentalists, we now face.

1.1 The extent of the environmental threat

How serious, then, are the environmental consequences of our present behaviour? We appear to be warming up the planet. If we do so to the extent that the polar ice-caps melt, then sea levels could rise by as much as 5 to 7 metres.[5] This would mean that many major cities would be flooded, as would highly populated low-lying regions such as the Netherlands and parts of Bangladesh. We have left unmapped toxic dumps, lying in wait like land mines, that may, one day, devastate the lives of the unsuspecting, such as happened at Love Canal in New York State. We are producing radioactive materials and allowing them to seep into the environment. Many of our cities are plagued by photochemical smog.[6] Acid rain from industry and power stations has been held responsible for killing the fish in Scandinavian lakes, acidifying soil and destroying forests in North America and Europe.[7] And we are threatening whole ecosystems with

4 As Charles Taylor writes: 'Theories with a false factual base in politics . . . are not just erroneous, but positively dangerous.' Charles Taylor, 'Neutrality in political science' in Peter Laslett and W. G. Runciman, *Philosophy, Politics and Society: Third Series* (Oxford: Blackwell, 1969), p. 34.

5 Norman Myers (ed.), *The Gaia Atlas of Planet Management* (London: Pan Books, 1985), p. 117.

6 For the classic account, see Barry Commoner, *The Closing Circle: Nature, Man, Technology* (New York: Alfred Knopf, 1971), pp. 69 ff.

7 In former West Germany, a 1984 government survey found half the forests there to be clearly sick, while 'serious damage to forests and trees is being reported from *all* countries in Europe.' Peter Bunyard and Fern Morgan-Grenville (eds), *The Green Alternative: Guide to Good Living* (London: Methuen, 1987), p. 23. As John Seymour and Herbert Girardet remark: 'It is clear now that the forests are simply unable to cope with the bad breath of industrial society.' John Seymour and Herbert Girardet, *Far From Paradise: The Story of Human Impact on the Environment* (Basingstoke: Green Print, 1988), p. 146.

the exorbitant use of pesticides,[8] just as we are endangering them by depleting the ozone layer.[9]

Meanwhile, the world population doubles in size every thirty-five years or so, with each additional person adding to the human impact on the environment and requiring resources whose finite nature is becoming ever more apparent.[10] This growth in population could eventually result in a greatly over-populated planet with insufficient resources to meet even the basic needs of humanity or, because of the individual actions of, literally, billions of humans, it could result in such large-scale damage being inflicted on the ecosystems upon which we all depend that the environment itself becomes harmful to human life. In either case, the end-result would be a catastrophic collapse in the human population and immeasurable global suffering in the process.[11] And in the view of many environmentalists, this is just to take the most fleeting peep into the planetary Pandora's Box.

Of course, some people think that there is no environmental problem of any significance. Some even go so far as to insist that environmental conditions are actually improving. However, John Dryzek has claimed that many of the apparent environmental improvements are, in fact, instances of re-locating the problem elsewhere. In his view, there are numerous examples where seeming environmental solutions have actually turned out to be cases of spatial, media and temporal displacements,[12] sometimes resulting in an exacerbation of the problem.

Consider energy production: Coal-fired power stations have been equipped

8 'There is ample evidence of the hazards of synthetic substances such as DDT, dioxin and PCBs on living systems. These are but the tip of a chemical time bomb. A recent count in the Great Lakes of North America identified 460 toxic chemicals, literally from A (Aldrin) to Z (Zytron). . . . The deaths of birds such as eagles and pelicans, at the top of the local food chains, is a warning bell for all species.' Sandy Irvine and Alec Ponton, *A Green Manifesto: Politics for a Green Future* (London: Optima, 1988), p. 33.

9 Insects, plants, aquatic micro-organisms and mammals are all harmed by any significant increase in the ultraviolet light which the ozone layer currently shields them from. See Jonathan Schell, *The Fate of the Earth* (London: Picador, 1982), pp. 79 ff.

10 For a devastating critique of the assumption that we can find enough substitutes for scarce resources and of the suggestion that we can solve the resource crisis by extracting minerals from the sea on an appropriate scale, see William Ophuls, *Ecology and the Politics of Scarcity: Prologue to a Political Theory of the Steady State* (San Francisco: W. H. Freeman, 1977), pp. 68 ff.

11 In fact, it could be argued that we have already committed such an assault on the integrity of the environment that a major and sudden collapse in human populations can now be envisaged. The sperm-count of western European males has, over the past fifty years, declined significantly. This appears to be the result of a massive release into the environment of 'Endocrine Disrupters', which can be found in plasticizers, industrial detergents, the lacquer on the inside of cans containing food, and pesticides, among other sources, and which are also to be found in sewage because of the use of the contraceptive pill. Moreover, such Endocrine Disrupters also seem to be responsible for testicular cancer, breast cancer, and, in some locations, wide-scale sexual transformations in wildlife.

12 See John S. Dryzek, *Rational Ecology: Environment and Political Economy* (Oxford: Blackwell, 1987), pp. 16–20.

with higher towers, which makes the nearby environment cleaner. But this results in the sulphur dioxide and the nitrogen oxides produced remaining in the atmosphere longer, thereby increasing the chemical reactions which they undergo, and thus, perhaps, producing even greater quantities of harmful acid rain, which would then precipitate in another location – a case of spatial displacement and actual increase in environmental damage (although it has the appearance of an environmental improvement for those who live near the power station).

As an alternative solution, some power stations have been fitted with 'scrubbers' (where the emissions are passed through a lime and water spray) in order to remove most of the sulphur dioxide. This certainly can be a genuine improvement, but it does lead to the production of a sulphurous sludge. If this is not processed but dumped, then the pollution simply changes from an airborne to a liquid-borne or solid-based form – a displacement of the problem from one medium to another. Moreover, the lime has to be mined, and that can lead to environmental problems in another medium.

A third apparent 'solution' consists in replacing coal-fired power stations with nuclear energy. But this leads to the creation of highly toxic radioactive products (such as plutonium), which are deadly for thousands of years. A greater environmental danger may thus be created, but it is foisted off onto future generations. The problem is not solved; it is displaced to the future, and exacerbated in the process.

Thus, much of what looks like environmental progress may, in fact, consist in mere surface improvements that are masking grave and long-term environmental deterioration.

1.1.1 Some environmental constraints on global food production

One difficulty that environmentalists frequently encounter in attempting to communicate their concerns is that many of the problems which they fear we face are rather diffuse and general in nature – perhaps too general and remote from immediate experience to elicit the degree of alarm that they feel is warranted. So, in order to appreciate some of the intricately connected elements of the ecological threat which environmentalists claim we face, let us concentrate on one vital area: our ability to feed ourselves.

The issue of global food production must be of concern to us all, and the recognition of its importance is growing. As Lester Brown writes:

> Environmentalists and scientists have long maintained that the population and environmental trends of the last few decades could not continue. Some thought environmental mismanagement would show up in the form of an epidemic of pollution-induced illnesses and wholesale rises in death rates. Others thought it might show up in the collapse of local ecosystems. Indeed, these may happen at the local level. But globally, food scarcity may soon become the principal manifestation of continuing population growth and environmental mismanagement. Rising food prices may be the first global

> economic indicator to signal serious trouble on the environmental front. For those who think the future may be a simple extrapolation of the past, there may be some surprises ahead.[13]

This remark contains a hint of irony, for many environmentalist concerns have been simply dismissed out of hand as 'neo-Malthusian'. Thomas Malthus argued that, whereas food production grows geometrically, human population grows exponentially.[14] Consequently, if we extrapolate into the future, population growth will eventually outstrip our ability to feed ourselves. As certain innovations in agriculture have led to rapidly increasing output, developments in global food production seem to have proven Malthus wrong. Some have taken this as proof that all claims about environmental limits are mistaken, and that we can, contrary to Malthus, extrapolate from present trends towards future abundance. Thus, many assume, in order to dismiss an environmentalist, it is sufficient to label him or her a 'neo-Malthusian'. It is imperative, therefore, that we consider the actual limitations which the environment can be argued to place upon continuing agricultural expansion.

1.1.1.1 Soil loss

Clearly, we cannot survive as a species if we destroy the land that we need to grow our food on. Unfortunately, fertile soil takes hundreds, if not thousands, of years to create, while at present we seem to be reducing its fertility at an alarming pace. Consider the loss of organic matter: 'Soil organic matter has fallen to dangerous levels in about 30% of UK soils, with serious implications for soil stability, water retention and nutrient holding capacity.'[15] Or consider the loss of topsoil due to erosion. Norman Myers claims that

> Europe, the continent least affected, is estimated to be losing close to one billion tonnes a year, while Asia, the worst affected, could be losing around 25 billion tonnes. The US loses well over one billion tonnes a year (net of natural replacement) from its grainlands – equivalent to more than 300,000 hectares of crop-growing potential.[16]

13 Lester R. Brown, 'The acceleration of history' in Lester R. Brown *et al.*, *State of the World 1996* (London: Earthscan, 1996), p. 7.

14 For a summary, see David Pepper, *Modern Environmentalism: An Introduction* (London: Routledge, 1996), pp. 175–7.

15 P. Bullock, quoted in Duncan McLaren, *Soils and Sustainability* (London: Friends of the Earth, 1994), p. 3.

16 Myers, *The Gaia Atlas of Planet Management*, p. 40. In the United Kingdom 'between 20 and 45 tonnes of topsoil [are] lost per hectare per annum on many cereal farms'. Bunyard and Morgan-Grenville, *The Green Alternative*, p. 73. In the mid-1980s it was reckoned that, at the then rate of topsoil loss, 'by the end of the [twentieth] century, there will be one-third less topsoil per person throughout the world than at present.' Michael Redclift, *Sustainable Development: Exploring the Contradictions* (London: Routledge and Kegan Paul, 1987), p. 32.

And according to recent calculations published by the Worldwatch Institute:

> Soil lost to wind and water erosion ranges from 5–10 tons per hectare annually in Africa, Europe and Australia to 10–20 tons per hectare in North, Central, and South America and nearly 30 tons per hectare in Asia. Because soil is created at roughly 1 ton per hectare a year, current rates of erosion are depleting the nutrient base of agriculture far faster than it is renewed. More than just unsustainable, this loss of topsoil is tragic: in just a few decades, human activity has squandered a natural patrimony that took thousands of years to accumulate.[17]

Over 50 million hectares (about one third) of the United States' grainlands are 'undergoing a marked decline in long-term productivity because of soil erosion'.[18] Worse still, 'official estimates in the USA give much of the mid-west only fifty years more productivity'.[19]

Globally, soil erosion, conversion of agricultural land to other uses, toxification[20] and desertification have been identified as leading to the loss of approximately 11 million hectares of arable land per year. In the mid-1980s it was calculated that it would take less that fifteen years for a further 18 per cent of the then remaining arable land to be lost.[21] Add to this the purported loss of 7 million hectares of grassland each year, and any continued faith in our ability to feed a growing world population by the prevailing agricultural system and with the present distribution of resources would seem to be irrational.

This is not to deny that many of our modern agricultural practices have, in fact, increased food production. However, often that increase is relative to labour as an input. Greater output for a lower input of labour is what more efficient production usually means, for in the developed countries labour is a significant cost. But

17 Gary Gardner, 'Preserving agricultural resources' in Lester R. Brown *et al.*, *State of the World 1996* (London: Earthscan, 1996), p. 83.

18 Myers, *The Gaia Atlas of Planet Management*, p. 40.

19 Bunyard and Morgan-Grenville, *The Green Alternative*, p. 75.

20 'There is . . . increasing concern about the accumulation of heavy metals in the soil, notably cadmium and lead. Cadmium reaches the soil via industrial emissions and also through the application of phosphate fertilizer.' Seymour and Girardet, *Far From Paradise*, p. 150. Consider former West Germany, where '7 per cent of the country's soil is now contaminated with heavy metals beyond the point where it should be used to grow crops for human consumption.' Bunyard and Morgan-Grenville, *The Green Alternative*, p. 24.

21 Myers, *The Gaia Atlas of Planet Management*, p. 40. 'It took modern agriculture only 70 years, from 1882 to 1952, to destroy half the topsoil on 38% of all cultivated land. During this period the amount of land which could no longer be cultivated increased by 3.45 billion acres. More than a third of the forests that were standing in 1882 have been razed (that is, 4.75 billion acres). Of the 3 billion acres currently under cultivation there are only 1.25 billion acres left of "good land".' André Gorz, *Ecology as Politics* (London: Pluto, 1980), p. 94. Most worryingly, as recently reported in an authoritative study undertaken by Friends of the Earth, it has been estimated that, within Europe alone, already an area the size of Belgium is 'extremely degraded and completely lost for agriculture.' Friends of the Earth Europe, *Towards Sustainable Europe: The Study* (London: Friends of the Earth, 1995), p. 61.

this does not always mean efficiency in the sense of the greatest output relative to land area. Ecological farming techniques, on the other hand, 'are highly productive (on a per-acre basis they can outproduce industrial agriculture), *but only when human labor is carefully and patiently applied*. Thus farming that is both productive and ecologically sound seems very likely to be small-hold, horticultural, essentially peasant-style agriculture finely adapted to local conditions'.[22] But the tendency, globally, is for food production to move in exactly the opposite direction: towards large agribusinesses with mechanized monocultural (single-crop) production that reduces the amount of human labour required and, along with it, ecological diversity. Moreover, and most importantly, a short-term increase in 'efficiency' cannot solve our long-term food requirements if the price of that increase is the destruction of the soil that is necessary for meeting them. But it is precisely such 'advanced' methods of agricultural production which, many argue, are so damaging to the sustainability of the soil.

The amount of food that can be grown is not only dependent upon the intensity with which the land is cultivated but also upon the area of land which is available for food production. However, with the world's population currently predicted to double in size to 10.5 billion by the year 2050,[23] and with ever-increasing migration from the rural areas, then the area of available agricultural land must inevitably decrease in size.[24] This 'increase in population and

22 Ophuls, *Ecology and the Politics of Scarcity*, p. 61. And as Susan George writes: 'Mechanization can be expected to increase productivity *per worker* – but not necessarily per hectare'. Susan George, *How the Other Half Dies: The Real Reasons for World Hunger* (Harmondsworth: Penguin, 1986), p. 318. Moreover, 'in Argentina and Brazil where vast latifundia reign supreme, the smallest family farms produce, per hectare, more than eight times as much as the largest estates. In Columbia . . . , the small producers are *fourteen times* as effective as the large ones in terms of output per hectare.' Ibid., p. 35. In short, in 'the three poor continents . . . *the largest holdings produce the least food*.' Ibid.

23 See Robert Garner, *Environmental Politics* (Hemel Hempstead: Harvester Wheatsheaf, 1996), p. 125. Incredibly, '[t]hose of us born before 1950 have seen more population growth during our lifetimes than occurred during the preceding 4 million years since our early ancestors first stood upright.' Brown, 'The acceleration of history', p. 3. And a growing world population has a growing demand for food. While increases in food production have, to some extent, been able to cater for this growing population up until now, 'neo-Malthusian' predictions seem to be starting to come true: 'In 1996, world carryover stocks of grain – the amount in the bin when the new harvest begins – are projected to drop to 245 million tons, down from 294 million tons in 1995. This third consecutive annual decline will reduce stocks to an estimated 49 days of consumption, the lowest level on record.' Ibid., pp. 7–8. Moreover, '[e]ven if the modest area of cropland that was set aside under farm commodity programs in the United States and Europe were in use, the 1995 harvest would still have fallen short of consumption. Grain stocks would still have declined.' Ibid., p. 8. And grain supplies over half of humanity's daily calories. See Gardner, 'Preserving agricultural resources', p. 80.

24 'Hong Kong . . ., South Korea, and Taiwan saw harvested grain area drop by more than 20 per cent between 1980–84 and 1990–94, while East Asia as a whole lost nearly 10 per cent of its harvested grain area.' Ibid., pp. 80–1. Given the requirements of global food production, this suggests that there are very real environmental limits on every poor country attempting to follow in the footsteps of those which have recently industrialized. How is it possible for

urbanization will put stresses on the food production sector and the threat of shortages will encourage ever-intensive agricultural practices causing further environmental damage.'[25] It would also appear to lead inevitably to an even greater rate of decline in long-term soil fertility.

1.1.1.2 Climatic impediments and 'natural' disasters

Our ability to grow food is not only dependent upon fertile soil, it is also dependent upon climate. According to many environmentalists, one of the greatest problems that we are creating for our ability to provide sufficient food in the future is the global warming that is argued to result from increasing the proportion of carbon dioxide in the atmosphere, partly as a result of burning fossil fuels. One consequence of the 'greenhouse effect' would be 'drier climates for some, especially Americans'.[26] Can we afford the 'breadbasket of the world' to dry up? 'What if the great grain belt of North America starts to become unbuckled, with less food not only for North Americans, but for dozens of countries that import grain from North America?'[27]

One shudders to think of the political ramifications should the world's most powerful, nuclear-armed state become unable to grow enough food to feed its population (or even should its economy, which is based upon grain production, collapse as a result of agricultural decline). This could easily herald a new era of the most disturbing political adventurism. And according to the 1996 Worldwatch Institute Report:

> The lack of growth of the world grain harvest since 1990 coupled with the continuing growth in world population and the increased likelihood of crop-damaging heat waves in the years ahead at least carries the potential of severe food shortages. The economic disruption that is likely to result could dwarf that which occurred when the Organization of Petroleum Exporting Countries engineered a tripling in the world price of oil in 1973. People can survive without oil, but not without food.[28]

---

every country to feed itself if the process of industrialization takes such a high proportion of arable land out of agricultural production, especially when there is expected to be a 64 per cent increase in global food demand over the next twenty five years? See ibid., p. 80. Even worse, as many cities are located close to the most productive land, it is prime agricultural land which tends to be lost when urban and/or industrial areas expand.

25 Garner, *Environmental Politics*, p. 125.

26 Myers, *The Gaia Atlas of Planet Management*, p. 44.

27 Ibid., pp. 44, 46. Also see Eugene P. Odum, *Ecology and our Endangered Life-Support Systems* (Massachusetts: Sinauer, 1989), p. 124.

28 Brown, 'The acceleration of history', pp. 17–18. 'When the US Department of Agriculture released its monthly world crop report in early September 1995, it reported a sharp drop in the estimated world grain harvest because of crop withering heat waves in the northern tier of industrial countries. Intense late summer heat had damaged harvests in Canada and the United States, across Europe, and in Russia.' Ibid., p. 15.

It was the oil shortage which prompted the US to create its Rapid Deployment Force. What might a global food shortage provoke?[29] Any widely experienced difficulty in obtaining necessary resources (in particular, food) could easily lead to conflict between the major powers; and that would herald a global catastrophe. War, and certainly nuclear war, 'is the ultimate pollutant'.[30]

In a word, the probable political consequences of looming environmental threats and increasing scarcity of resources are worrying in the extreme. Yet our industrialized way of life continues to demand more and more resources and pours into the atmosphere the carbon dioxide that threatens the climatic changes which could lead to major crop failures and thus to global food shortages.

Moreover, the destruction of the world's forests, which is currently being carried out on such an unprecedented scale, is also likely, in the opinion of many, to result in further – indeed catastrophic – climatic changes. For example:

> The Amazon basin . . . has a major influence on climatic patterns including the wind pattern that generates and sustains the Gulf Stream, which in turn makes the British Isles and the Nordic countries habitable on the present scale. . . . At the present rate it will be cleared in the next two to three decades; already in the last ten years an area the size of Europe has been cleared.[31]

Furthermore, it has been calculated that 'the Amazon Basin . . . consumes about 10 per cent of the gaseous carbon in the atmosphere.'[32] What is worse, it has been claimed that forest destruction[33] contributes nearly as much carbon dioxide to the atmosphere as all fossil fuel burning,[34] thus greatly adding to the greenhouse effect.

Tropical forests are also responsible for evaporating enormous quantities of water into the atmosphere, falling elsewhere as rain – a decrease in which would lead to even greater desertification and loss of productive land.[35] In fact, it has been claimed that 'much of the desertification in East Africa today has been

29 'Even as the pressure on cropland is mounting, the cumulative effects of soil erosion and aquifer depletion are making it more difficult to expand grain production. The economic manifestations of emerging food scarcity can be seen in rising seafood prices, falling grain stocks, and, most recently, rising grain prices. These and other trends suggest that the history of the next few decades will be defined by food, specifically by rising prices on both oceanic and land-based food products, [and] by a spreading politics of food scarcity'. Ibid., p. 7.

30 Irvine and Ponton, *A Green Manifesto*, p. 114.

31 Colin Lacey, 'Introduction' in Colin Lacey and Roy Williams (eds), *Education, Ecology and Development: The Case for an Education Network* (London: World Wildlife Fund/Kogan Page, 1987), p. 9.

32 Bunyard and Morgan-Grenville, *The Green Alternative*, p. 25.

33 Unbelievably, 'some 200,000 square kilometres of virgin rainforest are falling to the axe, fire and massive dam schemes every year.' Ibid., p. xiv.

34 Ibid., p. 157.

35 And it has been argued that there is worse to come. Desertification threatens 'about one-third of the world's remaining agricultural land'. Ibid., p. 75.

caused by cutting down forests in West Africa.'[36] And yet the chopping down of rainforest still continues at an unremitting rate, even though the benefits are extremely short-term. Although rainforests are the most intricate ecosystems known, they have very thin topsoil. When they are destroyed to make way for agriculture, the soil structure deteriorates rapidly, and within just a few years farmers have to move on and cut down more forest.

Worsening environmental conditions caused by human activity, such as clearing the land of tree cover, offer, in the opinion of many, a striking portent of what is in store for more and more people throughout the world:

> during the 1960s drought struck 18.5 million people every year; by the 1970s that figure had climbed to 24.4 million people annually. These studies were completed before the African drought and famines of 1984–5, which affected some 30 million people on one continent alone, and before the strangely less-publicized Indian droughts of 1985–6, which affected 100 million people in nine states. Drought has to do not only with annual rainfall, but with how much of the water which does fall is absorbed and held by the soil. Clearing the land of trees and bushes causes water to run off the soil quickly, making less water available for humans and their crops. The African and Indian droughts were thus directly related to the ways in which people had been using their land.[37]

But clearing the land of trees and bushes not only seems to be responsible for increases in the incidence of drought, it also appears to be the cause of ever more severe floods. During the 1960s, for example, '5.2 million people were affected by floods each year; by the 1970s the number had risen to 15.4 million. . . . The cause is the same: stripping the land of vegetation means that water runs off more quickly; rivers cannot absorb the excess, and in rainy areas the result is more, and fiercer, floods.'[38] Increasing flood damage in India and Bangladesh, for example, has, it would seem, been caused by deforestation in the Himalayas. Yet the trees are still being cut down relentlessly. And if current trends continue, all the world's primary forest is likely to have vanished within fifty years.

1.1.1.3 Decreasing biodiversity

The destruction of the world's forests has the added cost of severely reducing the available gene-pool. On one of the more conservative estimates, at the beginning of this decade, approximately one species became extinct every day, and by the year 2000 'we could be losing 130 species per day as the destruction of wild land

36 Ibid., p. 85.

37 Lloyd Timberlake, *Only One Earth: Living for the Future* (London: BBC Books/Earthscan, 1987), p. 20. Ethiopia, to take a dramatic example, 'once had 40 per cent forest; now it has 2 per cent.' Ibid., p. 18.

38 Ibid., p. 20.

accelerates',[39] with the prospect of a quarter of all species being lost by the middle of the twenty-first century.[40] This reduction in species diversity may well have tremendous significance for our continued ability to feed ourselves.[41] Our reliance on monoculture means that 75 per cent of the wheat Canada produces comprises only four varieties, with a single variety covering half the prairieland. Six varieties of soya bean provide the gene-pool for the United States' crop, while only four varieties of potato constitute nearly three-quarters of the US output.[42] The significance of this loss of diversity can be gleaned from

> the recent history of *Zea diploperennis*, a rare perennial maize discovered in 1978. Found in a few hectares of farmland in the Sierra de Manantlan, Mexico, this hitherto unknown variety was down to some 2,000 plants – and the elimination of its habitat continues. Yet its genes could open up the prospect of perennial maize production and increased resistance to at least four of the seven most important maize diseases. . . .[43]

The more we come to rely on a small number of varieties of plants for our food, the less secure we are in the face of ever more virulent pests. And yet we continue to destroy the fragile habitats of species after species.

Another source of our food is the sea. Yet if we consider the North Atlantic, for example, 'Americans and Western Europeans have contributed to a 40 per cent decline in stocks of herring, a 90 per cent decline in halibut, and similar depletions of haddock, cod, and several other prime species'.[44] According to the Worldwatch Institute, '[b]y 1989, all oceanic fisheries were being fished at or beyond capacity. Of the world's 15 leading oceanic fisheries, 13 are in decline.'[45] In the opinion of many environmentalists, what is ultimately in store is evident from the history of the Peruvian anchoveta, one of the world's great fisheries, which entirely collapsed in 1972 as a result of over-fishing.

39 Ibid.

40 Myers, *The Gaia Atlas of Planet Management*, p. 154.

41 It also deprives us of the potential medicines we might desperately need in the future. Something like 'one in four medicines in the West owes its origins to plants or animals in tropical rainforests.' Bunyard and Morgan-Grenville, *The Green Alternative*, p. 3. And As Timberlake informs us: 'Almost half our drugs and pharmaceuticals are based on the chemistry of wild plants; one obscure tropical forest plant, the rosy periwinkle, has saved the lives of countless Northern children suffering from leukaemia. But many plants vanish before they can be studied by scientists.' *Only One Earth*, pp. 19–20. What is more, new medicines will inevitably be required not just for healthy humans, but for healthy livestock as well.

42 Myers, *The Gaia Atlas of Planet Management*, p. 157.

43 Ibid., p. 156.

44 Ibid., p. 82.

45 Brown, 'The acceleration of history', p. 5.

1.1.1.4 A 'Green Revolution' or eco-catastrophe?

Of course, it is not only the finite nature of natural resources and our progressive degradation of them that seems to place limits upon our ability to feed the world's population. It is also the size of that population and the manner in which those resources are distributed within it. There is considerable disagreement as to how large a population the world could feed were food distributed more equally or were valuable land not devoted to the production of cash crops.[46] In the West, we consume large quantities of meat, when 'a significant proportion of the fodder fed to our livestock is imported from developing Third World countries – for example, oil seeds from India and tapioca from Thailand – which have turned over vast acreages of land to the export of cash crops.'[47] Furthermore, the consumption of animal protein involves tremendous waste, for it takes approximately seven kilograms of grain to produce one kilogram of feedlot beef. Consequently, it would seem that many more people could be fed were the rich to consume less meat.[48]

This notwithstanding, although present famines do not show that there is currently insufficient food produced in the world (for one can argue that what they instead show is the maldistribution of resources), it is clear that there must be some limit to the size of the population that our planet can support. Garrett Hardin, for example, has calculated that at present rates of growth it would take little over 600 years for the entire land surface of the planet to be occupied by human beings standing shoulder to shoulder.[49] It is surely absurd to think that the human population can grow forever on a finite planet.[50] Surely it is also absurd to think that we can wait until there is no longer any space left upon which to grow food before we will be unable to feed the world's population.

Nevertheless, it has been assumed that we can solve present global food problems by means of the 'miracle' high-yielding varieties of grains (HYVs) promoted in the inaptly named 'Green Revolution'. Moreover, in the view of some, 'high-yielding varieties' is equally a misnomer. In their view, 'high-responsive varieties' (HRVs) would be a far more accurate description as, it has been claimed, the new

46 See, for example, Susan George, *How the Other Half Dies*, and Frances Moore Lappé and Joseph Collins, *Food First* (London: Abacus, 1982).

47 Bunyard and Morgan-Grenville, *The Green Alternative*, p. 73.

48 See Gardner, 'Preserving agricultural resources', p. 93. Also see Frances Moore Lappé, *Diet for a Small Planet* (New York: Ballantine, 1971), pp. 4–9.

49 Cited in Paehlke, *Environmentalism and the Future of Progressive Politics*, p. 64.

50 And the suggestion that we could solve the problem of population growth by colonizing other planets is, surely, equally absurd: 'Suppose that we built rockets immeasurably larger than any in existence today – capable of carrying 100 people and their baggage to another planet. Almost 2000 of such monster ships would have to leave each day. The effects of their exhausts on the atmosphere would be spectacular to say the least.' Paul R. Ehrlich, 'The population explosion: facts and fiction' in H. D. Johnson (ed.), *No Deposit – No Return: Man and his Environment* (Massachusetts: Addison-Wesley, 1970), p. 41. This, of course, would mean that the Earth could support even fewer people. Two thousand such ships would be necessary because 'we would have to export [to other planets] 70 million people a year to keep our population constant.' Ibid. That was in 1970. Today, we add 90 million people a year to the global total.

varieties only produce a high yield when combined with large inputs of fertilizer, pesticide and water from irrigation schemes.[51] Otherwise 'they give yields inferior to most native cereal strains.'[52]

Not only has the introduction of HRVs been argued to have exacerbated world poverty,[53] and with it malnutrition, it also appears to pose massive environmental problems for the future. First of all, the nitrogen fertilizers required are made by and large from petrochemicals – an extremely scarce resource – and to 'push' such a package onto poor countries so that their production of food is addicted to a finite resource is surely a recipe for long-term famine.[54] Not surprisingly, then, it has been claimed that many modern farming techniques are 'simply unsustainable'.[55] Second, it can be argued that the large-scale use of fertilizers poses a massive pollution problem, both leading to the contamination of drinking water[56] and harming ecosystems on which we rely[57] – as, of course, would seem to be the case with the large-scale use of pesticides, though on an even vaster scale.[58] Third,

51 See Lappé and Collins, *Food First*, p. 104.

52 Ophuls, *Ecology and the Politics of Scarcity*, p. 54.

53 This is because only the richer farmers have been able to afford the whole package of seeds, fertilizer, pesticides and irrigation, thereby increasing their yield. As Susan George writes: 'When nothing is done to alleviate inequalities, the Green Revolution is guaranteed to worsen them.' *How the Other Half Dies*, p. 132. Thus, 'the "Green Revolution" has been a flagrant example of a "developmental solution" that has brought nothing but misery to the poor.' Ibid., p. 17.

54 Moreover, as Paul Ehrlich and John Holdren pointed out in 1968: 'if India were to apply fertilizer at the per capita level employed by the Netherlands, her fertilizer needs would be nearly half the present world output'. Paul R. Ehrlich and John P. Holdren, 'Population and panaceas: A technological perspective' in J. P. Holdren and P. R. Ehrlich, *Global Ecology: Readings towards a Rational Strategy for Man* (New York: Harcourt Brace Jovanovich, 1971), p. 12. And given that three tons of oil are needed to produce one ton of fertilizer, then as André Gorz adds: 'If the whole world were to use US agricultural methods on all the land currently under cultivation, agriculture alone would use up the known oil reserves in a matter of 29 years.' *Ecology as Politics*, pp. 95–6.

55 Timberlake, *Only One Earth*, p. 122.

56 'Nitrate pollution from artificial fertilizers now threatens one-third of [Britain's] water supplies.' Bunyard and Morgan-Grenville, *The Green Alternative*, p. 142. Yet our remedy for a global shortage of food is to make this problem universal.

57 And the use of fertilizer seems, in any case, to be subject to the law of diminishing returns: 'In 1949, an average of about 11,000 tons of fertilizer nitrogen were used *per USDA unit of crop production*, while in 1968 about 57,000 tons of nitrogen were used for the *same* crop yield. This means that the efficiency with which nitrogen contributes to the growth of the crop declined fivefold. Obviously, a good deal of the fertilizer nitrogen did not enter the crops and must have ended up elsewhere in the ecosystem.' Commoner, *The Closing Circle*, p. 150. Thus, 'it is literally impossible to obtain such high fertilizer-induced yields without polluting the environment.' Ibid., pp. 150–1. This led to the eutrophication of Lake Erie, to mention the most famous example, with a corresponding loss of fish.

58 'The pesticide story is quite similar: increased annual use, at reduced efficiency, leading to an excessive environmental impact.' Ibid., p. 151. And the reason for the loss in efficiency of pesticide use seems clear: the intake of pesticide becomes more concentrated as one moves from one trophic level to the next – thus the pests' natural predators are affected far more than the pests. 'By killing off natural insect predators of the target pest, while the latter tends to

as a result of over-use, fresh water appears to be in the process of becoming an increasingly scarce resource,[59] while badly thought-out irrigation schemes themselves could reduce long-term fertility through salinization of the soil.[60] In short, as Paul Ehrlich warns:

> Our desperate attempts to increase food yields are promoting soil deterioration and contributing to the poisoning of the ecological systems on which our very survival depends. It is a long and complex story, but the conclusion is simple – the more we strive to obtain increased yields by ill-considered means in the short run, the smaller the yields are likely to be in the long run.[61]

It seems clear, then, that we cannot, without substantial risk, simply carry on as usual.

> From 1984 to 1993, grain output per capita fell 11 percent. From 1989 to 1993, the world seafood supplies per capita fell 9 percent. From 1978 to 1993, per capita irrigated land, which plays a disproportionate role in meet-

---

become resistant, the new insecticides become increasingly inefficient. As a result, increasing amounts must be used simply to maintain crop yield. For example, in Arizona insecticide use on cotton tripled between 1965 and 1967 with an appreciable *drop* in yield – an agricultural treadmill, which forces us to move ever faster to keep in place. And again, the decreasing efficiency means an increasing release of pesticides into the environment – where they become a threat to wildlife and [hu]man[s].' Ibid., pp. 151–2. Unbelievably, from 1945 to 1989 the application of insecticides in the US 'increased tenfold, but crop losses to insects nearly doubled'. Gardner, 'Preserving agricultural resources', p. 89.

Moreover, any target pest's natural predator might also control what is, initially, a less harmful pest, but which, upon the loss of its predator, later becomes far more serious. As Gardner writes: '"secondary" pests – those originally found in small numbers in an ecosystem – often multiply when major pests are decimated. This happened in Indonesia, where the brown rice planthopper proliferated after its natural enemies were routed by pesticides. In a two-year feeding frenzy, this secondary pest ruined some $1.5 billion in rice.' Ibid. Furthermore, in the view of some: because HRVs 'require more "input" of pesticides (with all their deleterious ecological side effects), these crops may ultimately contribute to the defeat of other environment-related panaceas, such as extracting larger amounts of food from the sea.' Ehrlich and Holdren, 'Population and panaceas', p. 13.

59 'With water use exceeding the sustainable yield of aquifers in so much of the world, overpumping is now commonplace. Even at current levels of consumption, underground water tables are now falling in the southwestern United States, the US Great Plains, several states in India (including the Punjab, the country's breadbasket), in much of northern China, across northern Africa, in southern Europe, and throughout the Middle East.' Brown, 'The acceleration of history', p. 5. '[I]n the Indus Valley of Pakistan, groundwater is pumped at more than 50 per cent above the rate that will avoid salinated water.' Gardner, 'Preserving agricultural resources', p. 86. There seems little doubt that the populations of these divers parts of the world are thus dependent upon completely unsustainable agriculture.

60 There are, it has been estimated, 'about 1.5 million hectares of irrigated lands lost annually to salinization.' Michael Jacobs, *The Politics of the Real World: Meeting the New Century* (London: Earthscan, 1996), p. 16.

61 Ehrlich, 'The population explosion', p. 43.

> ing the world's food needs, fell 6 percent. If current trends continue, by 2010, per capita availability of rangeland will drop by 22 percent, seafood supplies by 10 percent, irrigated land by 12 percent, cropland by 21 percent and forest land by 30 percent. If current trends continue, by 2030, per capita grain availability levels will decline to those of 1950, before the introduction of the Green Revolution.[62]

In the meantime, the global human population will have multiplied several times over its 1950 total, and its deleterious impact on the environment will most likely have increased at an even more alarming rate.

If environmentalists are right, then, our recent pursuit of agricultural abundance will have failed to generate long-term benefits, and we will only have succeeded in depleting scarce resources and poisoning the environment. Thus, it would seem clear that we cannot rely on such 'technical fixes' as are currently on offer. For, in the opinion of many, to do so would be to invite an almost unimaginable catastrophe. It seems indubitable, therefore, that our present course of development must be altered.

But can't all of this simply be dismissed out of hand? Aren't such doom-laden warnings of (what some might regard as) hysterical environmentalists mere unsubstantiated clamourings which no rational person ought to take seriously? Interestingly, the authoritative study on the environment undertaken for the United Nations by the World Commission on Environment and Development (WCED) – *Our Common Future* – certainly takes such environmental warnings very seriously indeed. In fact, it pulls no punches in its description of our current predicament. But this is not the product of hysterical environmentalists. Rather, it consists in the conclusions reached by 'a group of 23 political leaders and scientists from both the developed and less-developed countries',[63] including the former British Conservative Prime Minister, Edward Heath, and chaired by the then Prime Minister of Norway, Gro Harlem Brundtland. Yet even such establishment figures as these are deeply worried about the environmental crises, for as they report:

> Each year another 6 million hectares of productive dryland turns into worthless desert. Over three decades, this would amount to an area roughly as large as Saudi Arabia. More than 11 million hectares of forest are destroyed yearly, and this, over three decades, would equal an area about the size of India. Much of this forest is converted to low-grade farmland unable to support the farmers who settle it. In Europe, acid precipitation kills forests and lakes and damages the artistic and architectural heritage of nations; it may have acidified vast tracts of soil beyond reasonable hope of repair. The burning of fossil fuels puts into the atmosphere carbon dioxide, which is causing gradual

62 James P. Sterba, 'Global justice' in William Aiken and Hugh LaFollette (eds), *World Hunger and Morality* (New Jersey: Prentice-Hall, 1996), p. 133.

63 Odum, *Ecology and our Endangered Life-Support Systems*, p. 262.

> global warming. This 'greenhouse effect' may by early next century have increased average global temperatures enough to shift agricultural production areas, raise sea levels to flood coastal cities, and disrupt national economies. Other industrial gases threaten to deplete the planet's protective ozone shield to such an extent that the number of human and animal cancers would rise sharply and the ocean's food chain would be disrupted.[64]

And they are quite clear about how urgent the situation is: 'Little time is available for corrective action. In some cases we may already be close to transgressing critical thresholds.'[65]

1.1.2 Inequality, political theory and the environment

This has been a very brief survey of only a few of the many grave environmental problems that numerous scientists and activists alike firmly believe now confront us, and which impinge upon at least one vital human interest: our continuing ability to feed ourselves.

What must be stressed, however, is that the environmental difficulties which we presently appear to face are not simply 'natural' disasters, such as earthquakes, volcanoes, or tidal waves. Rather, if we face an ecological catastrophe, it is human-made. More precisely, its causes are fundamentally economic, social and political in nature. For example, as Tim O'Riordan, writing in 1981, observes:

> The recent reports on the global environmental predicament . . . pinpoint the fact that a combination of population growth, neo-colonialism, national militarism, and multinational capitalism are both encouraging and forcing third-world economic elites and peasants alike to destroy vast areas of habitable rural and urban land through aggressive overexploitation and the dangerous addition of chemicals and other pollutants. In the case of many peasant communities, these forces are propelling them to destroy their only real asset – their land – often against their better judgement and certainly against their will.[66]

64 G. H. Brundtland *et al.*, *Our Common Future* (Oxford: Oxford University Press, 1987), pp. 2–3. Moreover, they are in full agreement with the above-mentioned concerns for future food production: 'Short-sighted policies are leading to degradation of the agricultural resource base on almost every continent: soil erosion in North America; soil acidification in Europe; deforestation and desertification in Asia, Africa, and Latin America; and waste and pollution of water almost everywhere.' Ibid., p. 125. For example, '[i]ndustry and agriculture put toxic substances into the human food chain and into underground water tables beyond reach of cleansing'. Ibid., p. 3.

65 Ibid., p. 35. For instance: 'New evidence of a possible rapid depletion of the ozone layer and a consequent increase in ultraviolet radiation poses a threat not only to human health but to ocean life. Some scientists believe that this radiation could kill sensitive phytoplankton and fish larvae floating near the ocean's surface, damaging ocean food chains and possibly disrupting planetary support systems.' Ibid., p. 264. Phytoplankton, of course, play a crucial role in maintaining the planet's oxygen supply.

66 Tim O'Riordan, *Environmentalism* (London: Pion, 1981), p. 386.

And such destruction is likely to have global effects which not even those in the richest countries would be able to escape.

Moreover, not only is the environmental threat acknowledged by those leading establishment figures who signed up to *Our Common Future*,[67] but the assessment that its causes are economic, social and political in nature is also acknowledged by them. For example, in their Tokyo Declaration, the WCED recognize that '[p]overty is a major source of environmental degradation which not only affects a large number of people in developing countries but also undermines the sustainable development of the entire community of nations – both developing and industrialized.'[68] And yet, even given this acknowledgement of the global consequences of Third World poverty, organizations such as the International Monetary Fund still insist on poor countries adopting policies of 'structural readjustment', which exacerbate that poverty. In fact, the 'gap between the richest 20% of the world's population and the poorest 20% has more than doubled in the last thirty years. 85% of world income now goes to the richest 20%, up from 70% in 1960. The share of the poorest 20% has fallen from 2.3 to 1.4%.'[69] Indeed, 'the net worth of the world's 358 dollar billionaires is equal to the combined annual income of the poorest 45 per cent of the world's population – some 2.3 billion.'[70]

Furthermore, it is not merely that environmental problems have been visited on the poor countries by the exploiting rich, only to threaten a return to the latter because of their seemingly universal consequences. The rich countries themselves engage directly in environmentally disastrous activities – the direct environmental impact of those who live in the rich countries being a function of their affluent lifestyle and their associated methods of production. For example, the industrialized countries comprise only 20 per cent of the world's population, yet they appear to be responsible for '93 per cent of global industrial effluents and 95 per cent of hazardous waste'.[71] In fact, it has been claimed that '500 million inhabitants of western Europe and North America currently cause the environment as much damage as 10 billion Indians would (if they existed).'[72] Thus, as

67 Tragically, a decade has now elapsed since the publication of *Our Common Future*, yet the conclusions reached by the WCED still stand, having been emphatically endorsed in a recent Worldwatch Institute Report: 'The demands of our generation now exceed the income, the sustainable yield, of the earth's ecological endowment. Since mid-century the sustainable yield thresholds of natural systems have been crossed in country after country. It is difficult, if not impossible, to find a developing country that is not losing tree cover. Every major food-producing country is suffering heavy topsoil losses from erosion by wind and water. . . . In every country in Africa, rangeland is being degraded by overgrazing. Forests all over Europe are suffering from air pollution and acid rain.' Brown, 'The acceleration of history', pp. 4–5.

68 Brundtland *et al.*, *Our Common Future*, p. 364.

69 Jacobs, *The Politics of the Real World*, p. 42.

70 McLaren, Bullock and Yousuf, *Tomorrow's World*, p. 27.

71 Jacobs, *The Politics of the Real World*, p. 32.

72 Gorz, *Ecology as Politics*, p. 96. Consider the globally inequitable use of resources: Currently, 5 per cent of the world's population, or thereabouts, 'utilizes about 70 per cent of the world's energy supplies'. Garner, *Environmental Politics*, p. 125. 'In 1980, every American

Barry Commoner insists: 'we are in an environmental crisis because the means by which we use the ecosphere to produce wealth are destructive of the ecosphere itself. The present system of production is self-destructive; the present course of human civilization is suicidal.'[73]

Now, environmentalists *might* have overstated the terrifying threat outlined above. Any one aspect might be amenable to some technical solution or might not in fact be as great as environmentalists fear. All of the statistics cited here are estimates and to some extent speculative. But even if each aspect is not as bad as is feared, and even if each can be responded to in some degree, the combined effect of all of these aspects, even if each is far less extreme than environmentalists argue, threatens major catastrophe.[74] The global ecosystem is a highly intricate and interconnected set of delicate relations[75] that is unlikely to withstand such a major and concerted onslaught.[76] So, given that the environment comprises intricate

---

consumed nearly 26,460 lbs, 12,000 kilograms, of "coal equivalent". West Germans about half that amount, Kenyans used 440 lbs and Ethiopians consumed 55 lbs. An American uses a thousand times more oil than a citizen of Rwanda. In 1975, each American used metals valued at 200 dollars, a Western European 120 dollars, an African 4 dollars. These figures do not only reflect different living standards but also different scales of ecological impact.' Seymour and Girardet, *Far from Paradise*, pp. 205–6.

Of course, one of the major polluters is widely recognized to be private motorized transport. 'In 1982, there were 385 cars for every 1000 West Germans, fifteen per 1000 Turks. If India wanted the same number of cars per inhabitant as the USA it would have 128 million, 237 times more than today. If all the countries in the world were to reach the production levels of the USA or West Germany, the global ecological consequences would be ruinous.' Ibid., p. 206. As Gorz pointedly observes: 'Hence the suspicion that when we ask the Third World for population control it may simply be so that we can continue to pillage the planet.' Gorz, *Ecology as Politics*, p. 96. Clearly, we cannot expect change in the poorer parts of the world if we are not prepared ourselves to reduce radically our own potentially disastrous environmental impact.

73 Commoner, *The Closing Circle*, pp. 294–5. And as Rudolf Bahro puts it: 'The global industrialization process not only devours and destroys its own preconditions, the resources which it soaks up in ever greater quantities, but also the natural foundations of human life, of the very biosphere which sustains us. The completion of this process on a world scale would be the ultimate natural catastrophe.' Rudolf Bahro, *Building the Green Movement*, trans. M. Tyler (London: Heretic Books, 1986), p. 12.

74 As Kirkpatrick Sale remarks: 'Sometimes it is comforting to quibble with this figure or that assumption or those lines of reasoning, to locate a contrary source, a different expert, to denigrate one professor's credentials, another's research techniques. But there is simply no escaping the rock-hard truths of the overall evidence of environmental peril in which our human society has plunged itself.' Kirkpatrick Sale, *Dwellers in the Land: The Bioregional Vision* (San Francisco: Sierra Book Club, 1985), pp. 36–7.

75 See Commoner, *The Closing Circle*, *passim*.

76 Consider the consequences of failing to alter the current course of development: 'Within the space of a generation, for example, China's present rate of combined population and economic growth will make it the largest economy in the world. With a per capita consumption level similar to that now enjoyed by South Korea, its carbon dioxide emissions will exceed those of all today's industrialized nations put together.' Jacobs, *The Politics of the Real World*, p. 28. How could the planet's life-support systems conceivably survive the onslaught of global development mirroring that of the industrialized nations?

interrelations, and given that it is being placed under stress from many directions, catastrophic eco-systemic collapse seems very likely indeed – and certainly it is sufficiently probable as to demand a radical alternative to the present course of human development.

Within our lifetime, then, eco-systemic collapse is not improbable. And it would mean that the species responsible – *Homo sapiens* – had effectively committed suicide. This hardly makes us as sapient as we like to view ourselves. But if we are to avoid further misguided complacency, we will have to engage in some serious critical reflection about the nature of our social and political arrangements, for it seems that the present course of human civilization must be radically altered if we are to have the least confidence in our ability to survive in the long-run as a species. It is the widening recognition of this desperate need for major changes that ultimately explains the nature of the radical political alternatives the green movement has proposed.

All of this has major implications for the future of political theory, for, as William Ophuls writes: 'the radically different conditions today virtually force us to be ecological theorists, grounding our analysis on the basic problems of human survival on a finite and destroyable planet with limited resources.'[77] If we are to address the political, economic, social and ideological causes of the environmental threat we now face, we need a political theory that will indicate which political practices are appropriate for our collective survival. But for that, we would need to understand the basic principles which govern the operation of the ecosphere, as our continued survival is utterly dependent upon it.

1.2 A brief guide to ecological thinking

That an ecological perspective must lie at the heart of any genuine green political theory seems obvious enough. But what, though, is ecology? 'Ecology' as a concept was first employed by Ernst Haeckel in 1868, and it refers to that science which deals with the way in which living organisms interrelate with other species and, more generally, with their environment. By studying the interrelationships between the parts of an ecosystem, ecologists have been able to gain some understanding of the ways in which ecosystems sustain themselves. But this also provides us with some understanding of the ecological problems that have already arisen and those that may soon appear on the horizon.

1.2.1 Commoner's four 'laws' of ecology

What, then, can ecologists tell us about the workings of ecosystems that we would need to take account of in developing a green political theory? Commoner has identified four 'laws' of ecology, none of which we can afford to ignore. The formulations are rather tongue in cheek, but they signify important features of ecosystems.

77 Ophuls, *Ecology and the Politics of Scarcity*, p. 11.

1.2.1.1 'Everything is connected to everything else'

The first 'law' is that everything is connected to everything else. It serves to signify the extent to which the parts of an ecosystem are interrelated, for life-forms are highly interdependent. Plants provide food for herbivorous animals. Herbivorous animals provide food for carnivores. Carnivores die and provide food for saprovores, which in turn provide the nutrients which plants require. At first glance this might seem a rather elementary circle, but the web of life is, in fact, tremendously complex. Moreover, it is the complexity of food chains which, it is argued, enables the self-compensating characteristic of rich ecosystems to work far more smoothly than very simplified ones.

To take an example: In a simple ecosystem where the population of one species of herbivore is kept in check by one species of carnivore, if the herbivore declines significantly in numbers because there are too many carnivores, then many carnivores will starve and their population will quickly decline. If the herbivores, now free of too many predators, begin to multiply rapidly and if the carnivores take a while to reach maturity, then the population of herbivores will explode until the population of carnivores begins to catch up. The process is therefore self-regulating, but because of the time delay caused by the slower maturation of the carnivore, there can be very wide fluctuations in the size of the populations in a very simple ecosystem. And if the herbivores are allowed to become too numerous, because of the time it takes for the population of carnivores to increase, and if they subsequently overgraze the land, then a dramatic collapse of both populations could occur.

Highly complex ecosystems, on the other hand, having a greater variety of species and thus different varieties of checks and balances, contain many more interdependencies (homeostatic mechanisms), which can significantly limit the extent of such fluctuations, and thus can operate much more smoothly. Hence, simplifying ecosystems can make them far less resilient by removing the forces and counterforces which dampen oscillations.[78] And though it is normal for oscillations around a point of balance to occur, too extreme an oscillation can lead to systemic collapse.

Another important ramification of the interdependence which is characteristic of ecosystems is that any damage inflicted on one part can have serious consequences elsewhere. Toxins which are introduced at the bottom of a food chain, for example, can have far more serious consequences higher up, as the concentration of toxins can increase tenfold from one trophic level to the next – a process of bioamplification. Hence, as Commoner summarizes:

> the [eco]system is stabilized by its dynamic self-compensating properties; these same properties, if overstressed, can lead to a dramatic collapse; the

78 It does not seem to be the case that greater diversity always leads to greater stability. However, a significant loss of diversity *is* likely to lead to the wild fluctuations in population size characteristic of the example given above of an ecosystem containing a single herbivore and a single carnivore.

complexity of the ecological network and its intrinsic rate of turnover determine how much it can be stressed, and for how long, without collapsing. . . .[79]

1.2.1.2 'Everything must go somewhere'

The second 'law' is that everything must go somewhere, and it serves to indicate that what is an output from one part of an ecosystem is an input for another part. With the exception of the incoming solar energy which drives the whole system, as it were, everything in an ecosystem is recycled. Recycling processes have been made possible because, as a result of natural selection (which has taken place over millions of years), organisms have evolved which can break down the products of other organisms. Hence, 'in nature there is no such thing as "waste".'[80] Everything that is naturally produced by living organisms can be made use of by some other organism. Thus, ecosystems are maintained by sustainable, cyclical processes. In consequence, as Eugene Odum puts it, 'the earth is *bioregenerative*: plants, animals, and especially micro-organisms regenerate, recycle, and control life's necessities.'[81]

This characteristic of ecosystems, however, means that the continual extraction of outputs from one part of an ecosystem, and their disposal to an inappropriate place, will interfere with the ecosystem's sustainability. For example, one cannot keep harvesting crops and transporting them to cities without returning nutrients to the soil. Nor can one keep dumping those nutrients (in the form of sewage) into lakes, for example, without seriously disrupting their ecosystems. To do so is to run the risk of a continued reduction in the fertility of the soil (which we only partly replenish with inorganic fertilizers) while over-feeding the algae in waterways which, when they die, are decomposed by bacteria that, in the process, can rob the water of oxygen, thus killing the fish – a process of eutrophication. Hence, as Commoner writes:

> One of the chief reasons for the present environmental crisis is that great amounts of materials have been extracted from the earth, converted into new forms, and discharged into the environment without taking into account that 'everything has to go somewhere'. The result, too often, is the accumulation of harmful amounts of material in places where, in nature, they do not belong.[82]

1.2.1.3 'Nature knows best'

The third 'law' is that nature knows best, and it serves to signify that 'any major [hu]man-made change in a natural system is likely to be *detrimental* to that

79 Commoner, *The Closing Circle*, p. 39.
80 Ibid., p. 39.
81 Odum, *Ecology and our Endangered Life-Support Systems*, p. 6.
82 Commoner, *The Closing Circle*, pp. 40–1.

system.'[83] The reason for this is that ecosystems, like watches, are extremely intricate and are unlikely to be improved by random tinkering. Moreover, 'the structure of a present living thing or the organization of a current natural ecosystem is likely to be "best" in the sense that it has been so heavily screened for disadvantageous components that any new one is very likely to be worse than the present ones.'[84] In other words, the individual species and the wider ecosystems that survive are the result of millions of years of screening out harmful mutations, or of developing organisms that can incorporate everything harmlessly into the biosphere. Thus, it can be very damaging suddenly to introduce (especially on a large scale) new substances, such as the products of industry, into an ecosystem, because it might take a very long time for an organism to evolve that can make use of that substance and assimilate it into the food chain, or, if it is a harmful substance, to convert it into a harmless one.[85]

1.2.1.4 'There is no such thing as a free lunch'

Finally, the fourth 'law' is that there is no such thing as a free lunch, and it 'is intended to warn that every gain is won at some cost'.[86] Clearly, we cannot just keep taking forever from nature without respecting the integrity of its ecosystems.[87] The outcome could certainly be ecological collapse. It is by ignoring

83 Ibid., p. 41.

84 Ibid., p. 43. However, as John Passmore argues: 'It is true enough . . . that every human intervention in an ecosystem is likely to disturb the workings of that system in a way that is detrimental to some member of it. So much is true of every change, [hu]man-induced or nature-induced. But it by no means follows, as [Commoner's] "law" might seem to suggest, that every such change, or even most such changes, will be detrimental to *human beings*. Unlike the watches to which he compares them, ecological systems were not designed for [human] use. When [humans] picked seeds off plants and sowed them on a cleared ground, they acted in a way that was detrimental to the organic life which was accustomed to feed on the fallen seeds. But only the most unreconstructed primitivist would suggest that the actions of our agricultural forefathers were destructive of human interests. A nature left entirely alone as "knowing best" would support only the dreariest and most monotonous of lives.' John Passmore, *Man's Responsibility for Nature: Ecological Problems and Western Traditions* (London: Duckworth, 1980), p. 185. On the desirability of an 'anthropogenic sub-climax', which contains less biomass than a climax ecosystem but which can support more humans, see Dryzek, *Rational Ecology*, pp. 44–6. This notwithstanding, as a rule of thumb it is certainly wise to avoid major and sudden alterations to ecosystems because we do depend upon them, and such actions might permanently damage their operation.

85 See Commoner, *The Closing Circle*, pp. 44–5.

86 Ibid., p. 46.

87 This point is all the stronger, given the expanding rate at which we take from nature: 'Since 1950, the need for grain has nearly tripled. Consumption of seafood has increased more than four times. Water use has tripled. Demand for the principal rangeland products, beef and mutton, has also tripled since 1950. Firewood demand has tripled, lumber has more than doubled, and paper has gone up sixfold. The burning of fossil fuels has increased nearly fourfold, and carbon emissions have risen according.' Brown, 'The acceleration of history', p. 4.

these 'laws' of ecology, many environmentalists claim, that we have severely disrupted the very ecosystems upon which we depend.[88] And of course, it is the risk of environmental disaster looming before us that vividly shows the need for an ecologically grounded political theory.

Obviously, the environmental risks adumbrated in Section 1.1, above, would appear to be, at least in part, the result of over-productive economies. But why, exactly, do the nations of the world have such seemingly profligate economies? This is one question that a green political theory needs to answer. Yet most prevalent political ideologies take for granted the need for continued economic growth and are thus unconcerned with this question. In short, the situation we now find ourselves in might be thought to render most political theories of the past *and the present* quite irrelevant as they currently stand. Clearly, the central problem that we face in developing a genuine green political theory is to work out how to situate ecological considerations within a coherent theoretical framework. This might, conceivably, require the formulation of a radically new theoretical approach in so far as virtually all mainstream political theory up to this day completely fails to take ecological consequences, never mind ecological theory, into account.

Thus the immense challenge confronting us – a challenge issuing from the risk of ecological disaster – shows the vital importance of developing an appropriate green political theory. We are forced by the threat of environmental catastrophe to develop a coherent and relevant political theory if we are to understand the deep-seated causes of, what environmentalists consider to be, the present crisis, for that is the first precondition of securing our escape from it. The question is: in order to develop a green political theory, which, if any, of the predominant traditions within the history of social and political thought are we to take as our starting point? In the next chapter, I consider what, at first glance, might appear to be the three most obvious candidates.

88 According to Odum: 'We are able to breath, drink, and eat in comfort because millions of organisms and hundreds of processes are operating in a coordinated manner out there in the environment.' *Ecology and our Endangered Life-Support Systems*, p. 8. Yet '[o]ur global life-support system that provides air, water, food, and power is being stressed by pollution, poor management, and population pressure.' Ibid., p. 1.

2 Three political perspectives

I have suggested that the environmental threat we presently face may render most previous and recent political theory irrelevant. Certainly, a political theory that can both explain the current predicament and offer a way out of it seems now to be of paramount importance. But surely, it will be objected, the mainstream political traditions can easily produce their own ecological variants. The three political perspectives that are most likely to be proposed as offering a potential basis for a green political theory, I presume, are: authoritarianism (in some right-wing manifestation), reformism and Marxism. A fourth – anarchism – will be discussed later. Each has its advocates. So, let me consider in turn the eco-political response each perspective suggests.[1]

2.1 Eco-authoritarianism

Britain, like many countries today, has an intensely authoritarian political culture. If told how great the environmental problems we face actually are, most members of the British public, when asked 'What is needed to respond to this environmental threat?', would probably reply: 'A strong leader.' As the potential of

1 A fifth – eco-feminism – might appear to be a glaring omission. However, to the extent that feminist responses take authoritarian, reformist, Marxist or anarchist forms, each such variety of feminism is subject to the respective analyses that follow. Obviously, this is not to exhaust all varieties of feminism. But while there are clear affinities between the attitudes of many males to women and to nature, as numerous eco-feminists have argued, it is far from certain that political theory can be reduced to explanations in terms of prevalent attitudes. Those attitudes themselves would seem to cry out for a social, economic and/or political explanation. Of course, it goes without saying that a solution to the inequality faced by women is of major importance. But so, too, is a solution to the inequality faced by ethnic minorities. And while racism has played a role in the proliferation of environmental problems (for example, apartheid policies resulted in blacks being forced to live in over-populated 'homelands', which caused environmental degradation in the midst of a relatively resource-abundant, white-controlled South Africa), it is unlikely to be the major explanation of the ecological catastrophe which environmentalists insist lies ahead. I confine my discussion of these important issues to these few cursory remarks because, unfortunately, not everything can be dealt with in one book. And eco-feminism has given birth to its own burgeoning literature.

environmental catastrophe appears to loom ever-larger and closer, the rise of right-wing eco-authoritarianism (even eco-fascism) becomes an ever-greater possibility.[2] And there are the seeds of eco-authoritarianism in the work of numerous environmentalists: for example, William Ophuls' hints at the need for a Hobbesian sovereign,[3] or Robert Heilbroner's demand for 'iron' governments.[4] One particularly extreme, right-wing response to the environmental crises is Garrett Hardin's infamous 'lifeboat ethics', which recommends that many in poorer countries should be left to starve to death so that the populations of those countries fall back to the carrying capacity of their lands. Hardin thus comes particularly close to eco-fascism in opposing both aid to poor countries and any immigration into the affluent nations.[5]

If we are to stand up to such a serious environmental threat as many insist we currently face, and if we need to respond to it quickly, isn't some highly authoritarian, centralized state that can enforce strict environmental policies the obvious solution? At its most attractive, eco-authoritarianism presents itself as a form of benevolent dictatorship – an environmentally benevolent dictatorship, as it were.

Unfortunately, as obvious a solution as eco-authoritarianism appears to be, its flaws seem equally obvious. As with any benevolent dictatorship, how can it be guaranteed that it will remain benevolent? It is difficult to see how whatever structures empower an authoritarian, centralized leadership to exercise power effectively will, at the same time, inhibit exercises of that power which take a non-benevolent form; unless it is the people themselves who constrain such a leadership. But then, why is a leader necessary in the first place? If a leader is necessary, it

2 What has loosely come to be called 'eco-fascism' is, basically, an authoritarian response to the environmental threat which puts one's own nation first. It is a label that applies as much to the New Right as to traditional fascists.

3 See William Ophuls, *Ecology and the Politics of Scarcity: Prologue to a Political Theory of the Steady State* (San Francisco: W. H. Freeman, 1977).

4 See Robert L. Heilbroner, *An Inquiry into the Human Prospect* (London: Calder and Boyars, 1975), especially p. 39.

5 See Garrett Hardin, 'Lifeboat ethics: the case against helping the poor' in William Aiken and Hugh LaFollette (eds), *World Hunger and Moral Obligation* (New Jersey: Prentice-Hall, 1977) and Garrett Hardin, 'Living on a lifeboat' in Jan Narveson (ed.), *Moral Issues* (Toronto: Oxford University Press, 1983). One important fact that Hardin appears to fail to take sufficiently into account is that the carrying capacity of the land is not fixed. Whereas some have objected that the carrying capacity of any region can be raised – see, for example, William Aiken, 'The "carrying capacity" equivocation' in William Aiken and Hugh LaFollette (eds), *World Hunger and Morality* (New Jersey: Prentice-Hall, 1996) – a far more serious objection would appear to be that a region's carrying capacity can be reduced. More specifically, poor people, while desperately trying to survive, frequently degrade their land, often turning it into desert, and deserts have a lower carrying capacity than the land prior to desertification. Hence, leaving the poor without aid, as Hardin advocates, can be argued to lead to a falling carrying capacity and loss of ecological diversity. In short, Hardin's 'solution' would likely exacerbate the problem. For a powerful response to eco-authoritarian 'solutions' to environmental problems, see Michael Taylor, *Anarchy and Cooperation* (London: John Wiley, 1976).

must be because he or she has real power,[6] and how can its exercise be guaranteed to remain benevolent? Even if a particular leader does turn out to be genuinely benevolent, even if he or she is not corrupted by the exercise of power or the need to retain it, how can it be guaranteed that those who inherit his or her position will be equally benevolent? Hierarchical structures, by their very nature, seem to make it easy for the most competitive, most ruthless and least caring to attain power. Moreover, the centralized exercise of authoritarian rule is an ever-attractive goal for would-be usurpers, whose vision is usually less pure than that of those whom they usurp, as the history of many coups can be argued to attest to.

In short, all of the arguments that have been rehearsed against ostensibly benevolent dictatorships appear equally pertinent to environmentally benevolent ones. If an autocrat wished to use his or her power to protect the environment, the structures which enabled that power to be exercised could, presumably, just as easily be used by his or her successors to degrade the planet further, or even at an accelerated rate, for their short-term or localized enjoyment. In fact, there is a powerful argument that can be deployed which seems to establish that *any* authoritarian response to the mounting environmental crises will accelerate them rather than provide a solution. But because of the theoretical assumptions underpinning that argument, it will have to wait until Chapter 6 before being presented, and until Chapter 7 before being deployed against eco-authoritarianism. Suffice it to say that we already have some reason to think that an effective long-term response to the ecological threat which environmentalists claim to have identified would require an alternative political theory to that propounded by eco-authoritarians.

2.2 Eco-reformism

Given the justified fears aroused by unconstrained leadership, even an ostensibly benevolent one, it is not surprising that much of the history of modern political thought, from the seventeenth century to today, has been concerned with the need for checks and balances on the exercise of power. This has led to the advocacy of constraints on any leadership that could implement genuinely radical policies, and to a widespread preference for reformist, piecemeal approaches to social and political change.

Now, reformism generally involves using what are perceived to be legitimate mechanisms within the existing political order. But then, '[t]he central question', as Andrew Dobson poses it, 'is whether a sustainable society can be brought about through the use of existing state institutions.' And in his opinion, that such a society could be so easily brought about is highly improbable, because

> political institutions are not best seen as neutral instruments that can be used by just any operator to achieve just any political ends. Political institutions are

6 For an appropriate view of 'power', see Section 3.3, below.

> always already tainted by precisely those strategies and practices that the green movement, in its radical pretensions, seeks to replace. An instance of this would be the way in which political institutions (in the Western world at least) have come already to embody the principles of representative forms of democracy. These institutions represent the formal abandonment of notions of mass participation in political life; they are indeed 'designed' to *preclude* the possibility of massive regular participation.[7]

And it might be added in support that if those who are the first to experience environmental degradation (usually the poorest members of a community) are excluded from political participation, then the environmental damage that most affects them is likely to go unrestrained.

Moreover, as Dobson maintains: 'political change is a matter of political and economic power. Even if we assume a Green party in government, we are still left with the problem of powerful sources of resistance in other institutions such as the bureaucracy, the financial centres and so on.'[8] Such a concern could easily be dismissed, though, for it might be objected that we all have a shared interest in avoiding environmental harm. In the words of Mary Mellor: 'At a superficial level environmentalism unites people of all political persuasions and levels of privilege.'[9] However, she continues: 'At a more fundamental level the environmental movement is an attack on the underbelly of dominant economic, military and national interests, as the blowing up of Greenpeace's ship *Rainbow Warrior* in Auckland harbour showed.'[10] Clearly, the sinking of the *Rainbow Warrior* by French secret agents in order to prevent Greenpeace from disrupting French nuclear tests in the pacific would seem to demonstrate beyond any reasonable doubt that environmental protection is not valued, and certainly not prioritized, by all state personnel.

Even if governments were to desist from the testing of nuclear weapons and other environmentally hazardous actions, there might still not be a shared interest in ending environmental damage. For example, as Dobson suggests: 'A significant and influential proportion of society . . . has a material interest in prolonging the environmental crisis because there is money to be made from administering it. It is utopian to consider these people to be part of the engine for profound social change.'[11] This point bites hardest when one considers the possible introduction of a 'polluter pays principle' (which is advocated by most green parties). Were a government to introduce such a principle – one that involved taxing those who polluted the environment – a reduction in pollution might then conflict with the

7 Andrew Dobson, *Green Political Thought: An Introduction* (London: Unwin Hyman, 1990), pp. 134–5.

8 Ibid., p. 135.

9 Mary Mellor, *Breaking the Boundaries: Towards a Feminist Green Socialism* (London: Virago Press, 1992), p. 20.

10 Ibid.

11 Dobson, *Green Political Thought*, p. 153.

state's own interests. For any government that received considerable revenue from a tax on polluting activities would have a material interest in that pollution continuing.

Irrespective of these objections to reformist strategies, the extent and nature of the ecological problems which environmentalists insist we face seem to militate against a reliance on gradual tampering with the present system from within. As Jonathon Porritt and David Winner write:

> tackling pollution, acid rain, famine in Africa, the annihilation of the tropical rainforests, nuclear poisoning, the destruction of the ozone layer and all the environmental crises which face us, is going to require solutions a good deal more radical than a spot of reformist tinkering with the self-same industrial system that got us into this mess in the first place. Reformist environmentalism, as practised by single issue pressure groups and advocated by environmentalists in the main political parties, is nowhere near enough. The danger lies not only in the odd maverick polluting factory, industry or technology, but in the fundamental nature of our economic systems.[12]

However, advocates of the free market might try to defend our economic system by claiming that the market is the most efficient method for meeting human needs. But, in response, it can be argued that it doesn't so much meet human needs as create perceived ones. If so, this would mean that market systems inevitably lead to over-consumption. Indeed, a case can be made that capitalism is actually premised upon over-consumption. Capitalism presupposes private property. And according to Marx, when the regime of private property obtains,

> each person speculates on creating a *new* need in the other, with the aim of forcing him to make a new sacrifice, placing him in a new dependence and seducing him into a new kind of *enjoyment* and hence into economic ruin. Each attempts to establish over the other an alien power, in the hope of thereby achieving satisfaction of his own selfish needs. With the mass of objects grows the realm of alien powers to which man is subjected, and each new product is a new *potentiality* of mutual fraud and mutual pillage.[13]

Under the capitalist system, producers have an interest in creating markets for the commodities they produce. This requires, in effect, the enslavement of potential purchasers to a perceived need for those products – or so Marx argues. Advertising, of course, would seem to serve just such a function. Moreover, in order to ensure that markets are not quickly saturated, producers have an interest in

12 Jonathon Porritt and David Winner, *The Coming of the Greens* (London: Fontana, 1988), p. 11.

13 Karl Marx, 'Economic and Philosophical Manuscripts' in *Early Writings*, intro. by Lucio Colletti, trans. Rodney Livingstone and Gregor Benton (Harmondsworth: Penguin, 1975), p. 358.

building obsolescence into their commodities. As Martin Ryle comments: '"long-life goods" are obviously preferable from the point of view of sensible resource use, but built-in obsolescence is preferable from the point of view of capitalist manufacture.'[14] In a world of finite resources and a finite capacity for absorbing pollutants, any such unnecessary production would certainly constitute a major part of the problem.

It can also be argued that limited lifestyle changes are quite inadequate with respect to the immensity of the challenge we face. We would not be able to save the planet simply by consuming greener commodities, for that would still entail far too much consumption. 'Green capitalism' would still involve excessive pollution and resource use, for it remains a variety of capitalism. 'Green producers' would require 'green consumers' and, therefore, would still need to create a perceived need for their products if they are to continue making any profit. *Any* capitalist system, radical critics would insist, leads inevitably to high consumption; and it is high consumption which has caused the environmental crisis, they would claim.

Nevertheless, advocates of the free market could still insist that it meets all needs, perceived or otherwise, better than any other system would. Perceived needs translate into demand, and markets satisfy demand. However, this argument rests on a confusion. It is not demand, but *effective market demand*, that markets meet. Markets only provide the goods that purchasing power demands. Those with little purchasing power can demand what they like, the market will not meet their needs – perceived or real. However, those with tremendous wealth generate a great deal of effective market demand. For example, if the rich would like a golf course in some exotic location, the market perceives a demand for it, while the demand of the poor for land to grow their own crops on is not registered.

So, if a demand arose due to environmental degradation that the market was able to satisfy in principle, it would only be effective market demand that was met, not what was demanded by the poor in genuine need. Consequently, to the extent that environmental harm most affected the poor, there would be little, if any, market response. But the market would respond to, and would continue to respond to, the demand of the wealthy, even if that was the cause of the environmental degradation. It would produce expensive cars for the rich to add to global warming, and ignore the needs of the poor for bore-wells when they then experience increased desertification.

There is, however, a response which is available to defenders of the free market: whatever the rich enjoy today will 'trickle down' to the poor tomorrow.

14 Martin Ryle, *Ecology and Socialism* (London: Radius, 1988), p. 49. To take one example, according to André Gorz: 'The first fluorescent lights put out in 1938 by Philips (Holland) had a lifetime of 10,000 hours. They could "burn" continuously for 14 months. Bad business, decided the Philips management, who, before putting the tubes on the market, carefully reduced the lifetime to 1,000 hours (42 days).' André Gorz, *Ecology as Politics* (London: Pluto, 1980), p. 82.

Unfortunately, this assumption does not hold in the case of 'positional goods'.[15] If, in a market economy, the principal value of education, for example, is that it serves, while few possess it, as a guaranteed passport to better employment, then that particular value cannot be enjoyed when it becomes available to all. A far more important objection to this response, however, is that there is reason to think that whatever 'trickles down' to the mass of people will not be environmentally benign.

Consider F. A. von Hayek's 'echelon advance' theory of economic growth.[16] According to this highly influential theory, rich people are required to provide the demand which acts as a spur to innovation. As the first of a new and innovative range of products will be very expensive to develop and then produce, no innovation would take place, it is argued, unless there were some rich people to buy new and expensive items. Later on, however, the production costs will fall and the innovative product will lower in price and become available to the mass of people – as happened with televisions, personal computers and holidays abroad, to take obvious examples.

But does the assumption that (positional goods aside) what the rich can enjoy today will be available for everyone tomorrow entail that the market will provide an appropriate response to the environmental crises facing us? Unfortunately, it does not. Certainly, a few environmentally-aware rich people might create the requisite initial demand for solar panels, say. But because a small minority of very rich people are not mass consumers, and as it is the sheer volume of polluting activity which constitutes a key feature of the environmental threat, then, while whatever it is that the rich consume is confined to a small number of people, it can be highly polluting or resource-demanding without causing an environmental catastrophe.

In which case, there is reason to believe that the products developed in an economy relying on 'echelon advance' would be far more environmentally damaging than those which would be developed if the aim were, instead, to meet the needs of society as a whole. For example, as the rich can afford 'gas-guzzling' sports cars, and as they could drive them without posing too severe a threat to the ecosphere, such cars will most likely be developed. But what would then 'trickle down' to the rest of society would be a highly polluting and resource-consumptive privatized form of transport, rather than an energy-efficient, public, mass transit system.

However, advocates of the free market might then try to defend our economic system by claiming that the market, if nothing else, is the most effective method for limiting resource use when resources become scarce. Unfortunately, this defence fails to take into account the delayed react-back time of a number of

15 For this objection, see Fred Hirsch, *Social Limits to Growth* (London: Routledge and Kegan Paul, 1977), *passim*.

16 For a concise summary and critique, see Raymond Plant, *Modern Political Thought* (Oxford: Blackwell, 1991), pp. 89–97.

human activities. For example, it is likely that the price of fish will rise when stocks become low. But often the price only rises after damage has been done to the ability of fish stocks to replenish themselves. Given that the consequences of many interventions into delicate ecosystems involve a time-lag, the effects of over-consumption frequently translate into higher prices long after major, and seemingly irreparable, harm has already occurred.

There is a further problem with market mechanisms regarding the delayed effects of environmentally harmful activities, and it concerns the discounting of the future which results from positive interest rates. As John Dryzek explains:

> any investment in the future has an opportunity cost: market rates of interest. Thus, economically rational actors must discount expected future benefits (and costs) by the rate of interest expected to prevail. Any positive rate of interest therefore shortens the time horizon of actors within the marketplace, and of the market as a whole. The higher the rate of interest, the more myopic the system becomes. At a rate of 10 percent, a dollar's worth of benefit or cost expected to be felt in 20 year's time is valued at 15 cents today. The major consequence is that any effects of present choices which will be felt in the moderate to distant future are accorded little weight in market social choices.[17]

This factor will inevitably lead to environmental problems being discounted, so long as their effects are not felt in the immediate future. In short, on this argument, the market will necessarily fail as a mechanism for preserving the integrity of the ecosystem.

It is not surprising, therefore, that radical critics insist that we cannot solve the key problem of high consumption without completely transforming the whole economic system that is based upon it.[18] And in their view, that means, not reform, but something much more revolutionary. Reformists, in relying on a gradualist approach to change, and in choosing to work within the present system, are thereby committed to the acceptance of a continuation of the environmental consequences of the present system – a system relying on market transactions – for however long it takes to transform it gradually. Thus, eco-reformism is only attractive when the environmental threat is presented as being

17 John S. Dryzek, *Rational Ecology: Environment and Political Economy* (Oxford: Blackwell, 1987), p. 74.

18 It is worth noting how much of the present economic system has been taken for granted by the leading liberal theorist, John Rawls, who justifies inequalities on the basis of its presumed benefits: 'The inequality in expectation provides an incentive so that the economy is more efficient, industrial advance proceeds at a quicker pace, and so on, the end result of which is that greater material and other benefits are distributed throughout the system.' John Rawls, 'Distributive justice' in P. Laslett and W. G. Runciman (eds), *Philosophy, Politics and Society: Third Series* (Oxford: Blackwell, 1969), p. 67.

considerably less pressing than the evidence suggests it to be.[19] Suffice it to say, then, that there is reason to think that an effective long-term response to that threat would require an alternative political theory to that of eco-reformism.

2.2.1 An environmentalist critique of private property

The above-mentioned, potentially disastrous, environmental consequences of the market – the expansion of manufactured wants, the production of built-in obsolescence, the satisfaction of ecologically destructive, effective market demand (while ignoring the needs of the poor), the delay in market response to the causes of certain critical environmental harms, and the discounting of future costs – thus appear to undermine a key concept at the heart of reformist liberalism: private property. This is because market exchanges are premised upon private property. Exchanges take place between the owners of commodities. But what could justify such exclusive ownership?

The most famous (and most convincing) attempt at justifying private property is undoubtedly John Locke's. His starting point is the observation that if all the fruits of the earth were held in common and each person needed to ask the permission of everyone else on the planet before consuming anything, we would all starve to death long before that permission was granted. Therefore, there must be some way of consuming goods without obtaining any such permission. Locke's solution is that as long as one does not take so much that it spoils before it can be put to use, and as long as there is 'enough, and as good[,] left in common for others', one may, by means of one's labour, remove things from 'the state of Nature'.[20]

But although this argument might work for a limited quantity of consumables, it is far from clear that it justifies the appropriation of large amounts of private property. There are many ways in which one could make use of items, with the notable exception of food, without making them exclusively one's own. Land could be farmed collectively and it could remain in common, even though the food produced upon it would have to be individually consumed. Works of art do not have to be kept in private collections; they can be displayed in public galleries. Books do not have to be privately owned; they can be kept in public libraries. In such cases, individual use is actually increased by alternatives to private property. Although the consumption of a meal necessarily implies the exclusion of anyone else from consuming it, it is not the case that exclusive use – a central feature of private property – is necessary for all other objects to be used or enjoyed. It is not certain, then, that the necessity of removing food from the common store entails that private property in non-food items is simultaneously justified.

19 It is also worth noting that supposedly environmentalist thinkers as diverse as Robert Paehlke and Boris Frankel downplay the extent of the environmental threat. See Robert C. Paehlke, *Environmentalism and the Future of Progressive Politics* (New Haven: Yale University Press, 1989) and Boris Frankel, *The Post-Industrial Utopians* (Cambridge: Polity, 1987), p. 237.

20 John Locke, 'An essay concerning the true original extent and end of civil government' in *Two Treatises of Government* (London: Dent, 1924), p. 130.

Rather, (what many take to be) the looming environmental crises seem to demonstrate that Locke's 'enough and as good' proviso[21] renders the wider institution of private property unjustifiable.[22] Private property in land has meant that farmers have to sell their products on the market, and if they can only remain profitable by undermining the long-term fertility of their soil, then they will be driven to do so. Moreover, as the land is considered to be their property, they are regarded as having the right to destroy it. But the inevitable outcome would be the inability of future generations to feed themselves. As private property in fertile land would thus prevent future generations from having 'enough and as good' for themselves, the private appropriation of land could not be justified by Locke's argument.[23] In fact, we could go further. If such consequences are indeed likely, the private appropriation of land must be morally wrong. And as all material commodities are, ultimately, extracted from the land, then the whole institution of private property would be indefensible. In short, the predicted environmental crises would mean that one of the core concepts of liberalism – private property – must be rejected.

Certainly, we need to appropriate in order to survive. But if the form that the appropriation takes itself threatens human life – as the institution of private property can thus be argued to – then it cannot be justified. And neither can any political philosophy (such as liberalism) which is premised upon it. In Chapter 1, I suggested that the present environmental crises might render most previous political theory irrelevant. We might now go further: they appear to show it to be philosophically bankrupt.

The predicted environmental crises would not only show eco-reformism to be centrally flawed, but also eco-authoritarianism. One of the most famous arguments in favour of centralized, coercive political institutions is 'the tragedy of the commons', re-introduced into political thought by Garrett Hardin.[24] In Hardin's example, herders graze their cattle on common land. When the number of cattle reaches the carrying capacity of the land, each farmer is argued to reason as

21 Jeremy Waldron denies that Locke insists on any such proviso. See Jeremy Waldron, *The Right to Private Property* (Oxford: Clarendon, 1988), especially p. 215. For a critique of Waldron on this point, see Alan Carter, 'The right to private property', *Philosophical Books*, Vol. 31, No. 3 (July 1990): 129–36.

22 For an extended critique of Locke along similar lines, see Tim Hayward, *Ecological Thought: An Introduction* (Cambridge: Polity, 1995), pp. 130–6.

23 Nozick's defence of private property would appear to fail for similar reasons. He claims that private appropriation is permissible as long as it does not leave others below 'the baseline condition', where the process of civilization would be, for them, a net loss. See Robert Nozick, *Anarchy, State and Utopia* (New York: Basic Books, 1974), pp. 178–9n. Were future generations to starve to death because of the environmental consequences of our private accumulation, the process of civilization would certainly be a net loss. A comprehensive critique of arguments purporting to justify private property can be found in Alan Carter, *The Philosophical Foundations of Property Rights* (Hemel Hempstead: Harvester-Wheatsheaf, 1989).

24 See Garrett Hardin 'The tragedy of the commons' in H. E. Daly (ed.), *Toward a Steady-State Economy* (San Francisco: W. H. Freeman, 1973).

follows: If I add one more cow to the common, it will begin to be slightly overgrazed. That will cause some harm to the common. However, it will be borne by all herders, and each, including myself, will individually pay a smaller cost than the benefit I alone will reap from the extra cow. As every herder reasons in this way, the common is flooded with extra cattle and the land is destroyed, causing disaster for all. What appears to be individually rational is collectively catastrophic. This, it is argued, proves that some coercive apparatus is required in order to prevent the addition of extra cattle.

But the problem only arises in the first place because the cows are privately owned by individuals. In other words, it can be argued that it is the institution of private property which causes the problem. If the cows were not privately owned, then there would be no reason for each herder to want to introduce an extra cow, for the benefit from that cow would not accrue to that individual alone and would not, therefore, outweigh for him or her the cost of putting that cow on common land which is already at its carrying capacity.

Thus, if private property, as defended by reformist liberals and right-wing authoritarians alike, is a cause of environmental problems, then some form of communism would appear to be the only possible solution. Moreover, many would argue, if the free market cannot deal effectively with the environmental challenge before us, then production must be organized according to a common plan. Many environmentally concerned radicals have thus argued, not surprisingly, for Marxist analysis to occupy a far more central location within green political thought.[25] Many argue that capitalism is the cause not only of social and political problems, but of environmental ones, too. And as Marxism claims to present the most powerful critique of capitalism, then it appears at first glance to be the obvious critical tool for radical greens.

Now, the vast majority of us live in capitalist societies. We have a first-hand familiarity with their workings, which provides us with considerable detailed knowledge. However, in general, the details of Marxist theory are far less well-known. Moreover, now that Marxist regimes have collapsed in Eastern Europe, many Marxists have turned their attention to the green movement. They have joined existing environmental organizations, set up their own, and produced theoretical analyses of the environmental threat, written from a Marxist standpoint. As to whether or not this is to be welcomed as an improvement in the level of analysis of green political thought or to be condemned as ideological infiltration merits careful consideration. Hence, for both of these reasons, in the remainder of this chapter I shall look at Marxism in some detail, as more and more are coming to take it very seriously as a possible grounding for a radical green political theory.

25 This plea has itself resulted in criticism of *Die Grünen*, in particular. See, for example, Charlene Spretnak and Fritjof Capra, *Green Politics* (London: Paladin, 1985).

2.3 Marxism as a basis for green political theory

Well, does Marxism provide an appropriate grounding for a green political theory? To answer this question we shall have to consider both Marxist theory and its practice. Historically, the most common Marxist practice has been some variety of Leninism. But before we look at the recommendations and experience of Vladimir Ilich Lenin, we first need to consider Karl Marx's theory of revolutionary transition and how his notion of class struggle fits into it.

2.3.1 Marx and the problem of class struggle

In his 'Preface to the critique of political economy' (the famous '1859 Preface'), Marx appears to present a theory of history which claims that a revolutionary transition from one epoch to another occurs because the forces of production (basically, technology) are prevented from further development[26] (or, perhaps, to be consistent with a transition to post-capitalism, from more efficient use). And this is, supposedly, because the prevailing set of relations of production (in other words, the economic structure of society, which could comprise, for example, master/slave, lord/serf or bourgeois/proletarian relations) has become a constraint on any further technological development (or, perhaps, on the optimal use of the currently available technology). At this stage, a revolution occurs which involves the introduction of new economic relations more appropriate to further technological development (or, perhaps, to more efficient use of technology). For example, according to the theory, when feudalism inhibits technological development and capitalism would further it, a revolution which brings in capitalist economic relations should occur, or when capitalism prevents the rational use of technology (because, being crisis-prone, it periodically forces factories to close down and throws workers into unemployment) whereas communism would, ostensibly, better employ the forces of production within a common plan, a revolution which brings in communist relations should occur.

However, according to 'The Communist Manifesto', revolution occurs because a subordinate class has grown in sufficient strength to enable it successfully to overthrow the 'ruling class'. How is this to be reconciled with the account given in the '1859 Preface', which explains revolution by reference to technological development?

The most plausible answer would seem to be that the ascendancy of different classes is tied to different stages of technological development. As technology develops, new classes arise and come into prominence as a result of this development. Moreover, it is clear that different classes benefit from different economic relations. Therefore, the transformation of the existing economic relations is accomplished when one of the classes engaged in class struggle is victorious,

26 See Karl Marx, 'Preface to the critique of political economy' in *Selected Writings*, ed. David McLellan (Oxford: Oxford University Press, 1977), p. 389.

overthrows the previously dominant class, and thus changes the economic relations to ones more suited to its own class dominance.

But for this to be fully consistent with what Marx writes in the '1859 Preface', the new economic relations which suit the new dominant class must be more appropriate than the old ones to furthering technological development (or, perhaps, to the optimal use of the available technology). In short, the claims made in the '1859 Preface' and those made in 'The Communist Manifesto' are consistent when the rise to power of a new class is appropriate to further technological development (or, perhaps, to the optimal use of technology). If Marx is correct, the rise to power of a class is, therefore, tied to technological development.

One immediate problem that this poses for greens is that if it is, in fact, the further development of the productive forces that new dominant classes are especially suited to, then we should expect the worst, for it is unrestrained technological development that, many environmentalists would argue, has brought us to the brink of ecological disaster. On the other hand, if it is the optimal use of the technology previously developed that new dominant classes are especially suited to, then greater use of the environmentally damaging technology that we have already developed seems just as bad. And yet Marx viewed favourably this process where classes would rise to ascendancy on the basis of their appropriateness to the further development, or optimal use, of the productive forces, for he saw capitalism as developing the material preconditions for an abundant communism, which the proletariat would then be able to benefit from.

Let us, then, see how such a process of class ascendancy could be described: With the growth of machinery and the corresponding increase in commodity production, the bourgeoisie – the capitalist class – rose in economic significance. However, the feudal economic system, which benefited the nobility, hindered the development of technology. As capitalist relations demand that the owners of the productive forces continually develop them so as to remain competitive, and as this is not true of feudal relations (which, rather, tend to impede development), capitalist relations are more suited than feudal ones to technological development. The bourgeoisie ultimately triumphed over the nobility and capitalist relations thus replaced feudal ones.

Marx argues, however, that capitalist economic relations will, ultimately, limit further technological development (or, perhaps, the optimal use of technology) because they give rise to periodic economic crises of increasing severity, which lead to productive forces standing idle or even being destroyed. This, in Marx's view, can only be overcome by replacing capitalist or market relations with communist ones. In other words, capitalism, too, comes to restrain technological development (or prevents the optimal use of technology), and this supposedly entails the ultimate triumph of the proletariat – and by 'proletariat' Marx usually means the industrial working class.

So, we are presented with an account of history where three major classes (the nobility, the bourgeoisie and a class comprising the serfs and incipient proletariat) reduce to two (the bourgeoisie and the proletariat) after the bourgeoisie triumphs in its struggle with the nobility. These two classes reduce to one (the proletariat) after the proletariat triumphs in its struggle with the bourgeoisie (though with only workers remaining, strictly speaking, they no longer constitute a class). Here is a clear historical pattern: three classes reduce to two, which then reduce to one.

But if we go slightly further back in time, we find that there were two major classes – the nobility and the serfs – and between them *emerged* the bourgeoisie, which later became dominant after a contest with the nobility. This left two classes – the bourgeoisie and the proletariat (the latter being what the class of serfs was transformed into). Why, though, given this pattern of an emerging middle class eventually becoming the dominant class, is it obvious that the two remaining classes must reduce to one? Why cannot this pattern be repeated? In other words, instead of three classes reducing to two and then to one, why, after the three classes have reduced to two, cannot a new class emerge between the two remaining classes, just as before, and then later achieve a position of dominance after overthrowing the second dominant class? And why cannot this pattern be reproduced again and again? Instead of a 3:2:1 progression in the number of classes, we could have a progression which goes 2:3:2:3, perhaps *ad infinitum*. If Marxists are to be justifiably confident in their expectations concerning an egalitarian post-capitalist society, they must be able to demonstrate that such a pattern will not be repeated.

What all of this means is that a new class might arise between the bourgeoisie and the proletariat, and if it were then to defeat the bourgeoisie, it would become the new dominant class. But what might such an emerging class look like? To be consistent with Marx's theory of revolutionary transformation, its emergence and rise in importance would have to be tied to technological development. Interestingly, Marx, apparently without realizing it, shows us in Chapter 14 of *Capital* and in 'The immediate results of the process of production' where such a potentially new dominant class might arise from.

In order to increase efficiency, the capitalist has divided the production of commodities into a series of detailed operations. Following Charles Babbage, Marx notes that it is cheaper to limit the number of skilled workers by employing them solely in skilled work than it is to have every worker capable of carrying out every single operation and all having to be equally skilled. As Marx writes of the capitalist labour process: 'there appears the simple separation of the workers into skilled and unskilled.'[27] One skill which some wage-earners acquire is the ability to design new technology required in order for the factory to remain competitive; another is the ability to organize other wage-earners in the most efficient way. This means that 'manufacture proper not only subjects the previously independent worker to the discipline and command of capital, but creates in addition a hierarchical structure amongst the workers themselves.'[28] Thus, a process of differentiation occurs within the class of wage-earners leading to a situation where, in Marx's words, 'some work better with their hands, others with their heads, one

27 Karl Marx, *Capital*, Vol. I, trans. B. Fowkes (Harmondsworth: Penguin, 1976), p. 470.
28 Ibid., p. 481.

as a manager, engineer, technologist, etc., the other as overseer, the third as manual labourer or even drudge.'[29]

Why, one might ask, can't this emerging group of managers, engineers, technologists and overseers constitute a new class? One thing seems clear: if it does constitute a new class, then its emergence is tied to technological development. Can we, then, identify this group as a class? Nicos Poulantzas has provided perhaps the most famous Marxist attempt to theorize a middle class situated between capitalists and proletarians. Poulantzas offers three criteria by which to isolate a class which he refers to as 'the new petty bourgeoisie'. And these three criteria identify managers (though Poulantzas would regard some as being within the actual bourgeoisie), engineers, technologists and overseers as being new petty bourgeois.

However, for Marx, the petty bourgeoisie is a class which does not grow in importance with capitalist development, and will, rather, tend to disappear as capitalist relations and industry advance. As it appears to be the case that the new petty bourgeoisie does grow in importance with such development, then 'petty bourgeoisie' seems an inappropriate component of the term. The term, as it stands, tends to suggest that it refers to an historically irrelevant class which just happens to find itself situated between the bourgeoisie and the proletariat. In order to avoid giving the impression that such an emerging class in advanced capitalism is historically irrelevant, and in order to indicate both its technocratic ('engineers and technologists') and bureaucratic ('managers and overseers') fractions, the term 'techno-bureaucracy' would seem more appropriate, and hence I shall adopt it in preference to Poulantzas' term 'new petty bourgeoisie'. This said, what are Poulantzas' criteria for delimiting this new, techno-bureaucratic class?

The first criterion is non-productive, as opposed to productive, labour. According to Poulantzas, one must produce surplus-value to be a proletarian. Given that this criterion, as it stands, is inseparable from Marx's labour theory of value, and given the lack of unanimity concerning the viability of this theory (even some leading Marxist theorists have rejected it), then the first criterion would be less problematic were its phrasing independent of Marx's disputed theory of value.

To take one possible alternative, following John Roemer we might, instead, consider a proletarian to be one who, in capitalism, cannot 'possibly command, through his [or her] purchase of goods, labour value equal to his [or her] contributed labour'.[30] Though 'labour value' is mentioned here, it is not presupposed that value is measured in terms of the quantity of socially necessary labour-time 'congealed' in a commodity, as it is for Marx. Roemer, in fact, sees the need for a definition of 'labour value' which, instead, 'renders values dependent on prices'.[31] On such an approach, all we need accept is that members of the techno-

29 Karl Marx, 'The results of the immediate process of production', appended to *Capital*, Vol. I, p. 1040.

30 John Roemer, 'New directions in the Marxian theory of exploitation and class', in John Roemer (ed.), *Analytical Marxism* (Cambridge: Cambridge University Press, 1986), p. 96.

31 John Roemer, *A General Theory of Exploitation and Class* (Massachusetts: Harvard University Press, 1982), p. 18.

bureaucracy, as well as the bourgeoisie, consume a greater value of products than they themselves produce. Or, in other words, the techno-bureaucracy lives off the surplus product of the true proletariat.

The second criterion is supervisory, as opposed to non-supervisory, labour. In the capitalist mode of production, supervisors aid the bourgeoisie in extracting the surplus product from the proletariat. In reward for carrying out this function, they are paid with a portion of that extracted surplus product. And one important aspect of supervisory labour is that it appears to lead to the workers having such a familiarity with subordination that it seems natural that they cannot organize themselves.[32]

The third criterion is mental, as opposed to manual, labour. And this is important because, as Poulantzas observes:

> The division of mental and manual labour . . . is . . . directly bound up with the monopolization of knowledge, the capitalist form of appropriation of scientific discoveries and of the reproduction of ideological relations of domination/subordination, by the permanent exclusion on the subordinated side of those who are deemed not to 'know how'.[33]

By means of these three criteria, true proletarians can be effectively distinguished from what I have chosen to call 'the techno-bureaucracy'. But then, the question that all this provokes is: Why cannot this new class, emerging *pari passu* with the advanced development of the forces of production in capitalism, eventually replace the bourgeoisie as the dominant class? It might be asked, why should it wish to do so when it is already relatively privileged within the capitalist mode of production? But one simple answer that can be offered is: For the same reasons that motivated the bourgeoisie to overthrow feudalism. In other words, so that its economic position would be less constrained (the techno-bureaucracy could easily claim that it could organize production better were it not for the vagaries of capitalist investors) and so that it would be even more privileged.

As the skilled techno-bureaucracy can plausibly claim that, were it to rise to power, it could organize production better than capitalists, then its victory over the bourgeoisie would be compatible with the Marxist claim that 'the class which rules through a period, or emerges triumphant after epochal conflict, is the class best suited, most able and disposed, to preside over the development of the productive forces at the given time'.[34] How, therefore, can Marx simply conclude that the future will be one where the proletariat has proved victorious in its struggle with the bourgeoisie? Such a conclusion seems unjustified, for the future could conceivably be one where the techno-bureaucracy has proved victorious.

32 See Erik Olin Wright, *Class, Crisis and the State* (London: New Left Books, 1978), p. 38.
33 Nicos Poulantzas, *Classes in Contemporary Capitalism* (London: Verso, 1978), p. 237.
34 G. A. Cohen, *Karl Marx's Theory of History: A Defence* (Oxford: Clarendon Press, 1978), p. 149.

And if a society dominated by the techno-bureaucracy and characterizable as a techno-bureaucratic mode of production is a future possibility, how can Marx justifiably claim that the 'bourgeois relations of production are the last antagonistic form of the social process of production'?[35] In a techno-bureaucratic mode of production the techno-bureaucracy would continue to enjoy the surplus product of the proletariat. Thus, techno-bureaucratic relations of production would be 'antagonistic' ones.

It would appear that Marx has four major reasons for assuming a proletarian victory. The first concerns economic crises in capitalism; the second concerns technological development; the third concerns the immiseration of the proletariat; and the fourth concerns the concentration of the proletariat. In order to ascertain whether or not Marx's conclusion is compelling, allow me to examine each of these in turn.

2.3.1.1 *Economic crises in capitalism*

According to Marx, the solution to economic crises is to replace the capitalist mode of production with a non-competitive mode. But why must a new mode of production which provides a solution to capitalist crises necessarily involve the triumph of the proletariat? Surely a mode of production in which the techno-bureaucracy were dominant could provide a solution to crises induced by competition? If a planned economy is the answer, as Marx assumes, surely it could as easily be planned by managers, engineers, technologists and overseers as by genuine proletarians? In fact, it could be argued that the techno-bureaucracy would probably be better suited than genuine proletarians to organizing a planned economy. And were the techno-bureaucracy in control of production, it is not difficult to imagine that they would be in a position to extract the surplus product of the proletariat. Thus, a need to avoid economic crises endemic to capitalism does not entail the triumph of the proletariat.

2.3.1.2 *The development of the productive forces*

Perhaps it is the inability of capitalism to further (or, perhaps, make the most efficient use of) technological development which demands the triumph of the proletariat? But if it were the case that capitalism no longer aided the optimal *development* of technology, surely it is engineers and technologists who are most likely to play a crucial role in any development of the productive forces, rather than the genuine proletariat? Surely it is the techno-bureaucracy which holds the required technical knowledge? On the other hand, if it is the most efficient *use* of the available technology which is significant, it is, again, the techno-bureaucracy which seems to provide the solution. Surely it is the managers and overseers – those who apply, for example, time and motion studies, and who have the greatest

35 Marx, 'Preface to the critique of political economy', p. 390.

knowledge of the organization of labour – who are the ones most able to ensure the most efficient use of the productive forces (at least in so far as the notion of 'efficiency' is commonly construed)?

2.3.1.3 *The immiseration of the proletariat*

A plausible reason, at least *prima facie*, for the triumph of the proletariat is that capitalism reduces the condition of the proletariat to one of increasing poverty.[36] The proletariat is thus *forced* to overthrow the bourgeoisie. But will it in fact do so? Some social psychologists have argued that the ever-increasing immiseration of the western proletariat is more likely to lead to ever-greater despair, than to revolutionary activity: witness the lack of militancy amongst the most hard-up in North America during the 1930s.

Moreover, were the proletariat forced to overthrow the bourgeoisie, would they necessarily do so in a manner that ensured a proletarian victory? The techno-bureaucracy could easily claim: 'Support us in our struggle with the capitalists, allow us to manage the economy without the capricious behaviour of bourgeois investors, and we will see to it that all poverty is eradicated.' And the proletariat might, conceivably, be misled into supporting the rise to power of the techno-bureaucracy in something like the manner in which it was led, so the story goes, into supporting the bourgeoisie when it announced: 'Support us in our struggle with the feudal nobility and everyone will be equal before the law, and, as a result, far better off.' If the proletariat backed or even just allowed the rise to power of the bourgeoisie, why assume it would resist the rise to power of the techno-bureaucracy? Besides, it would appear that by 1849 Marx had abandoned his absolute immiseration thesis.[37]

2.3.1.4 *The concentration of the proletariat*

Proletarians are geographically concentrated into, especially, factories, and they are linked together by means of a highly connected market, which is responsible for meeting their needs. But bringing proletarians together into a factory does not necessarily reveal that they have a common interest in overthrowing the bourgeoisie. For one thing, as Marx's discussion in *Capital* of commodity fetishism implies, capitalist relations of production are especially mystifying. What the concentration of proletarians into a factory and their linking together in a market economy might instead reveal to them is that they have a common interest against the unemployed who are competing for their jobs in a labour market, and against

36 See Karl Marx and Friedrich Engels, 'The Communist Manifesto' in Karl Marx, *Selected Writings*, ed. David McLellan (Oxford: Oxford University Press, 1977), p. 230.

37 Compare Marx's reliance on relative immiseration in 'Wage-labour and capital', published in 1849, with his use of absolute immiseration in 'The Communist Manifesto'. See Karl Marx, 'Wage-labour and capital' in *Selected Writings*, ed. David McLellan (Oxford: Oxford University Press, 1977), p. 259.

those in other factories whose rival products threaten their livelihood. The concentration of proletarians into one place of work might also reveal to them that they have a common interest in attracting investment to their factory, rather than to anyone else's. Certainly, proletarians *might* perceive a class interest vis-à-vis the bourgeoisie. But they might well perceive a more parochial interest, instead. So, again, we are not given a cogent reason for expecting the triumph of the proletariat.

2.3.2 Lenin and revolutionary practice

However, all is not lost. It is something like this last problem which Lenin primarily attempts to solve in *What is to be Done?* (written in 1902). He argues that the proletariat on its own will only develop a trade union consciousness which, if it engages in struggle with the bourgeoisie, is restricted to such things as wage demands. If the proletariat is to develop a revolutionary consciousness, then it must be aided in attaining that consciousness. Where is the help to come from? 'Proletarian' theory and organization must, according to Lenin, be introduced into the proletariat from without. Help must come from bourgeois intellectuals who align themselves with the proletariat and provide the revolutionary theory and perspective needed to transform society.[38] Help must also come from the Party – an institution created by those intellectuals to organize the proletariat[39] – which will appoint 'bodies of leaders for each urban district, for each factory district and for each educational institution, etc.'.[40] And concerning their 'professionalism', Lenin adds that they 'would become accustomed to being maintained entirely by the Party, would become professional revolutionaries and would train themselves to be real political leaders'.[41]

As the Party does not engage in actual material production, we can observe three features of the Party activists as they are described by Lenin:

(a) they live off the surplus product of the proletariat;
(b) they engage in supervisory activity; and
(c) they engage in mental labour and possess a privileged access to knowledge.

In short, in terms of the production of a new society, and in contrast with the genuine proletariat which will be employed to overthrow the capitalist class, Party members could be viewed as satisfying all three of Poulantzas' criteria for inclusion within what he calls 'the new petty bourgeoisie' or what I have preferred to label 'the techno-bureaucracy'.

It is not all that surprising, therefore, that post-revolutionary Russia should

38 See V. I. Lenin, *What Is to Be Done?* (Peking: Foreign Languages Press, 1975), p. 47.
39 See ibid., pp. 105–6.
40 Ibid., pp. 154–5.
41 Ibid., pp. 209–10.

have turned into a social formation easily characterizable as a techno-bureaucratic mode of production dominated by the techno-bureaucracy. Such an outcome comes as far less of a surprise when the very organization of revolutionary practice[42] is seen to be characterizable as embodying techno-bureaucratic relations. But any such outcome was inconceivable to the Bolsheviks because, at the time, they denied the very possibility of the techno-bureaucracy forming a class and producing its own corresponding ideology.[43] In short, the former Soviet Union can be viewed not as a 'contradiction' between socialism and capitalism,[44] but as a techno-bureaucratic mode of production – moreover, a techno-bureaucratic mode of production which had been brought into being as a result of Lenin's techno-bureaucratic political practice.

So, instead of Lenin providing the means for a proletarian victory over the bourgeoisie, his strategy, as it is espoused in *What Is to Be Done?*, can be viewed as providing the basis for a techno-bureaucratic triumph. On such an interpretation, rather than leading the proletariat to victory, Lenin's strategy would involve the proletariat remaining in a subordinate position, but this time one where it was subordinated to its new, techno-bureaucratic masters. Given that, at best, this would involve the proletariat being subject to those who, an eco-Marxist might hope, would proceed to organize society in an ecologically benign way, then this whole approach seems to reduce in important respects to a left-wing variant of eco-authoritarianism, subject to several of the criticisms which can be levelled against right-wing variants.

Any such interpretation of Leninism as a form of techno-bureaucratic practice would, of course, be a highly controversial one. So, is there any justification for it? What was Lenin's actual practice upon assuming power in Russia? According to Lenin: 'In every socialist revolution . . . there necessarily comes to the forefront the fundamental task of creating a social system superior to capitalism, namely, raising the productivity of labour, and in this connection (and for this purpose) securing better organization of labour.'[45] But many environmentalists would claim that it is the raising of labour productivity that has played such a central role

42 It should be noted that *What Is to Be Done?* is not the most centralist or dictatorial of Lenin's early writings. *One Step Forward, Two Steps Back* is more extreme. This work, written in 1904, also undermines a common defence of *What Is to Be Done?* – namely, that it describes the specific form the Party had to take in Russia alone because of the special conditions which prevailed there (such as the difficulty the Tsarist police posed to organizing a political party while in exile). But in *One Step Forward, Two Steps Back*, Lenin praised the highly centralized form taken by the German Social Democratic Party, which did not face the restrictions that the Russian Party experienced. Yet Lenin supported the same organizational form in both cases. See V. I. Lenin, *One Step Forward, Two Steps Back: The Crisis in Our Party* (Peking: Foreign Languages Press, 1976), especially pp. 260–3.

43 See Lenin, *What Is to Be Done?*, p. 48.

44 This is the interpretation offered in Leon Trotsky, *The Revolution Betrayed* (New York: Pathfinder, 1972), p. 244.

45 V. I. Lenin, *The Immediate Tasks of the Soviet Government* (Moscow: Progress Publishers, 1970), p. 22.

in precipitating the environmental crises. This notwithstanding, how is this better organization of labour to be achieved? As Lenin pronounces: 'We must raise the question of piece-work and apply and test it in practice; we must raise the question of applying much of what is scientific and progressive in the Taylor system'.[46] But who is to apply this scientific work organization? Surely, in practice, it would be the techno-bureaucracy.

However, Lenin, in *The State and Revolution* (which was written in 1917), indicates that certain restrictions would be placed upon the leaders of labour in order to prevent them from becoming bureaucrats: they would be elected and subject to immediate recall; their pay would not exceed that of an ordinary worker; and universal accounting procedures would be introduced to enable everyone to check the books. But are these restrictions sufficient, or even feasible, given the demand for increased productivity? If techno-bureaucratic organizers are put in charge of the production process and the organization of labour, and if incentives are to be introduced (as Lenin's remarks on piece-work suggest), who is to stop the organizers raising their own incomes? And are such skilled organizers in fact recallable? In 1918, Lenin admitted that he was forced 'to resort to the old bourgeois method and to agree to pay a very high price for the "services" of the top bourgeois experts'.[47]

It would appear from this admission that Lenin did not wish to give preferential treatment to the techno-bureaucracy, but was forced to do so. A common defence of Lenin claims that he had to introduce inegalitarian measures because of the backward nature of Russia. But Lenin claims that in *every* socialist revolution the productivity of labour must be raised. In which case, securing the services of the techno-bureaucracy cannot simply be a problem which is confined to an *undeveloped* economy. If highly productive labour is to be further developed, or at least retained, then the 'best organizers and top experts' must also be necessary for a *developed* industrial society. What is more, the inefficiency of capitalism is not, supposedly, due to its techno-bureaucratic managers, engineers, technologists and overseers, but to capitalist relations of production. Consequently, it can be argued that the preservation of the techno-bureaucracy in the former Soviet Union cannot be blamed on the backward nature of Russia at the time of the 1917 Revolution. It seems, instead, to be inextricably linked to the Marxist claim that socialism can only be built upon the highest levels of productivity. And here we can clearly see how fundamentally unsuitable Marxism/Leninism appears to be as a basis for a genuinely green political theory.[48]

What, though, would the actual role of the proletariat be after the seizure of power by the Party vanguard? Lenin replies: 'To *unquestioningly obey the single*

46 Ibid., pp. 23–4.

47 Ibid., p. 14.

48 As Lenin writes: 'Without the guidance of experts in the various fields of knowledge, technology and experience, the transition to socialism will be impossible, because socialism calls for a conscious mass advance to greater productivity of labour compared with capitalism, and on the basis achieved by capitalism.' Ibid., pp. 13–14.

will of the leaders of labour.'[49] If so, as Lenin asks, 'how can strict unity of will be ensured?' And his reply? 'By thousands subordinating their will to the will of one'.[50] This hardly seems consistent with the libertarian interpretation of Lenin which is based upon *The State and Revolution*. Moreover, it is likely to attract all of the criticisms which eco-authoritarianism invites.

So, what of the libertarian interpretation of Lenin? Was Lenin authoritarian at the time of writing *What Is to Be Done?*, and became libertarian later? Commentators such as Neil Harding, for example, stress Lenin's remarks which suggest that the proletariat will use its initiative, as well as stressing his focus upon Marx's claim that the Paris Commune would provide the model for 'even the smallest hamlet'.[51] This focus, Harding claims, proves that Lenin was a decentralist in 1917. As Harding writes: 'Marx's whole conception of the commune form was . . . extremely decentralist, even the smallest country hamlet was to organize itself as an autonomous unit'.[52]

But Harding, like others who regard Lenin as a libertarian, ignores his insistence that Marx 'purposely emphasized the fact that the charge that the [Paris] Commune wanted to destroy the unity of the nation, to abolish central authority, was a deliberate fake'.[53] How libertarian or decentralist is Lenin when he insists that 'central authority' is to be retained?

Libertarianism,[54] one would assume, is not to be measured in terms of the degree to which a central committee is willing to allow the proletariat to act on its own initiative if it is also presumed by those at the centre that proletarian actions will always be consistent with central directives. Had Jews voluntarily flung themselves into gas-chambers, the Nazi State would, surely, not have been more libertarian as a result. Surely, then, whether or not one is libertarian depends not on allowing initiative which fits in with one's directives, but *inter alia* on the manner in which one treats potential dissent. When Lenin does approve of local initiative, we find him adding: 'providing, of course, that it does not turn into eccentricity'.[55] But who is to judge what constitutes 'eccentricity'? If it is Lenin, then it is not clear that he was, in fact, genuinely libertarian.

So, how libertarian was Lenin? In 1918, we find him writing that '*unquestioning subordination* to a single will is absolutely necessary for the success of

49 Ibid., p. 33.

50 Ibid., p. 34.

51 Karl Marx, 'The Civil War in France' in *The First International and After* (Harmondsworth: Penguin, 1974), p. 210.

52 Neil Harding, *Lenin's Political Thought: Theory and Practice in the Socialist Revolution* (London: Macmillan, 1981), p. 122.

53 V. I. Lenin, *The State and Revolution* (Peking: Foreign Languages Press, 1973), p. 63

54 The term 'libertarian' was first introduced by anarchists in order to describe their own views when they were prevented from discussing anarchism in the press. My use of the term 'libertarianism' follows this original meaning, and it should not be confused with the right-wing economic libertarianism associated with the likes of Robert Nozick, who have usurped the term for their own purposes.

55 Quoted in Harding, *Lenin's Political Thought*, p. 175.

processes organized on the pattern of large-scale machine industry',[56] and this 'may assume the sharp forms of a dictatorship if ideal discipline and class-consciousness are lacking'.[57] Here, Lenin can hardly be attributing the lack of an ideal class-consciousness to the bourgeoisie. Consequently, he appears to be explicitly acknowledging the possibility of a dictatorship over the proletariat. These remarks are, in fact, consistent with his writings of the previous year if, at that time, Lenin believed that a proletariat which had attained a revolutionary class-consciousness would voluntarily subordinate itself to central directives, and that its initiatives would be compatible with those directives. Yet such a position would, surely, be neither genuinely libertarian, nor realistic.

But was this Lenin's view? Whilst the proletariat supported him, he was happy to regard it as having attained a revolutionary proletarian consciousness. However, when the proletariat began to object to Lenin's increasingly authoritarian measures, it did so by making, what Lenin described as, 'anarchist' and 'syndicalist' demands. What this revealed to Lenin was that the proletariat had, in the course of the Revolution, become 'declassed'.[58]

Thus, it seems that, for Lenin, to have a 'proletarian' consciousness is to choose to subordinate oneself to the Party. When one no longer accepts such subordination, then one is no longer proletarian.[59] There is, however, an alternative interpretation of what it is to be proletarian. Lenin was supported by the proletariat when he proclaimed 'All Power to the Soviets'. Yet this slogan is consistent with anarchism. Rather than the proletariat becoming de-classed and then, as a result, anarchist, perhaps it was always in essence anarchist? Perhaps a genuine revolutionary proletarian consciousness is, in fact, an anarchist one? If so, Lenin could believe that his position was proletarian because, initially, the proletariat backed him when he was not overtly distinguishable from an anarchist or a syndicalist. But when he became clearly distinguishable from an anarchist or a syndicalist, the proletariat made distinctly anarchist and syndicalist demands.

It can be argued, therefore, that Lenin, partly because he was first backed by the proletariat, believed his position to be genuinely proletarian when it was, in actual fact, techno-bureaucratic. Consequently, he projected onto the proletariat his own techno-bureaucratic ideology. And by assuming this to be 'proletarian', when the proletariat began to reject Lenin's position, he could no longer consider them to be proletarian. But whether or not this analysis is correct, what we clearly see is that Lenin appeared to have no time for initiative by proletarians which fell outside his scheme of things. In other words, it is difficult to conclude that Lenin was genuinely libertarian. Consequently, it is not difficult to claim that, because of Lenin's approach, the Party adopted and then retained an exploitative, supervisory role, which was ostensibly justified by its privileged access to revolutionary theory.

56 Lenin, *The Immediate Tasks of the Soviet Government*, p. 33.
57 Ibid.
58 See Harding, *Lenin's Political Thought*, pp. 278–9.
59 See ibid., p. 278.

Lenin's actual practice was, as he himself admits, 'to build up and successfully maintain the strictest centralization and iron discipline'.[60] In industry, this involved replacing the factory committees, which the workers had set up themselves, with 'one-man management'. It is not difficult to argue, therefore, that the final result of Lenin's actual practice was the consolidation of a techno-bureaucratic society in the former Soviet Union.

Let me conclude this section by positing four (what to Marxists will appear) heretical claims which the above discussion suggests: First, Lenin was neither a bourgeois intellectual nor a proletarian; rather he was a member of the techno-bureaucracy (or, in Poulantzas' terminology, new petty bourgeoisie).[61] Second, far from being genuinely proletarian, the Marxist/Leninist Party is a techno-bureaucratic organization. Third, its practice is and was techno-bureaucratic. And fourth, its theory – Marxism/Leninism – is not proletarian science, but, in actual fact, techno-bureaucratic theory – a theory designed to put into control of the economic forces a class that can most effectively increase production.[62] Clearly, if there is any justification for this fourth claim, then Marxism/Leninism is especially unsuitable as a grounding for a genuinely green political theory.

This raises a key question. Is this possible criticism just limited to Lenin and his practice, or is it also applicable to Marx? Well, consider Marx's attitude to agriculture:

> What we require is a daily increasing production and its exigencies cannot be met by allowing a few individuals to regulate it according to their whims and private interest, or to ignorantly exhaust the powers of the soil. All modern methods, such as irrigation, drainage, steam ploughing, chemical treatment and so forth, ought to be applied to agriculture at large. But the scientific knowledge we possess, and the technical means of agriculture we command, such as machinery, etc., can never be successfully applied but by cultivating the land on a large scale.[63]

60 V. I. Lenin, *Left-Wing Communism, An Infantile Disorder* (Peking: Foreign Languages Press, 1975), p. 7.

61 And in terms of family background, so were Lukács, Gramsci, and many other leading Marxists. So, too, was Marx. Engels, however, was quite different. To revert to Poulantzas' terminology, there was nothing 'petty' about Engels' bourgeois credentials.

62 Although I have relied on Poulantzas' criteria for delimiting a rising middle class, the above argument could just as easily have been based on John Roemer's theorization. See Roemer, *A General Theory of Exploitation and Class*. It seems to me that any realistic Marxist approach that can identify a rising middle class will be subject to this argument, and any version of Marxism that cannot identify a rising middle class is not worth considering.

63 Karl Marx, 'The nationalization of the land' in Karl Marx and Frederick Engels, *Selected Works in Three Volumes*, Vol. II (Moscow: Progress Publishers, 1969), pp. 288–9. Engels' view was similar. As he declares: 'The productivity of the land can be *infinitely* increased by the application of capital, labour and science.' Quoted in John Passmore, *Man's Responsibility for Nature: Ecological Problems and Western Traditions* (London: Duckworth, 1980), p. 150. Clearly, at the time, Engels had no real conception of ecological limits.

What Marx is arguing for are precisely the developments that have caused the apparent crisis in agricultural production described in Section 1.1, above. From an ecological perspective, then, Marxism is a theory fundamentally flawed due to its insistence that communism requires the highest levels of productivity.

In short, how can a theory designed to liberate by a reliance on high productivity be an appropriate basis for a genuine green political theory? Moreover, the authoritarianism which seems to be implicit in Marxist/Leninist theory and overt in its practice means that any environmentalist version of it would be subject to the charge that, apart from claiming to be internationalist rather than nationalist, it would, in essence, be scarcely different from the eco-authoritarianism discussed earlier in so far as it, too, would boil down to an environmentally benevolent dictatorship. Why this might be so will start to become clearer after an attempt has been made to clarify the concept 'power' in Section 3.3, below.

2.3.3 Analytical Marxism

But perhaps this is unfair. Not all Marxists are Leninists, and perhaps not all of the above arguments are pertinent to all Marxists. For one thing, not all Marxists have to accept all of Marx's recommendations. This notwithstanding, all Marxists *qua* Marxists do have to look back to Karl Marx to some degree. But Marx is capable of many different interpretations. Unfortunately, the fact that it is not immediately transparent what Marx was arguing has led to some very powerful criticisms being made of his theory. Analytical philosophers, for example, seem to have had no difficulty in showing common understandings of Marx's theory to be fundamentally incoherent.[64]

However, in recent years a cogent restatement of Marx's theory has been presented by G. A. Cohen, which has given rise to a whole new school of Marxism – namely, analytical Marxism. This has proved to be a particularly fecund school of thought, and it offers insights which are extremely valuable in understanding the various elements which combine together to generate the environmental threat facing us. In the remainder of this book, I attempt to develop a comprehensive environmental political theory in the light of certain clarifications presented in Cohen's work. Consequently, I shall now discuss Cohen's theoretical approach in considerably greater detail than the approaches discussed up until now, for Cohen's work is a necessary prelude to the theoretical approach which follows.

Cohen's highly acclaimed attempt to defend Marx's theory of history is especially unusual in that it succeeds in conforming to the rigorous requirements of analytical philosophy. In other words, Cohen has bolstered up Marxism to the point where it is capable of withstanding the critical techniques deployed by twentieth-century philosophers. What Cohen persuasively demonstrates is that

64 See, for example, H. B. Acton, *The Illusion of the Epoch* (London: Routledge and Kegan Paul, 1962) and John Plamenatz, *German Marxism and Russian Communism* (London: Greenwood Press, 1975).

Marx's theory of history is far from incoherent when it is interpreted as employing a form of functional explanation. And by offering a rigorous account of functional explanation, Cohen convincingly rescues Marx from the charge of incoherence.

2.3.3.1 The need for functional explanations

Marx's theory of history is most succinctly adumbrated in his suitably famous '1859 Preface'. It is in this pivotal text that he draws his controversial distinction between base (or foundation) and superstructure. Cohen provides an invaluable service by clarifying what Marx is there asserting. According to Cohen, the superstructure consists of 'a set of non-economic institutions, notably the legal system and the state'[65] – in other words, legal and political institutions – whereas the base is the economic structure and is composed of the relations of production.[66] By 'relations of production', Cohen means relations of, or relations presupposing, effective control of the forces of production.[67] And by 'forces of production', Cohen means labour-power (that is, the strength, skill, knowledge, etc. of the producing agents) and means of production (that is, tools, machines, premises, raw materials, etc.). Specific to Cohen's interpretation of Marx is the claim that the base – the economic structure of society – does not include the forces of production within it.

With the clarifications Cohen has provided, we are now in a better position to make sense of the following crucial passage from Marx's '1859 Preface':

> At a certain stage of their development, the material productive forces of society come in conflict with the existing relations of production, or – what is but a legal expression for the same thing – with the property relations within which they have been at work hitherto. From forms of development of the productive forces these relations turn into their fetters. Then begins an epoch of social revolution. With the change of the economic foundations the entire immense superstructure is more or less rapidly transformed.[68]

Here, Marx seems to be arguing that a change in the forces of production is responsible for a change in the relations of production, which in turn is responsible for a change in the superstructure. Cohen's clarifications thus suggest an architectural model comprising three tiers. On the top floor is the superstructure of legal and political institutions, which rests on the structure of economic relations – the base – which in turn rests on the productive forces – in other words, on the degree of technological development. And the relationship between these

65 Cohen, *Karl Marx's Theory of History*, p. 216.
66 See ibid., pp. 28–9.
67 See ibid., pp. 34–5.
68 Marx, 'Preface to the critique of political economy', p. 389.

levels is as follows: the level of technological development explains the kind of economic relations which obtain, and they in turn explain the kind of legal and political institutions which prevail. Hence, in the '1859 Preface', Marx seems to offer a theory of historical transition which is a form of technological determinism.[69]

Unfortunately, elsewhere in Marx's corpus, such as in 'The Communist Manifesto', the claim seems to be that the relations of production affect the development of the productive forces – either the argument is that competition between capitalists or, as Wal Suchting argues, the need to control the work-force demands the introduction of new productive techniques.[70] To take one example, in 'The Communist Manifesto' we find Marx writing: 'The bourgeoisie cannot exist without constantly revolutionizing the instruments of production'.[71] The reason why the bourgeoisie must revolutionize the forces of production might be that competition, which is intrinsic to market relations, ensures that a producer will go out of business if he or she does not keep up with the latest technological developments. Moreover, a producer will get ahead of his or her competitors if he or she is the first to modernize the productive forces. In this case, capitalist relations of production would be responsible for innovation – for the development of the productive forces. Yet this seems to contradict 'vulgar' technological determinism, which insists that it is the forces of production which influence the relations of production, rather than vice versa.

Furthermore, in *Capital*, Marx claims that the (superstructurally imposed) Factory Acts promulgated in his day led to the search for and implementation of new machinery. By banning cheap child labour, the Acts forced factory owners to reduce their costs by introducing labour-saving technologies. Here, it appears to be the superstructure that has explanatory primacy. In other words, both 'The Communist Manifesto' and *Capital* appear, at first sight, to contradict the '1859 Preface'. Of what use to greens is a self-contradictory theory?

Well, there are two common 'Marxist' responses to this apparent contradiction in Marx. The first, following from Engels' later letters (written ten years after Marx's death), is to attenuate the explanatory primacy of the productive forces so that they are claimed to be determinant only 'in the last instance'. Not only could this be viewed by Marxists as a later weakening of the theory on Engels' part, it is not fully clear from the letters what 'in the last instance' is supposed to mean. Theories of history are certainly not improved by reducing their clarity. This criticism is even more applicable to the second common 'Marxist' response, which describes the relationship between the forces and relations of production, or between the base and superstructure, as 'dialectical'. What the term 'dialec-

69 The appearance of technological determinism is even stronger in *The Poverty of Philosophy*: 'The hand-mill gives you society with the feudal lord; the steam-mill, society with the industrial capitalist.' Karl Marx, *The Poverty of Philosophy* (Peking: Foreign Languages Press, 1978), p. 103.

70 See Wal Suchting, *Marx: An Introduction* (Brighton: Wheatsheaf Books, 1983).

71 Marx and Engels, 'The Communist Manifesto', p. 224.

tical' often tends to cover for in such a response is a vague notion of interaction. And if Marxist theory reduces itself to the claim that there is an interaction between forces and relations of production, or between base and superstructure, then it is difficult to see what is distinctly 'Marxist' about it. In short, it can be argued that all the term 'dialectical' does in this case is hide confused and trite claims under the mask of mystification – a mystification which suggests to the uncomprehending some deeper, more profound meaning.

In the light of all this, Cohen's interpretation of Marx has three obvious advantages. First, it is not '*vulgar*' technological determinism. Second, it is consistent with the bulk of Marx's pronouncements. And third, it provides an admirably clear account of a strong theory which is free of mystification. How does it do so?

Central to Cohen's account is what he refers to as the Primacy Thesis. However, it is possible to formulate quite different primacy theses. In Chapter 4, I shall propose an alternative. Hence, in order to distinguish Cohen's Primacy Thesis from any other, I shall refer to his as 'the Techno-Primacy Thesis', for it considers (what is basically) technology to have explanatory primacy. Cohen formulates it this way:

> (T-P Thesis) The nature of a set of production relations is explained by the level of development of the productive forces embraced by it (to a far greater extent than *vice versa*).[72]

Because Cohen places the Techno-Primacy Thesis at the core of his defence of Marx's theory of history, I shall call Cohen's interpretation 'the Techno-Primacy Theory'.

Now, the problem Cohen needs to solve is that, on the one hand, he must defend the Techno-Primacy Thesis in order to retain the technological determinist element in Marx's theory. But on the other hand, he must accommodate the claim that economic relations have an influence on technological development, for Marx argues that capitalist economic relations drive technological innovation. The solution, therefore, consists in reconciling two of Marx's apparently contradictory premises:

(i) the productive forces have explanatory primacy; and
(ii) the relations of production significantly affect the development of the productive forces.

Cohen insists that only by invoking 'functional explanation' is it possible to reconcile these two premises in a manner which is compatible with the majority of Marx's pronouncements. Thus, the need for understanding the relationship between the three levels in Cohen's model as relying on some kind of functional

72 Cohen, *Karl Marx's Theory of History*, p. 134.

explanation arises because a straightforward form of technological determinism is not consistent with the claims that Marx makes about the economic relations having an effect on the development of technology.

2.3.3.2 The nature of functional explanation

What, then, are functional explanations? According to Cohen, functional explanations are a sub-set of consequence explanations, and consequence explanations relate to consequence laws. Consequence laws take the form:

(1) If (if *Y* at t_1, then *X* at t_2), then *Y* at t_3,

where '*X*' and '*Y*' are types of events, and where 't_1' is some time not later than t_2, and where 't_2' is some time not later than time t_3. For a functional explanation to relate to (1), then *Y* would have to be functional for *X*. An example of a relevant consequence law:

(2) If it is the case that if birds were to develop hollower bones then they would be able to fly better, then they would come to develop hollower bones.

Cohen argues that consequence laws do not commit the apparent fallacy of the effect preceding the cause, as one might assume they do, because the actual cause is not the later effect, but a prior disposition. For example, (2) does not claim that being able to fly better is what *caused* the development of hollower bones. That would be a case of the effect preceding the cause. On the contrary, it claims that birds develop hollower bones in a situation where birds which have developed hollower bones have their flight facilitated.

One problem with such functional explanations is that they are clearly incomplete. To be fully convincing, they require 'elaborating'.[73] (2) could be elaborated by means of a theory of genetics which accounted for chance variation within the species and hence the development of hollower bones by particular birds (and perhaps heavier bones by others), combined with a Darwinian account of the survival of the fittest whereby only those birds which developed hollower bones (and thus flew better) survived being caught by predators. Thus, because hollower bones are functional for flight, birds come to develop them. Nevertheless, Cohen controversially maintains that 'a consequence explanation may be well confirmed in the absence of a theory of *how* the dispositional property figures in the explanation of what it explains'[74] and, correlatively, 'Marxian functional-

73 'A satisfactory elaboration provides a further explanation and locates the functional fact within a longer story which specifies its explanatory role more precisely.' Ibid. p. 286.

74 Ibid., p. 266.

explanatory claims . . . may be rationally tenable before suitable elaborations are available.'[75]

One difficulty with this is that it is always possible for the disposition and its apparent effect to be jointly explained by an independent cause. In which case, the consequence explanation would be false if it were not the disposition which explained its apparent effect, but the third feature which independently explained *both* the disposition *and* its apparent effect. But a more important difficulty is that, even if the disposition did have an influence, that influence might only hold under certain conditions – conditions which might not be evident until a full elaboration was provided. For example, if a species of bird had no natural predator, then those that were unable to fly would survive. Hence, as flightless birds could evolve in such circumstances, it would not always be the case that if hollower bones were functional for flight, birds would develop them. And unless one possessed the appropriate elaboration, it would be impossible to predict when birds would and when they would not develop hollower bones. Consequently, there should be an onus on anyone offering functional explanations to attempt to provide elaborations.

It would seem likely that the most common kind of elaboration which might be offered of consequence explanations regarding social developments would be *purposive* ones – in other words, elaborations arguing that an actor's intention to introduce a state of affairs (which he or she rightly believed to be in his or her own interest) led to the introduction of that state of affairs. Not only is a purposive elaboration usually a complete account, people often *know* (Freud notwithstanding) why they have acted. In addition, with a purposive elaboration there is clearly no problem about causes being preceded by their effects. It is not the future state of affairs which is the cause of an action; what is of most significance is the actor's present belief about the desirability of a future state of affairs. Furthermore, purposive elaborations which identify people as the cause of social transformation avoid any questionable acceptance of 'free-floating intentions, purposes that can be held by no specific actor,'[76] and which is characteristic of functionalism.

However, it might be objected that purposive elaborations are incompatible with functional explanations. In order to attempt an answer to this objection, let us engage in a little thought-experiment. Consider the following case of a rare species of bird which came to develop hollower bones. The development of hollower bones is functional for flight. And (2) is a consequence law explaining such developments. Here, then, is a functional explanation. But now imagine that the theory of chance variation had been categorically falsified and replaced by some variation on Lamarck's evolutionary theory,[77] and that the following elaboration

75 Ibid., p. 271.

76 Jon Elster, *Making Sense of Marx* (Cambridge: Cambridge University Press, 1985), p. 17.

77 Jean Baptiste Pierre Antoine de Monet de Lamarck (1744–1829) was a French biologist who tried to explain evolution by means of the assumption that characteristics which an organism acquired during its life-time could be inherited by its offspring.

for the development of hollower bones within this particular species of bird were to be provided. Some ecologically-minded ornithologist who wished to preserve the species (which had become threatened with extinction because of the introduction of a non-indigenous predator – the house cat) drilled holes in the bones of some individual birds so that they could fly better and thereby escape being eaten. Hollower bones were then inherited by the offspring of those birds that had been surgically manipulated by the ornithologist. Thus the species came to develop hollower bones, for only those birds with hollower bones evaded being caught by cats.

Now, even though this is just what the ornithologist purposively intended, the elaboration provided still supports a functional explanation: the species developed hollower bones because such a development is functional for flight. As this fits perfectly Cohen's account of what a functional explanation consists in, then, surely, it remains a functional explanation even though the development would not have taken place without the intended activity of the ornithologist. Consequently, purposive elaborations do not, in fact, seem to be inconsistent with functional explanations, as many have presumed. They would only be obviously incompatible if functional explanations presupposed some variety of structural functionalism that precluded any account which emphasized the intentions of individual actors. But Cohen is adamant that one does not have to be any such functionalist in order to subscribe to functional explanations.[78]

2.3.3.3 Functional explanation in Marx's theory of history

If all this is so, how does Cohen reconcile (i) and (ii)? He holds that 'the character of the forces [of production] *functionally* explains the character of the relations.'[79] In the context of Marx's theory of history, the following consequence law is thus suggested:

> (2′) If it is the case that if new relations of production were to be selected then the productive forces would develop further, then they would come to be selected.

And this would underpin a functional explanation from one particular mode of production to another when the new relations of production which had been selected were functional for the further development of the productive forces.

78 There is a great deal of widespread confusion on this issue. Structural functionalism is a theory claiming that the presence of social features is to be explained by their being functional for the preservation of the social form. Cohen's theory, on the contrary, is a theory of *revolutionary change*. Revolution occurs, on Cohen's account, because an element of the overall structure of society has become *dysfunctional*. Cohen is most certainly not a structural functionalist. It is, therefore, immensely confusing to describe him, as some nevertheless do, as a 'functionalist Marxist'.

79 Cohen, *Karl Marx's Theory of History*, p. 160.

Moreover, as Cohen points out: 'the bare fact that economic structures develop the productive forces does not prejudice their [that is, the productive forces'] primacy, for forces select structures according to their capacity to promote development.'[80] Specific economic relations, then, are 'selected' because they are functional for the development of the forces of production. Consequently, the use of functional explanation allows the claim that it is technological development which has explanatory primacy to be reconciled with the apparently contradictory claim that the economic relations significantly affect technological development.

Similarly, Cohen's account of the relationship between the base and superstructure involves functional explanation. Specific legal and political institutions are 'selected' because they stabilize the economic relations. Just as the effect of the economic relations on technological development is acknowledged in Cohen's account, so is the effect of the political relations – the structure of legal and political institutions – on the economic relations. (See Figure 2.1.)[81]

Thus, Marx's theory of history can briefly be stated as follows. Certain economic relations are, for a while, functional for technological development. But at a certain point in time they become dysfunctional for further development. A revolution then occurs whereby the structure of legal and political institutions is transformed into one which stabilizes new economic relations which *are* functional for technological development beyond the present level. Moreover, the new structure of legal and political institutions is chosen precisely because it stabilizes the new economic relations which are functional for developing technology further. (Or, perhaps in the case of a transition to post-capitalism, a revolution occurs when the existing economic relations become dysfunctional for the optimal *use* of the prevailing technology. The structure of legal and political institutions is then transformed into one which stabilizes economic relations which *are* functional for utilizing that technology. Moreover, in such a scenario, the new legal and political structure would be chosen precisely because it stabilized economic relations which were functional for the optimal use of available technologies.)

Cohen's interpretation of Marx's theory of history, then, consists in a conjunction of functional explanations. But what elaboration can Cohen provide in its support? He argues that there is a tendency for the forces of production to develop through history (what he calls 'the Development Thesis'). This is due to three main factors:

(a) human rationality;
(b) a situation of scarcity; and
(c) human inventiveness.

80 Ibid., p. 162.

81 In Figure 2.1, X_1 selects Y_1 because Y_1 is functional for X_1, and X_2 selects Y_2 because Y_2 is functional for X_2.

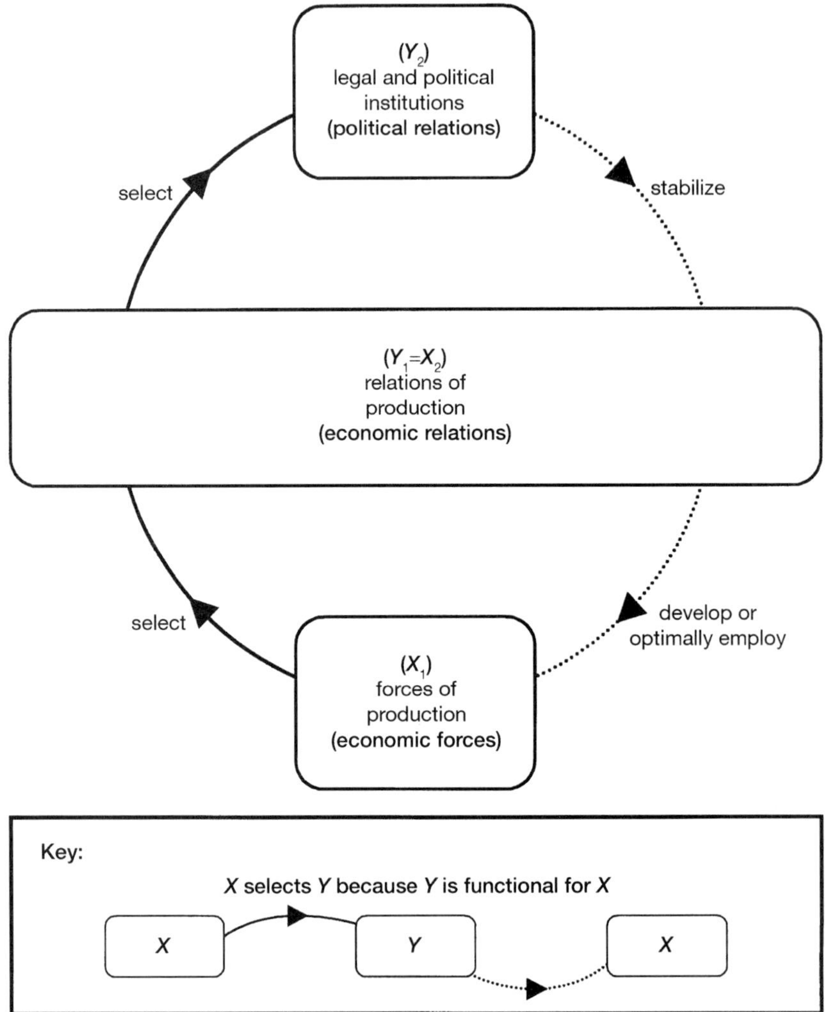

Figure 2.1 A Marxist Techno-Primacy Model

It is assumed (albeit controversially) that human beings are rational and that they face a situation of scarcity. It is also assumed, and this is uncontroversial, that it is within the capability of some to apply their intelligence to the task of inventing new technologies. As it appears rational for individuals in a situation of scarcity to seek to develop technology further in order to increase production and thereby provide for their needs, then it can be assumed that there will be a tendency for technological development to take place. If, in order to develop technology further or faster, it is necessary to select economic relations (e.g. capitalist relations) which would be functional for that development, then it would appear rational for such relations to be selected. And if the legal and political institutions must change so that the required economic relations can be stabilized, then it is rational to select new, and more appropriate, legal and political institutions. Thus, Cohen seems to have presented a cogent elaboration of his functional explanations. And as it involves choices that rational actors could be expected to make in order to bring about a future they would prefer, then Cohen's elaboration appears, in actual fact, to be a purposive one.

2.3.4 The state as instrument or as actor?

In arguing that the structure of legal and political institutions is 'selected' in order to stabilize economic relations, this Techno-Primacy Theory of historical development fits in well with the common Marxian claim that the state is an instrument of the dominant economic class. Although Engels acknowledged that in certain circumstances – for example, when there are two equally-strong economic classes contesting for power – the state might act as if it were free from either of them, Marx insisted that even the exceptional Bonapartist state acted so as to protect the long-term interests of the bourgeoisie. And given that the modern state does tend to protect bourgeois interests, it is not surprising that Marx should assume that the 'executive of the modern State is but a committee for managing the common affairs of the whole bourgeoisie.'[82]

But does the fact that the modern state tends to protect bourgeois interests provide adequate justification for an instrumentalist theory of the state? No, because the modern state may well protect the interests of the bourgeoisie for some other reason than that it is an instrument of that class. If it were the case that the state had its own distinct interests, for example, then this would give a simple explanation for why it is that the state provides welfare services, etc. – services which force Marxists to accord, inelegantly, a 'relative autonomy' to the state. If the state has its own interests, including an interest in preserving order and maintaining a healthy labour force (that it does not directly exploit), then it would not be surprising if the state were, at times, to increase taxes levied on the bourgeoisie in order to improve the condition of the workers. But a mere instrument of the bourgeoisie would be unlikely to do this in so far as the bourgeoisie is preoccupied with maximizing direct exploitation in the short term.

However, such actions as lead to an improvement in the condition of the working class would stabilize the political order, and would ensure a constant supply of labour. Such actions are, therefore, in the long-term interest of the bourgeoisie. But this fact does not entail that this is the reason why the state carries out such actions. The bourgeoisie needs the subordinate classes to be kept at work so as to produce profit. The state needs the subordinate classes to be kept

82 Marx and Engels, 'The Communist Manifesto', p. 223.

at work so as to create the wealth which it must tax in order to pay its personnel.[83] But this latter fact is sufficient to account for the state's behaviour; and to the extent that it is the state which acts to stabilize the relations of production, then the principle of parsimony suggests that the needs and interests of the bourgeoisie be omitted from the explanation of why it is that the relations of production are preserved. For it can be argued that the state would, in any case, continue to behave in a manner which, as a matter of contingent fact, protected the interests of the bourgeoisie, but only so long as this manner of behaving facilitated the production of the wealth the state requires.

So, if the state acts in a manner which protects the interests of the bourgeoisie, it might well do so when and because bourgeois and state interests happen to coincide[84] (which, it can be argued, is usually the case, given that both the state and the bourgeoisie require that the production of wealth be maximized, and given that the bourgeoisie is highly efficient at maximizing it). In other words, Marxists could very well have mistaken a contingent correspondence between state and bourgeois interests for an instrumental relationship. In which case, the modern state would not, as many Marxists have thought, be the instrument of the bourgeoisie; rather it would act so as to carry out its own interests – interests which just happen usually to correspond to those of the bourgeoisie.

Interestingly, Cohen seems to commit himself implicitly to the view that a state can have its own interests when he discusses the possibility of an authoritarian socialist state, for its own political reasons, being responsible for increasing production well above meeting scarcity.[85] But this possibility does not seem to follow from his purposive elaboration. Moreover, what Cohen especially fails to notice is that this possibility fits in with an alternative functional explanation – namely, that *the state backs economic relations which facilitate increased production because the latter is functional for the state.* And this alternative functional explanation could easily be given a purposive elaboration of its own: state personnel choose to stabilize specific relations of production which they believe to be in their interests. In the example of authoritarian socialism, the state would be increasing production because increased production was functional for its rule. Yet in such a case, it would be the state, not the productive forces, which had explanatory primacy. I return to such an alternative functional explanation in Chapter 4, below.

One implication of Marx's theory, including Cohen's interpretation, is that if states are selected by inegalitarian economic relations in order to preserve them, then if there are no inequalities to be preserved, no state will be required. If egalitarian economic relations are attained, then the state will, to use Engels'

83 See, for example, Theda Skocpol, *States and Social Revolutions: A Comparative Analysis of France, Russia and China* (Cambridge: Cambridge University Press, 1979), p. 30.

84 Consider: 'When completing his report to the British Poor Law Commission in 1842 urging an improvement in the sanitary conditions of the poor, Lord Chadwick noted that a healthy labouring class was likely to be more productive and politically contented.' Tim O'Riordan, *Environmentalism* (London: Pion, 1981), p. 20.

85 See Cohen, *Karl Marx's Theory of History*, p. 315.

famous phrase, 'wither away'.[86] Unfortunately, the Russian Revolution, which did most to raise the standing of Marxism on the Left, does not seem to corroborate this theory – but not because egalitarian relations failed to appear. In fact, it can be argued that egalitarian economic relations *did arise*, for factory committees, run by the workers themselves, emerged within Russian industry. But rather than this leading to the state withering away, the Bolshevik state replaced the factory committees with inegalitarian 'one-man management'. What is especially interesting is Lenin's justification for this. Within a year of coming to power, Lenin proclaimed: 'All our efforts must be exerted to the utmost to . . . bring about an economic revival, without which a real increase in our country's defence potential is inconceivable.'[87] In other words, the needs of the state dictated that worker control be replaced by managerial (techno-bureaucratic) control. Ironically, then, the revolution in Russia, led by Marx's followers, seems to contradict Marx's theory of history, for rather than the economic relations determining the form of the state, it can be argued that the state determined the form of economic relations that came to preponderate – and as the 1930s demonstrated to many who were previously uncritical supporters of the 1917 Revolution, the eventual outcome in Russia was highly authoritarian and extremely inegalitarian.

2.3.5 An ecological interpretation of Marx

So, does Marxism provide the basis for a radical green political theory? It certainly doesn't seem to. Of what use is a theory that seems to be contradicted by its own adherents' political practice? Moreover, to the extent that Marxist theory has failed so dramatically in all of its predictions for a future desirable society,[88] then

86 See Frederick Engels, *Anti-Dühring, Herr Eugen Dühring's Revolution in Science* (Peking: Foreign Languages Press, 1976), p. 363.

87 Lenin, *The Immediate Tasks of the Soviet Government*, p. 6.

88 David Pepper denies my claim that Marx's theory of history seeks to make predictions. See David Pepper, *Eco-Socialism: From Deep Ecology to Social Justice* (London: Routledge, 1993), p. 75. Now, Marx does describe class struggle throughout history as 'a fight that each time ended either in a revolutionary re-constitution of society at large or in the common ruin of the contending classes.' Marx and Engels, 'The Communist Manifesto', p. 222. However, this refers only to the past and appears to be a mere *ad hoc* remark to deal with apparent counter-examples to his theory, such as the fall of the Roman Empire. At no time does Marx indicate that the outcome of the class struggle between the proletariat and the bourgeoisie will not be a communist society. Consider Marx's explicit self-assessment delivered to Weydemeyer: 'no credit is due to me for discovering the existence of classes in modern society or the struggle between them. Long before me bourgeois historians had described the historical development of this class struggle and bourgeois economists the economic anatomy of the classes. What I did that was new was to prove: (1) that the existence of classes is only bound up with particular historical phases in the development of production, (2) that the class struggle necessarily leads to the dictatorship of the proletariat, (3) that this dictatorship itself only constitutes the transition to the abolition of all classes and to a classless society'. Karl Marx to Joseph Weydemeyer, 5 March 1852, in Karl Marx, *Selected Writings*, ed. David McLellan (Oxford: Oxford University Press, 1977), p. 341. If the claim 'Event *A* (which is now occurring) necessarily leads to event *B*' is not a prediction, what is?

its claim to provide the theory greens require seems rather weak. And in any case, a theory geared to human liberation on the basis of high productivity hardly seems the most appropriate foundation for green political practice.

But why did Marx come to place so much faith in ever-increasing productivity? His theory of history begins with the claim that for society to reproduce itself, it must produce its means of subsistence. But because Marx took production to play the primary role in social reproduction, he began to focus upon production to the point where, it can easily be argued, he ended up paying insufficient attention to other factors. And it can further be argued that the result was such a slide from the conditions of *social reproduction* to the conditions of *social production* that the ecological conditions essential for humanity to continue reproducing itself were ignored or downplayed. This has resulted in a political philosophy which, it might be concluded, lays so much stress on developing production that it has become as much of a threat to the survival of humanity as right-wing authoritarianism and liberal reformism, with their stress on private property. In short, the environmental crises apparently unfolding before us can be considered to reveal Marx's political philosophy to be as outdated today as both right-wing authoritarian and liberal reformist thinking.

To some, the incipient threat lying within Marx's political philosophy has been made manifest in those Eastern European regimes which formerly laid claim to his intellectual heritage. There, under centralized state control,

> managers were rewarded for fulfilling their plans and severely penalized for not doing so. The entire political and economic system was geared towards production regardless of cost, leaving managers unaccountable for the amount of inputs used. The result was considerable waste, notably of energy resources, and with it pollution on a massive scale.[89]

But this outcome is unsurprising, given (what can be argued to be) Marx's unbalanced emphasis on production. Why, then, should anyone have considered Marxism as a candidate for grounding a green political theory in the first place?

Consider Reiner Grundmann. In the most academically respectable attempt to produce an eco-Marxist theory which retains at least some semblance of fidelity to Marx's thought,[90] Grundmann attempts a reconstruction of Marx that would seem to make him relevant for illuminating environmental problems. Grundmann begins by arguing that dominating nature is desirable. This might sound profoundly unecological, but, as he writes: 'Powers which turn into an existential threat for the power-holder do not contribute to domination.'[91] In other words, ecological problems actually result from insufficient domination of nature, their

89 Michael Waller and Frances Millard, 'Environmental politics in Eastern Europe', *Environmental Politics*, Vol. 1, No. 2 (1992), p. 164.

90 See Reiner Grundmann, *Marxism and Ecology* (Oxford: Clarendon Press, 1991).

91 Ibid., p. 15. However, one could reply that in commanding one's slaves to do something not in one's interests, one still, nevertheless, dominates them.

presence demonstrating 'the absence of such a domination.'[92] 'Communism', on the other hand, means society's common conscious control of its relationship with nature. As Grundmann declares: 'a communist society must be a society which regulates its interchange with nature in a rational way; this is to say that the existence of severe ecological crises would inhibit one from calling such a society "communist".'[93]

But this argument seems to rest on a confusion regarding the '*meaning*' of 'communism'. If we are unable to describe a society with ecological problems as 'communist', then Grundmann would have to be using 'meaning' to mean 'the necessary condition'. But what 'communism' *means*, in this sense of 'means', is, according to Marx, something like 'the absence of private property' or 'the collective control over social relationships' or even 'the collective control over the productive forces'. Surely, this is how Marx defines 'communism'. Surely, he doesn't *define* it as 'the collective control over the whole of nature', and he certainly doesn't *define* it as 'the absence of severe ecological crises'. That Marx believed humans would have greater control over nature in a communist society was, for Marx, surely a *consequence* of communism – what communism '*means*' in the sense of '*causes*'.

In other words, Marx appears to have defined 'communism' as something like 'the absence of private property', believing this to *enable* control over the natural world. As Grundmann himself acknowledges: 'Marx . . . seemed to believe that with the abolition of private property all other points would follow more or less automatically. . . .'[94] Grundmann makes Marx appear valuable to ecological thought simply by *redefining* Marx's goal as the solution to ecological problems. This kind of verbal sleight-of-hand hardly provides any substantial basis for a green political theory, especially when there is no reason to believe that the theory of how to arrive at a communist society has any relationship whatsoever to solving ecological problems. In fact, it seems rather the converse, given that increased productivity is viewed by Marx as a precondition for a successful communist society, and it is now widely regarded that increased productivity is the cause of so many of the environmental problems that we appear to face.[95]

In my view, such revisionary apologetics serve only to obfuscate the central-

92 Ibid., p. 232.

93 Ibid., p. 279.

94 Ibid., p. 182.

95 In Marx's view, increased productivity is required principally because a communist society will have to be an abundant one if conflicts are not to re-emerge. But there is a second sense in which increased productivity is assumed by Marx to be a precondition for communism: 'in big industry the contradiction between the instrument of production and private property appears for the first time and is the product of big industry; moreover, big industry must be highly developed to produce this contradiction. And thus only with big industry does the abolition of private property become possible'. Karl Marx and Friedrich Engels, 'The German Ideology' in Karl Marx, *Selected Writings*, ed. David McLellan (Oxford: Oxford University Press, 1977), p. 176. But this is just the kind of industry which, many environmentalists believe, has brought us to the verge of ecological collapse.

problem.[96] I want to suggest that, surprising as it might seem, the central problem is obscured because Marx focuses our attention on the economy and on technology. This will appear a surprising claim because, as so many now accept, current economic relations and technology *are*, clearly, environmentally damaging. Nevertheless, I want to argue the following. Because Marxism focuses our attention primarily on the economy, it is particularly dangerous as a *political* theory. In so directing our focus, it diverts our attention away from what may be the central, underlying cause of the environmental problems that we seem to face. And it does so for the same reason that the Marxist Techno-Primacy Theory is apparently contradicted by Lenin's political practice – namely, by underplaying the importance of the state and political power in general. That this might well be the case will only become plausible after the concept 'power' has been discussed in the next chapter and after a very different theory of history has been outlined in Chapter 4, below.

Nevertheless, enough has already been said to cast some doubt on the suitability of either right-wing eco-authoritarianism, middle-of-the-road eco-reformism or left-wing eco-Marxism as serving as the basis of compelling green political theories. We thus have reason to feel that there is some justification for the suspicion voiced in the previous chapter that a very different political theory may well be required in order to ground a truly radical green politics – a political practice capable of meeting the challenge environmentalists insist lies threateningly in our path. But before any such theory could be developed in full, some general problems would need to be examined first: problems about power (for eco-authoritarianism, eco-reformism and eco-Marxism can all be argued to fail, in the last resort, because of inadequate conceptions of 'power') and about the nature of social relationships in general. These issues will be the subject of the next chapter.

96 There are, of course, ecological variants of Marxism other than Grundmann's. However, they appear less unacceptable only to the extent that they move further and further away from Marx's views. Rather than discuss every possible variant, it might be more fruitful simply to try an alternative tack. That is what I now proceed to attempt.

3 Interrelationism, freedom and power

Having considered the three most common theoretical responses to the threat identified by environmentalists, we have been led to conclude that their cogency is in some doubt. So let us now embark upon the development of an alternative green social and political theory.

Two issues must be broached right at the outset. First, a green social theory, like any other, needs to be clear about the nature of society. Second, a green political theory must understand, amongst other things, the ecological ramifications of political power, for political theory is about politics and politics is about power. En route to clarifying how environmentalists might best conceptualize 'power', I shall consider how 'freedom' might be best conceptualized, for freedom and political power are intimately related. Political power, of course, is itself social. Being relational, it is not the property of isolated individuals. But neither, I shall suggest, is it a causal effect that collective entities exert upon their parts, as some structuralists seem to think.[1]

3.1 Individualism or collectivism?

In Section 1.2, it was noted how a number of ecologists understand the workings of ecosystems. Does this have any significance for how we might most profitably comprehend the workings of society? And could this be used to ground a social and political theory that allowed us to be less potentially self-destructive by enabling us to refrain from harming the environment upon which we depend? Could

1 For one such example, see Louis Althusser and Étienne Balibar, *Reading Capital* (London: New Left Books, 1977), pp. 186–7. The ostensible justification for such structuralist Marxism is the following methodological pronouncement by Marx in his Preface to the First Edition of *Capital*: 'I do not by any means depict the capitalist and the landowner in rosy colours. But individuals are dealt with here only in so far as they are the personifications of economic categories, the bearers [*Träger*] of particular class-relations and interests. My standpoint, from which the development of the economic formation of society is viewed as a process of natural history, can less than any other make the individual responsible for relations whose creature he remains, socially speaking, however much he may subjectively raise himself above them.' Karl Marx, *Capital*, Vol. I, trans. B. Fowkes (Harmondsworth: Penguin, 1976), p. 92.

such a political theory suggest which social form might best sustain the environmental preconditions of its own survival? In short, what kind of approach to the understanding of society would be most consistent with an ecological perspective? The three political standpoints that were considered in the previous chapter (eco-authoritarianism, eco-reformism and eco-Marxism) tend to occupy fairly clear positions within the debate between individualism and collectivism. Eco-reformism, especially when it takes a liberal form, is usually individualist, eco-Marxism is collectivist, while eco-authoritarianism (including eco-fascism) could take either an individualist form (in its New Right guise) or a collectivist form (were certain neo-Hegelians to concentrate upon environmental issues). But do either individualism or collectivism really correspond with ecological thinking? If they do not, then it would no longer be surprising that present eco-authoritarian, eco-reformist and eco-Marxist attempts at solving the environmental threat might well be wholly inadequate.

Now, a great deal of ink has been spilled over the debate between individualism and collectivism. Accusations have been levelled by each camp against the other, only to meet the response that the various objections have missed the mark. Moreover, the discussion has now become so voluminous that it is difficult to ascertain clearly the details of the respective positions. With the hope of introducing some clarity into this topic, I shall view 'individualism' and 'collectivism' not in a way which respects the favourable categorizations chosen by their respective supporters – for that has only served to obscure the differences between each position – but, rather, in a manner which isolates each position as the object of criticism derided by those who reject it. Adopting this unusual strategy will ensure that the various criticisms which have been levelled against each position do hit a target.

But adopting such a 'principle of uncharity' might, at first glance, appear to be a signally odd approach to take. What could possibly justify defining a standpoint not in the terms of those who argue for it, but in the terms of those who oppose it? Surely, it will be objected, if a position is to be criticized, then it should be criticized in its strongest form? And its characterization by those who show it little or no sympathy can hardly be its most favourable presentation. This is undoubtedly true. However, participants in the debate between individualism and collectivism have attempted to define their respective positions as mutually exclusive and jointly exhaustive.[2] Thus, both camps have ruled out in advance all possibility of any common ground being shared between them. And this is especially confusing when the various belligerents occasionally appear to argue from a standpoint which *does* seem to be common to both positions.

Hence, if one attempts to define 'individualism' and 'collectivism' in the terms of the defenders of each, then it is impossible to specify adequately each to the exclusion of the other in a manner which is agreeable to all parties concerned. So, if one cannot satisfy both parties simultaneously, why satisfy either of them when

2 See, for example, J. W. N. Watkins, 'Historical explanation in the social sciences' in John O'Neill (ed.), *Modes of Individualism and Collectivism* (London: Heinemann, 1973), p. 168.

that would mean giving one party an unfair advantage? And if, instead, 'individualism' and 'collectivism' are defined in the terms of the opponents of each position, then it becomes possible to isolate a middle ground – a middle ground from whose standpoint the untenable claims made by each party could, in principle, be rejected. What is more, the middle ground that would remain might prove to be not only the position which alone is viable (being devoid of the unacceptable trimmings of both individualism and collectivism), but also one which the various disputants were prepared to accept and, perhaps, even come to regard as their own.[3] It is this possibility of isolating an acceptable middle ground which might justify the adoption of a principle of uncharity in this specific case.

How, then, are we to view individualism and collectivism? I shall concentrate on methodological individualism and methodological collectivism. Let me begin with methodological individualism.

3.1.1 Methodological individualism

It must be stressed at the outset that if methodological individualism is to be rejected, not everything which might fall under the rubric 'individualism' is necessarily to be dismissed along with it. Steven Lukes has listed a number of features of individualism, which might be thought to form a family.[4] These are listed (a) through (k) in the left-hand column of Table 3.1. Not all versions of individualism will possess all these 'family resemblances'.[5] In a family, mother and daughter might share the same hair colour, father and son might have similar builds, and siblings might have the same coloured eyes, while no feature is shared by all members of the family. Nevertheless, if an individual possesses one or more

3 For example, Derek Parfit defends a form of 'atomism' (individualism), which he distinguishes from 'holism' (collectivism) in the following manner: 'With respect to many types of thing, we may take one of two views. We may believe that the existence of this type of thing does not involve anything more than the existence of certain other (interrelated) things. Such a view can be called "atomistic". We may instead believe that the things in question have a quite separate existence, over and above that of these other things. Such a view can be called "holistic".' Derek Parfit, 'Later selves and moral principles' in J. Rachels (ed.), *Ethical Theory 2: Theories About How We Should Live* (Oxford: Oxford University Press, 1998), p. 167. On the other hand, Fritjof Capra, while defending a form of 'holism' (or collectivism), remarks: 'The universe . . . is a unified whole that can to some extent be divided into separate parts, into objects made of molecules and atoms, themselves made of particles. But here, at the level of particles, the notion of separate parts breaks down. The subatomic particles – and therefore, ultimately, all parts of the universe – cannot be understood as isolated entities but must be defined through their interrelations.' Fritjof Capra, *The Turning Point: Science, Society, and the Rising Culture* (London: Fontana, 1983), p. 70. In other words, both Parfit (a defender of 'atomism') and Capra (an avowed 'holist') seem to consider interrelationships as core constituents of their respective ontologies. Consequently, an emphasis on interrelations might be expected to provide the basis for an ontology which both individualists and collectivists could readily accept.

4 See Steven Lukes, *Individualism* (Oxford: Blackwell, 1973).

5 On 'family resemblances', see Ludwig Wittgenstein, *Philosophical Investigations*, trans. G. E. M. Anscombe (Oxford: Blackwell, 1974), pp. 31–2.

Table 3.1 Individualism, interrelationism and collectivism

	Individualism	*Interrelationism*	*Collectivism*
a)	The individual is considered to possess supreme and intrinsic value or dignity.	Individuals are considered to possess value or dignity in their relations with others.	The collective is considered to possess supreme and intrinsic value or dignity.
b)	The individual is autonomous. Uninfluenced by others, he or she is self-directed.	Individuals are self-directed, while being significantly influenced by others.	The individual is subject to the totality of social forces. He or she is directed by the collective.
c)	The individual ought to be left a private sphere of thought and/or action immune from the incursions of others or a wider 'public'.	The individual ought to think and act not only with regard to himself or herself but also with regard to respecting the needs of others.	The individual ought to think and act solely with the collective in mind. The thoughts and actions of the collective are of ultimate value.
d)	The individual can and ought to promote his or her own self-development, and can do so alone.	Individuals can and ought to develop together, and ought to avoid attempting to do so at the expense of others.	The collective can and ought to experience self-development, irrespective of its individual members.
e)	The individual is pictured as possessing interests, wants, purposes and needs, etc., independently of any social context.	The individual's interests, wants, purposes and needs, etc. are affected by his or her relations with others, and so cannot be abstracted from those relations.	The individual's interests, wants, purposes and needs, etc. are the result of his or her relation to the collective, and so cannot be abstracted from it.
f)	If there is political authority, only individuals could be the source of it.	If there is political authority, only related individuals could the source of it.	Political authority obtains, and the collective is the only source of it.
g)	The individual should produce in order to satisfy his or her desires in his or her own way without regard for the needs of others.	The individual should produce in a way which takes into account not only his or her own needs and desires but also those of others.	The individual should produce in order to satisfy the desire of, and according to a plan which has been dictated by, the collective.
h)	The individual is responsible only for his or her own destiny.	Individuals are responsible for their own destinies and for the destinies of others.	The collective is responsible for its own destiny and for the destiny of its members.
i)	The individual is the source of all moral principles.	Interpersonal relations are the source of moral principles.	The collective is the source of all moral principles.

Individualism	*Interrelationism*	*Collectivism*
j) The individual is the only source and depository of knowledge.	Related individuals are the source of knowledge, and it is dispersed among them.	The collective is the source and depository of knowledge, providing the criteria of truth.
k) The individual (especially his or her psychology) is the basis of all explanations of social phenomena.	Related individuals are the basis of all explanations of social phenomena (for it is their relations which constitute it).	The collective, with its own laws, is the basis of all explanations of social phenomena.
l) Only individuals really exist. Society is a fiction.	Individuals exist in relations with others (thus forming societies).	Only collectives really exist. The individual is a fiction.

of these features, it might be obvious which family he or she belongs to. This is also true of different versions of individualism. It might be the case that no particular feature is present in all versions. However, a necessary condition of being a variety of individualism is that one or more of the features listed is present.

Although these features do not mutually entail each other, and although not every feature listed is accepted by all individualists, they often *do* go together and form what might be called a 'cluster' comprising, *inter alia*, political, economic, religious, ethical and epistemological – as well as methodological – individualisms. One reason why they often go together is that there is a close relationship between these elements and an element which Lukes does not list as a genuine 'family feature' of individualism–namely, ontological individualism. For example, if in seeking the explanation of social phenomena one entertains the view that society must be explained by the beliefs and dispositions of individuals alone, then an 'ontological individualism' might very well be what is being presupposed. It is clear that if one thinks that only individuals really exist, then one must also think that they are the basis of the true explanation of any social phenomenon. Ontological individualism (l) thus completes the left-hand column of Table 3.1. Moreover, an ontological individualist can easily argue not only for (k) – methodological individualism – but also for (a) through (j) in the left-hand column of Table 3.1 on the basis of his of her belief that only individuals really exist. A different ontology (for example, one that claims individuals exist within significant relations) might suggest a quite different set of family resemblances.

Now, adherents of methodological individualism often deny that it focuses upon individuals alone,[6] while frequently making claims that seem to imply the

6 Joseph Agassi, for example, denies that Karl Popper (who is considered by many to be the archetypal methodological individualist) is only concerned with isolated individuals. See Joseph Agassi, 'Methodological individualism' in O'Neill (ed.), *Modes of Individualism and Collectivism* (London: Heinemann, 1973), p. 188.

contrary. F. A. von Hayek, for example, states clearly enough that an individual's relationships are of relevance. But that notwithstanding, there is a pronounced tendency in most individualists to omit mention of relationships at crucial points in their explanations. Consider the following from Hayek: 'The structure of Men's mind, the common principle on which they classify external events, provide us with the knowledge of the recurrent elements of which different social structures are built up and in terms of which we can alone describe and explain them.'[7] Here, the ultimate explanation turns out to be the psychology of individuals. Relationships, rather than playing any crucial explanatory role, have to be explained in psychological terms. Instead of constituting a genuine element in social explanation, social relationships appear to be evaporated away by a reductionist methodology. Hence, there does seem to be some justification for attacking methodological individualism on the grounds that it is, in essence, psychological individualism, even though methodological individualists often vociferously deny the charge.[8]

It is all very well saying that relationships are significant, but when they come to be ignored at crucial points, then the position which frequently so ignores them can justifiably be criticized on that count, irrespective of its protestations of respect for social relationships. I shall, therefore, uncharitably characterize 'methodological individualism' as the attempt to explain social phenomena by reference to individuals' beliefs and dispositions, rather than by focusing upon the social relationships in which they arise.[9] This position can easily be associated with the ontological presupposition that there are no collective social entities, only individual human beings.

As there is a wealth of objections that have been raised against methodological individualism more generally construed,[10] I shall confine myself to one or two objections. Methodological individualists often attempt to explain certain social phenomena by reference to individuals holding beliefs in collective entities. For example, someone might claim to have made a sacrifice for the nation. Methodological individualists would have to reduce the nation to the attitudes of

7 F. A. Hayek, 'From *Scientism and the Study of Society*' in O'Neill (ed.), *Modes of Individualism and Collectivism*, p. 35.

8 Watkins, while denying that his individualism is reducible to 'psychological individualism', writes: 'The methodological truism which underlies this paper [is] that the social scientist can continue searching for explanations of a social phenomenon until he has reduced it to psychological terms.' Quoted in K. J. Scott, 'Methodological and epistemological individualism' in O'Neill (ed.), *Modes of Individualism and Collectivism*, p. 219.

9 This is justified in that one cannot claim that the *ultimate* explanations of social phenomena are individuals' beliefs, and then seriously discuss the social *causes* of those beliefs. To do so would imply that those causes explained the supposed ultimate explanations, which could not then be *ultimate* explanations.

10 See, for example, the criticisms of methodological individualism found in Lukes, *Individualism*, and in Part 4 of O'Neill (ed.), *Modes of Individualism and Collectivism*.

individuals.[11] But even if it is possible to explain much of what someone does in terms of a motivation engendered by his or her belief in a collective entity, and even if such an ostensibly *sui generis* entity does not exist, it does not follow that the individual is not situated in a network of objective social relationships which have explanatory primacy. That a supra-individual nation might not exist would not rule out the possibility that people who claimed to act in its name stood to others in concrete, coercive relationships or that those relationships might have primacy with regard to explaining individual behaviour. Methodological individualism, as I am characterizing it, should, it seems, thus be rejected in favour of a position which admits the ontological claim that a society is more than just individuals. A society is, surely, at the very least a collection of *related* individuals.

Individualists frequently claim that the whole is merely the sum of its parts. And it is usually stated by collectivists that the whole is more than the sum of its parts. But what do these respective claims mean?[12] When one adds up the parts of anything, one does not need to do so with those parts arranged in any special order. So, for example, the sum of the parts of an unassembled chair is the same no matter how those parts are laid out. In other words, the sum of the parts of a group ignores the relationships between those parts. But a whole cannot be understood without reference to such relationships. A chair is quite different to an unassembled heap of chair-parts. But the sum of the parts is the same irrespective of whether the chair is assembled or awaiting assembly. A chair has the same parts as those of an unassembled chair, but the assembled chair differs in so far as its parts are related to each other in specific ways – the legs must be joined to the seat, and so on. As Andrew Brennan remarks in *Thinking about Nature*: 'unless the word "sum" is being used in a special sense, a whole is never merely a sum of its parts, for it needs to be integrated and structured' in the relevant ways.[13] This is not a mere pedantic point, for unless one understands how a whole is structured, one will not be able to understand why it possesses the properties it does:

> certain wholes, those that are unified and causally integrated, will be more than merely the sum of their parts, for they have properties – powers – which their parts lack, that is, properties that are not inherited from any part on its own. A mere sum of parts, by contrast, only has those powers

11 Watkins: 'Whereas physical things can exist unperceived, social "things" like laws, prices, prime ministers and ration-books, are created by personal attitudes. (Remove the attitudes of food officials, shop-keepers, housewives, etc., towards ration-books and they shrivel into bits of card-board.) But if social objects are formed by individual attitudes, an explanation of their formations must be an individualistic explanation.' J. W. N. Watkins, 'Ideal types and historical explanation' in O'Neill (ed.), *Modes of Individualism and Collectivism*, p. 150.

12 For one analysis of the claim that the whole is more than the sum of its parts, see Ernest Nagel, *The Structure of Science: Problems in the Logic of Scientific Explanation* (London: Routledge and Kegan Paul, 1961), pp. 380–97.

13 Andrew Brennan, *Thinking about Nature: An Investigation of Nature, Value and Ecology* (London: Routledge, 1988), pp. 82–3.

> which it inherits from its various parts alone, and has no powers in its own right.[14]

But does any of this really have any relevance for developing a green political theory? That it certainly seems to will become apparent if we consider the methodology employed by Thomas Hobbes in his attempt to justify an absolute sovereign power – an argument upon which most eco-authoritarianism is ultimately based.

3.1.1.1 Hobbesian individualistic methodology

Hobbes, writing at the time of the English Civil War, was preoccupied with the breakdown of his society. His project in *Leviathan*[15] was to identify the requirements of a stable political order. And the method he chose purported to be scientific in so far as it mirrored the approach taken by the School of Padua – the resolutive/compositive method[16] – which has been described as the most successful scientific methodology of its day. This consisted in a two-part procedure: if one wishes to understand how something works, first of all, take it to pieces (the way of resolution), have a good look at its parts, and then put them back together again (the way of composition), taking note of how the various parts fit with one another. So, if one's aim is to discover how a clock works, one must take it apart, examine its spring or its weights, its winding mechanism, and so on, and then put it all back together. Hobbes' project was rather like repairing a clock that one did not understand. First, take it to bits, and then see how these bits should fit together if the clock is to work properly. As Hobbes thought that the motion of individuals in society was, in its fundamentals, little different from mechanical motion – individuals, in his view, move because of attraction and repulsion (desires and aversions) – then society could be understood and repaired in an analogous way.

Of course, Hobbes couldn't actually take his society apart in a real empirical experiment, but he had accounts of its collapse during the Civil War, and he could dismantle society in a thought-experiment. If one's goal is to understand how a currently broken-down society *should* work, imagine its component parts in isolation, study their properties, and then fit them together into a working whole. The first step is Hobbes' state of nature.

But is this really an appropriate methodology for comprehending how society works? While the resolutive/compositive method might have value in understanding simple mechanics, more recently developed sciences would find it

14 Ibid., p. 87.

15 Thomas Hobbes, *Leviathan*, ed. Richard Tuck (Cambridge: Cambridge University Press, 1991).

16 See J. W. N. Watkins, *Hobbes's System of Ideas* (London: Hutchinson, 1973), p. 32. However, that Hobbes adopted the resolutive/compositive method is challenged in Tom Sorell, *Hobbes* (London: Routledge, 1986), pp. 17–18. For a reply to Sorell, see Alan Carter, 'The method in Hobbes' madness', forthcoming.

wanting. Certainly, scientists can test a component when removed from its ordinary situation, but not, usually, in a vacuum all on its own without any outside influences. This method might have some value for understanding the workings of a very simple mechanical clock. It would be useless as a method for understanding how a modern, electronic, digital watch works. One would never understand how it worked by looking at its parts in isolation. Unless the parts were within an electrical circuit, one would be quite unable to understand any of their significant properties, never mind how the watch as a whole works.

Similarly, an ecologist would balk at the suggestion that ecosystems can be adequately comprehended by studying individual members of component species in isolation. Ecology is not elementary biology. One will simply fail to understand the properties of an ecosystem, an ecologist would insist, if one views it as a mere agglomeration of unconnected individuals. The parts of an ecosystem are not only interrelated, but interdependent. Key properties of any ecosystem are symbiosis and diversity – mutually beneficial relationships between diverse parts of the system. Is a society more like an old clock? Or is it more like an ecosystem? Well, it certainly isn't like an old clock! In short, the most persuasive and popular justification of authoritarian political philosophies employs what seems to be a completely inappropriate methodology, which assumes an apparently defective individualistic ontology. Such an individualism can be argued to be not only inadequate for understanding social relationships but also disastrous when it comes to ecological ones. A major reason for the environmental problems that we seem to be confronted with is the lack of awareness of, or plain disregard for, the highly complex relations within the ecosphere, as was indicated in Chapter 1. Trying to understand society without considering all of its interconnecting relationships is likely to be just as disastrous, as the subsequent chapters will attempt to show.

Now, it can be argued that much of the confusion regarding the individualism/collectivism debate arises because of the different ways in which the claim 'the whole is more than the sum of its parts' can be construed. If an individualist means by this claim 'the whole is more than the sum of the *related* parts', then he or she is right to reject it. If a collectivist means by the claim 'the whole is more than the sum of its *unrelated* parts', then he or she is right to assert it. But then, they would seem to be agreeing with the same proposition while rejecting what each takes to be other's statement of it. If this were the case, then there would indeed be a common ground. However, once the argument between individualists and collectivists gets under way, it soon becomes apparent that they are defending quite different propositions. Often, individualists very soon begin to make claims that assume the whole to be *less than* the sum of its *related parts* (namely, the whole is extensionally equivalent with the sum of its unrelated parts), while collectivists frequently very soon begin to make claims that assume the whole to be *more than* the sum of its *related parts.*

In other words, methodological individualism usually tacitly assumes an individualist ontology which holds that society can be understood to be less than the sum of related individuals (i.e. it is just the sum of individuals), and methodological collectivism usually assumes a collectivist ontology which holds that a society is to be understood as being more than the sum of the related individuals which make up that society. And if ontological individualism and ontological collectivism are conceived of in these two ways, then it becomes quite apparent that, although they are mutually exclusive, they are not jointly exhaustive – for a society can be taken to be no more and no less than the sum of the related individuals who compose it. And methodological individualism and methodological collectivism, which usually presume these respective ontologies, are not exhaustive either – they too allow of a middle way.

Hence, if by 'part' is meant 'an unrelated part', the collectivist would be correct to argue that wholes are more than the sum of their parts. Any whole must also include the relationships between its parts. That many who claim to be methodological individualists sometimes subscribe to the view that society is a collection of *related* individuals is beside the point. They frequently take a position which does not sufficiently stress this relational aspect. It is for this failing that methodological individualism must be rejected. My uncharitable characterization of methodological individualism, by effectively pin-pointing the target, enables such objections to be levelled clearly and decisively. But before I suggest a middle way between my uncharitable characterizations of individualism and collectivism, let me first turn to consider methodological collectivism.

3.1.2 Methodological collectivism

Many of those who subscribe to the view that methodological individualism is untenable regard themselves as methodological collectivists, even though they claim to reject such typically collectivist, supra-individual entities as 'group minds',[17] and so on. However, while many collectivists claim to deny the existence of such problematic supra-individual entities, I wish to contend that they often revert to an analysis which tacitly presupposes them.

How, then, are we to characterize methodological collectivism?[18] Collectivists, whether consciously or otherwise, frequently go so far as to claim that the behaviour of social individuals is determined by the whole. As it is this view which I especially wish to contest, in accordance with my principle of uncharity, I shall characterize 'methodological collectivism' as the attempt to explain social phenomena in terms of totalities determining their parts. As an example of this sort of view, Maurice Mandelbaum remarks: 'By holding that there is a necessary direction of change in a society as a whole, and by holding that form of global law which states that the whole is so related to its parts that the parts are determined by the whole, a law of change concerning a specific institution follows.'[19] Here,

17 Whether or not Rousseau's 'General Will' is to be construed in this way is a matter of some debate, but Hegel's *Geist* (which seems rather like the General Will discovering itself to be God) would seem to presume the existence of such an entity.

18 For one attempt, see Watkins, 'Ideal types and historical explanation', pp. 149–50.

19 Maurice Mandelbaum, 'Societal laws' in O'Neill (ed.), *Modes of Individualism and Collectivism*, p. 244.

Mandelbaum is clearly arguing that the whole determines its parts. He would not claim to subscribe to the view that society is a supra-individual entity like a 'group mind'. Yet I would suggest that his position is actually tantamount to the acceptance of such supra-individual entities, as I now attempt to show.

Because methodological collectivists tend to argue that individuals can only be understood in terms of their position within the social structure, they are prone to make the following claim: in order to understand an individual, one must understand the way in which that individual is related to society as a whole. For example, Mandelbaum writes: 'All of these types of law would be instances of an attempt to state global laws of the fundamental type, i.e., laws which involve the relation of its components to the concrete nature of a system considered as a whole.'[20] Hence, collectivists tend to focus on both individuals and groups simultaneously. If one is to understand a social individual, then one must understand how that individual is related to the whole which he or she is situated within. This might be regarded, for our purposes, as the paradigm response of collectivists to the problem of social relations. Now, this response could be taken to mean one of two things. It could mean that in order to understand a social individual, one must understand his or her logical relation to the whole, or it could mean one must understand the causal relation obtaining between the whole and the individual.

Let me begin with the logical relation between the individual and the whole. For methodological collectivists, if one is to understand how social individuals are related to each other, then one must look at their relations to the whole within which they are situated. In order to understand how a mother is related to her daughter, one needs to know how both are related to the whole – in this case, the family. But if, as this position claims, it is necessary to postulate a relation to a third entity in order to theorize the relation between particulars, how is one then to theorize the relation between the individual and the postulated third entity (the whole) which gives meaning to the relations between individuals? What must be posited to mediate between the individual and the third entity (the whole) which the individual is supposedly related to? A fourth entity? But that leads to an infinite regress.

X may be considered to be related to *Y* when they are similar in some respect – for example, by their membership of a class. *X* is related to *Y* when they are members of the same class *Z*. But if *Y* is a class which includes *X*, talk of the relationship of *X* to *Y* will, if one has certain relationships in mind, be highly problematic – what Gilbert Ryle has called a 'category mistake'[21] will be committed. To talk of the relationship of a particular mother to a particular daughter is to talk of a relationship within a particular family. But what of the relation of the mother to the family? The mother could be significantly related to another family; but what about the family of which she is a member? As the family she belongs to

20 Ibid., p. 242.

21 See Gilbert Ryle, *The Concept of Mind* (Harmondsworth: Penguin, 1963), pp. 17 ff.

includes herself, to talk of her relation to the family is, at least in part, to talk of her relation to all the members of the family. But, as she is one of those members, this is, *inter alia*, to talk of her relation to herself. And to ask questions concerning her relation to herself is somewhat odd, except when the relation is one of inclusion or identity or of the more general form '*X* is the same *Z* as *Y*'. But these can hardly be the *significant* relations between the whole and its parts which collectivists have in mind. Thus, the logical relation between a whole and its parts does not look like a promising basis for social explanations.

Let me, therefore, turn to the ostensible causal relation between the whole and the individual. David Hume, in his *Treatise of Human Nature*, argued that what we mean by the terms 'cause' and 'effect' entails that a cause and its effect be contiguous in space and time, and that a cause be prior to its effect.[22] Were Hume correct (and his approach to causation has certainly been very influential), then if society as a whole were thought to exert a causal influence on an individual (as most methodological collectivists assume), it would have to precede that individual. This can be argued to be so. Individuals are born into societies that have existed long before they were born. So, the cause having to be prior to the effect is not, apparently, too problematic for an established society.

What about spatial contiguity, though? One problem with such contiguity is that it rules out effects from a distant object. Let us side-step that problem by interpreting 'contiguity' as including both direct and indirect connections. In other words, an effect must be connected either directly or indirectly to its cause. So, given the requirement of contiguity, for a society to exert a causal influence on its members, then they would have to be conjoined to it in some direct or indirect way. But, contrary to common parlance, individuals are not conjoined to their society. *They are conjoined together so as to constitute a society.* Individuals are conjoined *to the rest* of their society – i.e. to their *complement. They are not conjoined to the society as a whole.* My contention is that the assumption that they are is the major error commonly committed by collectivists.

Consider group or class *G* and individual *A*, who is a member of *G*. One can talk coherently about *G* and *A*. For example, one could talk about *G*, then about *A*. One can talk about *G* and about *A* being included in it. But the 'and' conjoins claims about the group with claims about the individual. It does not conjoin the group with one of its members. If *G* consists of *A*, *B*, *C* and *D*, then talk of *G* being conjoined to *A* is no less than to talk of *A*, *B*, *C*, *D* and *A*. But this is to conjure up an extra *A* out of thin air. The conjunction is between the part and the whole of which it is a part, and the part thus occurs twice in any such formulation. Quite simply, wholes are not conjoined to their parts nor *vice versa*. For example, a dog's tail is not conjoined to the dog unless it has been severed from it. An unsevered dog's tail is conjoined to *the rest of the dog*, not to the dog. Whereas

22 See David Hume, *A Treatise of Human Nature*, ed. L. A. Selby-Bigge (Oxford: Clarendon, 1951), pp. 75–6. In Hume's view, if a cause were not temporally prior to its effect, then time would be impossible.

individualists often speak as if a tail were not joined to the rest of a dog, collectivists often speak as if a tail were joined to a dog which already has one.

Most importantly, this fallacy of thinking that a whole is conjoined to its parts can lead to a politically dangerous conclusion. When we talk about a whole being conjoined to its parts, and if we take each part in turn, then we have every part being conjoined to the whole which includes every part. A complete extra whole appears from nowhere as if by magic. This is particularly worrying in political philosophy when the magically arising whole is deemed to be what is of fundamental importance – for example, when all of the people can be sacrificed for the nation, or when all of the workers can be sacrificed for the proletarian class.[23] Moreover, there can also be very worrying implications when this fallacy is committed by those who purport to be ecologically aware. Consider the following:

> I believe that the universe is one being, all its parts are different expressions of the same energy, and they are all in communication with each other, therefore parts of one organic whole. (This is physics, I believe, as well as religion.) The parts change and pass, or die, people and races and rocks and stars; none of them seems to me important in itself, but only the whole.[24]

It is easy to move from this to the view that only 'Gaia' matters, and not the individual people, animals or plants who live within it. The political implications are serious indeed, for such a collectivist approach could cash out into the most abhorrent variety of eco-fascism.

But all of this seems to rest on a conceptual mistake. Quite simply, as it makes no sense at all to talk of parts being conjoined to their whole, or to talk of a whole being conjoined to its parts (because the whole just *is* the related parts), then it is bizarre to think that the whole matters and the parts are irrelevant.

Furthermore, as wholes are not conjoined to their parts, talk of causal relations between wholes and their parts would also appear to be incoherent. Collectivist social explanations would seem, therefore, to be, in effect, completely barren. Moreover, it is generally thought that for anything to affect causally or to determine something else, not only must it be (directly or indirectly) connected to it, it must be distinct from it. But if we take group *G* and its parts *A*, *B*, *C* and *D*, then *G* (which includes *A*) is not distinct from *A* in the relevant sense. So how can *G* affect causally or determine *A*? To talk of the whole causally affecting or determining one of its members is tantamount to setting up the whole as an entity distinct

23 With regard to classes as supra-individual entities, Marx and Engels write: 'the class, in its turn, achieves an independent existence over against the individuals, so that the latter . . . become subsumed under it.' Quoted in Richard Schmitt, 'What classes are: Bolshevism, democracy and class theory', *Praxis International*, Vol. 2, No. 4 (1983), p. 394.

24 Robinson Jeffers, quoted in Bill Devall and George E. Sessions, *Deep Ecology: Living as if Nature Mattered* (Salt Lake City: Peregrine Smith, 1985), p. 101. On such 'ecological holism', see Appendix C, below.

from its parts. To talk of the whole causally affecting or determining its parts is, therefore, tacitly to presuppose a supra-individual entity over and above the parts, and quite distinct from them. This, I suggest, is what many collectivists actually do, even while claiming that they entertain no beliefs in such supra-individual entities.

But in doubting the need to resort to supra-individual entities, am I not denying those properties which are only found in groups and not in isolated individuals? Not at all. I am not defending an ontology that comprises only *isolated* individuals, but one that contains *related* ones. And it is in relations that new properties emerge. Furthermore, as Brennan writes: 'There is no reason why we should not use the term "emergent" to apply to properties displayed by wholes that are not simply inherited from their parts. Use of the term, however, should not be taken to imply that emergent properties are in some special way novel or unpredictable.'[25] Take, for example, certain kinds of group behaviour. Individuals often behave differently in crowds than they do on their own. There might be considerably more bravado displayed in a group, for example. But this isn't because the group has some property of bravado over and above its members. The members relate to each other in such a way that bravado is displayed. For example, they show off to each other. Isolated individuals have no one to show off to. When individuals find themselves in relations, therefore, their behaviour often changes. This is one sense in which groups behave differently. Hence, as Brennan insists:

> To argue that the whole is more than the sum of its parts, and to deny ontological privilege to any special class of things is still compatible with maintaining that the properties, or powers, of wholes are explicable, at least to some extent, in terms of the properties and interaction of their parts. There is nothing either terminologically or ontologically reductionist about taking this line on explanation.[26]

Now, to deal with one objection that might be raised against what I am arguing, Mandelbaum insists that social institutions must be referred to when describing certain relationships: 'it is impossible to escape the use of societal concepts in attempting to understand some aspects of individual behaviour: concepts involving the notions of status and role cannot themselves be reduced to a conjunction of statements in which these or other societal concepts do not appear.'[27] But my behaviour towards a male bank teller, to take one of Mandelbaum's examples, is not determined by his status, but by what I take to be his status. If I think he is a bank robber, then I will react differently to him than if I think he is a bank teller. Furthermore, if I happen to walk into a bank just after a well-dressed bank robber has tied up the bank clerks, and if he happens to be standing behind the counter at the time, I will no doubt take him to be a bank teller and behave towards him

25 Brennan, *Thinking about Nature*, p. 88.
26 Ibid., pp. 87–8.
27 Mandelbaum, 'Societal laws', pp. 224–5.

accordingly. Certainly, a bank teller is situated within the institution of banking, but this example shows that individual psychological attitudes which are directed towards objects which do not necessarily exist as conceptualized *can* go a long way towards explaining 'social' behaviour.

Nevertheless, some relations clearly are social. Our conception of the bank teller needs to be explained in terms of the institution of banking. But all that it is necessary to admit is that there is taken to be an institution only within which certain delineated behaviour makes sense, rather like saying that there is a game only within which the behaviour of the players makes sense. And to understand this, all that is required is to comprehend the fact that the players restrict and define their behaviour with reference to a certain set of rules.[28] No supra-individual causal entity need be postulated. There is no need to regard a game as a supra-individual entity which *causes* the behaviour of its players. The need to refer to the institution of banking in order to comprehend the status of a supposed bank teller is the need to specify a role which makes sense given a certain set of rules, and not the need to summon forth a supra-individual entity which exerts power over those who are situated within the institution of banking either as officials or as customers.

To say that, of course, is not to deny that those within the institution exert a causal influence over each other. In fact, to say this is precisely to identify the relevant causal relations. It is not that the whole causally affects its parts, as, for example, several Marxist structuralists seem to think. It is that the parts causally affect each other[29] and, most importantly, it is to say that a part is causally affected by its *complement* within the whole which they together constitute.

3.1.2.1 The appeal of methodological collectivism

Why, then, should such problematic relationships to totalities of which one is a member ever have been posited in the first place? The most compelling reason for assuming that collective entities causally affect or determine their parts is the existence of certain features which are only present in groups, and not in isolated individuals – for example, group pressure or group feeling. As Ernest Gellner writes: 'That all members of [a] unit feel the *esprit de corps* is a generalization (which is seldom true); but that *esprit de corps* has influenced an individual is not to say that he has been influenced by isolable individuals or their acts.'[30] What,

28 For a seminal discussion of how structures are produced and reproduced, and how their rules are both enabling and constraining, see Anthony Giddens, *New Rules of Sociological Method* (London: Hutchinson, 1976).

29 What about organic entities? Does a dog not cause its legs to move? Strictly speaking, it does not. An electrical stimulus is sent from one part of the dog to another part. The muscles in the dog's legs contract when they are stimulated by a message which comes from another part of the dog. The different parts causally affect each other. The whole does not causally affect its parts.

30 Ernest Gellner, 'Explanations in history' in O'Neill (ed.), *Modes of Individualism and Collectivism*, p. 258.

though, are we to make of such an *esprit de corps*? Consider *A*, *B* and *C* to constitute a society, and regard them as exerting social pressure on one another. They are each subject to the same social pressure. Is this social pressure not a total force exerted on each individual?

To think that it is would be to fall prey to yet another confusion. *A* is subject to the pressure *x* exerted by *B* and *C*, but *B* is subject to the pressure *y* exerted by *A* and *C*, while *C* is subject to the pressure *z* exerted by *A* and *B*. Now, *x*, *y* and *z* may be the same *type* of pressure, but they are different *tokens*. Yes, it is true to say that everyone is subject to the same social pressure. But not because there is one total pressure exerted on all the individuals. Instead, it is because there is one type of pressure which each is subject to. The token of pressure exerted on any individual is the resultant (the 'vector') of the pressure exerted by his or her complement, and each complement must be a different token vis-à-vis each individual. The assumption that there is one concrete group pressure which each is subject to arises, in this case, out of confusing type with token. I suggest it is confusions such as this which lead to assumptions about the existence of supra-individual totalities that, supposedly, causally determine their parts.

A second kind of group feature which can give rise to beliefs in peculiar supra-individual entities is the occurrence of 'statistical effects'. If person *A* measures the length of a hockey pitch, he or she is likely to under- or over-estimate its length by some small amount. The same is true of person *B* and so on. Some will under-estimate, others will over-estimate. It is conceivable that no single person will actually arrive at the correct measurement. However, when we consider some large group of people measuring the pitch, then the results of those who seriously under-estimate will be balanced by the results of those who seriously over-estimate, the results of those who marginally under-estimate will be balanced by the results of those who marginally over-estimate, and therefore the group's average estimate will probably be correct (unless there is some factor present which leads to a systematic under or over-estimation – for example, if everyone uses the same inaccurate tape-measure).

Collectivists might at this point be inclined to think that, as no individual was correct but as the group as a whole produced the right answer, there must be a group over and above the various individuals. But what if, instead of many different individuals measuring the hockey pitch, one individual, say person *A*, measured the pitch every day of his or her life? Some days he or she under-estimates its length, other days he or she over-estimates it. The collection of results obtained throughout *A*'s life will exhibit exactly the same statistical effect as that exhibited by the collective results of a group of different people. But, surely, we would not want to claim that there was a group of person *A* which had an existence over and above that person! And we would be even less inclined to think that it exerted a casual influence over him or her! Clearly, then, such statistical effects are no grounds for assuming the existence of highly questionable kinds of supra-individual entities.

However, there is, apparently, one supra-individual entity that many do believe in: the nation. And the fact that different individuals throughout history have been members of the same nation suggests that something like a supra-individual entity – the 'nation' – exists. If there is no such entity, how are people known to be and to have been members of the same nation? Surely it is in virtue of being members of the same nation that these individuals are seen to be related?

Certainly, it appears that the nation must be posited for such relations to make any sense. But how do we actually ascertain that individuals belong to or have belonged to the same nation? We refer to relations of a geographical nature, modes of behaviour, parents, shared ideals, loyalty to certain leaders and their successors, allegiance to common institutions, and so on. These are the sorts of relationships we cite in order to show that individuals belong to or have belonged to the same nation.

However, factors such as allegiance to common institutions indicate that we need to take into account what we might call 'second order' relationships. Synchronically, nationals interrelate economically and politically such that specific economic and political structures are thereby constituted. Diachronically, those structures of economic and political relationships might change. They might do so gradually, or the transition might be revolutionary. Nevertheless, even in the case of revolutionary transformations, there remains some relationship between previous, present and future economic and political structures within any given territory. Consequently, at any moment in time, nationals interrelate economically and politically with, *inter alia*, other living nationals, thereby constituting structures of political and economic relations, which themselves relate to previous economic and political structures within which former nationals interrelated, while also relating to future economic and political structures within which future nationals will interrelate. Given that such second order relationships succeed in providing the necessary linkage between past, present and future nationals, the nation, construed as an extra supra-individual entity, is not required to provide it. In which case, Occam's razor should cut it down to size.

But, it might then be objected, nations can do things that ordinary individuals cannot. Nations can make treaties, for example. However, the followers of certain religions could, no doubt, believe that their God was bound by the promises which His or Her representatives claimed that He or She had made; but that hardly constitutes an argument for the existence of their God, never mind for His or Her existence as a causal entity. Thus, such reference to nations does not require the positing of a supra-individual entity which exerts a causal influence upon its members (although some claiming to be its agents frequently exert, in its name, a causal influence over others). As Joel Feinberg writes:

> A corporate entity, of course, is more than a mere collection of things that have some important traits in common. Unlike a biological species, an institution has a charter, or constitution, or bylaws, with rules defining offices and procedures, and it has human beings whose function it is to administer the rules and apply the procedures. When the institution has a duty to an outsider, there is always some determinant human being whose duty it is to do

> something for the outsider, and when the state, for example, has a right to collect taxes, there are always certain definite flesh and blood persons who have rights to demand tax money from other citizens. We have no reluctance to use the language of corporate rights and duties because we know that in the last analysis these are rights or duties of individual persons, acting in their 'official capacities'. And when individuals act in their official roles in accordance with valid empowering rules, their acts are imputable to the organization itself and become 'acts of state'. Thus, there is no need to posit any individual superperson named by the expression 'the State' (or for that matter, 'the company', 'the club', or 'the church').[31]

In short, methodological collectivism appears to provide no improvement on methodological individualism. Both seem to be equally untenable.

3.1.3 Methodological interrelationism

I have rejected both methodological individualism and methodological collectivism as I have uncharitably characterized them. My characterizations have been suggested by the criticisms of each position by its respective adversaries. However, this might, after all, not be as unfair a practice as it initially appears, because the adherents of each standpoint *do* seem to display a tendency to fall into those positions which are the objects of criticism. And adopting this uncharitable procedure enables us to rule out the positions which, upon examination, do not appear to be viable. If methodological individualism is thought of as involving the belief that to understand the individual in society it is merely necessary to understand the individual abstracted from his or her social relations, and if methodological collectivism is thought to involve the belief that, in order to understand the individual in society, one must theorize a causal relation between that individual and his or her society as a totality, then these two positions can be rejected in favour of a 'third path': it is possible to understand the individual in society by focusing, not on an isolated part, nor on a part as if it were significantly related to a whole, but on that individual as a part so related to the other parts that a whole of a specific sort is constituted. This third approach, I shall call 'methodological interrelationism'.[32]

31 Joel Feinberg, 'The rights of animals and unborn generations' in W. T. Blackstone (ed.), *Philosophy and Environmental Crisis* (Georgia: University of Georgia Press, 1974), pp. 56–7.

32 One ramification of interrelationism is worth drawing out: In a society *S* consisting of *A*, *B* and *C*, the extension of '*A* who is socially related to *B* and *C*, who are themselves so related to the others' is the same as 'Society *S*'. It is thus misleading to claim that in order to understand a society one must understand the socially related individuals, and it is also misleading to claim that in order to understand the socially related individuals one must understand the society. To understand one *is the same thing* as understanding the other.

If a society is the same thing as the socially related individuals who compose it, then the

Even though both methodological individualists and methodological collectivists make claims we can assent to, they each appear to have their own excesses. The methodological individualist is in error when he or she omits relevant relational features. I shall call this error '*the individualist fallacy*'. At the other extreme, the illicit attempt to explain certain facts about social individuals in terms of their relations to the totality of which they are a part, I shall call '*the collectivist fallacy*'. And such illicit attempts arise when the totality is thought to affect causally or to determine its parts.[33] By dismissing both methodological individualism and methodological collectivism because of their excesses, we can lay claim to the common-sense, common ground.

So, by 'methodological interrelationism', I mean a perspective which attempts to understand social individuals in terms of the way that these individuals who comprise a collectivity so relate to each other (and not to the collectivity) that the specific collectivity is constituted.[34] By 'methodological individualism', I mean a perspective which attempts, overtly or covertly, consciously or unconsciously, to understand social individuals in isolation from each other. And by 'methodological collectivism', I mean a methodological perspective which attempts, overtly or covertly, consciously or unconsciously, to understand social individuals in terms of the way that those individuals who comprise a collectivity are determined or causally affected by that collectivity.

Earlier, I mentioned that there are a 'cluster' of views which are 'individualist'. It is possible to construct an antithetical cluster of views which are 'collectivist', as in the right-hand column of Table 3.1. However, a 'middle way' between the individualist and collectivist clusters is also possible. One such interrelational

---

following attempted solution to the apparent individual/society problem fails: 'So-called methodological individualists hold that the behaviour of individuals causes society to display certain features or characteristics (and thereby fully explains these characteristics or effects) – hence, how society works, and what it is, can be explained and accounted for, in terms of the behaviour of the individuals, which make up society and constitute its cause. So-called collectivist theorists reverse the causal order, and hold that it is society which causes individuals to behave in certain ways. Hence, society is the cause and individual behaviour the effect. The truth of the matter may be more complex than either side assumes – as the processes of interaction between individuals and society are open-ended and loopish, the one (the individuals) has effects upon the other (society), just as surely as the latter has effects on the former.' Keekok Lee, *Social Philosophy and Ecological Scarcity* (London: Routledge, 1989), p. 56.

33 For example, while Fritjof Capra sounds distinctly interrelationist in the quotation in note 3, above, in the very next paragraph he writes: 'atomic phenomena are determined by their connections to the whole'. Capra, *The Turning Point*, p. 70. And a few pages later he adds: 'it is the whole that determines the behaviour of the parts.' Ibid. p. 76. One problem with New Age thinking in general is a common reliance on the confused notion of 'holism', which seems to slide indiscriminately between interrelationism and collectivism, and which is liable to engender the collectivist fallacy.

34 C.f.: 'we would expect the doings of nations to be reducible to the inter-related doings of people in them'. Simon Blackburn, *Spreading the Word: Groundings in the Philosophy of Language* (Oxford: Oxford University Press, 1984), p. 166.

cluster is presented in the central column of Table 3.1. Given an acceptance of ontological interrelationism (namely, that individuals so relate to each other that a society of a specific form is constituted – in other words, a society just *is* interrelated individuals), it is not too difficult to construct arguments for (a) through (k) in the middle column of Table 3.1. Suffice it to say that my preference is, by and large, for the interrelationist and against the individualist and collectivist clusters.

How, then, do methodological individualism, methodological collectivism and methodological interrelationism sit with ecological thinking? In committing the individualist fallacy, methodological individualism would, clearly, be inappropriate. As was remarked earlier, any serious ecologist would grimace at the thought that ecosystems could be understood by studying individual members of a species outside of their relations to others within their wider environment. In short, neither the component parts of ecosystems nor social individuals can be properly understood outside of the relations in which they are embedded.

On the other hand, rigorous ecologists do not commit the collectivist fallacy, either. They do not make the kind of fallacious connections between wholes and their parts that methodological collectivists frequently espouse. Ecologists, by and large, take a 'systems theory' approach to the study of the ecosphere. They study how individual parts relate so that an ecosystem is constituted. And it is worth observing how often ecologists refer to the interrelations between the parts of an ecosystem. For example, as Neil Evernden writes: 'The really subversive element in Ecology rests not on any of its more sophisticated concepts, but upon its basic premise: interrelatedness.'[35]

In a word, the methodology of ecologists would appear to be interrelationist. Hence, in an effort to provide the foundations for a genuinely green political theory, I shall endeavour to work within an interrelationist perspective, given that it seems to be the methodological approach most in accord with ecological thinking. In the following chapter, I offer an interrelationist theory of history, and in Chapter 6, I indicate how the interrelations between the elements identified in that theory would appear to produce disastrous environmental consequences, such as those briefly outlined in Chapter 1.

3.2 Freedom

Thus far, I have focused upon *methodological* individualism, collectivism and interrelationism. But individualism and collectivism as clusters contain significant *political* differences. This is most evident in their different conceptions of freedom.

In developing a green political theory, the question of freedom is one which

35 Neil Everndon, quoted in Devall and Sessions, *Deep Ecology*, p. 48. And it is worth noting that Haeckel originally defined 'ecology' as 'the study of all the complex interrelations referred to by Darwin as the conditions for the struggle for existence.' Quoted in Lee, *Social Philosophy and Ecological Scarcity*, p. 46.

cannot be avoided, for environmentalists have often been accused of wishing to inhibit everyone's freedom. If this were indeed true of all environmentalists, then it would make green political practice unappealing in a world which values freedom so highly. And if green political practice were to lack any appeal, then it would be even more difficult to solve environmental crises effectively. Thus, it might be concluded that if we are to answer the environmental challenge, green political practice requires a far wider appeal. And if it is to have widespread appeal, then it would benefit from being genuinely liberatory, rather than unpalatably inhibitory. In which case, any political theory informing such practice would have to pay adequate attention to the question of freedom.

But could an effective green political practice turn out to be liberatory? Or is it doomed to be oppressive? To answer this question, we first require a clear understanding of what 'freedom' means. And without doubt, the most influential discussion of 'freedom' and its cognate 'liberty' is that of Isaiah Berlin, who draws a famous distinction between what he terms 'negative' and 'positive' freedom.

3.2.1 Negative freedom

Negative freedom is the object of concern when answering the question: 'What is the area within which the subject – a person or group of persons – is or should be left to do or be what he [or she] is able to do or be, without interference by other persons?'[36] There is a clear basis for this conception of freedom, for freedom is often associated with absence of interference. On this conception, freedom can be regarded as 'simply the area within which a man [or woman] can act unobstructed by others'.[37] If one is prevented by others from doing what one would otherwise be able to do, then one is unfree. And the less one is interfered with by others, the freer one is.

Clearly, if one were to be free from all interference, then one would be able to interfere in what others wished to do. So, if everyone is to be as free as possible from interference by others, then certain constraints are required on each person's behaviour. But such constraints should, it is often argued, only prevent a person from interfering with others. The classical liberal tradition, for example, insists that 'there ought to exist a certain minimum area of personal freedom which must on no account be violated'.[38] In other words, liberals insist that there ought to be a wide range of activities which individuals should be free to pursue without interference by the wider public or, especially, the state. For the state to interfere in the area of private behaviour would be despotic. Hence, 'the defence of liberty consists in the "negative" goal of warding off interference.'[39]

36 Isaiah Berlin, 'Two concepts of liberty' in Anthony Quinton (ed.), *Political Philosophy* (Oxford: Oxford University Press, 1967), p. 141.

37 Ibid.

38 Ibid., p. 143.

39 Ibid., p. 146.

Where this has been most stressed is in the assertion that the owner of private property should be free to enjoy it without any interference. Significantly, one of the eleven 'incidents' which, in his influential discussion of property rights, A. M. Honoré lists as comprising 'full liberal ownership' is the right – the 'liberty' – to destroy what one owns.[40] The freedom of the owner of private property to use his or her property as he or she sees fit, with minimal interference from others, thus has potentially disastrous environmental consequences, for it can cash out (and, many would say, has already cashed out) into the 'right' of landowners to degrade their land and the 'right' of factory owners to pollute the environment – the latter harm tending to be ignored as an 'externality'. And, of course, it is the suggestion that these activities ought to be curtailed which has incurred the charge that greens are antithetical to freedom.

3.2.2 Positive freedom

Whereas negative freedom can be loosely characterized as consisting in freedom *from*, positive freedom can be loosely characterized as consisting in freedom *to*; and it is positive freedom which is the object of concern when answering the questions: 'By whom am I ruled?' or 'Who is to say what I am, and what I am not, to be or do?'[41] Or, put another way, a concern with positive freedom is what lies behind the question: 'What, or who, is the source of control or interference, that can determine someone to do, or be, one thing rather than another?'[42] This conception of freedom derives from wanting to be one's own master. Being free in this sense consists in acting in accordance with one's own reasons, rather than being dictated to or being subject to others. In a word, being free is to be self-directed.

The conception of positive freedom developed in a very different direction to that of negative freedom. Whereas the latter has come to be what liberal individualists espouse, positive freedom has come to be what many collectivists ostensibly promote. Moreover, it has come to be associated with totalitarianism. How has this come about? According to Berlin, the notion of self-mastery came to be understood as not being a slave to anything – for example, not being a slave to nature or to one's passions. The latter can be interpreted as entailing that one possesses a rational, higher self, which brings one's unbridled passions under control. One is free when one acts according to reason, say, and not according to one's passing desires. The higher, rational self then came to be identified with the community. Consequently, the higher self is supposedly revealed when one acts in accordance with the collective's purposes, rather than when one follows one's individual preferences. So, whereas the concept 'negative freedom' tended to

40 See A. M. Honoré, 'Ownership' in A. G. Guest (ed.), *Oxford Essays in Jurisprudence* (London: Oxford University Press, 1961), p. 13.

41 Berlin, 'Two concepts of liberty', p. 148.

42 Ibid., p. 141.

become very individualistic, the concept 'positive freedom' tended to become collectivist.

In short, as the conception of positive freedom developed historically – through Rousseau and Hegel – freedom came no longer to consist in identifying with one's passing individual desires, but with the community as a whole. As Berlin writes:

> This entity is then identified as being the 'true' self which, by imposing its collective, or 'organic', single will upon its recalcitrant 'members', achieves its own, and, therefore, 'higher' freedom. The perils of using organic metaphors to justify the coercion of some [people] by others in order to raise them to a 'higher' level of freedom have often been pointed out. But what gives such plausibility as it has to this kind of language is that we recognize that it is possible, and at times justifiable, to coerce men [and women] in the name of some goal (let us say, justice or public health) which they would, if they were more enlightened, themselves pursue, but do not, because they are blind or ignorant or corrupt. This renders it easy for me to conceive of myself as coercing others for their own sake, in their, not my, interest. I am then claiming that I know what they truly need better than they know it themselves.[43]

And in claiming that individuals have a true, higher self, it can be argued that by making someone do what his or her higher self would want were it not subordinate to, say, passing desires, one is making that person more free. It is in this way that the conception of positive freedom can easily lead to totalitarianism. As Berlin continues:

> Once I take this view, I am in a position to ignore the actual wishes of men [and women] or societies, to bully, oppress, torture them in the name, and on behalf, of their 'real' selves, in the secure knowledge that whatever is the true goal of [hu]man [beings] (happiness, fulfilment of duty, wisdom, a just society, self-fulfilment) must be identical with this freedom – the free choice of his [or her] 'true', albeit submerged and inarticulate, self.[44]

Berlin acknowledges that the concept 'negative freedom' could be similarly abused. However, as a matter of historical fact, it is the concept 'positive freedom' which has developed in this particular way. And whereas the desire to be master of oneself might imply that if a people is to be master of itself, then it requires democratic institutions, the concept of positive freedom has so developed that it has been used to justify tyranny.

In order to see how positive freedom can lead to a justification of totalitarianism, consider Christopher Caudwell, who insists that if they are merely slaves to

43 Ibid., pp. 150–1.
44 Ibid., p. 151.

their environment, then people are not free. Rather, freedom requires being able consciously to control one's environment; and that requires knowledge. Hence, to be free, one needs to understand the laws of nature. Such knowledge allows one, for example, to utilize a lever in order to move a stone. Thus, one is free to move a large stone only if one has the requisite knowledge of natural laws. Hence, according to Caudwell, freedom is not opposed to determinism. Instead, it is 'a special form of determinism – namely, the consciousness of it'.[45] The more knowledge one acquires of causal processes, the more free one becomes. Moreover, if the stone is very large, and if it is to be moved successfully, then it is necessary for many individuals to work collectively with the lever. Clearly, social organization is required for certain kinds of activity – most importantly, in Caudwell's view, for the social production which creates the community's means of subsistence. Social organization, therefore, makes people free. It enables them to produce the things they need in order to do whatever it is that they want to do.

However, social organization requires certain restrictions. As Caudwell writes: 'all "constraints", "obligations", "inhibitions", and "duties" of society are the very means by which freedom is obtained by men [and women].'[46] But 'constraints', 'obligations', 'inhibitions', and 'duties' are frequently considered to curtail freedom. To assert that they entail freedom seems at first glance to be paradoxical, at best, if not just plain false. Nevertheless, social constraints *can* be seen to be consistent with freedom if one employs the concept 'positive freedom', rather than the concept 'negative freedom'. For example, such constraints enable social forces to be used to create the wealth that allows society to do more than it would otherwise have been able to do.

Now, as (in Caudwell's view) state-communism understands 'the causality of society',[47] it makes possible a far greater freedom, because freedom requires knowledge of causal processes. The bourgeoisie, acting within a capitalist system, on the other hand, do not understand social causation. Hence, they are trapped within market relations which they are unable to control. Thus, there is very limited freedom in capitalist societies:

> Any definition of liberty is humbug that does not mean this: liberty to do what one wants. A people is free whose members have liberty to do what they want – to get goods they desire and avoid the ills they hate. What do [people] want? They want to be happy, and not to be starved or despised or deprived of the decencies of life. They want to be secure, and friendly with their fellows, and not conscripted to slaughter and be slaughtered. They want to marry, and beget children, and help, not oppress each other. Who is free who cannot do these things, even if he [or she] has a vote, and free speech? Who

45 Christopher Caudwell, *The Concept of Freedom* (London: Lawrence and Wishart, 1977), p. 61.
46 Ibid., p. 64.
47 Ibid., p. 73.

> then is free in bourgeois society, for not a few [people] but millions are forced by circumstances to be unemployed, and miserable, and despised, and unable to enjoy the decencies of life?[48]

All this sounds like an admirable criticism of the lack of freedom which, it can be argued, many people in capitalist societies face.

Unfortunately, Caudwell doesn't stop here. Only a couple of pages later we find him adding the following:

> And as Russia shows, even in the dictatorship of the proletariat, before the classless State has come into being, [a person] is already freer. He [or she] can avoid unemployment, and competition with his [or her] fellows, and poverty. He [or she] can marry and beget children, and achieve the decencies of life. He [or she] is not asked to oppress his [or her] fellows.[49]

Caudwell is arguing that because people in Russia at the time he was writing – two decades on from the 1917 Revolution – were free to work, to marry, and to enjoy an acceptable standard of living, they lived in a relatively free society. But as Richard Norman points out:

> The regime which Caudwell is trying to justify here is the Stalinist regime of the thirties, with its purges, show trials, forced labour and forced collectivization of agriculture. Whatever we may count as the achievements of that regime, the promotion of freedom is hardly likely to figure prominently in the list. . . .[50]

To describe such a situation – one in which people were so coerced – as one embodying freedom would only be possible if negative freedom (in particular, when it is construed as freedom from coercion) were not valued at all.

Moreover, the collectivist regimes which Caudwell is defending have, in the view of many, proven to be ecological disasters. The collective purpose has been so emphasized in state-communist societies that its unbounded pursuit of industrialization has led to (what many consider) serious environmental deterioration in Eastern Europe (for example, Romania's 'black town' – Copsa Mica – arguably competes with Brazil's Cubatão for the title of 'the world's dirtiest town'),[51] as

48 Ibid., pp. 72–3.

49 Ibid., p. 74.

50 Richard Norman, *Free and Equal* (Oxford: Oxford University Press, 1987), pp. 33–4.

51 See Steven Yearley, *The Green Case: A Sociology of Environmental Issues, Arguments and Politics* (London: Routledge, 1992), p. 183n. '[T]he ecological problems created by industrialization in the Soviet Union and Eastern Europe are fearsome. Indeed, in most respects industrialization under "state socialism" has been more environmentally damaging than under capitalism. . . . At present, the capitalist West looks environmentally far superior to the state-dominated East.' Ibid., pp. 105–6. However, as Yearley surmises: 'this may be because

well as in the urban districts of China. Collectivists have so valued the collective that many of them have been relatively unconcerned with harm befalling individuals. Not surprisingly, then, collectivist regimes appear to have been quite happy to sacrifice both individual people and their environment.

3.2.3 A triadic conception of freedom

That there is something unacceptable about rejecting negative freedom and opting instead for positive freedom seems clear from the unpalatable conclusion Caudwell reaches. But the problems he identifies with negative freedom seem to show that there is something equally unacceptable about rejecting positive freedom and opting instead for negative freedom.

One can only regard a situation lacking external interference, but where many are unable to do very much, as one of freedom if positive freedom is not valued at all. Nevertheless, as unacceptable as this appears, one frequent rejoinder to proponents of positive freedom is the assertion that one is only free when one is free from interference, and that this is all that freedom involves. Were this so, negative freedom would be a sufficient condition for being free. In which case, the lack of freedom to do the things that one could not afford to do could be disregarded. According to many advocates of the capitalist system, we live in a free society – that everyone is not free to enjoy what the wealth of the few can purchase is, in their view, of no account.

But can it be assumed that one is free solely on the grounds of being free from any interference with whatever little one might own? By analogy, if, while strolling in a university college, one noticed a sign warning that students were prohibited from walking on the grass, one would surely not conclude that students were prohibited! Being *prohibited from* something does not necessarily mean that one is *prohibited sans phrase.* Similarly, that one is free from something should not, therefore, simply be assumed to entail that one is free. Hence, merely being free from interference with one's property should not be taken to entail that one is free, especially when one might possess so little property that one finds oneself unable to do very much. On the other hand, by analogy, pointing out to obnoxious intruders that they were welcome to leave certainly would not mean that they were welcome! Being *welcome to* do something does not necessarily mean that one is *welcome.* Similarly, that one is free to do something should not, therefore, simply be assumed to entail that one is free. Hence, merely being free to partake of the benefits of a state-communist society should not be taken to

some of the environmental costs of the West's wealth are borne by the Third World, whereas the Soviet Union, for example, has to a larger extent felt the effect of its own drive for industrialization.' Ibid., p. 106. In comparing the West with the East, the enormous costs of the West's affluence on the South ought, surely, to be itemized on the West's balance sheet. If such accounting were practised, then the likely result would be that the individualist West and the collectivist East were shown to be roughly as bad, in environmental terms, as each other.

entail that one is free, especially when one might be subject to considerable coercion and prevented even from leaving the country.

So, on the one hand, if one is free from interference by others with the enjoyment of one's property, but one has so little property in a propertarian society that one can achieve few of one's aims, then it is unlikely that one is enjoying much freedom. But, on the other hand, if one is free to partake of the benefits of a particular society, but one is constantly subject to constraint or coercion, then one would not seem to have much freedom there, either. The problem would appear to be that, while proponents of negative freedom seem to have come to regard individuals as isolated entities who ought to be kept as separate as possible, contained within the boundaries of their property rights, many proponents of positive freedom have come to regard the collective as all-encompassing and all-important, so much so that those acting in its name may interfere in the lives of others to whatever degree they wish. Both negative and positive freedom can thus be regarded as displaying in a particularly pernicious form the dichotomy between individualism and collectivism. Both appear to be unacceptably one-sided. And, it can be argued, both approaches have proven to be politically and environmentally disastrous.

Instead, what seems to be required is a far more interrelationist approach – one that is not indifferent to the harmful relations which can result from the promotion of either negative or positive freedom on its own, while being able to synthesize whatever remains of value in both conceptualizations. This can be accomplished by considering negative and positive freedom not as sufficient conditions, but as *necessary conditions*, for being free. In fact, Gerald MacCallum Jr. goes so far as to argue against the very distinction between negative and positive freedom. Both are dyadic relations – one concerns the freedom of an agent or agents *from* interference, the other concerns the freedom of an agent or agents *to* do something – whereas, MacCallum argues, the freedom of agents is in fact a triadic relation:

> Whenever the freedom of some agent or agents is in question, it is always freedom from some constraint or restriction on, interference with, or barrier to doing, not doing, becoming, or not becoming something. Such freedom is thus always *of* something (an agent or agents), *from* something, *to* do, not do, become, or not become something; it is a triadic relation. Taking the format '*x* is (is not) free from *y* to do (not do, become, not become) *z*,' *x* ranges over agents, *y* ranges over such 'preventing conditions' as constraints, restrictions, interferences, and barriers, and *z* ranges over actions or conditions of character or circumstance. When reference to one of these three terms is missing in such a discussion of freedom, it should only be because the reference is thought to be understood from the context of the discussion.[52]

52 Gerald C. MacCallum, Jr., 'Negative and positive freedom' in P. Laslett, W. G. Runciman and Q. Skinner (eds), *Philosophy, Politics and Society: Fourth Series* (Oxford: Blackwell, 1972), p. 176.

In other words, the freedom of agents always involves those agents being free *from* some interference so that they are able *to* do something. Freedom concerns a relationship between three terms, not just two. Hence, according to MacCallum, the distinction between negative and positive freedom fails to differentiate between two genuinely alternative kinds of freedom. Neither is an authentic variety of freedom, for 'freedom' is a relational concept requiring three terms, whereas both negative and positive freedom only relate two of those terms. At best, in MacCallum's view, the distinction over-emphasizes one or other feature of every example of freedom concerning agents. As such, both the negative freedom espoused by individualists and the positive freedom espoused by collectivists seem partial and inadequate. Surely, then, being genuinely free requires both positive and negative sides to be satisfied.

This implies, *inter alia*, that a respect for freedom requires a rejection of inegalitarian distributions of private property, because the disproportionate power of the wealthy, which is purchased at the expense of the poor, means that freedom can only be maximized throughout society by rendering the wealthy less potent. If inequalities in power are the result of inequalities in wealth, the latter would have to be opposed. Quite simply, a respect for liberty surely does not mean a respect for the freedom of one group at the total expense of another. It means, surely, freedom for all. The power of the wealthy is located within a zero-sum game. The property holder's power to do with his or her property as he or she wishes is exercised at the expense of those who are excluded from so doing. We cannot afford to overlook such relations between people. Thus, we require a conception of freedom that is considerably more interrelational than the individualistic one. The triadic conception succeeds in taking more of the relations between individuals into account by drawing attention to those things which it is in their power *to* do or not, as the case may be. And that requires us to consider what it is that property relations allow some, but not others, to enjoy, perform, accomplish, and so on.

On the other hand, if genuine freedom requires both positive and negative sides to be satisfied, valuing freedom would imply opposing the coercion of individuals in the name of a supposedly all-important collective. The triadic conception of freedom draws attention to whatever it is that, in order to be free, one needs to be free *from*. And that includes coercion as an instance of power exercised by some over others in the name of the collective. In other words, the triadic conception of freedom turns out to be more interrelational than the collectivist one, for, unlike the latter, it does not leave certain coercive power relationships out of account. And this has important political implications. For when political power is a zero-sum game – in other words, when some can only have power to control others within any society at the cost of those others lacking that power – valuing genuine freedom would entail an opposition to unequal distributions of power. Valuing freedom thus seems to imply valuing political equality. In other words, it is not only economic equality that genuine freedom seems to demand but also some form of genuine democracy.

Moreover, from the standpoint of the more interrelational, triadic conception of freedom (where the relationships involved in being free from interference and the relationships involved in being free to do various things are all taken into account), it could be argued that if democracy is necessary to protect freedom, and if there are economic preconditions for freedom as well as political ones, then it is necessary for democracy to be extended to the production process – to the sphere of work – so that the economic preconditions of freedom can likewise be safeguarded. To secure freedom, the economic structure, too, would have to be democratized. All of this suggests that if green political practice is to be genuinely liberatory and have the widest possible appeal, then it must seek to further freedom, increase equality and establish genuinely democratic decision procedures, both at the political and the economic level.

Of course, in most societies, including our own, economic relations are most certainly not democratically controlled. Furthermore, democratic control of the workplace is something that most proponents of negative freedom vehemently oppose, because they consider it to be an infringement on the freedom of the enterprise's owner. But, given the above analysis, this reaction must be taken either to rely on an inadequate concept of 'freedom' or to display a complete disregard for the freedom of all but the wealthy minority. Most people experience very little freedom regarding their work – even though it constitutes a major part of their lives – and are, instead, subject to considerable power exerted over them, often quite arbitrarily, by others.[53]

However, whereas 'power over' is a zero-sum game, there is another kind of power – the kind Caudwell draws our attention to with his example of several individuals pulling together on a lever in order to move a large stone. This is not a zero-sum form of power, for it is not a variety of power which is only increased at another's expense. Rather, the power to move a stone is of a kind which can be increased for all by means of cooperation. So, whereas 'power over' is always maximized at another's expense and is, therefore, a zero-sum game, 'power to' can be maximized through cooperation. And as an interrelational analysis thus seems to imply, freedom is maximized by minimizing another's power over one, while maximizing one's power to do what one chooses to do. In Chapter 7, I outline some of the features of a cooperative form of society that could reconcile freedom, democracy and equality, and, in the process, avoid bringing about the devastation which appears to have been wreaked on the environment by individualist and collectivist societies, alike. In short, I attempt to show that green politics can, in practice, be genuinely liberatory and thus highly appealing.

Now, an interrelationist perspective – the perspective which seems to be most consistent with ecological thinking – focuses upon the way in which things interrelate. This involves how one thing affects another. And politically, one most affects another ordinarily through the exercise of power, or so it would appear. Hence, if we are to understand fully how people interrelate, we require an

53 For an instructive example of this, see Michael Walzer, *Spheres of Justice* (New York: Basic Books, 1983), pp. 295–303.

adequate conception of power. Moreover, in order to develop a green *political* theory, it is necessary to focus upon the relations that are of most concern to political theorists: namely, power relations. (And of course, the question of freedom cannot be divorced from an analysis of the exercise of power if it is indeed true that valuing genuine freedom entails opposition to unequal distributions of power.) Thus, having isolated a general perspective to adopt for the study of society – an interrelationist one – and having seen what an adequate conception of freedom seems to involve, let us now focus on a key notion for any political theory: the concept of 'power'. For an analysis of power will, I suggest, add more weight to the claim that eco-authoritarianism, eco-reformism and eco-Marxism are inadequate political theories, and must, ultimately, be rejected.

3.3 The dimensions of power

Let me begin by noting some common characterizations of the concept 'power'. As with 'freedom', the various conceptualizations of 'power' that have been proposed have tended to fall within quite distinct political traditions. This is not surprising in so far as different conceptions of 'power' isolate different kinds of behaviour as instances of the exercise of power, and it is different kinds of behaviour which different political traditions consider to be problematic. But the inability to identify some behavioural forms as instances of the exercise of power has invited the criticism that the conceptualization of 'power' in question is thereby deficient.

Thus, it has been argued that certain pluralists,[54] for example, have conceptualized 'power' in such a way that agenda-setting can easily be overlooked as an instance of power, and on that ground is deficient. It has also been argued that certain more critical and reformist liberals[55] have conceptualized 'power' in such a way that agenda-setting is identified as an exercise of power, but the foisting onto others of an ideology fails to be so identified – making it a deficient conceptualization. It has further been argued that a radical 'semi-Marxist' such as Steven Lukes,[56] on the other hand, has conceptualized 'power' in such a way that both agenda-setting and the foisting onto others of an ideology might be identified as exercises of power, but that the paternalistic practice of the Bolshevik Party can easily be overlooked, and this renders Lukes' conceptualization deficient. In this section, I attempt to go beyond Lukes' conceptualization of 'power' by seeking a standpoint from which one would be able to identify all of these seemingly significant varieties of power.

54 See, for example, Robert A. Dahl, *Who Governs? Democracy and Power in an American City* (New Haven: Yale University Press, 1961) and Nelson W. Polsby, *Community, Power and Political Theory* (New Haven: Yale University Press, 1963).

55 See, for example, Peter Bachrach and Morton S. Baratz, *Power and Poverty: Theory and Practice* (New York: Oxford University Press, 1970).

56 See Steven Lukes, *Power: A Radical View* (London: Macmillan, 1974).

Lukes has developed his three-dimensional (3-D) view of power in contrast with what he describes as two-dimensional (2-D) and one-dimensional (1-D) views. Let me briefly review each approach.

3.3.1 The one-dimensional view of power

On the 1-D conceptualization of 'power', power is being exercised when one out of two or more conflicting policies prevails. This means that conflicting policies have to be in visible contest with one another. The person (or persons) whose policy triumphs has (or have) power over the others, i.e. those whose policies fail. Such a view of power focuses upon actual decision-making with respect to key issues. It requires observable conflict based upon different, subjectively-perceived interests which are formulated as policy preferences in the course of political participation – preferences that are publicly aired.

Clearly, it would seem, one dimension of power *is* identified by this conceptualization: namely, an exercise of power is revealed when one's preferred policy prevails against competing and conflicting policies which come up for debate on political committees. As it is not always the policy preferred by one particular group which prevails (some of the policies preferred by other groups are occasionally enacted), those who subscribe to this view of power consider whatever power there is to be fairly evenly distributed throughout society.[57] It is not surprising, therefore, that those who hold this view also consider power to be far from prevalent or pervasive. But this view of power rules out many other examples of what we would intuitively consider to be power. Hence the need for a further dimension.

3.3.2 The two-dimensional view of power

On the 2-D conceptualization of 'power', it is not only those whose policies that have come up for discussion and have prevailed who exercise power, it is also those who are able to influence the decision as to which policies receive a public hearing.[58] Power, on this view, involves not only being able to decide between proposed policies, but also being able to prevent certain policies from being discussed – 'nondecision-making'.[59] Thus, for those who hold the 2-D view, potential issues, as well as issues which have in fact been placed on the political agenda, are of importance. This means that conflict can be covert, and not just overt.

It also seems clear that this view of power succeeds in identifying a dimension of

57 See Polsby, *Community, Power and Political Theory*, pp. 132–3.

58 As Bachrach and Baratz write: 'to the extent that a person or group – consciously or unconsciously – creates or reinforces barriers to the public airing of policy conflicts, that person or group has power.' Bachrach and Baratz, *Power and Poverty*, p. 8.

59 On 'nondecision-making', see ibid., p. 44.

power which the other view overlooks.[60] Consequently, there appears to be more power around when one adopts this second conceptualization. Moreover, as it could be argued that it is the political committees themselves which usually set the agenda, this second view of power would seem to suggest that power is more concentrated than is implied by the first view. However, it is possible to add a still further dimension.

3.3.3 The three-dimensional view of power

On the 3-D conceptualization of 'power', both decision-making and nondecision-making concerning observable overt and covert conflict are acknowledged, as in the 2-D view, but latent conflict is also stressed. Lukes does so by referring not only to subjective interests (i.e. what one perceives to be one's interests) but also to *real* interests. According to Lukes, the 1-D and 2-D views of power overlook what is the most insidious form of power. This is, rather than possessing the ability to have one's policies enacted, or the ability to prevent others' policies from being included on the agenda, having the ability to inhibit others from even seeing which policies are in their real interests. In other words, the third dimension of power isolated by this view concerns the ability (sometimes of institutions) to form persons' preferences so that what they perceive to be in their interests is not in actual fact what is in their real interests. The foisting of an ideology onto others is a case in point. Clearly, this third view of power suggests that power is far more pervasive than is suggested by either of the other views.

The relevance of this for green political theory should be clear to those familiar with Matthew Crenson's pioneering work. For Lukes' 3-D conceptualization of 'power' was, in large part, motivated by Crenson's discussion of why the issue of air pollution remained suppressed for a considerable time in certain North American cities which, nevertheless, were perceived to suffer greatly from such pollution.[61] Crenson's study seems to demonstrate that an understanding of the relationship between the political process and environmental problems requires a different conception of 'power' from either the 1-D or the 2-D view.

Now, it seems that Lukes is right to be concerned about preference formation, for certain forms of advertising and ideological activity are widely accepted to be instances of some having power over others. Moreover, given the role that advertising plays in over-consumption, which itself adds to environmental degradation, any genuinely green political theory would have to take this dimension of power into account. But his 3-D view of power, although apparently wider in its extension than the other views, faces two significant difficulties: First, how can it be

60 Bachrach and Baratz are, therefore, in a position to observe that the 1-D view possesses the following important defect: 'the model takes no account of the fact that power may be, and often is, exercised by confining the scope of decision-making to relatively "safe" issues.' Ibid., p. 6.

61 See Lukes, *Power*, pp. 42–5.

ascertained *what* someone's real interests are when individuals have been prevented from seeing them themselves? And second, how can it be ascertained *who* is in a position to be able to identify the real interests of those who are prevented from seeing them? Both of these problems indicate that it is difficult to operationalize Lukes' conceptualization of 'power'.

One ready answer to the second of these problems is highly significant: if the oppressed cannot perceive their real interests, then the Party is necessary to reveal their real interests to them. Just as the 1-D view of power supports pluralists' seeming indifference to the power of the state in 'pluralist' societies, and just as the 2-D view of power supports liberal critics in their limited critique of the state, Lukes' 3-D view of power (albeit unintentionally) appears to support the (frequently paternalistic) political practice of Marxism/Leninism. For one implication of the 3-D view is that if the proletariat does not perceive its own real interests, then it is others who must speak, or act, or make their decisions for them.

If the Party, for example, claims to be privileged in having the scientific theory which enables it to identify the real interests of the proletariat,[62] or claims to have a privileged epistemological standpoint from which it is able to impute to the proletariat what it *should* identify as its real interests,[63] then it can claim to know better than the proletariat what the latter ought to do in order to realize its real interests.[64] And if the proletariat has been prevented from perceiving its real interests (because it only has a 'trade-union consciousness'), then it is but a short step to arguing that the proletariat ought to obey the Party if it is to realize its real interests. Most importantly, Lukes cannot, on his 3-D view of power, identify as a power relation the proletariat being forced to obey the Party if the present interests of the proletariat are served by it obeying the Party. Different conceptualizations of 'power' are not without substantive political implications.

Nevertheless, Lukes does draw attention to what appears to be a vitally important instance of power – the foisting onto others of an ideology. And any radical's view of power must be able to draw attention to ideology, especially if it is both one of the more insidious forms of power and the form most obstructive to the emergence of a revolutionary consciousness amongst the oppressed. Furthermore, if it is a consumerist ideology that has been foisted onto the mass of the

62 Cf. V. I. Lenin, *What Is to Be Done?* (Peking: Foreign Languages Press, 1975), especially p. 29.

63 Cf. Georg Lukács, *History and Class Consciousness* (London: Merlin, 1971), especially p. 51. For a critique of Lukács, see Alan Carter, *Marx: A Radical Critique* (Brighton: Wheatsheaf Books, 1988), Section 4.8.

64 Marx: 'I have always defied the momentary opinions of the proletariat. If the best a party can do is to just fail to seize power, then we repudiate it. If the proletariat could gain control of the government the measures it would introduce would be those of the petty bourgeoisie and not those appropriate to the proletariat. Our party can only gain power when the situation allows it to put its own measures into practice.' Karl Marx, 'Speech to the Central Committee of the Communist League' in *Selected Writings*, ed. David McLellan (Oxford: Oxford University Press, 1977), p. 299.

people, then it seems essential that the power responsible be challenged if we are to avoid what many environmentalists fear to be an imminent environmental catastrophe.

What is evidently required, then, is to avoid the paternalistic implications of Lukes' 3-D view, and yet retain its insights. Can this be achieved? If we are to answer this question affirmatively, we need to be clear about precisely what it is that is problematic about Lukes' conceptualization of 'power'.

Both of the major problems with Lukes' view – the problem of identifying the real interests of any person or group, and the problem of identifying those who are able to perceive the real interests of any person or group – arise because of his stress on *real* interests. Given that, on the 3-D view, the oppressed have been prevented from perceiving their real interests, there can always be a dispute as to where their real interests lie.[65] Similarly, there can always be a dispute as to who is best placed to perceive the interests of the oppressed. A requirement for a workable, radical approach to power is thus being able to avoid the difficulty Lukes' view experiences in actually identifying the third-dimension of power. For if the real interests of the oppressed are in dispute, then so is the 'power' which affects those mooted interests. It seems, therefore, that radicals would be well advised to avoid having to identify real interests when trying to expose power relations.

3.3.4 New foundations for a radical conception of power

One attempt to provide new foundations for a 3-D view of power is that offered by David West, who recognizes the necessity of avoiding any reference to real interests. Interestingly, he has deliberately sought to retain Lukes' insight that shaping preferences is an instance of power, while trying to avoid the paternalistic implications of Lukes' view. West's proposed solution is to isolate the third-dimension of power as 'whatever intrudes on the formative practice of individuals. In other words, power occurs when *A* affects *B* in a way which intrudes on the formative practice of *B* or contrary to *B*'s autonomous formation of interests.'[66] The main advantage of this proposal is that real interests are not referred to. Thus, the paternalism of those who claim to know the interests of the oppressed better than the oppressed themselves is precluded.

However, as West admits: 'any critique of power along these lines presupposes some account of the free formation of wants, desires or projects.'[67] But in requiring such an account, West's view is at no greater disadvantage than that of Lukes. Unfortunately, by having to describe how *B*'s wants, desires or projects *would have developed* had *A* not intruded into their formation (for, without such an

65 For example, if capitalism allows the proletariat a high standard of living, whereas state-communism failed to deliver it, capitalists can argue successfully against Marxist revolutionaries by asserting that supporting capitalism is in the proletariat's real interests.

66 David West, 'Power and formation: new foundations for a radical concept of power', *Inquiry*, Vol. 30, Nos. 1–2 (1987), p. 142.

67 Ibid., p. 143.

account of autonomous development, how can it be ascertained that *A* has significantly intruded?), West is, in this respect, *in no better position than Lukes is*. An account of the counterfactual formation of someone's wants, desires or projects is as speculative and contentious as an account of another's misperceived, real interests.

There is a further, and more serious, difficulty with West's view of power. How is he to deal with 'intrusions' which do not affect an individual's formation? These could not, on his view, be instances of power. Alternatively, if all 'intrusions' *are* to be described as power, that would entail considering everything that an individual does or experiences as 'formative'. But in this case, the notion of 'formative practice' would become vacuous.

Now, West is surely right to be concerned about the paternalistic implications of Lukes' view. Perceptively, he observes that Lukes' conceptualization of power has the added problem of inhibiting a critique of paternalism:

> Not only does Lukes' account provide a possible justification for paternalism. Its form also makes it conceptually *blind* to the paternalistic exercise of power. According to Lukes' definition, a person *A* exercises power over another person *B* if *A* affects *B* in a significant manner and in a way which is *contrary to B's interests*. But surely, a person may be affected by power without being affected adversely: e.g. when I am forced to do something for my own good.[68]

West is surely correct to point out that one can be forced to do something which is in one's interests. But if this does not intrude on the formation of one's wants, desires or projects, then it is not identified as power on West's view, either. Lukes, however, would go so far as to deny that this is an instance of *power*. As West himself observes: 'Intrinsic to Lukes' favoured concept of power . . . is the idea that power *harms* the people on whom it is exercised.'[69] This, clearly, has paternalistic implications. If what the Party does is not harming the proletariat, then the Party cannot, on this view, be exercising power over them.

But there is reason to think that this is false. Consider: It is World War II. The place is North Africa. You are a soldier fighting against Rommel's army. Your tank has been burnt out by a German shell. For two days you have been walking through the desert under the burning sun. At last you discover an oasis. But just as you bend down to drink the crystal-clear water, a German officer suddenly steps out from behind a palm tree and, pressing the barrel of his Lüger against your head, orders you to drink the water.[70] According to Lukes' considered view, this could not be an exercise of power, for it does not go against your real

68 Ibid., p. 141.

69 Ibid., p. 139.

70 Why does he act in this manner? Perhaps he can see that you desperately need a drink, but he has been trained to ensure that prisoners of war only do what they have been ordered to do. Instead of allowing you to drink, he orders you to drink.

interests. And it is difficult to see how the action of the German officer non-vacuously intrudes in any formative practice you are engaging in. So, on West's view, too, this could not be an exercise of power. Yet, intuitively, it seems indubitable that you are in the officer's power – that the officer has power *over* you.[71]

Neither Lukes nor West have a conception of 'power' which deals with this kind of case. The officer is not going against your wish to drink. He is not going against your real interests. Nor is he interfering in your formative practices. Yet, surely, he has power over you. Why? Two reasons could be given: (i) were it the case that you did not in fact wish to drink the water, or were it the case that it was not in fact in your real interests to drink it,[72] then you would be forced to drink it anyway; and (ii) were it the case that the officer, instead, ordered you not to drink the water when it was in your subjective and/or real interests to drink it, then you would not be able to drink the water.

This example seems to demonstrate that I may wish to do something and it is in my (either subjectively-perceived or real) interests to do that thing, yet I actually do it *because* I am ordered to do it.[73] And it seems to be the case that the person who orders me to do it has power over me when and because I am forced to do it *irrespective of my wishes or interests.* This means that it is possible to develop an approach to power which is independent of both subjective[74] and real interests, and which does not have to rely on having to specify an individual's autonomous formation.

Thus, I suggest the following way of conceptualizing the relationship of possessing power over someone: *there is a power relation when an individual or group*

71 Compare Robert Nozick's discussion of person *P* coercing person *Q* into refraining from performing act *A*: '*Q* may have refrained from doing *A* because of the threat even though he formed the intention of not doing it before learning of the threat. For example, *Q* intends to visit a friend tomorrow. *P* threatens him with death if he doesn't go. *Q* then learns that his friend has a communicable disease such that were it not for the threat, *Q* wouldn't visit him. But *Q* goes because of *P*'s threat, though he formed the intention of going before learning of the threat, and never lost this intention. . . . *P* coerced *Q* into going.' Robert Nozick, 'Coercion' in P. Laslett, W. G. Runciman and Q. Skinner (eds), *Philosophy, Politics and Society: Fourth Series* (Oxford: Blackwell, 1972), p. 102 n. My claim is that, in visiting his friend, *Q* would be acting under *P*'s power even if he hadn't learned that his friend had a communicable disease.

72 The German officer might, in this case, know that the water is poisoned. In such a case, perhaps he orders you to drink the water because he is a sadistic member of the SS?

73 Interestingly, Nozick concludes that, '[i]n the case where *Q*'s whole reason for not doing *A* is to avoid or lessen the likelihood of *P*'s threatened consequence (ignoring his reasons for wanting to avoid this consequence), *P* coerces *Q* into not doing *A*', adding: 'Even if *Q* has other reasons for not doing *A*. We distinguish between "*Q* has a reason *r* for not doing *A*," and "*r* is (part of) *Q*'s reason for not doing *A*."' Ibid., p. 134.

74 The need to develop a theory of power which, unlike the 1-D and 2-D views, is independent of subjective interests is made clear by Berlin: 'For if to be free – negatively – is simply not to be prevented by other persons from doing whatever one wishes, then one of the ways of attaining such freedom is by extinguishing one's wishes.' Isaiah Berlin, *Four Essays on Liberty* (Oxford: Oxford University Press, 1969), p. xxxviii. This would be an absurd consequence of a theory of political power.

of individuals can ensure[75] *that another or others do or do not do something, want or do not want something, believe or do not believe something, irrespective of the latter's (subjective or real) interests.* However, for a 'significant' power relation, then whatever it is that individuals are forced to do, want or believe would also have to be 'significant'. Ascertaining what is significant, of course, could generate some disagreement. But there is no reason why 'power', like 'baldness', should not have some vagueness in its application, nor give rise to disagreement concerning its applicability in certain cases.[76]

Now, it might be objected that this conception of 'power' confuses actual with potential power. Perhaps the German officer would only be exerting power over you when you preferred not to drink the water. Until then, his power would only be potential. But, surely, that cannot be right. If the officer orders you to drink and you want to drink, the officer's power would, on such a view, only be potential. If you suddenly changed your mind, then his power would become actual. It is surely implausible to claim that the officer's power changes from being potential to actual merely because a different thought runs through your head, without any change in the officer's capacity to make you do what you do not want to do.

Another possible objection might run as follows: It is Lukes' opinion that we cannot distinguish between benign and malevolent exercises of influence unless we refer to some notion of interests. Does this not entail that 'power' must contain a reference to interests? But, in reply, the inclusion of interests within the conception of 'power' is only required if we assume, as Lukes does, that exercising power necessarily means harming someone. I would agree with Lukes that there are reasons to think that the exercise of power tends to be harmful; but, if true, this is an empirical matter, not a tautology. It is surely not self-contradictory to say that power can be exercised benignly. If we are to be able to distinguish between the *use* and *abuse* of power, then harm cannot be part of our conceptualization of 'power'.

One of the things that might be thought to be particularly dangerous about the possession of power is that, even if another is currently being forced to do what is in his or her interests (the benign use of power), this ability to so force another – the '*power*' – could be used at a different time to force him or her to do what is not in his or her interests (the malevolent use or the abuse of power). And it is precisely this potentiality that makes both eco-authoritarianism and Marxism/Leninism appear so dangerous. If power constitutes an ever-present, potential threat, then its concentration ought to be avoided. But what should be noted is that it is not even possible to argue this point (especially against those who would wish to exercise power in what they consider to be a benign manner) unless power is not definitionally related to harm.

75 And if one wishes to prevent rational persuasion from being identified as an exercise of power, then 'ensure' has to be so construed that rational persuasion is excluded.

76 Lukes, for one, is happy to consider the concept of 'power' to be an 'essentially contested concept'. See Lukes, *Power*, p. 26.

Surely, we would want to say that there are times when *A*'s ability to command *B* effectively (*A*'s '*power*') is potentially problematic, and it ought to be possible to highlight that. But the best that Lukes and West can do, given their views of power, is claim that when *A* acts against *B*'s interests or intrudes in his or her formation, then power arises. But it is an extremely restrictive and restricting notion of 'power' which is then being employed, because *A*'s ability to act against *B*'s interests or intrude in his or her formation *is only identified as power when that potential is actually being realized*,[77] and then it is often too late to do anything about it.

3.3.5 Four dimensions of power

As the case of the German officer seems to show, the alternative approach to power proposed here identifies exercises of power overlooked by the other views. But it also identifies what the 1-D, 2-D and 3-D views seek to identify. It is, therefore, a *four-dimensional* (4-D) *view of power*.

The 4-D view of power claims that *A* exerts power over *B* when *B* is unable to do, want or believe *b* irrespective of whether or not *B* wishes to or irrespective of *B*'s interests, and *B* is unable to do, want or believe *b* because, perhaps *inter alia*,[78] *A* ensures that it is so. Clearly, this view of power identifies as power the kind of decision-making which the 1-D view of power focuses upon, because *A*, having his or her policy enacted rather than *B*'s, inhibits *B*. Furthermore, the 4-D view of power also identifies agenda-setting as an exercise of power, because *A*'s nondecision-making inhibits *B* if *B* could have acted otherwise had his or her suppressed policy been voted on, instead.

But it is when we come to the 3-D views of power (both Lukes' and West's) that the 4-D view is especially interesting. It will be recalled that the 3-D views of power seem difficult to operationalize. This is because real interests and the counterfactual course of autonomous preference formation are hard to pinpoint uncontroversially. The 4-D view of power cannot identify as a specific set what the 3-D views hope to identify – namely, cases where *B* is unable to do what is in his or her real interests because of *A*, or engage in formative practices without significant intrusion by *A*. This is because the 4-D view claims no special privilege in being able to pinpoint real interests or the counterfactual course of autonomous preference formation.

However, everything that the 3-D views relevantly attempt to identify as power is actually so identified by the 4-D view. In particular, the foisting by *A* of belief *a*

77 It is not without significance that West should write: 'Interests can only be either formed or discovered in actual processes of formation. They cannot be anticipated or revealed in a purely intellectual discussion.' West, 'Power and formation', p. 152. This approach, with its excessive focus on the present, could easily lead to the undermining of any attempt to predict the future outcomes which would result from choosing certain political strategies – which, ironically, is a very good way of blundering into Stalinism.

78 *B*'s constraint may be overdetermined.

(ideology) on *B* irrespective of *B*'s wishes or interests is a clear case of power according to the 4-D view, as is any inhibiting or manipulation by *A* of *B*'s autonomous development. In other words, the cases which the 3-D views attempt to identify as a third dimension of power can be successfully identified as power by the 4-D view because they form a sub-set of what the 4-D view identifies. But in so far as what the 1-D, 2-D and 3-D views identify does not exhaust what the 4-D view identifies, the 4-D view does indeed have an extra dimension of power.[79] And just as the 1-D, 2-D and 3-D views of power have their own political implications, so does the 4-D view. On this latter view, *all paternalistic political practice is revealed to be potentially problematic.* If concern about inequalities of power make the 1-D view pluralist, the 2-D view critical liberal, and the 3-D view Marxist, it would seem to make the 4-D view more radical than any of these – perhaps even anarchist in its implications.

Nevertheless, the ability of the 4-D view to isolate as power what the 3-D views attempt, but apparently fail, to isolate is a clear advantage of the former. Moreover, Lukes' 3-D view appeared, at first glance, to be important for green political theory because it purports to present a conceptualization of 'power' that enables us to identify as an exercise of power the suppression of politically significant environmental issues, such as air pollution. But in failing to be operationalizable, the 3-D view fails to deliver what it promises. However, with the 4-D view, the existence of insidious power is not put into question in advance because of the problematic nature of ascertaining real interests or the counterfactual course of autonomous preference formation. Hence, it has the potential for successfully exposing as a power relation the prevention by insidious means of the raising of environmental issues.

Furthermore, those who are wary of Lukes' view because it suggests that the social critic is a better judge of the circumstances of the oppressed than the oppressed themselves need have no such suspicions of the 4-D view, even though it succeeds in identifying as instances of power what the 3-D views attempt to isolate (though, it appears, with little success).

But does this 4-D view of power not experience a problem because it, too, seems to require a specification of counterfactual situations? Does it not need us to know what *B could* have done were it not for *A*? How, then, can this problem be dealt with? And does this not make the 4-D view no better than West's version of the 3-D view? First, it certainly makes the 4-D view no worse than West's view,

79 It should be noted that those who claim to subscribe to each view of power are often concerned in practice about forms of power which fall outside of their stated theoretical views. Dahl's observations of power in New Haven go beyond what his 1-D conceptualization suggests. Bachrach and Baratz often fall into a position which is half-way between the 2-D and 3-D views, though they claim to subscribe to the 2-D view. West, though attempting to provide new foundations for Lukes' 3-D view by drawing attention to *some* paternalistic practices, in fact occupies a position somewhere between the 3-D and 4-D views. The theoretical formulations of the various views are often far neater than the practice of those who claim to subscribe to them.

while nevertheless succeeding in being more inclusive a theory of power than West's – and this is the basis of West's claim to having a superior view to Lukes. Second, it is not, in fact, a criticism of the 4-D view to describe it as a '*counterfactualist*' conceptualization of power. This is because, although it has to say something about counterfactual situations, it appears to be superior to West's view in having to say less about them, as I now attempt to show.

In order to claim that power has been exercised, West has to be able to give an account of how the individual *would* have developed autonomously, if he is to show that any intrusion in that development is significant.[80] But all that a holder of the 4-D view need cogently claim is that the individual *could* have done, wanted or believed something different were it not for the powerful.[81] According to the 4-D view, power can be identified, not by reference to what *B would* in fact have done were it not for *A*, but by reference to a reasonable expectation of what *B might* have been able to do were it not for *A*. Telling *any* convincing story about what *B* could have done were it not for *A* is all that the holder of the 4-D view need do in order to persuade another that a power relation obtains. However, West, it would seem, has to show *exactly* how *B* would have developed (and Lukes has to identify *exactly* what *B*'s real interests are).

This requirement of the 4-D view – telling a convincing story – is not a serious limitation, for if one cannot persuasively describe what *B* might reasonably be expected to have been able to do were it not for *A*, then there is little scope for a convincing critique of *A*'s power over *B*. In other words, no matter what theory of power is preferred, there is a serious possibility of condemning *A*'s power over *B* only when one is able to give a cogent account of what *B* might alternatively have been able to do. Restricting one's capacity for identifying power to cases where a persuasive alternative scenario can be contemplated is no hindrance to the radical critic, because any other cases would be irrelevant with regard to serious political debate. And it is this minimal restriction which is placed on the operation of the 4-D view.

But what are the advantages, if any, of a 4-D view of power? West claims four advantages for his view: First, it is possible to identify as exercises of power paternalistic interventions in formative practices. Second, his view is consistent with libertarian political practice as no assumption is made about knowing better than others where their real interests lie. Third, the oppressed can ascribe their own interests, leading to less inequality between them and social analysts. And fourth:

80 Recall that West admits of his view that 'any critique of power along these lines presupposes some account of the free formation of wants, desires or projects'. Ibid., p. 143.

81 West writes: 'The operation of power can be identified, on Lukes' preferred view, where a counterfactual of the following form can be verified: that, but for some other agent *A*, *B* would have performed action *b* rather than *a*.' Ibid., p. 139. As was noted earlier, West gives as Lukes' definition of power: 'a person *A* exercises power over another person *B* if *A* affects *B* in a significant manner and in a way which is *contrary to B's interests*.' Ibid., p. 141. Yet in the first passage he makes no reference to *B*'s interests. Inadvertently, West, in this passage, comes very close to discussing the theory of power proposed here. The difference is that, on the 4-D view, but for some other agent *A*, *B could* (not would) have performed action *b* rather than *a*.

'[p]ower can be identified without having to know what people would actually choose to do if power were not being exercised upon them. The concept of power, therefore, can be employed in empirical research – it is operationalizable.'[82] However, the 4-D view of power also appears to possess these four advantages. Moreover, the 4-D view does not seem to suffer from the inadequacies which appear to be present in West's conceptualization. As the more comprehensive approach, and at the same time arguably the less problematic, it is the 4-D view of power which seems to be the more acceptable. And from the standpoint of the 4-D view, power is even more pervasive than the 3-D views suggest. For, on the 4-D view, paternalistic parties acting in the name of the oppressed whilst not intruding into their formation also exercise power.

Moreover, it can be argued that it is this area of power which particularly needs to be highlighted, and which the 4-D view alone reveals, for it is where power is least visible – namely, when it is not presently going against the wishes, or interests, or intruding into the formative practices of the powerless, while remaining an ever-present threat. And eco-authoritarianism, eco-reformism and eco-Marxism all display complacency with respect to such power. By describing as a power relation a situation where individuals who want x and where x is in their interests are forced by another or others to do x, attention is drawn to the fact that if x were not in the interests of the powerless or if it ceased to be in their interests, then they would be forced to do it anyway. Such power is least evident because its problematic nature lies in its *potential* misuse.

Yet it is in situations involving the potential misuse of power where radicals hold out most hope – revolutionary situations – and, consequently, where they can be most disappointed. It is in such situations that parties which ostensibly represent the oppressed are most able to abuse their power, for it is then that they are most powerful and most able to secure their own private interests. If the oppressed must obey the Party even when it is no longer in their interests to do what it dictates, then such a situation is fraught with danger. At the very least, we require a conceptualization of 'power' that sensitizes us to this potential danger by allowing us to identify the power which some have and could later misuse. Only the 4-D view seems suited to this essential task.

Similarly, eco-authoritarianism, when it takes the form of an environmentally benevolent dictatorship, underplays the serious potential that any dictatorial form of power has for misuse. Hence, regarding the potential abuse of power, ecologically orientated Marxist/Leninist and eco-authoritarian approaches seem not to be significantly different. In addition, it can be argued that eco-reformism also fails to take sufficiently seriously the problem of power, in so far as it views its exercise by the state as far less problematic than, arguably, is in fact the case. Just how

82 Ibid., pp. 143–4. However, as we have seen, it is doubtful that West's view of power actually is operationalizable. Though West does not have to know what people would, counterfactually, choose to do, it appears that he does have to know how people would, counterfactually, develop.

problematic state power might actually be, even in a society headed by a reformist government, will only become apparent after considering, in the next chapter, the nature and behaviour of the state, and in Chapter 6, the likely environmental consequences of that behaviour. Only then will it become fully clear how inadequate eco-authoritarian, eco-reformist and eco-Marxist approaches might well turn out to be in the face of ever-worsening ecological crises.

In this chapter, however, we have focused on how best to conceptualize social relations, freedom and power in order to provide the necessary conceptual building blocks for an environmental political theory. All forms of (4-D) social power, which curtail the (triadic) freedom of others, arise in interrelations between individuals. The extent of the power individuals hold over others is a function of the capacity of those who possess it and the vulnerability of those who are subject to it.[83] Power can arise within institutions (where behaviour is enabled and constrained by the prevailing rules) when some are more enabled and some are more constrained than others. One major source of devastating ecological damage is widely agreed to be economic activity. That seems to be determined by unequal *economic power*. But from where do the rules governing that power derive? The answer would appear to be from a particular structure of institutions: namely, the state, which is the primary locus of *political power*. It is the state which defines and protects property rights, for example. And it is at the level of the state where most power seems ultimately to be concentrated and exercised. Hence, it is to the question of how best to theorize the state that we must now turn.

83 And power may be increased either by making that capacity more visible or by increasing the visibility of the subjects. By drawing on Bentham's Panopticon as an analogy, Foucault has explored the way in which increased susceptibility to surveillance has led to increased subjection to power. For example, as he writes: 'The scarcely sustainable visibility of the monarch is turned into the unavoidable visibility of the subjects.' Michel Foucault, *Discipline and Punish: The Birth of the Prison* (Harmondsworth: Penguin, 1979), p. 189. And power can be most easily exercised when the awareness of visibility is internalized by the subjects. As Foucault adds: 'He who is subject to a field of visibility, and who knows it, assumes responsibility for the constraints of power; he makes them play spontaneously upon himself; he inscribes in himself the power relation in which he simultaneously plays both roles; he becomes the principle of his own subjection.' Ibid., pp. 202–3. Foucault's account of various micro-foundations of power is instructively interrelationist.

4 The State-Primacy Theory

The last chapter suggests that the authoritarianism characteristically advocated by the Right, the reformism standardly defended by the Centre and the Marxism typically upheld by the Left, even when taking seemingly environmentally-aware forms, all rest upon deficient conceptions of 'power'. Such deficient conceptions are likely to cash out into inadequate theories of the state. In this chapter, I begin by arguing that the two most common views of the state may well fail to give it sufficient weight. Then, I propose an alternative approach to theorizing the state – one that seems anarchist in its implications.

Thus, we now come to consider anarchism and some of its theoretical foundations. In developing a green political theory, anarchism deserves special consideration, for, as Tim Hayward acknowledges:

> a strong current of opinion maintains that ecological politics must in fact be a form of anarchism. Certainly, from a historical perspective, it seems to be the case that the most searching ecological questions were raised – long before questions of environment and ecology were of widespread public concern – by anarchists more than by thinkers of other political colours.[1]

But why should we even bother to consider anarchism today, given that it was historically superseded by Marxism? Anarchism might have been the major radical alternative in the nineteenth-century to authoritarian socialism; but it is certainly not regarded so now.

However, after (what many would regard as) the long-overdue demise of state-communism in Eastern Europe, the political theory of the radical Left seems to lack any clear direction. It could be argued that because of the initial success of a group of Marxist revolutionaries in Russia – the Bolsheviks – Marxism rose to ascendancy on the Left. Yet it was the subsequent fate of Bolshevism that so demoralized and discredited the radical Left as a whole. Some, however, see this as an opportunity for a streamlined version of Marxism to race ahead unhindered, now that it has jettisoned the heavy burden of Stalinism. Some, on the other

1 Tim Hayward, *Ecological Thought: An Introduction* (Cambridge: Polity, 1995), p. 189.

hand, feel that a wrong turning was taken when the Left rushed headlong into a Marxist cul-de-sac instead of coasting along (what they might view as) the open freeway of anarchism. With such divergent views emerging, it would seem that the time is ripe to reconsider these two theories side-by-side, for contrasting these alternative revolutionary approaches could, I suggest, shed light on which route political theory in general would most profitably take.

Anarchism and Marxism have, since the middle of the nineteenth century, strenuously competed for the minds of the Left. Hence, much of anarchist theory has evolved in opposition to Marxist theory, while much of Marx's thought evolved in opposition to a number of anarchist thinkers.[2] The major strength of anarchism has corresponded with the most obvious weakness of Marxism – namely, the prediction (remarkably successful in the case of anarchism, unsuccessful in the case of Marxism) of the nature of a post-capitalist society brought into being by a revolutionary party seizing control of the state. Anarchists, such as Marx's principal antagonist – the Russian Mikhail Alexandrovitch Bakunin (1814–1876) – have insisted that the state cannot be used by revolutionaries in order to bring about a classless or non-oppressive society. They have argued that any attempt to use the state will inevitably frustrate such a goal. And the experience of 'actually existing socialism' would appear to offer some support for the anarchist claim. It is somewhat ironic, therefore, that it is Marxist theory which came to dominate left-wing thought, especially as the revolution which catapulted Marxism into theoretical ascendancy appears, as we saw in Chapter 2, to contradict the most coherent version of Marxist theory – namely, G. A. Cohen's.

But there is another reason for the theoretical scales having tipped in favour of Marxism – namely, the apparently ahistorical nature of much of anarchist theory. It is here that the major strength of Marxism and the apparent weakness of anarchism correspond. Whereas anarchists have often been content to confine their attention to the state, Marx was able to develop a comprehensive theory that seems to account for the major economic transformations which have been evident as societies have moved from one historical epoch to the next. But is it the case that anarchism is unable to offer an equally informative theory of historical transition? It is my contention that a theory of historical change can be developed which not only underpins the anarchist critique of the state (thus successfully supporting Bakunin in his controversy with Marx, and accurately predicting the nature of 'actually existing socialism') but also manages to explain the changes in the economic relations that Marxist theory so impressively seems to explain. And I would further contend that such an anarchist theory of history might be exactly

2 See Paul Thomas, *Karl Marx and the Anarchists* (London: Routledge, 1980) for an account of how Marx's thought was primarily shaped by his antagonistic attitude to a series of anarchist thinkers: Max Stirner, Pierre-Joseph Proudhon and Mikhail Bakunin. Thomas does, however, provide a somewhat unbalanced assessment, given his uncritical acceptance of Marx's views and his explicit bias against anarchism.

what is required to provide the theoretical underpinning which green political practice so desperately requires.

This alternative theory will be contrasted with Cohen's 'Techno-Primacy Theory', for his is widely recognized to be the most cogently argued interpretation of Marx's theory of history. And just as Cohen has provided clearer foundations for Marxist theory, what follows aims to provide clearer foundations for anarchist theory. Moreover, just as Cohen has developed his clarifications within the tradition of analytical philosophy, the following is also to be located within that tradition. Consequently, as Cohen has given us analytical Marxism, what follows could be regarded as 'analytical anarchism'.

As was noted in Chapter 2, by interpreting Marx's theory of history as one employing functional explanations, Cohen rescues Marx from the charge of incoherence levelled against him by analytical philosophers. However, although Cohen's rigorous account of functional explanation convincingly defends Marx against this charge, is it the case that functional explanation is most suited to rescuing Marx's theory of history, or is there an alternative theory which could employ functional explanations even more successfully? In what follows, I argue in favour of the latter by presenting an alternative theory of history – one based upon functional explanations – which, I would argue, is more robust, while better conforming to certain key historical events, than Marxist theory. Hence, by developing a clear account of functional explanation, Cohen has made possible an alternative theory of history to that of Marx – one which, ironically, may well pose a more threatening challenge to Marxism than the charge of incoherence levelled by 'bourgeois' analytical philosophers. This is because, although the charge of incoherence can be avoided, the alternative theory of history throws into question fundamental Marxist assumptions about the nature and development of post-capitalist society – precisely the goal to which Marxists strive.

This problem arises for Marxist theory because of the very nature of the model which Cohen presents. In his model, it will be recalled, the development of technology affects the economic relations, while the economic relations affect technological development. Similarly, the economic relations affect the political relations, while the political relations affect the economic relations. In other words, Cohen situates these elements within a model which is bi-directional. The model is recognizably Marxist because one particular direction of explanation (that from the bottom to the top – from technological developments through changing economic structures to political transformations) is taken to be primary, while the other is, presumably, secondary. This is depicted in Figure 2.1, where the unbroken line represents the primary direction of explanation and the broken line represents the secondary direction.

In what follows, I am able to offer an alternative model as a result of exploring the possibility – one which is inherent in any such bi-directional model – that what Cohen takes to be primary is, in fact, secondary, and that what he takes to be secondary is actually primary. Now, although this might seem a rather pedestrian manoeuvre, the ramifications are extremely important. For, as will become apparent, rather than the reversal of the primary direction of explanation being trivial, it turns out that it has significant implications for revolutionary strategy and seriously threatens to undermine the Marxist revolutionary project. It also provides the possibility of a theory of history that can effectively explain the causes of our present environmental predicament. And understanding its causes is the precondition for its solution. But before I proceed to expound an anarchist theory of history which can be employed to ground the core claims of a radical green political theory, certain assumptions about the state need to be examined.

4.1 Two views of the state

Until recently, few theorists of the modern nation-state (Machiavelli, who is 'often regarded as the first theorist of the modern state',[3] is one such notable exception) have regarded it as anything other than an instrument, in some sense or other, of civil society. This can be brought out by briefly considering the two opposing theories that have the widest support amongst political theorists today: pluralism and Marxism. According to pluralist theory,[4] the state serves to reconcile competing interests within civil society.[5] According to traditional Marxist theory, the modern state serves to secure the interests of one particular class within civil society – the bourgeoisie.[6]

Unfortunately, it can be doubted whether either theory provides a satisfactory account of why the state should be confined to whichever role it is supposedly allocated. Certainly, pluralists have argued that a political party seeking to attain or remain in office will have to satisfy as many interest groups as it can. But a government only need do that as long as it continues to offer itself for re-election. This is not something that all democratically elected governments have chosen to do – Hitler's didn't, to take one obvious example. In other words, merely claiming that governments have to reconcile conflicting interests in civil society begs the question of why they must do so.

Now, there are reasons why a democratically elected government might offer itself for re-election. But they do not necessarily show the state to be an instrument of civil society. One reason suggested by Anthony de Jasay is that a

3 David Held, *Models of Democracy* (Cambridge: Polity, 1987), p. 43.

4 The most influential account is that presented in Robert A. Dahl, *A Preface to Democratic Theory* (London: University of Chicago Press, 1956).

5 This only appears plausible given a very restricted notion of interests and how they are revealed – precisely that underlying the 1-D view of power. It is not surprising, then, that one of the leading pluralist theorists – Dahl – is also one of the authors of the 1-D view of power.

6 As has been noted previously, Marx and Engels claim that '[t]he executive of the modern State is but a committee for managing the common affairs of the whole bourgeoisie.' Karl Marx and Frederick Engels, 'The Communist Manifesto' in Karl Marx, *Selected Writings*, ed. David McLellan (Oxford: Oxford University Press, 1977), p. 223. However, although the majority of pluralists and Marxists have employed a 'cipher image' of the state, not all have done so. For an overview of the various standpoints that have been taken, see Patrick Dunleavy and Brendan O'Leary, *Theories of the State: The Politics of Liberal Democracy* (London: Macmillan, 1987).

government might place constitutional limits on governmental activities, and abide by its own self-imposed limits, not because the state

> mistrusts *itself* and would rather not have levers or powerful tools lest it should misuse them. It knows that *it* could not possibly be tempted to misuse power. It is its rivals for state power who would, by the nature of their ambition, misuse it. . . . [Thus] fearing its capacity for wrong-doing in profane hands, the capitalist state is rational in adopting the contours of the minimal state.[7]

Moreover, should the government be defeated, an incoming government could reason in the same way and similarly choose to remain limited or to respect constitutional restrictions. So, as an example, governments could *choose* to have their power constrained by an 'independent' judiciary. And as Jasay remarks: 'The judiciary is definitely a safeguard against the executive as long as the executive lets it be'.[8] The problem is that the judiciary 'has no powers to enforce its own independence'.[9] In which case, governments might only be constrained as long as it suits them to be.

A more plausible reason for governments' accepting constitutional limits, among which is the requirement of periodic elections, is that they allow the state to purchase consent rather than having to rely on force to secure its rule.

> Agreeing to constitutional guarantees, then, is an intelligent move, a gesture to reassure the minority that nothing really harsh is going to be done to them. As disarming the mistrust of the prospective minority is, so to speak, a condition for getting everybody's signature on the social contract, there may very well occur historical conjunctures where it is *rational for the state actually to suggest* limits to its own power if its purpose is to maximize it. It has long been known that it can be rational for the wolf to put on sheep's clothing and to refrain for a while from eating sheep.[10]

However, as this means that it is the state which binds itself with constitutional guarantees, it would always be the state's prerogative as to whether or not it chose to remain bound.[11]

It would seem, though, that an even more plausible reason for governments' agreeing to stand for re-election is that another part of the state (the civil service or the military, for example, on which the government depends for its continued rule) might insist that the government offer itself periodically for re-election. Jasay fails to consider this possibility, perhaps because of his tendency to view the state as a single entity, rather than as a supra-institution comprising sometimes

7 Anthony de Jasay, *The State* (Oxford: Blackwell, 1985), p. 31.
8 Ibid., p. 68.
9 Ibid., pp. 68–9.
10 Ibid., p. 191.
11 See ibid., pp. 192–3.

conflicting institutions (such as central government, local government, the police, the military, and so on). In any case, none of the reasons considered establish that the state is an instrument of civil society. What they all suggest is simply that the state rationally chooses to present itself as such.

Marxists, on the other hand, have usually accorded such explanatory primacy to economic factors that they have often merely taken it for granted that the state will be a reflection of civil society and, in particular, of its class nature. Nevertheless, some Marxists have offered theories which purport to explain why the state has to secure bourgeois interests. For example, the state has been described as 'the factor of cohesion between the levels of a social formation'.[12] On this view, the state is where class struggle is condensed, and its function is to secure the interests of the bourgeoisie.

But it is not clear that this is an *explanation* of the state's behaviour, because either it appears to be a variety of structural functionalism in disguise, which simply takes for granted the reproduction of the social and political order, or, alternatively, it takes seriously class struggle as a mechanism but appears simply to assume that class struggle condensed at the level of the state will always result in the securing of bourgeois interests. Surely, class struggle could only be expected to result in the securing of bourgeois interests while the bourgeoisie were, in some significant sense, the strongest political entity? But the assumption that this is so seems to rest on the implausible view that the state has no independent power. For such structuralist Marxists, only classes are deemed to have power.[13] But this claim appears persuasive only when a very limited (and, most likely, defective) conception of 'power' is being employed.

Other Marxists have assumed that the economic power of the bourgeoisie will inevitably constrain the state. But as with pluralist theory, this seems to beg the question. The bourgeoisie might only be strong as a class and only able to use their economic power to constrain the state while the state lets them.[14] Certainly, the bourgeoisie can harm the state by failing to invest. But they might only be able to do so as long as the state chooses not to appropriate bourgeois property.

12 Nicos Poulantzas, *Political Power and Social Classes* (London: New Left Books, 1973), p. 44.

13 'State apparatuses do not possess "power" of their own, but materialize and concentrate class relations, relations which are precisely what is embraced by the concept "power". The state is not an "entity" [with] an intrinsic instrumental essence, but it is itself a relation, more precisely the condensation of a class relation.' Nicos Poulantzas, *Classes in Contemporary Capitalism* (London: Verso, 1978), p. 26. In other words, whereas '[c]lass relations are relations of power . . .', '[w]hen we speak, for example, of *state power*, we cannot mean by it the mode of the state's articulation and intervention at the other levels of the structure; *we can only mean the power of a determinate class* to whose interests (rather than to those of other social classes) the state corresponds.' Poulantzas, *Political Power and Social Classes*, pp. 99–100. Thus, '[t]he various social institutions, in particular the institutions of the state, do not, strictly speaking, have any power. Institutions, considered from the point of view of power, can be related only to *social classes which hold power*.' Ibid., p. 115. For a critique of this view, see Alan Carter, *Marx: A Radical Critique* (Brighton: Wheatsheaf Books, 1988), pp. 203–4.

14 In other words, Marxists may well overlook this possibility because of a blindspot regarding the fourth dimension of power.

And states have, of course, occasionally nationalized private property. Alternatively, the bourgeoisie can harm the state by transferring their capital to another country. But again, they might only be able to do so as long as the state allows them to, for states have been known to impose currency restrictions and prevent the export of large amounts of capital.

Why, then, should the state ordinarily secure bourgeois interests and thereby constrain itself? One reason could be that doing so serves the interests of state actors. For example, as John Dearlove and Peter Saunders observe of Britain:

> the commitment of senior civil servants to the preservation of the established economic order is perhaps revealed in their spectacular migration to jobs in private industry which has gathered pace over the last two decades. . . . Most Senior Permanent Secretaries now expect a clutch of new jobs after they retire at 60 and this may well have implications for the way in which they choose to conduct official business.[15]

If senior state actors, whether politicians, military personnel or civil servants, can expect to benefit from a later move into the private sector, then it is rational for them to secure the capitalist order. And it is perhaps worth noting that, in 1990, '373 Ministry of Defence officials and officers in the armed forces left to take jobs in industry, the bulk of them with arms contractors'.[16] Most importantly for developing a green political theory, if the businesses that state actors can expect to move into make their profits from environmentally damaging activities, then the commitment of the state to pollution control, for instance, must be in some doubt. Interestingly, in 1992, to take one example, 'a new chief of British Nuclear Fuels Limited was appointed: his former job was Chief Permanent Secretary in the Department of Energy'.[17] But, it must be stressed, this does not make the state the instrument of a class in civil society. For what these examples might imply instead is merely that a contingent correspondence holds between the interests of state actors and those of the bourgeoisie, as was suggested in Chapter 2.

Hence, both pluralist and Marxist theories seem to offer inadequate accounts of the state.[18] What is remarkable is that both theories, when they fail to identify a convincing mechanism that would reduce the state to an instrument of civil society or to a class within it, appear to end up regarding state actors as if they were a different kind of species from the rest of humanity. Those who are

15 John Dearlove and Peter Saunders, *Introduction to British Politics: Analyzing a Capitalist Democracy* (Cambridge: Polity, 1984), p. 125.

16 David Pepper, *Eco-Socialism: From Deep Ecology to Social Justice* (London: Routledge, 1993), p. 210.

17 Ibid.

18 As Jasay observes: 'Neither provides any good ground for supposing that the state, once it has the monopoly of force will not, at times or forever, use it *against* those *from* whom it received it. Neither is a theory of the state in the proper sense, i.e. neither really explains why the state will do one thing rather than another.' Jasay, *The State*, p. 34.

occupied in the economy are perceived, by and large, as rational actors pursuing their own self-interests. They are viewed as members of *Homo oeconomicus*. But state actors are supposed either to serve the public by reconciling conflicting interests in civil society or to serve a particular class. Neither theory seems to take sufficiently seriously the possibility that all humans belong to the same species, and that state actors are also pursuing their own rational self-interest. While we in civil society are to recognize ourselves as self-serving, we are, nevertheless, to assume state actors to be predisposed to serving others. Our masters appear to us as our servants. Whether or not we are all self-interested, the time has surely come for political theorists to take the state seriously.[19]

19 Whereas neo-pluralists have come to take economic relations more seriously than pluralists did (see Dunleavy and O'Leary, *Theories of the State*, pp. 293–7 and Held, *Models of Democracy*, pp. 203–4), there has been a growing awareness on the Left of the need to accord greater theoretical independence to the state. Much of the initial impetus has come from Claus Offe, who has observed that, '[s]ince the state *depends* on a process of accumulation which is beyond its power to *organize*, every occupant of state power is basically interested in promoting those conditions most conducive to accumulation.' Claus Offe and Volker Ronge, 'Theses on the theory of the state' in Anthony Giddens and David Held (eds), *Classes, Power, and Conflict: Classical and Contemporary Debates* (London: Macmillan, 1982), p. 250. Thus the state is not allied to the bourgeoisie, nor is it subject to the political power of the capitalist class. Rather, the state has 'an institutional self-interest in guaranteeing and safeguarding a "healthy" accumulation process upon which it depends'. Ibid. Nevertheless, despite this theoretical development, Offe still regards the state as basically 'reactive' (see Held, *Models of Democracy*, p. 212). For example, he claims that 'the state is *denied* the power to control the flow of those resources which are indispensable for the *use* of state power'. Offe and Ronge, 'Theses on the theory of the state', p. 250. But this fails to recognize that the state might not be denied control of accumulation. Rather, it may well, for its own reasons, choose to forgo exerting that control.

A further theoretical development is made in Fred Block, 'Beyond relative autonomy: state managers as historical subjects' in R. Miliband and A. Saville (eds), *The Socialist Register 1980* (London: Merlin, 1980), where the state is granted even more of an active role. Block argues that 'state managers collectively are self-interested maximizers, interested in maximizing their power, prestige, and wealth'. Ibid., p. 229. Moreover, he adds that at certain historical conjunctures, states have greater freedom in relation to the dominant economic class. Hitler, for example, took 'advantage of the dynamics of an exceptional period to free [himself] of constraints imposed by the capitalists'. Ibid., p. 233. However, Block fails to note the extent to which Hitler could have been responsible for such an exceptional period.

Yet more autonomy is granted the state, though from opposing theoretical standpoints, in the work of Theda Skocpol and, more recently, in that of Michael Taylor. See Theda Skocpol, *States and Social Revolutions: A Comparative Analysis of France, Russia and China* (Cambridge: Cambridge University Press, 1979). Also see, for example, Michael Taylor, 'Rationality and revolutionary collective action' in Michael Taylor (ed.), *Rationality and Revolution* (Cambridge: Cambridge University Press, 1988). The state is taken most seriously as an independent actor in Jasay, *The State* and, from a diametrically opposite political standpoint, in Carter, *Marx: A Radical Critique*. Whereas the former takes private property for granted, the latter is concerned not only about the power of the state, but also about the problems posed by inegalitarian economic relations. For a critique of propertarian views (the holding of which distinguishes the libertarian Right from the libertarian Left), see Alan Carter, *The Philosophical Foundations of Property Rights* (Hemel Hempstead: Harvester-Wheatsheaf, 1989).

4.2 Re-thinking the state

How, then, might the state be taken seriously? Let me begin by drawing some distinctions. G. A. Cohen, as we have seen, distinguishes between a 'superstructure' of non-economic institutions (in particular, legal and political institutions) and the structure of relations of production that comprise the 'base' or 'foundation', in Marx's terminology. For brevity's sake, we can regard this as a distinction between a set of political relations and a set of economic relations. Cohen further distinguishes between the relations of production and the forces of production. The relations of production are relations of, or relations presupposing, effective control of the productive forces. And it is the development of these forces of production which explains historical transition, according to Cohen's Techno-Primacy Theory. Within the forces of production, Cohen distinguishes between the labour-power of the producing agents and the means of production (which are primarily tools and raw materials). What develops when the forces of production develop, therefore, is labour-power in the form of skill and knowledge, on the one hand, and tools and machinery, on the other. For convenience, I shall refer to this as 'technological development'.

But why does Cohen define the economic structure as a set of relations of, or presupposing, effective control of the productive forces, rather than as it is standardly conceived – namely, as a set of ownership rights? He does so because a common objection raised by analytical philosophers against Marx's theory of history is that the base cannot be effectively distinguished from the superstructure because economic relations are legal relations, and legal relations are superstructural. By defining economic relations in a *rechtsfrei* manner, Cohen side-steps this objection.

But construing economic relations as relations of, or presupposing, effective *control* of the productive forces gives rise to the question of how such control is enabled and preserved. Just as Cohen argues that it is a mistake to confuse *rechtsfrei* economic relations with legal ones, it could equally be argued that it is at least as serious an error to fail to separate economic relations, when construed as relations of, or presupposing, effective control, from whatever the ability to exercise that control rests upon. Such an ability cannot just be taken for granted. It requires power. How, then, is that ability enabled and preserved? Partly, one presumes, by the coating of legality it has been sprayed with – in other words, by a general acceptance of the legal standing of the economic relations. But also, surely it is enabled and preserved coercively by agents of the state: by those actors deemed responsible for securing economic control – namely, the police and, in the last resort, military personnel. But these *agents* are neither economic forces, economic relations nor legal or political relations (although they might be situated within political relations, just as the economic forces are situated within economic relations).

In short, Cohen distinguishes between the political and the economic, on the one hand, and between relations and forces, on the other. But the set of categories he thereby employs appears to be incomplete, for he only employs economic forces, economic relations and political relations. But we can easily draw a distinction within the political sphere that parallels the one drawn within the economic. Let us therefore complete the set of political and economic categories by distinguishing between both the political and the economic instances, and between their respective relations and forces. This gives us the four categories summarized in Table 4.1. Rotating clockwise, they consist of: political relations, economic relations, economic forces and political forces. And this new category – *political forces* – can be construed as containing what we might call 'forces of defence'.

Table 4.1 Political and economic relations and forces

	Political	*Economic*
Relations	Relations of, or presupposing, political control	Relations of, or presupposing, economic control
Forces	Forces employed to maintain relations of political control	Forces employed within relations of economic control

So, on the one hand, following Cohen, we can distinguish between relations of production and forces of production – a distinction between economic relations and economic forces. The set of economic relations, constituting the economic structure, comprises relations of, or presupposing, effective control over production and exchange.[20] Relations of production, specifically, are relations of, or presupposing, effective control of the productive forces. And these economic forces – the forces of production – comprise economic labour-power (that

20 I include within the category 'economic relations' the relations of control not just over production but also over exchange because, it can be argued, the common Marxist view that exploitation in capitalist societies only occurs at the point of production and only results from an employer/employee relationship misses what is perhaps the most important kind of exploitation in the world today – namely, that of the Third World by the advanced countries. Such exploitation can, surely, take place without the First World as a whole employing the Third World, and without First World firms employing Third World workers. Surely, exploitation can take place because the First World, having a dominant position in the world market, can effectively insist on a high price for its products and a low price for what is produced elsewhere. By the First World selling its products dear and buying Third World goods cheap, the surplus-product of the Third World is thus transferred to the First World. This would not be a case of the exploitation of employees by employers, nor would it be a case of the Third World exploiting itself. It would be a case of *market exploitation*. For a theory of exploitation purportedly better able to deal with this problem than the theory employed by traditional Marxists, see John Roemer, 'New directions in the Marxian theory of exploitation and class' in John Roemer (ed.), *Analytical Marxism* (Cambridge: Cambridge University Press, 1986). On Roemer's theory, exploitation 'can be accomplished, in principle, with or without any direct relationship between the exploiters and the exploited in the process of work' (ibid., p. 95), and his theory therefore allows us to comprehend the exploitation of the Third World by the First through 'unequal exchange'. (See ibid., p. 112.)

capacity which the agents of production supply) and the means of production (for example, tools and machinery).

On the other hand, going beyond Cohen, we can further distinguish between political relations and political forces. As the ability to control effectively the economic forces seems to rest upon both the accepted legality of the economic relations and their preservation by the political forces, then any such ability appears to be dependent upon relations of power – in particular, political relations – involving:

(i) the power to enact laws which are then viewed as legitimate;
(ii) the power to enforce them; and
(iii) the power to defend the community against external aggression and to engage in external aggression when the latter is deemed appropriate.

Thus, the set of political relations, constituting the political structure, and required, it would seem, for enabling and preserving the relations of control over production and exchange, includes those relations which are embodied in the various legal and political institutions. The political institutions, specifically, can be viewed as relations of, or presupposing, effective control of the defensive forces. In the modern state, such political forces – the forces of 'defence' (which are, of course, more often offensive than genuinely defensive) – are coercive in nature. And such forces of coercion can be described as comprising political labour-power (that capacity which, for example, agents of coercion supply – in other words, the work offered by soldiers, police and so on for payment) and means of coercion (for example, weapons, prisons, even instruments of torture). With these various distinctions in mind (and as mapped out in Table 4.2), we might now possess the conceptual apparatus necessary to reach a better understanding of the actual behaviour of the modern state.

4.2.1 Rationality and competing groups

According to Cohen's Techno-Primacy Model, represented in Figure 2.1, technological development is key in understanding historical change. In other words, on Cohen's account, central to Marx's theory of history is the development of the forces of production. These economic forces explain the nature of the economic relations, which in turn explain the nature of the political relations. However, we have identified a fourth category – one that is omitted from the Marxist Techno-Primacy Model – namely, political forces (the forces of defence or, more usually, of coercion). How might these political forces be fitted into a model of historical transition that includes political relations, economic relations and economic forces?

It is apparent from even the most cursory glance at history that one consequence of the development of the productive forces has been the generation of a surplus which has allowed the development of the coercive forces in order to provide greater security – in other words, historically, there has not just been a

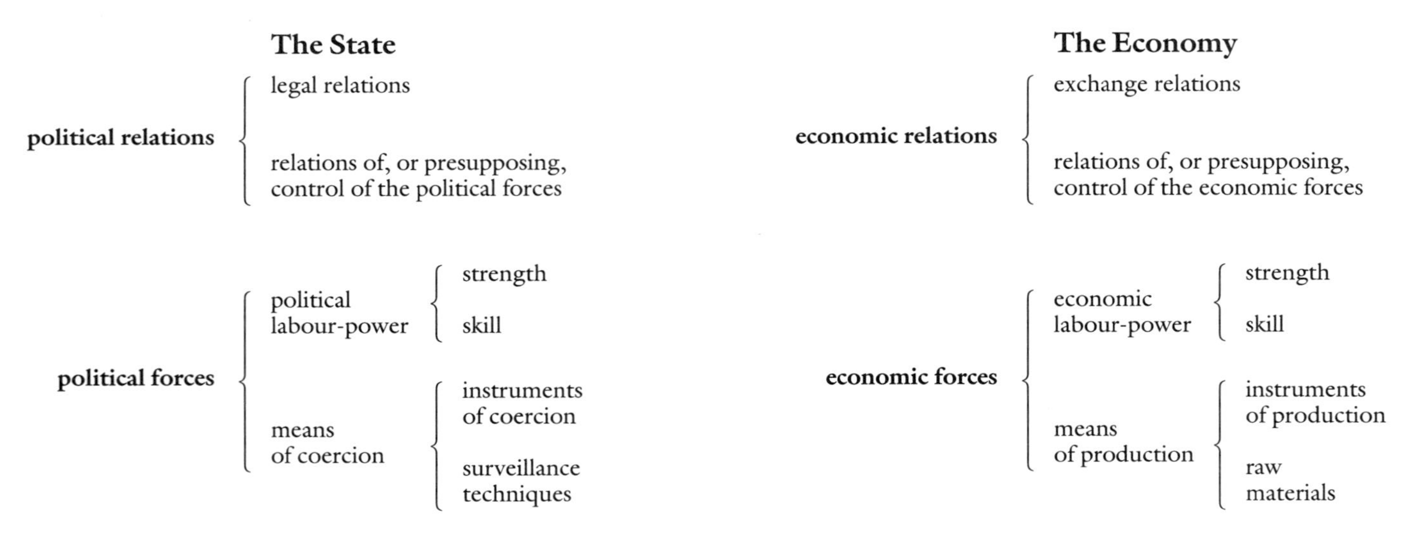

Table 4.2 The state and the economy

	The State			The Economy	
political relations	legal relations		**economic relations**	exchange relations	
	relations of, or presupposing, control of the political forces			relations of, or presupposing, control of the economic forces	
political forces	political labour-power	strength	**economic forces**	economic labour-power	strength
		skill			skill
	means of coercion	instruments of coercion		means of production	instruments of production
		surveillance techniques			raw materials

development of the productive forces but 'defensive' development, too. And this defensive development, along with the growth of nationalistic sentiments, would seem to be at least part of the explanation of the emergence and expansion of antagonistic nation-states.

Now, it is widely accepted that Marxist theory, because of its emphasis on the economic, has proved itself to be inadequate with regard to analysing convincingly the phenomenon of nationalism. Cohen, for one, doubts the ability of traditional Marxism to account for this fundamentally important social feature. (Other crucial features which pose similar difficulties are ethnicity, gender relations and religion). In Chapter 2, above, it was noted that three factors – human rationality, a situation of scarcity and human inventiveness – motivate his Techno-Primacy Theory. In order to deal with phenomena such as nationalism, Cohen has, since the publication of his seminal work *Karl Marx's Theory of History: A Defence*, been led to introduce a fourth important factor, which he introduces as follows:

> Marxist philosophical anthropology is one-sided. Its conception of human nature and human good overlooks the need for self-definition, than which nothing is more essentially human. And that need is part of the explanation of the peculiar strength of national and other self-identifications, which Marxists tend to undervalue.[21]

Perhaps by taking this fourth factor into account, along with (a) rationality, (b) scarcity, and (c) inventiveness, Marxists might be in a position to explain the features of society (e.g. nationalism) which otherwise appear to fall outside the ambit of historical materialism. This fourth important factor can be characterized as:

> (d) self-definition within a community.

But for Cohen to introduce this factor as an afterthought, as it were, is, surely, a rather questionable procedure. It will be recalled from our discussion in Chapter 2, that his theory of history is constructed on the basis of only three motivating factors: (a), (b) and (c). Factor (d) was not present in the formation of the theory. A later introduction into Marxist theory of this fourth factor is problematic because, with this factor in operation but ignored in the theory's presentation, we no longer know that it can still be constructed in a convincing manner. Let me, therefore, return to Cohen's purposive elaboration of the Techno-Primacy Theory, except that this time let us see what happens when factor (d) is also brought into play.

Cohen argues that it is rational to invent and develop technology in a situation

21 G. A. Cohen, 'Restricted and Inclusive Historical Materialism', *Irish Philosophical Journal*, Vol. 1, No. 1 (1984), p. 25.

of scarcity. If only factors (a), (b) and (c) are in play, the Development Thesis – that the productive forces tend to develop through history – can easily be supported. When individuals are faced with a situation of scarcity, it does appear rational to develop the productive forces and increase production. But the significance of factor (d) is that different individuals identify with different groups. Individuals often define themselves in terms of exclusive communities.[22] And it is within such different groupings that rational individuals face scarcity. Now that factor (d) has been introduced, we need to know whether or not it is always rational for individuals who identify with different, and possibly conflicting, groups to develop the productive forces.

Unfortunately for the theory, it appears that it is not always rational for them to do so. For example, on the one hand, one's group might, conceivably, reduce undesirable toil and solve the problem of scarcity with less effort by plundering the produce of another group. On the other hand, if some other group has decided to plunder rather than produce, then an increase in one's production capability might make one more likely to be plundered. In a situation where some have chosen to plunder, it might be extremely unwise to make oneself a more attractive target by increasing production. When factor (d) is in play, then, it can no longer just be assumed that it is rational to develop the productive forces. Factor (d) – self-definition within a community – therefore interferes with the construction of the Techno-Primacy Theory.

However, those who wish systematically to consume the surplus produced by others would benefit greatly from the development of political forces – in particular, forces of coercion. And forces of coercion can only be developed if the productive forces have reached a level of development which creates a surplus above mere subsistence. Once such a level has been attained and coercive forces have been developed by one grouping, they could systematically force another group to produce more and consume less than they might otherwise. The resulting surplus could then be extracted continually from the subordinate group. This can be thought to be exemplified in class-divided societies. But in time, the individuals within such a society, through living together, might come to define themselves as members of one nation and, collectively, wish to oppress others. This would be rational for all within the nation because oppressing a foreign group would offer the possibility of increased wealth for all nationals, thus reducing the need for coercion within the national community, while simultaneously increasing the overall surplus available to those in control of the political forces (just as long as a considerable surplus can be extracted from foreigners).

As it is rational for such groupings to form and behave thus in order to meet scarcity, then all four factors, combined together, contribute to an explanation of class-divided, imperialist nation-states. (In fact, such a process of expanding self-definition could, plausibly, continue further, for the peoples of oppressed nations,

22 See Frank Parkin, *Marxism and Class Theory: A Bourgeois Critique* (London: Tavistock, 1981), pp. 44–73 for a pertinent Weberian theory of 'social closure as exclusion'.

through living with their colonial administrators, might come to define themselves in their masters' terms, thus giving rise to a genuine empire or, later, a commonwealth.)

Furthermore, it is rational not only to oppress another group and impose upon it greater toil so as to reduce one's own labour, but also to resist the imposition of greater toil. And in order to resist another nation determined to impose greater toil upon one's own community, it appears, at first glance, beneficial to develop the forces of coercion. Hence, such resistance equally seems to require the production of a surplus above subsistence requirements, so that the coercive forces might be developed.

On both imperialist and defensive counts, then, it is quite understandable that within nations some of the population should have come to be expertly engaged in producing the society's wealth, part of which goes to others who have become expertly engaged in 'defence' and, in consequence, are themselves no longer employed directly in production. It is quite understandable that workers, fearing that their nation might be subjugated by another, should support those who are charged with their defence. And it is quite understandable that those who are in effective control of the productive forces (the dominant economic class) should support those exercising political control, when the latter choose to stabilize relations of production which simultaneously develop the productive forces and increase the private wealth of those in control of production. Moreover, it is quite understandable that those exercising political control should back those economic relations which develop the productive forces that create the very surplus which they consume.

In short, it can be argued that the development of the productive forces creates the surplus which is needed to finance a standing army and a police force, for weapons research, etc., and that these forces of coercion are precisely what enable the state to enforce the relations of production that lead to the creation of the surplus which the state requires. Moreover, it can further be argued that, given its need for the development of such forces of coercion, and given that, unlike other groups, it is not primarily engaged in production, the state can be expected to have its own interests vis-à-vis the rest of society.[23] And being in control of the instruments of coercion, the state would be in a position both to protect and to further its own interests. What is significant about all this is that any account along these lines would most likely support anarchist suspicions about the wisdom of employing any form of state as a means for bringing about political and economic equality.

23 On the speculative history outlined above, as states are theoretically conjectured to have originated out of exclusionary groupings formed in order to prey on the surplus produced by others, and as states have continued to extract such surplus for their own requirements, then states would clearly have interests different from (indeed, have certain interests against) the other groupings within their territories.

4.3 The State-Primacy Model

Having indicated how the state might thus be regarded as possessing its own interests, I am now in a position to present, in outline, a possible anarchist theory of history. I shall commence by showing how an alternative to Cohen's Techno-Primacy Model might be formulated.

Cohen's model, it will be recalled, claims that economic forces select economic relations which develop, or optimally employ, the economic forces, and the economic relations that are selected themselves select political relations which stabilize those economic relations. (See Figure 2.1.) It will also be recalled that Cohen's model is restricted to these three principal categories because he draws no distinction between the political relations and the political forces – the forces of defence or, in present-day circumstances, of coercion. In contraposition to Cohen's, the proposed alternative model employs as its principal categories not only the economic forces, economic relations and political relations but also the political forces, and, in so doing, it further separates conceptually the relations of economic control from the means by which that control is secured.

How, then, might these four categories – the political relations, the economic relations, the economic forces and the political forces – be combined? Generally, according to the model I now propose, the political relations ordinarily select economic relations which develop, or optimally employ, the economic forces because that facilitates the development of the political forces, which usually empower the political relations. Moreover, the political forces stabilize the economic relations that are selected – relations which themselves support the development of the political forces by providing the surplus needed to finance it. This is depicted in Figure 4.1.[24]

Put another way, the claim is that, in the modern era, the legal and political institutions enact and implement legislation which determines a specific economic structure because, except in special circumstances, it is functional for those institutions by encouraging the development of, or by optimally employing, the forces of production – principally productive skills and technologies – which are needed to produce the ever-growing surplus which is required for further development of the forces of defence, for it is precisely this defensive development which the power of the legal and political institutions ultimately seems to be premised upon.

It is further claimed that when those individuals who are, *de facto*, in direct control of the defensive forces are not those who are at the head of the legislature, it is normally in the interests of the former to empower the latter, because the latter both confer legitimacy upon the former (they might even be taken by the former to possess legitimacy) and are responsible for managing the revenue which the state as a whole requires, including that which those in direct control of the defensive forces need for their forces' development. In addition, it is claimed that

24 In Figure 4.1, as in Figure 2.1, X_1 selects Y_1 because Y_1 is functional for X_1, and X_2 selects Y_2 because Y_2 is functional for X_2.

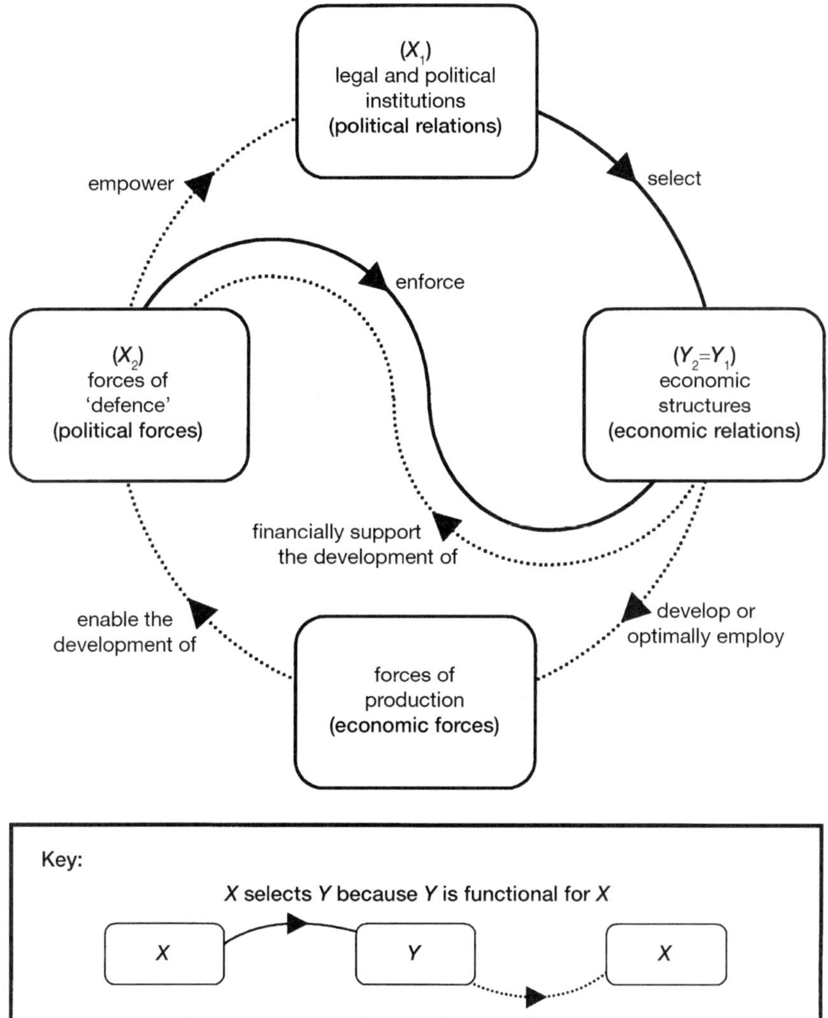

Figure 4.1 An anarchist State-Primacy Model

it is this defensive development (usually in the form of ever-more sophisticated forces of coercion) which preserves the economic structure selected – an economic structure that is also functional for defensive development by providing it, through taxation, with the financial resources it requires.

In short, according to the alternative model being proposed, *ordinarily, a structure of political relations selects economic relations that are functional for it. And, ordinarily, the political forces stabilize those economic relations which are simultaneously functional for the development of the political forces by producing the surplus their development requires.*

Here, then, is an alternative model that employs functional explanations, just like the Techno-Primacy Model, but which reverses their direction. Whereas the principal direction of explanation in the Marxist model (Figure 2.1) is from the bottom to the top – from the economic to the political – the alternative model (Figure 4.1) reverses the direction of explanation. In Cohen's model, it is technological development which has explanatory primacy; in the alternative model, it is the structure of legal and political institutions combined with the defensive forces. And in the modern era, the structure of legal and political institutions ordinarily deploying the political forces is *the state*. It seems appropriate, therefore, to label this alternative 'the State-Primacy Model'.

On the basis of this State-Primacy Model, how might a State-Primacy Theory of history be formulated? It could briefly be stated as follows: Certain economic relations, by furthering technological development, are, for a while, simultaneously functional for both the structure of legal and political institutions, on the one hand, and the political forces, on the other. But, at a certain point in time, they come to constrain any further development, and thus become dysfunctional. (Or, perhaps in the case of a transition to post-capitalism, they become dysfunctional by preventing the optimal use of the prevailing technology.) A revolution then occurs which involves, at some point, the state choosing to stabilize new relations of production which *are* functional for it in so far as they further, beyond the present level, the development of technology. (Or, perhaps, the new economic relations are functional for the state in so far as they allow the current technology to be optimally employed.)

Moreover, the new economic relations which the state chooses to stabilize are selected precisely because, in furthering technological development, they are functional for the state. (Or, alternatively, they might be selected because they are functional for the state in so far as they encourage the optimal use of the prevailing technology.) And with new economic relations, the legal and political institutions are free to alter their form to one which appears more appropriate.[25] Like Cohen's interpretation of Marx's theory of history, this, too, is a complex of functional explanations.

In Chapter 2, it was noted that Marxian functional explanations from one mode of production to another are underpinned by something like the following consequence law:

(2′) If it is the case that if new relations of production were to be selected

25 The form could come, eventually, to have the appearance of being, for example, pluralist or even corporatist. Regarding the latter, for an account (drawing on the work of M. J. Smith and assuming state autonomy) of how it was functional for the British state to invite the National Farmers' Union 'into government' by according it 'a statutory right to be consulted over agricultural policy', thus ensuring that its relationship with the Ministry of Agriculture, Fisheries and Food (MAFF) was a privileged one, see Robert Garner, *Environmental Politics* (Hemel Hempstead: Harvester-Wheatsheaf, 1996), pp. 158–60. For some of the seemingly grave environmental consequences that resulted from this privileged relationship, see ibid., pp. 157–8.

then the productive forces would develop further, then they would come to be selected.

Interestingly, (2′) is as consistent with the State-Primacy Theory as it is with the Techno-Primacy Theory. Hence, if the reason for choosing the Techno-Primacy Theory is that it coheres with (2′), then that constitutes no reason for preferring it to the State-Primacy Theory. Both theories claim that new relations of production tend to be selected when they are functional for furthering technological development. The difference between them is that, according to the State-Primacy Theory, it is the state which selects the new relations of production, and it does so to promote its own interests.

Now, as was also noted in Chapter 2, one of the claims that Cohen most wishes to defend is the Techno-Primacy Thesis, which, it will be recalled, he puts as follows:

> (T-P Thesis) The nature of a set of production relations is explained by the level of development of the productive forces embraced by it (to a far greater extent than *vice versa*).[26]

This Techno-Primacy Thesis lies at the heart of Cohen's Techno-Primacy Theory. I also remarked in Chapter 2 that I would later forward a quite different primacy thesis. I now make good on that promise. And the alternative thesis that I now wish to propose I shall call 'the State-Primacy Thesis', which can be stated thus:

> (S-P Thesis) The nature of a set of production relations which prevail in a society is (ultimately) explained by state interests.

Just as the Techno-Primacy Thesis lies at the heart of the Techno-Primacy Theory, the State-Primacy Thesis lies at the heart of the State-Primacy Theory.

Thus, the State-Primacy Thesis is one of the State-Primacy Theory's core claims, and it could be supported by the following elaboration: State actors can only continue to enjoy their positions while the state remains secure. It is, therefore, in the interests of state actors to ensure that their nation's economy is as productive as those of neighbouring states. If their economy were weaker than one of their neighbouring states', then the state would not be able to fund the development of its defensive capability to the same degree as that neighbouring state could, and, in the long-run at least, would be unable to defend itself. In order to retain power, therefore, state actors have an interest in selecting and stabilizing appropriate economic relations. Hence, it could be concluded, the state will ordinarily select economic relations that it regards as appropriate to developing further the productive forces beyond the level of development they

26 G. A. Cohen, *Karl Marx's Theory of History: A Defence* (Oxford: Clarendon, 1978), p. 134.

have so far reached, because that is in its interests. The State-Primacy Theory can, therefore, be supported by a purposive elaboration of its own.

4.3.1 The nature of state interests

However, any such elaboration immediately gives rise to the following question: Is it *the state as a structure* that selects economic relations which are in *its interests* or is it *state actors* that act in *their own interests*? In other words, it appears as if the State-Primacy Model (represented in Figure 4.1) could be interpreted in one of two mutually exclusive ways. For example, we could regard the structure of legal and political institutions literally as what selects the economic relations. This would provide us with the basis for a 'structuralist anarchism'. Alternatively, we could take it to mean that the politically dominant actors select an economic structure that is in their interests. This would provide the basis for a methodological individualist anarchism.[27]

But these two positions are not jointly exhaustive, for it is possible to steer a middle course. And the interrelationist perspective outlined in the previous chapter suggests just such a middle course. An interrelationist perspective would not view collectives as entities in themselves with causal effects on their members, as many methodological collectivists are prone to regard them. Nor would it reduce social explanation to the psychology of unrelated individuals, as numerous methodological individualists tend to do. Rather, an interrelationist middle course might, instead, attempt to explain social phenomena in terms of the rational choices taken by individuals who act within certain relationships to one another. The causal influences, on this approach, would be recognized to be from one individual or group of individuals to another, and not from a collective entity to its parts, while individuals would, nevertheless, still be regarded as being related within a structure. In other words, taking this middle course would not entail a simple reduction of all structures to mere collections of individuals.

As an interrelationist approach seems to be more compatible with ecological thinking, and as my intention is to offer the State-Primacy Theory as a tool for shedding light on the environmental threat, allow me to adopt such an interrelationist standpoint in order to offer some refinements to the State-Primacy Model. On this favoured approach, then, when it is claimed in Figure 4.1 that the legal and political institutions select economic relations, that claim should be construed as 'the *agents acting within the structure of legal and political institutions* select for stabilization one set of economic relations in preference to another'. Moreover, when it is simultaneously claimed that the forces of defence enforce economic relations, that claim should ordinarily be construed as 'those *agents* who live by means of their coercive labour-power use the means of

27 This parallels the famous disagreement in Marxist circles between Nicos Poulantzas and Ralph Miliband. See their respective contributions in Robin Blackburn (ed.), *Ideology in Social Science* (London: Fontana, 1972).

coercion at their disposal to protect specific economic relations in preference to others'.

However, this explication necessitates a further refinement. As the various state actors will occupy different positions within the state, all their choices are unlikely to push in exactly the same direction. Furthermore, their individual powers to determine any outcome are likely to be differently weighted according to their different locations within the state. But viewing the decisions of state actors in these terms allows us to conceptualize what the state decides to select and enforce as *a vector of these variedly directional and weighted decisions*. Let such a vector signify the 'collective decision of state actors'.

In other words, we can regard '*state interests*' as a resultant '*parallelogram of forces*' resolving the numerous interests of state actors with their differing powers for promoting their interests. What would enable us still to talk of 'state interests' in this sense – as if they were the interests of the state conceived of as a collective entity – is that, although the relevant individual interests push in different directions (army personnel might prefer more state revenue allocated to them than to the police, for example), all state actors would seem to share a common interest in preserving the state. Nevertheless, although all state actors appear to have interests pushing in that direction, there remains the possibility of fracturing within the state because of other interests taking diverging directions.

Now, the State-Primacy Model claims that states ordinarily select economic relations which serve their interests by developing the technology that increases the surplus available to the state. As all state actors appear to have an interest in preserving the state, does this mean that every agent of the state will necessarily be committed to selecting economic relations that are optimal for maximizing the state's revenue? Were this the case, then at least part of the State-Primacy Model could apparently be established *a priori*. Unfortunately for the theory, matters are not so simple. There is a debate within the theory of the firm which bears upon this question. The debate concerns whether managers seek to maximize the profits of their companies or whether they are content with levels of profit that will be satisfactory to their shareholders – thus allowing the managers to keep their jobs. A parallel question could be raised concerning senior state actors. Are they maximizers or satisficers with regard to state revenue?

It might be thought that those non-elected state actors who are secure in their positions or who lack ambition will be content to behave as satisficers, whereas those seeking promotion will wish to impress by acting as maximizers. If such maximizers were the most successful at obtaining promotions, it might safely be assumed that they would be the ones who would come to occupy the most senior posts. Senior state actors surely have greater power with respect to the execution of their decisions than juniors. In other words, surely the decisions of the former carry greater weight. Hence, it might be concluded that the state will act so as to maximize its revenue, and it will do so because of how the hierarchical structure of its various internal institutions determines which personality-type of state actor rises highest within them.

However, 'pushy' state actors seeking promotion by adopting a maximizing stance could, alternatively, be viewed as risky appointments who were likely to 'rock the boat'. This might make them less likely to attain senior positions than 'dependable' and 'reliable' satisficers. Moreover, maximizers who obtained senior positions within the state would, in fact, only have effective power to the extent that those below them in the chain of command complied with, rather than chose to frustrate, the execution of their decisions. Thus, the likelihood that maximizers would obtain senior positions or that, having attained them, they would be able to act effectively will depend upon the particular culture of the state in question. Hence, whether the state decision-vector would always select optimal or satisfactory economic relations is an open question and cannot be decided *a priori*. This seems to vitiate to some degree the immediate plausibility of the State-Primacy Theory.

There is another feature of the process effecting promotion within the structure of legal and political institutions which might be thought to undermine the plausibility of the State-Primacy Theory. Eligibility for promotion is determined not by those seeking it, but by those higher up the management chain. Those who occupy senior positions, and thereby determine the criteria by which an individual's suitability for advancement within a state institution is to be judged, will already have risen within that structure and are likely to value the 'older' approaches which they are familiar with. Moreover, they are likely to display personalities and adopt approaches which met the approval of an earlier generation of state actors occupying senior positions. One might conclude, therefore, that there will tend to be a conservative bias at work in filtering out those deemed appropriate for promotion. The probable result is that those who come to be senior state actors will lean strongly towards traditional perceptions of, and means for securing, state interests. And that suggests that they might not be too inclined to select new economic relations.

However, all of this assumes that state actors have a significant measure of power. But do they? How powerful are state actors? In particular, how powerful are non-elected state personnel? Consider the United Kingdom: Dearlove and Saunders describe a British 'secret state' consisting of 'state institutions which are *non-elected*, which enjoy substantial *autonomy* from the control of government and Parliament (no matter what constitutional theory might assert), and which tend to be *closed and secretive* as to the ways in which they exercise their very *substantial powers*.'[28] Within this 'secret state' they list: 'the civil service; the nationalized industries (including the Bank of England); the judiciary; the police; the security services; and the military.'[29] And in their view, if one examines the behaviour of the civil service, never mind the other institutions of the 'secret state', it soon becomes apparent that it

> tends to serve as a powerful conservative force within the state machine. It is

28 Dearlove and Saunders, *Introduction to British Politics*, p. 116.
29 Ibid.

> sceptical of the case for change; committed to continuity and ordered, steady, progress, and so is eager to contain the wilder excesses of party politicians keen to implement their manifestos with practical talk of the need to attend to 'reality' and 'the facts'. The civil service is organized in such a way that it is best able to exert a negative power which blocks the cry for innovation. It is keenly attuned to the maintenance of established policy (after all, it did much to establish the policy over the years), and the recruitment and socialization of senior civil servants suggests that the service is likely to be concerned to maintain the essentials of the established society and economy.[30]

If this is so, then, clearly, the power of such state actors has to be taken very seriously, indeed – a lesson the radical British politician Tony Benn claims to have learnt, for his 'experience as Energy Minister in the 1974–9 Labour administration led him to the belief that civil service "mandarins" exert extremely strong political influences on environmental decision making'.[31] Thus, it seems that any cogent green political theory would, obviously, have to take such power into account. Now, whereas Marxists tend to de-emphasize it, because of their stress on economic factors, the State-Primacy Theory does at least assign a central place to the power of state actors, even if the conservative tendencies of such agents might be thought to diminish the plausibility of the theory as an explanation of revolutionary transformations.

However, while the high probability that senior state actors will display conservative tendencies seems to provide a major objection to the State-Primacy Theory, it does have clear implications for green political theory in general. It suggests there is little likelihood that a radical green who perceived state interests to lie in facilitating a transition towards a sustainable society, and away from the highly productive economic relations which have satisfied state requirements up until now, would ever rise to a genuinely powerful position within the state. It also seems likely that if a person concealed his or her radical green views and thereby attained a position of power, he or she would soon feel isolated and lacking support once he or she made any move to act upon those views. Hence, there is reason to think that he or she would not enjoy any genuine power. In short, there are grounds for thinking that environmentally motivated individuals acting outside of the structure of legal and political institutions will inevitably be far more radical in their conception of the need for change and the form that it must take than any state actor enjoying significant power.

4.3.1.1 *A preliminary defence of the State-Primacy Theory*

Nevertheless, although a high probability of conservative tendencies on the part of senior state actors does suggest that the state cannot be relied upon to bring

30 Ibid., p. 125.

31 David Pepper, *The Roots of Modern Environmentalism* (London: Routledge, 1989), p. 179.

about an environmentally benign economic structure, it does not, in fact, mean that the State-Primacy Theory should be rejected as a theory of revolutionary transition. For, all the above considerations notwithstanding, there is a very powerful and overriding argument which can be deployed in support of the State-Primacy Theory. No matter how conservative senior state personnel turn out to be, the desire to select economic relations optimal for providing the state with revenue could be expected with considerable certainty when the state finds itself in a situation of military competition with another state, for otherwise it would simply not survive. Yet this is precisely the situation which states usually find themselves in.

Moreover, should the state behave irrationally by not attending to its defence requirements, it could expect its nation to be incorporated into a territory controlled by one of the more militarily successful states – in other words, one which did attend to the economic requirements of an expanding military capacity. But then, the former territory of the defeated state would most likely have economic relations imposed upon it which served the interests of the militarily successful state. Clearly, the only way for even the most conservative of states to be at all sure of avoiding what for them would be such a disastrous outcome is for them to select those economic relations which, at that time, were most suited to technological development. Thus, it can be argued that, by a 'Darwinian' mechanism, the states that survive will tend to be those which the State-Primacy Theory describes. In short, there is good reason to think that the State-Primacy Theory successfully describes the behaviour of existing states.

But there is a further, and seemingly decisive, argument available to the State-Primacy Theory. The theory is offered in order to explain the outcome of epochal transitions. It serves to account for the form taken by economic and political structures following a period of revolutionary change. And revolutions are highly significant events not only for the societies revolutionized but also for neighbouring states. A popular revolution within a country might give rise to a revolutionary zeal which spurred on its state to invade other territories, perhaps in order to effect similar structural changes within them. Neighbouring states are thus likely to fear invasion from any seemingly zealous revolutionary state. Any such perceived threat would lead to the increasing militarization of threatened neighbouring states as well as of the revolutionary society. One obvious example is the period of the Napoleonic Wars. Perhaps another is the period dominated by the rise of fascism.

Alternatively, if neighbouring states did not fear invasion from a revolutionary state, they might still dread infection from its revolutionary ideals, which might spread contagiously through their territories. Hence, the threat a revolutionary society poses to the stability of neighbouring states might provoke one of them to assist an invasion or to arm insurgents or to invade it themselves (as happened to Cuba, Nicaragua and Granada, respectively). In order to deter any such threat, the revolutionary state would need to build up its military capability, and that would necessarily effect its choice of economic structure.

A third possibility is that the revolutionary society might be weakened because of internal conflicts which had come to prominence during the course of its revolution, thereby making it an attractive target for imperialist neighbours (as happened to Russia immediately after the 1917 Revolution). And resistance to aggressive intervention by neighbouring states would require the revolutionary state to expand its military capacity, which would force it to choose an economic structure able to support its military needs.

For these reasons, it can be argued that periods of revolutionary change are most likely to lead to increasing militarization. Most importantly, then, a revolution thus seems to require any revolutionary state which it brings into being to concentrate upon its military requirements and to stabilize whichever economic relations are appropriate for supporting its military needs. In other words, it is during revolutionary periods that the State-Primacy Theory is most likely to apply. But, surely, such periods are precisely those which determine the economic and political structure of the following epoch. In short, the State-Primacy Theory is likely to be the most appropriate theory to employ when seeking to understand precisely those periods which it most needs to explain.

Thus, to recapitulate some of the argument so far: according to Cohen's Techno-Primacy Model, economic forces select economic relations that select political relations. But this is to leave out a key category: the political forces. They can be fitted into a coherent model by reversing the direction of explanation. This provides us with the State-Primacy Model: political relations select economic relations that develop economic forces which enable the development of the political forces – these political forces enforcing economic relations which provide them with the surplus they require. And the State-Primacy Model can be provided with the following purposive elaboration: in order to oppress another national group and meet scarcity, or in order to resist another national group threatening to impose greater scarcity, the actors dominant within the state will collectively decide to stabilize specific economic relations which encourage the development of the productive forces (technological development) and thus allow a surplus to be extracted which finances the development of the forces of coercion (defensive development) necessary for those state actors to protect or further their interests. In this alternative model, the state selects relations of production so as to develop the productive forces, and does so for its own politically-motivated reasons. Hence, the cogency of Cohen's model, which accords explanatory primacy to the productive forces over the economic relations and the superstructure, must be cast into some doubt when a complex of functional explanations which accords primacy to the 'superstructure' over the economic relations and the productive forces can just as easily be forwarded.

In fact, it is possible to go further in criticizing Cohen. Not only can the State-Primacy Model be formulated as clearly as Cohen's, but there is also reason to consider the former to be conceptually superior, for it does not rely on a dubious metaphor. When Cohen develops his Techno-Primacy Model, he writes of the forces of production 'selecting' specific relations of production because the latter are functional for their development. As he puts it: 'forces select structures according to their capacity to promote development.'[32] But 'select' must, in this instance, be metaphorical. Technology neither acts nor has intentions. Consequently, even though Cohen denies that he is a functionalist, he leaves himself open to the charge that he is relying on the 'free-floating intentions'[33] associated with functionalism. One considerable advantage of according explanatory primacy to the state is that state personnel, unlike technology or economic relations, do have intentions and are the sorts of entities that can make selections – thus allowing a genuinely purposive elaboration of the State-Primacy Model.

However, given that I have been focusing upon state actors – agents acting within the state – one obvious question needs to be answered. What exactly is the state? The question can be answered intensionally or extensionally. The most famous intensional reply is that of Max Weber, who defines 'the state' as 'a human community that (successfully) claims the *monopoly of the legitimate use of physical force* within a given territory.'[34] Probably the most famous extensional reply is Ralph Miliband's, who identifies the state as a system of institutions which comprise: 'the government, the administration, the military and the police, the judicial branch, sub-central government, parliamentary assemblies',[35] etc. From the perspective of the State-Primacy Model, it is precisely from within these various institutions that differently weighted decisions coming from differently positioned agents with correspondingly different interests are taken.[36]

4.3.1.2 Two further objections

There are, however, a couple of further objections (besides the potentially conservative bias of state actors) that might be raised against the State-Primacy Theory and which need to be answered immediately. The first is that the theory seems to presuppose state personnel knowing which economic relations will encourage the development of, or will optimally employ, the forces of production. This is certainly a questionable assumption. What is likely is that, in a revolutionary period, state personnel[37] will back the relations of production which they

32 Cohen, *Karl Marx's Theory of History*, p. 162.

33 Jon Elster, *Making Sense of Marx* (Cambridge: Cambridge University Press, 1985), p. 17.

34 Max Weber, 'Politics as a vocation' in *From Max Weber*, ed. H. Gerth and C. Wright Mills (London: Routledge and Kegan Paul, 1970), p. 78.

35 Ralph Miliband, *The State in Capitalist Society* (London: Quartet, 1973), p. 50. And as Dunleavy and O'Leary add: 'The state is a recognizably separate institution or set of institutions, so differentiated from the rest of its society as to create identifiable public and private spheres.' Dunleavy and O'Leary, *Theories of the State*, p. 2.

36 Given that the state comprises various institutions, then there are likely to be conflicts of interests between them. In fact, the institutions themselves may well contain fairly severe internal fractures. Hence, it would be a mistake to regard the state as monolithic or homogenous. This notwithstanding, all state institutions, like all state actors within them, seem at least to be united in having an interest in the preservation of the state.

37 Perhaps the most significant would be new state actors coming to prominence as a result of the overthrow of the previous government.

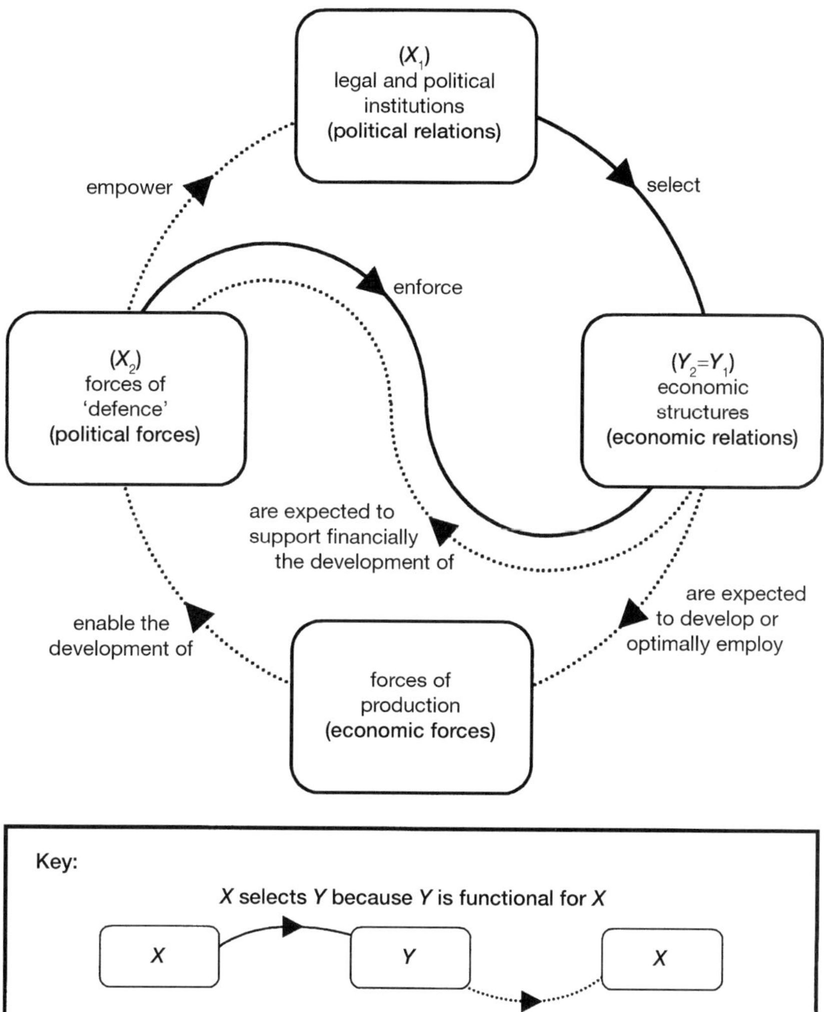

Figure 4.2 An anarchist State-Primacy Transitional Model

believe would be most conducive to serving their interests. This is represented in Figure 4.2.

This also suggests a modification to the State-Primacy Thesis, which I shall call the short-term variant:

(S-P Thesis$^{S\text{-}T}$) The nature of a set of production relations in a society is explained by the state's perception of how most effectively to promote its interests at that time.

But if the new relations of production are stabilized and then fail to serve the interests of the state satisfactorily, new relations of production might then be tried (also Figure 4.2).[38] The relations of production that in the long term would most likely come to be stabilized would be those which, at that level of development of the productive forces, prove in fact to serve the interests of the state, for then there would no longer be a pressing reason to change them. This is what Figure 4.1 actually represents. In which case, the long-term process schematically represented in Figure 4.1 can be elaborated by reference to the short-term process schematically represented in Figure 4.2 – the short-term process being motivated by the beliefs of state personnel.

What this means is that this alternative theory of history is not only a rational-choice explanation[39] but also, as I indicated earlier, 'Darwinian'. It is a rational-choice theory in so far as it focuses on the rational choices of state actors occupying their particular state roles. Thus, variations in the economic relations are explained by changing state beliefs about their efficacy, given changing political situations and changing perspectives. It is a Darwinian theory in so far as it claims that the relations of production which tend to prevail are those which are, in fact, most suited to survive in an environment determined by militarily competing states. And by emphasizing the roles agents occupy within such a complex of relationships, the State Primacy Theory is clearly interrelationist.

A second possible objection against the State-Primacy Theory focuses on the apparent fact that some elected governments carry out programmes which protect bourgeois interests, while other governments carry out programmes which better protect the interests of the workers. Does this not demonstrate that governments reflect their (economic) class bases, and are, therefore, to some extent at least, the instruments of classes? And does this not undermine the claims of the State-Primacy Theory, which presumes independent state interests? Evidently, some elected governments do side with the bourgeoisie more than others, and some may even side slightly more with the workers than with the bourgeoisie. But, as was remarked when discussing the nature of the vector of state interests, all state actors appear to have one interest in common: state preservation. Thus, even both extremes of government would seem to share a common interest in the continuation of the state. The different programmes may serve different economic classes, but all the programmes chosen appear to serve the state, as well as a particular economic class.

In other words, although certain policies may change from one government to the next (one policy aiding one group in society, another aiding a different group), there would seem, nevertheless, to be an overlapping area which is consistent. And that overlapping area concerns the state's interests. Even if at different times different economic classes manage to get their representatives elected, and even if the representatives remain on the side of their electors, on assuming

38 The fact that formerly communist states have allowed market relations to develop would suggest that planning did not serve the state as well as it was originally believed it would do.

39 See Elster, *Making Sense of Marx*, p. 9.

state power the elected also then have an interest in protecting state power, and consequently, could be expected to act so as to protect it. (Though it may well be the case that representatives originating from different economic classes have different visions of how best to do so.) Moreover, the elected usually have limited scope for changing policy, which, it seems, is more often than not determined by those state personnel who are career civil servants.[40] And the latter have a very good reason for ensuring that state interests are continually protected.

4.3.2 From feudalism to capitalism

The State-Primacy Model (Figure 4.1) is clearly the inverse of the Marxist Techno-Primacy Model (Figure 2.1), for it regards as determining what the latter takes to be determined. But does it have as much explanatory power as Marxist theory?

Consider an account, informed by the Techno-Primacy Theory, of the transition from feudalism to capitalism: In feudalism, the surplus-product of the serf had to be extracted by the constant threat of force. Capitalist relations emerged alongside technological developments. These relations, being more productive than feudal ones, became dominant, and they allowed a surplus to be extracted without the constant threat of force. All the state was then required to do was protect property rights. This meant that *the state was allowed a measure of autonomy from the economy.* The Marxist theory can, therefore, explain technological developments, the ascendancy of capitalist relations of production, and the liberal appearance of the state in capitalist societies.

Now consider an account informed by the State-Primacy Theory: In feudalism, the surplus-product of the serf had to be extracted by the constant threat of force. Capitalist relations emerged alongside technological developments. These relations, being more productive than feudal ones, eventually came to be backed by those who exerted coercive power. As capitalist relations allowed a surplus to be extracted without the constant threat of force, the state restricted its actions within the nation to protecting property rights. This meant that *the economy was allowed a measure of autonomy from the state.* The alternative theory can, therefore, also explain technological developments, the ascendancy of capitalist relations of production, and the liberal appearance of the state in capitalist societies.

Both the Marxist Techno-Primacy Theory and the alternative State-Primacy Theory can explain the same historical events. However, it is not necessary to claim that the alternative theory correctly applies to the transition from pre-capitalist to capitalist social formations. It might be the case that it is the Marxist

40 According to Miliband: 'even where the political executive is strong and stable, top administrators are still able to play an important role in critical areas of policy by tendering advice which governments often find it very difficult, for one reason or another, to discount. However much argument there may be over the nature and extent of bureaucratic power . . . the range of possibilities must exclude the idea that top civil servants can be reduced to the role of mere instruments of policy.' Miliband, *The State in Capitalist Society*, p. 48.

theory which provides an accurate explanation of the transition from feudalism to capitalism. But it might also be the case that in the capitalist epoch the state grows to such importance[41] that, in order to understand further developments, the state would have to be conferred explanatory primacy. The Techno-Primacy Model would thus need to 'flip over' and convert to the State-Primacy Model. Hence, were such a 'flip-over' in explanatory primacy to become necessary, then, if we are to understand and predict the transition to post-capitalism, we would need the alternative theory of history rather than the Marxist one. Yet it was primarily in order to illuminate the transition to post-capitalism that Marx presented his theory of history.

This notwithstanding, the appropriateness of employing the State-Primacy Theory to understand pre-capitalist periods is supported by an argument presented by Robert Brenner for the growing importance within feudalism of the political relations and their need to expand their political forces – the latter being a core feature of the State-Primacy Theory. Brenner reasons:

> In view of the difficulty, in the presence of pre-capitalist property relations, of raising returns from investment in the means of production (via increases in productive efficiency), the lords found that if they wished to increase their income, they had little choice but to do so by *redistributing* wealth and income away from their peasants or from other members of the exploiting class. This meant they had to deploy their resources towards building up their

41 According to Marx: 'The executive power with its enormous bureaucratic and military organization, with its ingenious state machinery, embracing wide strata, with a host of officials numbering half a million, besides an army of another half million, this appalling parasitic body, which enmeshes the body of French society like a net and chokes all its pores, sprang up in the days of the absolute monarchy, with the decay of the feudal system, which it helped to hasten. The seigniorial privileges of the landowners and towns became transformed into so many attributes of the state power, the feudal dignitaries into paid officials and the motley pattern of conflicting medieval plenary powers into the regulated plan of a state authority whose work is divided and centralized as in a factory. The first French Revolution, with its task of breaking all separate local, territorial, urban and provincial powers in order to create the civil unity of the nation, was bound to develop what the absolute monarchy had begun: centralization, but at the same time the extent, the attributes, and the agents of governmental power. Napoleon perfected this state machinery. The Legitimist monarchy and the July monarchy added nothing but a greater division of labour, growing in the same measure as the division of labour within bourgeois society created new groups of interests, and, therefore, new material for state administration. Every common interest was straightway severed from society, counterposed to it as a higher, general interest, snatched from the activity of society's members themselves, and made an object of government activity, from [a] bridge, a schoolhouse and the communal property of a village community to the railways, the national wealth and the national university of France. Finally, in its struggle against the revolution, the parliamentary republic found itself compelled to strengthen, along with the repressive measures, the resources and centralization of governmental power. All revolutions perfected this machine instead of smashing it. The parties that contended in turn for domination regarded the possession of this huge state edifice as the principal spoils of the victor.' Karl Marx, 'The eighteenth Brumaire of Louis Bonaparte' in *Selected Writings*, ed. David McLellan (Oxford: Oxford University Press, 1977), p. 316.

> *means of coercion* by investment in military men and equipment. Speaking broadly, they were obliged to invest in their politico-military apparatuses. To the extent they had to do this effectively enough to compete with other lords who were doing the same thing, they would have had to maximize both their military investments and the efficiency of these investments. They would have had, in fact, to attempt, continually and systematically, to improve their methods of war. Indeed, we can say the drive to *political accumulation*, to *state building*, is the *pre-capitalist* analogue to the capitalist drive to *accumulate capital.*[42]

But once the state's coercive capacity had been built-up to a certain level, then it is conceivable that it would have had the means to secure capitalist economic relations as the revolutionary outcome following on from feudalism, were capitalist relations more in its interests.

Moreover, there is corroboratory evidence that the State-Primacy Theory provides the correct explanation for the transition from feudalism to capitalism.[43] For example, as Samuel Huntington, commenting on European history, observes: 'The prevalence of war directly promoted political modernization. Competition forced the monarchs to build their military strength. The creation of military strength required national unity, the suppression of regional and religious dissidents, the expansion of armies and bureaucracies, and a major increase in state revenues.'[44] And in order to increase state revenues it was occasionally necessary to introduce a new mode of production – one which was more productive. As Huntington remarks: 'The centralization of power was necessary to smash the old order, break down the privileges and restraints of feudalism, and free the way for the rise of new social groups and the development of new economic activities. In some degree a coincidence of interest . . . exist[ed] between the absolute monarchs and the rising middle classes.'[45]

42 Robert Brenner, 'The social basis of economic development' in John Roemer (ed.), *Analytical Marxism* (Cambridge: Cambridge University Press, 1986), pp. 32–3.

43 Note that Marx acknowledges that the state, during the period of the absolute monarchy, 'helped to hasten' what he describes as 'the decay of the feudal system'. Marx, 'The eighteenth Brumaire of Louis Bonaparte', p. 316.

44 Samuel P. Huntington, *Political Order in Changing Societies* (New Haven: Yale University Press, 1968), p. 122. And as he adds: 'War is the great stimulus to state building. . . . The need for security and the desire for expansion prompted the monarchs to develop their military establishments, and the achievement of this goal required them to centralize and to rationalize their political machinery.' Ibid., p. 123.

45 Ibid., p. 126. For example, it has been claimed that various European monarchies backed the cities (where capitalist relations were developing) in order to subvert the power of feudal lords. In other words, they backed a change in the relations of production because it was in their interests to do so. Moreover, Michael Taylor argues that it was state actors who were responsible for selecting new relations of economic control in France from the fifteenth century and this was due to their need to obtain increased tax revenue because of 'geopolitical-military competition'. See Michael Taylor, 'Structure, culture and action in the explanation of social change', *Politics and Society*, Vol. 17, No. 2 (1989), pp. 124–6.

Backing a new mode of production would favour new classes, and a new dominant class would thus emerge whose interests were likely to correspond to the current interests of the state. This is because the selection and then preservation of new relations of production that offer a greater revenue to the state would also serve the interests of whichever class most benefits from the new economic relations. But acting in a manner which would benefit a new dominant economic class would not entail that the state was the mere instrument of a class which had up until then failed to achieve dominance, for it need only mean that at that time state interests and the interests of that class corresponded.[46] And they might not always do so, which is precisely why the state could not be relied upon always to protect the interests of the dominant economic class, and why the Marxist notion of a 'ruling class' may well be so misleading. Surely, classes do not rule; states do.

4.3.3 Towards post-capitalism

Even if the State-Primacy Theory had not been able to account for the transition from feudalism to capitalism, the possibility that the growth of the state through history might require the replacement of Marxist theory by the State-Primacy Theory is sufficient to cast in serious doubt the value of the Techno-Primacy Theory as a tool for analysing the transition from capitalism to post-capitalism. This is for the reason that, although the two theories can equally explain the transition from feudalism to capitalism, they imply very different predictions regarding the transition to post-capitalism.

What, then, is the significant difference between the two theories when they are employed to cast light on the transition from capitalism to post-capitalism? The Marxist theory, as was noted in Chapter 2, in claiming that superstructures are 'selected' according to their ability to stabilize the relations of production, implies that if egalitarian relations of production arise and, therefore, do not require coercive legal and political institutions to stabilize them, then the state will no

46 There is a lacuna in the argument in Section 2.3, above. There, I suggested that it should have come as no surprise when post-revolutionary Russia turned to a new techno-bureaucratic mode of production, given that the Bolshevik Party can be characterized as 'techno-bureaucratic' with respect to the production of a new society. But 'production' here means *political production*. The new mode of production appears to have contained techno-bureaucratic relations with respect to *economic production*. Now the hiatus can be filled. Lenin's mind-set, perhaps deriving from his techno-bureaucratic background, was such that he believed that the most appropriate way of organizing a party was managerially. Given that mind-set, he believed that the best way of organizing the economy was also managerially. Furthermore, given that Lenin sought managerial chains of command in the polity, and given that the economy had to be fitted into a state-planned order, then managerial lines of command within the economy better fitted Lenin's conception than independent factory committees. What needs stressing, therefore, is that the Bolshevik state can be seen to have chosen managerial relations because they made sense to it and appeared to be in its interests, rather than because it was the mere instrument of techno-bureaucratic managers. However, while this explanation would account for short-term change, the long-term stability of those relations would need to be explained in a Darwinian manner.

longer be required, and will wither away. But the withering away of the state cannot be presumed if one adopts, instead, the alternative State-Primacy Theory. And this difference between the two theories parallels Bakunin's dispute with Marx and Engels, which is characterized by Engels as follows:

> While the great mass of Social-Democratic workers hold our view that state power is nothing more than the organization with which the ruling classes – landlords and capitalists – have provided themselves in order to protect their social prerogatives, Bakunin maintains that . . . the capitalist has his capital only *by grace of the state*. And since the state is the chief evil, the state above all must be abolished; then capital will go to hell of itself. We, on the contrary, say: Abolish capital, the appropriation of all the means of production by the few, and the state will fall of itself. The difference is an essential one. . . .[47]

This certainly is an essential difference, for the State-Primacy Theory, in claiming that the state selects and enforces relations of production according to their suitability to serving the state's interests, implies that if egalitarian relations of production arise and do not offer an adequate surplus to the state, then the state will impose new relations of production more to its liking. This is in stark contrast to Engels' prediction that the state will wither away. In short, the crucial difference between the two theories consists in their respective predictions about the potential power and subsequent behaviour of the post-capitalist state. And as the Bolshevik state did not wither away but, instead, imposed 'one-man management'

47 Frederick Engels to Theodor Cuno, 24 January, 1872 in Karl Marx and Frederick Engels, *Collected Works*, Vol. 44 (Moscow: Progress, 1989), pp. 306–7. Bakunin puts the dispute this way: 'To support his programme for the conquest of political power, Marx has a very special theory, which is but the logical consequence of [his] whole system. He holds that the political condition of each country is always the product and the faithful expression of its economic situation; to change the former it is necessary only to transform the latter. Therein lies the whole secret of historical evolution according to Marx. He takes no account of other factors in history, such as the ever-present reaction of political, juridical, and religious institutions on the economic situation. He says: "Poverty produces political slavery, the State." But he does not allow this expression to be turned around, to say: "Political slavery, the State, reproduces in its turn, and maintains poverty as a condition for its own existence; so that to destroy poverty, it is necessary to destroy the State!" And strangely enough, Marx, who forbids his disciples to consider political slavery, the State, as a real cause of poverty, commands his disciples in the Social Democratic party to consider the conquest of political power as the absolutely necessary preliminary condition for economic emancipation.' Michael Bakunin, *Bakunin on Anarchy*, ed. Sam Dolgoff (London: George Allen and Unwin, 1973), pp. 281–2. Compare Bakunin's characterization of Marx's view with what Marx and Engels write in *The German Ideology*: 'The material life of individuals, which by no means depends merely on their "will", their mode of production and form of intercourse, which mutually determine each other – these are the real basis of the State, and remain so at all the stages at which division of labour and private property are still necessary, quite independently of the will of individuals. These actual relations are in no way created by the State power; on the contrary they are the power creating it'. Quoted in David McLellan, *Karl Marx: His Life and Thought* (St. Albans: Granada, 1973), p. 149.

on industries which had created their own proletarian factory committees, then, surely, of the two it is the State-Primacy Theory that is corroborated.

Moreover, how did Lenin justify the suppression of egalitarian economic relations and their replacement by inegalitarian ones? As we saw in Chapter 2, by citing the need to increase production in order to increase the state's military capacity. This choice by the state of inegalitarian economic relations in order to increase production for military purposes fits the State-Primacy Model exactly. And in so doing, ironically, the revolution in Russia, headed by a vanguard of 'Marxist' revolutionaries, contradicts the Marxist Techno-Primacy Theory, while corroborating the State-Primacy Theory.

4.4 Fettering and revolutionary change

Now, consideration of revolutionary transitions provokes a question which has given rise to some debate within analytical Marxism. Marx, in the '1859 Preface',[48] posits that revolutions from one mode of production to the next occur because the economic relations prevalent in a society have become constraints on technological development. In Marx's terminology, they have ceased being forms of development of the productive forces and have turned into '*fetters*' on that development. In the language of Cohen's interpretation of Marx – the Techno-Primacy Theory – epochal change occurs when the prevailing economic relations have become dysfunctional for the further development or optimal use of the productive forces. But the State-Primacy Theory also makes this claim. The difference between the two theories, as spelled out earlier, is that, according to the State-Primacy Theory, it is state interests which explain why it is that economic relations which have become incompatible with further technological development are replaced by certain others. So, on both the Techno-Primacy Theory and the State-Primacy Theory, change occurs from one mode of production to the next when the forces of production are fettered by the economic structure.

The question this provokes is: How, precisely, should this 'fettering' of the productive forces by the economic relations be construed? Cohen analyses three plausible construals of 'fettering': Development Fettering, Use Fettering and Net Fettering. He also discusses a stronger notion: that of 'Forfeiture'.[49] Let us examine each of these in turn.

48 See Karl Marx, 'Preface to the critique of political economy' in *Selected Writings*, ed. David McLellan (Oxford: Oxford University Press, 1977), p. 389.

49 See G. A. Cohen, 'Fettering' in *History, Labour and Freedom* (Oxford: Clarendon, 1988). Cohen observes an ambiguity in the term 'development' (see ibid., p. 115). For example, 'development' could refer exclusively to producing new knowledge and skills or it could also refer to expanding the use of current techniques. Consequently, on the second, wider construal, Development Fettering, Use Fettering and Net Fettering all fetter what could be subsumed under the term 'development'. However, the term 'Development Fettering' in what follows is confined to the first, narrower construal.

4.4.1 Development Fettering

The most obvious construal of 'the fettering of the productive forces by the economic relations' is Development Fettering, which consists in the relations of production inhibiting the development of new productive techniques, skills or knowledge. And Development Fettering would certainly appear to be what Marx had in mind in the '1859 Preface', which Cohen regards as the canonical text.

However, Cohen mentions two constraints that any adequate conception of fettering must meet. The first – *the predictability constraint* – asserts that 'it must be plausible to suppose that, under continued development of the productive forces, relations do, sooner or later, become fetters.'[50] The second – *the revolution constraint* – asserts that 'it must be plausible to suppose that when relations become fetters they are revolutionized.'[51] And following Richard Miller, Cohen notes that Development Fettering can take two forms: Absolute Stagnation and Relative Inferiority. When there is Absolute Stagnation, 'fettering relations prevent all further improvement in productivity', whereas when Relative Inferiority obtains, 'existing relations are not optimal for further development of the productive forces.'[52]

Unfortunately, neither variety of Development Fettering appears to meet both constraints. It is, at least, plausible that Absolute Stagnation would motivate a revolution to a social form capable of expanding productivity. But it is hard to imagine that capitalism could ever reach a stage where it prevented *any* further technological development. Hence, Absolute Stagnation might meet the revolution constraint but it seems to fail the predictability constraint. Relative Inferiority is the exact opposite. It is certainly plausible that, at some future time, a different social form could increase technological development at a greater rate than the present form is capable of (thus the predictability constraint is satisfied). But it is difficult to believe that such a consideration would lead to the mass of people embarking on a revolution. In other words, Relative Inferiority fails the revolution constraint:

> For the costs and dangers of revolution, both to those initiating it and to those who follow them, make it unreasonable to expect a society to undergo revolution just because relations which are better at developing the productive forces are possible, especially when those relations have not already been formed elsewhere and been seen to be better.[53]

We could add that in order to develop at a greater rate, more resources would

50 Ibid., pp. 109–10.

51 Ibid., p. 110.

52 Ibid., p. 109.

53 Ibid., p. 111. It seems even more unreasonable to expect this when the sub-optimal relations are still expanding the productive forces at an ever-increasing rate. As Cohen asks: 'Would workers overthrow a capitalism which has reduced the length of each computer generation to one year because socialism promises to make it in nine months?' Ibid.

need to be diverted away from consumption. Hence, the price of faster development is likely to be relatively lower consumption in the immediately foreseeable future, and who would revolt simply for that?

4.4.2 *Use Fettering*

If Development Fettering fails in both of its forms, what about Use Fettering? Use Fettering consists in the economic relations inhibiting the use of the productive forces, and on Cohen's view it also takes two forms: Absolute Use Fettering, which 'means a complete unemployment of all factors of production';[54] and Relative Use Fettering, which means that an alternative set of economic relations would better employ the factors of production. Absolute Use Fettering could meet the revolution constraint. With no production whatever, revolution might seem likely – unless, that is, everyone had starved to death! (Alternatively, and not unrealistically, the mass of the population might have become so weak through poverty that rebellion was beyond them.) But Absolute Use Fettering seems to fail the predictability constraint severely. It is surely inconceivable that any economic structure could prevent the employment of *all* factors of production.

Relative Use Fettering, on the other hand, might well meet the predictability constraint. That any class-divided society will, at some stage, be sub-optimal for the use of the productive forces is likely, given certain assumptions about economic relations being optimal for the development of the productive forces only within a specific range of their level of development. But if Relative Use Fettering manages to meet the predictability constraint, how well does it meet the revolution constraint? Cohen's view is that

> Relative Use Fettering meets the revolution constraint better than Relative Development Fettering does, since the discrepancy between capacity and use is more perceptible than, and is, therefore, a more potent stimulant of unrest, protest, and change than, the shortfall in the rate of development implied by Relative Development Fettering.[55]

This might work for a transition to post-capitalism, if it is clear that post-capitalism would use the productive forces better than capitalism does. If one believes, as Marx did, that the market system is inherently inefficient by producing periodic economic crises that throw people out of work, close down factories and thus lead to factors of production lying idle, then a post-capitalist system that was not subject to such crises would seem far preferable. (However, that the planned economy in the former Soviet Union was better able to use the productive forces than market economies is far from universally agreed!) But Marx's theory of history is a general theory. It is supposed to apply to

54 Ibid., p. 113.
55 Ibid., p. 114.

other epochal transitions, too. What about the transition from feudalism to capitalism?

Surprisingly, Cohen thinks that Relative Use Fettering is applicable here, as well. He writes:

> Early modern forms of division of labour in what Marx called 'manufacture' demanded the concentration in one place of large numbers of workers. Such concentration was variously forbidden and hampered by feudal and semi-feudal bonds and regulations, which tied producers to particular lords and masters in dispersed locations. Here, then, the relations of production fettered the use of the productive forces and, moreover, those relations came under pressure for that reason. Change occurred because of the gap between what *could* be achieved and what *was* being achieved, rather than because of the gap between how fast capacity was improving and how fast it could be improved: the second gap existed but it is hard to believe that it was comparably powerful as a precipitant of social change.[56]

However, recall that, for Cohen, two of the underlying motivational factors for epochal change are human rationality and a situation of scarcity. Certainly, it can be rational for individuals facing a situation of scarcity to seek economic relations that better use the productive forces. But only if *they* benefit from such use. It is far from clear that the workers benefited shortly after the rise of capitalism to a degree that would provide a rational motivation for revolution.

Consider what historians tell us about the enclosure movement: originally, at least, peasants didn't flood off the land to find preferable well-paid work in the factories; rather, they were driven off their land often into unemployment and starvation. That was not a rational use of the factors of production *for them*. They had enjoyed access to land and they were prevented from using it. For them, that factor of production – land – along with another – their labour – was prevented from being put to use. Others were forced to work in conditions that made feudalism look idyllic – conditions Engels so graphically describes.[57] Capitalism was hardly a mode of production that it was rational for those workers to fight for. Those who did appear to obtain better use from the land and from the factories were not the mass of people, but the landowners and the mill-owners.

Now, it might be argued that the workers didn't know that capitalism would be so bad for them in its early stages (and still is for workers in less developed countries). But what about countries that became capitalist later? Cohen suggests that 'new relations would . . . display their superiority, and consequently, through imitation, be generalized'.[58] But superior for whom? Not for those labouring in

56 Ibid., p. 113.

57 See Frederick Engels, *The Condition of the Working Class in England* (Harmondsworth: Penguin, 1987).

58 Cohen, 'Fettering', p. 111 n.

early capitalist factories. Consider what Marx thought about the introduction of capitalist relations into India:

> The British . . . destroyed [Hindu civilization] by breaking up the native communities, by uprooting the native industry, and by levelling all that was great in the native society. The historic pages of their rule in India report hardly anything beyond that destruction. The work of regeneration hardly transpires through a heap of ruins. Nevertheless it has begun.[59]

And as he famously remarks: 'Has the bourgeoisie . . . ever effected a progress without dragging individuals and peoples through blood and dirt, through misery and degradation?'[60] This is hardly a prospect for the future exploited workers to be the first to revolt for and even less to imitate. For *them* to engage in a revolution to bring about capitalism and, with it, such a use of the productive forces would be highly irrational.

Consequently, Relative Use Fettering seems implausible as an explanation of epochal transition, unless it is to be construed as referring to the motivation of those who will attain control of the productive forces and who thereby stand to gain by removing the fetters to using the productive forces imposed by the current economic relations. But if we say that it is those who will be in control of the productive forces after the revolution that are relevant, that would leave Marxists having to claim that it was the bourgeoisie who revolted prior to capitalism and the workers prior to state-communism. But it is doubtful that the workers ended up with any meaningful control in Russia. They seemed to be in control for a while – when they took over the factories and set up their own factory committees. But the Bolshevik state took control away from them when it imposed 'one-man management'. Hence, it can easily be argued, once the Bolshevik state attained sufficient power, it was there where control really lay. It was the Bolshevik state that came to be in *ultimate* control of the productive forces after the revolution, and certainly not the workers. This route would surely lead us to the State-Primacy Theory, not to the Techno-Primacy Theory.

4.4.2.1 ACRU Fettering

What if, instead, we were to say that it is those who *expect* to be in control of the productive forces after the revolution that are the relevant agents? The workers in pre-Revolutionary Russia might have expected to become the new dominant class. In which case, here we have a new variety of Relative Use Fettering – let us call it 'Anticipated Control and Relative Use Fettering' or 'ACRU Fettering', for short – where the productive forces are fettered when there is the possibility of an

59 Karl Marx, 'The future results of British rule in India' in *Selected Writings*, ed. David McLellan (Oxford: Oxford University Press, 1977), pp. 332–3.

60 Ibid., p. 335.

alternative set of economic relations that would better use the productive forces that the revolutionary class could expect to be in control of.

But this possible construal of 'fettering' would pose major problems for the Techno-Primacy Theory. For, while ACRU Fettering might well tell us when a revolution would occur, it would fail to predict the outcome. Just prior to the Russian Revolution, for example, it might have told us that if, at that time, the proletariat expected to gain control of better used productive forces after a revolution, then the time was ripe for one. What it would signally have failed to tell us is that the state would later deprive them of that economic control. Such a theory on its own – telling us only that the time for revolution was ripe – could do the Left far more harm than good. Furthermore, what about the revolution that brought in capitalism? The workers of later entrants into the capitalist mode of production would not expect to control the productive forces, so the relevant revolutionary class would have to be the bourgeoisie. But then, the rationality of the mass of the people would be irrelevant for explaining historical transitions.

This is far from being a minor point, for a key feature of Cohen's Techno-Primacy Theory is that it requires exogenous motivation. If it is the fettering of the development (widely construed) of the productive forces which explains revolution, if their development 'bursts asunder' the economic structure, then, in Cohen's view, it cannot be the prevailing economic relations which explain that rupturing development. For they could only take the development of the productive forces up to the point where rupture was possible. They could not explain the actual rupturing.

For the rupturing of the economic relations to be explained, it is necessary to identify factors that drive the development of the productive forces beyond their present constraints – constraints imposed by the prevailing economic relations. This is the role that human rationality and a situation of scarcity play for the Techno-Primacy Theory. They are two of the exogenous factors – the third being inventiveness – that add considerable plausibility to the Development Thesis (which, as we have noted, asserts that there is a tendency for the productive forces to develop through history). And it is rationality and a situation of scarcity, in particular, which are employed by Cohen to explain the motivation behind the further development of the productive forces such that new economic relations are required. However, if it is not the mass of the population that ACRU Fettering is relevant to, then their rationality and the scarcity they face fail as exogenous motivating factors. But if it is the bourgeoisie that are the relevant actors in the transition from feudalism to capitalism, then further development can simply be explained by the incipient capitalist relations. In which case, no exogenous factors are required, and the whole basis of Cohen's argument disappears. If rationality and a situation of scarcity are not what actually motivate technological development, if, instead, economic relations explain all such development, then the productive forces do not have explanatory primacy, and the Techno-Primacy Theory collapses.[61]

61 I return to the question of exogenous motivation in Chapter 6.

One would then be left placing key actors in the economy at the centre of one's explanation, rather than the development of the productive forces. But why is it only the rationality of members of an economic class that counts? What of the rationality of state actors? This is likely to be ignored by many Marxists because of their reductionist tendency to explain state behaviour in terms of the interests of the dominant economic class. But Lenin's behaviour surely cannot be reduced in this way. Yet in much of Marxist theory the interests of state actors are reduced to the interests of others.

But if we return once again to the transition to communism, who ended up in *direct* control? It can be argued that it was a rising managerial and technical class – the techno-bureaucracy – who ended up in *direct* control of the productive forces in post-revolutionary Russia.[62] But they were not the major actors who brought about that revolution. Surely, the workers and the Bolshevik Party were. Hence, it appears that those who attained direct control of the productive forces were neither those who expected to gain it nor those who engaged in revolutionary practice. In which case, focusing upon key actors in the economy does not seem to provide us with the explanation for epochal change that we are seeking.

4.4.3 Net Fettering

Use Fettering thus seems insufficient. However, Cohen does consider a third kind of fettering – Net Fettering – which he elucidates with the following example:

> Social form *A* is arguably superior to social form *B* if, although *A* uses the forces to degree .6 and *B* to degree .95, *A* develops them so much faster than *B* that comparison of their trajectories shows a net effect of greater used productive power in *A*. *A* might, indeed, need to underuse the forces in order to develop them as quickly as it does. . . .[63]

What is to be maximized, on this conception of economic superiority, is 'used productive power', and that is 'a multiple of level of development and degree of use'.[64] Net Fettering is what occurs, then, when some other set of economic relations at given future times would harness greater used productive power than the current economic relations would. And as Cohen argues: 'it would be irrational to prefer society *A* to society *B*, if *B* is use fettering relative to *A* but *A* is net fettering relative to *B*.'[65] But Net Fettering is vulnerable to the same criticism that was earlier levelled against Development Fettering in the form of Relative Inferiority: namely, development requires resources to be diverted away from consumption, and the mass of people are unlikely to run the risks of revolution simply for what *they* are likely to experience as a relatively worsened condition in

62 See Carter, *Marx: A Radical Critique*, Ch. 4.
63 Cohen, 'Fettering', p. 117.
64 Ibid.
65 Ibid., p. 118.

the immediately foreseeable future. Net Fettering thus seems to fail the revolution constraint, certainly with respect to explaining the transition to capitalism.

4.4.4 Forfeiture

There is, though, a fourth possible explanation for revolutionary motivation that Cohen entertains: John McMurtry's notion of 'Forfeiture'. 'Forfeiture' is not simply a constraint on development (however construed), but the actual loss of productive capability. It 'means that revolution occurs when, in its absence, the forces would not only not grow in power, but actually decline.'[66] Yet this would hardly provide for a general theory of revolution. Who, in feudalism, would have predicted the forfeiture of the level of development of the productive forces had that mode of production not been replaced by capitalism? Surely not the mass of the people.

Thus, it appears that neither Development Fettering, Use Fettering, Net Fettering nor Forfeiture is adequate for enabling Cohen to present a general explanation of epochal transitions. And even were it the case that his Techno-Primacy Theory could provide cogent explanations of all transitions by employing different varieties of fettering to explain different revolutions, it is difficult to see what resources there are in the theory for predicting which variety of fettering would be relevant when. Hence, it can be argued to fail as an adequate theory of history. In short, the most rigorous version of Marxist theory founders due to the apparent intractability of one of its central explanatory concepts.

4.4.5 Fettering and state-primacy

The Techno-Primacy Theory appears seriously and irredeemably flawed because all of the plausible variants of fettering (those that satisfy the predictability constraint) seem ultimately to fail the revolution constraint. But the State-Primacy Theory, in contrast to the Techno-Primacy Theory, assumes a very different mechanism to be operating behind a transition to new economic relations, and, as such, has very different implications. According to the State-Primacy Theory, a state which is engaged in military competition with other states will select economic relations which increase productivity because that is functional for that state, quite irrespective of who expected to benefit from or end up in control of the forces of production. Hence, the State-Primacy Theory does not need to claim that there is any correspondence between those who revolt and those who come to control the productive forces or to benefit from their development or more efficient use. In other words, the lack of any such correspondence (which renders the Techno-Primacy Theory implausible) does not affect the

66 Ibid., p. 121.

State-Primacy Theory. Consequently, neither Development Fettering, Use Fettering, Net Fettering nor Forfeiture seems to pose the slightest problem for the State-Primacy Theory, as I now attempt to show.

Consider the three forms of fettering. Consider, first, Development Fettering in the form of Relative Inferiority: If there is the prospect of military competition in the future, then it is rational for a state to replace current economic relations that are sub-optimal for the development of productivity with relations that aren't. Second, consider Use Fettering: If there is an immediate and severe military threat from another state, such as during wartime, then it is rational for the state to replace current economic relations that are sub-optimal for the use of the productive forces with relations that aren't (for example, by switching from a laissez-faire to a command economy).[67] Consider, finally, Net Fettering: If a state faces an immediate, but not too severe, military threat from another state, and if that situation is likely to continue far into the future, then it is rational to balance use and development, so that a surplus for military requirements is maximally available at any time in the future. Economic relations that do not allow that will be guilty of Net Fettering, and it is rational, in such a situation, for a state to replace them. Moreover, even this brief discussion shows that, from the standpoint of the State-Primacy Theory, it could easily be predicted when Development Fettering, Use Fettering or Net Fettering would precipitate change.

Forfeiture is even easier to deal with than the three variants of fettering: Relations of production that would lead to a lower level of productive power would damage the state's military competitiveness, and the state, if it is to survive, would have to replace them with relations that did not threaten productivity. In fact, *if it were perceived that workers' control would most likely result in greater consumption by, and less productivity from, the workers, the state might very well consider it to be a case of Forfeiture and, just as the Bolshevik state did, replace direct control by the workers with less egalitarian economic relations.*

Given how central the issue of fettering is for Marxist theory, given the problem it poses for that theory, and given the ease with which the State-Primacy Theory deals with it, then the State-Primacy Theory would appear to be far superior.

4.5 The implications for radical political strategy

We have good reason, then, to prefer the State-Primacy Theory to the Techno-Primacy Theory – good reason to think states select and stabilize relations of

67 Consider the role of women: Sometimes the state encourages economic relations that confine them to the home. During wartime, however, it very quickly re-locates them in munitions factories. When the war is over, it goes to some lengths to persuade them to return to the home. Consequently, the State-Primacy Theory could be employed to ground a certain kind of feminist critique.

economic control that are in *their* interests. And it is the deployment of the coercive forces that, it can be argued, enables state actors to select or stabilize the economic relations which serve their purposes.[68]

One implication of the State-Primacy Theory is that if the state chooses to stabilize capitalist economic relations[69] and thereby adopts the role of guarantor of bourgeois interests, it is not, as pluralists seem to think, because civil society as a whole has allocated to it such a role, nor, as Marxists often assume, because the bourgeoisie have so decided, but because it is in the interests of state actors to assume such a role. On this alternative theory, *such a role is self-chosen by the state*. In other words, those who enjoy a dominant position within the relations of economic control do so on the sufferance of state actors, for it is in the interests of the latter that the former retain economic control. And why might this be so? Because those who are allowed to retain economic control are well-suited to organizing the accumulation process that the state requires.

Such a consideration is likely to be paramount when the modern state finds itself, as it ordinarily does, located within an international system of competing states.[70] In order to compete militarily and secure or further its interests, the state needs to develop its coercive forces. But this is only possible if the productive forces are developed sufficiently to provide the surplus that the development of the coercive forces requires. Hence, it is in the interests of state actors to select or stabilize a structure of economic relations (and thereby support the class dominant within it), which is especially conducive to developing the productive forces. Thus, it can be argued, state actors will tend to stabilize relations of economic control[71] that benefit the bourgeoisie if, and so long as, those economic relations seem to be in the interests of the state. Although this has the appearance of the state being an instrument of a particular class, the state is, on this State-Primacy account, an autonomous entity. Of course, this is not to say that there aren't real economic constraints which the state has to take into account. Nevertheless, even granted these constraints, it is still the

68 As the overthrow by the Chilean military of Allende's government all too clearly shows, it is not always governments that are in control of 'their' political forces. I return to the subject of military coups in the next chapter.

69 It can be argued that such stabilization is accomplished by repressive state apparatuses (RSAs) and by ideological state apparatuses (ISAs), both of which 'function' by violence and by ideology, although the former are considerably more repressive. See Louis Althusser, 'Ideology and ideological state apparatuses' in *Lenin and Philosophy and Other Essays* (London: New Left Books, 1977), p. 138.

70 See Skocpol, *States and Social Revolutions*, pp. 30–2.

71 Of course, states are not always successful at stabilizing the prevailing order. For an illuminating account of when they are likely to be successful and when they are not, see J. Goodwin and T. Skocpol, 'Explaining revolutions in the contemporary Third World', *Politics and Society*, Vol. 12, No. 4 (1989): 489–509.

political instance rather than the economic that, on this theory, has explanatory primacy.[72]

Thus, from the standpoint of the State-Primacy Theory, it is this *appearance* of the state being an instrument of the dominant economic class that has so misled Marxists. Moreover, because they have assumed that the state is, by and large, a mere instrument of the dominant economic class, they have tended to regard the state as being relatively unimportant. Their attention has, therefore, focused heavily on the economy. And the result of this, it can be argued, is that the highly problematic nature of the state has been ignored, both theoretically and in revolutionary practice, with disastrous consequences both for radical theory and for radical politics. From the standpoint of the State-Primacy Theory, it is clear that it was the inadequate view of state power that Marxists promote which led to the sorry outcome of the Russian Revolution – an outcome which has so wounded and disabled the Left as a whole. Because post-revolutionary state power was viewed as unproblematic, no constraints were placed on the Bolshevik state. Thus, from the standpoint of the State-Primacy Theory, Stalinism was an inevitable outcome. It was not, on this view, just the product of Lenin's authoritarian practice. It was also the progeny of Marx's seriously deficient theoretical approach. And the tragic history of the Soviet Union has done far more to discredit the Left than anything else.[73]

72 The principal purpose of Marx's theory of history is the prediction of a certain kind of post-capitalist society. Thus, it is in this respect that the productive forces should be deemed to have explanatory primacy. However, the post-capitalist state imposed inegalitarian economic relations rather than withering away. Hence, in this regard, the productive forces do not, it would seem, have explanatory primacy. Instead, the state can be thought to have explanatory primacy to the extent that it selected economic relations that were perceived to be functional for it. It is for this reason that I refer to the generalized account advanced here as 'the State-Primacy Theory'. Moreover, while the State-Primacy Theory employs a purposive variety of functional explanation, just like the Techno-Primacy Theory it is not functionalist, either. As mentioned earlier, functionalism is a theoretical approach focusing primarily on the preservation of the existing order. Both the State-Primacy Theory and the Techno-Primacy Theory are, fundamentally, theories of ***historical transition***.

73 One response has been to embrace a post-modernist, theoretical nihilism. It is instructive that 'many of those now associated with poststructuralism and postmodernism were previously Marxists. . . . This background is important, because Marxism is arguably the most frequent, if not always the explicit, target of postmodernist critics of modernism. Warnings about the dangers of "totalizing" theory, and scepticism about the unfounded pretensions of the philosophy of history are most plausibly read as references to Marxism.' David West, *An Introduction to Continental Philosophy* (Cambridge: Polity, 1996), p. 193. Some might feel inclined to argue that because one's particular theory has degenerated into gibberish is no reason for renouncing theory and embracing gibberish, or, slightly less uncharitably, that the mere fact that one's Marxist 'grand narrative' has turned out to be a fairy tale is no reason for announcing the end of all grand narratives – at least not without first considering what resources can be found in anarchist theory, especially when it was the apparent success of the now abandoned Marxist theory which played such a role in the eclipsing of anarchism. If Marxism has indeed turned out to be a cul-de-sac, then perhaps we should retrace our steps to the point where we veered into a dead-end, rather than abandon the journey completely.

It is vitally important, therefore, that the state be given the attention it deserves. And there is good reason to think that Marxist theory has paid it insufficient attention. This is why the State-Primacy Theory might well be of such consequence, for it returns our attention to the potentially problematic nature of the state. Nevertheless, a complete account of revolutionary transformations would require an explanation of why the mass of people occasionally revolt. I am inclined to argue that *Anticipated Control and Relative Use (ACRU) Fettering could be employed to explain what precipitated the changes in Russia in 1917, while the State-Primacy Theory should be employed to explain the nature of the final outcome.*

Now, one implication of accepting the State-Primacy Theory in preference to Marxist theory is of the greatest importance. It is that any claim about a 'transitional' revolutionary state withering away must be rejected. State personnel, according to the alternative theory, back inegalitarian relations of production because it is in their interests to do so. If the workers were in control of production themselves, then they would most likely increase their consumption, or work less, rather than increase the surplus available to the state. Hence, that the state would ever back genuinely libertarian and egalitarian economic relations is far too improbable an assumption for any effective political strategy to be based upon it. What the state might well do, as the State-Primacy Theory implies, is choose new relations of production – for example, techno-bureaucratic ones – which offer the possibility of an even greater surplus to the state than is offered by capitalist relations. What the state would be very unlikely to do is choose egalitarian relations that significantly reduced the surplus available to it. Thus, neither a vanguard seizing state power (and becoming new state personnel) nor setting up a new so-called 'transitional state' could be relied upon to lead to an egalitarian society. And it is precisely this issue of the so-called 'transitional state' which has traditionally distinguished anarchist and Marxist political theory and their respective political practices.

This leaves us with a problem: Given the alternative theory, how is the mass of the population to gain meaningful control of production and of society as a whole? One thing is clear. A necessary (though not necessarily a sufficient) condition for human emancipation and equality would have to be the abolition of the state by the citizens themselves. It is the only plausible means by which the process, identified by the State-Primacy Theory, which perpetuates inegalitarian relationships could be terminated. Marxists, by considering the use of state power as an acceptable means towards equality and freedom, advocate a course of action which, from the standpoint of the State-Primacy Theory, would perpetuate the extensive inequalities they ostensibly oppose.[74] And they are led to advocate such

74 As Bakunin so prophetically writes: 'Now it is clear why the dictatorial revolutionists, who aim to overthrow the existing powers and social structures in order to erect upon their ruins their own dictatorship, never are or will be the enemies of government, but, on the contrary, always will be the most ardent promoters of the government idea. They are the enemies only

a course because their theory denies the fundamental importance of the state and state power – the result being the promotion of a strategy which, it can thus be argued, inadvertently perpetuates unfreedom and inequality.

So, an anarchist theory of historical transition can be developed which is at least as effective as Marxist theory in explaining technological, economic and political developments, but which has the added advantage, by drawing attention to the tremendous power which the state can exert, of predicting accurately the outcome of vanguardist revolutions. This is in stark contrast with Marxist theory, which, through underemphasizing the power of the state because of an arguably unbalanced stress on the economic, has created such a potentially dangerous pitfall for the Left. By stressing the technological and the economic, Marxists have distracted attention from the state. This, it can be argued, proved disastrous in the Russian Revolution, the Chinese Revolution, numerous revolutions in the Third World, and will do so time and time again if Marx's theory of history is not decisively rejected by the Left. As I remarked at the beginning of this chapter, the deceptively simple procedure of reversing the direction of explanation in Cohen's model allows the formulation of an alternative theory of history – one which has profound implications for political strategy. For its acceptance, to put it bluntly, would require nothing less than the total rejection of Marxism as a theory of history and as a form of revolutionary practice.[75]

4.5.1 The scope of the State-Primacy Theory

But the State-Primacy Theory will, inevitably, fall prey to some misunderstandings. So, in concluding this chapter, allow me to deal with one major misconception that the argument so far might have given rise to – a misconception about the scope of the theory's reliability. Let me attempt to clarify the limits of what the State-Primacy Theory actually asserts. This is, perhaps, best done by contrasting it, once again, with Marx's theory of history.

---

of contemporary governments, because they wish to replace them. They are the enemies of the present governmental structure, because it excludes the possibility of their dictatorship. At the same time they are the most devoted friends of governmental power. For if the revolution destroyed this power by actually freeing the masses, it would deprive this pseudo-revolutionary minority of any hope to harness the masses in order to make them the beneficiaries of their own government policy.' Bakunin, *Bakunin on Anarchy*, p. 329.

75 The alternative model is the opposite of the Marxist model. Consequently, if the alternative model is taken to underpin anarchist political theory, then current talk of a synthesis between anarchist and Marxist theory reveals a profound failure to understand precisely what it is that, from an anarchist standpoint, is problematic about Marxist political theory. Or, perhaps, such a synthesis is supposed to involve the acceptance of Marx's economic theory? But the fact that Bakunin accepted it is no reason why anarchist theory as a whole needs do so. Even Cohen, who has provided such an impressive defence of Marx's theory of history, considers it best to ditch Marx's labour theory of value. See G. A. Cohen, 'The Labour Theory of Value and the Concept of Exploitation' in Ian Steedman *et al.*, *The Value Controversy* (London: Verso, 1981).

There are many who think that if Marx is right, he must be able to explain everything in terms of class struggle or the development of technology. But for Marx to be a significant political theorist he need do no such thing. The essential features of Marx's theory of history, as summarized in the '1859 Preface', can be abstracted from his understanding of the French Revolution of 1789 – the 'lighthouse of all revolutionary epochs'.[76] Marx believed that the prospects for technological development were fettered in feudalism. A rising class, the bourgeoisie, would be able to develop production further, but only if it overthrew the feudal system and replaced it with a capitalist one. Marx understood the French Revolution to be one where a rising bourgeoisie, whose ascendancy was intimately related to the development of the society's productive capacity, seized political power so that it could transform the economic relations to one's in its interests. Moreover, those interests corresponded at the time to what was appropriate for further technological development. The feudal system was, therefore, transformed because it fettered technological development.

What Marx appears to have done was abstract from this portrait of the French Revolution a general theory of historical transition. As we have seen, Cohen presents it as follows: productive development explains the selection of economic relations which further that development, and those economic relations, in turn, explain the selection of the legal and political institutions which stabilize those relations. This, if Cohen has correctly expounded it, is Marx's major claim. And it is all that Marx has to defend in order to be a significant political theorist. Marx does not, in actual fact, have to explain any of the numerous events that happen in society within an epoch. Marx has given us a theory of *epochal* transition. All that he really has to defend is the claim that technological or economic interests are key in determining the basic structure of society as it moves from one epoch to the next. In other words, when it comes to a period of revolution, the next dominant class will have arisen as a result of economic development and it, or the mass of the population, will select economic relations in the new epoch that are conducive to further economic development. This fits in with Engels' later characterization of his and Marx's position as economic determination 'in the last instance'.

However, even though that is all Marx need defend, this on its own suggests that economic factors are powerful ones. Hence, this provides us with a heuristic. If one wants to understand what is going on in society, then it would be appropriate, given the importance that economic factors supposedly have in epochal transitions, to begin by ascertaining what economic interests are involved. But if economic interests do not explain the particular intra-epochal social fact under consideration, then the theory of epochal transition remains unaffected.

Now, there are clear parallels between these aspects of Marx's theory and the State-Primacy Theory. The latter was initially abstracted from a certain portrait of

76 Marx, quoted in Alan Gilbert, *Marx's Politics: Communists and Citizens* (Oxford: Martin Robertson, 1981), p. 30.

the Russian Revolution of 1917. In that revolution, the Bolshevik state chose to replace with 'one-man management' the egalitarian economic relations that had arisen in the course of the revolution. As egalitarian economic relations seem to have been supplanted because they did not correspond with state interests, and as 'one-man management' seems to have prevailed because it was in the interests of the state, this suggests that it is state interests which are key in determining the basic economic structure of society as it moves from one epoch to the next. The State-Primacy Theory, therefore, could be regarded as a general theory abstracted from key features of the Russian Revolution. And the really key feature appears to be that, when it came to the crunch, state interests shaped the economic structure of the coming epoch. In which case, the State-Primacy Theory could be characterized as 'political determination in the last instance'.

The State-Primacy Theory, then, makes a far smaller claim than one might think. It doesn't claim that all events have to be explained by means of state interests. For example, during the Russian Revolution there was a period in which the state had virtually collapsed. During that time, historians tell us, all sorts of remarkable things happened. The workers took control of certain industries and ran them by means of their own factory committees. They formed soviets so that they could control the local polity themselves. A guerrilla army was organized to fight successfully the invading white troops in the Ukraine. It would be ludicrous to claim that everything which occurred at that time was in accord with state interests.

But the State-Primacy Theory is committed to no such claim. First of all, the State-Primacy Thesis – that the nature of a set of production relations which prevail in a society is (ultimately) explained by state interests – refers to epochal, not intra-epochal, changes. Second, it only holds when there is a state to have interests. Third, the State-Primacy Thesis is also conditional upon the state having sufficient compliance by enough of those whose compliance is significant.[77] When the Bolshevik state was constituted and acquired enough power to advance its

77 In the past, large numbers of people with a comparatively low level of technical skill – soldiers – seem to have been required when the general population did not wish to comply with the state. The compliance of numerous soldiers, who then appeared especially significant, would have been necessary for the State-Primacy Thesis to hold. However, for the state to demonstrate its power, there has been a tendency through history for fewer significant people to be required, but for them to be more technically skilled. This is because of the development of the instruments of social control and coercion: from television cameras and other forms of electronic surveillance to nuclear weapons fired by the turn of a key. Operatives of sophisticated surveillance equipment might be viewed as especially significant when there is a crisis of legitimacy among the population at large. If the State-Primacy Thesis usually holds, however, it might be because of a wide compliance among the population, which thereby empowers the state. But in which case, when the state lacks compliance, the State-Primacy Thesis would not hold. The important issue is, surely, not whether the State-Primacy Thesis is true or not. Rather, the important issue is how to ensure that it doesn't hold in the future. Unfortunately, when even revolutionaries argue for a post-revolutionary state, then future compliance with the state is less likely to dissolve, and it is more likely that the State-Primacy Thesis *will* hold.

interests, then it appears to have shaped the Russian economic structure in conformity with those interests. And this seems to explain the economic relations within the Soviet bloc during the epoch following the 1917 Revolution.

But doesn't talk of the Bolshevik state being *constituted* raise a central problem for the State-Primacy Theory? If a new state arises after a revolution, in what sense has *the state* chosen new relations of production? Isn't a new state now being referred to? In reply, first of all, in most transitions from a pre- to a post-revolutionary state there is likely to be a considerable continuity in state personnel. For example, Lenin had to employ within the state structure a large number of those who had previously occupied positions in the Tsarist state, partly because they formed a minority in knowing how to read and write and how to fill in bureaucratic forms. But second, even if there were to be a complete discontinuity between pre- and post-revolutionary states, and even if a new state were to be created completely from scratch, those who came to occupy positions within the new state structure would, because of their new roles within a set of interrelationships involving differential distributions of power, acquire new interests.[78] In particular, they would acquire a new interest in the preservation of the state. Hence, they would acquire a new interest in the economic preconditions of the state's survival. In which case, the new state could be expected to act according to the State-Primacy Model. All of this follows from adopting an interrelationist perspective which focuses upon an agent's rational pursuit of his or her interests as they arise from his or her location within a structure of power relations. And the interests that arise for those who come to occupy positions within a post-revolutionary state are rationally pursued by stabilizing whichever economic relations are best suited to meeting the state's needs – namely, those which, in such a situation, would characterize a new mode of production and thus a new epoch.

However, although the State-Primacy Theory only need explain epochally significant structural transformations, because the state seems to be *so important* in this regard – important enough to determine revolutionary outcomes – then its interests may explain other social facts, as well. Hence, just as with Marx's theory of history, the State-Primacy Theory can be applied heuristically: if one wants to understand a social occurrence, then don't forget state interests. In fact, looking at the interests of the state would be an appropriate place to start, given how significant state interests seem to with respect to transitions from one epoch to another. (At least, that is what the experience of the Bolshevik state seems to show.) But if a social fact within an epoch is not illuminated by the State-Primacy

78 C.f.: 'men who were democrats and rebels of the reddest variety when they were a part of the mass of governed people, became exceedingly moderate when they rose to power. Usually these backslidings are attributed to treason. That, however, is an erroneous idea; they have for their main cause the change of position and perspective.' Michael Bakunin, *The Political Philosophy of Bakunin: Scientific Anarchism*, ed. G. P. Maximoff (New York: The Free Press, 1964), p. 218.

Theory, then that is not fatal for the theory, because it is fundamentally concerned with epochal transitions.[79]

It should be clear, then, that when the State-Primary Theory is limited to epochal change, it makes a very small claim. It only says that, in the last instance, the economic structure of the coming society will coincide with state interests. This is a *very* small claim. But it is also a very big one. It is small in content but huge in significance. It doesn't say very much, but the implications are immense. To show this, all that is needed is the additional claim that what is ultimately in the interests of the state will not ultimately be in the interests of the mass of the world's population. And substantiating that claim will be the burden of the following chapters. Should such a claim prove to be established successfully, and were the State-Primacy Theory accepted and pursued to its logical conclusion, then an identification with the interests of the mass of the world's population would lead to anarchism. It would lead to the advocacy of anarchist societies and anarchist political practice to attain them. In other words, although the State-Primacy Theory says very little, its implications include (if one sides with the mass of the world's population rather than with those who oppress them, that is) the rejection of all authoritarian, reformist and Marxist political theory and practice. Quite simply, if the interests of the mass of the world's population lie in an ecologically secure planet, and if, as I shall proceed to argue, immediate state interests compromise that, then the solution cannot be eco-authoritarianism, eco-reformism or eco-Marxism, but, rather, eco-anarchism.

In Chapter 6, I show how the State-Primacy Theory can provide the core of a radical green political theory. First, however, an area where the State-Primacy Theory might be thought to be signally unconvincing needs to be examined – namely, that concerning the relationship between states in less developed countries and transnational capital. And this is an issue of immense importance to greens, for many of today's environmental problems appear most visible in the poorer countries, and currently seem to have the most devastating impact upon their peoples.

79 These features of the State-Primacy Theory might help to deter its too hasty rejection by mistakenly thinking that it has to explain a lot more than it plausibly does explain. Moreover, the State-Primacy Theory is more robust than might at first be thought, even when it is taken as more than a heuristic with respect to the explanation of intra-epochal social facts, because ascertaining whether or not state interests are being satisfied is not always as straightforward as it might seem. There are, no doubt, occasions when the state fails to do something that would, at first glance, appear to be in its interests. But anything the state chooses to do will have opportunity costs. Doing one thing might mean that something more important could not be done, and the balance of state interests might therefore rule it out.

5 Development or underdevelopment

Few informed people today doubt that a great deal of the environmental damage seemingly being perpetrated around the globe is directly caused by the activities of transnational corporations (TNCs). These tremendously powerful institutions often have turnovers exceeding the gross national products of many Third World countries. Consequently, states in less developed countries (LDCs) seem powerless to prevent these giant corporations from plundering their resources and polluting their lands. Isn't this an obvious case where the State-Primacy Theory is clearly wrong? Isn't it transparent that Third World states are the mere puppets of TNCs? And doesn't this mean that it is transnationals within the global economy that determine what states do, rather than state interests explaining the nature of Third World economies?

But is it really all that clear-cut? Global inequality is, certainly, of fundamental importance. Not only does its degree appear to many as pernicious in itself but it also seems to exacerbate what environmentalists would regard as the currently disastrous human impact on the environment. While those in the rich countries squander resources, many in the poorer regions of the world seem to have no alternative but to degrade their environment even further merely in order to survive. And it can be argued that, by repatriating profits, TNCs add to the excessive affluence of the rich nations, while increasing poverty in the Third World. This ought to be of paramount importance for environmentalists and Third World development theorists alike if, as Michael Redclift observes, '[h]uman poverty makes physical environments poorer, just as poor physical environments make for greater human poverty.'[1] But are we really sure of the

1 Michael Redclift, *Development and the Environmental Crisis: Red or Green Alternatives?* (London: Methuen, 1984), p. 79. As he adds: 'For too long social scientists have ignored the environment in the construction of development theory, while those interested in environmentalism have scarcely addressed the theoretical problems which their commitment raises.' Ibid., p. 6. And as the World Commission on Environment and Development note: 'Poverty is a major cause and effect of environmental problems. It is therefore futile to attempt to deal with environmental problems without a broader perspective that encompasses the factors underlying world poverty and international inequality.' G. H. Brundtland *et al.*, *Our Common Future* (Oxford: Oxford University Press, 1987), p. 3.

actual dynamic that lies behind all this? In short, what theoretical perspective will best clarify Third World political and economic developments?

The most influential work from a 'bourgeois' perspective has undoubtedly been *Political Order in Changing Societies* by Samuel Huntington. Huntington's approach is, perhaps, best seen as falling within the tradition of elite theory. However, in opposition to 'bourgeois' approaches there arose a 'neo-Marxist' critique emphasizing either 'the development of underdevelopment' or dependency in the poorer countries. This became the orthodoxy of the Left in the 1970s and is, perhaps, best viewed as falling within the tradition of class theory, as its primary focus is on exploitation. Both views have since come to be regarded as inadequate.[2] Unfortunately, at present there is no widely-held, alternative theoretical perspective that seems capable of providing a satisfactory account of political developments in the Third World.[3]

In this chapter I begin by arguing that while much of what Huntington claims is correct, much of it is inadequate. In a similar vein, I then argue that while much of what the underdevelopment theorists claim is correct, much of it, too, is inadequate. Most importantly, I argue that, by omitting the inadequate claims of both positions, while accommodating their positive features within a general theory of revolutionary change, the State-Primacy Theory, in effect, sublates them both. And the reason why such a sublation has not been widely developed is, possibly, because the vitriolic opposition between supporters of elite theory and class theory has obstructed any meaningful synthesis of these seemingly antithetical standpoints.

2 As James Manor notes, 'political development' and 'dependency', which are 'the two paradigms or schools of thought that have dominated the study of Third World politics over the last quarter-century[,] have encountered serious difficulties'. James Manor, 'Politics and the neo-liberals' in Christopher Colclough and James Manor (eds), *States or Markets? Neo-liberalism and the Development Policy Debate* (Oxford: Clarendon, 1991), p. 306.

3 However, '[s]ome economists looked to the neo-liberal paradigm for the study of economic systems, which gained influence just as the "political development" and "dependency" schools were encountering difficulties. . . . But analysts of Third World politics have shown scarcely a flicker of interest in this body of ideas. This is partly because the neo-liberal economists, like the earlier and more optimistic generation of development economists against whom they are reacting, lack a theory of the state.' James Manor, 'Introduction' in James Manor (ed.), *Rethinking Third World Politics* (London: Longman, 1991), pp. 9–10 n. And as Manor also remarks: 'State structures, political institutions, or even ruling cliques often possess considerable complexity and material substance, which means that they generate their own imperatives and possess their own internal logic.' Manor, 'Politics and the neo-liberals', p. 311. But '[t]he neo-liberal paradigm has little to say on these matters. It is hardly surprising, then, that political scientists find it wanting.' Ibid. In fact, it can be argued that, from an interrelationist perspective, the nature of the relationships which constitute state structures will determine the interests of state actors – for example, within the Third World state, such complex relationships can be seen to explain the need to satisfy certain clients if state actors in the Third World are to remain in power.

5.1 Thesis: an elite theory approach

In the previous chapter, Huntington was cited as providing evidence in support of the State-Primacy Theory and against G. A. Cohen's Techno-Primacy Theory. Perhaps, then, Huntington's theory of societal change as it stands is an adequate alternative to Marxist theory? With this possibility in mind, let me commence with Huntington's political realism, which was a response to the seemingly unwarranted optimism of modernization theory.

It had been assumed by modernization theorists that societies contained traditional and modern sectors – the 'dualist hypothesis' – and that they were moving from being predominantly 'traditional' to being predominantly 'modern'. Although the goal was, apparently, to bring about liberal democracies in the developing world, it had been recognized that this process of 'modernization' could, at times, be facilitated by an authoritarian elite that might decide to retain power.[4] Nevertheless, among modernization theorists it was widely assumed that there did exist a general process of transition towards pluralist, democratic polities built upon developed, capitalist economic relations. In other words, the assumption was that economic modernization would bring in its train political modernization and the stability characteristic of the advanced western democracies.

5.1.1 The problem of modernization

In the 1960s this optimism was shattered by the growth of authoritarian regimes and revolutionary struggles in the Third World. Huntington's response was to point out the destabilizing effects of transition and to indicate the contrasting stability of both undeveloped and developed societies. Whereas both traditional and modern societies were stable, transitional societies were, in his view, highly unstable. Huntington's principal thesis is that major violence and instability is 'in large part the product of rapid social change and the rapid mobilization of new groups into politics coupled with the low development of political institutions.'[5] As he amplifies:

> Social and economic change – urbanization, increases in literacy and education, industrialization, mass media expansion – extend political consciousness, multiply political demands, broaden political participation. These changes undermine traditional sources of political authority and traditional political institutions; they enormously complicate the problems of creating new bases of political association and new political institutions combining legitimacy and effectiveness. The rates of social mobilization and the expansion of

4 See, for example, Gabriel Almond, 'Introduction: a functional approach to comparative politics' in Gabriel Almond and James Coleman (eds), *The Politics of the Developing Areas* (New Jersey: Princeton University Press, 1960), p. 53.

5 Samuel P. Huntington, *Political Order in Changing Societies* (New Haven: Yale University Press, 1968), p. 4.

> political participation are high; the rates of political organization are low. The result is political instability and disorder. The primary problem of politics is the lag in the development of political institutions behind social and economic change.[6]

The failure of modernization theory can thus be attributed to a disjunction between economic and political development, for although economic 'modernization' involves the breakdown of the traditional polity, it does not always result in a modern political order. So, Huntington concludes, 'modernity breeds stability, but modernization breeds instability.'[7]

Huntington therefore accepts a version of the dualist hypothesis, but adds that a transition from a pre-modern to a modern society is likely to result in violence and disorder. And this leads him to some rather drastic conclusions. For example:

> Reform, it can be pointed out, may contribute not to political stability but to greater instability and indeed to revolution itself. Reform can be the catalyst of revolution rather than a substitute for it. Historically, it has often been pointed out, great revolutions have followed periods of reform, not periods of stagnation and repression.[8]

One implication that some might draw from this is that it is better to put up with a reactionary, authoritarian regime than to risk any reform that could prove to be destabilizing.[9]

However, Huntington does not, in fact, simply reject all revolutions. For, in his view, they are sometimes necessary in order to bring about a stable polity:

> The successful revolution combines rapid political mobilization and rapid political institutionalization. Not all revolutions produce a new political order. The measure of how revolutionary a revolution is is the rapidity and the scope of the expansion of political participation. The measure of how successful a revolution is is the authority and stability of the institutions to which it gives birth.[10]

Nevertheless, although there are successful revolutions on occasion, failed attempts at producing a stable modern society are common.

6 Ibid., p. 5.
7 Ibid., p. 41.
8 Ibid., p. 363.
9 Interestingly, Colin Leys, commenting on Huntington, deplores the fact that '[t]hroughout his work there runs a strong current of dislike for the confusing, disturbing, and contradictory aspirations of the masses, and an admiration for any "elite", bureaucracy, or "leadership" capable of containing, channelling, and if necessary suppressing them.' Colin Leys, 'Samuel Huntington and the end of classical modernization theory' in H. Alavi and T. Shanin (eds), *Introduction to the Sociology of 'Developing Societies'* (London: Macmillan, 1982), p. 335.
10 Huntington, *Political Order in Changing Societies*, p. 266.

One such failure is what Huntington refers to as a 'praetorian' society, where different social groups become politicized in the face of a paucity of effective political institutions capable of mediating between them or moderating their behaviour. The result is a society characterized by 'naked' confrontation; and various direct methods are then employed to influence political outcomes:

> Each group employs means which reflect its peculiar nature and capabilities. The wealthy bribe; students riot; workers strike; mobs demonstrate; and the military coup [*sic*]. In the absence of accepted procedures, all these forms of direct action are found on the political scene. The techniques of military intervention are simply more dramatic and effective than the others because, as Hobbes put it, 'When nothing else is turned up, clubs are trumps.'[11]

Hence, in Huntington's view, when there is no consensus, and when social groups do not accept constraints on their action, governments will ultimately have to resort to force, with the army emerging as the most successful group in society because it controls the means of coercion. And this problem is considered to arise because, as a result of economic modernization, new social groups emerge with rising expectations and come to demand political participation. But they cannot be incorporated into the polity because of its undeveloped political institutions. And given that the prevailing elite will wish to restrict any such participation, praetorian societies are especially violent, conflictual and authoritarian. Nevertheless, although Huntington identifies praetorian societies as a pitfall on the road to development, his goal is clearly the attainment of modern liberal democracies.

5.1.2 The priority of order

One possible problem with Huntington's approach is that, while he regards political modernization as involving 'the rationalization of authority, the differentiation of structures, and the expansion of political participation',[12] he assumes that it is necessary to bring them about in the order in which he lists them:

> The primary problem is not liberty but the creation of a legitimate public order. Men may, of course, have order without liberty, but they cannot have liberty without order. Authority has to exist before it can be limited, and it is authority that is in scarce supply in those modernizing countries where government is at the mercy of alienated intellectuals, rambunctious colonels, and rioting students.[13]

11 Ibid., p. 196.

12 Ibid., p. 93.

13 Ibid., pp. 7–8. It would appear that the value Huntington places on authority visibly strays into authoritarianism when he writes: 'Societies, such as Sparta, Rome, and Britain, which have been admired by their contemporaries for the authority and justice of their laws, have also been admired for the coherence and discipline of their armies. Discipline and development go hand in hand.' Ibid., pp. 23–4.

But, it can be objected, even if political authority were a priority, that is not to say that it must come chronologically prior. It would be a non sequitur to argue *a priori* that, as one cannot have limited authority without having authority, then one must first of all establish an authority and then limit it. This is obviously fallacious, for it is logically possible to construct a polity with limited authority right from its inception. Hence, it would simply be confused to claim *a priori* that authority *must* be established chronologically prior to its being constrained.

Huntington nevertheless presumes that the powerful state must come not just first in importance but first in temporal order. In his view, power must first be concentrated so as to transform the traditional society. Then the system must evolve in order to assimilate those demanding participation. Finally, political checks and a wider dispersion of power will be demanded, and (hopefully) provided.[14] However, a potential problem with this strategy is that if power were to be centralized and concentrated first, without prior regard to the instituting of any checks and balances, then those exerting that power might easily discover that they possess the ability to retain control, and they might become exceedingly authoritarian in order to ensure that they retain it.

Yet Huntington is well aware of the problems of military intervention. In fact, he goes so far as to produce his own typography of various kinds of military coup: A '*breakthrough coup*' is deemed to occur when a group of army officers – usually young, educated, westernized officers – seize power in order to rid society of a traditional monarch who is holding up modernization. Such officers are perceived to identify with the newly emerging middle classes arising as a result of capitalist development. Should the military choose to institute a civilian, middle-class government, what Huntington calls a '*guardian coup*' may well occur at some time in the future if the government were to find itself in crisis and be viewed as incompetent or corrupt. After a short while, perhaps, the military might allow new elections and a return to a civilian government. But a '*veto coup*' may well occur later should a new social force, perhaps the workers or the peasants, seek political power and elect an administration sympathetic to them. The new administration might thus be deposed by the military, which, Huntington assumes, would seek to protect the middle class interests it ostensibly identifies with. Clearly, at this point, the military would be preventing an increase in political participation and would have become overtly reactionary in Huntington's own terms.[15]

However, Huntington also argues that the expansion of democracy in the Third World will lead rural groups to elect into power those who back agrarian

14 See ibid., pp. 145–6.

15 As he writes: 'the more backward a society is, the more progressive the role of its military; the more advanced a society becomes, the more conservative and reactionary becomes the role of the military.' Ibid., p. 221.

rather than industrial development.[16] As this would not seem to be in the interests of a modernizing military, we should expect it, given Huntington's analysis, to engage in a veto coup in order to preserve the system it prefers. Interestingly, all of this is consistent with the short-term variant of the State-Primacy Thesis (formulated in the previous chapter), which implies that state personnel select economic relations that are perceived to promote their interests. For it would be surprising if military officers valuing a 'modern' economy were to allow rural groups to impede industrial development, especially when such development is required for the military to 'modernize' its equipment. More interestingly still, numerous veto coups are just what Huntington's own theory would lead one to expect.

Thus, on the basis of his own argument, Huntington's whole strategy of first centralizing power before expanding participation seems of necessity to lead to military regimes seizing control. And this means that his approach to modernization appears to have extremely reactionary implications, even in his own terms. Rather than offer us some prospect of liberal democracy, it seems to lead us only in the direction of dictatorship. It is not surprising, therefore, that many of those who had hoped for Third World polities to take the form of western liberal democracies should have come to feel so despondent in the 1970s. What is more, the whole 'bourgeois' approach can be regarded as seriously flawed not only in its prescription for how to create a liberal order but also for its failure to theorize growing global inequality and for its complete disregard for the environmental costs of 'modernization'. For as Redclift insists: 'The costs of development are expressed not only in terms of class conflict and economic exploitation, but also in the reduction of the natural resource base on which the poor depend for their livelihoods.'[17]

5.2 Antithesis: a class theory approach

So, if the most influential 'bourgeois' approach is flawed, let me turn to a major critique of 'bourgeois' approaches – namely, underdevelopment theory, which emerged in the late 1960s. Underdevelopment theory could be regarded as superior to Huntington's approach in so far as it adopts a more global perspective. It takes far greater cognizance of international linkages, and stresses the systemic inequality in the global economy, focusing on the sustained exploitation of the

16 See ibid., p. 245. And as he adds: 'The upshot of democracy is to disperse power among a plurality of more traditional elites. By increasing the power of rural groups democracy also tends to promote policies aimed at rural and agrarian rather than urban and industrial development.' Ibid. In which case, it is difficult to see why a modernizing military would be committed to democracy.

17 Redclift, *Development and the Environmental Crisis*, p. 18. And even if one were to be rather generous in one's assessment of the motives behind political modernization, the fact still remains that 'unless the environmental crisis is averted, no other important social goals will be achieved.' Ibid., p. 56.

less developed areas by the more developed. If capitalism consists of a world system – a view made famous by Immanuel Wallerstein – then it is surely inadequate to focus upon any country in isolation.

5.2.1 Developing underdevelopment

Wallerstein refers to the relation between developed and less developed areas as one of core and periphery. In his view, as a result of concentrating on manufacturing industry, and as a consequence of the forms of labour specialization and organization associated with it, the countries of Western Europe were able to develop a relatively strong form of state. It is these countries, along with the USA, which are regarded as forming the core. In contrast, the less developed regions are viewed as having adopted a form of production which required relatively little skill. Thus, they became the exporters of primary products, and form the periphery. But because the core countries have strong state machines, they are able to extract surplus from the weaker regions at the periphery, and this leads to the further strength of the core states, and the increased weakness of the periphery. For example, thanks to their strong position, the core states can impose terms of trade on the peripheral areas which are to the advantage of the core. Hence, according to Wallerstein, capitalist development does not develop the peripheral regions, but weakens and exploits them, widening global economic and social differences.[18]

André Gunder Frank describes the relationship between the advanced areas and the less developed in a slightly different way, using the terms 'metropolis' and 'satellite'. In his view, capitalism has expanded into a world-wide system of exchange where monopolies in the metropolis have become dominant and are able to exploit the satellites. Thus, surplus is continually extracted from various satellites by the metropolis, leading to a progressive polarization between the developed parts of the world – the metropolis – and the underdeveloped parts – the satellites.

Frank goes on to argue not only that the relation between the developed parts of the world and the less developed is a metropolis/satellite relationship but also that each satellite is itself a metropolis, of a kind, with its own respective satellites. And perhaps they, too, have their own satellites. The model is, thus, one of a chain of linkages with a major metropolis at the centre, which feeds off the surplus from a number of satellites, each a sub-metropolis, as it were, which in turn extracts surplus from its satellites. As Frank puts it, capitalism 'generates at once economic development and underdevelopment on international, national, local and sectoral levels'.[19] And the result of all this is that the satellites are starved of

18 See Immanuel Wallerstein, *The Modern World-System: Capitalist Agriculture and the Origins of the European World-Economy in the Sixteenth Century* (New York: Academic Press, 1974), especially p. 350.

19 André Gunder Frank, *Capitalism and Underdevelopment in Latin America: Historical Studies of Chile and Brazil* (New York: Monthly Review Press, 1967), p. xi.

capital and stagnate or even decay, while the advanced countries have an even greater surplus to invest and can therefore develop very quickly. In a word, Frank does not see capitalism as developing the satellites, but as 'underdeveloping' them. And whereas 'undevelopment' signifies that a region has simply failed to develop, 'underdevelopment' means that it has been inhibited from developing or has even regressed because of persistent exploitation by the metropolis. In short, what modernization theory has regarded as development, Frank sees as 'the development of underdevelopment'. Thus, the backwardness of underdeveloped countries is not seen as the result of any internal deficiency. Rather, it is international capitalism which is deemed responsible. Clearly, this is in stark contrast to modernization theory.

One perceived consequence of all this is that if satellites do ever develop, then they will 'experience their greatest economic development if and when their ties to their metropolis are weakest'.[20] And apparent confirmatory evidence of the hypothesis that development only occurs in poor areas when they are de-linked from the rest of the world system comes from those periods of crisis in the 'world metropolis' caused by war or depression which led to satellites being isolated. As Frank believes that it was because of 'the consequent loosening of trade and investment ties during these periods' that 'the satellites initiated marked autonomous industrialization and growth',[21] then he concludes that breaking these links is the prerequisite for genuine development in the poor regions.

In fact, the exploitation of satellites by the metropolis has been taking place since the sixteenth century, on Frank's view – from the time of the Spanish and Portuguese conquests of South America. As it is difficult to regard the internal relations of production within sixteenth-century Latin America as 'capitalist', Frank claims that any region which is linked in any way to the world market is part of the capitalist system and is, thereby, capitalist.[22] And he supports this claim by attempting to show how the internal economies of Latin America have been significantly shaped by the effects of capitalist penetration.

What this implies is that, if all regions are tied to the international capitalist system, and if all sectors of each region are similarly tied, then there is little point in arguing for further capitalist development. On this neo-Marxist analysis, the whole world is now, in a sense, capitalist. The solution that is proposed, instead, is to seize control of the Third World state in a revolution and de-link from the

20 André Gunder Frank, 'The development of underdevelopment', *Monthly Review*, Vol. 41, No. 2 (June 1989), p. 44.

21 Ibid., pp. 44–5.

22 The claim by underdevelopment theorists that Latin America has been capitalist since the sixteenth century has been the subject of much controversy. See, especially, Ernesto Laclau, 'Feudalism and capitalism in Latin America', *New Left Review* 67 (May/June 1971): 19–38. Much of the disagreement concerns the issue of whether exploitation is based solely in production or also in exchange. On this latter point, see John Roemer, 'New directions in the Marxian theory of exploitation and class' in John Roemer (ed.), *Analytical Marxism* (Cambridge: Cambridge University Press, 1986).

exploitative, capitalist world system. Only then, it is claimed, will capital no longer be drained away from the poorer regions and development become possible there.[23] Hence, for both Frank and Wallerstein, capitalism is regarded as a global system of exploitation, which must be radically transformed if genuine development is to take place.

But there does appear to be an obvious objection that can be raised against underdevelopment theory: some areas of the Third World have clearly undergone marked development. Thus, it is not surprising that underdevelopment theory has been subject to considerable criticism. In particular, it has been vehemently opposed on the Left by those who prefer a 'classical' Marxist approach – the most influential being Bill Warren.[24] Classical Marxists have always viewed capitalism as progressive in so far as it supposedly develops the material preconditions for a highly abundant socialism. Consequently, underdevelopment theory, in claiming that certain regions will simply not develop, poses something of a threat to the whole classical Marxist tradition.

However, the fact that some areas in the Third World have developed fails to refute the general thrust of underdevelopment theory. For example, a sub-metropolis might have developed because less capital was transferred out of it than it extracted from its satellites. But this would provide no grounds for thinking that its satellites would be able to develop. Quite possibly, the development of the newly industrializing countries (NICs) has been purchased at the price of a greater underdevelopment of the hinterland they themselves directly or indirectly exploit.

Nevertheless, the fact that some development has been observed in certain regions has led to a modification of underdevelopment theory – namely, what has come to be called 'dependency theory'. As one of its leading proponents,

23 However, the view (see Frank, *Capitalism and Underdevelopment in Latin America*, pp. 119–20) that super-exploitation of the Third World will eventually drive its peoples to rebel seems rather optimistic. As Huntington points out: 'The simple poverty thesis falls down because people who are really poor are too poor for politics and too poor for protest. They are indifferent, apathetic, and lack exposure to the media and other stimuli which would arouse their aspirations in such manner as to galvanize them into political activity.' Huntington, *Political Order in Changing Societies*, p. 52. This implies that if underdevelopment is in fact taking place, then the prospects for revolution might be even grimmer than they would be otherwise. Also see J. C. Davies, 'Towards a theory of revolution', *American Sociological Review* 27 (1962): 5–19.

24 See Bill Warren, 'Imperialism and capitalist industrialization', *New Left Review* 81 (September/October 1973): 3–44. Also see Bill Warren, *Imperialism: Pioneer of Capitalism*, ed. J. Sender (London: New Left Books, 1980). For criticisms of Warren, see Arghiri Emmanuel, 'Myths of development versus myths of underdevelopment', *New Left Review* 85 (May/June 1974): 61–82, and Philip McMichael, James Petras and Robert Rhodes, 'Imperialism and the contradictions of development', *New Left Review* 85 (May/June 1974): 83–104. Many of Warren's conclusions appear to depend upon misleading aggregations of data. Moreover, his prescription is one of unhindered capitalist expansion as a prelude to socialism. And many might well think that a more environmentally irresponsible strategy is hard to imagine.

F. H. Cardoso, writes: '*dependency*, *monopoly capitalism* and *development* are not contradictory terms: there occurs a kind of *dependent capitalist development* in the sectors of the Third World integrated into the new forms of monopolistic expansion.'[25] In other words, there is, occasionally, development in the poorer areas, but the development that takes place there is regarded as skewed because of the influence of international capital. Moreover, Third World states are seen as dependent states, serving international capital. This is thought to be the case even with military dictatorships, although Cardoso acknowledges that 'new political analyses are needed to explain the bureaucratic-technocratic form of authoritarian state which serves the interests of the internationalized bourgeoisie and their allies.'[26]

5.2.2 The independence of the state

But is it acceptable to regard Third World states as mere instruments of international capital, as many Marxists and neo-Marxists do? It would appear not, for as Warren emphasizes:

> Third World states have shown the ability to take punitive action against foreign firms located in their territories, e.g. the forcible nationalization of oil in Iraq, Egypt's nationalization of the Suez Canal, Uganda's take-over of British assets, the often unilaterally declared acquisition of majority shareholdings in foreign firms, such as timber and mining in Ghana.[27]

Moreover, '[t]he potential threat of such punitive action is often just as effective, and probably more often used, than the action itself.'[28]

In addition, Third World states have called for a New International Economic Order, they have attempted to reduce the amount of capital transferred out of their countries, they have formed agreements amongst themselves concerning the trade in commodities they export, and they have imposed numerous constraints on transnational corporations. For example, as Stephen Krasner observes: 'Governments have promulgated rules regarding the establishment of affiliates, repatriation of profits, debt financing, transfer payments, employment of nationals, disclosure of information, and tax rates.'[29] In short, according to Krasner:

25 Fernando Henrique Cardoso, 'Dependency and development in Latin America', *New Left Review* 74 (July/August 1972), p. 89.

26 Ibid., p. 94.

27 Warren, 'Imperialism and capitalist industrialization', p. 12.

28 Ibid.

29 Stephen D. Krasner, *Structural Conflict: The Third World against Global Liberalism* (Berkeley: University of California Press, 1985), p. 181. Krasner's study is essential reading for anyone who subscribes to the unquestioned belief that Third World states are the mere playthings of transnationals. Quite simply, in Krasner's view, they behave 'the way states have always behaved; they are trying to maximize their power – their ability to control their own destinies.' Ibid., p. 12.

> Third World states have pursued a wide variety of goals. These include economic growth, international political equality, influence in international decision-making arenas, autonomy and independence, the preservation of territorial integrity from external invasion or internal fragmentation, the dissemination of new world views at the global level, and the maintenance of domestic regime stability. They have used a wide variety of tactics to promote these objectives, including international commodity organizations such as OPEC and CIPEC (*Conseil Intergouvernment des Pays Exportateurs Cuivre*), regional organizations such as the Organization of African Unity (OAU) and the Association of Southeast Asian Nations (ASEAN), universal coalitions such as the Group of 77 (G-77) at UNCTAD and the United Nations, alliances with major powers, local wars to manipulate major powers, irregular violence such as national liberation movements, bilateral economic arrangements, national regulation of multinational corporations, nationalization of foreign holdings, foreign exchange manipulation, and international loans.[30]

The pursuit of such goals and the employment of such tactics would, surely, be patently inconsistent with the view that the Third World state is merely an instrument of international capital.

On the other hand, if Third World economies have expanded most rapidly when the imperialist chain has been severed, why do they not remain de-linked? That the chain is re-forged when the metropolis is no longer in a political or economic crisis surely demonstrates that the Third World state is not an instrument of indigenous capital, either – especially when re-linking leads to the transfer of capital from the satellite to the metropolis. In addition, states in LDCs often seem to have deliberately encouraged the incursion of transnational capital to the detriment of indigenous capital, which is something an instrument of indigenous capital obviously would not do. In fact, it has been noted that states in LDCs have gone so far as to lower environmental regulations in order to attract transnational capital – a likely consequence, of course, being major environmental deterioration.[31]

But there is a further, and far more serious, theoretical problem with viewing the state as a mere instrument of the economy or, more specifically, of classes. As Teodor Shanin objects, states have, on occasion,

> produced class structures, transformed them, or made them disappear, as when a bourgeoisie or a peasantry has been created by deliberate state policy, as in Kenya, Pakistan, Tanzania, or Brazil. Nor has this happened only in states of the capitalist era. In the China of Chin Shih (third century BC), to cite one example, a state-initiated agrarian reform effectively abolished the

30 Ibid., pp. 13–14.

31 See, for example, Steven Yearley, *The Green Case: A Sociology of Environmental Issues, Arguments and Politics* (London: Routledge, 1992), pp. 157–60.

> rural proletariat-cum-serf classes that the polarization and debt-enslavement of the peasantry had created, returning China to 'square one,' i.e., to a gigantic system of small-holder agriculture serving the imperial interest – a revolution from above in clear contradiction to the immediate interests of the dominant class of the large landowners.[32]

But if states choose to support new economic relations that will give rise to a new dominant class, then *states cannot be the instrument of the present dominant class*, whatever it is taken to be. Shanin's examples clearly entail the inadequacy of any instrumentalist theory of the state – precisely the theory that, by and large, pervades Marxism, and which is especially evident in underdevelopment theory and dependency theory.

Marxism has, for the most part, reduced the interests of the modern state to those of the bourgeoisie. At most, mainstream Marxism has regarded the state as having a 'relative autonomy'. However, as Wallerstein acknowledges: 'To be a partly autonomous entity, there must be a group of people whose direct interests are served by such an entity: state managers and a state bureaucracy.'[33] But if state actors have interests of their own, why assume that the state is only partly autonomous? The state could act in the interests of a particular class even if it were fully autonomous. For instance, as argued in Section 2.3.4, above, it could do so when its own independent interests corresponded with those of that class. Of course, the state could not be more than partly autonomous unless it had the power to pursue its own interests. But Wallerstein evidently believes that core states have considerable power, for he claims that 'the development of strong states in the core areas of the European world was an essential component of the development of modern capitalism.'[34] Nevertheless, he explicitly rejects the view that states in the periphery are of much significance.[35]

But some theorists working within the Marxist tradition have argued that this will not do at all. Instead, they have insisted that states in the periphery are extremely powerful with respect to their internal economic relations. Consider

32 Teodor Shanin, 'Class, state, and revolution: substitutes and realities' in H. Alavi and T. Shanin (eds), *Introduction to the Sociology of 'Developing Societies'* (London: Macmillan, 1982), p. 316. Even a leading dependency theorist notes that, '[p]aradoxically, the military have taken upon themselves the task of modernization.' T. Dos Santos, 'The crisis of development theory and the problem of dependence in Latin America' in Henry Bernstein (ed.), *Underdevelopment and Development: The Third World Today* (Harmondsworth: Penguin, 1976), p. 70. In addition, Ralph Miliband, a major Marxist theorist of the state, when discussing post-colonial countries, admits that 'the relation between economic and political power has been inverted'. See Ralph Miliband, *Marxism and Politics* (Oxford: Oxford University Press, 1977), pp. 108–9. In other words, the moment one examines the Third World, it becomes apparent that Marxist theory has everything upside down.

33 Wallerstein, *The Modern World-System*, p. 355.

34 Ibid., p. 134.

35 See ibid., p. 349.

Hamza Alavi, who argues that the task of the metropolitan bourgeoisie in the colony is

> to create [a] state apparatus through which it can exercise dominion over *all* the indigenous social classes in the colony. It might be said that the 'superstructure' in the colony is therefore 'over-developed' in relation to the 'structure' in the colony, for its basis lies in the metropolitan structure itself, from which it is later separated at the time of independence. The colonial state is therefore equipped with a powerful bureaucratic-military apparatus and mechanisms of government which enable it through its routine operations to subordinate the native social classes. The post-colonial society inherits that overdeveloped apparatus of state and its institutionalized practices through which the operations of the indigenous social classes are regulated and controlled. At the moment of independence weak indigenous bourgeoisies find themselves enmeshed in bureaucratic controls by which those at the top of the hierarchy of the bureaucratic-military apparatus of the state are able to maintain and even extend their dominant power in society, being freed from direct metropolitan control.[36]

Certainly, this could be viewed as a significant improvement on Wallerstein, who, like other underdevelopment and dependency theorists, seems seriously to undervalue and, consequently, undertheorize states in the periphery.[37] Yet, ironically, Alavi can be accused of undervaluing these states, too. For he remains within a Marxist perspective in regarding the state as an instrument of the economy – except his central proposition is that the state is not the instrument of one class; instead, it is the collective instrument of several.[38] But, it could be argued, this is still to undervalue both the power and the interests of the state, because, as we observed Shanin to insist, states do not merely preserve the dominant mode of production; sometimes they use their power to create new modes of production. What Marxists could thus be charged with is having systematically failed to take seriously state power and state interests. Hence, the whole class theoretical approach can easily be considered to be as inadequate in its own way as elite theory appears to be.

36 Hamza Alavi, 'The state in post-colonial societies: Pakistan and Bangladesh' in Harry Goulbourne (ed.), *Politics and State in the Third World* (London: Macmillan, 1979), pp. 40–1.

37 A point noted by John Saul: 'The problem of "the state" as it presents itself in the context of "underdevelopment" has been undertheorized and little researched.' John S. Saul, 'The state in post-colonial societies: Tanzania' in Ralph Miliband and John Saville (eds), *The Socialist Register 1974* (London: Merlin, 1974), p. 349.

38 See Alavi, 'The state in post-colonial societies', pp. 41–2.

5.3 A theoretical synthesis: the state-primacy approach

The elite theory approach of Huntington seems to be clearly inadequate in failing to take into sufficient account the international exploitation of the poorer countries. This is negated by the class theory approach of Frank and Wallerstein, which does emphasize international exploitation. However, this latter approach seems also to be clearly inadequate in reducing the state to an instrument of capital. Yet both the elite and class theoretical approaches draw attention to important phenomena that must be recognized in any adequate theory. The task, therefore, is to retain what is of value in elite theory and class theory while discarding what is problematic. In other words, the task is to sublate both approaches by, in a sense, containing and negating them. And such a sublation could be made possible by a 'negation of the negation': by a theoretical position that 'negates' the 'negation' of the state, while including a class analysis that is able to highlight international exploitation.

5.3.1 The nature of the Third World state

If Third World states are as significant as they appear to be, how exactly are we to theorize them? The first thing we must keep in mind is that they are *post-colonial states.* They are located within countries that were formerly colonies of advanced states, themselves now western liberal democracies, and it is those states which originally imposed state structures on their colonies. Why, then, have so many post-colonial states failed to develop the democratic institutions and practices modernization theory expected? Christopher Clapham sheds light on this problem by usefully describing the Third World state as 'neo-patrimonial'.

Clapham draws on Max Weber's distinction between rational-legal, charismatic and traditional types of authority. Authority in the modern state is widely considered to be of the first kind. There is a distinction between public and private life whereby one is supposed to be impartial while acting in the public sphere, but free to pursue one's own interests in the private sphere. The bureaucrat, when acting as a bureaucrat, is to disregard the fact that someone is his or her friend or relative, and treat everyone alike. While acting in an impartial manner within a rational-legal institution, the official possesses rational-legal authority. The modern state is supposedly based on this sort of rational-legal approach.

Charismatic authority – the second type – is based upon some personal characteristic (often messianic) of a rising leader, who usually wishes to change the social order in some way. However, when a successful charismatic leader comes to power, the society will tend to institutionalize the new authority structure, and so charismatic leadership will frequently turn into the rational-legal kind.

The third kind of authority is traditional authority, and this usually takes a patrimonial form. Authority resides in a particular person, such as the village head or chief, rather than in an office. And as the word 'patrimonialism' implies, the relationship between the leader and the rest is like that of a father to his children. Unlike the case of the charismatic leader, the person who has traditional authority possesses it simply because of the prevailing social and political order, which he or she does not challenge. Authority is based on tradition – for example, by being the child of the previous ruler when tradition requires that succession follows on that basis. Most importantly, the authority structure is one where those with authority lower down the chain have it by virtue of a grant from those above. And this differs from the rational-legal form where one is deemed to have authority by virtue of one's position in a rational-legal institution. In a patrimonial system, anyone lower down the chain has authority because it has been given, ultimately, by the ruler.

Clapham argues that in order to understand Third World states patrimonial authority is the key. But such states are not simply patrimonial, rather they are, in his view, '*neo-patrimonial*'. This is

> a form of organization in which relationships of a broadly patrimonial type pervade a political and administrative system which is formally constructed on rational-legal lines. Officials hold positions in bureaucratic organizations with powers which are formally defined, but exercise those powers, so far as they can, as a form not of public service but of private property.[39]

Thus, to describe post-colonial states as neo-patrimonial is to imply that, from a rational-legal standpoint, corruption is rife within them. Officials often see their positions as a source of wealth, and use them accordingly. As state personnel within a neo-patrimonial order regard themselves as owning their positions, they think they can do what they like with them, so long as it does not offend whoever has given them their positions. And as positions are bestowed, nepotism may also be rife.

What this suggests is that modernization theory is perhaps right in drawing attention to a duality between a traditional sector and a modern sector which has been introduced by colonial powers. But if there is justification in describing a Third World polity as neo-patrimonial, then modernization theory would be only partly right, because the colonial legacy would not consist in the modern sector having modernized the rest of society. Rather, it would be more accurate to regard traditional norms and behaviour as having crept into a system that was ostensibly rational-legal. And although the old traditional norms might have worked well enough formerly, their amalgamation with a modern political structure would invariably lead to a disastrous political system characterized by extensive corruption. Whereas modernization theory assumed that the modern sector would dominate and replace the traditional one, instead the traditional sector can be viewed as having profoundly influenced the nature of the post-colonial state.

The colonial state can, of course, be regarded as an instrument originally designed to maximize the extraction of wealth from the colony. Hence, it would not be surprising if the possession of an official position in the post-colonial state

39 Christopher Clapham, *Third World Politics* (London: Croom Helm, 1985), p. 48.

allowed the extraction of considerable resources from its people. And a state which is geared to maximize the extraction of wealth from its people is obviously going to be a coercive and an extremely powerful one. But the post-colonial state only appears powerful in one sense. In another sense it seems extremely fragile. Because controlling the state can be a great source of wealth, it is a very attractive prize for any potential usurper. Not surprisingly, then, coups are common in Third World countries; and the Third World state, while appearing highly coercive, can simultaneously be regarded as highly unstable. As Marylin Waring calculates: 'By 1985, 57 out of 114 independent developing states were militarily controlled. There had been 138 successful coups between 1960 and 1985.'[40] One thing is clear: a state whose officials regard themselves as owning their positions and who view them as a means of enrichment, and which is such an attractive prize to individuals that it is subject to periodic coups, cannot simply be reduced to an instrument of any economic class in civil society.

If an instrumentalist theory of the state will not do, how are we to make sense of the state's actions? Recall Shanin's observation that, although they usually preserve the existing mode of production, states occasionally back new ones. The most cogent explanation for why states sometimes introduce a new mode of production and sometimes stabilize the prevalent one which benefits existing dominant classes or class amalgams would appear to be that in each particular case *the course of action taken is in the interests of the state.* In Section 4.3.1, above, I argued that we might best understand 'the interests of the state' as a vector – a 'parallelogram of forces' – of the weighted powers of state actors to pursue their interests. This means that a parsimonious explanation for why states act as they do is that state actions are in the interests of certain state actors. And military coups, evidently, would appear to be in the interests both of those state actors who seize power and of those who support them.

Now, all state actors would seem to have an interest in the state obtaining revenue. Thus, a plausible reason for why the preservation of the prevailing economic order is often in the interests of the state is that the state obtains its revenue from a functioning economy. And by obtaining revenue, it is in a position to develop its coercive capacity. As Samuel Finer notes:

> Military forces call for men, materials, and, once monetization has set in, for money, too. To extract these has often been very difficult. It has become easier and more generally acceptable as the centuries have rolled on. . . . Troops extract the taxes or the forage or the carts, and this contribution keeps them in being. More troops – more extraction – more troops: so a cycle of this kind could go on widening and deepening.[41]

40 Marylin Waring, *If Women Counted: A New Feminist Economics* (London: Macmillan, 1989), p. 171.

41 Samuel E. Finer, 'State- and nation-building in Europe: the role of the military' in Charles Tilly (ed.), *The Formation of National States in Western Europe* (New Jersey: Princeton University Press, 1975), p. 96. This process is also acknowledged by Wallerstein: 'A state

The state could then employ its developing coercive capacity to preserve the existing economic structure. On the other hand, the state might employ it to transform the economic structure. But why, exactly, would a state precipitate such a transformation? And when would it do so?

This is precisely what the State-Primacy Theory purports to explain. It is a general theory of revolution[42] which identifies the state as having explanatory primacy with respect to the determination of a mode of production. According to this theory, the state tends to select relations of production which develop or optimally employ the productive forces, for that is in its interests. If the prevailing mode of production offers adequate revenue to the state, then the state has an interest in preserving it. As I argued in Section 4.4.5 (when discussing how the State-Primacy Theory can easily deal with different varieties of 'fettering'), one reason why a state might introduce a new mode of production is because that new mode is perceived to be, in some sense, more productive than the old, and thus presents the possibility of offering greater revenue to the state. If and when the prevailing mode of production does not offer adequate revenue to the state and an alternative would be practicable – in other words, when the economic relations 'fetter' in some way the development or use of the productive forces – then the state has an interest in promoting a new mode of production. And when states find themselves in military competition with other states, as they usually do, then there is good reason to think that they will be driven to obtain as much revenue as possible in order to fund the massive costs of remaining militarily competitive. That might mean, in certain circumstances, that they have no choice but to transform the prevailing economic relations to ones that are more productive.

In short, states would ordinarily preserve relations of production that are in their interests. But when new economic relations were perceived to be more in their interests, then states would act rationally in selecting those new relations. And given that we can translate 'state interests' into 'a vector of the weighted powers of state actors to pursue their interests', then the State-Primacy Theory claims, in effect, that when new economic relations are perceived to be more in the interests of certain state actors, those new relations are selected.

---

machinery involves a tipping mechanism. There is a point where strength creates more strength. The tax revenue enables the state to have a larger and more efficient civil bureaucracy and army which in turn leads to greater tax revenue – a process that continues in spiral form.' Wallerstein, *The Modern World-System*, p. 356.

42 In this respect, the State-Primacy approach can be regarded as a theoretical advance on Huntington; for as Leys points out, Marx's conception of revolution refers to a transition 'from an epoch dominated by one mode of production (such as feudalism or capitalism) to a new epoch dominated by a new mode of production. For Huntington, however, "revolution" refers . . . simply to any "rapid, fundamental, and violent change."' Leys, 'Samuel Huntington and the end of classical modernization theory', p. 346. Unlike Huntington's far less specific approach and realist approaches in general, the State-Primacy Theory *is* a theory of revolution in Leys' sense.

Clearly, this is compatible with Huntington's account of breakthrough coups, where a modernizing military promotes the development of capitalist relations. Moreover, as it would not appear to be in the interests of the military to have state funds wasted by inept civilian governments or to have too high a proportion of state revenue diverted into the bank accounts of corrupt government officials, the State-Primacy Theory is compatible with Huntington's account of guardian coups, as well. Furthermore, as it would appear that states in military competition with other states do not have an interest in reverting to less productive economic relations (the phenomenon of 'Forfeiture'), the State-Primacy Theory is also compatible with Huntington's account of veto coups, where the military prevents political developments that would put a brake on industrialization. The State-Primacy Theory is thus consistent with what seems to be of most value in Huntington's account. But, as we have seen, Huntington leaves out international exploitation. How, then, can a State-Primacy approach deal with this question? It must be able to do so if it is to be a genuine sublation of elite theory and class theory.

5.3.2 State-Primacy and underdevelopment

Can the State-Primacy Theory provide an account of underdevelopment? To begin with, the short-term variant of the State-Primacy Theory (see Figure 4.2) prioritizes the perceived interests of state actors. Ordinarily, economic growth would seem to be in their interests. However, as James Manor remarks:

> People in authority in Third World political systems – politicians and bureaucrats – generally accept the need for economic growth, but they often have other, more compelling political concerns that take precedence. They are usually more anxious about the security of their regime and sometimes of the state than about development. . . .[43]

Like Manor, Robert Bates believes that state interests can, on occasion, clash with development, and that states in less developed countries put politics before economics. Interestingly, Bates holds a position that, at first glance, seems to resemble the State-Primacy Theory:

> Instead of simply reflecting the dominant mode of production, [the state] can also seek to transform it. In addition, rather than securing the fullest realization of the productive potentialities at society's command, the state can in fact both fetter and undermine them. The African case . . . compels recognition of the possibility that political forces may be fully autonomous

43 Manor, 'Politics and the neo-liberals', p. 311.

> and, as a consequence, may act at the cost of economic rationality and solely in service of themselves.[44]

In what way, then, can state actors be seen to sacrifice economic rationality? Cash crops play a major role in many Third World economies. In Africa, where Bates conducted his research, the majority of governments 'maintain publicly sanctioned monopsonies for the purchase and marketing of these crops'.[45] Rural producers seem to have little choice but to sell their produce to them at a domestic price set below the international one. Bates regards the difference between these prices as tantamount to taxing agricultural producers. As he calculates: 'In most cases, [producers] obtained less than two-thirds the potential sales realization. And, in many cases, they received less than one-half.'[46] Significantly, 'the marketing agencies have become the source of over a third of the revenues of some of the states of Africa.'[47]

In addition, African governments, like those in many poor countries, frequently choose to overvalue their currencies, and this is also tantamount to taxing rural producers:

> By overvaluing their currencies, governments in Africa seek to make it easier for industries to import capital equipment; they thereby attempt to promote domestic industrialization. But in so doing they also lessen the purchasing power of those who earn their incomes in foreign markets. For, with the overvaluing of their currency, earnings of foreign exchange convert into lesser amounts of local 'dollars'. The maintenance of an overvalued currency thus represents a tax on exports; export agriculture is hurt in an effort to assist the growth of the industrial sector.[48]

This could, of course, be explained by the more powerfully expressed interests of the urban classes, whom states in LDCs have an interest in placating in order to avoid riots. And admittedly, it *is* usual, or so it would seem, for such states to keep the price of food low. But, as Bates insists, the behaviour of African states is explained neither by the interests of the urban classes nor by an attempt to reconcile the interests of all groups within society. In other words, the implication is that neither Marxist-style class theory nor pluralist theories can account for many of the policies adopted by states in LDCs: for example, Bates lists the toleration of inefficient projects, the subsidizing of farm inputs as opposed to alternative means

44 Robert H. Bates, *Essays on the Political Economy of Rural Africa* (Cambridge: Cambridge University Press, 1983), p. 147.

45 Ibid., p. 109. 'By one estimate, at the time of independence, government marketing agencies handled 90 per cent of the exports of palm kernels, 80 per cent of the exports of coffee, 65 per cent of the exports of tea, and 60 per cent of the exports of raw cotton.' Ibid.

46 Ibid.

47 Ibid., p. 110.

48 Ibid., pp. 110–11.

of keeping down food prices, a preference for rationing, and, in general, discriminatory treatment within the sector of rural production.

However, the policies of African governments become quite understandable when the interests of state actors are taken into account. Consider inefficient projects:

> public officials are frequently less concerned with using public resources in a way that is economically efficient than they are with using them in a way that is politically expedient. If a project fails to generate an adequate return on the public investment, but is privately rewarding for those who build it, provision it, staff it, or hold tenancies in it, the political officials may none the less support it. For it will serve as a source of rewards for their followers and as an instrument for building a rural political constituency.[49]

Similarly, part of the revenue obtained from marketing agencies can be used to subsidize inputs for particular rural producers, just as a system of rationing allows government officials to allocate resources or permits to a selected few. In this way, not only can state actors purchase loyalty but the opposition groups may also be weakened through division. In short, agricultural policies are one of the instruments African governments can employ to stay in power and control their populations. Such policies are often economically inefficient and, 'in many cases, the inefficiencies persist *because* they are politically useful; economic inefficiencies afford governments means of retaining political power.'[50] Or so Bates argues.

Now, while all of this is compatible with the State-Primacy Theory, it is more a theory of *undevelopment* than of *underdevelopment*. If one views Third World state actors as simply parasitic on their nation's economy, or if one views them as so preoccupied with retaining or extending their support within the country in order to hold onto power that they will preserve economic relations or pursue policies that benefit their supporters while fettering development, then one is merely presenting an account of a lack of development resulting from internal failings. Although this would explain stagnation in certain countries, it is less consistent with a focus on international exploitation, and fails to explain why states should transform modes of production. So, while Bates' account is, no doubt, part of the story, it would seem to be, at best, only a part.

Clearly, the key to understanding the behaviour of Third World states would appear to lie in attending to the problems they face in obtaining sufficient revenue. This might be thought to be evidenced in many of the environmentally disastrous courses which they pursue. For example, states in LDCs, in order to acquire foreign exchange, have, it is charged, encouraged the dumping within their territories of highly toxic wastes produced in the developed countries.[51] Why

49 Ibid., p. 127.

50 Ibid., p. 128.

51 'Large deals of this sort may offer impoverished, small countries the chance nearly to double their annual national incomes.' Yearley, *The Green Case: A Sociology of Environmental Issues, Arguments and Politics* (London: Routledge, 1992), p. 36.

should states in LDCs often resort to practices outlawed elsewhere? The answer would seem to be: because of the lengths to which they must go if they are to gain adequate income. And this would itself seem to be for the reason that much of their economies comprise subsistence production, and much of the exchange that takes place does so in the informal sector. Unlike the formal economy which transnational corporations operate within, a large part of the economies of Third World countries appears to offer only a limited source of revenue to their states. Can this observation be used in an extended analysis to explain not only cases of undevelopment but of underdevelopment or dependent development, too?

5.3.2.1 The rationality of underdevelopment

By suffering the taxing of their profits, TNCs provide 'metropolitan states' with revenue – revenue such states could be expected, obviously, to seek to protect. If a Third World state were to be offered military aid from a 'metropolitan state' for preserving economic relations that the latter benefited from – in other words, if a 'satellite' were to be offered military assistance for allowing TNCs to do virtually what they liked within its territory – then it would be rational for the 'satellite state' to accede, as it would enable it to bypass the normal difficulties it would encounter in obtaining sufficient revenue to meet its military requirements. In such a situation, the underdevelopment of its economy would not be a major concern for the 'satellite state'. (See Figure 5.1.) Such a possibility provides one good reason why states should not be viewed in isolation – and viewing them in isolation is, I have contended, one of the weaknesses of Huntington's approach.

But what of those states that do not receive military aid from 'core states'? Well, surprising as it might at first seem, even in these cases it would frequently be rational for 'peripheral states' to stabilize economic relations that led to the exploitation of their own citizens by TNCs. States, it can be argued, choose to stabilize economic relations that benefit one class rather than another because, by so doing, states maximize their incomes. For example, stabilizing capitalist relations would both underpin the exploitation of one class by another and promote the high productivity that states usually require. However, it has been claimed that, given the extent of both subsistence production and the informal economy within the Third World, the most effective way for 'peripheral states' to obtain revenue is usually by imposing tariffs. As Michael Todaro points out: 'Duties on trade are the major source of government revenue in most LDCs, since they are a relatively easy form of taxation to impose and even easier to collect.'[52] Consequently, Third World states often have an interest in maintaining international

52 Michael P. Todaro, *Economic Development in the Third World*, 3rd ed. (New York: Longman, 1985), p. 414. In other words, 'given administrative and political difficulties of collecting local income taxes, fixed percentage taxes on imports (*ad valorem* tariffs) collected at a relatively few ports or border posts often constitute one of the cheapest and most efficient forms of raising government revenue. In many LDCs, these foreign trade taxes are thus a central feature of the overall fiscal system.' Ibid., p. 412.

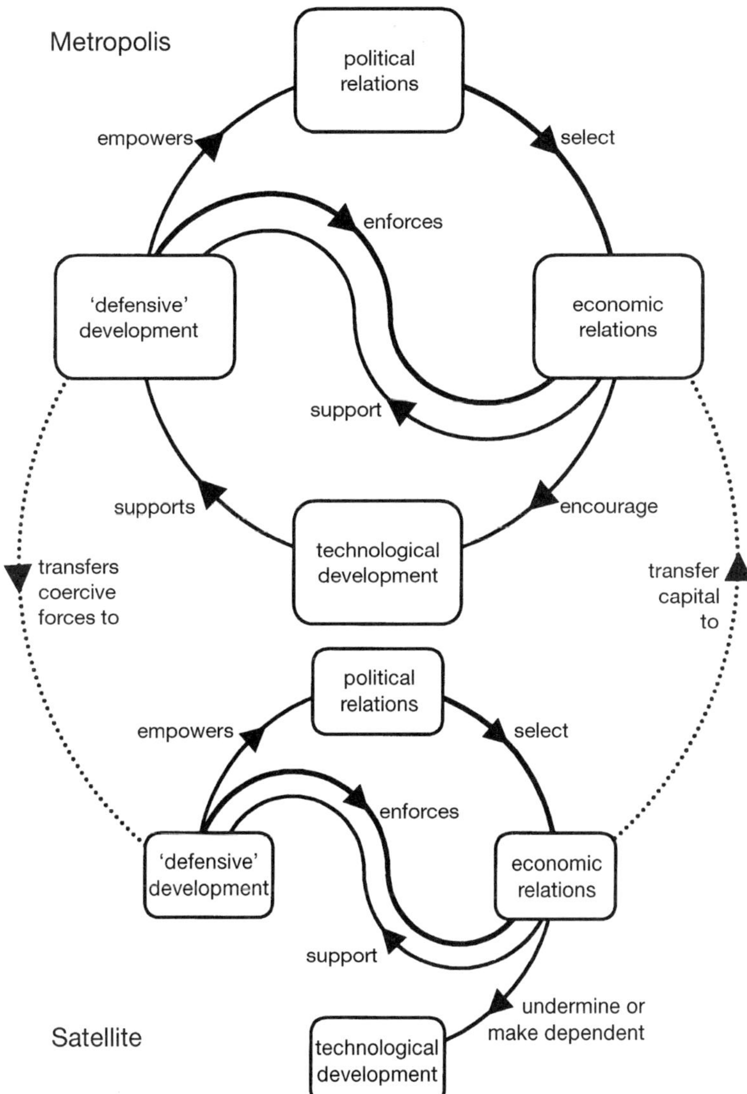

Figure 5.1 Metropolis and satellite

trade, even when that would lead to the underdevelopment of their economies, because such trade would at least allow those states to finance themselves.

There is another possible advantage to 'peripheral states' which might ordinarily be expected to result from their cooperating with TNCs. As Tim O'Riordan notes: 'Emerging nations are especially prone to invest precious resources in costly military programmes and prestigious arms buying (missiles, supersonic flight aircraft, and sophisticated electronic equipment) despite the existence of widespread malnutrition and social suffering.'[53] And as the World Commission on Environment and Development (WCED) add: 'defence expenditure is one of the most import-intensive of activities, usually creating a large secondary demand for imported spares, ammunition, servicing, training, and fuel.'[54] What is more, such advanced military equipment necessitates a vast, technological infrastructure. Hence, much of the 'development' in Third World countries can be viewed as geared to providing the background requirements of the military, rather than meeting the needs of their peoples. All of this requires advanced technology – a precondition of Third World states maintaining their military competitiveness – and the prospect of more advanced technology is just what TNCs offer.[55]

Of course, the prioritization of military requirements, with an accompanying profligate expenditure on armaments, would likely cause not only human suffering but also terrible environmental damage in order to cash in on the natural resources needed to pay for it. In addition, it is widely believed that arms build-ups often lead to wars. 'Yet', as O'Riordan observes, 'despite the profound human suffering and ecological devastation that are caused even by relatively small-scale wars, most nations persist in maintaining a credible military posture.'[56]

Inevitably, such a 'credible military posture' will pose a perceived threat to neighbouring states. The probable result is a treadmill of exorbitant military costs and a complicity in devouring the local economy in order to pay them, for

> when a nation's security is actually threatened, there is no real limit to the diversion of resources to ensure survival. The Middle Eastern countries (such as Israel and Jordan) currently invest about three-fifths of their national budgets (some 25% of total national wealth) in military expenditures even though this leads to high inflation and economic depression.[57]

Consequently, with such a proportionately astronomical demand for resources to satisfy their military preoccupations, if Third World states were to obtain

53 Tim O'Riordan, *Environmentalism* (London: Pion, 1981), p. 21.

54 Brundtland *et al.*, *Our Common Future*, p. 299.

55 In the words of the Brandt Report: 'It is a terrible irony that the most dynamic and rapid transfer of highly sophisticated equipment and technology from rich to poor countries has been in the machinery of death.' Willy Brandt *et al.*, *North–South: A Programme for Survival* (London: Pan, 1980), p. 14.

56 O'Riordan, *Environmentalism*, p. 22. Clearly, the environmental and social opportunity costs of military expenditure are massive: 'Four of the most urgent global environmental requirements – relating to tropical forests, water, desertification, and population – could be funded with the equivalent of less than one month's global military spending.' Brundtland *et al.*, *Our Common Future*, p. 303. Meanwhile, '[t]he plants that manufacture weapons, the transport of those weapons, and the mining of minerals for their production all place enormous demands on energy and mineral resources and are a major contributor to pollution and environmental deterioration.' Ibid., pp. 297–8.

57 O'Riordan, *Environmentalism*, p. 22. Remarkably, '[g]lobal military spending in 1985 was well in excess of $900 billion. This was more than the total income of the poorest half of humanity.' Brundtland *et al.*, *Our Common Future*, p. 297.

substantial revenue or new technology as a result of the activities of TNCs, or if they were to obtain military assistance from 'metropolitan states' that benefit from them, then it would be rational for such 'satellite states' to support these activities. Thus, *Third World states frequently have an interest in being complicit in the underdevelopment of their country's economy.* This only becomes apparent when one realizes that what is in the interests of Third World states is not necessarily what is in the interests of Third World peoples. Instead, it is often, though not always, what is in the interests of TNCs. In short, the interests of Third World states and those of transnationals often contingently correspond.[58]

However, if a Third World state is complicit in the underdevelopment of its own country's economy because of the income it expects to be able to derive from trade, and should the potential revenue fail to be realized because the TNCs operating within its borders are engaged in practices such as transfer pricing,[59] then it would be rational for such a state occasionally to object – sometimes to the point of threatening to nationalize TNCs' assets. Thus, it can be argued that sense can only be made both of the apparent complicity of Third World states in the underdevelopment of their country's economy by TNCs and of their occasional hostility to transnationals by taking seriously Third World states as autonomous agents rationally pursuing their own interests.

It can also be argued that most TNCs ultimately derive their power from the 'core states' who, in benefiting from their activities abroad, provide them with protection, both defensively and aggressively.[60] And when a 'core state' supports domestic capital, that does not entail that it does so because it is the instrument of such capital, for it is in the interests of states to protect the capital they obtain revenue from.[61] In the opinion of Stephen Krasner, states are 'the basic actors in the international system. The behavior of other actors, including multinational corporations and international organizations, is conditioned and delimited by state decisions and state power.'[62]

58 Cf.: 'During the last decade there has been mounting criticism of the role of transnational corporations (TNCs) in the "development" of the South. Most of this criticism has focused on the "irresponsibility" of TNCs which put profits before nature conservation and, for that matter, human livelihoods. Criticism tends to overlook the essentially rational and systematic way in which TNCs operate, *usually with the support or complicity of national governments in less developed countries.*' (Emphasis added.) Michael Redclift, *Sustainable Development: Exploring the Contradictions* (London: Routledge, 1987), p. 73.

59 When transnationals own chains of subsidiaries which purchase goods from each other, capital can be extracted from Third World countries by selling a good (for example, a capital good such as machinery) produced by a subsidiary located in the advanced country at a greatly over-inflated price to a subsidiary (for example, a producer of cash-crops) located in a poorer country. It is this practice which is referred to as 'transfer pricing'.

60 See Robin Murray, 'The internationalization of capital and the nation state', *New Left Review* 67 (May/June 1971), pp. 91–2.

61 However, it has been claimed that advanced states do not act as they do with respect to the Third World simply in order to benefit their own capitalists. As the Brandt Report insists: 'The major powers sell weapons mainly to suit their own foreign policy or to maintain regional balances, rather than to benefit their economies.' Brandt *et al.*, *North–South*, p. 120.

62 Krasner, *Structural Conflict*, p. 28.

So, as both 'core states' and 'peripheral states' obtain revenue from TNC activity, the underdevelopment of Third World economies can thus be seen to be in the interests of both. And correlative to any such underdevelopment would be the more rapid development of the economies of the 'core states'. Hence, there would be global technological development; but it would be aggregative, not universal. Certainly, the 'peripheral state' would thereby lose out in competition with the 'core state' that benefited most from capital extraction. But this would still be rational for the 'peripheral state', for in managing to obtain revenue, it would benefit vis-à-vis its immediate military competitors – namely, neighbouring 'peripheral states'. Furthermore, the revenue it would obtain would also allow it to retain control over its own nationals, which is surely one of any state's primary concerns.

Thus far, I have argued that it is rational for a weak state lacking its own significant formal economy and relying on the export of cash crops or raw materials to be complicit in the underdevelopment of its own country's economy. But it is also rational for a weak state to support transnational-financed industrial development, when offered, even if the development is 'dependent' or skewed, because such development makes more advanced technology available and could provide a basis for later, wider-scale industrialization that holds out the promise of greater revenue. Consequently, the State-Primacy Theory can accommodate not only some of the insights of underdevelopment theory, but of dependency theory, as well.

But, most importantly, it can go further than either. For a stronger Third World state has an interest in developing its own industry within its own 'modern' formal economy when it is in a position to do so, because that would offer it the greatest revenue.[63] Consider the NICs Taiwan and South Korea. As James Manor

63 This can be used to help explain international economic crises. States have an interest in developing their own 'strategic industries', which enable 'military self-sufficiency and national economic independence'. Gautam Sen, *The Military Origins of Industrialization and International Trade Rivalry* (London: Frances Pinter, 1984), p. 6. As Sen writes: 'Since the benefits of economies of scale, both static and dynamic, can be reaped by longer production runs the latecomer countries will . . . need to establish a level of capacity, when they industrialize, that allows them to reach the competitive threshold already prevalent in the firstcomer countries, with the attendant need for adequate export markets as well. Thus, they in turn may establish a level of productive capacity in excess of local consumption levels and hope to carve out a share in the international market. A further element which accentuates the problems of excess capacity is the need to ensure the ability to produce adequate quantities during war-time. Thus, the planned capacity may well exceed strictly national peacetime needs.' Ibid., p. 8. Such an account could be expanded to explain 'Kondratieff cycles', which Robert Gilpin insists lack a convincing causal mechanism. See Robert Gilpin, *The Political Economy of International Relations* (New Jersey: Princeton University Press, 1987), pp. 100–106. In the run-up to major wars, the productive capacity in each country's strategic industries would rise to a point where global overproduction ensued. If industry remained intact after the war, then there would be a global surplus and a recession would follow until excess capacity was cut back. If, on the other hand, industry was severely damaged during the war, then there would be space for growth. This might explain why high growth occurred after the second of the two World Wars, but a depression fell between them.

observes: 'The Taiwan government has long possessed formidable coercive powers, but in recent times it has demonstrated a capacity to assist the private sector in achieving spectacular export success.'[64] Moreover, the 'tradition of centralized government control over the private sector' in South Korea is 'pervasive',[65] while the same was, apparently, true of Japan.[66] In other words, the State-Primacy Theory can also account for the rise of the NICs, whereas underdevelopment theory is clearly inadequate in so far as it 'neither anticipated nor explained the rise of newly industrializing countries on the "periphery" of the international economic system'.[67] For this important reason, the State-Primacy Theory seems to be far superior.

5.3.3 Four problem areas

Clearly, then, the State-Primacy Theory appears to have greater explanatory power than the alternative theories. But, surely, it will be objected, there are obvious cases that it would have difficulty in explaining. Let me therefore consider four highly contrasting, apparent counter-examples to the appropriateness of applying the State-Primacy Theory to the Third World: Islamic fundamentalism, revolutionary Third World states, 'quasi-states' and global neo-liberalism. Rather than stray too far into tangential considerations, the following remarks will, unfortunately, be cursory; however, they do indicate how the State-Primacy Theory could plausibly respond to such ostensible difficulties.

5.3.3.1 Fundamentalist Islamic states

From the end of the 1970s, several Third World states have espoused and promoted Islamic fundamentalism. Often this has seemed to go hand in hand with a rejection of capitalist values and the undermining of capitalist economic relations. This would suggest economic regression. Yet the State-Primacy Theory would lead one to expect states to seek economic progress when practicable. Does this not pose a problem for the theory?

It certainly appears to be a difficulty, but the State-Primacy Theory has the resources to deal with it. We have already seen that state interests can explain

64 Manor, 'Politics and the neo-liberals', p. 309.

65 John Toye, quoted in ibid.

66 '[I]n the case of Japan, industrialization was engendered by the state's efforts to create a domestic defence industry during the third quarter of the nineteenth century.' Sen, *The Military Origins of Industrialization and International Trade Rivalry*, p. 9. Interestingly, it would appear that the state has also played a major role in the changes taking place in China: 'Economic liberalization in China has . . . been attended by the shrinkage of certain party and state agencies and roles, but also by the very substantial growth of the state, both as an arena within which capitalism can operate and as an enabler of private enterprises.' Manor, 'Politics and the neo-liberals', p. 309.

67 Manor, 'Introduction' in *Rethinking Third World Politics*, p. 2.

undevelopment. But fundamentalist Islamic states are a special case. Most are oil exporters, and their oil industries are, by and large, state-controlled. This means that such states can obtain considerable revenue directly. As a consequence, it can be argued, they do not have the need that most states have for a highly productive capitalist economy. In which case, they can promote forms of social control requiring values that do not appear homologous with capitalism. If social control could be better managed by propagating anti-capitalist values, then it would be in the interests of oil-rich states to propagate them at the expense of redundant capitalist relations.

Moreover, oil-rich states seem to possess sufficient economic strength for them to be neither 'satellites' nor 'dependent states'. Hence, they could afford to be far more explicit in their opposition to, or condemnation of, imperialism than weaker states who are dependent upon the activities of transnationals or 'metropolitan' military aid. An oil-rich state could be thought to have the luxury of being free not only to denounce the West and all its values but also to employ the anti-imperialist opposition that is thereby generated to enhance its position with respect to its own people, and thus render its internal control more secure. For a state in such a situation, the promotion of Islamic fundamentalism would be quite rational. This is not to deny that the leaders of such states are sincere in their religious beliefs. It is only to point out that promoting such beliefs does not necessarily conflict with their interests.

5.3.3.2 Revolutionary states in the Third World

What, though, of a country like China during the Cultural Revolution or, to take a more lurid example, Kampuchea under the Khmer Rouge? In their purging of intellectuals, such countries appear highly regressive with respect to development, yet they were certainly not oil-rich in the way that certain Middle Eastern states are.

Let me first consider China. Mao came to power at the head of a peasant-based, guerrilla army. The initial strategy adopted by the Chinese Communist Party on gaining control of mainland China in 1949 was to follow the Soviet model of development. However, with even less centralized industry than in the early Soviet Union, China switched to a course of small-scale, rural industrialization, which reached its peak in the Great Leap Forward, launched in 1958. However, with the failure of the Great Leap Forward, Mao lost face in the Party. The Cultural Revolution of the 1960s, which involved, among other things, numerous experts being sent to work in the fields in order to be 're-educated', is, perhaps, best seen as a temporary return by Mao to his power base – the peasantry and the Red Army – in response to a power struggle in which he was embroiled within the Party.

Can the State-Primacy Theory deal with Kampuchea, though? In particular, can it deal with the de-urbanization strategy of the Khmer Rouge, which led to de-industrialization in the short term? Pol Pot has been regarded as a Maoist who believed that he was moving directly to a cultural revolution of his own. This could be viewed as an irrational, blind adherence to a certain interpretation of Maoism, *or it could be seen as the most rational strategy for a leader of a peasant, guerrilla army*. However, it can also be argued that the price of Kampuchea's de-industrialization was an inability to maintain its defensive capability – in particular, an inability to defend itself adequately against a Vietnamese invasion mounted in response to the threat the Khmer Rouge posed to all neighbouring countries. And it can further be argued that the economic relations which ultimately prevailed in Cambodia were those imposed by Vietnam in its own interests, and which currently support the (now independent) Cambodian state – a state which has continued to be harassed by the Khmer Rouge.

This possible explanation of the economic relations that came to prevail in Cambodia employs one of the Darwinian features of the long-term variant of the State-Primacy Theory: countries controlled by political agents that (perhaps irrationally) select economic structures which fail to support their defence requirements will tend to be defeated by those that have chosen more appropriate economic structures. And the latter can be expected to impose on the former economic relations more suited to serving the (imperialist) state's interests. Hence, by a Darwinian mechanism, the nature of such a set of production relations can ultimately be explained by state interests – which is precisely what the State-Primacy Thesis claims.

So, the State-Primacy Theory can, in fact, deal with even the most problematic of Third World revolutionary states. What is worth stressing, though, is the problem revolutionary states in general pose for Marxist theorists. Consider Gordon White:

> the pre- (and post-) revolutionary context of military threat and conflict . . . contributes to a pervasive militarization of society, ideologically and institutionally, a heavy security consciousness which tends to retain its strength when the actual level of threat has [receded]. The heavily statist nature of Third World socialist societies both reflects and reinforces these tendencies, a fact which helps to explain the weakness of 'socialist internationalism' and the frequency of wars *between* socialist countries over the past decade.[68]

While struggling to explain the often unsavoury behaviour of 'Marxist' regimes in the Third World, some Marxists thus offer explanations that seem far more compatible with the State-Primacy Theory than with the primacy Marxism accords to economic factors.

68 Gordon White, 'Revolutionary socialist development in the Third World: an overview' in Gordon White, Robin Murray and Christine White (eds), *Revolutionary Socialist Development in the Third World* (Brighton: Wheatsheaf, 1983), p. 6.

5.3.3.3 'Quasi-states'

However, given that the State-Primacy Theory emphasizes state interests, how can it explain the creation and persistence of post-colonial states that seem barely capable of defending themselves internationally? Robert Jackson has dubbed such states 'quasi-states', and views them more as supported 'by international law and material aid' than as 'self-standing structures with domestic foundations.'[69] How could such weak states have escaped colonial control and remained sovereign entities?

One possible defence of the State-Primacy Theory might run as follows: Decolonization did not reach its peak until after the Second World War. The United States entered the war after the great European powers had begun to exhaust themselves in mutual conflict. Thus it emerged from the war as the world's strongest military and economic power. In order to become the 'hegemon'[70] of the 'free world', the USA had an interest in the decline of British and French imperialism – perhaps most palpably revealed in its response to the Suez invasion. Given that the European powers had created in their colonies the foundations for independent capitalist countries, given that US economic power could be employed to exploit such independent countries without the need for direct military control, and given that the direct military take-over of the former European colonies would have been impracticable and needlessly costly, US interests were best served by supporting an international system of sovereign states. While the USA was at its economic peak and could effectively exploit independent nations, it had a clear interest in leading a 'free world' in which the sovereignty of states (that might otherwise have succumbed to Soviet imperialism) would be guaranteed by 'the international community'. Of course, the sovereignty of states that appeared to threaten US interests, such as Cuba, Nicaragua, Granada or Kampuchea, failed to attain an equal measure of recognition. In short, the emergence and persistence of so-called 'quasi-states' can be explained by reference to the interests of the world's most powerful state.

In addition, it can be argued that many states desire to expand their military capabilities not because they intend to invade their neighbours, but because they fear that their neighbours have imperialist designs on them. Clearly, it would be rational for such weak states to support an international regime that purported to recognize and preserve each state's 'right' to sovereignty.

5.3.3.4 Globalization

But surely, it will be objected, doesn't global neo-liberalism, so-called, indicate that it is right to accord economics explanatory primacy? In response, closer

69 Robert Jackson, *Quasi-States: Sovereignty, International Relations and the Third World* (Cambridge: Cambridge University Press, 1990), p. 5.

70 See Gilpin, *The Political Economy of International Relations*, pp. 72–80 for a summary of the theory of hegemonic stability.

inspection of the process of globalization might actually reveal that it is not, in fact, incompatible with the State-Primacy Theory. According to Leo Panitch, for example:

> capitalist globalization is a process which . . . takes place in, through, and under the aegis of states; it is encoded by them and in important respects even authored by them; and it involves a shift in power relations within states that often means the centralization and concentration of state powers as the necessary condition of and accompaniment to global market discipline.[71]

In short, Panitch claims that any 'international constitutionalization of neo-liberalism has taken place through the agency of states'.[72] It would not be difficult, therefore, in defence of the State-Primacy Theory, to argue that any such development is in the interests of those states responsible for it.

Nevertheless, a number of theorists who have been influenced by Marxism have concluded that a process of economic globalization must be undermining the nation-state as an institution world-wide. But, it can be argued, this thesis is highly dubious, for as Michael Mann observes:

> The world . . . remains conflict-ridden, with a substantial place for 'hard' geo-politics. Consider this list: rising ethnic separatism, conflict between potentially nuclear states like India and Pakistan or the two Chinas, China's geo-political role incommensurate with its real strength, the instability of Russia and some smaller well-armed Powers, the prevalence of military regimes in the world, the likely proliferation of nuclear weapons and the largely uncontrolled current spread of chemical and biological weapons through the world. Who knows what eco-tensions, resulting from water shortages, foreign-dominated exploitation of a country's habitat etc. might lurk around the corner? It is unlikely militarism or war will just go away. All these threats constitute serious obstacles to the diffusion of transnational and universal global networks.[73]

71 Leo Panitch, 'Globalization and the state' in Ralph Miliband and Leo Panitch, *Socialist Register 1994: Between Globalism and Nationalism* (London: Merlin, 1994), p. 64. And as he continues, those who stress 'the "nebuleuse" that is global capitalist governance usually fail to appreciate that capitalism has not escaped the state but rather that the state has, as always, been a fundamental constitutive element in the very process of extension of capitalism in our time.' Ibid., p. 87.

72 Ibid.

73 Michael Mann, 'The global future of the nation-state', revised version of a paper presented at the conference on 'The Direction of Contemporary Capitalism', University of Sussex, 26–28 April 1996, pp. 18–19. Furthermore, there is reason to think that there is a limit to how far genuinely capitalist economic relations will be able to spread. For example, '[t]hough a far broader range of goods are now bought and sold, many of the most important ones are not actually sold as commodities on free markets. In defence the [US] government is a monopolistic customer for hi-tech weapons systems and it decides what other states (friendly ones) will

If neither militarism nor war will 'just go away', then neither, one must assume, will the state. And, according to Mann, it is the domestic market within the state's national boundaries that over 80 per cent of world production is still destined for; it is within their 'home' states that the research and development, assets and, indeed, ownership of transnationals are, in the main, located; and it is under those states' laws that transnationals' accountancy procedures and even the sale of their shares are governed. In short, it can be argued that, even in a period of apparently global financial movements, the state nevertheless remains determinant.[74]

5.3.4 The transcendence of elite theory and class theory

Thus, the State-Primacy Theory *can*, it seems, and without falling to obvious and decisive objections, explain political and economic developments in the Third World. And unlike other theories, it manages to cast light on the relationship between the interests of Third World states and the development, dependent development, undevelopment or underdevelopment of their economies, rather than obscure it. According to the extended State-Primacy Theory, Third World states are neither the instruments of international capital nor of an indigenous bourgeoisie. Rather, they are rational actors who will industrialize their economies when practicable, but who often find it in their interests to be accomplices in the dependent development or even underdevelopment of their own economies. And the reason primarily has to do with the difficulties such states experience in obtaining sufficient revenue. Furthermore, it is by focusing on the independent interests of Third World states that the State-Primacy Theory is able to explain why it is that they sometimes threaten to take punitive action against TNCs – an action inconsistent with neo-Marxist underdevelopment theory.

Clearly, if the Marxist view does, indeed, undertheorize the state, then it is necessary to negate that approach. But the State-Primacy Theory not only emphasizes the role of the state, it simultaneously highlights the exploitative nature of Third World societies and explains the frequent underdevelopment or dependent development of their economies. And, it can be argued, this underdevelopment or dependent development not only has disastrous human consequences but also disastrous environmental ones. Yet these features of the Third

---

be allowed as customers; supply is not very competitive (sometimes only one manufacturer will "tender" and sometimes profit is calculated on a cost-plus basis). The weapons embody more "use" than "exchange" value – the US *must* have them, almost regardless of cost, and the corporation can produce them without much thought of market risk.' Ibid., pp. 14–15. And even if '[c]apitalist transformation seems to be somewhat weakening the most advanced nation-states of the North yet successful economic development would strengthen nation-states elsewhere.' Ibid., p. 19.

74 Moreover, it can be argued that current assumptions about globalization rely upon taking an exceptional period of state intervention as the yardstick by which to measure the supposed recent weakening of the state. See S. Bromley, 'Globalization', *Radical Philosophy* 80 (November/December 1996), pp. 2–5.

World are underplayed and undertheorized both by modernization theory and by Huntington's approach – which is why they, too, deserve to be negated. In short, the State-Primacy Theory appears to solve the intractable problems in Wallerstein and Frank, on the one hand, and in Huntington, on the other, by transcending their theoretical positions. It purports to combine effectively the valuable insights that can be gleaned from Huntington's more state-centred analysis with those from underdevelopment and dependency theory, while leaving behind the flaws characteristic of these divergent approaches.[75]

But the State-Primacy Theory doesn't just stop there. Both modernization theory and underdevelopment theory, although in very different ways, place their faith in the Third World state. The State-Primacy Theory, however, indicates that it would be a grave mistake to place much faith in the state as the solution to Third World problems. What the theory claims to reveal is that *both 'core states' and 'peripheral states' bear responsibility for the oppression and exploitation of the world's poor and the environmental degradation that accompanies this.* For example, it can be argued that bi-lateral aid primarily serves to prop up regimes that are complicit in the exploitation of their people and the destruction of their environment. On such an account, support for the oppressed people of the world is, therefore, not the same as wanting a better deal for the disadvantaged states that oppress them. Hence, from the standpoint of the State-Primacy Theory, it would be a mistake to rely either on rich states or on poor ones for genuine liberation. Rather, it is to the people's of this world (not their states) and to the non-governmental organizations (NGOs) which help them to help themselves that we would have to look for a future that was non-exploitative of people and the planet.[76]

5.3.5 *An alternative to 'modernization'*

I have argued that one reason why Third World states might support TNC activities within their countries is because of the technology that is thereby introduced. But if the people living in the Third World are to be in control of production themselves, then they require a technology which is appropriate to that, and not a technology which is imposed upon them by the needs of their states, advanced states or their capitalist corporations. This suggests that Third World peoples

75 As Redclift insists: 'the resource crisis in the South is also a development crisis. . . . [Both] the development strategies based on the experience and interests of western capitalist countries, and those based on an alternative Marxist perspective, are seriously inadequate. Neither type of strategy is capable of generating better livelihoods for poor people from existing resources, without taking an unacceptable toll on the environment.' Redclift, *Development and the Environmental Crisis*, p. 2.

76 See B. Pratt and J. Boyden (eds), *The Field Directors' Handbook: An Oxfam Manual for Development Workers* (Oxford: Oxford University Press, 1985) and Robert Chambers, *Rural Development: Putting the Last First* (London: Longman, 1983) for alternative approaches to 'development'.

would be better off pursuing a policy of self-sufficiency than relying on transnationals diffusing western technology to the Third World.

Moreover, any long-term solution to the problems faced by the Third World must be ecologically viable. No meaningful development can be based upon technologies which either destroy the environment or consume vast quantities of finite resources. Yet both 'bourgeois' and Marxist theorists assume that any development in the Third World will require the transfer of capitalist technology to LDCs – a technology which environmentalists claim has reaped and continues to reap environmental havoc and which, being capital-intensive, is highly consumptive of finite resources. But as the Third World is short of capital while being well-endowed with labour, less resource-consumptive and more labour-intensive technologies seem far more appropriate.

Such an alternative to high-technology approaches to development has been most famously promoted by E. F Schumacher:

> As Gandhi said, the poor of the world cannot be helped by mass production, only by production by the masses. The system of *mass production*, based on sophisticated, highly capital-intensive, high energy-input dependent, and human labour-saving technology, presupposes that you are already rich, for a great deal of capital investment is needed to establish one single workplace. The system of *production by the masses* mobilizes the priceless resources which are possessed by all human beings, their clever brains and skilful hands, *and supports them with first-class tools.* The technology of *mass production* is inherently violent, ecologically damaging, self-defeating in terms of non-renewable resources, and stultifying for the human person. The technology of *production by the masses*, making use of the best of modern knowledge and experience, is conducive to decentralization, compatible with the laws of ecology, gentle in its use of scarce resources, and designed to serve the human person instead of making him [or her] the servant of machines. I have named it *intermediate technology* to signify that it is vastly superior to the primitive technology of bygone ages but at the same time much simpler, cheaper, and freer than the super-technology of the rich. One can also call it self-help technology, or democratic or people's technology – a technology to which everybody can gain admittance and which is not reserved to those already rich and powerful.[77]

77 E. F. Schumacher, *Small is Beautiful: A Study of Economics as if People Mattered* (London: Abacus, 1974), p. 128. And as he adds: 'the poverty of the poor makes it . . . impossible for them successfully to adopt our technology. Of course, they often try to do so, and then have to bear the most dire consequences in terms of mass unemployment, mass migration into cities, rural decay, and intolerable social tensions. They need, in fact, the very thing . . . which we also need: a *different* kind of technology, a technology with a human face, which, instead of making human hands and brains redundant, helps them to become far more productive than they have ever been before.' Ibid.

In Schumacher's work, we can see the main values embedded in today's green movement: a society and a technology which develops individuals rather than stultifying them; a technology that is both environmentally sound and controllable by the individual; one that is labour-intensive rather than capital-intensive; a strategy of low-growth or sustainable growth presupposing conservation and recycling rather than one requiring a high consumption of resources; a less-consumptive lifestyle in general; geographical and political decentralization; grass-roots or bottom-up initiative rather than top-down direction; an emphasis on small-scale, self-sufficiency and self-help. And given these values, what seems to be required are 'methods and equipment . . . cheap enough so that they are accessible to virtually everyone', that are 'suitable for small-scale application', and that are 'compatible with [humanity's] need for creativity.'[78]

This is all very different from the dominant approaches to development. Like modernization theorists, Schumacher does, in fact, accept a notion of dualism – that there are traditional and modern sectors – but unlike those who assume that the modern sector will modernize the traditional, Schumacher argues that it creates enormous problems for the traditional sector, which then react back on the modern. Development is concentrated in the cities, and this leads to the destruction of the traditional sector in the rural areas, and then people are driven to migrate to the cities, where they cannot find work and are forced to live in shanty towns. And this uncontrolled growth of the cities then causes problems for the modern sector. Thus, as Schumacher writes:

> It is necessary . . . that at least an important part of the development effort should by-pass the big cities and be directly concerned with the creation of an 'agro-industrial structure' in the rural and small-town areas. In this connection it is necessary to emphasize that the primary need is workplaces, literally millions of workplaces.[79]

So, in opposition to orthodox development theory, which argues for the latest, highly-productive technology to be transferred to the Third World, and which, being very sophisticated, is extremely expensive per job created, Schumacher argues for a technology which is relatively cheap. Investing a great deal in a technology which is highly productive, but which employs few people for the amount invested, will, it is argued, do nothing to help the poor who comprise the majority: capital-intensive technology will either cater for the local rich, or it will be geared to export. On the other hand, a cheaper technology which was more widely distributed would, the argument continues, provide the basis for local employment, increase local demand, stimulate an indigenous development, and be of real relevance to those most in need.

In other words, the orthodox assumption is that the technology which the

78 Ibid., p. 27.
79 Ibid., p. 145.

developed countries are able to benefit from is also that which LDCs require. As Schumacher puts it:

> The ruling philosophy of development over the last twenty years has been: 'What is best for the rich must be best for the poor.' This belief has been carried to truly astonishing lengths, as can be seen by inspecting the list of developing countries in which the Americans and their allies and in some cases also the Russians have found it necessary and wise to establish 'peaceful' nuclear reactors – Taiwan, South Korea, Philippines, Vietnam, Thailand, Indonesia, Iran, Turkey, Portugal, Venezuela – all of them countries whose overwhelming problems are agriculture and the rejuvenation of rural life, since the great majority of their poverty-stricken peoples live in rural areas.[80]

Given this analysis, the classical Marxist approach exhibits the same problem as orthodox development theory, for it, too, fails to distinguish between appropriate and inappropriate technologies. The assumption of both classical Marxism and modernization theory is that the more sophisticated technology is, the better it is. But, Schumacher argues, industry that 'has arisen in societies which are rich in capital and short of labour . . . cannot possibly be appropriate for societies short of capital and rich in labour.'[81] Modern factories lying idle in LDCs because they are short of spare parts from the developed world and short of experts who can repair their machinery can thus be viewed as the tangible result of the orthodox assumption. What Schumacher argues for in opposition to this is a technology which the poor can use and repair themselves, and by means of which they can improve their own lives. Thus, in Schumacher's view, what they really need are not technologies such as huge nuclear power stations, but relatively small-scale tools.[82]

In contrast to the prescriptions of both modernization theory and classical Marxism, then, what is argued to be needed is not industrialization in the Third World, but a form of small-scale, decentralized development based on intermediate technology that will lead to greater creativity and self-development by the mass of the people, and which will also, it is claimed, ward off the environmental threat that endangers humanity. The problem is, however, that intermediate technology seems to be in the interests neither of transnational capital (which appears to require employees and consumers, rather than small-scale autarkies) nor of states desiring economic modernization as a precondition for developing their military capabilities – a development that seems to have proved very costly

80 Ibid., pp. 139–40.

81 Ibid., p. 146.

82 '[I]ntermediate technology would also fit much more smoothly into the relatively unsophisticated environment in which it is to be utilized. The equipment would be fairly simple and therefore understandable, suitable for maintenance and repair on the spot. Simple equipment is normally far less dependent on raw materials of great purity or exact specifications and much more adaptable to market fluctuations than highly sophisticated equipment. [Workers] are more easily trained; supervision, control, and organization are simpler; and there is far less vulnerability to unforeseen difficulties.' Ibid., p. 151.

indeed; so costly, in fact, that the creation of a massive international debt can be regarded as its direct consequence.

5.3.6 State-Primacy and Third World debt

Allow me, then, to conclude this chapter by briefly considering the issue of Third World debt – an issue that I have reserved till last, for it seems, at first glance, to pose even more of an insurmountable problem for the State-Primacy Theory than the mooted condition of underdevelopment.

The State-Primacy Theory claims that states select economic relations that are functional for meeting their interests. In other words, ordinarily, a state will select a set of economic relations which is conducive to developing the productive forces because that allows the development of its coercive capacity by means of which it is able to defend itself. However, we have seen that it can sometimes be rational for a Third World state to be complicit in the underdevelopment of its country's economy. There are occasions when allowing TNCs to plunder its country's resources seems to be the most effective way for a Third World state to obtain revenue. Even in accounting for cases of underdevelopment, then, the State-Primacy Theory emphasizes the central role played by states. But, it might be objected, doesn't Third World debt show that it is economics that rules the world, not states? In order to answer this objection, I shall borrow heavily from a writer who has done much to publicize Third World debt and to whom many NGOs and their supporters show considerable respect – Susan George.

Third World debt is, without doubt, an issue of immense importance to those concerned about the plight of LDCs. It has been calculated that, in 1986, the debt owed by Third World countries exceeded $1 trillion,[83] with a crippling effect on the world's poorest people, who, it has been claimed, shoulder the burden of repaying that debt.[84] The obvious response, one would think, is to demand that the debt be, unconditionally, written off[85] – a demand made by organizations as diverse as the World Development Movement, Oxfam and Friends of the Earth. But before jumping hastily to any conclusions, no matter how glaringly obvious they might seem, it would be wise to consider the reasons for Third World debt.

A number of factors seem to have led to the debt accumulated by LDCs

83 It is worth bearing in mind that, apparently, in the same year the United States' public debt exceeded $2 trillion. See Susan George, *A Fate Worse than Debt* (Harmondsworth: Penguin 1990), p. 12.

84 'In the five years between 1982–87 Third World countries as a group, including the most impoverished and crisis-ridden in Africa, sent us $220 billion more than we sent them. . . . Never before in history have the poor financed the rich on such a lavish scale.' Susan George, 'Several Pounds of Flesh', *New Internationalist* 189 (November 1988), p. 18.

85 For one defence of the unconditional cancellation of Third World debt, see Barry Wilkins, 'Debt and underdevelopment: the case for cancelling Third World debts' in Robin Attfield and Barry Wilkins (eds), *International Justice and the Third World: Studies in the Philosophy of Development* (London: Routledge, 1992).

reaching colossal proportions. The price of oil rose sharply. Northern banks were keen to lend the capital they had accumulated, and were seemingly happy to invest it in quite inappropriate projects in poorer countries, such as the Marong nuclear power station. As George commented in 1989 on this insane scheme, which was ordered in 1976 at an initial estimate of $2.1 billion:

> The debt incurred for this plant alone cost the Philippines at least $350,000 *a day* in interest payments – a figure that jumped to $500,000 in 1987 when debt to the US Ex-Im Bank fell due. The reactor is ready to go; that it is not yet operating is perhaps just as well. The building site chosen is in the middle of the 'fire-rim' earthquake zone at the foot of a volcano.[86]

At first, the interest rates were so favourable (initially less than the rate of inflation) that Third World states would have acted irrationally in not taking advantage of the offers of loans. But then interest rates rose sharply. And the apparent reason for the huge increase is particularly interesting. It surely wasn't a plan by the Northern banks to wreck financially Third World economies. And, one must assume, it certainly wasn't a plan by transnational capital to instigate a global economic crisis. World interest rates rocketed up primarily, it would seem, as a result of the tremendous borrowing requirements of the United States in order to fund its 'star wars' programme. It appears that, in order to attract sufficient revenue, the United States' government had to offer investments at very high rates of interest. And for the commercial banks to keep the savings coming in, their interest rates had to keep up. The result of this, it has been argued, was a crippling burden of repayments for those countries which had taken advantage of loans at what were originally low rates of interest. In other words, far from the debt being a simple matter of economics, its burdensome nature is, it would seem, intimately linked to the military needs of the world's strongest state. And this is quite consistent with the State-Primacy Theory, of course.

Another purported reason for the huge debt burden was capital flight out of LDCs. It has been charged that corrupt government officials in Third World states were, in many cases, able to acquire considerable wealth by transferring capital out of their countries and into private bank accounts abroad.[87] Again, as the State-Primacy Theory emphasizes the interests of state actors, this, too, is not inconsistent with the theory.

However, one of the most significant direct causes of Third World debt appears to have been military expenditure by states in LDCs. There seems to be a clear correlation between the size of the debt and per capita military expenditure, for, it

86 George, *A Fate Worse than Debt*, p. 18.

87 Consider the case of Somoza in Nicaragua: 'Somoza pocketed most of the international loans meant for the reconstruction of Managua after the 1972 earthquake and continued to steal from his country right up to the moment he was finally forced out in 1979. When he fled the country, he left all of $3 million in the treasury. Nicaragua's outstanding debt is $4 billion, three-quarters of which was contracted under the Somoza regime.' Ibid., p. 118.

has been noted, it is the poorest countries with the largest debts that have tended to spend, proportionately, the most on 'defence'.[88] Moreover, it has also been noted that, when the IMF has demanded draconian measures be imposed on civil spending by LDCs, 'arms budgets remain untouched.'[89] As George remarks: 'It is not coincidental that those countries that today find themselves in the deepest debt trouble were those that yesterday bought the most weapons.'[90]

It should also be borne in mind that states in LDCs did not have to pay for all of the armaments that they accumulated. It has been calculated that, in 1972, for example, 40 per cent of the arms acquired by non-oil exporting countries were gifts from the United States, while the Soviet Union gave them 8 per cent of their arms. In 1982, however, the Soviet Union appears to have increased its donation to 12 per cent of those countries' armaments, while the United States seems to have decreased the proportion it gave away to 2 per cent of the arms they acquired. Still, it has been observed, 14 per cent were received by Third World states free of charge. 'The catch was that they were expected to pay for the rest, and the rest, in 1982, came to $12 billion.'[91]

The alleged consequences of trying to repay the debt are not simply that many people in LDCs suffer appallingly – UNICEF has estimated that, in 1989, 500,000 people died because of the debt.[92] It has also been claimed that there are devastating environmental consequences. Friends of the Earth, for example, have calculated that 'deforestation in the Ivory Coast has reached . . . 15% per year due to measures taken to try to pay the debt.'[93] And reasons for why dire environmental consequences will inevitably attend both Third World borrowing and the subsequent attempts to repay the debt incurred are not difficult to provide:

> There are two debt/environment connections. The first is borrowing to finance ecologically destructive projects. The second is paying for them – and all the other elements of debt-financed modernization – by cashing in natural resources. The two are necessarily intertwined. Many of the grandiose projects that helped to put Third World countries on the debt treadmill to begin with are environmental disasters in their own right. Mega-projects are part of the standard development model; they pay no heed to future penalties for present recklessness.[94]

88 See ibid., p. 22. Consider Ethiopia: 'Its GNP is $4.3 billion, which works out to about $110 per Ethiopian, the lowest per capita GNP anywhere in the world, according to World Bank figures. This does not prevent Ethiopia from spending $13 per head and per year on its military but only $7 on health and education combined.' Ibid.

89 Ibid. And as several commentators have observed, the IMF and the World Bank act 'as accessories to US policy'. Robert Cox, quoted in Panitch, 'Globalization and the state', p. 69.

90 George, *A Fate Worse than Debt*, p. 23.

91 Ibid. It is worth noting that, '[s]ince the early 1960s, military spending in developing countries as a whole has increased fivefold.' Brundtland *et al.*, *Our Common Future*, p. 298.

92 The World Development Movement, *Piggy Banks* (London: WDM, 1991), p. 12.

93 Ibid.

94 George, *A Fate Worse than Debt*, p. 156.

Many of these projects were, apparently, related directly to military requirements. (And it should not be forgotten that in Africa, for example, at a recent count, 60 per cent of the countries had military rulers.) Moreover, much of the remaining development funded by the debt was, it would seem, to provide infrastructural support for the military. Thus, if one considers not only direct military expenditure, but the indirect, too, then Third World debt seems, in fact, to pose no problem for the State-Primacy Theory. Quite the contrary, for an appreciation of its ostensible causes actually draws attention to precisely the state interests that the State-Primacy Theory focuses upon.

Now, given the seeming correlation between arms expenditure and indebtedness, is it still so clear that the answer to this immense problem of Third World debt is *unconditional* cancellation? If military expenditure has been a major, if not *the* major, cause of the debt accumulated by states in LDCs, isn't it quite likely that one result of simply writing off the debt would be an increase in military spending by certain states? But that would not only mean greater repression for the people who live in those countries, it would also mean regional destabilization. Neither consequence is in the least to the benefit of the mass of people who live in the poor countries.

5.3.6.1 *Confusing the conditions*

One possible confusion at the heart of the concerted calls for unconditional debt cancellation would consist in the failure to differentiate between a necessary condition and a sufficient condition for improving the lot of Third World peoples. It certainly appears to be a necessary condition for their lives to improve that the debt be cancelled. But it is, surely, not a sufficient condition. What is more, if debt cancellation were mistakenly regarded as if it were a sufficient condition, and if it were effected without other accompanying changes, then the situation could, in certain cases, actually be made worse. The liberation of General Mobutu Sese Seko from a debt burden of $6 billion so that he could have spent even more on oppressing the people of Zaire would hardly have been in their or their neighbours' best interests. Thus, unless debt cancellation goes hand in hand with genuine popular control, it cannot be guaranteed in every situation to be more of a solution than a problem.

A second possible confusion at the heart of the concerted calls for unconditionally writing off the debt concerns the conditions that should be set for its cancellation. Because the governments of the advanced countries would be likely to impose conditions that are of dubious benefit to Third World peoples (for example, when at their best, by insisting on the implementation of a political system that relies on, what might be regarded as, an impoverished conception of 'democracy'),[95] radicals have frequently opposed any suggestion of setting conditions.

95 See Carole Pateman, *Participation and Democratic Theory* (Cambridge: Cambridge University Press, 1970) for what might be thought of as a considerably less elitist conception of democracy.

Certainly, there is reason to think that the governments of the advanced countries cannot be trusted to act in a way that is beneficial to the mass of the world's population, even when they seem to be acting in the most benign manner and for the purest motives. As an example, it has been claimed that, when other countries have complied with its foreign policy, the United States has, while appearing to aid them, deliberately attempted to alter their diets in order to make them dependent on American grain.[96] Furthermore, it is commonly argued that most food aid has the effect of discouraging 'local production aimed at self-sufficiency'[97] and increasing dependency. As George insists: 'Food aid is a means for developing markets, for helping agribusiness, for gaining a stranglehold on the policy decisions of needy governments and for promoting US foreign policy and military goals.'[98] This is quite explicit in the case of PL 480:

> Public Law 480 (now also called the Food for Peace Law) [was] passed by the US Congress in 1954 with these stated purposes: '*An Act to increase the consumption of United States' agricultural commodities in foreign countries*, to improve the foreign relations of the United States and for other purposes.' The Congress further specifically declared that one goal was 'to develop and expand export markets' for American products.[99]

And, it can be argued, increased sales of American products abroad simultaneously develops other countries' dependency upon, while raising the potential revenue available to, the United States.

However, when other countries have not complied with its foreign policy, the United States appears to have been quite happy to practise low intensity conflict (LIC), which, following the debacle in Vietnam, was, it seems, its preferred policy prior to the muscle flexing of the Gulf War.

> Unlike conventional warfare, LIC does not seek to eliminate an enemy physically. It seeks instead to isolate him internally and externally, to exclude him from the international community (and from its aid), to delegitimize his government (or his political influence in the case of a popular government). Support for *contras* in various parts of the world is one part of LIC. Making

96 See Frances Moore Lappé and Joseph Collins, *Food First* (London: Abacus, 1982), p. 287.

97 Susan George, *How the Other Half Dies: The Real Reasons for World Hunger* (London: Penguin, 1986), p. 206.

98 Ibid., p. 212. As she adds: 'Charity indeed begins at home. Any 10-per-cent increase of per capita income in a country receiving food aid is estimated to result in 21 per cent more sales of US farm products.' Ibid., p. 198.

99 Ibid., p. 196. To see how good an investment the Food for Peace Programme turned out to be for the United States, consider the case of Japan: 'From the beginning of the Programme in 1954 Japan got not quite $400 million worth of food aid, but by 1975, had *bought* over $20 *billion* worth of food. Its purchases of food imports alone are now worth over $2 billion a year to the US.' Ibid., p. 198.

> economies 'scream' or 'cry uncle', to use Reagan administration terminology, is another – realized through blockades, sabotage and other forms of economic intimidation.[100]

Moreover, it has been claimed, the advanced states have been able to use *the debt* as a tool for waging what is in effect a form of LIC on numerous Third World states. And this, too, is quite consistent with the State-Primacy Theory.

Radicals are surely right, then, to be suspicious of any conditions imposed by the advanced states on LDCs. But this is not a reason for rejecting conditionality outright. Because the conditions that the advanced states would impose may well be problematic is no reason for tacitly giving unconditional support to every military dictatorship in the poorer parts of the world. This is precisely why it is essential that the interests of the peoples of LDCs and those of their states must not be confused.

What I have been arguing should not, in any way, be taken as endorsing the debt, excusing it or belittling its importance. But it cannot just be taken for granted that its unconditional cancellation is the best possible strategy *in all cases*, without any measures pursued in tandem to establish genuine popular control that can protect and further the interests of the poor. Surely, it *is* imperative that the poor peoples of the world do not have to shoulder any of the burden of Third World debt. But, surely, it is also imperative that they be liberated from the burdens imposed upon them by oppressive political regimes in their own countries. If so, then radicals need to be fighting just as hard for the poor to be politically in control of their own lives as for them to be in control of their own lives economically. Yes, radicals must, surely, call for the cancellation of the debt because of the terrible harm that it is doing. But they must demand a lot more, as well. Quite simply, if an appropriate response is to be forthcoming, debt cancellation must not be viewed in isolation.

In fact, it can be argued that most political theory and practice is often wholly inappropriate precisely because, in failing to take a genuinely interrelational perspective (namely, one that sees how all of the issues are interlinked), it tends to view issues in relative isolation. But as Brian Tokar writes: 'As ecology describes the interconnections among all living things, an ecological politics needs to embrace the interconnectedness of all aspects of our social and political lives and institutions.'[101] Following the above defence of the State-Primacy Theory – a theory which purports to be genuinely interrelational – the time has now come to try to make explicit the connections between our political and economic institutions and their seemingly disastrous social and environmental effects.

Most of the pieces of the theoretical jigsaw puzzle now lie before us. Thus, the time has come to attempt to fit them together into a genuinely interrelational, green political theory. This will be the task of the next chapter.

100 George, *A Fate Worse than Debt*, p. 233.

101 Brian Tokar, *The Green Alternative: Creating an Ecological Future* (California: R. and E. Miles, 1987), p. 56.

6 The state and nature

The groundwork has now been laid allowing the central features of a genuinely interrelationist theory to be keyed together. In particular, the arguments presented in the preceding chapters act in concert to suggest a comprehensive theoretical edifice – one which is capable of indicating the possible interlinking of political, economic, technological and military developments, and which also seeks to explain the cause of their attending social and environmental problems, thereby constituting a radical green political theory.

But if a green political theory is to be both comprehensive and consistent, then all of its core features must cohere together. What precisely, then, are the core features of green political thought – features that must be reconciled with one another if the theory is to be neither incomplete nor self-contradictory?

6.1 Radical green values: feminist, socialist and anarchist

There is, of course, one value which all greens embrace in some form or other: namely, environmental protection. But as most greens (and certainly, those who are members of green parties) never tire of insisting, their concerns extend much further than that. However, because of the considerable diversity within the green movement, not all greens embrace every value which many of their number consider to be central. Nevertheless, the most strongly defended elements of radical green political thought[1] commonly include decentralization, participatory

1 In seeking to identify these features, I here abstain from examining the core features of green *moral* thought. There has been a recent tendency in some circles to regard green political theory as indistinguishable from environmental ethics. But this obfuscation makes green political theory unnecessarily vulnerable to the lack of agreement between those advocating greater concern for animal welfare, those seeking to justify animal rights, and those wishing to provide a moral theory that accords intrinsic value to species. On this divide, see, especially, J. Baird Callicott, 'Animal liberation: a triangular affair' in Robert Elliot (ed.), *Environmental Ethics* (Oxford: Oxford University Press, 1995). Green politics, on the other hand, has been most concerned with the practical question of how to save the planet. The present book is fundamentally concerned with developing a political theory capable of informing *that* task. And conveniently for the theory here proposed, if it should turn out to be the case that there

democracy, egalitarianism, self-sufficiency (or, perhaps more realistically, self-reliance), alternative technology, pacifism and internationalism.[2] Radical greens tend to value these as core features of their political thought partly because each element is widely considered, ultimately, to serve the end of environmental protection. Yet none of these elemental values is confined to the green movement. Many have their sources in earlier political traditions. In particular, feminism, socialism and anarchism between them espouse all of these values. What is more, each of these traditions has made its own significant contribution to the development of green political thought.

Feminism has contributed much to green thinking, having exerted a particularly strong influence on *Die Grünen*, where policies designed to combat patriarchy were incorporated into their 1983 election manifesto.[3] One requirement for which many feminists have convincingly argued is for more participatory and less hierarchical political structures.[4] Many have also emphasized the need for a consensual rather than a conflictual approach to decision-making. And not only have feminists contributed a general critique of patriarchy (as well as of the domination of nature, which many eco-feminists tend to see as related to the domination of women),[5] they have also been especially active in the peace movement, where they have managed to stimulate a considerable re-birth of interest in pacifism.[6] However, it should be noted that some feminists have been critical of certain tendencies within the green movement – in particular, criticisms have been levelled against those who are seen as coming from a 'macho' socialist background[7] and who, it has been asserted, are thus insufficiently sensitive to a more consensual approach.

---

is a dynamic which is driving us to harm human beings, while simultaneously driving us to ignore the welfare or rights of nonhuman animals *and* to reduce biodiversity, then an opposition to that dynamic could be justified either by a concern for human well-being, animal welfare, animal rights or species preservation. In which case, it may well be possible to sidestep this whole debate, which is currently raging within the domain of environmental ethics. Nevertheless, for one attempt at developing a moral theory that might explain and resolve all of these ethical concerns, see Alan Carter, 'Humean nature', paper presented at the conference on 'Environmental Ethics', University of London, 5 December, 1997.

2 For some justification of this list, see Appendix A, below.

3 See *Die Grünen*, *Programme of the German Green Party* (London: Heretic Books, 1983).

4 It is, perhaps, not surprising that it was a feminist who wrote the seminal book arguing for participatory democracy: Carole Pateman, *Participation and Democratic Theory* (Cambridge: Cambridge University Press, 1970).

5 For example, see Vandana Shiva, *Staying Alive: Women, Ecology and Development* (London: Zed, 1988). Moreover, a sustainable society is surely one 'which is "reproductive" rather than simply "productive".' Chiah Heller, 'Toward a radical eco-feminism' in John Clark (ed.), *Renewing the Earth: The Promise of Social Ecology* (London: Green Print, 1990), p. 170. For a particularly attractive, degendered response to patriarchal values, see Val Plumwood, 'Women, humanity and nature', *Radical Philosophy* 48 (Spring 1988): 16–24.

6 Feminist opposition to nuclear weapons, for example, took a highly visible form at the women's peace camp at Greenham Common.

7 For an example of one such criticism, see Charlene Spretnak and Fritjof Capra, *Green Politics* (London: Paladin, 1985).

This notwithstanding, the socialist tradition has also contributed much to green thinking. The egalitarian stress on the need for redistribution in order to alleviate poverty and the demand for a global, internationalist perspective both have their roots in nineteenth-century socialism. However, some socialists, too, have expressed criticisms of the green movement. They have characterized it as, amongst other things, 'petit bourgeois radicalism'[8] concerned solely with middle-class issues that do not deal adequately with the problems faced by the proletariat.[9] For such socialists, greens are viewed as theoretically naive – especially those with anarchist inclinations – and it is frequently argued that the only remedy is to inject a large dose of Marxist theory into the green movement.

Nevertheless, anarchism, too, has contributed a great deal to green thinking. The stress on self-sufficiency and the insistence on decentralization[10] both have their roots in the nineteenth-century anarchist movement. However, anarchists have tended to be rather purist, frequently rejecting all compromise with the state, and, as a result, repeatedly denigrating the parliamentary tactics adopted by sections of the green movement. The concessions elected green politicians have made while in office have attracted particular criticism from anarchists, who have been especially scathing in their denunciations of '*Realos*',[11] whom they see as 'trying to turn their movement into a completely reformist parliamentary party.'[12] And the willingness of *Realos* to cooperate with social democrats has certainly incurred considerable hostility from anarchists.

Is it clear, then, that there *is* a distinctive green political theory, when greens seem merely to have borrowed values from earlier traditions? Unquestionably, one reason for the existence of tensions within the green movement is that these contributory traditions have often been highly antagonistic towards one another. Anarchists and Marxists, for example, have a long history of enmity. In addition,

8 See, for example, Klaus Eder, 'The "new social movements": moral crusades, political pressure groups, or social movements?', *Social Research*, Vol. 52, No. 4 (1985): 869–90.

9 This criticism is most famously expressed in H. M. Enzensberger, 'A critique of political ecology', *New Left Review* 84 (1974): 3–31.

10 For an enormously important and comprehensive defence of decentralization, see Kirkpatrick Sale, *Human Scale* (London: Secker and Warburg, 1980).

11 The '*Realos*' in *Die Grünen* claimed to be 'realists' by adopting what they considered to be a pragmatic approach, in contrast to the '*Fundis*', whom their opponents characterized as extreme fundamentalists refusing to compromise any of their beliefs.

12 Murray Bookchin, 'New social movements: the anarchic dimension' in David Goodway (ed.), *For Anarchism: History, Theory and Practice* (London: Routledge, 1989), p. 273. Bookchin is, undoubtedly, the most internationally famous eco-anarchist, and many of the central features of radical green thinking can be traced directly to his 1965 essay 'Ecology and revolutionary thought'. For example, consider the following passage: 'It cannot be emphasized too strongly that the anarchist concepts of a balanced community, a face-to-face democracy, a humanistic technology and a decentralized society – these rich libertarian concepts – are not only desirable, they are necessary. They belong not only to the great visions of [humanity's] future, they now constitute the preconditions for human survival.' Murray Bookchin, 'Ecology and revolutionary thought' reprinted in *Post-Scarcity Anarchism* (London: Wildwood House, 1974).

the difference between anarchist and Marxist political strategies parallels the division in the environmental movement between, what Tim O'Riordan has labelled, 'technocentric' and 'ecocentric' modes of thinking. 'Ecocentrism', according to O'Riordan, 'argues for low impact technology (but is not antitechnological); it decries bigness and impersonality in all forms (but especially in the city); and demands a code of behaviour that seeks permanence and stability based upon ecological principles of diversity and homeostasis.'[13] In contrast, 'technocentrism', in O'Riordan's view, 'is almost arrogant in its assumption that [humanity] is supremely able to understand and control events to suit [its] purposes.'[14]

One thing *is* clear, however: such conflicting traditions cannot easily be combined without the threat of contradictions emerging. Any cogent green political theory, if one can be devised, would have to be extremely judicious in its selection of elements drawn from often competing traditions if it is to be at all consistent. One cannot just help oneself randomly to parts of different political ideologies without running the very real risk of producing something which is incoherent. It is far too likely that such self-service, cafeteria politics would prove to be totally indigestible. What needs to be ascertained, then, is whether or not such diverse elements as those listed above – decentralization, participatory democracy, egalitarianism, self-sufficiency, alternative technology,[15] pacifism and internationalism – actually form the basis of a coherent political theory. Can they be clearly and cogently related? Or, alternatively, is radical green thinking little more than a random hotchpotch of inconsistent values?

I shall argue that a definite reply can be given: that green values are intimately related. Additionally, I shall attempt to show that the values radical greens espouse can be combined coherently in a quite distinctive way. If this is so, then green political theory is not just derivative; it offers an entirely new perspective. But if such an affirmative reply is to stand any chance of sounding convincing, we must return to a fundamental question in political theory: How are we to theorize the state – the current locus of concentrated political power? Except that now we must frame this question in what, today, seems to have become its most urgent form: How are we to theorize the behaviour of the state with respect to understanding the environmental threat towering before us?

13 Tim O'Riordan, *Environmentalism* (London: Pion, 1981), p. 1.

14 Ibid. For an example of a technocentric view, see Reiner Grundmann, *Marxism and Ecology* (Oxford: Clarendon, 1991).

15 The need for an alternative technology has been argued for by certain feminists, socialists and anarchists, though their visions of an alternative technology have not always been identical. See, for example, C. Thomas, 'Alternative technology: a feminist technology?' in Leonie Caldecott and Stephanie Leland (eds), *Reclaim the Earth: Women Speak out for Life on Earth* (London: The Women's Press, 1983), William Morris, *News from Nowhere* (London: Routledge and Kegan Paul, 1970), and Peter Kropotkin, *Fields, Factories and Workshops Tomorrow*, ed. Colin Ward (London: George Allen and Unwin, 1974).

6.2 An environmentally hazardous dynamic

A clue to how one might be able to link the state to severe environmental degradation – and likewise, a clue to how important it might be to expose such a linkage – is to be found in the tremendous acceleration of environmental problems that occurred during and immediately following the Second World War. According to Barry Commoner, writing in his path-breaking 1971 book *The Closing Circle*:

> Many pollutants were totally absent before World War II, having made their environmental debut in the war years: [photochemical] smog (first noticed in Los Angeles in 1943), [hu]man-made radioactive elements (first produced in the wartime atomic bomb project), DDT (widely used for the first time in 1944), detergents (which began to displace soap in 1946), synthetic plastics (which became a contributor to the rubbish problem only after the war).[16]

Is it a mere coincidence that numerous environmental problems (or, at least, what many now perceive as environmental problems) originated at the same time, and during war-time, at that?

It would seem not. The reason, it would appear, for the release into the environment of huge quantities of such potentially dangerous substances was the considerable expansion in output of new products required for the successful conduct of the war. Commoner:

> The last fifty years have seen a sweeping revolution in science, which has generated powerful changes in technology and in its application to industry, agriculture, transportation, and communication. World War II is a decisive turning point in this historical transition. The twenty-five years preceding the war is the main period of the sweeping modern revolution in basic science, especially in physics and chemistry, upon which so much of the new productive technology is based. In the approximate period of the war itself, ***under the pressure of military demands***, much of the new scientific knowledge was rapidly converted into new technologies and productive enterprises. Since the war, the technologies have rapidly transformed the nature of industrial and agricultural production. The period of World War II is, therefore, a great divide between the scientific revolution that preceded it and the technological revolution that followed it.[17]

16 Barry Commoner, *The Closing Circle: Nature, Man, Technology* (New York: Alfred Knopf, 1971), p. 128.

17 Ibid., p. 129. (Emphasis added.) C.f.: 'The countryside has been exploited for centuries and very little true wilderness now remains. For some deep ecologists this, by itself, would lead to condemnation even though human impact need not necessarily be destructive. The problem is that much modern farming *is* environmentally destructive. These modern agricultural practices date back to the Second World War when the development of intensive farming methods coincided with the desire for Britain to be self-sufficient in food.' Robert Garner, *Environmental Politics* (Hemel Hempstead: Harvester-Wheatsheaf, 1996), p. 157.

The conclusion one might therefore draw is that the period building up to the Second World War was one of frantic research into the scientific preconditions of the technologies that would be needed during the approaching conflict, while the war-time period itself was one where those technologies were developed and then marshalled at the fastest possible rate in order to aid the war-effort. This resulted in vast amounts of toxic materials being produced. And, as we noted in Chapter 1, it is precisely the sudden introduction of massive quantities of new substances into the environment that, in Commoner's view, causes it so much harm, for there is insufficient time for natural mechanisms to evolve that can incorporate those substances harmlessly into the ecosystem. All of this suggests that states' military requirements play a key role in ever-worsening environmental deterioration.

As the State-Primacy Theory, in its effort to explain the outcome of historical developments, assigns a central role to the state and its military requirements, it is not unlikely that it would be able to shed light on the underlying causes of the environmental threat. Given its emphasis on military competition, and given the apparent role of military competition in environmental degradation, the theory certainly appears well-placed to do so. Hence, if there is a causal mechanism driving us towards environmental destruction, perhaps the State-Primacy Theory can be employed in order to reveal it.

The State-Primacy Theory, it will be recalled, is premised upon the following abstract model: Ordinarily, those individuals who enjoy a dominant position within the structure of legal and political institutions select or stabilize economic relations that are especially suited to developing technology, the form and productivity of which support the development of the forces of 'defence'. And these defensive forces usually empower those who are dominant within the structure of legal and political institutions. Furthermore, it is the various forces of defence that ultimately preserve and enforce the relations of economic control – economic relations which, on this model, are also selected or stabilized because they are conducive to supporting the forces of defence by, for example, extracting the surplus upon which the defensive forces rely. (See Figure 4.1.)

Let us see how this abstract model could be thought to be instantiated in a modern, capitalist social formation. One not wholly implausible description might go something like this: a pseudo-representative, quasi-democratic[18] legisla-

18 For an account of how elitists have usurped the term 'democracy', which previously referred to what is now called 'direct democracy', see Anthony Arblaster, *Democracy* (Milton Keynes: Open University Press, 1987). And as Jane Mansbridge writes: 'Every American schoolchild knows that when you set up a democracy you elect representatives – in school, the student council; later, senators, representatives, councilmen, assemblymen, and aldermen. When you do not agree, you take a vote, and the majority rules. This combination of electoral representation, majority rule, and one-citizen/one-vote *is* democracy. Because this conception of democracy assumes that citizens' interests are in constant conflict, I have called it "adversary" democracy.' J. J. Mansbridge, *Beyond Adversary Democracy* (Chicago: University of Chicago Press, 1983), p. 3. However, as Mansbridge points out: 'Every step in this adversary process violates another, older understanding of democracy. In that older understanding, people who disagree do not vote; they reason together until they agree on the best answer. Nor do they

tive located within, and ostensibly at the head of, a massive, centralized, impersonal bureaucracy ordinarily acts so as to stabilize competitive, inegalitarian economic relations which develop 'non-convivial',[19] environmentally-damaging, 'hard'[20] technologies, for their productivity supports the (nationalistic and militaristic) coercive forces that empower the state as a whole. The technologies chosen thus serve the interests of the centralized, impersonal bureaucracy – as well as serving the interests of the dominant economic class, which benefits directly from the economic relations the bureaucracy chooses to stabilize. Moreover, the competitive, inegalitarian economic relations that are stabilized are ones which maximize the surplus available to the state, and thereby allow it to finance its weapons research and pay for its standing army, secret service and police (i.e., the coercive forces).

Thus, those state personnel who constitute the human element within the coercive forces have an interest in empowering the centralized bureaucracy because it possesses the institutional mechanisms required for obtaining, through taxation, a proportion of the wealth produced by the competitive, inegalitarian economic relations – a significant part of which going to the nationalistic and militaristic coercive forces. Hence, personnel organized as forces of coercion serve their own interests by enabling the state to preserve the inegalitarian relations of production it has chosen to stabilize, while the centralized bureaucracy serves its own interests by supporting economic relations which maximize the surplus available to it and to the coercive forces.[21]

The State-Primacy Model, with its political relations, political forces, economic relations and economic forces thus described, indicates an interrelational,

---

elect representatives to reason for them. They come together with their friends to find agreement. This democracy is consensual, based on common interest and equal respect. It is the democracy of face-to-face relations. Because it assumes that citizens have a single common interest, I have called it "unitary" democracy.' Ibid.

19 The application to technology of the term 'non-convivial' derives from Ivan Illich: 'a society, in which modern technologies serve politically interrelated individuals rather than managers, I will call "convivial". . . . I have chosen "convivial" as a technical term to designate a modern society of responsibly limited tools.' Ivan Illich, *Tools for Conviviality* (London: Fontana, 1975), p. 12.

20 The distinction between 'hard' and 'soft' technologies derives from Amory Lovins: 'There exists today a body of energy technologies that have certain specific features in common and that offer great technical, economic, and political attractions, yet for which there is no generic term. For lack of a more satisfactory term, I shall call them "soft" technologies: a textual description, intended to mean not vague, mushy, speculative, or ephemeral, but rather flexible, resilient, sustainable, and benign.' Amory B. Lovins, *Soft Energy Paths: Toward a Durable Peace* (New York: Harper and Row, 1979), p. 38.

21 Accordingly, the interest which the coercive forces have in empowering the legislative would surely be lessened were its intention to redirect the state's budget towards environmental or social programmes and away from defence expenditure. From this perspective, then, it is understandable that the Secret Service in Britain should have engaged in 'dirty tricks' campaigns against socialist politicians and even previous Labour governments. It can easily be argued, therefore, that elected environmentalists should expect to meet the same fate.

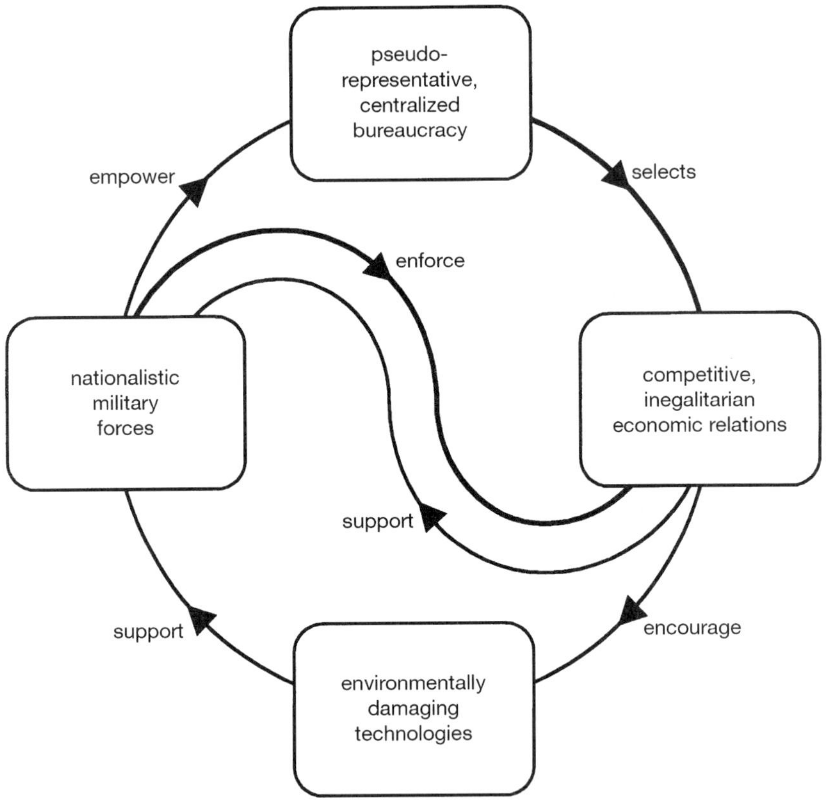

Figure 6.1 An environmentally hazardous dynamic

self-reinforcing ***dynamic***. (See Figure 6.1.) And it is clear that any such dynamic would be environmentally hazardous in the extreme. On this instantiation of the State-Primacy Model, actors located within a centralized bureaucracy, with sham representation and little real accountability, could be expected to enact and implement legislation in support of inegalitarian relations of production (that developed the productive forces) in order to benefit from the surplus and the technology thereby produced, both of which are essential for the development of the forces of coercion, which must be developed continually if the state is to remain competitive within an arms race.[22] Not only might such an arms race result

22 And this is not just a requirement from a western perspective. While he was a dissident in former East Germany, Rudolf Bahro argued: 'Above all . . . the measure of accumulation needed for socialism is not determined within the system itself, but rather in so-called economic competition with capitalism. . . . The arms race is the real issue at stake in "economic competition".' Rudolf Bahro, *The Alternative in Eastern Europe*, trans. D. Fernbach (London: New Left Books, 1978), p. 134.

in one state appearing to have developed a first-strike capability, which could force another state into launching a pre-emptive strike as its only 'defence', thereby precipitating a nuclear war – as environmentally catastrophic a scenario as can be imagined[23] – but also, and irrespective of whether or not it ever resulted in nuclear conflict, *the dynamic* described *demands ever-increasing productivity, entailing a high consumption of resources and an equally high output of pollution.*

Were the likely environmental consequences of such a dynamic not bad enough in themselves, they would serve also to reinforce the dynamic, spinning us into an ever-worsening spiral. For example, as the World Commission on Environment and Development (WCED) point out:

> Environmental stress is both a cause and an effect of political tension and military conflict. Nations have often fought to assert or resist control over raw materials, energy supplies, land, river basins, sea passages, and other key environmental resources. Such conflicts are likely to increase as these resources become scarcer and competition for them increases.[24]

What is more, such an environmentally hazardous dynamic would not require that any state actually has imperialist designs on another state or on its resources. The mere worry that some other state might have imperialist designs on one's territory or resources would be sufficient to drive the dynamic. In order to defend its territory against other states which it views as potential aggressors, the state needs to remain militarily competitive. And this need can be expected to shape the means of social control that are employed, the nature of the economic relations that are chosen, and the kind of technology that is developed. For example, technologies such as nuclear power, which provides plutonium for nuclear weapons, and which also facilitates centralized, authoritarian control, will tend to be preferred – as will the economic relations capable of producing such technologies. In short, the imperative motivating the dynamic would shape and leave its imprint on every one of its interrelating aspects. And each of those aspects would, as a result, present a serious danger to the environment.

Additionally, given a perceived need to remain militarily competitive, not only will the technologies that can be expected to be developed be designed for maximum productive output but also the economic relations that can be expected to be chosen will be as exploitative as practicable in order to maximize the state's revenue. Furthermore, the means of social control that can be expected to be employed will be in conformity with the state's military requirements. Consequently, such a dynamic can be assumed to have, of necessity, profoundly

23 See Jonathan Schell, *The Fate of the Earth* (London: Picador, 1982). And as the authors of the Brundtland Report exclaim: 'The likely consequences of nuclear wars make other threats to the environment pale into insignificance.' G. H. Brundtland *et al.*, *Our Common Future* (Oxford: Oxford University Press, 1987), p. 295.

24 Ibid., p. 290.

destructive consequences for people as well as for the planet. If any such dynamic were to obtain, then those concerned about the environmental threat facing humanity would simply have no alternative other than to attempt to undermine it.

For an indication of just how destructive any such dynamic would most likely be, consider its implications for industry and agriculture. By taxing the sale of commodities (as well as the various stages of their production and distribution), states can obtain revenue. Therefore, states have an interest in economic relations which maximize the output of commodities so that they can maximize their revenue. Hence, states might be expected to favour an economic system which forces producers to maximize their output in order to survive economically.

With respect to industrial goods, this would cash out in manufacturers finding themselves compelled to take measures to preserve their markets. And in order to avoid market saturation, they would need to build obsolescence into their products. If the public turned out not to be so stupid as to purchase badly made items that didn't last (for example, certain clothes), then they could, perhaps, be manipulated into throwing away perfectly good ones in order to keep pace with ever-changing, artificially induced fashions. The result would be a ridiculously wasteful use of resources (including human labour) and a needlessly high emission of pollutants.

With respect to agricultural produce, in order to survive in the marketplace, farmers would find themselves compelled to maximize their short-term output. This would require the massive use of inorganic fertilizers and pesticides, with the subsequent contamination of the soil (and of the environment in general), and the deployment of heavy farm machinery to save labour, with subsequent damage to the structure of the topsoil upon which our collective survival depends. Farmers would simply be unable to afford to farm in a way that preserved the soil – the very basis of their livelihoods – for if they were to go out of business as a result of failing to be profitable in the short term, then they would have no long-term future as farmers anyway.[25]

In short, according to the State-Primacy Theory, in order to meet state interests, the most demanding economic relations will inevitably have to be chosen and retained – relations which promote the development and employment of environmentally destructive technologies and productive practices. And this applies just as much to agriculture as to manufacturing industry. Most worryingly, current industrial and agricultural practices appear to provide corroboratory evidence that just such an environmentally hazardous dynamic obtains – a dynamic incorporating the most demanding of economic relations, which strenuously promote the development and use of (what most environmentalists view as) environmentally destructive technologies and productive practices.

25 It can also be argued that having to regard farming as a business, just like any other which must operate within the marketplace, undermines the norms of stewardship; and the resulting lack of care for the land will inevitably lead to a loss of soil fertility in the long term.

Furthermore, the seemingly destructive farming techniques practised today are obviously not a consequence of straightforward ignorance. Every British schoolchild is taught that one of the major agricultural innovations in history was the introduction of crop-rotation to prolong soil fertility. But where can one find the system of crop-rotation being practised today? All that one usually sees in the British countryside is field after field of monoculture. Even worse, what one often sees is field after field of winter wheat, which, because of the time of year it is planted, leaves the soil highly vulnerable to soil erosion – a potential ecological disaster which currently seems to be unfolding on an unprecedented scale. But if farmers do not plant winter wheat, if, instead, they try to preserve their soil, then they run the very real risk of going bankrupt. In other words, it is not ignorance, but the structure of economic relations, stabilized by the state, which seems to be what *forces* farmers to act as they do; and they appear to do so against their own better judgement. And there must be little doubt that any agricultural system geared to the short-term maximization of output will eventually prove to be an ecological catastrophe.

Given the protracted military competition in Europe in the first half of the twentieth-century, given the prolonged military competition between the Western powers and the Soviet Bloc in the second half of the twentieth century, and given the continued military escalation in much of the Third World, the State-Primacy Theory is certainly not wholly implausible. But in the modern world, the State-Primacy Theory would seem inevitably to cash out into an environmentally hazardous dynamic. Given the major problems which environmentalists have described (some of which were listed in Chapter 1, above), and given that their apparent causes seem to corroborate the claim that just such a dynamic obtains, then there is reason to conclude that ***it is precisely the environmentally hazardous dynamic, as portrayed in Figure 6.1, which has shaped recent history and brought us to the brink of eco-catastrophe.***

6.2.1 ***State-Primacy and the Development Thesis***

Interestingly, focusing upon the development of (what would appear to be) environmentally destructive industrial and agricultural technologies brings to the fore a significant difference between the State-Primacy Theory and the Techno-Primacy Theory defended by G. A. Cohen. It will be recalled from Chapter 2, above, that the second of Cohen's two principal theses – the Development Thesis – asserts that the productive forces tend to develop through history. The Development Thesis is not too controversial unless interpreted in a certain way, for clearly there appears to have been a *tendency* overall for the productive forces to develop over time, even if there have been periods in history when there was little, if any, technological 'progress'.

The problem arises because, as Cohen admits, the elements within his Techno-Primacy Model do not, on their own, account for the Development Thesis. As was discussed in Chapter 4, above, revolution is to be explained, according to Marx's theory of history, by the fettering of the development of the productive forces by the prevailing economic relations. But, according to Cohen, those prevailing economic relations cannot themselves be what cause the technological development which 'bursts asunder' the economic structure. Some external factor or factors must drive technological development beyond its present economic constraints. Hence, in Cohen's view, exogenous factors – rationality, scarcity and inventiveness – have to be added to supplement the model in order to underpin the Development Thesis. (See Figure 6.2.)

But this is likely to lead to the Development Thesis being interpreted in a way that is more than a little contentious. If technology develops because rational individuals are seeking to solve the problem of scarcity, then the technology that is developed is likely to be viewed, as many Marxists do indeed view it, as socially and politically neutral. If technology is developed in order to meet scarcity, then if it is not behaving as a benign technology, it must, on such an account, be because of the social relations within which it is employed. In short, if human rationality and the desire to avoid scarcity are the motivations behind technological 'progress', then it would appear that most technological development can safely be assumed to be appropriate to satisfying human needs in general. In other words, when situated within Cohen's model, the Development Thesis is likely to be so construed that the possible social and political implications of certain directions that technological 'progress' might take will tend to be downplayed.[26]

The State-Primacy Model, when it is considered to be instantiated in the environmentally hazardous dynamic of Figure 6.1, need involve no such assumptions, for such a dynamic could be propelled internally. To take one possibility: Those who are oppressed or exploited might develop means of resistance, and the state, in response, might need to develop more sophisticated mechanisms of repression, which might then lead to novel forms of resistance, which might then demand even more refined techniques of social control, and so on. The outcome could easily be an increasingly expensive and exceedingly vicious circle. Or, to purchase continuing support and thereby avoid the need for repressive measures, the state might encourage the production of sweeter and sweeter bread and evermore lavish circuses. And keeping pace with the expectations such a policy would engender could well be sufficient to motivate the dynamic.

But the usual motivation for the environmentally hazardous dynamic would be that the military development of another state was viewed as a threat. This means that the State-Primacy Theory ordinarily assumes a complex system comprising a dual dynamic – where one state is locked in its own dynamic because of the parallel dynamic the competing state is locked within. Both dynamics roll on with reference to each other. (See Figure 6.3.)

26 That Cohen has a rather contentious view of technological development is clear from the following observation by André Gorz: 'Nuclear energy, for example – whether "capitalist" or "socialist" – presupposes and imposes a centralized, hierarchical, police-dominated society.' André Gorz, *Ecology as Politics*, trans. P. Vigderman and J. Cloud (London: Pluto, 1980), p. 19. If Gorz is correct, then the claim that technology is socially and politically neutral seems highly implausible.

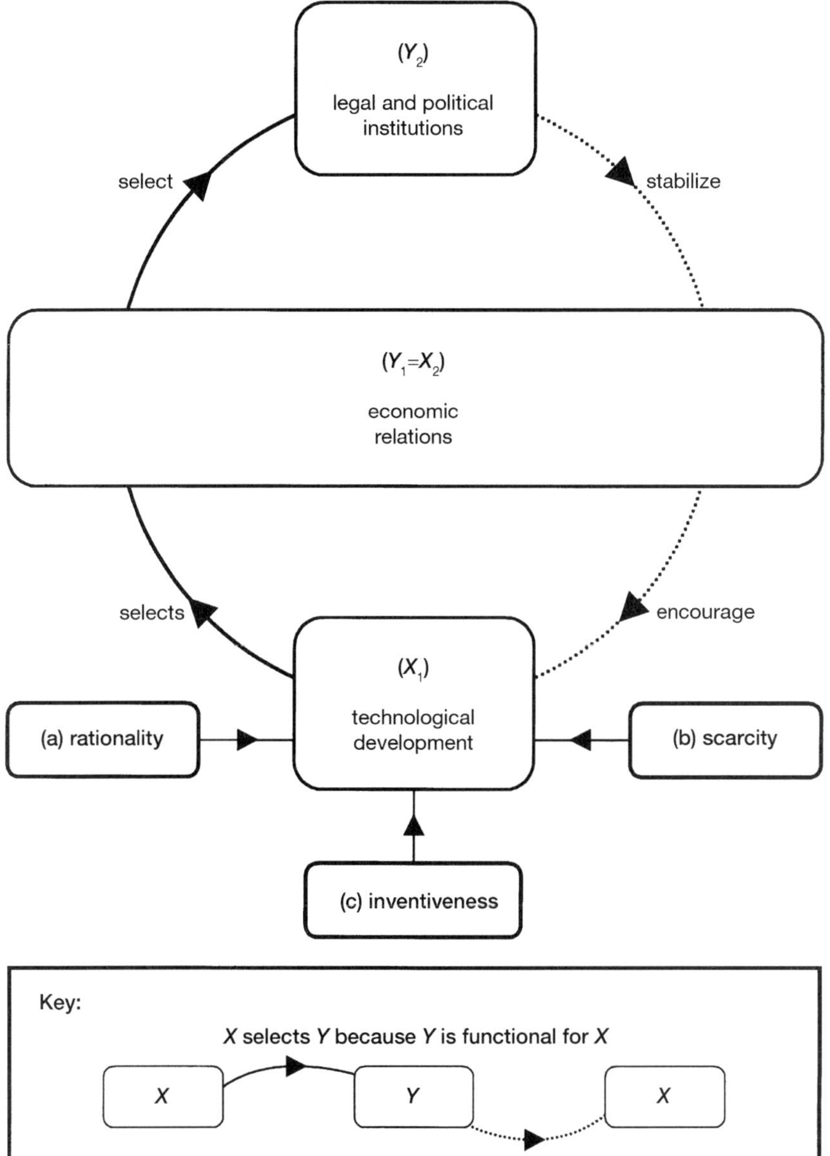

Figure 6.2 A Marxist model with exogenous factors

From the perspective of the State-Primacy Theory, then, all of the motivation that explains the Development Thesis is endogenous to this dual system. The mass of the people within an advanced society facing a situation of scarcity (and by that Cohen means working longer than they would otherwise choose to) is not required as an exogenous factor, for military competition will suffice to drive

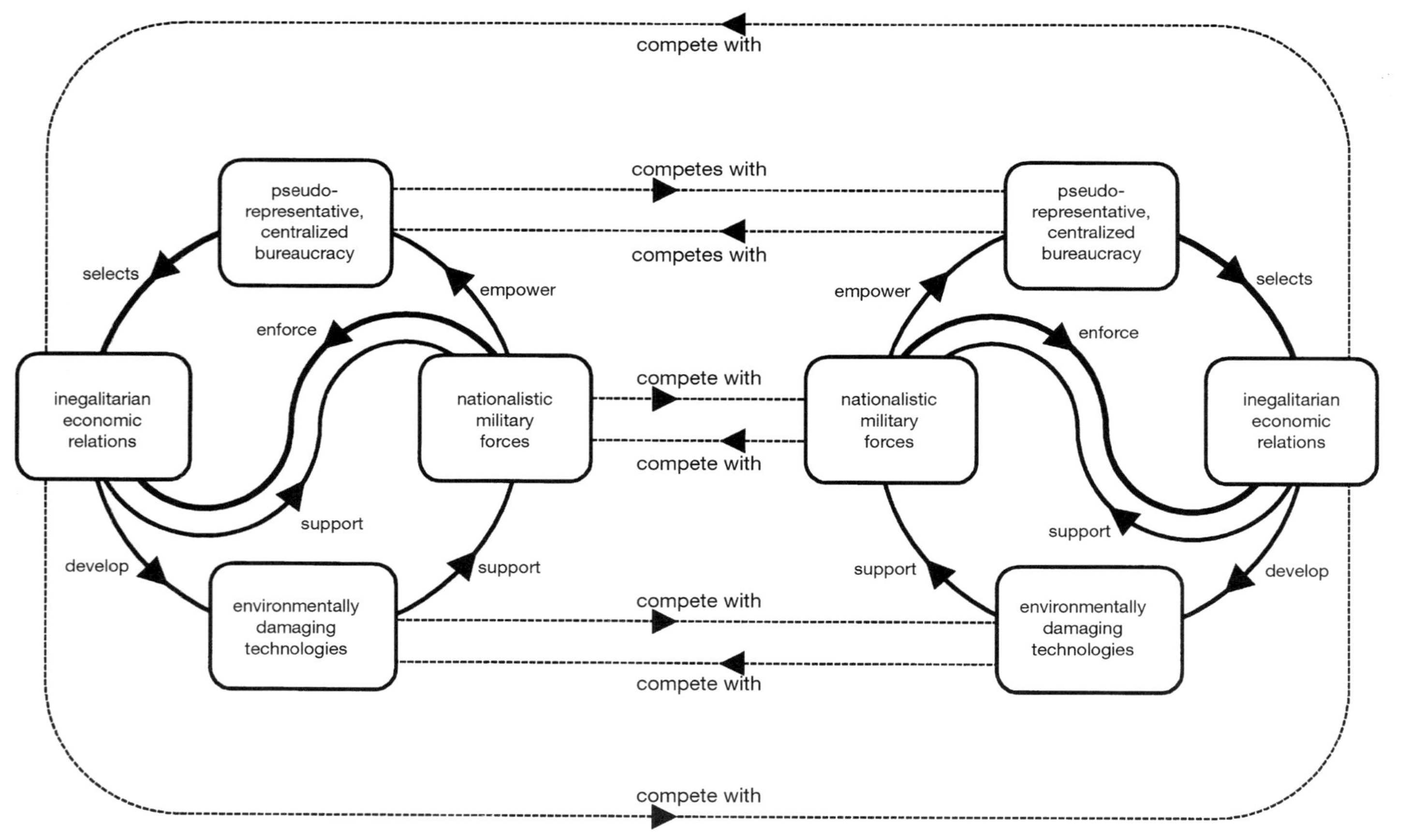

Figure 6.3 An endogenously motivated dual dynamic

technological development – even to drive it 'through' fettering economic relations. Hence, from the standpoint of the State-Primacy Theory, there is no need to assume that the technology developed is rational for meeting the scarcity which individuals within a society face. One need only assume that in some direct or indirect way the technology chosen ultimately serves the perceived interests of the state.

So, a crucial difference between the State-Primacy Theory and the Techno-Primacy Theory is that, according to the latter, the technological development which occurs is rational for meeting scarcity; whereas the State-Primacy Theory indicates that a very different kind of technology might develop – one that satisfies state interests without necessarily being rational for meeting scarcity at all. Of course, according to the State-Primacy Theory, labour-saving technology is likely to be introduced; but not because the workers would rather work less (if that is their preference), nor because they experience scarcity in some other way. Rather, it is because labour-saving technology makes agriculture and industry more profitable and thereby offers the possibility of greater revenue to the state. Which theory, then, gives the most plausible interpretation of the Development Thesis?

In attempting to decide between these two theoretical approaches, let us consider, for example, nuclear power as opposed to wave energy: As a result of newspaper and television exposés, it is now common knowledge in Britain that a wave-energy device (Salter's Duck) was known to be economic, and yet the figures were misreported so that it appeared uneconomic. This, it has been claimed, was to prevent resources being diverted towards alternative technology and away from nuclear power. At the same time, the books were cooked so that the highly uneconomic nuclear power programme was made to appear economic (for example, by not factoring in the massive de-commissioning costs nuclear power stations will eventually incur).

This sort of manipulation in order to direct research funding from cost-effective projects to uneconomic ones is certainly not rational with respect to meeting scarcity, never mind (given the environmental threat which nuclear power is widely held to pose) with respect to safeguarding the environment for future welfare. It is, on the other hand, rational with respect to meeting the needs of future warfare. What the nuclear power programme was undoubtedly rational with respect to was the provision of weapons-grade plutonium for nuclear weapons[27] (as well as undermining the economic and political power of the mineworkers). Such support for the nuclear programme seems to make no sense at all on the Techno-Primacy Theory. But it is perfectly comprehensible on the

27 It is also fairly common knowledge in Britain that the first two nuclear reactors constructed for the so-called 'Atoms for Peace' programme never provided electricity to the general public. But, it has been alleged, they did provide fissile material for nuclear weapons. What about nuclear fusion as opposed to fission, though? Surely fusion is a peaceful technology? Interestingly, R. Gillette, in *Science*, 'reports that the US nuclear fusion program is geared primarily to military needs, not to the peaceful use of abundant energy.' Cited in O'Riordan, *Environmentalism*, p. 22.

State-Primacy Theory.[28] Moreover, it appears to provide clear corroboration for the environmentally hazardous dynamic, for state interests appear to have resulted in a preference for the environmentally hazardous over the environmentally benign.

Of course, it might be objected that what is being argued here implies an extremely uncharitable view of how states behave. Modern western states, with the exception of 'aberrant' examples (such as Thatcher's Britain), are more than happy to provide all sorts of welfare services for their citizens, the objector might continue.

But consider the following observation: 'as army recruitment at the time of the Boer War demonstrated, many young working-class males were not even fit and healthy enough to offer their lives in the service of their country, for thousands had to be turned away on grounds of ill-health'.[29] Thus, John Dearlove and Peter Saunders conclude: 'the introduction of school meals in 1906 . . . was largely a response to the horrifying evidence of working-class malnutrition thrown up by recruitment for the Boer War.'[30] Was this out of concern for the poor condition of the working class, or out of concern for the quality of future coercive and economic labour-power? Perhaps some state actors *are* concerned about the condition of the poor. But, it could be argued, states are far more likely to act when it is their own interests that are at stake. It can thus be argued that when the condition of the poor is improved, it is usually when that improvement is not only in the interests of the impoverished but also in conformity with state interests. This would be unproblematic, of course, if the interests of the poor and those of their states always corresponded. But there is ample reason to think that this is not the case. And if state interests *do* diverge significantly from those of the mass of the world's population, it ought to be a matter of grave concern.

So, is there a convergence or a divergence of interests between states and the

28 There is a further reason for preferring the State-Primacy Theory. Earlier, I remarked that the Development Thesis, in describing a *tendency* for the productive forces to develop, is less controversial than it would otherwise have been, for although there have been periods when technology 'progressed' little, if at all, there does appear to have been an overall tendency for technological development to have taken place. However, cases of a society becoming technologically stagnant while another society, formerly less advanced, became the technological 'torch-bearer', as it were, while supporting the claim that there has been a tendency through history for the forces of production to develop, do, nevertheless, seem to pose something a problem for the Techno-Primacy Theory. The State-Primacy Theory, on the other hand, appears to face no insurmountable difficulty in explaining 'relay-race' developments. Because of the requirements imposed by military competition, a state in a position to select the least fettering economic relations will do so, even if its current technology is less advanced than another state. In due course, it may then become the economically and militarily dominant one. And then, in order to explain the nature of the set of economic relations which come to prevail, the Darwinian feature of the State-Primacy Theory can be deployed. See Section 4.3.1.1, above.

29 John Dearlove and Peter Saunders, *Introduction to British Politics: Analyzing a Capitalist Democracy* (Cambridge: Polity, 1984), p. 302.

30 Ibid., p. 306.

mass of the world's population? According to the State-Primacy Theory, states select economic relations which develop the economic forces, for that is functional for 'defensive development'. However, this doesn't mean that states should be expected to concentrate solely on what is indirectly required for developing the means of coercion. Given the assumptions which the State-Primacy Theory is premised upon, states would, at times, also have an interest in developing political (or coercive) labour-power directly. Consequently, the following observation might be thought to provide some support for this aspect of the theory:

> the advocates of a large population have not uncommonly seen in such a population the source of a nation's 'greatness', defined in military terms. This brings out one difficulty in the concept of an optimum population. It is always optimal *in respect of some particular end*; it maximizes some specific property. The optimum economic population – the population which gives the highest per capita real income – will certainly not coincide with the population which gives a country its maximum power or the leaders of that country *their* maximum power. For the maintenance of power requires resources to be set aside for that purpose – an army, armaments – which will raise the numbers of the population necessary to produce any particular distributable income. That is why expansionist powers are commonly pro-natalist.[31]

It would seem that this potential problem is not confined to poor countries. There are grounds for thinking that it also applies to the historical development of Britain. For example, as Tim O'Riordan reminds us: 'the (first) British census of 1801 revealed an alarmingly higher population than was anticipated', which, O'Riordan thinks, should have surprised no one 'as successive British governments had consistently encouraged population growth so that they could open up their colonies, man their armies, combat the population explosion in France, and have an abundant reservoir of low-cost labour.'[32]

Sadly, it would seem that this is not a problem which is confined to the past, either, for as the Brandt Report bemoans: 'There are still countries which limit rather than promote access to family planning and whose population growth is believed to be a source of national or ethnic strength.'[33] In other words, even the Brandt Report – hardly a radical document – expresses the view that states often promote population growth because it is functional for meeting state interests.

Unfortunately, population growth will inevitably lead to greater poverty in a world of finite resources and increasing environmental devastation, or so one must assume. Environmental impact is a function of the form and level of

31 John Passmore, *Man's Responsibility for Nature: Ecological Problems and Western Traditions* (London: Duckworth, 1980), p. 134.
32 O'Riordan, *Environmentalism*, p. 41.
33 Willy Brandt *et al.*, *North–South: A Programme for Survival* (London: Pan, 1980), p. 107.

production, the form and level of consumption, and the size and make-up of the population. Clearly, if states have an interest in developing production, in furthering consumption (that can be taxed) and in increasing the size of the population (in order to expand both political and economic labour-power), then their interests are profoundly anti-ecological. And in the long-run, ecological damage will surely harm people. In short, there are very strong grounds for believing that the interests of states and those of the mass of the world's population most certainly do not correspond.

6.2.2 State-primacy and ideology

Thus far I have focused upon ways in which economic relations and technological development can be regarded as being functional for the state. But there are other potentially functional relationships which an expanded State-Primacy Theory could evoke. Such a theory could claim, for example, that a state will select *ideological apparatuses* that are functional for serving its interests. These might comprise a particular institutionalized religion, certain favoured organs of mass media and a specific kind of educational system.

Is there any reason to think that states select ideological apparatuses which are functional for meeting their interests? Consider the educational system in Britain. As Dearlove and Saunders reveal:

> beneath the formal curriculum of science, geography and religious instruction there is a 'hidden curriculum' which never appears on the timetable but is nonetheless significant for that. What we learn in school – though are rarely taught – is how to sit still, to speak when addressed, to stand in rows, to divide our time into 'work' and 'play' or 'free time', to be punctual, to treat learning as a means to an end (i.e. passing an examination), to control our exuberancy and channel our aggression, to respect authority, to be passive, to be subordinate. When most of us at 16 come to exchange our school uniform for blue overalls or a grey suit, and to exchange our school desk for an office desk or a factory bench, we are already well equipped with all the unwritten yet crucial knowledge which we are required to have if the economic system and the social order . . . are not to crumble under the strain of an undisciplined workforce and an active citizenry.[34]

And as they conclude:

> It really does not need 11 years to teach most of the elementary maths, the smattering of geography and the rudimentary English grammar with which we eventually pass out of school, but it needs all of 11 years to mould individuals into a largely unthinking and non-reflexive orientation to the world

34 Dearlove and Saunders, *Introduction to British Politics*, p. 348.

> around them in which the present mode of organizing our society is taken as given.[35]

Certainly, if the real purpose of the educational system is not to learn facts nor to develop the powers of critical thinking but, rather, to learn docility and obedience, then it would certainly appear to be just the kind of ideological apparatus the state requires if it is to retain power.

According to the State-Primacy Theory, then, and if it is given the widest of construals, states tend to select for stabilization and further development whatever accords, directly or indirectly, with their interests. If the promotion among the population of the ideology of unquestioned discipline and passivity enables the state to retain control and to keep the labour force at work, then it is in the interests of the state to establish and maintain the institutions that can promote such an idcology. And if the promotion of the ideology of consumerism is functional for developing the purchasing power and the correlatively high productive output which, through taxation, maximizes state revenues, then states have an interest in promoting that ideology. In other words, states have a very real interest in promoting attitudes and modes of behaviour that are likely to be environmentally disastrous in their effects.

Now, from the perspective of such a wide reading of the State-Primacy Theory, it could be argued that ideology is able to operate even more insidiously than is often realized. Take, for example, one particular ideological tool which appears to be both functional for states and ecologically disastrous. There are many possible indicators that could be employed to measure social well-being or improvements in the quality of life. However, as Michael Redclift declares: 'The crudest, and most familiar, indicator of development is gross national product (GNP).'[36] But for environmentalists, 'GNP is a particularly inadequate guide to development since it treats sustainable and unsustainable production alike and compounds the error by including the costs of unsustainable economic activity on the credit side, while largely ignoring processes of recycling and energy conversion which do not lead to the production of goods or marketable services.'[37]

Herman Daly gives a number of examples of how inappropriate a measure GNP is for those concerned either about the condition of the planet or about its people: 'Is the water table falling? Dig deeper wells, build bigger pumps, and up goes GNP! Mines depleted? Build more expensive refineries to process lower grade ores, and up goes GNP! Soil depleted? Produce more fertilizer, etc.'[38] Not surprisingly, then, environmentalists often denounce mainstream economists for their

35 Ibid.

36 Michael Redclift, *Sustainable Development: Exploring the Contradictions* (London: Routledge, 1987), p. 15.

37 Ibid., p. 16.

38 Herman E. Daly, 'The steady-state economy: toward a political economy of biophysical equilibrium and moral growth' in Herman E. Daly (ed.), *Toward a Steady-State Economy* (San Francisco: W. H. Freeman, 1973), p. 150.

preoccupation with GNP. What is more, environmentalists often talk as if GNP is simply an irrational measure that intelligent people should have more sense than to use. But is it really an irrational measure? GNP can be argued to be a *very* rational indicator. The problem is what it is rational for.

GNP and GDP (gross domestic product) form the basis of the United Nations System of National Accounts (UNSNA), the basic concepts of which have remained unchanged since 1953. The person mainly responsible for developing UNSNA was Sir Richard Stone, who obtained the Nobel Prize in Economics in 1984 in recognition. Stone was asked by John Maynard Keynes to join him in the British Treasury shortly after the outbreak of World War II, and they jointly wrote a paper entitled 'The national income and expenditure of the United Kingdom, and how to pay for the war'. According to Marylin Waring, this paper 'formed the foundation of Stone's further work, during peacetime, to develop the uniform accounting system subsequently adopted by the United Nations.'[39] Note, as Waring is at pains to stress: this uniform method of accounting was 'developed to measure the national income *of a country at war*'.[40]

Moreover, in 1941, Milton Gilbert became chief of the National Income Division of the US Department of Commerce, and 'strongly supported the use of GNP as the *proper measure in analyzing the economic relationship between defence expenditures and total output*'.[41] in a paper that was 'the first, clear, published statement of Gross National Product'.[42] As Waring, a former member of the New Zealand Parliament, comments: 'national income estimates everywhere continue, to this day, to be an assessment of *how to pay for the war*.'[43]

GNP, then, is not a completely irrational measure, after all. It is a measure originally designed to serve certain state purposes. If someone builds a block of flats, GNP rises. If someone then knocks them down before anyone has lived in them, GNP rises further. This might *appear* an utterly irrational indicator. But if a state is primarily interested in taxing economic activity, then GNP is, in actual fact, a rational instrument for it to use. The state can tax the builders, and then it can tax the demolition workers. In other words, GNP is an indicator of the government's access to revenue. It is a concept designed from the outset to enable the state 'to pay for the war'. And the ideological advantage to the state of selling 'GNP' as a measure of a society's well-being or level of development should be obvious.

It can thus be argued that when mainstream political parties advocate an increase in GNP, their whole conceptual apparatus confines them within the environmentally hazardous dynamic of Figure 6.1 to a degree that they are not even aware of. In other words, they are more subtly, yet more centrally, trapped in

39 Marylin Waring, *If Women Counted: A New Feminist Economics* (London: Macmillan, 1989), pp. 54–5.
40 Ibid., p. 55.
41 Ibid., p. 56.
42 Ibid., pp. 55–6.
43 Ibid., pp. 56–7.

the dynamic than they would ever dream. And in furthering discourse organized around the concept 'GNP', the state would be furthering its military interests. On this argument, the pursuit of state interests results in a society-wide preoccupation with 'growth' defined in terms of GNP, and the prime consequence of this, it can further be argued, is environmental degradation on an almost unimaginable scale. The needs of the state would thus be met at the expense of both the mass of the world's people and their environment.

In short, according the State-Primacy Theory in its widest form, when the state selects economic relations, or ideological apparatuses, or forms of acceptable behaviour, it selects what is functional for it, even though what is selected is far from what is functional for the preservation of the environment. Hence, in the modern world, the State-Primacy Theory can be assumed invariably to cash out into the environmentally hazardous dynamic portrayed in Figure 6.1. Moreover, because states are usually in military and economic competition with some state or other, then, from the standpoint of this theory, they can be seen to be *driven* to take courses of action that are functional for their military and economic needs, while being severely dysfunctional for the ecosphere and, in the last resort, for every human and non-human animal who depends, or who will come to depend, upon it.

6.2.3 *State-primacy and the superpowers*

The State-Primacy Theory, if it succeeds in accurately depicting the most important causal relationships propelling various developments in the modern world, thus reveals the state to be centrally implicated in an environmentally hazardous dynamic – a dynamic with potentially catastrophic consequences of global significance. But one fairly obvious objection that might be raised against buying into this account is that states in Europe seem to be uniting under a federal system which is reducing their individual autonomy; and, furthermore, the European Parliament has even succeeded in passing some environmentally benign legislation.

However, the actual reality is not necessarily incompatible with the State-Primacy Theory, nor does it entail that we ought to conclude that an erstwhile environmentally hazardous dynamic has since subsided. Most of the states in the European Union formerly had empires, which, by and large, they regret having lost. Britain and France are nuclear powers, while Germany, suffering constraints on its military development following its defeat in the Second World War, possesses a large army. But European states, yearning after their past 'glory', can no longer, on their own, remain militarily competitive with the two major powers: the United States and Russia. Consequently, it is not irrational for European states to unite, at the cost of their sovereignty, in order to form a new superpower. However, it can be argued that this would be a second-best strategy for many leading personnel in independent states. Hence, from the standpoint of the State-Primacy Theory, it is not surprising that the centralization of political power within the European Union has been resisted and that 'The Union' still lacks any united military force, with Britain and France pursuing their own 'independent' nuclear policies.

Rather than military and political union, what has been far easier to pursue for most member states is a measure of economic union. And this is consistent with the State-Primacy Theory. For it can be argued that the decline in the military competitiveness of most European states has proceeded in large part because of a decline in their economic competitiveness. And in order to improve comparatively the economies of the European countries, collective measures against the major economic powers – the United States and Japan – have been sought. Thus, by providing the possibility of greater revenue to the European states, an improved European economy increases their independent power; whereas political union, while increasing their collective power against the superpowers, decreases the individual power of the majority of existing state agents. Thus, from the perspective offered by the State-Primacy Theory, it should come as no surprise that moves towards economic union have developed at a greater pace and with less resistance than the genuine surrender of state sovereignty within a federal European superstate.

Moreover, while the European Parliament has succeeded in passing some environmental legislation (which, given the apparent extent of the current global predicament, most environmentalists would regard as barely cosmetic), this has been constrained by the interests of individual states and, at best, half-heartedly enacted in member countries – Britain, having simultaneously the most extreme and anachronistic military pretensions, being one of the major culprits. But what might be thought to reveal the European Union, incontrovertibly, to be still enmeshed within the environmentally hazardous dynamic of Figure 6.1 is its ecologically-disastrous Common Agricultural Policy. This particular policy, with its heavy emphasis on intensive farming practices (arising from the interests member states appear to have in over-production), and with its highly wasteful, bureaucratically-imposed standardization (resulting from administrative centralization), has, in its overall effects, been far more environmentally damaging than European environmental legislation has been benign. Or so many environmentalists would claim.

However, mention of the superpowers might give rise to another fairly obvious objection against the State-Primacy Theory: namely, do not recent developments in relations between the two major powers vitiate any analysis suggested by the theory? Do these developments not indicate that states are more benign than the theory presumes? And do these developments not show that, even if there was an environmentally hazardous dynamic once, we have now escaped from it?

Yet consider the following: What if two militarily competing states were to select different relations of economic control, and one set of relations turned out to be more productive than the other? Given the processes described by the State-Primacy Theory, the state with the less productive economic relations, if it is it to remain militarily competitive, would have to select more efficient relations of production, divert an ever-increasing proportion of its society's wealth to military expenditure or attempt to decelerate the arms race. The Soviet Union, in its dying breath, seems to have attempted to pursue all three courses simultaneously. Hence, it can be argued that its behaviour was not, in actual fact, inconsistent with the State-Primacy Theory. Rather, it provides the theory with further corroboration.

Moreover, although the United States appears to have won the arms race because of its more powerful economy, the cost seems to have been an unsustainable burden on that economy. Just consider the extent of this burden:

> The US military budget . . . is larger than the GNPs of all but eight countries in the world. (The budget of the US Department of Defence is the largest centrally planned economy outside the [former] Soviet Union.) In 1986, the Pentagon was spending nearly \$1 billion a day, \$41 million an hour, \$700,000 a minute. This statistic does not include expenditure for the manufacture of nuclear fuel and all things nuclear, which in the United States is paid for by the Department of Energy.[44]

Between 1980 and 1985 the United States' national debt doubled, and, it has been claimed, this was 'due more to the growth in military expenditures than to any other factor'.[45] It is not surprising, then, given the cost of military competition with the former Soviet Union, that the United States should have entertained a new détente. As Waring observed just prior to the Eastern Bloc's disintegration: '*Both of the superpowers*, the United States and the Soviet Union, devote twice the amount of public money to weapons research as they spend on research for all civilian needs combined.'[46]

Nevertheless, the collapse of the Soviet Union did not mean an abandonment of weapons research. For example, James Sterba informs us that 'the United States . . . is still spending \$3.8 billion on SDI (Strategic Defense Initiative) even after the demise of the Soviet Union.'[47] Moreover, it has been estimated, annual global military expenditure is in excess of \$1,000 billion,[48] with more still being spent per capita on armaments than 'on food, water, shelter, health, education, or ecosystem protection'.[49] Furthermore, a temporary deceleration of the arms race

44 Ibid., p. 9.

45 Ibid., p. 169.

46 Ibid., p. 168.

47 James P. Sterba, 'Introduction' in *Earth Ethics: Environmental Ethics, Animal Rights, and Practical Applications* (New Jersey: Prentice-Hall, 1995), p. 14.

48 Brundtland *et al.*, *Our Common Future*, p. 7.

49 Waring, *If Women Counted*, p. 167. And as one British politician has noted: 'in 1980 the per capita military expenditure in developing countries was nearly three times the per capita expenditure on health. . . .' Simon Hughes, 'The environmental crisis' in Felix Dodds (ed.), *Into the Twenty-First Century: An Agenda for Political Re-alignment* (Basingstoke: Green Print, 1988), p. 72. The opportunity costs of military research are even more disturbing: 'Half a million scientists are employed on weapons research world-wide, and they account for around half of all research and development expenditure. This exceeds the total combined spending on developing technologies for new energy sources, improving human health, raising agricultural productivity, and controlling pollution.' Brundtland *et al.*, *Our Common Future*, p. 298.

while the economies of the major powers recovered would provide no evidence for the cessation of an environmentally hazardous dynamic.[50] More disconcertingly, it remains a distinct possibility that the Russian military might reject the present road their government is taking and stage a coup d'état. Alternatively, in order to remain in power, the future Russian leadership might transform their policies into those more in line with the military's liking. Either possibility could result in an unprecedented escalation of the arms race. Worse still, the possibility of conflict between the nuclear-armed former Soviet territories, or their becoming implicated in further nuclear proliferation, could be thought to constitute a menacing expansion of the environmentally hazardous dynamic. It is not surprising, therefore, that faced with such possibilities, some western states (most notably Thatcher's Britain, with its insistence on going ahead with Trident) should have refused to participate in any serious disarmament, and thereby, it can thus be argued, have continued to fuel the dynamic.

6.2.4 Inhibiting the environmentally hazardous dynamic

We have good reason, therefore, to take the State-Primacy Theory seriously, and no conclusive reason, it would seem, for doubting that we are trapped within the environmentally hazardous dynamic represented in Figure 6.1 – a dynamic which the theory implies.

However, although the State-Primacy Theory has allowed the environmentally hazardous dynamic to be identified, the specific set of interrelationships the theory describes might only constitute a sufficient condition and *not a necessary condition* for the environmentally hazardous dynamic. In fact, thus far, I have placed considerable emphasis on the importance of the state because, it can be argued, certain previous theorists have over-emphasized economic factors. In short, it can be argued that before a more balanced view could be obtained, we first needed to redirect our attention towards the role that the state may well play in the environmental crises seemingly before us.[51] And if the State-Primacy Theory constitutes a sufficient rather than a necessary condition for the environmentally hazardous dynamic, then there is greater reason for considering ourselves trapped within the dynamic than there is for accepting the State-Primacy

50 It should also be noted that the countries which were prevented, following the Second World War, from devoting comparable proportionate expenditures to military needs have since been able to develop the economies most capable of supporting their future military requirements – namely, Japan and Germany. And it is ironic that this is precisely *because* they were temporarily relieved from the drain such expenditure would otherwise have imposed on their economies,

51 C.f.: 'Marx and I are ourselves partly to blame for the fact that the younger people sometimes lay more stress on the economic side than is due to it. We had to emphasize the main principle vis-à-vis our adversaries, who denied it, and we had not always the time, the place or the opportunity to give their due to the other elements involved in the interaction.' Frederick Engels to J. Bloch, 21 September 1890, in Karl Marx and Frederick Engels, *Selected Works in One Volume* (London: Lawrence and Wishart, 1970).

Theory, because the rejection of the theory would not require the abandonment of the belief that we are entrapped within the environmentally hazardous dynamic.[52]

Now, it is usually considered rational to maximize expected utility – to weigh the benefits multiplied by the probability of enjoying them against the costs multiplied by the probability of incurring them. For example, on this conception of rationality, it is irrational to pursue a possible benefit that one was unlikely to enjoy rather than a similar benefit one stood a greater chance of gaining. Likewise, it is irrational to pursue a possible benefit in preference to a greater benefit that one has an equal chance of enjoying. How rational it is to pursue a possible benefit or to avoid a possible cost will thus depend upon its probability and its magnitude. It is therefore rational to avoid a very great cost, even if there is some doubt about whether or not it will be incurred.[53] But *eco-catastrophe is a cost of the greatest magnitude*. It could well result in our collective suicide. Thus, only the *certainty* that we are not en route to it would make it collectively rational not to take steps to avoid it.[54]

If, then, we *are* presently confined within the environmentally hazardous dynamic portrayed in Figure 6.1 (and everything we have considered up until now strongly points in that direction), it is imperative that it be prevented from driving us collectively towards our own suicide. But even if some doubt remains concerning our entrapment within such a dynamic, the possibility that we are so entrapped, combined with the extreme magnitude of the costs of remaining within such a dynamic, makes it collectively rational to behave as if we *are* confined within the dynamic, as well as making it collectively rational to do what would be necessary to escape from it or, at the very least, to slow it down considerably. More to the point, collectively, it would be highly irrational to act as if we were not trapped within the dynamic and continue with business as usual.

How, though, might such an environmentally hazardous dynamic – a dynamic seemingly capable of propelling us towards oblivion – be inhibited? If, as seems highly likely, we are currently entrapped within this suicidal dynamic, or if, as the above argument suggests, it would, in any case, be collectively rational for us to behave *as if* we were confined within it, then the question of how we might escape from the dynamic becomes, without a shadow of a doubt, by far the most important question facing humanity today. It is to this crucial question that I now turn.

52 Although it might require the elements of the dynamic to be given a different or more equal weighting.

53 If one agrees with Rawls that it is rational to adopt the pessimistic approach underlying his defence of maximin, then disaster avoidance is certainly the most rational strategy. See John Rawls, *A Theory of Justice* (Massachusetts: Harvard University Press, 1971).

54 As humanity could, conceivably, colonize other worlds in the far distant future before our sun eventually dies, then an eco-catastrophe could prevent an infinite number of human lives from being enjoyed. In which case, we could regard the cost as infinite in its magnitude. Consequently, it would only be collectively rational for us to ignore it if the probability of eco-catastrophe were infinitesimal.

6.2.4.1 Changing the legal and political institutions

In order to halt the environmentally hazardous dynamic, perhaps all that we need do is replace the present government with a more environmentally aware one? But any state serving its own interests, and having to remain within an arms race (given that the employment by the state of coercive methods of controlling its own population will inevitably pose a threat to other states), would, as a result, most likely find itself locked within this dynamic irrespective of its level of environmental concern. For, as the Brandt Report points out: 'there are sometimes considerations which overshadow mutual interests. This is nowhere clearer than in disarmament where . . . the great common interest of mankind in reducing the cost and the growing risk of armaments is thwarted by mutual suspicion between states or groups of states.'[55] In other words, it might be in every state's interest for all states to disarm (although one wonders what the justification for the privileged position of certain state personnel would then be), but finding themselves in an international Prisoners' Dilemma, they might be unable to.[56]

In which case, were an elected green government to try to disarm, it is extremely unlikely that the rest of the state would be enthusiastic about aiding it in what would appear to be the undermining of state power. State institutions have, for example, obstructed and even undermined British Labour governments whose policies were far less radical than those which committed greens would attempt to enact. Hence, the election of a green government would seem to be insufficient for bringing about a green society. One conceivable response to the election of such a government is the military rejecting that government, as it is unlikely to accept quietly a green government slashing its budget and dispensing with its traditional role. It is worth bearing in mind Dearlove and Saunders' comments on modern British history:

> In the mid-seventies, there was informed speculation as to the prospects for a military coup in Britain: the country was seen as harder to govern; the unions were 'too' powerful; a variety of new movements made for unrest on the streets; and the politicians were regarded as failing to get a grip. Men in the shadows regarded authoritarian rule with favour, and, for many, democracy went out of fashion. In fact, practice has shown that it would not take a coup to bring British troops onto the streets and into a position of political prominence. Moreover, we should remind ourselves that no revolution in Britain would be left wing, for the army are the men with the guns, and, like many

55 Brandt *et al.*, *North–South*, p. 66.

56 In Sections 6.3.2.1 and 6.3.2.2, below, I spell out the Prisoners' Dilemma, and some of its implications for green political theory.

other parts of the secret state, they are committed to the essentials of the status quo – and to the status quo as once was at that.[57]

If a radical change of government within one state alone would invite a military coup, how about the creation of an environmentally concerned, centralized, global state as the solution? But can one really imagine all nuclear powers agreeing either to one of them becoming such a super-state or to their joint subordination to a state above them all?[58] The history of the United Nations attests to the implausibility of the latter.[59] Moreover, surely it is sufficient to recall that the

57 Dearlove and Saunders, *Introduction to British Politics*, p. 162. It is worth remembering that, even in the second half of the twentieth century, several European countries have been ruled by military governments, from Greece in the east through Germany in the middle to the Iberian Peninsula in the West.

58 Yet one still hears recommendations that the following, or something very like it, be instituted: 'a world governmental agency . . . imposing mutually beneficial enforceable international strategies, with teeth, for environmental protection.' Luke Martell, *Ecology and Society* (Cambridge: Polity, 1994), p. 61. Martell insists that, in order to assuage liberal fears of potential totalitarianism and tyranny, such an agency's remit should not extend beyond environmental regulation. But if it is to have 'teeth', then it is difficult to see how it could be prevented from ever overstepping its remit. On the other hand, if it is incapable of overstepping its remit, and if it is supposed to be the principal means of our environmental salvation, it is difficult to see how it would possess sufficient, or sufficiently sharp, 'teeth'.

59 The United Nations seemed to show most promise in the build-up to the 1992 United Nations Conference on Environment and Development (UNCED) – the Rio Summit – which culminated in the acceptance of Agenda 21 – a radical programme initiated by a combination of NGOs and supported by UN staff working independently of any direct state control. One of the most interesting aspects of Agenda 21 is the decentralist assumptions lying behind Ch. 28. This called for local authorities to 'have undertaken a consultative process with their populations and achieved a consensus on "a local Agenda 21" for the community' by 1996. Joyce Quarrie (ed.), *Earth Summit 1992: The United Nations Conference on Environment and Development*, intro. by Boutros Boutros-Ghali (London: Regency, 1992), p. 200. Suffice it to say, most local authorities have not pursued this enthusiastically. As Voisey *et al.* summarize on the basis of case studies in Norway, Germany and the United Kingdom: 'The vast majority of local authorities in the three countries detailed have yet to respond to global environmental considerations or to undertake sustainable development at a local level.' Heather Voisey, Christiane Beuermann, Liv Astrid Sverdrup and Tim O'Riordan, 'The political significance of Local Agenda 21: the early stages of some European experience', *Local Environment*, Vol. 1, No. 1 (1996), p. 48. Moreover, in Britain, while the previous Conservative government was ostensibly committed to LA21, the quality of environmental services appears to have *declined* because of its policies with regard to local authorities, particularly the imposition of Compulsory Competitive Tendering. As Alan Patterson and Kate Theobald conclude from their interviews of local authority staff: 'current forms of local government restructuring are creating a political framework, an increasingly market-orientated "hollowed out" local state, that is incapable of responding adequately to the demands of Local Agenda 21, because the means by which the principles of sustainability, subsidiarity and strategy can be implemented are being weakened or removed.' Alan Patterson and Kate S. Theobald, 'Local Agenda 21, Compulsory Competitive Tendering and local environmental practices', *Local Environment*, Vol. 1, No. 1 (1996), p. 18.

From the perspective of the State-Primacy Theory, the extent to which the Earth Summit *of nation-states* failed, in reality, to deliver any genuine environmental commitment was quite

major human, large-scale catastrophes (with their deleterious, environmental consequences), which relief organizations such as Oxfam have dealt with since World War II (for example, Bangladesh, Biafra, Ethiopia, the Balkans), were all wars of secession. Such conflict would surely increase were a centralized, global super-state created.[60] We have seen the consequences of colonial powers arbitrarily drawing lines on maps of Africa and subjecting different peoples to the same government. The post-colonial legacy in numerous countries has been that of one ethnic group finding itself subject to rule by another – irrespective of whether or not the society became a majoritarian, representative democracy. And the outcome has often been savage ethnic conflict. The consequences of global government could easily turn out to be Rwanda (or former Yugoslavia, if one believes Europe to be completely unlike Africa) on a massive scale. And either wars of secession or the need to quell ethnic conflict would provide an internal drive for a global environmentally hazardous dynamic.

This is why, even if the 'Russian threat' were to disappear completely, it is possible for the United States to fuel such an internally driven, environmentally hazardous dynamic by offering itself as a global protection agency, for such a 'mercenary state' (to use Noam Chomsky's perceptive phrase) could be expected to demand payment from all beneficiaries of its services. We have seen the US make such demands over the Gulf War; and (possibly trumped-up) threats, for example, of 'upstart' Third World states or Islamic fundamentalism, would provide the apparent need for its continued services. This might prove to be especially attractive to the US state, for it would enable it to expand, or perhaps simply remain at, a size well beyond what its own ailing economy can support.

Perhaps, then, if neither current governmental structures nor a new global government would suffice to inhibit the environmentally hazardous dynamic, we will have to think more radically. What if we were to transform the structure of

---

comprehensible. And it is not surprising that what came to be issued instead turned out to be a declaration of mere 'manifesto rights', given the extent to which 'Western, particularly American, administrations blocked, resisted and stonewalled the following proposed measures in preliminary negotiations' prior to UNCED: 'reference in any treaty to safety standards in developing new biotechnology products; endorsement of the Bamako Convention banning toxic waste shipments across international borders; agreement on deadlines to reduce CO_2 emissions; reference to the West's overconsumption as a cause of environmental degradation; [and] a proposal that transnational corporations should accept environmental liability for the 70 per cent of the world trade which they control'. David Pepper, *Eco-Socialism: From Deep Ecology to Social Justice* (London: Routledge, 1993), p. 94. It would thus appear that the interests of the advanced states came before agreement on global environmental concerns.

60 Interestingly, Rawls seems to agree: 'a world government – by which I mean a unified political regime with the powers normally exercised by central governments – would be either a global despotism or else a fragile empire torn by frequent civil strife as various regions and peoples try to gain political autonomy.' John Rawls, 'The law of peoples' in S. Shute and S. Hurley (eds), *On Human Rights: The Oxford Amnesty Lectures 1993* (New York: Basic Books, 1993), pp. 54–5.

legal and political institutions from (what could be characterized as) a sham representative, centralized bureaucracy into a genuinely participatory democracy? Maybe that would be sufficient because the people as a whole would, conceivably, have less of an interest in remaining within an environmentally hazardous dynamic.

But would they, in actual fact, choose to leave such a dynamic? Theorists of competitive elitism have argued that ordinary individuals are at the mercy of political persuasion. They are less rational in their choices of political policies than in their choices of consumables, for they do not suffer the direct consequences of their policy choices in the near future, and therefore do not learn from their mistakes. They do not take the trouble to inform themselves of the various options, as they do when purchasing some expensive item. Hence, they live in a political fantasy world about what is desirable and possible. When they assess different policies, they degenerate to an irrational level where they act on the most basic emotions. And they respond on the basis of prejudice and sheer impulse, rather than on considered and informed thought. In short, the argument goes, the general public are politically irresponsible, and it is fortunate, in the view of several theorists of competitive elitism, that they are politically apathetic. To quote the most influential of these theorists, Joseph Schumpeter: 'the typical citizen drops down to a lower level of mental performance as soon as he [*sic*] enters the political field. He argues and analyses in a way which he would readily recognize as infantile within the sphere of his real interests. He becomes a primitive again.'[61]

However, theorists of participatory democracy have claimed to have seen a route out of this problem. If the average citizen is a 'political primitive', it is, in their view, as a result of being prevented from participating in political decision-making. So, although politically responsible behaviour has to be learnt, it can be. As Carole Pateman writes:

> The existence of representative institutions at national level is not sufficient for democracy; for maximum participation by all the people at that level socialization, or 'social training', for democracy must take place in other spheres in order that the necessary individual attitudes and psychological qualities can be developed. This development takes place through the process of participation itself. The major function of participation in the theory of participatory democracy is therefore an educative one, educative in the very widest sense, including both the psychological aspect and the gaining of practice in democratic skills and procedures. Thus there is no special problem about the stability of a participatory system; it is self-sustaining through the educative impact of the participatory process. Participation develops and fosters the very qualities necessary for it; the more individuals participate the better able they become to do so. Subsidiary hypotheses about participation

61 Joseph Schumpeter, *Capitalism, Socialism and Democracy* (London: George Allen and Unwin, 1987), p. 262.

> are that it has an integrative effect and that it aids the acceptance of collective decisions.[62]

Unfortunately, the theorists of participatory democracy would appear to be trapped in something of a vicious circle, for as C. B. Macpherson – one famous advocate of participatory democracy – admits, a change in consciousness and a reduction in social inequality are both prerequisites for participatory democracy. 'Hence the vicious circle: we cannot achieve more democratic participation without a prior change in social inequality and in consciousness, but we cannot achieve the changes in social inequality and consciousness without a prior change in democratic participation.'[63] However, Macpherson does think that there are some loopholes which allow the possibility of society escaping from this apparently vicious circle.

The first possible loophole is that the environmental costs incurred by our society are making some people question the consumer mentality. Environmental problems arising from a worship of consumption draw attention to the need for some notion of public interest. And it is clear that the public interest is not adequately served by consumers merely pursuing their own private interests regardless of others. The very serious ecological costs of the consumer mentality can thus lead more and more people to reject that mentality – or so Macpherson argues.

The second possible loophole is that the costs of apathy are, in Macpherson's view, becoming more obvious. There is a price to be paid for remaining apathetic – for example, being dominated by massive corporations. This, Macpherson believes, explains recent demands for workers' control. And workers' control can lead to demands for greater participation elsewhere. Individuals are also dominated by large-scale corporations at the level of the neighbourhood – hence the demand for greater local control, whether it concerns the dumping of nuclear waste, the siting of factories or airports, or whatever.

The third possible loophole is the apparent inability of the capitalist system to meet consumer expectations. It is Macpherson's contention that the present system will be unable to deliver continually the various goods which its consumer mentality requires in ever-greater abundance. And it certainly will be unable to deliver them to everyone who wants them. The system will either break down or there will be growing demands for a more equal distribution of goods. And this

62 Pateman, *Participation and Democratic Theory*, pp. 42–3. In other words: 'The advocates of the contemporary theory [competitive elitism] argue that certain personality traits (the "authoritarian" or "non-democratic" character) have to be taken as given – the active participation of such individuals would be dangerous for the democratic political system. The participatory theory, on the other hand, argues that the experience of participation itself will develop and foster the "democratic" personality, i.e. qualities needed for the successful operation of the democratic system, and will do so for all individuals.' Ibid., p. 64.

63 C. B. Macpherson, *The Life and Times of Liberal Democracy* (Oxford: Oxford University Press, 1977), p. 100.

will lead, Macpherson thinks, to workers demanding greater participation in political affairs.

The major problem, however, is that, although a genuine participatory democracy, once established, could persist because it would have citizens with the right consciousness, it is difficult to see how it would arise without people of the right consciousness. And as the theorists of participatory democracy themselves admit, we do not have such people at present. Most people today do not seem to have a sufficient sense of community, or sufficient confidence in their ability to participate in decision-making, and so on. Where, then, could citizens obtain the necessary experience of participating in decision-making? Theorists of participatory democracy reply that the experience must be gained at the local level and, most importantly, in the workplace.

But if this is so, then one cannot merely introduce a participatory democracy at the political level. That, on its own, would be insufficient. One would also have to introduce more participatory and egalitarian economic relations.

6.2.4.2 Changing the economic relations

If the introduction of more participatory and egalitarian relations of economic control are required for a more participatory political system, would introducing such economic relations suffice to inhibit the environmentally hazardous dynamic portrayed in Figure 6.1? More to the point, could we expect participatory and egalitarian relations to prevail in present circumstances?

First, it is doubtful that they would arise on a large scale, for those who benefit from the existing inequality in society are unlikely to risk any genuine participation by the less privileged.[64] Were the latter granted such participation, then they might very well do something about the prevailing inequality. And it is the state itself that is one of the beneficiaries of inegalitarian economic relations, as they provide it with the surplus it requires. Is it likely, then, that those who are at present benefiting from the relations of economic control would undermine their own privileged position by sanctioning any developments that would lead to a more active and demanding citizenry? This is doubtful. Hence, it is highly implausible that a non-participatory state would endorse the introduction of significantly participatory or egalitarian relations of economic control.

Second, it has been claimed that centralized states have, in recent years, been taking away the very local control which would be necessary to make participation in local decision-making meaningful. Dearlove and Saunders:

> Precisely because it has in the past represented (to some extent) a democratic enclave within the state system, and has thus proved a constant irritant to those in positions of power elsewhere in the system, local government has

64 This is why a reduction in social inequality is considered to be one of the prerequisites for participatory democracy.

> been neutered. The emaciation, restriction and, ultimately, abolition of troublesome local councils has been nothing less than a deliberate attempt to close up the one democratic chink in the state's armour, the Achilles heel of the state apparatus.[65]

Third, and particularly disturbing, however, is the fear that if egalitarian and participatory workplaces did manage to arise on a significant scale, then the state would simply re-impose inegalitarian economic relations upon the workers. This fear is not unjustified, because if the workers themselves were in control of their workplaces, they might choose to work less hard and make less surplus available to the state. As we saw in Chapter 2, such a replacement of egalitarian economic relations is precisely what the Bolshevik state enforced within a year of Lenin coming to power.

Fourth, and perhaps the most intractable problem, is that non-convivial, hard technologies do not appear to be suited to a more democratic workplace.[66] Nuclear power stations, for example, do not seem ideally suited to being converted into workers' cooperatives – not least because they seem to require stringent security measures. For genuine workers' control, technologies quite different to the prevailing ones would surely have to be developed and introduced on a wide scale. This is one important reason why theories which downplay the social implications of technology may prove to be extremely dangerous.

6.2.4.3 Changing the nature of technological development

Perhaps, then, it is the introduction of alternative (or 'appropriate') technologies[67] – 'convivial', 'soft' technologies – which would provide an effective answer to the environmentally hazardous dynamic? But how would such technologies come to be developed and implemented? Such alternative technologies do not appear to support the coercive forces required by the state (for they would make everyone more independent, thereby undermining central control and offering

65 Dearlove and Saunders, *Introduction to British Politics*, p. 392.

66 Indeed, it has been convincingly argued that certain means of production were developed precisely in order to facilitate hierarchical control within the workplace. See Harry Braverman, *Labor and Monopoly Capital: The Degradation of Work in the Twentieth Century* (New York: Monthly Review Press, 1974) and S. A. Marglin, 'What do bosses do? The origins and functions of hierarchy in capitalist production' in André Gorz (ed.), *The Division of Labour: The Labour Process and Class-Struggle in Modern Capitalism* (Brighton: Harvester Press, 1976). Also see D. Elliott and R. Elliott, *The Control of Technology* (London: Wykeham Publications, 1976).

67 For a brief discussion of alternative technology, see R. Clarke, 'Technology for an alternative society' in R. Clarke (ed.), *Notes for the Future: An Alternative History of the Past Decade* (London: Thames and Hudson, 1975). For more comprehensive accounts, see Godfrey Boyle and Peter Harper (eds), *Radical Technology* (London: Wildwood House, 1976) and David Dickson, *Alternative Technology and the Politics of Technical Change* (London: Fontana, 1974).

the state less surplus). Hence, neither research into them nor their implementation on a major scale can be expected to be backed enthusiastically by any state pursuing its own interests. And to the extent that such technologies undermined the existing relations of economic control, it is unlikely that they would be funded by those who presently benefit directly from inegalitarian relations, and who own the private capital which would be needed for the development and production of convivial technologies on any scale if the state had no interest in promoting them.

It is also worth noting that when the state or private business does support renewable forms of energy, it seems to prefer the most centralized forms – ones that maximize the possibility of centralized control. The choice is not ordinarily for, say, small windmills scattered around the countryside, powering local communities and adding to their independence, but, instead, tends to be for very large concentrated schemes that are far less attractive and more likely to meet concerted local opposition.

6.2.4.4 Changing the nature of 'defence'

This leaves us with the final element of the environmentally hazardous dynamic: the militaristic coercive forces. Certainly, unless there is a significant reduction in arms spending, none of the measures necessary to prevent further environmental degradation or to ameliorate their causes are likely to be viewed as affordable. As Boris Frankel remarks: 'There can be no development of "appropriate technology", no guaranteed minimum income, no transformations in the centralized state and corporate structure, so long as the existing military arms race continues.'[68] As an alternative form of defence, were the development of the coercive forces to be replaced by a widespread commitment to pacifism and the wide-scale adoption of non-violent direct action (NVDA) against any potential aggressor, would this not fundamentally inhibit the dynamic? This seems the most promising suggestion so far.

But how would NVDA come to be promoted on a large scale? If the population were highly trained in non-violent resistance and non-cooperation with an aggressor, then such a population would probably be viewed as ungovernable. However, that would apply to rule not only by an external aggressor but also by their present state. Consequently, it is highly improbable that proof of NVDA working effectively as an alternative defence strategy would be forthcoming, for as Richard Routley acutely observes:

> Nonviolent resistance is . . . unlikely to be put to the test in any adequate way in present state-determined circumstances. No state would be prepared to risk training its populace in full nonviolent action techniques (civil defense is different). It would then be all too easy for them to 'rout' the police: civil

68 Boris Frankel, *The Post-Industrial Utopians* (Cambridge: Polity, 1987), p. 117.

> obedience, for example, could no longer be ensured by customary violent means.[69]

As Routley's observation seems to establish, because pacifist techniques have the clear potential of undermining the power exerted by the state over its own populace, it is highly improbable that state personnel would ever sanction their widespread adoption, never mind promote such techniques. Yet as their adoption appears to be a prerequisite for escaping an arms race (itself, it would appear, a precondition for inhibiting the environmentally hazardous dynamic), then it would seem to be necessary to oppose the state as an institution. In other words, the full ramifications of pacifism might well be considerably more radical than is usually assumed – certainly much more radical than that of mere passivity.[70]

Moreover, unless there is a greater sense of community and trust among the population, then any attempted use of collective NVDA would probably be severely constrained. But there is reason to think that a general feeling of community and shared trust is unlikely to arise in a hierarchical or an inegalitarian society, with its tremendous social divides.[71] Hence, pacifism on its own does not, *prima facie*, appear to be a completely satisfactory response to the environmentally hazardous dynamic. If all this is so, and if our very survival as a species depends upon stopping such a dynamic, what is to be done?

6.3 An environmentally benign interrelationship?

A possible answer, rather than regarding each of the proposed radical solutions as sufficient to inhibit the environmentally hazardous dynamic, is to see them as necessary conditions which might be jointly sufficient. For it is the absence of the other conditions being met that seems to render each condition insufficient. And this is because of the interrelational, mutually-reinforcing nature of the dynamic. In other words, it would not do to negate a pseudo-representative, centralized bureaucracy or inegalitarian, competitive economic relations or non-convivial, hard technologies or nationalistic and militaristic coercive forces without also negating the other elements of the dynamic. And interestingly, when all of these elements are simultaneously negated, a different and stable interrelationship could conceivably be produced – one that is environmentally benign. Consider, then, such a set of interrelationships in an established, environmentally benign society.

One possible negation of the first element of the environmentally hazardous dynamic – a pseudo-representative, centralized bureaucracy – might consist in a

69 Richard Routley, 'On the alleged inconsistency, moral insensitivity and fanaticism of pacifism', *Inquiry* 27 (1984), p. 132.

70 On the important distinctions between pacificity and passivity, and between acting forcefully and acting violently, see ibid., p. 128 and pp. 118–19, respectively.

71 See John Baker, *Arguing for Equality* (London: Verso, 1987), Ch. 4.

decentralized, participatory democracy. For the people to remain in political control, they would have to ensure the perpetuation of the egalitarian relations of production that are one of its preconditions (if the theorists of participatory democracy are right). But it is at least plausible that a population of equals,[72] participating in a participatory democracy, would be more politically informed and would want to retain their egalitarian economic relations both for their own sake and because they were understood to be a precondition for the continuance of their participatory democracy. Moreover, a more consensual democracy would mean that those who would lose out from inegalitarian economic relations would be able to veto their introduction. In short, it could be argued that, whereas a centralized, authoritarian state chooses to preserve inegalitarian economic relations because they are functional for it, egalitarian economic relations are functional for a participatory democracy, which might, therefore, be expected to choose to preserve them.

However, it is likely that inegalitarian economic relations will only be avoided if local economic control is retained (as economic control from afar would probably end up being exploitative and environmentally damaging, for the owners would not have to live in that locale). This would require each locality to be as self-sufficient (or, at least, as self-reliant) as possible. But it is also plausible that this is what the mass of people (being more informed as a result of equal economic control) would insist on, given that they would, in all likelihood, wish to remain in control of the productive forces. And more self-sufficient, egalitarian economic relations negate the second element of the environmentally hazardous dynamic – inegalitarian, competitive economic relations.

But there is reason to believe that egalitarian relations will only be preserved if the workers employ a convivial technology. Non-convivial technologies, by definition, serve to preserve and further inegalitarian and authoritarian relations. Convivial technologies, on the other hand, provide liberation from 'experts'. As a possible example of a convivial technology, consider small-scale aerogenerators (or windmills): Whereas the aerodynamics of their design, if they are to be maximally efficient, can involve extremely complex calculations, once designed they can be easy to construct and even simpler to maintain. They can add to self-sufficiency and, in consequence, facilitate autonomy. They can be used by everyone, and therefore do not, inherently, lead to inequality. In contrast to a convivial technology such as small-scale windpower, consider a seemingly non-convivial technology such as large-scale, conveyor belt production: In this system, the production process has been designed so that the work-rate of the employees labouring on the production line can be controlled from a distance, with minimal supervision, by managers simply turning the speed of the conveyor belt up or down. Such a technology, it would seem, has been specifically designed to increase the control of managers and to decrease the autonomy of the workforce.

It seems not unlikely that the majority of informed workers situated within

72 For an appropriate conception of 'equality', see ibid.

egalitarian economic relations which they themselves controlled would insist on convivial technologies – ones that facilitate equal control – rather than technologies that make a few workers privileged and the rest subservient. There is considerable evidence to suggest that those who have enjoyed dominant positions within the relations of economic control have introduced non-convivial technologies to serve their own purposes.[73] Thus, with equality in the workplace, it is less likely that non-convivial technologies would be chosen to replace convivial ones. And, of course, convivial technologies negate this third element of the environmentally hazardous dynamic – non-convivial technologies.

Now, it can be argued that convivial technologies, in so far as they are incompatible with authoritarian, central control, and in so far as they offer less surplus to fuel any potential development of militaristic coercive forces, would not support an arms race, and their employment could thereby inhibit its re-emergence. What is more, it can be argued that the employment of convivial technologies would make the society less of a threat to its neighbours, which might eliminate the need to participate in an arms race altogether and, in the process, remove the need to develop those technologies which are required to support an arms race.[74]

Thus, a participatory democracy could feel that it had an interest in using convivial technologies. And, unlike a coercive, centralized state, it could regard itself as being in a position to be able to afford to do without less convivial ones (which a coercive state seems to require simply in order to retain power), because within a participatory democracy the citizens would exercise collective control over themselves. In addition, the sharing and trust that convivial working arrangements would most probably foster is widely regarded as a condition for pacifist defence and non-violent social control. To the extent that this would be far less confrontational and conflictual, it could facilitate the development of a less nationalistic perspective – something which an awareness of the global nature of environmental crises also seems to promote.

Furthermore, the less it was confined to a single nation, the more effective would a pacifist approach probably be. Hence, there are good reasons for such a society wishing to promote pacifism internationally. And a population with a more global, international outlook prepared and able to employ pacifist methods in their own defence (and in defence of the environment) negates the fourth

73 See Marglin, 'What do the bosses do?'; also see Braverman, *Labor and Monopoly Capital.*

74 One often-heard, and seemingly cogent, argument against nuclear disarmament is that nuclear weapons, once invented, cannot be uninvented. However, although the knowledge of how to manufacture them is unlikely to be lost completely, if the technological preconditions of their manufacture (e.g., nuclear power stations) are replaced with convivial technologies, then the argument is considerably weakened. If one knows, in principle, how to make nuclear weapons but lacks the technological means for manufacturing them, then one poses far less of a threat to one's neighbours. Thus, world peace and genuine global security seem to require convivial technologies, for, it can thus be argued, only when such technologies preponderate will the potential threat that drives the arms race have subsided.

element of the environmentally hazardous dynamic – nationalistic and militaristic coercive forces.

Finally, it can be argued that a widespread ability to engage in collective NVDA would empower a participatory democracy and enable it to preserve egalitarian economic relations. In addition, if the citizens of a participatory democracy wished to enjoy their own produce rather than supporting expensive coercive forces, then they would have good reason to develop cheaper, non-violent methods of defence (methods that seem to be unavailable to authoritarian states). And a more egalitarian society would most likely have less need of coercive forces as there would be fewer inequalities in need of protection. Furthermore, an egalitarian, non-violent democracy would be less able to force exploitative relations onto other (for example, poorer) countries, thereby playing its part in a more egalitarian world. This would involve it having to be more self-sufficient. And were there greater self-sufficiency, less international competition and exploitation, and consequently no apparent need to remain within an arms race, there would be no seemingly inescapable dynamic forcing the squandering of resources, the unhindered pollution of the environment, or the headlong rush into nuclear holocaust.

In which case, were such an alternative interrelationship (as illustrated in Figure 6.4) to be realized, it could offer those living within it the luxury of being able to exist in an environmentally benign way, unlike the dynamic (depicted in Figure 6.1) that appears to have taken us to the brink of ecological catastrophe. And because we can now see the potential consequences of entering such an environmentally hazardous dynamic – potentially horrific repercussions which could not easily have been foreseen at an earlier time (possibly when humanity first entered such a dynamic) – we might expect those who, from the present-day onwards, chose to live within such an environmentally benign interrelationship to ensure that they did not re-embark on the seemingly disastrous voyage undertaken by statist societies.

Nevertheless, given that the decision whether or not to enter an environmentally hazardous dynamic might remain a possible choice, the major difference between the environmentally hazardous dynamic and this environmentally benign interrelationship is that, whereas the former appears to be *driving* us towards collective suicide irrespective of our wishes, the latter would seem to allow us to live in harmony with the rest of the biosphere upon which we depend. And as all the elements of this benign society are so interrelated, as are those of the environmentally hazardous dynamic, then an appropriate political strategy would be to oppose the latter on all fronts – in fact, if indeed we are entrapped within such a dynamic, and if it were not transformed on all fronts, then, as the above arguments suggest, it would simply re-establish itself.

This is not to say that *only* a sudden revolution would provide a solution. A transition could be gradual. But all elements of the environmentally hazardous dynamic would, if the above arguments hold, have to be transformed in tandem. Moreover, the environmentally hazardous dynamic and the environmentally benign interrelationship are clearly 'ideal types'. As such, if they possess any

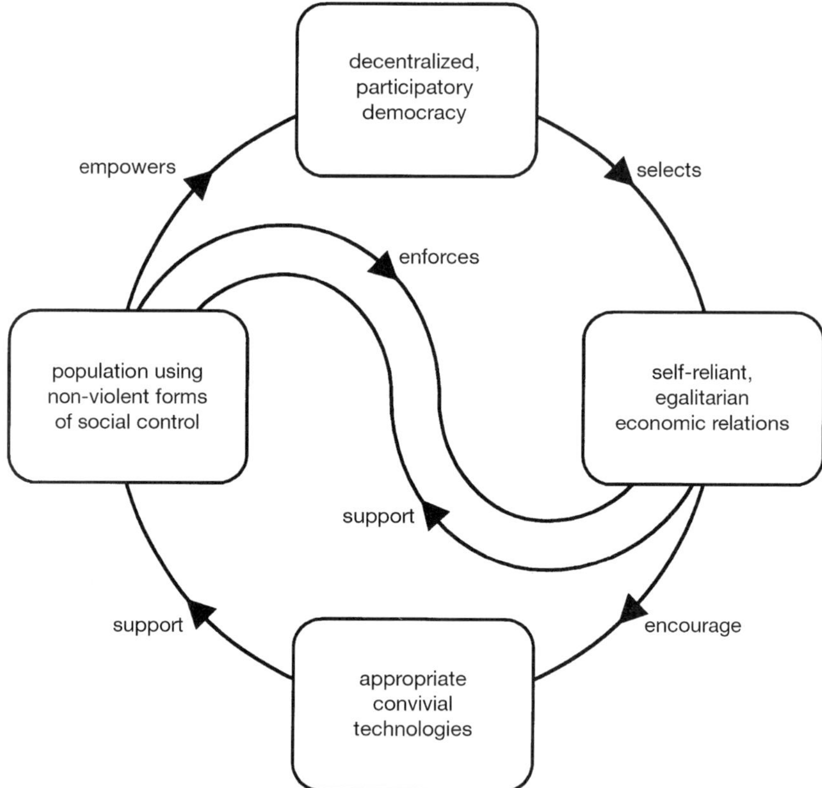

Figure 6.4 An environmentally benign interrelationship

descriptive or explanatory value, then societies would tend to fall between them: some would be more environmentally hazardous, some more benign.[75] Interestingly, those societies that today appear to be relatively less hazardous (for example, Denmark) not only have more soft technologies, they also tend to have more political participation, to be less militaristic and to be more egalitarian. What seems to be needed, generally, then, is a move considerably further from the hazardous and much more towards the benign.

75 What might explain why it is that states have evolved differently? One possible explanation which fits the State-Primacy Theory is suggested by Patrick Dunleavy and Brendan O'Leary: 'it is important to note that a critical influence on the degree to which each state is centralized, hierarchical and bureaucratic is whether or not its society experienced Feudalism. North America did not have a feudal era. Compared with Western European societies, the USA, Canada and countries with similar histories have in some respects relatively undeveloped central "states". It is also evident that revolutions, wars, and the place countries occupy in international military, diplomatic and economic systems have profound consequences on how their state structures evolve.' Patrick Dunleavy and Brendan O'Leary, *Theories of the State: The Politics of Liberal Democracy* (London: Macmillan, 1987), p. 3.

6.3.1 Moving towards the benign

However, if the State-Primacy Theory effectively describes prevailing social and political interrelationships, then the state would surely resist any attempt to oppose the environmentally hazardous dynamic on all fronts, as that dynamic would be intimately related to the serving of its interests. How, then, could this dynamic be effectively opposed? How might we move from the hazardous to the benign?

Were it in fact the case that the coercive forces are insufficient to preserve state power on their own,[76] and were the state partly empowered by the compliance of its people, then it might be possible to provide an answer. Just as it appears rational for the state to back economic relations which develop the productive forces that provide the surplus it requires, and just as it appears rational for members of the dominant economic class to support the state in so far as it stabilizes the economic relations they benefit from, it also appears rational for subordinate economic classes to back the state in defending their nation from being subjugated by another, for such subjugation would probably lead to an even greater burden being imposed upon them. It is not surprising, therefore, that nationals comply with their state and, perhaps, thereby empower it.

However, if this support for the state results in an environmentally hazardous dynamic posing an even greater threat than that posed by imperialist aggressors (real or imagined), then it is no longer rational to continue backing the state. As the World Commission on Environment and Development despairingly reported to the United Nations (itself a body of states!):

> The deepening and widening environmental crisis presents a threat to national security – and even survival – that may be greater than well-armed, ill-disposed neighbours and unfriendly alliances. . . . The recent destruction of much of Africa's dryland agricultural production was more severe than if an invading army had pursued a scorched-earth policy. Yet most of the affected governments still spend far more to protect their people from invading armies than from the invading desert.[77]

Unfortunately, it is doubtful that states spend their revenue on protecting their people. Rather, they seem to spend it on protecting themselves. (For example, the purchase of torture equipment is of dubious benefit to civilians when its use is

76 Given that each element of the environmentally hazardous dynamic can be regarded as playing a role in its continuation, then the dynamic could be described in a manner which accorded each element a more equal role than is found in the State-Primacy Theory, which accords explanatory primacy to the state. This would depend, in part, upon whether the soundness of the State-Primacy Theory were regarded as a necessary or a sufficient condition for accepting that we are situated within an environmentally hazardous dynamic.

77 Brundtland *et al.*, *Our Common Future*, p. 7.

targeted principally towards internal opposition.) Hence, this prioritization of expenditures would not seem to be as irrational for states as it first appears.

But if this is the situation, then it is highly irrational for the mass of the world's population to go on accepting it. For, as Jonathon Porritt writes:

> Everything that once served to enhance both individual and collective security now serves to undermine it: larger defence budget, more sophisticated weaponry, the maximization of production and consumption, higher productivity, increased GNP, the industrialization of the Third World, expanded world trade, the comprehensive exploitation of the Earth's resources, an emphasis on individualism, the triumph of materialism, the sovereignty of the nation-state, uncontrolled technological development – these were once the hallmarks of success, the guarantors of security. Collectively they now threaten our very survival.[78]

Hence, if the state is empowered not only by its coercive forces but also by the compliance of its people (who have hitherto considered it rational to support the state in their own defence), then an increasing perception that it is irrational to maintain that support could provide an answer to the environmentally hazardous dynamic. In other words, widespread individual non-cooperation with the state, undertaken as a response to the growing need to take action against the increasingly threatening environmental crises the state seems to be centrally implicated in, could conceivably disempower it.

In short, the extent of the environmental problems that we appear to face could provide the rationale and motivation for the disempowering of the state through non-cooperation. And this could begin to undermine any environmentally hazardous dynamic we might currently be imprisoned within. In which case, the disempowerment of the state by non-violent civil disobedience, and the correlative empowerment of those practising it,[79] seems the most promising place to start undermining the environmentally hazardous dynamic. And the recent history of Eastern Europe certainly suggests that widespread non-cooperation with the state can be an effective strategy for radical transformation.[80]

Now, whereas the changes in Eastern Europe might, at first glance, be thought

78 Jonathon Porritt, *Seeing Green: The Politics of Ecology Explained* (Oxford: Blackwell, 1984), p. 217.

79 Thus NVDA can be viewed as providing appropriate support for participatory democracy, for as Bookchin argues: 'direct action is literally a form of ethical character-building in the most important social role that the individual can undertake: active citizenship. . . . Direct action is at once the reclamation of the public sphere by the ego, its development toward self-empowerment, and its culmination as an active participant in society.' Murray Bookchin, 'New social movements', p. 339.

80 Interestingly, Michael Waller and Frances Millard do not find it in the least surprising that 'the environmental degradation of Eastern Europe fuelled the movements of dissent that were the harbinger of change in the region.' Michael Waller and Frances Millard, 'Environmental politics in Eastern Europe', *Environmental Politics*, Vol. 1, No. 2 (1992), p. 182.

to show that states are capable of more radical transformation than the State-Primacy Theory suggests, to the extent that the changes were brought about through the undermining of state power by a disaffected citizenry, they seem, instead, to offer evidence for the possibility of a move towards a more benign interrelationship.[81] Unfortunately, given the extent to which the peoples of Eastern Europe look towards western political and economic models, unless they soon recognize the probable environmental costs of adopting them, the future looks bleak indeed. Clearly, what is appealing to many in Eastern Europe is the level of affluence enjoyed in the West – precisely the feature of western societies which environmentalists regard as a major cause of environmental crises.

This raises an important issue. States can, perhaps, remain in power not just by the threat of force but also by appearing to be able to offer the material goods demanded by their populace. Materialism could, conceivably, seduce a whole population to such an extent that a need for change was deflected or prevented from even being perceived. This possibility means, as was noted earlier, that there could be an internal drive to the environmentally hazardous dynamic – an impetus which did not require the presence of any external military threat. For example, it could be argued that if materialist values prevail, then in order to retain power, states would have to sustain the material productivity necessary to keep their peoples seduced, and thus introduce or preserve those economic relations most conducive to sustaining it. And to the extent that this was successful, states would have an interest in maintaining materialist values.

Nevertheless, such materialism could be challenged by demonstrating that its environmental costs make it counter-productive to pursue it – a task made easier the more those costs become apparent. This is one possible explanation for the rise of post-materialist values, whereas the standard explanation sees post-materialism as arising once affluence has been enjoyed.[82] If either explanation is correct, then values which would undermine an environmentally hazardous dynamic might be expected to spread and deepen as the dynamic progressed. Up until this point in the argument, however, I have relied solely on rational choice explanations because they predominate in current political theory. The introduction of ideological values greatly complicates the issue. On the one hand, ideological inertia makes change more difficult. On the other hand, the costs of materialism seem to be becoming ever-more apparent, dissatisfaction with

81 This does, however, raise an interesting philosophical point. Certain phenomena which might appear problematic for the analysis presented here are not necessarily evidence for the mooted environmentally hazardous dynamic being other than described, but, arguably, instances of a move towards something more environmentally benign. In other words, although the analysis is based on contrary ideal types, its refutation is not straightforward, because apparently disconfirmatory evidence with respect to the nature of the hazardous will often tend to be corroborative evidence for the plausibility of the benign.

82 See R. Inglehart, 'Post-materialism in an environment of insecurity', *The American Political Science Review* 75 (1981): 880–900; also see D. Elgin, *Voluntary Simplicity* (New York: William Morrow, 1981). For more on this topic, see Appendix B, below.

materialism has emerged in the latter half of the twentieth century, and the subsequent growth of post-materialist values could provide a new motive for radical transformation.

6.3.2 Pacifism, decentralization and egalitarianism

The argument thus far suggests the need for widespread, non-violent, non-compliance with any state locked within an environmentally hazardous dynamic in order that society be radically transformed. But any such pacifist response might give rise to the following worry: Wouldn't the rejection of violence, and with it the coercive state, imply that justice could no longer be enforced effectively?[83] This does not, in fact, follow. It only implies that justice would have to be enforced by non-violent means. And it can be argued that the best way of avoiding injustices is to establish societies which, unlike hierarchical and inegalitarian ones, do not require violence in order to perpetuate themselves.

It is, therefore, worth stressing some of the problems that can be thought to result from viewing violence 'as the ultimate instrument of justice', especially in the international realm. As H. J. N. Horsburgh points out:

> First, the financial costs are huge. Billions of dollars are thrown away on arms and armed forces that might have been directly applied to the relief of suffering and the remedying of injustice. Secondly, these preparations are constantly aggravating and multiplying disputes, partly through deepening fear and suspicion, and partly through causing crises, shortages and revised priorities. Thus, it is violence and preparations for violence as much as anything else which produce the situations in which violence is said to be necessary. Thirdly, preparing for violence has harmed the environment in innumerable ways, including the testing of nuclear weaponry, the appropriation and spoliation of large tracts of beautiful country, and the world-wide industrial expansion which it has necessitated or promoted. Finally, the quest for new and superior weaponry and counter-weaponry has acted as a lopsided spur to the development of science and technology, setting us mounting problems that we are less and less able to meet.[84]

In short, we have diverted vast resources to the development of the means of mass

83 Such an objection occurs in Jan Narveson, 'Pacifism: a philosophical analysis' in James Rachels (ed.), *Moral Problems: A Collection of Philosophical Essays* (New York: Harper and Row, 1971). A cogent reply is contained in Routley, 'On the alleged inconsistency, moral insensitivity and fanaticism of pacifism.' We might include within our idea of 'justice' the prevention of, and compensation for the effects of, environmentally damaging behaviour in so far as it causes harm to others. On the increasingly apparent limitations of tort law with respect to environmental 'accidents', see Richard H. Gaskins, *Environmental Accidents: Personal Injury and Public Responsibility* (Philadelphia: Temple University Press, 1989).

84 H. J. N. Horsburgh, 'Reply to Kai Nielsen', *Inquiry* 24 (1981), pp. 66–7.

destruction, such as nuclear weapons, and seriously threatened the environment in the process because, it would seem, military goals which serve the state's purposes have taken priority.[85]

Now, the argument thus far suggests not only a pacifist response to the environmental crises we presently appear to face but a decentralist one, too. For the political reasons indicated above, in order to escape the environmentally hazardous dynamic – a dynamic entailed (or, perhaps, exposed) by the State-Primacy Theory – we would seem to require direct, participatory democracies. But it is commonly argued that they are only possible in small-scale communities. It is interesting, therefore, that many environmentalists argue on straightforward environmental grounds that moving from large-scale, urban communities to small-scale, decentralized ones is essential if we are to reduce our environmental impact – a precondition, in the view of many, for our very survival. This is because, in the words of one such environmentalist, Eugene Odum, '*the city is a parasite on the natural and domesticated environments*, since it makes no food, cleans no air, and cleans very little water to a point where it could be reused.'[86] As Kirkpatrick Sale amplifies:

> Certainly there is no question that the city of a million people, or even half a million most probably, has gone beyond the ecological balance point at which it is able to sustain itself on its own resources. Cities, particularly modern industrial cities, are like colonizers, grand suction systems drawing their life from everywhere in the surrounding nation, indeed the surrounding world, long since having gone past the point of adjusting to the carrying capacity of either their own territory or the nearby regions. A city of 1 million, it has been calculated, takes in 9,500 tons of fossil fuel, 2,000 tons of food, 625,000 tons of water, and 31,500 tons of oxygen *everyday* – and puts out 500,000 tons of sewage, 28,500 tons of carbon dioxide, and great quantities of other solid, liquid, and gaseous wastes. The contemporary high-rise city, in short, is an ecological parasite as it extracts its lifeblood from elsewhere and an ecological pathogen as it sends back its wastes.[87]

85 And as Horsburgh asks: 'Is it not possible – even likely – that the acceleration of nuclear conflict may prove fatal to our species?' In which case, the value of non-violence should be obvious, for 'only the non-violent can inherit the earth: the violent can only deny them a world to inherit.' Ibid., p. 73. For the fullest discussion of pacifist methods, successes and theory, see Gene Sharp, *The Politics of Nonviolent Action*, 3 vols. (Massachusetts: Porter Sargent, 1973).

86 Eugene P. Odum, *Ecology and our Endangered Life-Support Systems* (Massachusetts: Sinauer, 1989), p. 17. Moreover, as O'Riordan points out: 'There is ample reason to believe that, beyond a certain size, the costs of urban services, such as waste treatment, solid residuals collection, transportation, police and fire protection do rise disproportionately faster than the rate of population growth.' O'Riordan, *Environmentalism*, p. 78.

87 Kirkpatrick Sale, *Dwellers in the Land: The Bioregional Vision* (San Francisco: Sierra Book Club, 1985), p. 65.

Contrast this with the small community, which, Sale insists, 'has historically been the most efficient at using energy, recycling its wastes, reducing drawdown, and adjusting to carrying capacity.'[88]

Why, then, did human societies become geographically centralized in the first place? Because, or so it has been argued, such centralization is in the interests of those who exert political control, for '[w]e can find no instance of significant city-building through commerce alone. . . . We must, if we are to explain the growth, spread and decline of cities, comment upon the city as a mechanism by which a society's rulers can consolidate and maintain their power';[89] or in the terminology preferred by Anthony Giddens: 'The city is the generator of the authoritative resources out of which state power is created and maintained.'[90] Clearly, this explanation provides added corroboration for the State-Primacy Theory.

Even though the ecological advantages of geographical decentralization appear to be quite evident, many still oppose it. Consider Robert C. Paehlke, for example, whose hostility to decentralization has been extremely influential: Paehlke argues that urban areas can use more efficient forms of transport.[91] But in a decentralized society, where people were more self-sufficient (and, especially, where they grew their own food within walking distance of their abodes), it is unlikely that there would be such a need for transport. There would surely be far less need for transport if people did not live in cities which produced little or no food and had to have it brought in, often from thousands of miles away.

Paehlke also argues that urban populations must be 'contained' in order to protect agricultural land. But this seems to indicate a very confined view of what an ecological future might need to look like. To reduce energy consumption and the emission of greenhouse gases, it seems imperative that we use more labour-intensive farming methods, as well as less transport. But surely, that also requires people living closer to the land. Paehlke assumes that less agricultural land would then be available and less food production would result. But this is simply to ignore both what many consider to be the ecological preconditions for sustainable food production and the possibilities thrown up by certain forms of eco-architecture – for example, earth-covered buildings, which use up virtually no land surface at all.[92] If a society were to decentralize, it would have to create new dwellings, and a sane society would surely build ecologically-appropriate ones. A

88 Ibid. '*Drawdown* is the process by which the dominant species in an ecosystem uses up the surrounding resources faster than they can be replaced and so ends up borrowing, in one form or another, from other places and other times.' Ibid., p. 24.

89 G. Sjoberg, quoted in Anthony Giddens, *A Contemporary Critique of Historical Materialism: Volume I: Power, Property and the State* (London: Macmillan, 1981), p. 145.

90 Giddens, ibid.

91 See Robert C. Paehlke, *Environmentalism and the Future of Progressive Politics* (New Haven: Yale University Press, 1989), pp. 247–50.

92 For example, see J. Baldwin and S. Brand (eds), *Soft-Tech* (Harmondsworth: Penguin, 1978), pp. 102–11.

decentralized, environmentally benign society is not a world of 1980s-style suburban housing estates!

Now, small-scale, participatory democracies not only seem to require geographical decentralization but also imply political decentralization. But a common objection against political decentralization is, as Robert Goodin puts it, that global problems require global solutions, and that means, he thinks, that we have to look beyond the actions of individuals or local responses. Goodin rejects decentralization because, in his view, decentralized communities would face serious coordination problems and, in order to solve the pressing environmental challenge that lies before us, 'a central agency will . . . prove essential'.[93] However, Goodin's argument appears to rest upon a confusion. Acting locally is not the same as acting solitarily, as Goodin's objection appears to presume. Certainly, the coordination problems of getting everyone to carry out some collective action are indeed real. Starting up a production line, for example, requires a degree of coordination. But the global problems environmentalists are most concerned with, and which Goodin prioritizes – ozone depletion and climate change[94] – do not appear to be of this sort. They all seem to require us to *stop* doing certain things. Each of us stopping work on a production line, for example, requires far less coordination than is needed for us all to begin work. The relevant solutions to environmental problems appear to be of a different kind to organizing collective *actions*, and thus do not seem to be, technically, so intractable. Most importantly, it can be argued that it is far easier for non-violent activists to disrupt polluting practices than it is to engage in large-scale coordinated activities.

This provides one possible answer to the objection that decentralized communities would continue to pollute as long as they believed that the pollution they emitted affected another community and not their own. Acid rain might be thought to be one environmental problem which could be expected, on this reasoning, to continue unabated. But polluters could expect to attract justifiable non-violent direct action from environmentally concerned members of their own community, as well as from other communities (including, of course, those affected). Given a mounting concern for the condition of the environment in response to increasing ecological destruction, polluting industries could expect to suffer more and more from a growing willingness by activists to engage in ecologically-motivated sabotage – or 'ecotage', as it has come to be known in some circles. This could easily reach a stage where pollution simply would no longer pay. (In addition, it has been claimed that whereas many countries had formerly assumed that the air pollution produced within their frontiers would not produce noticeable effects inside their own borders, but only in countries 'down wind', many are now seeing the effects of their own emissions on their own forests and buildings. Few pollutants only affect others and not those who produce them.)

93 Robert E. Goodin, *Green Political Theory* (Cambridge: Polity, 1992), p. 167.
94 See ibid., p. 157.

Furthermore, if decentralized communities were not forced to damage their environments by national or global economic relations, then they might be expected to stop dirtying their own backyards. And if they were thereby to stop contributing to global problems that then react back on them, such local action would be a global solution. There is no inconsistency at all between global problems and local actions taken in order to solve them. To think there is would be to fall prey to a false local/global dichotomy. It would be a variety of the collectivist fallacy: failing to see how the local parts make up the global whole.[95] What is more, the likelihood that decentralized communities would stop contributing to environmental problems is certainly no more improbable than that of a centralized agency far from the source of pollution being sufficiently concerned with it or having the detailed local knowledge (especially of the bioregion) necessary to deal with it appropriately.

Most significantly, Goodin opposes decentralized solutions, yet signally fails to answer the arguments that numerous greens have forwarded highlighting the many potential problems of centralization – including the extent to which centralized decisions-makers with real power might take decisions that are in their own interests and not in those of the mass of humanity – precisely the problems which the State-Primacy Theory brings into sharp focus. In short, by hanging onto a centralized political structure, Goodin could be criticized for failing to offer any real escape route from the environmentally hazardous dynamic we have reason to believe we are presently entrapped within.[96]

95 Goodin even insists that we ought not to feel obliged to live green lifestyles. In justification of his (potentially ecologically disastrous) view, he begins by confusing New Age beliefs – for example, the 'worship of tree spirits' (Goodin, *Green Political Theory*, p. 79) – with genuine green proposals (such as organic farming), and then offers the following core argument: If we are too like that which provides the larger context, then it will not prove 'to be satisfying or even meaningful.' (Ibid., p. 81). Nature should be the larger context that gives meaning to our lives. Hence, we should not be too green in our lifestyles. As he further explains: 'For one thing to be "in harmony" with another, you need to have two separate things.' (Ibid.) In other words, we shouldn't be too 'natural' or we will not be sufficiently separate from nature for it to provide the required meaning. This is analogous to arguing that, were society to provide that larger context, then if one wished to preserve the status quo that one valued, one should campaign for public policies which are designed to preserve it, while, in order not to be too like the status quo, behaving as a nonconformist and dissident in one's private life. It is difficult to imagine a more absurd argument. Goodin's argument also seems to be hopelessly confused with respect to how parts are related to wholes, and appears to reveal a tendency to commit the collectivist fallacy by failing to see how wholes are not separate from their parts. On this fallacy, see Sections 3.1.2 and 3.1.3, above.

96 It should be noted that Goodin has since wholly re-assessed his position: 'There may be something about ecological issues, as such, that necessarily make them unsuited to central, authoritative decision-making. Complexity, uncertainty, local variability conspire to undermine such solutions. A regime of Environmental Guardians, even if it might have more enlightened values, has less capacity to act efficaciously on them in aid of environmental urgencies. Some decentralized mechanism would be structurally better suited to environmental necessities, and among decentralized mechanisms small-scale participatory democracies seem the most likely to be guided by the environmentally most suitable values.' Robert E.

The same can be said for another respected critic of decentralization, Boris Frankel, who offers the following choice:

> Either one aims for a stateless society – possibly organized around 'basic communes' – and argues the feasibility of this post-industrial utopia; or else, one is forced to recognize that state institutions are not mere political-administrative apparatuses (that is, there is much more to states than the parties, bureaucrats, etc., who make the laws), and will continue to be heavily involved in many social relations normally defined as belonging to 'civil society'.[97]

And in support of the latter, state-centred option, Frankel adds that 'there is a need to clarify the difference between the exercise of power within state institutions (by one-party or multi-party rule, military and bureaucratic personnel), and the state-organized socio-economic and cultural practices which constitute an indispensable part of the contemporary social reproduction of everyday life',[98] and which, Frankel thus assumes, require the retention of the state. In short, Frankel thinks that there is, in fact, no real choice at all.

In order to respond, we would need to distinguish between the political, economic and social aspects of the modern state. The distinction can be drawn not only conceptually, but also in reality. How else could the Thatcher government in the UK have privatized so much that was formerly part of the state, unless what was privatized was not purely political? And everything that was privatized, clearly, was not a *necessary* component of the state.[99] Consequently, Frankel might be criticized for seeming to ignore the fact that what is genuinely 'an indispensable part of the contemporary social reproduction of everyday life' does not have to be a state institution at all. Such a criticism becomes easier to make if one employs Weber's conception of the state. Weber, considering the state to be in competing military relations with other states, conceptualized it partly in terms of coercion.[100] But given a Weberian conception, there is no reason at all to think

---

Goodin, 'Introduction' in Robert E. Goodin (ed.), *The Politics of the Environment* (Aldershot: Edward Elgar, 1994), p. xvii. It is ironic, therefore, that much of the recent work on green political theory should have swallowed uncritically Goodin's previous dismissal of decentralization, given that Goodin himself has now lost confidence in his earlier centralist proposals and accompanying rejection of decentralization. For examples of an uncritical acceptance of Goodin's attack on decentralism, see Martell, *Ecology and Society*, pp. 59–60 and Garner, *Environmental Politics*, p. 40.

97 Frankel, *The Post-Industrial Utopians*, p. 203.

98 Ibid., pp. 204–5.

99 Note: I am *not* arguing that welfare services (especially health) are better run as private profit-making businesses.

100 See Max Weber, 'Politics as a vocation' in *From Max Weber*, ed. H. H. Gerth and C. Wright Mills (London: Routledge and Kegan Paul, 1970), p. 78.

that what is essential to social reproduction has to be a part of *the state*. Moreover, it is certain that the state, however conceived, didn't always play a central role in social reproduction, for states have only a relatively recent history.[101] Frankel could thus be criticized for obfuscating the issue by linking all necessary social institutions conceptually with 'the state'. And in so doing, he makes it all too easy for highly coercive and authoritarian apparatuses to creep back in.

6.3.2.1 The game-theoretical critique of decentralization

However, it is possible to mount a far stronger critique of decentralization than has so far been addressed, and it derives from an application of the Prisoners' Dilemma, which lies at the core of the modern game-theoretical approach to political philosophy.

The Prisoners' Dilemma takes the following form: Two criminals, call them 'Margaret' and 'Ronald', are caught red-handed committing a minor offence, for which they could each expect to serve one year in prison. However, the local sheriff knows that they have committed a far more serious crime, which, if they could be convicted, would carry a sentence of twenty years imprisonment. Unfortunately, the sheriff lacks any evidence, which would stand up in court, of their having committed the serious crime. Moreover, Margaret and Ronald have previously agreed to cooperate with each other in remaining silent about the serious offence. So, the sheriff locks them up in separate cells and offers Margaret a deal. If she were to testify that Ronald committed the serious offence, then the sheriff would drop the minor charge against her. Moreover, were Ronald to testify against Margaret, she would be convicted of the serious offence, but by testifying against him, she would have five years of her sentence commuted. The sheriff then offers a similar deal to Ronald.

Each prisoner proceeds to reason as follows: Either my partner in crime will continue to cooperate with me in keeping our agreement to remain silent or will defect from that agreement. If both my partner and I stick to our agreement, then we will be convicted of the minor offence and will both serve one year in prison. But if my partner sticks to our agreement and I renege on it, then my partner will serve twenty years in prison, but I will get off scot-free. So, if my partner continues to cooperate, it is better for me to defect. On the other hand, if my partner breaks our agreement and I stick to it, then my partner will get off scot-free and I

101 However, it can be argued that 'with [the] consolidation of national power . . . the state *makes itself necessary* by destroying the other organizations that were supplying public services to the citizenry before it came along. . . . It happened all over, and it went on for centuries. As the size of the state increased and its control over localities grew, the instruments of self-sufficiency and cooperation by which these communities had come to live began to wither. As they withered, the state took upon itself the task of intervening to supply those services left undone, thereby justifying its existence by remedying the problems that its existence caused. Simple, circular – and devastating.' Sale, *Human Scale*, pp. 123–4.

will serve twenty years in prison. But if we both break it, then we will both serve only fifteen years in prison. So, if my partner reneges on our agreement, it is better for me to do so, too. Either way, it is better for me to defect, and so I shall. Hence, they both defect and both serve fifteen years in prison, even though they would both have been better off by cooperating together in remaining silent and thereby only serving one year each.

In this example, the Prisoners' Dilemma is set up in terms of disbenefits – years served in prison. But it can also be presented in terms of benefits. Imagine that mutual cooperation pays $150 each, mutual defection pays $50 each, and when one defects while the other cooperates, the defector receives $200 and the cooperator gets nothing. This produces the following matrix:

	If Ronald cooperates	If Ronald defects
If Margaret cooperates	150, 150	0, 200
If Margaret defects	200, 0	50, 50
	Margaret, Ronald	Margaret, Ronald

If the other player cooperates, it is better to defect (for one obtains $200 instead of $150), and if he or she defects, it is also better to defect (for one comes away with $50 instead of being left empty-handed). Thus, again, no matter what the other player does, it is better to defect. But the outcome is that both players defect and only receive $50 instead of the $150 which they would have been paid had they both cooperated together.

What the Prisoners' Dilemma, just like the Tragedy of the Commons, seems to demonstrate is that what is individually rational can be collectively irrational. And neo-Hobbesians take this to show that individuals require some coercive agency, such as the state, in order to force them to cooperate, for cooperation is what is in their interests. Hence, if there is no centralized state to force individuals to cooperate with respect to refraining from individually rational, but collectively irrational, environmentally destructive behaviour, then they will degrade the environment. Thus, environmental problems seem to demand the state for their solution.

However, very few human interactions take the form of a one-off Prisoners' Dilemma game (where individuals are allowed only one move each). Usually, an individual finds himself or herself continually interacting with another person.

And as Michael Taylor and Robert Axelrod[102] independently seem to establish, whereas a one-off Prisoners' Dilemma game appears to suggest that cooperation is individually irrational unless imposed by an external agent, the most rational strategy to adopt in a series of iterated games (a supergame) is one of conditional cooperation.

As we have seen, in a Prisoners' Dilemma game (with only one move per player), the pay-offs resulting from the available moves are such that it is individually rational for each player to behave uncooperatively, but collectively irrational to do so. By each attempting to maximize his or her individual pay-off, each obtains less than he or she would obtain by cooperating. However, in a supergame (which involves a continuous series of moves in response to each other player), where past cooperation can be observed and the benefits of future cooperation foreseen, it is individually rational to cooperate while the other cooperates, for this produces a far greater pay-off both individually and collectively. Thus, in a supergame, the rational strategy is one of conditional cooperation.

Conditional cooperation (technically, C-tit-for-tat), where the strategy is to cooperate on the first move and from then on imitate the other player's previous move, produces the highest pay-off for the following (admittedly, over-simplified) reason. Consider three strategies: never cooperate (D^{∞}), always cooperate (C^{∞}), and conditionally cooperate (C^{TFT}). When D^{∞} plays D^{∞}, the pay-off for every round is poor ($50 each, on the second example given above). When C^{∞} plays C^{∞}, the pay-off for every round is good ($150 each). But when C^{∞} plays D^{∞}, the pay-off is very poor for C^{∞} (who comes away with nothing), while it is excellent for D^{∞} (who gets $200). Thus, when some refuse to cooperate and others always cooperate, the former ('free riders') do extremely well, while the latter ('suckers') get badly stung.

How do conditional cooperators fare within the supergame? When C^{TFT} plays D^{∞}, D^{∞} (being paid $200) scores as highly on the first round as he or she does against C^{∞}. But on every following move C^{TFT} refuses to cooperate and D^{∞} scores the same as against another D^{∞}. In other words, poorly (only getting $50). C^{TFT}, on the other hand, is stung on the first move (coming away with nothing), but from then on does no worse against D^{∞} as another D^{∞} would do (getting $50). When C^{TFT} plays C^{∞}, every move is mutually cooperative and each enjoys a good pay-off ($150 each). And when C^{TFT} plays another C^{TFT}, the outcome is the same as two C^{∞}s playing together (each obtaining $150). In short, conditional cooperators enjoy the benefits of cooperation without continually falling prey to free-riders.

To see how this can make conditional cooperation the most rational strategy,

102 See Michael Taylor, *Anarchy and Cooperation* (London: Wiley, 1976), Michael Taylor, *Community, Anarchy and Liberty* (Cambridge: Cambridge University Press, 1982) and Robert Axelrod, 'The emergence of cooperation amongst egoists', *The American Political Science Review*, 75 (1981), pp. 306–18.

imagine a community containing a free-rider (D^{∞}), a sucker (C^{∞}) and a conditional cooperator (C^{TFT}). If one were to join this community, which strategy would it be rational to adopt? If one were to act as a free-rider, then on the first move one would obtain $50 from playing against the other free-rider, $200 from playing against the sucker, and $200 from playing against the conditional cooperator (who would cooperate on the first move). This would give a total of $450. But on every subsequent round, one would obtain $50 from playing against the other free-rider, $200 from playing against the sucker, and only $50 from playing against the conditional cooperator (who would defect on the second round, and continue to defect on every subsequent round, as a result of one's previous defection). This would give a total of $300 per round. So, by the end of the third round, one would have accumulated $1,050, and by the end of the fourth, $1,350.

If, however, one were to act as a sucker, then on every round one would obtain nothing from playing against the free-rider, $150 from playing against the other sucker, and $150 from playing against the conditional cooperator (who would never have any reason to defect, as all one's previous moves would have been cooperative). This would give a total of $300 per round. And by the end of the fourth round, one would have accumulated $1,200. Clearly, free-riding is a better strategy.

What, though, if one were to act as a conditional cooperator? On the first round one would obtain nothing from playing against the free-rider, $150 from playing against the sucker, and $150 from playing against the other conditional cooperator. This would give a total of $300. On every subsequent round one would still obtain $150 from playing against the sucker and a further $150 from playing against the other conditional cooperator (for conditional cooperators never have reason to defect on each other). However, after the first round, one would have stopped cooperating with the free-rider, and one would obtain $50 for every further round played against him or her. This would give a new total of $350 per round. So, by the third round, one would have accumulated $1,050, and by the end of the fourth, $1,400. In other words, by the end of the third round one would have equalled the amount one would have obtained by acting as a free-rider, and from then on one would continue to exceed by a further $50 per round the amount one would have obtained by so acting. Hence, the rational strategy in such a supergame – a series of iterated games comprising several players – would be conditional cooperation.

Now, as environmental problems are, except in very unusual circumstances, the result of ongoing activities, it would seem that they are better modelled by a supergame than by a one-off Prisoners' Dilemma. And what supergames appear to demonstrate is that cooperation would arise, without any centralized coercion, even among purely self-interested, economically rational actors, for conditional cooperation is the most economically rational strategy.

This also seems to suggest that the coordination between decentralized communities is not anywhere near as hopeless a task as many presume. The arguments of Taylor and Axelrod concerning the rationality of strategies of conditional cooperation and the emergence of cooperation between individuals could, in principle, be extended to the relationships between communities.[103] If one extends to communities the analysis of what constitutes the most rational behaviour for individuals within a supergame, then the conclusion which seems to follow is that communities behave most rationally by adopting strategies of conditional cooperation towards one another. And the outcome might then be expected to be cooperation between communities without any need for external coercion or a central agency.

Now, the strategy of conditional cooperation is usually less rational the greater the number of players in any game.[104] This implies that coordination between individuals would more likely arise within small communities. Hence, we appear to have a clear justification for decentralization, for it would appear to allow the easiest coordination between individuals. However, the smaller the communities are in size, the greater will be their number. But that seems to imply that the coordination between decentralized communities will be all the more problematic. And here seems to lie the most powerful objection against decentralization.

6.3.2.2 A game-theoretical reply

This objection, as powerful as it at first seems, can be argued to rest upon a confusion, however. For it is surely not the number of players per se which undermines the rationality of conditional cooperation. Rather, it is what a large

103 John Dryzek, however, asserts, without supporting argument, that '[c]ollective entities cannot feel moral obligation, or suffer ostracism, or share a sense of community, or even adopt consistent conditional strategies.' John S. Dryzek, *Rational Ecology: Environment and Political Economy* (Oxford: Blackwell, 1987), p. 228. But each of these assertions is, surely, false – unless, that is, a confused notion of 'collective entity' is being presumed (such as the collectivist notions criticised in Sections 3.1.2 and 3.1.3, above). Some workers' cooperatives (especially wholefood shops) feel morally obliged to send money to poor communities in other parts of the world. Many communities, such as Jewish ghettos, have been ostracized. Benedictine monasteries feel a sense of community with the rest of the Church. And many communities cooperate with one another just so long as the benefits are mutual – an interrelationship which has been exceedingly common among tribal peoples. Dryzek agrees that small-scale, decentralized communities are the most ecologically rational. But he points out that it is difficult for them to survive in a world of states. He also agrees that states are far from ecologically rational. However, surely their mooted ecological irrationality provides a very good reason why each of us should seek to free ourselves from them.

104 Conditional cooperation is also less rational the more one discounts the future. (But see Chapter 7 for an argument which attempts to establish the immorality of discounting the harms we might inflict on future generations.) There are, of course, other factors that I have not mentioned which can make cooperation less rational than it would otherwise be: for example, considerably higher pay-offs for defection. On the mathematics of this and other factors, see Taylor, *Anarchy and Cooperation*. However, there are also factors which make cooperation far more rational than it would otherwise be: for example, when conditional cooperators are not evenly distributed and 'cluster'. See Axelrod, 'The emergence of cooperation amongst egoists'.

number of players ordinarily implies: namely, a large number of one-off Prisoners' Dilemma games and very few iterated supergames. As an example, consider a con-artist operating within a big city. By defecting on agreed transactions, the con-artist acts as a free-rider. But he or she will only get away with conning each person once. Fortunately for the free-rider, in a big city, where there are many individuals, he or she will be able to move on, time and time again, to a new transaction with a different person – one who does not know that the other player is a con-artist. By behaving in this way, the con-artist maximizes his or her pay-off.

What should be noted is that continuous defection becomes the rational strategy not because there is a large number of players, but because of what that allows in such a situation: in particular, anonymity and few interactions between the same people.[105] It is surely these features of city life which can effectively turn potential supergames into a series of one-off Prisoners' Dilemmas, and that make defection the most rational strategy. For if everyone knew who the con-artists were, then no one would cooperate with them. And conditional cooperation would then, it seems, provide the best pay-off. Moreover, if there were countless individuals whom one could play against, but, nevertheless, one had to keep playing against the same players, then again conditional cooperation would appear to be a more rational strategy than free-riding. Hence, or so it would seem, it is not actually the number of players involved which poses the potential difficulty for strategies of conditional cooperation.

Of crucial importance in assessing the game-theoretical critique of decentralization, therefore, is whether or not the existence of a large number of small communities would, in fact, invite free-riding. And it seems clear that the situation of sedentary communities contrasts dramatically with that of the urban con-artist. Ordinarily, no community would be in a position to deal with each of the others once only, and then move on to dealings with other communities that lacked all knowledge of which communities always defected on agreements. For one thing, any community is likely to have many interactions with its neighbours, and they will either be cooperative or uncooperative interactions. Clearly, this constitutes a supergame, within which the rational strategy is, apparently, conditional cooperation. Consequently, it would seem to be irrational to export one's pollution to other communities, for it is likely to incite defection on their part.

Moreover, a community which defects on agreements to behave in an environmentally benign way will, because of its detectable pollution, most likely be viewed by all eco-communities as a defector. Such a community would not then be able to move on to interactions with other communities in the way that free-riders within a city can move on to other innocents. Any defecting community would likely face non-cooperation from all environmentally benign ones. And one form that non-cooperation with a defector might take is ecotage

105 This claim can easily be supported by elementary thought experiments. For two relevant examples, see Alan Carter, 'Game theory and decentralization', *Journal of Applied Philosophy* (forthcoming).

conducted by individuals residing in affected communities (or even by environmentally-aware activists from within its own midst).

In short, sedentary communities are in a very different situation from that which makes free-riding rational. The assumption that there is an intractable problem of coordination between decentralized communities can, therefore, be seen to result from a confusion between the number of actors and what that ordinarily implies for mobile individuals – namely, anonymity combined with the possibility of very few iterated interactions. But sedentary communities are neither anonymous nor free from continuing interactions with their neighbours. Hence, it can be argued that they do not face the coordination problems that many critics of decentralization presume; and thus, it can be further argued, environmentally benign communities have no need of the state.

Rather than placing our hope in the state, what seems to be required in order to escape the environmentally hazardous dynamic we may well be trapped within are institutions genuinely controlled by the people themselves – by people living in communities that could mandate recallable delegates to reach decisions with other communities, subject to each community ratifying any decision taken. Small communities could coordinate confederally. They could network horizontally, rather than subordinately. On such a decentralist model, no coercive state appears necessary. In fact, as Peter Kropotkin was fond of remarking, the European rail and postal networks operated in such a fashion – precisely the sorts of institution that Boris Frankel seems to view as indistinguishable from the state. Moreover, on such a decentralist model, local communities would remain in control of their locales, so that their environments would not be degraded (as they appear to be at present) by those who exercise power over distant communities while not having to live in them. I shall call such a cooperative yet autonomous relationship between communities (or an analogous one between individuals) '*cooperative autonomy*' – discussion of which I leave till the final chapter.

Now, the argument presented in this chapter suggests not only a pacifist and a decentralist response but also an egalitarian one. But this invites the obvious objection that any decentralist proposal is bound to be incompatible with egalitarian demands. As there are different levels of resources in different parts of the world, wouldn't a centralized, global super-state be necessary to redistribute from the rich to the poor? And doesn't this show decentralization, self-sufficiency and egalitarianism to be incompatible? In response: first, the most effective organizations with respect to environmentally benign development (albeit on far too small a scale) seem to be non-governmental organizations such as Oxfam, which attempt to help the poor to help themselves; and second, the *major* problem is surely not a lack of redistribution, but the redistribution currently practised – namely, from the poor to the rich.

Merely ending international exploitation would not, of course, provide global equality, but it might be the best practicable, wide-scale approach, given that terminating underdevelopment, for example, would most likely be far more egalitarian and less problematic than allowing a global super-state to redistribute resources, when a significant proportion would almost certainly be redistributed in its own direction in the process.[106] Moreover, to the extent that egalitarians are most concerned to reduce inequalities arising from exploitation, then self-sufficiency and de-linking from the world economy as an answer to under-development would be egalitarian. And we saw in the previous chapter how the State-Primacy Theory underpinning the analysis presented here is not incompatible with a theory of underdevelopment, as might at first be assumed.

6.4 The coherence of green political thought

In this chapter I have tried to weave together the threads of a radical green political theory. The State-Primacy Theory seems to cash out in the modern world into an environmentally hazardous dynamic. And the identification of such a dynamic appears to shed light on all of the major problems greens have focused upon. Thus, we now have an answer to our question concerning the coherence and distinctiveness of radical green political thought: *What can be considered to link together theoretically the various aspects of radical green political theory* – decentralization, participatory democracy, egalitarianism, self-sufficiency, alternative technology, pacifism and internationalism – *is the need to inhibit the environmentally hazardous dynamic that we appear currently to be imprisoned within.*

In short, then, *the various elements of radical green political thought can be seen to consist in the systematic negation of every element of the environmentally hazardous dynamic.* Pacifism (or, alternatively, the 'defensive defence' proposed by Johan Galtung[107]) can be considered to negate the apparent present need to

106 In the view of John Clark, 'to the extent that redistribution is a necessity, it will be encouraged more by the practice of mutual aid through free federation than by the continuation of action by nation-states or by the creation of a world state.' John Clark, *The Anarchist Moment: Reflections on Culture, Nature and Power* (Montreal: Black Rose, 1984), p. 152. What is more, the US is surely the present state most likely to form the basis of any possible world-state. Yet '[i]n the United States, a nation with the greatest concentration of wealth and one of the longest traditions of liberal democracy, there appears to be virtually no redistribution taking place between economic strata and only a fraction of 1% of the GNP is devoted to aid to poorer countries.' Ibid., p. 153. By contrast, however, if one examines 'the federations established by the anarcho-syndicalists in Spain in 1936', one finds that 'the redistribution which has been largely absent over generations in liberal and social democratic countries took place in a period of a few months in collectivized areas, primarily as a result of the institution of self-managed industry and agriculture. In the short time that the collectives were able to act autonomously, they began to expand this egalitarianism beyond the limits of the individual collectives.' Ibid. This is evidenced by 'such programs as disaster relief, redistribution of fertilizer and machinery from the wealthier to the poorer collectives, and cooperative seed production for distribution to areas in need.' Ibid.

107 Galtung sees four dimensions to a genuine security. The first is '*the extent to which the country has a credible non-provocative defence*, and not an offensive military capacity.' The second is 'non-alignment, *the degree of decoupling from the superpowers.*' The third is '*the extent to which the country itself has inner strength*, by being reasonably self-reliant in essentials (food, energy, health, defence); not being too centralized; having some reservoir of

develop militaristic forces of coercion. Negating such a perceived need also seems to require a more internationalist approach. Convivial, soft technologies can be thought to be the negation of those technologies (such as a civil nuclear power programme) appropriate to supporting the arms race. The replacement by egalitarian economic relations and greater self-sufficiency (also a feature of Galtung's 'defensive defence') of those competitive and inegalitarian relations of production which offer a surplus to the state can be viewed as the negation of those relations. And finally, a decentralized participatory democracy can be viewed as the negation of a pseudo-representative, centralized bureaucracy. The employment of the State-Primacy Theory thus makes it possible to unite the core values of radical green political thought into a coherent whole.

Of course, there are independent environmental reasons that can be provided for preferring decentralization, self-sufficiency, egalitarianism, alternative technology, pacifism and internationalism. For example, as was mentioned earlier, it has been claimed that decentralized, small-scale, self-sufficient communities have a far lower environmental impact.[108] It has also been argued that only greater equality can prevent the poor (never mind the excessively affluent) from destroying the environment – for example, by being driven onto marginal land that cannot sustain them.[109] Only alternative technology seems to allow an environmentally sustainable economy.[110] Unlike dropping Agent Orange on complex

---

intermediate technology to fall back on; not being too easily fragmented by class, ethnic and other conflicts; above all by being autonomous.' The fourth, and most problematic, is '*the extent to which the country is useful to others* if left in peace, so that belligerents prefer to leave it intact.' J. Galtung, *There Are Alternatives! Four Roads to Peace and Security* (Nottingham: Spokesman, 1984), pp. 12–13.

108 See Edward Goldsmith *et al.*, *A Blueprint for Survival* (Harmondsworth: Penguin, 1972), pp. 50–3. Moreover, as Dryzek argues, centralized administrative systems seem to be particularly unsuited to solving ecological problems. See John S. Dryzek, 'Ecology and discursive democracy: beyond liberal capitalism and the administrative state' in Robert E. Goodin (ed.), *The Politics of the Environment* (Aldershot: Edward Elgar, 1994), especially pp. 400–1.

109 'Environmental stress has often been seen as the result of the growing demand on scarce resources and the pollution generated by the rising living standards of the relatively affluent. But poverty itself pollutes the environment, creating environmental stress in a different way. Those who are poor and hungry will often destroy their immediate environment in order to survive: They will cut down forests; their livestock will overgraze grasslands; they will overuse marginal land; and in growing numbers they will crowd into congested cities. The cumulative effect of these changes is so far-reaching as to make poverty itself a major global scourge.' Brundtland *et al.*, *Our Common Future*, p. 28.

110 Since the WCED report, the concept 'sustainable development' has gained common currency. But there is considerable confusion with respect to what the concept means. The authors of the report themselves define 'sustainable development' in their Tokyo Declaration 'simply as an approach to progress which meets the needs of the present without compromising the ability of future generations to meet their own needs.' Ibid., p. 364. But does this mean, in effect, 'sustained development'? There are many who wish to interpret the notion in this way. But that we can go on developing our productive capacity forever on

ecosystems or exploding nuclear devices, non-violent direct action is usually environmentally harmless. Moreover, environmentally benign technologies seem to be most suited to small communities.[111] And although decentralized, small-scale, self-sufficient communities would have to act locally, ecologically-aware ones might feel more inclined than present states to take into account the global implications of their actions.

In this chapter, however, I have been concerned principally with the political interrelationships between the various elements of radical green thinking. And as the State-Primacy Theory enables them to be linked together systematically through an analysis of contemporary society that takes into account both political and economic inequalities, then green political theory does not have to be Marxist for it to avoid being theoretically unsophisticated or inherently biased towards the middle classes.[112]

So, the values that radical greens espouse can be linked together coherently and in a quite distinctive manner. It is the urgent need to answer the threat posed by the very real possibility of being entrapped within an environmentally hazardous dynamic which provides the most compelling of motivations for embracing decentralization, participatory democracy, egalitarianism, self-sufficiency, alternative technology, pacifism and internationalism. It appears, then, that radical green political thought isn't, after all, a fast-food, cafeteria political ideology, grabbing from here and there without any rhyme or reason; instead, it seems well-balanced and wholesome. And it's top of today's menu.

---

a finite planet is highly implausible. Consequently, it would be preferable if 'sustainable development' were taken to mean 'development for sustainability' – i.e., developing and introducing the technologies and social practices which are appropriate for a sustainable society. For example: 'The woman who cooks in an earthen pot over an open fire uses perhaps eight times more energy than an affluent neighbour with a gas stove and aluminium pans. The poor who light their homes with a wick dipped in jar of kerosene get one-fiftieth of the illumination of a 100-watt electric bulb, but use just as much energy. These examples illustrate the tragic paradox of poverty.' Ibid., p. 196. In short, a degree of *appropriate* development appears to be a precondition for sustainability.

111 'Most renewable energy systems operate best at small to medium scales, ideally suited for rural and suburban applications. They are also generally labour intensive, which should be an added benefit where there is surplus labour.' Ibid., p. 194.

112 It should be noted that the political theory offered here is neutral with respect to anthropocentric, biocentric or more spiritual environmental approaches. Whether one's concern is for one's grandchildren, other species or a greater spiritual identification with nature, the eco-anarchist theory here adumbrated is equally applicable. And this is because remaining trapped within the environmentally hazardous dynamic depicted in Figure 6.1 would most likely cause immeasurable harm to one's grandchildren, other species and natural systems. Consequently, escaping from such a dynamic should be a priority for all environmentalists, irrespective of whether their environmentalism is anthropocentrically, biocentrically or more spiritually motivated.

7 Towards a cooperative autonomy

If the environmental threat looming on the horizon is as great as it appears to be, and if, as we have reason to believe, we are presently trapped within an environmentally hazardous dynamic (or, at the very least, if it would be collectively rational for us to act as if we were so entrapped), then what political practice is required of us? The environmentally hazardous dynamic depicted in Figure 6.1 follows from the State-Primacy Theory (modelled in Figure 4.1). But in identifying the state as the principal problem, and in thereby requiring as a solution its abolition, the theory is an anarchist one. This might suggest that it is some form of anarchist political practice that is required of us.

Unfortunately, 'anarchism' has had a very bad press; and not surprisingly, for it is hardly in the interests of the state to have its panoply of ideological apparatuses portray it in an attractive light. We have seen in the previous chapter that the State-Primacy Theory could employ functional explanations to account for prevailing ideologies. If, as such an extended State-Primacy Theory would claim, the educational system and the mass media[1] chosen are functional for the state, then they are unlikely to paint an anti-state approach *couleur de rose*. And from this perspective, it is unsurprising that a common stereotype of anarchists as bomb-throwing maniacs should predominate. Certainly, a small number of anarchists have, in the past, subscribed to 'propaganda by deed'. But, historically, it would seem that a far greater number of bombs have been thrown by nationalists, not to mention the uncountable number that have been dropped on civilians by states. Moreover, many anarchists are pacifists. And it would be a great injustice simply to denounce *them* as murderous terrorists, especially when it has been suggested by more than one historian that the most infamous acts of terrorism attributed to

1 One frequently heard claim is that, in the West, we enjoy a 'free press'. But not only are the organs of the media either owned by a small number of very rich individuals (whose interests appear to correspond with those of leading state personnel) or by the state itself, the media is often directly controlled by the state in ways that many members of 'the public' do not seem to realize. In Britain, for example, news items may easily be suppressed by the serving of a 'D-Notice' if their publication is deemed not to be in the national interest (read: 'not in the state's interest'). I have heard journalists claim that reporting of environmentally-motivated direct action has, on occasion, been suppressed, just as news of race-riots has been. One might suspect, just as in the latter case, in order to avoid the spread of 'copy-cat' actions.

anarchists, such as the Haymarket bombing in Chicago on 4 May 1886, were actually carried out by agents provocateurs.[2]

Nevertheless, given that attitudes towards anarchism are, in the main, extremely negative, calling a perspective 'anarchist' is a sure-fire way of inviting a quick dismissal. Anarchist arguments are frequently dismissed, often far too quickly, because of common perceptions of what 'anarchism' signifies. But most common conceptions of 'anarchism' are, it can be argued, misconceptions. So, let me begin this final chapter by trying to assuage one or two of the fears and suspicions that the label 'anarchist' might evoke. I shall attempt to do this in the course of addressing several philosophical issues which arise as a result of certain claims made by some who describe themselves, or are described by others, as 'anarchists': One is the actual definition of 'anarchism'. A second is the relationship between anarchy and chaos. And a third is the relationship between anarchists and other parts of the political spectrum – in particular, economic 'libertarians' such as Robert Nozick.[3]

7.1 Some comments on 'anarchism'

First of all, the word 'anarchy' derives from the Greek word αναρχία, which itself derives from the negative prefix αν (meaning 'without') and αρχή (meaning 'rule' or 'government'). Just as 'monarchy' means 'government by one', and 'oligarchy' means 'government by the few', so 'anarchy' literally means 'without government' or 'government by no one'. Hence, an anarchy would appear to be some form of stateless society. It would seem to be a society where no group has sustained power over another group (with possible exceptions, such as children or the mentally disabled).

This much at least seems clear. But 'anarchy' is often identified with 'chaos'. Yet given that 'anarchy' derives from 'without government', and not from 'chaos', the common presupposition that 'anarchy' means chaos is not an uncontested definition; rather, it is a *political conclusion*. 'Anarchy' is often assumed to mean chaos because it is usually presumed uncritically that without government, chaos would follow. Put another way, many simply assume that a condition without government would, of necessity, *cause* chaos. But given that many tribal peoples seem to have lived for thousands of years in some measure of peace and harmony without being subject to anything which most western political theorists would regard as a government,[4] such a political conclusion cannot simply be taken for

2 See, for examples, James Joll, *The Anarchists* (London: Methuen, 1979), p. 124 and George Woodcock, *Anarchism* (Harmondsworth: Penguin, 1975), p. 438.

3 See Robert Nozick, *Anarchy, State and Utopia* (New York: Basic Books, 1974).

4 On acephalus societies, see J. Middleton and D. Tait (eds), *Tribes without Rulers: Studies in African Segmentary Systems* (London: Routledge and Kegan Paul, 1970); also see Michael Taylor, *Community, Anarchy and Liberty* (Cambridge: Cambridge University Press, 1982), as well as Harold Barclay, *People Without Government* (London: Kahn and Averill with Cienfuegos Press, 1982).

granted. However, it is clearly in the state's interests that its citizens do take such a political conclusion for granted.

Of course, from the standpoint of the State-Primacy Theory extended to incorporate ideological state apparatuses within its complex of functional explanations, it would not be surprising if educational systems and mass media functional for the state were to attempt to inculcate into its citizens the belief that 'anarchy' should be defined as chaos, for that would be an effective method of prejudicing them in advance against anarchy. And by conceptually restricting political discourse, ideological state apparatuses could rule out by definitional fiat many of the most radical criticisms which might otherwise be levelled against the state. This suggests that if we are to retain the possibility of exploring certain radical criticisms of the state, we should resist *defining* 'anarchy' as chaos.

As 'anarchy' is thus a contested term, considerable disagreement abounds concerning what exactly an anarchist is (and not least among people who call themselves, or are called by others, 'anarchists'). *Minimally, an anarchist would appear*, at first glance, *to be one who approves of anarchy*. And, as we have just seen, from the standpoint of an extended State-Primacy Theory, it is understandable that many people (including a number who call themselves anarchists) should identify anarchy with chaos. Thus, whereas statists, not surprisingly, often conflate an absence of government with an absence of order, and hence have a tendency to label as 'anarchists' many of those whom they disagree with regarding the level of authority which should be imposed upon society, even some self-styled 'anarchists' identify anarchy with chaos – the difference being that they happen to like the idea of chaos. But if the presupposition that a lack of government would necessarily lead to chaos is false, then any such notion of what it is to be an 'anarchist' is simply confused. In which case, confusion might be avoided by labelling those with a penchant for disorder 'nihilists', instead of 'anarchists'.

Certainly, those who happen to like the idea of chaos could cite, in justification for calling themselves anarchists, an everyday, ordinary language definition of 'anarchy' which simply equates it with chaos. But, as we have seen, this might be the result of ideological manipulation. Moreover, the Oxford English Dictionary, which sees some value in identifying the roots of English words, includes the definition 'absence of government'. Hence, even relying on (what might be viewed as) an establishment-biased definition would still make the advocates of chaos at most only one kind of anarchist. Furthermore, they would comprise a kind with which it is difficult to have much sympathy, for the simple reason that few of us would want to see our fellow human beings subjected to chaos. It is doubtful that many of them would benefit from it.

Restricting the use of the term 'anarchist' to those I have suggested would better be labelled 'nihilists' seems unhelpful, then, for there is no reason why those who have a predilection for disorder should own a monopoly on the word 'anarchist', especially when they may well claim their monopoly on the basis of ideological circumscription, definitional confusion or a lack of familiarity with ethnographies of acephalus societies (or of accounts of Andalusian and Catalonian Spain during 1936 – another case often cited by anarchists as evidence for the possibility of a social order without government).

On the other hand, those who are part of the organized anarchist movement – 'fully paid-up anarchists', as it were – have a tendency to restrict the use of the term 'anarchist' to other active members. In other words, they tend to confine the description 'anarchist' to members of anarchist groups. Such groups seek to bring about a society in which there is no government – a society which these groups believe will be a considerable improvement on the present one. But limiting the label 'anarchist' to members of anarchist groups might also be thought to be too restricting because it does not seem that there is anything self-contradictory about referring to those who oppose the state, yet choose not to belong to an anarchist organization, as anarchists. For example, if someone dislikes those who happen to be in the movement (perhaps because certain misconceptions of 'anarchy' attract towards anarchist groups some people with personality disorders), and so does not join an anarchist organization, yet argues for and/or fights for a condition of anarchy, then it seems odd not to call him or her an anarchist just because he or she refuses 'to join the club'.

However, it is possible to have not just restricted[5] but also wider notions of 'anarchist'. Having argued against two restricted definitions of 'anarchist', I am left seeking a wide definition[6] – but not wide in the sense employed by several statists. I see no reason for including everyone who is not an outright authoritarian under the rubric 'anarchist'. It is useful to be able to distinguish between

5 John Clark prefers what is, perhaps, the most restrictive conception of 'anarchism', while allowing that those excluded might be 'anarchists' in a looser sense: 'In order for a political theory to be called "anarchism" in a complete sense, it must contain: (1) a view of an ideal, noncoercive, nonauthoritarian society; (2) a criticism of existing society and its institutions, based on this antiauthoritarian ideal; (3) a view of human nature that justifies the hope for significant progress toward the ideal; and (4) a strategy for change, involving immediate institution of noncoercive, nonauthoritarian and decentralist alternatives.' John P. Clark, 'What is anarchism?', *Freedom*, Vol. 40, No. 3 (1979), p. 13. Clark is surely right that anarchism as a coherent political philosophy is likely to comprise four such elements. And, admittedly, if the political theory in question is to be regarded as a variety of anarchism, then it must assume that 'noncoercive, nonauthoritarian and decentralist alternatives' to the state are possible. But it is doubtful that all varieties of anarchism have to assume that such alternatives can, in practice, be introduced immediately. Surely, one could, conceivably, subscribe to a gradualist version of anarchism. Moreover, couldn't one be an anarchist of a sort (or liberal, or conservative, for that matter) without having either a coherent or a fully comprehensive political philosophy?

6 Given a wide definition of 'anarchist', then anarchists can be divided into many different varieties. Eltzbacher, for example, identifies (a) anarchist teachings as in general genetic, critical, idealistic, eudemonistic, altruistic or egoistic; (b) anarchist prescriptions for the future as federalistic or spontanistic; (c) anarchist notions of law as anomistic or nomistic; (d) anarchist views of property as indoministic or partly dominístic (the latter being partly individualistic or partly collectivistic); and (e) anarchist strategies as reformatory or revolutionary (the latter being renitent or insurgent). See P. Eltzbacher, *Anarchism: Exponents of the Anarchist Philosophy* (New York: Libertarian Book Club, 1960), pp. 200–202.

different political creeds, and lumping together too many different colours of the political spectrum can hardly serve the cause of clarity. Some liberals are not too fond of excessive government; but that does not mean that they are complete opponents of the state.

7.1.1 Anarchism and the minimal state

However, mention of liberals gives rise to an important issue. It is often assumed that anarchists must always be closer to liberals than to state socialists. For example, consider the following remark by Henry David Thoreau: 'I heartily accept the motto, – "That government is best which governs least; " and I should like to see it acted up to more rapidly and systematically. Carried out, it finally amounts to this, which I also believe, – "That government is best which governs not at all" '.[7] This might be taken to imply that having a minimal state is the next best thing to having no state.

Yet, in a number of ways, many anarchists can be closer to those who desire a very large state than to those who desire a minimal state. Many state socialists desire economic equality. They often seek a large state in order to redistribute wealth and to cater for the needy. Many anarchists are also egalitarian with regard to the distribution of wealth. However, they usually believe that the state exists to protect inequalities or to serve itself. Such anarchists frequently claim that if the state were to be abolished, then great inequalities could not so easily be perpetuated, and society would be much more equal. State socialists are thus criticized by many anarchists because the latter usually believe that if the state is employed ostensibly to create equality, then it will serve its own interests in the process. And equality will not be the end result.[8]

What is worth noting is that many anarchists thus appear nearer to state socialists with respect to the goal of economic equality than they are to those who desire a minimal state in order to allow the private accumulation of wealth. (This is why it might not be wholly misleading to place most anarchists on the left of the political spectrum.) A state which merely existed to protect property rights, and which did nothing about redistribution towards equality, would probably bring about a situation (namely, considerable inequality) which was far worse than that produced by the welfare state. In other words, as paradoxical as it might at first

7 Henry David Thoreau, 'Civil disobedience' in *Walden and Other Writings* (New York: Bantam, 1971), p. 85.

8 Some also argue that the institutionalization of care is counterproductive, and that a genuine community care would be far more beneficial than anything offered by faceless, professional bureaucrats, who merely do a job without any real feeling for their clients – a point acknowledged, for example, in Peter Singer, 'Reconsidering the famine relief argument' in Peter G. Brown and Henry Shue (eds), *Food Policy: The Responsibility of the United States in the Life and Death Choices* (New York: The Free Press, 1977). Genuine community care, of course, would be very different from providing no care under the guise of placing care back into the hands of the community.

seem, many anarchists are in a number of important ways closer to maximal statists than they are to minimal statists.

One implication of this is that it is not true that for all anarchists the less state the better. For those who are extremely concerned about inequality,[9] more state action (if it is a welfare state) could be regarded, in certain circumstances, as preferable to less state action (if it is a state like Nozick argues for – one that is restricted primarily to the protection of private property).[10] But clearly, the most preferable condition for anarchists would be that of no state at all. Nevertheless, regarding economic equality, a condition of 'no-state' could be considered to be closer to one of 'more state' than either would be to one of 'less state'. And that is one very good reason for not confusing anarchists with liberals or economic 'libertarians' – in other words, for not lumping together everyone who is in some way or other critical of the state. It is also a good reason for thinking that calling the likes of Nozick an 'anarchist' is highly misleading.[11] In other words, genuine anarchists do not just argue for less state. Ultimately, they are content with nothing less than no state.

It is also worth noting that just as 'anarchy' is not coextensive with 'chaos', neither does it necessarily imply being able to do anything one likes. There are, apparently, a number of self-styled 'anarchists' who assume that this is precisely what all anarchist doctrines justify. For them, being an anarchist involves doing whatever they please without restriction and without taking others into account. Certainly, if one wishes to be free to do as one likes, then (unless one happens to be at the head of the state) one cannot consistently desire any effective government. But that is not to say that a society without government has to be one in which anyone is free to do anything he or she likes irrespective of anyone else. Just as it is difficult to have much sympathy for nihilists, it is difficult to sympathize with those who regard anarchism as a justification for their own self-centredness. One reason for having sympathy with the anarchist position is that if anarchists are

9 Kropotkin, for one, regards equality as the fundamental principle of anarchism. See Peter Kropotkin, 'Anarchist morality' in *Kropotkin's Revolutionary Pamphlets* (New York: Dover, 1970).

10 Nozick's minimal state is confined to providing security, enforcing contracts and preserving property. This is only minimal with respect to the number of its functions. In failing to provide welfare, it would most likely require a massive coercive apparatus to protect the inequalities that would inevitably arise. Hence, ironically, a minimal state might end up having more personnel and being more costly than a welfare state. And in being more coercive, a minimal state would be all the more objectionable to anarchists. I am grateful to Jerry Cohen for drawing my attention to this point.

11 See, for example, David Miller, *Anarchism* (London: Dent, 1984), which is one of the most academically respected books on anarchist thought, yet which includes an account of Nozick. Interestingly, certain Marxists have been content to call Nozick an 'anarchist' and have also been happy to allow him and so-called 'anarcho-capitalists' to appropriate the term 'libertarian'. (On the origin of this term within anarchist discourse, see Chapter 2, note 54, above.) To have anarchists who are economic egalitarians lumped together with Nozick is clearly functional for state-socialism. For just as the 'capitalist state' has an interest in fostering misconceptions of its critics, so, too, does the 'socialist state'.

right in believing that the state causes the major social and environmental problems which we seem to face, then anarchy might allow improved relations between people and their environment. And wanting that is rather different from not wanting to have to take others into account.

7.1.2 An alternative conception of 'anarchism'

How, then, ought we to understand the term 'anarchism', in the sense of a political belief system? As 'anarchy' literally means 'without rule' (thus signifying a situation in which no person rules over another), then a condition of pure anarchy might be thought to consist in a complete equality of political power – perfect political equality, as it were. But, many would object, if anarchists seek pure anarchy in this sense, then, quite simply, they are seeking the unattainable. In any practicable social arrangement, some people are bound to possess more power than others.

However, anarchism is not the only political belief system which appears at first sight to be incoherent in so far as its adherents seem to be seeking the unattainable. Egalitarianism has been dismissed on similar grounds. If egalitarians are seeking perfect equality (which, it is often assumed, means that everyone is to be made exactly the same), then, many would object, they are seeking the unattainable. However, John Baker has challenged the view that egalitarians *are* seeking perfect equality (in this sense). Rather, in his view, egalitarians merely oppose certain substantive inequalities.[12] And if 'egalitarianism' is construed as the opposition to certain substantive inequalities, then it is not so easy to dismiss.

Perhaps, then, 'anarchism' should be interpreted in a similar way. Perhaps, not all anarchists should be dismissed out of hand for attempting to bring about pure anarchy. Rather, anarchists might perhaps be more profitably viewed as those who oppose certain substantive *political* inequalities, and not merely economic ones. For anarchists usually most oppose certain inequalities in political power, just as ordinary egalitarians usually most oppose certain inequalities in economic power. And the most significant political inequalities, for

12 The principles of equality which, according to Baker, egalitarians generally wish to defend are the following: First, everyone's basic needs ought to be met. Second, everyone deserves sufficient respect for snobbery and patronizing attitudes to be unacceptable. Third, massive income differentials should not exist, and some should not be forced to spend their lives confined to unpleasant work. Undesirable tasks ought, instead, to be shared out. Fourth, power should be more equal so that those who are presently powerless have greater control over their own lives. Fifth, different treatment based on colour, sex, culture, religion or disability ought to be opposed. In Baker's opinion, egalitarians usually wish to defend these five principles. Thus, in his view, the demand for equality is not a demand for one simple thing, such as the same income for everyone. Rather, it is a demand for a number of substantive inequalities to be removed. See John Baker, *Arguing for Equality* (London: Verso, 1987), pp. 4–5. However, while Baker does mention inequalities in power, which includes political power, most egalitarians have tended to focus their opposition on inequalities in economic power.

anarchists, would seem to be those which flow from centralized, authoritarian forms of government.

This suggests that 'anarchism', as a political belief system, might best be construed as having both a normative and an empirical component. Anarchism could be viewed as containing a *normative* opposition to certain substantive political inequalities, along with the *empirical* belief that political equality (in the sense of an absence of specific, substantive political inequalities) is inevitably undermined by state power.[13] Given the normative component, anarchism can thus be regarded as a form of egalitarianism – political egalitarianism. However, many of those who advocate representative democracy would also regard themselves as political egalitarians. It is the second feature which would distinguish anarchists from others who claim to value political equality – namely, the empirical belief (which most of those who describe themselves as 'anarchists' tend to hold) that centralized, authoritarian forms of government (including varieties of representative democracy) cannot deliver political equality.

Thus, given the conceptualization of 'anarchism' proposed here, *for an individual to be an anarchist, he or she would have to hold both the normative opposition to certain substantive political inequalities and the empirical belief that they principally derive from, or are preserved by, or are embedded within, certain centralized forms of power.*[14] Hence, all anarchists, on the proposed definition, oppose the state. But that should not be confused with an opposition to society. Nor should it be confused with a rejection of all of the rules that a society might need – for example, moral rules. In fact, most anarchists are highly moral.[15] Consequently, when discussing anarchism, it is extremely important to realize that 'without rule' does not have to signify 'without rules', nor does it have to mean a lack of structure. What is surely crucial to any version of anarchism worth its salt is that

13 It is interesting that Joseph Raz should emphasize 'the intrinsic desirability of people conducting their own life by their own lights', and then proceed to admit that 'the validity of a claim to authority . . . is hard to make.' However, as he immediately adds, 'if anarchists are right to think that it can never be made, this is for contingent reasons and not because of any inconsistency in the notion of authority, nor in the notion of authority over moral agents.' Joseph Raz, *The Morality of Freedom* (Oxford: Clarendon, 1988), p. 57. I am in complete agreement that if anarchists are right in this respect, then it is, as Raz points out, because certain of their empirical claims are true.

14 And it seems to me that this conception of what it is to be an 'anarchist' captures all of the classical anarchist theorists, including William Godwin, Max Stirner, Pierre-Joseph Proudhon, Mikhail Bakunin and Peter Kropotkin, as well as more recent anarchists such as Paul Goodman, Noam Chomsky, Colin Ward, Nicholas Walter and Murray Bookchin. Moreover, it avoids anarchists having to offer attempted defences of seemingly indefensible views, such as feeling compelled to advocate a society without any power relations or authority whatsoever.

15 For one interpretation of several of the major anarchist theorists which stresses the central role of morality in their thought, see George Crowder, *Classical Anarchism: The Political Thought of Godwin, Proudhon, Bakunin and Kropotkin* (Oxford: Clarendon, 1991). However, Crowder's claim that the classical anarchists subscribed to the positive conception of freedom seems to me to be mistaken. See my review of Crowder's book in *Political Studies*, Vol. 43, No. 1 (1995), p. 216.

the anarchist structures it proposes be empowering to those within them, and do not lead to a centralization of power or decision-making. Even with those restrictions, the possibilities for anarchist social organization are clearly far greater than most opponents of anarchism realize or than is portrayed in popular stereotypes of anarchist practice.

7.2 Creating cooperative autonomy

Let me, then, turn to the question of anarchist social organization. A common view of anarchism is that, as it assumes that we would have a far better society without a state, then it is a political philosophy which concludes that in order to bring about a desirable society, it is merely sufficient to abolish the state.[16] This is an assumption which deserves examining, as does a closely related one – namely, that the state must be abolished prior to any effort at embarking on the formation of a truly desirable society.

Anarchists have forwarded impressive reasons in defence of the claim that a society without a state would be preferable to the one which we presently inhabit. They have provided telling criticisms of statist societies and statist solutions to social problems.[17] They have pointed out that when states are employed to provide a solution, they usually give rise to far greater problems than they are designed to solve. Many statists have argued that without a state, it would be impossible to settle disputes. Anarchist theorists have replied that there are far simpler solutions to such problems (for example, by rotating arbitrators), and that permanently armed bodies charged with the task of settling disputes inevitably settle them in a way which is to their own advantage and to the disadvantage of those who are subsequently rendered powerless.[18] Many authoritarians have argued that without a state there would be nothing to keep order, and violence would be widespread. Anarchists have justifiably insisted that it is difficult to imagine greater violence or disorder than that resulting from warring states. Institutionalized violence is probably the most worrying kind. Besides, the study of

16 This is a perception shared by a number of those who today call themselves 'anarchists'. It is particularly common among several self-styled 'anarchists' who have little familiarity with the complexity of nineteenth-century anarchist thought. Moreover, given that this is a popular stereotype of anarchism, it merits consideration.

17 See, for example, April Carter, *The Political Theory of Anarchism* (London: Routledge and Kegan Paul, 1971).

18 Anarchists would add that this problem is not merely confined to the concentration of coercive forces in a few hands. It also extends to the concentration of expertise. As Bakunin writes: 'A scientific body to which had been confided the government of society would soon end by devoting itself no longer to science at all, but to quite another affair; and that affair, as in the case of all established powers, would be its own eternal perpetuation by rendering the society confided to its care ever more stupid and consequently more in need of its government and direction.' Michael Bakunin, *God and the State* (New York: Dover, 1970), pp. 31–2. Bakunin had in mind socialist state-planners, but his criticism might equally apply to a body of ecological experts in whom society had entrusted its governance.

stateless societies seems to show that a feeling of community and mutual trust is what is needed in order to reduce violence.[19] And the institutionalization of social relations appears to undermine any genuine community and feelings of altruism,[20] and thus it seems to impair what is quite possibly the only solution to the problem of social disharmony – the very problem which states profess to answer.

Moreover, almost any small, decentralized, self-governing community would be far more peaceful than societies plagued by military death-squads. Anarchist theorists have, therefore, argued cogently that to solve the problem of disorder by setting up military rulers is to create a far greater potential problem than that which the 'solution' is supposed to solve. Many statists have then resorted to the claim that human beings are naturally bad and need a state to keep them in order. Anarchists have pointedly replied that even if it were the case that people are naturally bad, then that on its own would provide no justification for the state. For if people are naturally bad, then the worst thing that one could do is to set up a centralized, authoritarian structure for one of them to control. Effective states magnify the power of those at their centre. Hitler without the state would have been an irrelevant little man. At the head of the Nazi state-machine, he was one of the twentieth century's greatest nightmares.

Anarchists, then, would prefer a society where people govern themselves. And they usually insist that a self-governing society where no one can impose sustained, arbitrary authority over another and where all have equal powers of decision-making would be the ideal social form. But, I have argued, an anarchy does not have to be quite so pure. Rather, we could consider an anarchist society to be one where power is distributed and dispersed as widely as is practicably possible. On the conceptualization of 'anarchism' propounded in Section 7.1.2, such a society would count as anarchist just so long as no substantive political inequalities prevailed. But, many self-styled anarchists argue, for *any* anarchist society to arise, the state (which is the locus of centralized power, and thus is regarded as the cause, not solution, of social antagonisms) must first be smashed. To create the new harmonious order, it is sometimes claimed, we must begin by destroying the old, oppressive society. Destruction, then, is the prelude to the real 'millennium', as it were.

However, such an anarchist position could rest upon a fallacy. When we talk about creating something, usually it is a new form that is created. We do not ordinarily create new matter. What we do is re-arrange matter so as to produce a different form. And when re-ordering matter into a new form, we necessarily

19 See Ashley Montagu (ed.), *Learning Non-Aggression: The Experience of Non-literate Societies* (Oxford: Oxford University Press, 1978).

20 It can also be argued that the commodification of previously altruistic social relations can undermine them. See, for example, Richard M. Titmuss, *The Gift Relationship: From Human Blood to Social Policy* (London: George Allen and Unwin, 1970). Also see Peter Singer, 'Altruism and commerce: a defense of Titmuss against Arrow', *Philosophy and Public Affairs*, Vol. 2, No. 3 (1973), pp. 312–20. To the extent that the state plays a role in such commodification, anarchists could legitimately deploy this argument.

destroy its old form. Creation necessarily implies destruction. We cannot create without destroying. In order to create, it is necessary to destroy. This seems uncontentious. The mistake that can be made lies in assuming that this truism necessarily refers to a chronological, rather than to a logical, order. The fallacy arises when one jumps to the conclusion that if one is to create, then one must *first* destroy. But that is not entailed by the proposition:

(D-C) In order to create it is necessary to destroy.

This proposition does not entail that destruction must precede creation, for the reason that the old form could be destroyed quite simply *by* an act of creation. It is not that one must be destructive *before* one can be creative, because one can be destructive by being creative.[21] Of course, it might be the case that certain institutions prevent the creation of a new form, and that the only way that a new institution could arise *is* by first destroying the restricting institution. But whether or not this is so is an empirical matter. It cannot be presumed *a priori* that all of the old institutions have to be destroyed before a new form can arise, simply because creation necessitates destruction. In certain cases, it is conceivable that the prior destruction of the old form would make it more difficult, if not impossible, for a particular new form to arise.

Are certain self-styled anarchists right, then, to presuppose that destruction of the old social order must precede, rather than be an aspect of, the setting up of a new social form? They are not right to presuppose it *a priori* on the basis of creation necessitating destruction, as we have seen. What empirical claims, then, could they offer in support of their belief that destruction must precede creation?

One argument common amongst many anarchists is that human beings are naturally good or cooperative, and that they are only evil or uncooperative because of the society in which they live.[22] Specifically, the existence of the state is argued to engender uncooperative behaviour. To take one example, the state protects private property, and the institution of private property can be argued to result in persons viewing each other as isolated property holders, rather than as sharing members of a community. Private property and the market can easily be argued to result in competitive and uncaring behaviour. Were the state (which enforces the institution of private property) to be removed, so the argument goes, then people would naturally cooperate. Or, to take another example, people are not usually made more caring and cooperative by being conscripted into an army and then trained to hate and kill other people.

However, if we are to feel confident that just abolishing the state is adequate for

21 In Hindu mythology, the Dance of Shiva signifies the perpetual round of destruction and creation, and 'Maya' means the illusion of the world. Hence, if the Dance of Shiva is presumed by necessity first to have destructive and then to have creative movements, it would indeed appear to be a form of Maya.

22 See, for example, Peter Kropotkin, *Mutual Aid: A Factor of Evolution* (Boston: Extending Horizons Books, n.d.).

a new and desirable order to arise safely, then we would have to *know* that people are naturally cooperative, otherwise something which is even worse than a statist society might arise in its place – perhaps real chaos. But how could the claim that people are naturally cooperative be established? We do not have any examples of individuals outside of any society (except, perhaps, for children who have been brought up by wolves – but they seem more to exhibit the characteristics of wolfish society than natural human behaviour, whatever that is). How, then, can we ascertain what a 'natural' human being is like? More to the point, if people are made competitive because of the state, as this anarchist argument suggests, then social forces must affect human behaviour. Furthermore, the fact that people in different cultures behave in a different manner must suggest that socialization plays, at the very least, a significant role in character formation. How, then, can it be presumed that were the state to be abolished, people would be naturally anything other than that which the state had encouraged them to be while it existed – namely, as many anarchists allege, uncooperative, hierarchical and authoritarian?[23]

Hence, the problem is that if competitive and statist societies produce uncooperative people, how can it be assumed that, merely by smashing the state, such products of undesirable societies will automatically cooperate? One possible argument is that, even in competitive societies, a great deal of cooperative behaviour takes place when institutions do not get in the way.[24] There certainly are impressive examples of cooperation without, and even in spite of, the state. Unfortunately, any number of positive examples is insufficient to prove that without a state people would be able to cooperate satisfactorily. This is because the logic of the social situation is such that one bad example seems to weigh far more than a hundred good ones. Consider the need for mutual trust and honesty if a society is to operate in an acceptable manner. Today, in our society, we cannot leave our doors unlocked just because a large number of our neighbours reveal a remarkable degree of honesty. *One* dishonest neighbour is sufficient to ensure that distrust, rather than trust, abounds. Similarly, any number of impressive examples of cooperative behaviour are insufficient to establish that, without the state, people would naturally cooperate to the necessary degree.

As examples of cooperative behaviour are insufficient to establish that abolishing the state is all that is required, where does that leave us? If people are not all

23 Kropotkin argues: 'Equality in mutual relations with the solidarity arising from it, this is the most powerful weapon of the animal world in the struggle for existence.' Kropotkin, 'Anarchist morality', p. 99. According to Kropotkin, for the species to survive, people have naturally evolved into cooperative individuals. Thus, a sense of solidarity would prevail were it not for the social structures that we inhabit and which pervert us. But this is to acknowledge that we are, to some extent at least, socially conditioned. In fact, Kropotkin clearly admits this when he discusses the case of Jack the Ripper, whom Kropotkin sees as the product of circumstances. But in this case, how are we to ascertain what is natural? If people are to some extent the product of social circumstances, how are we to know what they would be like naturally?

24 See Kropotkin, *Mutual Aid*. Also see Colin Ward, *Anarchy in Action* (London: Freedom Press, 1982).

naturally good and cooperative, that doesn't mean that they are naturally evil and uncooperative. Surely, the many examples of cooperative societies show that this is not the case. People appear to be socialized into being either cooperative or uncooperative depending upon the social structures into which they are born and in which they live and work – in other words, depending upon how other members of their society relate to them. In our society, most people are socialized into being very uncooperative. In that case, it does seem rather utopian to assume that such individuals will naturally cooperate once the state is smashed.

7.2.1 Anarchism and pre-figurative forms

Ought we, therefore, to reject anarchism? That would be over hasty. Certainly, we ought to doubt the assumption made by some who claim to be anarchists that smashing the state is sufficient for a cooperative anarchist society to emerge. When most of the great anarchist theorists were writing – such as Godwin, Proudhon and Bakunin – the majority of Europeans were peasants, and the state played a relatively insignificant part in their lives. As their behaviour at harvest time indicates, peasants were obviously able and willing to organize themselves cooperatively. That is not obviously true of most of us today. Society has changed fundamentally since the middle of the nineteenth century. We have all been subject to state education, for one thing. For another, we are all used to state provisions for health, as well as state provisions for security. And interestingly, such state provisions are clearly functional for the state in so far as they encourage its citizens to believe that the state is essential for their well-being.[25] Thus, many individuals, faced with the collapse of the state, would undoubtedly want nothing better than for a new one to arise, and would probably fight to establish a new state. But even so, that does not leave anarchists in a hopeless position. All it means is that anarchists ought to think carefully about the destruction of the state.

Let me return to the assumption that in order to create one must first destroy. I argued that one can, instead, destroy *by* creating. And there, perhaps, lies the answer. By creating prefigurative anarchist forms – by creating new social organizations which incorporate anarchist social relations – then the old order could, perhaps, be challenged. In short, to the extent that particular social forms were effective in socializing people towards cooperation and autonomy, then they could be expected to develop individuals who would neither support the state nor seek a new one should the present order be abolished.

So, although the destruction of the state is unlikely, on its own, to result in a

25 It might also be argued that, in 'late capitalism', capitalist relations are functional for the state in so far as they seem to require a measure of overall planning, which serves to justify the states' existence. It is perhaps not all that surprising, therefore, that those seeking governmental office should so often prioritize their claim to be the politicians most suited to managing the economy effectively.

desirable anarchist society, the creation of social forms which socialized people towards cooperation and autonomy could allow them to evolve into precisely the sort of individuals capable of creating a viable anarchist society.[26] If individuals seek their own autonomy, but in asserting their autonomy find themselves incapable of working together, then their desire for an anarchist society is bound to be frustrated. Just as any attempt to set up a participatory democracy seems to require of us that we learn democratic skills, *any* workable anarchy seems to require the acquisition of cooperative skills. If people are not naturally cooperative anarchists, then perhaps what anarchists should be doing is not just trying to smash the state, but, instead, organizing alternative social structures which socialize people towards cooperation and autonomy. In other words, anarchists might actually serve anarchism more effectively by constructing social structures which would enable those individuals who chose to enter them voluntarily to cooperate together on a free and equal basis. If people are not naturally cooperative anarchists, then simply abolishing the state would not be the fundamental task for anyone sympathetic to anarchism. Rather, it would first be to create the conditions most appropriate for a desirable form of anarchy – what might be called a '*cooperative autonomy*'.

What prefigurative anarchist forms might serve such a purpose? Possible candidates for appropriate organizations and structures are workers' cooperatives, communes and municipal direct democracies, where individuals can freely choose to organize themselves on a cooperative basis, and where many serious anarchists are active. These structures could, conceivably, provide the preconditions for a workable anarchy.[27]

But one objection that is likely to be raised against this line of reasoning is that the state would, as a matter of empirical fact, prevent the emergence of prefigurative anarchist forms. The state does not, at present, prevent the formation of workers' cooperatives or communes. But that is not to say that, were the anarchist potential of these cooperatively autonomous forms to become more evident, the state would not inhibit their formation.

However, if such cooperatively autonomous structures were seen by the mass of the population as offering the only viable escape route out of the environmentally hazardous dynamic portrayed in Figure 6.1, then the state might be unable to prevent their proliferation. On the other hand, if the state deliberately and overtly inhibited the growth of prefigurative anarchist structures, then the

26 C.f.: '"That government is best which governs not at all; " and when men are prepared for it, that will be the kind of government which they will have.' Thoreau, 'Civil disobedience', p. 85.

27 I should point out that I am not, of course, assuming that all economic and political problems can be overcome merely by the workers forming cooperatives. Nevertheless, for some defence of workers' coops against a number of criticisms, see Alan Carter, '"Self-exploitation" and workers' cooperatives', *Journal of Applied Philosophy*, Vol. 6, No. 2 (1989): 195–9 and Alan Carter, '"Institutional exploitation" and workers' cooperatives', *The Heythrop Journal*, Vol. 33, No. 4 (1992), pp. 426–33.

people might feel that they had no alternative but to reject the state. In order to survive, they might feel compelled to abolish it, or, at the very least, to resist it through engaging in civil disobedience.

Most importantly, collective civil disobedience directed against the state – for example, *environmentally-motivated, non-violent direct action* (NVDA) – could conceivably empower those engaged in it while simultaneously disempowering the state. When practised in a certain way, engaging in NVDA can, by itself, lead to autonomous cooperation becoming the norm among activists. One means of engaging in civil disobedience which has been favoured by many within the environmentally motivated direct action movement, and which might be thought especially appropriate for socializing individuals towards cooperative autonomy, is participation within 'affinity groups' – small groups of activists who know each other well, reach collective decisions about actions, and who offer each other mutual support. As Graham Baugh, one proponent of such groupings, writes:

> While the affinity group constitutes the most basic unit of an ecological society, direct action constitutes the social practice by which individuals assert their ability to control their own lives. Direct action is not just a tactic, but the political expression of individual competence to directly intervene in social life and manage social affairs without any mediation or control by bureaucrats or professional politicians. The individual takes direct action instead of relying on someone else to act for him or her. The action encompasses a wide range of activities, from organizing cooperatives to engaging in non-violent resistance to authority. The affinity group structure often provides an excellent vehicle for direct action, which places moral commitment above positive law. It is not meant to be a last resort when other methods have failed, but the preferred way of doing things. It enables people to develop a new sense of self-confidence and an awareness of their individual and collective power. Founded on the idea that people can develop their social competence and ability for self-rule only through practice, it proposes that all persons directly decide the important issues facing them.[28]

28 Graham Baugh, 'The politics of Social Ecology' in John Clark (ed.), *Renewing the Earth: The Promise of Social Ecology* (London: Green Print, 1990), pp. 100–101. And as Baugh adds: 'In the political sphere, this implies the practice of direct democracy. Instead of relying on elected representatives, people make political decisions themselves in general assemblies.' Ibid., p. 101. Some of the advantages affinity groups offer those engaged in non-violent direct action are the following. When individuals act within a team of friends sharing similar views, who remain in very close proximity to each other during an action: (1) it is less likely that individuals will be picked off by police or security guards and arrested or assaulted; (2) it is far more difficult for agents provocateurs to infiltrate an action or, should they successfully join an affinity group, cause trouble while participating in the action, for they would more likely be restrained by the rest of their affinity group; (3) it is less likely that the level of violence would escalate, for activists would not feel lost and isolated within a hysterical crowd and would be far less likely either to panic or to engage in inappropriate displays of bravado; rather, they could expect to experience mutual support from the rest of their group; and (4)

In short, self-organized environmentalist opposition to the state can, in the process, generate prefigurative anarchist forms capable of socializing individuals towards a cooperative autonomy.

All of the above argument is consistent with anarchist goals, even though it raises a number of objections to certain assumptions held by some self-styled anarchists. But are the above considerations consistent with the major tenets of anarchist political theory? Probably the most central theoretical claim made by numerous anarchists is that the state is the cause of the major social ills which we encounter. But does the claim that it is not necessarily sufficient to smash the state entail that the state is not, in fact, their cause, and, therefore, that anarchist theory is mistaken? No, because the state may well be the *immediate cause* of major social problems, even if it is not their *ultimate cause.*

Causal relations are, ordinarily, transitive. If *A* causes *B*, and *B* causes *C*, then it is usually permissible to regard *A* as causing *C*. Hence, anarchists may well be right to consider the state as the cause of major social problems. But it might also be the case that the state itself is the effect of other factors. And these factors could well cause the state to arise, which, once having arisen, would then be the cause of the major social ills. If this is in fact the case, then abolishing the state (the *immediate cause*) without getting rid of the *ultimate cause* may prove to be an ineffective strategy. For such an ultimate cause could either reconstitute the state, or give rise to even greater problems than those which we currently experience. In which case, any effective strategy would need to focus on the ultimate cause, for doing so could simultaneously address both the immediate cause (the state) and the problem of the re-emergence of those social problems which the state itself causes.

Well, what might be the ultimate, rather than the immediate, cause of social ills? What is it that gives power to the state? It would seem that there are a number of factors, rather than one straightforward ultimate cause. One possible factor underpinning state power is the authoritarian and hierarchical attitudes which prevail in our society. Not only do these attitudes support the state, their persistence would most likely lead to the re-emergence of the state or some even worse phenomenon were the state just simply to be smashed without such attitudes being transformed. Hence, it is not surprising that anarchists have laboured hard to challenge authoritarian and hierarchical attitudes, especially through their work in the field of libertarian education.[29]

Another possible factor underpinning state power is the situational logic which

---

the more volatile individuals would tend to be calmed down by the more sober group members. For a brief account of the useful role affinity groups can play in civil disobedience, see the direct action handbooks produced for the attempted occupations of the construction site of the Seabrook nuclear power station. For a comprehensive account of the theory and practice of NVDA, see Gene Sharp, *The Politics of Nonviolent Action*, 3 vols. (Massachusetts: Porter Sargent, 1973).

29 See, for example, Michael P. Smith, *The Libertarians and Education* (London: Unwin, 1983), Joel Spring, *A Primer of Libertarian Education* (Montreal: Black Rose, 1975), and Paul Goodman, *Compulsory Miseducation* (Harmondsworth: Penguin, 1971). Also see Ivan Illich, *Deschooling Society* (Harmondsworth: Penguin, 1971).

appears to act upon state personnel. Even those in a conscript army usually feel obliged to obey their commanders. This might be the result of the individual isolation which individuals can find themselves experiencing within such organizations. Hence, those occupying powerful positions within repressive state apparatuses might ordinarily be able to rely on each subordinate disciplining any other because of their mutual 'diffidence' (to borrow a term from Hobbes). If no one can trust anyone else not to report him or her out of fear of also being reported (and then executed), who would dare suggest rebellion? Consequently, it is not surprising that many anarchists have worked within the pacifist movement, promoting non-violent alternatives to militarized forms of 'defence'.

Yet another possible factor underpinning state power is the technology, and the desire for the technology, which the state can utilize. Not only does weapons technology support state power but also certain 'peaceful' forms of technology seem to have statist implications. An anarchist society based on nuclear power would strike few of us as being particularly feasible. There is little doubt that the nuclear police, with the special powers they have been granted, are not a purely accidental phenomenon. The risk of terrorists stealing plutonium, for example, appears to justify repressive measures and levels of secrecy that would be difficult to defend otherwise. Indeed, given the clear social implications of 'peaceful' nuclear technology, it is not surprising that the state should actively support the development of it, for in appearing to demand a secret, 'expert', hierarchical state, it is functional for just such a state. Not surprisingly, therefore, many anarchists have been active in the 'alternative technology' movement,[30] and in environmental politics generally.

Each of these factors – ideology (which can be fostered through certain ideological apparatuses, such as the state educational system), situational logic (which pertains to the state's repressive apparatuses), and particular forms of non-convivial technology – appears to be functional for the kind of state which could be expected to be implicated in the environmentally hazardous dynamic of Figure 6.1. Their presence would thus seem to require the acknowledgement of additional interrelations within any theory attempting to model the state system, for state power can be argued to be perpetuated by all three factors (see Figure 7.1).[31] And anarchists thus have grounds for opposing each of them.

What all of the above suggests is that if we want to be sure of surviving within a society comprised of autonomous, cooperating individuals, living in an environmentally benign and sustainable way, then not only would we have to reject the state, we would also have to render inoperative whichever factors give rise to it

30 See, for an historical example, Peter Kropotkin, *Fields, Factories and Workshops Tomorrow* (London: Unwin, 1974), and for a modern one, Murray Bookchin, 'Towards a liberatory technology' in idem., *Post-Scarcity Anarchism* (London: Wildwood House, 1974).

31 In Figure 7.1, X_1 selects Y_1 because Y_1 is functional for X_1, X_2 selects Y_2 because Y_2 is functional for X_2, and X_3 selects Y_3 because Y_3 is functional for X_3. For a discussion of this possible 'substructural' support of the state, see Alan Carter, *Marx: A Radical Critique* (Brighton: Wheatsheaf, 1988), Ch. 6.

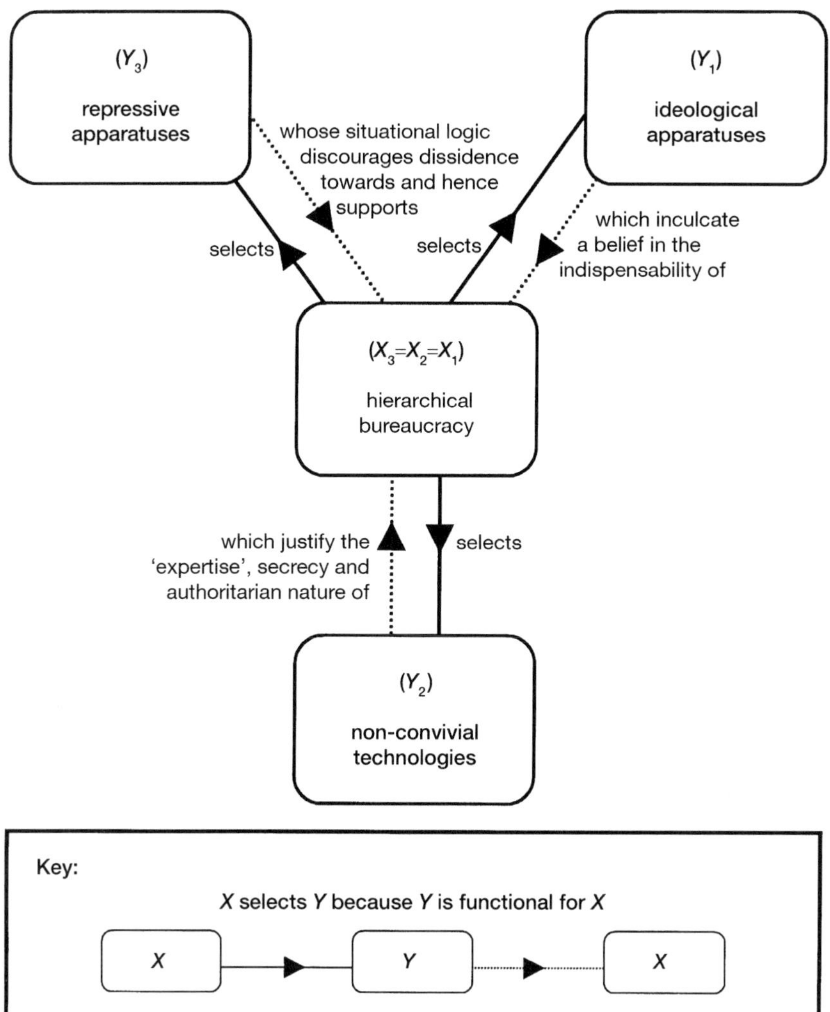

Figure 7.1 Three factors perpetuating the state

and perpetuate it. It thus seems that we would have to undermine authoritarian and hierarchical notions. It seems that we would have to build up trust and community so that it would be more difficult for the powerful to base their power on our mutual diffidence. And it seems that we would have to think very seriously about what kind of technology is appropriate not just to an environmentally sustainable society but also to an anarchist one. Without the factors that support the state, it is difficult to see how the state could persist. With such factors remaining in play, it is easy to see how a state, once dismantled, could later reconstitute itself. But then, if indeed we are entrapped within the environmentally hazardous dynamic depicted in Figure 6.1, the reconstitution of the state would start the dynamic rotating all over again.

How, then, should we respond to these factors? As there is reason to think that they would tend to be undermined by the prefigurative anarchist forms mentioned earlier, then if we are to reduce the risk of any continuing ensnarement within an environmentally hazardous dynamic, it seems that we ought to promote such forms. Participating in both workers' cooperatives and environmental direct action, for example, can lead to the rejection of authoritarian and hierarchical attitudes and practices. It can create mutual trust and overcome the diffidence we feel towards each other.

In short, that a desirable anarchist society could be created by merely smashing the state without first creating such prefigurative forms, or, more realistically, without employing them in the process of dismantling the state, would seem to be wishful thinking. By creating such prefigurative anarchist forms, we may well thereby dismantle the state. But were we to dismantle it without creating such prefigurative forms, we would probably just end up producing another state. Thus, instead of asserting that we must destroy in order to create, certain self-styled anarchists might serve the anarchist cause better by directly seeking to create.[32] And that is something which several of the classical anarchist theorists seem to have been well aware of.

7.3 A green vision

What kind of a society, then, should we be trying to create? In order to elude the environmentally hazardous dynamic depicted in Figure 6.1, and on the basis of the arguments deployed in previous chapters, it seems that we require a society which is simultaneously libertarian and egalitarian. Only such a society would appear to be a genuinely environmentally benign one. But is such a society even conceivable? To many people, the epithet 'libertarian' seems to suggest an individualist society, while 'egalitarian' suggests a collectivist one. Can this apparent contradiction be reconciled? I suggest that it can, but only within a genuine cooperative autonomy.

Political individualism has, of course, stressed the importance of the individual. Individualist political philosophers have tirelessly defended the individual and his or her rights against the incursions of oppressive and interfering governments or trade unions. But many in the individualist tradition have not stressed the importance of *all* individuals. Individuals have often been treated in isolation. And this has had disastrous consequences for some of them. As was argued in Chapter 3, the relations which obtain between individuals tend not to be given sufficient weight by individualists. Thus, individualists often espouse conceptions of free-

32 But, clearly, whatever structures anarchists might create with the intention of prefiguring an anarchist society, if they are to have any chance of successfully leading to such a society, then they cannot embody power relationships that would prove to be problematic later.

dom, for example, where one person might be free to squander resources, while another is free to starve.[33]

The usual justification for this is the right to do what one likes with one's private property, of course. But property is not simply private to an isolated person. Rather, it consists in a triadic relation – a *relation between persons with respect to things*. Private property consists of a relation principally concerning one's rights against others, and the obligations they owe one, with respect to one's exclusive use of a good.[34] Moreover, because of the use of private property, one person might be free to pollute profitably, while another has to incur the costs of the former's externalities. Viewing the individual in isolation, therefore, is unlikely to provide the basis for a socially and environmentally benign vision of the future.

Political collectivism, on the other hand, is not without its own problems. In setting up the collective as the object of fundamental importance, countless individuals can be sacrificed in its name – whether the worshipped collective entity be the Third Reich or the Proletarian State.

So, on the one hand, a socialist such as C. E. Vaughan had no trouble denouncing the individualism of the nineteenth century. At the beginning of the twentieth century, Vaughan could easily look back at all the horrors of the industrial revolution and attribute them to rampant individualism. As he wrote at the time, the results of individualism are

> writ large in the slums of our industrial cities, in the hovels which still disgrace many of our villages. [They are] writ larger yet in the monstrous conditions under which . . . our whole industrial system was allowed to grow up, and which were allowed to remain unchecked and unreproved for half a century: and all this under the 'all-atoning name of liberty,' of the sacred right of the master to buy his labour in the cheapest market, of parents and 'guardians' to sell the labour of their children for what it would fetch in a market which they themselves had artificially flooded.[35]

Whereas, on the other hand, at the close of the twentieth century, looking back over the past hundred years *we* cannot help but see the horrors of the totalitarian state, calling for its army of Stakhanovites, unquestioned conformity, the sacrifice of minorities, and the suppression of individuality, while its supporters insist that the only valid expression a person can make is through the state.

Neither individualism nor collectivism seems any longer to offer us a worthwhile vision. Surely, we cannot just consider individuals regardless of their

33 See, for example, F. A. von Hayek, *The Constitution of Liberty* (London: Routledge and Kegan Paul, 1960), Ch. 1.

34 See Alan Carter, *The Philosophical Foundations of Property Rights* (Hemel Hempstead: Harvester-Wheatsheaf, 1989).

35 C. E. Vaughan, intro. to Jean-Jacques Rousseau, *Principles du Droit Politique* (Manchester: The University Press, 1918), pp. xlix–l.

relations, nor can we afford to make such a god of the collective that individual people no longer matter. What we seem to require, instead, is an approach which values individuals within their relationships. But, surely, we would also need the relationships between individuals to be valuable, and for individuals to value each other. But if individuals are to value each other, then, it can be argued, they must respect each other's autonomy. But, on the other hand, how many people want to live the life of a hermit? A cooperative autonomy may well provide the solution to this apparent dichotomy. How? By each individual autonomously choosing to cooperate with others, while retaining his or her individual autonomy and respecting theirs. But what might count as living within a cooperative autonomy?

One possibility is living within a society where access to the land and to the means of production is individually enjoyed on a usufruct basis. An individual could then produce what he or she needed and share his or her work and its products with the others in the community. Individuals would thus be able to retain their autonomy at work, while enjoying the possibility of free cooperation. And within such an arrangement, it would no longer make sense to produce goods which had obsolescence built into them. Who would choose to waste his or her life working all day to produce things that others would soon have to replace so that he or she could buy their equivalent soon-to-be-replaced products? It would no longer make sense needlessly to squander resources and pollute the environment. Individuals who produced primarily for themselves and their local *community* wouldn't need such contrivances as fashion, for they would not depend upon getting others to throw perfectly good things away so that more of their goods could be sold.

In short, individuals living in a community which they controlled themselves would have no need to engage in completely unnecessary work. They would have no need to work in a factory that was unnecessarily poisoning the air they breath or on a farm that was unnecessarily destroying the fertility of the land they require to survive.

Perhaps work and other aspects of living might have to be institutionalized a little more than this. But there is no reason to think that a state is required to provide what is necessary for social reproduction, as Boris Frankel, for one, appears to assume.[36] In the 1980s, in its heyday, some of the most successful industries in Spain belonged to the Mondragon group of workers' cooperatives.[37] They had their own bank, their own university, their own technical college, their own schools, their own research institute and their own social security system. The workers controlled the factories themselves and they enjoyed an extremely egalitarian pay-structure. Institutions which supplied the factories with services, such as the bank, the university and the research institute, were second-degree cooperatives. Whereas all the board of directors of an industrial coop in the Mondragon group were elected by that cooperative's workers, a second-degree coop

36 See Boris Frankel, *The Post-Industrial Utopians* (Cambridge: Polity, 1987), pp. 204–5.
37 See Alastair Campbell, *Mondragon 1980* (Leeds: ICOM, n.d.), Pamphlet No. 9.

had some of the board elected by its workers, but the majority were elected by the industrial cooperatives which it served.

This successful model of second-degree cooperatives could provide a possible alternative to the capitalist system. Workers' coops are usually far more benign than ordinary factories. But they could, in principle, be just as polluting if the workers were desperate to remain competitive in a free market.[38] This notwithstanding, that the workers were in control of their own factories in the Mondragon group, and also benefited from relatively equal wages, was, in the view of many, a clear advance on capitalists' exploiting employees for profit. Today, while many of the original features of the Mondragon group still remain, the rates of pay display greater differentials than previously. This appears to have been a result of trying to attract and retain certain professionals. Such a problem is likely to persist while cooperatives have to work within a capitalist economic structure. And the problem of being forced to pollute in order to stay competitive is also likely to persist within such an economic structure.[39]

So, consider the following alternative: the second-degree cooperative structure is extended to all production units within a society so that the workers within each workplace, producing its share of the community's subsistence requirements, elect a minority of its board to represent their interests, while the community elects the majority to ensure that in doing the best for the workers, the enterprise does not, at the same time, harm the community or the environment. Such a structure might then meet the working requirements of its workers and the needs of both the local community and its environment.

Well, what kind of technology would such a self-directed community comprising such workplaces choose? Would it choose a form that contaminated the land and poisoned its children? Would it choose machines that individuals couldn't understand and which left them at the mercy of experts? Or would it prefer, instead, a technology that was 'user-friendly' and easy to repair and maintain? Would the technology chosen squander finite resources? Or would it tap the free, non-polluting energy of the sun, the wind and the sea? Would it pipe its waste onto its beaches? Or might it prefer, instead, to store it in biogas tanks, and then put it to use as fertilizer and as a source of energy?

Where would the members of such a cooperative autonomy choose to work? Would they choose to travel for hours each week just to get to their workplaces, and needlessly build roads all over the country in order to do so? Would they happily continue threatening to alter the global climate so that they could waste so much time getting nowhere in a permanent traffic jam? Would they build even

38 Moreover, a particular cooperative, being a collective, could turn out in practice to be a tyranny of the majority. Nevertheless, democratic control of production does at least allow the possibility of meaningful self-management, which is not the case with the economic dictatorship workers usually confront.

39 See Neil Carter, 'Worker cooperatives and green political theory' in B. Doherty and M. de Geus (eds), *Democracy and Green Political Thought: Sustainability, Rights and Citizenship* (London: Routledge, 1996) for several criticisms of Mondragon from a green perspective.

more roads to supply themselves with some product insignificantly different from their own? Or, instead, would they live close to their work and close to the land, meeting their own needs as far as possible themselves?

How would the members of such a community under their own control choose to work? Would they spend all day long in the same mindless routine within a working environment that excludes children and is therefore prejudiced against parents with infants? Or, instead, might autonomous individuals cooperating together prefer a less formal working arrangement? But to respect each individual's autonomy while facilitating their cooperation, the community would seem to require as participatory and consensual an approach to decision-making as possible – an approach that valued both autonomy and the desire to cooperate. But for this, a community would surely need to display certain characteristics. It would most likely have to be small, face-to-face and as self-sufficient or self-reliant as possible.

Moreover, there is no reason why such autonomous communities couldn't choose to cooperate with other communities, and they could, in principle, cooperate together by means of a structure paralleling that of their own internal social relations. For example, each community could send delegates to seek cooperative agreements with the other communities, subject to individual ratification. The communities would thereby voluntarily comprise a confederal system in which all the communities were respected as equals, as autonomous, and as willing to cooperate for the mutual benefit of all. And where might the mutual benefit of all be expected to lie? Surely, it would be found in a sustainable way of life that respected the integrity of the ecosphere upon which all depend. In short, such a cooperative autonomy would exhibit the ecological values of diversity and symbiosis. Such a way of life would be simultaneously green, anarchist and communist.

7.4 Two justifications of civil disobedience

But, of course, such a green anarcho-communist vision has not yet been realized in modern societies. What, then, should individuals do *now*, faced, as they appear to be, with an approaching environmental catastrophe? Earlier, it was claimed that environmental activism can provide a training ground for cooperative autonomy. Engaging in environmental protest can empower individuals and create a sense of solidarity between them. In other words, were it sufficiently widespread, environmental protest might provide the foundations required for the proliferation of green anarcho-communes, while simultaneously halting the most environmentally damaging developments. Perhaps, then, it is in individually motivated, cooperatively organized, non-violent civil disobedience that our future salvation lies?

However, there is a moral and political problem of paramount importance which this suggestion immediately gives rise to. Certainly, in the face of unjust and oppressive political regimes, the long tradition of non-violent civil disobedience has often been viewed as a noble one, with such milestone advocates as

Thoreau,[40] Tolstoy[41] and, of course, Gandhi.[42] In recent times, the question of civil disobedience re-surfaced dramatically during the 1960s, first with the civil rights movement in the United States, and then with widespread opposition to the Vietnam War. Civil disobedience played a prominent role in the transformations in Eastern Europe in 1989. Presently, non-violent civil disobedience is practised in Britain by animal liberationists,[43] most notably in opposition to the export of live animals and to bloodsports such as fox-hunting, and by environmentalists more widely construed, especially in protest against further road-building.[44]

The problem is this: Many people today would regard opposition to racist regimes as justifiable. A large number would sanction the refusal to fight in an unjust war. The majority would approve of the refusal to cooperate with a totalitarian dictatorship. But many of the protests currently being undertaken by environmentalists are directed against seemingly just and democratic institutions within liberal societies. In the West, few people regard themselves as living under oppressive regimes. If liberal democratic polities choose to degrade their environment, isn't that up to them? Isn't it their choice and no one else's business? In a word, can the often extreme disobedience undertaken by environmental protesters really be justified? In particular, do currently respected justifications of civil disobedience adequately support environmentally-motivated protests or, if such protests are indeed morally praiseworthy, is a new justification required?

7.4.1 A justification on the grounds of fairness

Probably the most prominent recent justification of civil disobedience is that propounded by John Rawls. And if anyone is widely regarded as having provided the theoretical underpinnings for modern liberal democratic societies, it is Rawls. His discussion of civil disobedience would therefore seem to be the obvious place to start.

By 'civil disobedience' Rawls means 'a public, nonviolent, and conscientious

40 For the classic discussion, see Thoreau, 'Civil Disobedience'.

41 Tolstoy's major writings on civil disobedience can be found in Leo Tolstoy, *On Civil Disobedience and Non-Violence* (New York: Signet, 1968).

42 For a thorough exposition of the views of Mohandas K. Gandhi, see Raghavan Iyer, *The Moral and Political Thought of Mahatma Gandhi* (New York: Oxford University Press, 1973).

43 The most influential discussion is, of course, Peter Singer, *Animal Liberation: A New Ethics for Our Treatment of Animals* (New York: Avon, 1975). More concise justifications of the moral stance of animal liberationists can be found from utilitarian and deontological perspectives in Peter Singer, 'All animals are equal' in Peter Singer (ed.), *Applied Ethics* (Oxford: Oxford University Press, 1986) and in Tom Regan, 'The case for animal rights' in Peter Singer (ed.), *In Defence of Animals* (Oxford: Blackwell, 1985), respectively.

44 'Landmark' campaigns have recently been 'fought' in Britain at Twyford Down, Oxlees Wood, the extension of the M11 and Newbury.

act contrary to law usually done with the intent to bring about a change in the policies or laws of the government'.[45] In order to see why Rawls thinks that civil disobedience is justifiable in certain circumstances, we first need to consider his account of political obligation, for civil disobedience can be argued to be, in effect, a conditional denial of political obligation. In other words, to justify such a denial, it seems that it is necessary to understand the limits of political obligation. Clearly, this is an issue of central importance to anarchists.

Why, then, ought we to regard ourselves as falling under political obligations? Rawls answers as follows:

> We should comply with and do our part in just and efficient social arrangements for at least two reasons: first of all, we have a natural duty not to oppose the establishment of just and efficient institutions (when they do not yet exist) and to uphold and comply with them (when they do exist); and second, assuming that we have knowingly accepted the benefits of these institutions and plan to continue to do so, and that we have encouraged and expected others to do their part, we also have an obligation to do our share when, as the arrangement requires, it comes our turn.[46]

But when are social arrangements just? In Rawls' view, when they accord with the principles that each would choose under a 'veil of ignorance' – in what Rawls calls 'the original position'.[47] The core idea is that a society is just if the principles assigning those goods which are necessary for whatever plan of life a person might decide upon are fair. And their fairness can be established by their acceptability to all who do not know what social position they will come to occupy or what talents luck will allocate to them or even what their preferred plan of life will turn out to be. Thus, the original position, from which the principles governing social institutions are hypothetically chosen under a veil of ignorance, is designed to rule out all bias, and the principles chosen in such a situation will therefore be fair.[48]

45 John Rawls, 'The justification of civil disobedience' in James Rachels (ed.), *Moral Problems: A Collection of Philosophical Essays* (New York: Harper and Row, 1971), p. 132.

46 Ibid., p. 126. The second reason is Hart's 'mutuality of restrictions', which can be regarded as giving rise to special rights. See H. L. A. Hart, 'Are there are natural rights?' in Anthony Quinton (ed.), *Political Philosophy* (Oxford: Oxford University Press, 1967). Rawls' views on political compliance have since undergone a process of evolution, culminating in John Rawls, *Political Liberalism* (New York: Columbia University Press, 1996). Sadly, the implications of his recent work seem to be less liberal and more of a justification of the status quo than Rawls would care to admit. Unfortunately, it would involve too much of a digression to defend this charge here.

47 See John Rawls, *A Theory of Justice* (Massachusetts: Harvard University Press, 1971), pp. 136–7.

48 In Rawls' view, the following principles would be chosen in the original position and would be fair (hence just) because everyone ignorant of their share of talents or social standing would, he assumes, agree to them: 'first, each person is to have an equal right to the most

On the basis of such principles, we are able to judge whether the laws which have been passed in a democratic society are just or not. Unfortunately, in Rawls' view, even the best practicable political procedure could result in the enactment and enforcement of unjust laws and policies, for he assumes that 'the best constitution is some form of democratic regime affirming equal political liberty and using some sort of majority (or other plurality) rule'.[49] Clearly, if we have to rely on majority rule, then unjust laws could very easily be passed, because majorities are far from infallible. In short, because their sense of justice is imperfect, the majority can occasionally pass laws which exceed acceptable limits. Should this happen, Rawls argues, civil disobedience may be permissible. And when it is, conscientiously contravening the law[50] serves to implore the majority, by appealing to its sense of justice, to reconsider its decisions. Furthermore, it acts as a warning that the dissenters firmly believe that the conditions upon which social cooperation rest are being contravened.

This defence of civil disobedience thus takes protesters to be addressing the shared conception of justice upon which the democratic constitution is, supposedly, premised. Civil disobedience is justified, in Rawls' view, when constitutionally valid decisions gravely flout that shared conception of justice, because that nullifies the basis for the obligations protesters would otherwise have to the constitution. Consequently,

> persistent and deliberate violation [of] basic liberties over any extended period of time cuts the ties of community and invites either submission or forceful resistance. By engaging in civil disobedience a minority leads the majority to consider whether it wants to have its acts taken in this way, or whether, in view of the common sense of justice, it wishes to acknowledge the claims of the minority.[51]

Moreover, in Rawls' opinion,

> if the appeal against injustice is repeatedly denied, then the majority has declared its intention to invite submission or resistance and the latter may

extensive liberty compatible with a like liberty for all; second, social and economic inequalities (as defined by the institutional structure or fostered by it) are to be arranged so that they are both to everyone's advantage and attached to positions and offices open to all.' Rawls, 'The justification of civil disobedience', p. 128.

49 Ibid., p. 130.

50 Rawls thinks that those who engage in civil disobedience, even when justified in doing so, should expect and accept both arrest and punishment without resistance because, by their willingness to pay the penalty for their actions, they manifest their respect for legal procedures. By willingly availing themselves of legal retribution, dissenters show that their opposition to a law remains faithful to law, thereby demonstrating that their actions are intended to address the sense of justice of the majority, follow from sincerely held convictions and are undertaken for conscientious reasons.

51 Ibid., p. 132.

> conceivably be justified even in a democratic regime. We are not required to acquiesce in the crushing of fundamental liberties by democratic majorities which have shown themselves blind to the principles of justice upon which justification of the constitution depends.[52]

There seems to be no reason why we could not extend this argument to those cases where persons suffer harm as a result of others' polluting activities. Thus, there would come a time when a refusal to desist from those activities would invite justifiable resistance. And one such form of resistance which Rawls' argument so extended would thus appear to justify is ecologically-motivated sabotage – 'ecotage'.

However, Rawls proceeds to spell out three conditions which he insists must be met if one is to be justified in engaging in civil disobedience. The first is that the injustice protested against must have been more or less deliberately inflicted for some length of time in spite of the protesters having already followed more conventional routes for expressing opposition to that injustice (for example, by lobbying politicians). The second is that the injustice must clearly violate the liberties involved in equal citizenship. And the third is that unacceptable consequences should not result from a general tendency to engage in civil disobedience whenever a case of similar standing arises. If there were too great a tendency to be civilly disobedient, then social cooperation would be impossible.

Nevertheless, if an instance of civil disobedience were to satisfy all three conditions, then, in Rawls' view, it would be legitimate. In other words, if the conditions of social cooperation are persistently flouted through the violation of liberties which are necessary for equal citizenship, and when the usual channels for expressing disapproval have been exhausted, then civil disobedience may be permissible – but not to the extent that a willingness to resort to it would make social cooperation too difficult, and thereby itself undermine the conditions of social cooperation.

In addition, Rawls argues that justified civil disobedience not only leads to greater fairness, it actually plays a stabilizing role in democracies; for

> [i]f straightway, after a decent period of time to make reasonable political appeals in the normal way, men [and women] were in general to dissent by civil disobedience from infractions of the fundamental equal liberties, these liberties would, I believe, be more rather than less secure. Legitimate civil disobedience properly exercised is a stabilizing device in a constitutional regime, tending to make it more firmly just.[53]

Of course, those who exercise political power tend to regard civil disobedience as, at best, a disturbance of the peace – which should come as no surprise, given that

52 Ibid., pp. 133–4.
53 Ibid., p. 136.

disobedience is usually directed against those in power and constitutes a challenge to their authority. But in Rawls' view, 'if civil disobedience seems to threaten civil peace, the responsibility falls not so much on those who protest as upon those whose abuse of authority and power justifies such opposition.'[54] Rawls thus seems to have gone quite a long way in justifying civil disobedience.

7.4.2 A justification on the grounds of non-participation and a failure of compromise

However, Peter Singer thinks that Rawls hasn't gone far enough, and offers an even more extensive justification of civil disobedience. He sees two problems with Rawls' account which lead to it being too limited.

The first problem is that Rawls thinks that dissenters have to appeal to the community's shared sense of justice. But Singer wonders why any such appeal to the community must be restricted to the principles of justice which it presently accepts. If its sense of justice is imperfect, surely civil disobedience could be undertaken not merely to induce the majority to reconsider whether or not its decisions satisfy the principles of justice it currently values but also to reconsider whether or not its conception of justice is adequate. As Singer is one of the foremost defenders of animal liberation, then one area where he strongly feels that our society's conception of justice is defective is in its lack of regard for the welfare of non-human animals. And some humans might firmly believe themselves to be justified in engaging in civil disobedience in order to induce the majority of our community to reconsider its attitude to, and treatment of, other species. Moreover, in protesting on behalf of other species, such humans clearly would not be acting in their own self-interests, but conscientiously.

The second problem with Rawls' account is that he thinks that civil disobedience is justified in terms of justice, rather than in terms of a wider morality. If we consider the case of non-human animals again, he seems to believe that although cruelty to animals is immoral, this notwithstanding, humans cannot treat them unjustly. But as Singer remarks: 'If we combine this view with the idea that the justification of civil disobedience must be in terms of justice, we can see that Rawls is committed to holding that no amount of cruelty to animals can justify disobedience.'[55] Yet clearly there are a large number of people, Singer being one of them, who feel that non-violent direct action in defence of animals *is* legitimate. But Rawls' account of civil disobedience is incapable of allowing such protest. Hence, it is not surprising that Singer should want to go further than Rawls in his defence of civil disobedience.

To this end, Singer focuses upon the question of whether or not civil disobedience is less justified in a democratic society than in an undemocratic one. This is surely a key question, for many feel that, while undemocratic societies are often

54 Ibid., p. 140.
55 Peter Singer, *Democracy and Disobedience* (Oxford: Oxford University Press, 1973), p. 90.

illegitimate, democratic ones ought to command our allegiance. Justifications of political obligation which provide no reason for being more obedient to a democratic than to an undemocratic regime would seem to oblige one to any effective regime, no matter how unsavoury – a conclusion few rational people would accept.[56]

However, Singer thinks it is clear that the obligation to obey the laws of even a democratic society cannot be absolute; for, as he asks: 'Could anyone plausibly maintain that if the Nazis had received majorities in free elections, and allowed freedom of speech, association and so on, this would have made it right to obey laws designed to exterminate Jews? To maintain this would require fantastic, and surely misguided, devotion to democratic laws.'[57] Thus, in Singer's view, the obligation to obey the law, is *prima facie* (or, perhaps better, *pro tanto*). We must attach some importance to political obligation, but any such obligation is defeasible. It is an obligation which can be overridden, rather like the way a promise can be overridden, by a more important moral consideration.

What, then, would count as a good reason for obeying the laws of a democratic society?[58] One reason which Singer believes to be valid is the following: The problem of a dissenter refusing to obey the law and deliberately flouting what the majority have decided is that the dissenter has, in effect, a greater say than the others. But the rest could equally demand a greater say. If everyone is sincere in his or her opinions, and if they cannot reach agreement, then it is far preferable that some compromise is accepted, rather than everyone doing what they individually decide is best. Anything other than accepting a compromise would be unacceptable to some, and would undermine any peaceful decision-procedure.

56 For a powerful refutation of Hobbesian arguments concerning the supposed need for an authoritarian, centralized power in order to ensure cooperation, see Michael Taylor, *Anarchy and Cooperation* (London: Wiley, 1976).

57 Singer, *Democracy and Disobedience*, p. 6.

58 Singer convincingly rejects the threat of law and order breaking down, the receiving of benefits from society, the existence of 'settled methods' for promulgating and abrogating laws, and tacit consent as reasons for being under an obligation not to disobey the laws (see ibid., pp. 6–24). Among other problems with these attempts at establishing political obligation, they fall to the following objection: if successful, they would all justify too much – namely, obedience to any regime, no matter how undemocratic. Perhaps the most plausible reason for obedience in a democratic society rests on the widely held assumption that all persons equally have the right to govern themselves. Hence, only those political forms which grant to each an equal say ought to be obeyed. Unfortunately, as Singer points out: 'equality is not a completely satisfactory basis for explaining why we ought to obey the law in a democracy. For the assumption or prescription can be turned against the purpose for which it is being used. It can be taken as showing, not that there is a special obligation to obey democratic authority, but that there can be no obligation to obey any authority except oneself. In other words, it may be denied that the equal rights of all to govern themselves are satisfied by majority government over the minority. What reason is there for supposing that "equal rights" can be added up in such a way that the side with more has the right to prevail over the side with less? Equal rights to a cake would not be satisfied if the majority walked off with the whole cake.' Ibid., p. 28.

Singer's view is that a democratic decision-procedure giving an equal say to all members of the community (who abide by the decision reached) constitutes a fair compromise. Moreover, in allowing disputes to be settled peacefully rather than by force, such a compromise is clearly a beneficial one. And this provides a reason for obeying democratic rather than undemocratic laws, according to Singer, for

> it is only in [a democratic] association that the nature of the decision-procedure makes it possible for everyone to refrain from acting on his [or her] own judgement about particular issues without giving up more than the theoretical minimum which it is essential for everyone to give up in order to achieve the benefits of a peaceful solution to disputes. It is the fairness of the compromise by which force is avoided that gives rise to the stronger reason for accepting the decision-procedure of [a democratic] association.[59]

So, in order to arrive at an agreement, individuals must compromise; and that means each having to abandon some of what he or she wanted. But arriving at such an agreement is preferable to trying unsuccessfully to have one's own way completely and experiencing conflict instead. As Singer writes: 'the essence of the fair compromise [is] that everyone gives up his [or her] own claim to have more than an equal say in deciding issues, but retains his [or her] claim to have an equal say. In that way every member can have the maximum influence compatible with a peaceful settlement.'[60] Disobeying the settlement would constitute a refusal to accept a fair compromise. It would be to deny others an equal say. Moreover, it would leave them with no other option than a recourse to the use of force – and force is what we would all like to avoid.

A second reason, which Singer accepts as valid, for obedience to laws resulting from a democratic procedure is that choosing to participate in such a procedure can incur an obligation to abide by its outcome. Singer argues that if one participates in a decision-procedure alongside others of differing views, but who would abide by the decision should it go against them, then by participating in that procedure one creates in the others the reasonable expectation that one will similarly abide by decisions contrary to one's preferred outcome; and one thereby acquires the obligation to accept the decision reached. Singer refers to this as an example of 'quasi-consent', which he thinks incurs obligations just as much as actual consent does. The example he provides is that of being in a group where everyone is taking turns to buy a round of drinks. Even if you did not actually consent to buying anyone else a drink, you would still incur the obligation to reciprocate if you had happily accepted drinks from the others and behaved so as to give them the expectation that you would buy a round when it came to your turn.

Singer thinks that voting is very similar, for anyone who understands that an

59 Ibid., p. 32.
60 Ibid., pp. 45–6.

election serves to enable a group decision to be reached, and who voluntarily participates in the voting procedure to decide an issue, thereby leads the others to believe that he or she has accepted the voting procedure as an appropriate means for arriving at a group decision. In this way, participation in a decision-procedure, something much more common in democratic than in undemocratic societies, incurs an obligation to accept and obey its outcome – or so he argues. Hence, Singer concludes that both fair compromise and participation can provide greater reasons for obeying democratic rather than undemocratic laws.

However, Singer points out that there are clear limitations to any such obedience. If a fair compromise is not the outcome, then one may legitimately engage in disobedience with the aim of obtaining a more appropriate decision-procedure – one in which a fair compromise *would be* represented. And when there is a permanent minority, for example, then majoritarian voting procedures relying on equal voting rights will not guarantee a fair compromise between all interested parties. The permanent majority will be able to do virtually what it likes, and no compromise will obtain between their preferences and those of the minority. In other words, whenever there is any systematic tendency towards unfairness regarding the passing of laws or their operation, those who suffer that unfairness lack the reason fair compromise would otherwise provide for obedience.

Hence, Singer argues, minorities (or those otherwise disempowered, or potentially disempowered) need to have rights against the majority. If there is any restriction on their freedom of speech, for example, then fair compromise would not obtain. If some cannot argue their case, then there is less chance that others will be converted to their view and vote for their preferred choice, or even take it sufficiently into account. The same is true of any other right that would need to be safeguarded for a democratic decision-procedure to arrive at a fair compromise. This would include rights such as 'the right to vote or stand for office, or the right to freedom of association and peaceful assembly',[61] among others. Should anyone's democratic rights be violated, then he or she would be justified in engaging in civil disobedience, because the reasons for obeying the outcome of the democratic process would no longer apply.[62]

Civil disobedience may also be justified, in Singer's view, when one side of the debate on an important moral issue has failed to receive a fair hearing. Civil disobedience, in this case, attempts to remedy the defects in the political system by striving to bring about a more equal presentation of views – something which is essential if a fair compromise is to be reached. However, Singer thinks that any

61 Ibid., p. 67.

62 Who is to decide whether or not anyone's democratic rights have been infringed? Singer's view is that it has to be the individual who experiences the mooted violation. The reason is obvious: If the rights of the minority were to be infringed by the majority, then the democratic process could not reliably be employed to ascertain that this was the case, because the majority could easily decide not only to violate the minority's rights but also to conclude that their rights had not been violated. Consequently, when one feels that one's democratic rights have been violated, one can justifiably engage in civil disobedience in defence of those rights.

such protest must be non-violent, otherwise it would be a case not of persuasion, but of coercing or intimidating the majority.

Civil disobedience may also be justified, Singer holds, in order to make a plea for reconsideration. Democratic procedures can fail to take into account the intensity of feeling of different groups. The intensity of the minority's feelings can be revealed to the majority by the minority engaging in civil disobedience. As Singer remarks:

> A majority may act, or fail to act, without realizing that there are truly significant issues at stake, or the majority may not have considered the interests of all parties, and its decision may cause suffering in a way that was not foreseen. Disobedience, and especially disobedience followed by acceptance of punishment, may make the majority realize that what is for it a matter of indifference is of great importance to others.[63]

Civil disobedience, in this case, too, attempts to remedy a defect in the political system.

The justifications of civil disobedience which Singer expounds would apply even to the most democratic of societies – for example, societies which were direct and participatory – never mind representative democracies. But as Singer regards the democratic credentials of the existing 'democracies' to be dubious in the extreme, then, in his view, civil disobedience is certainly justified in the present circumstances in order to obtain a fair compromise. In the so-called democracies, the electorate is presented with a small number of 'package deals' by the major political parties (which are highly oligarchical organizations possessing considerably more power than is compatible with a fair compromise being reached), and none of the package deals on offer might accord with the actual preferences of the electorate. In addition, as the control of newspapers, or simply great differences in wealth, cash out into considerable differences in the ability to fight elections or to apply political pressure, then, in Singer's opinion, the so-called democracies are a long way from offering the prospect of a fair compromise.

All of this suggests that any obligation to obey the laws of the so-called democracies is highly doubtful. None of us lives in anything like as democratic a society as would provide us with the reasons Singer offers for obeying the laws. Our present societies are, evidently, nowhere near the embodiment of a fair compromise and, consequently, cannot justifiably command our obedience. Hence, if political obligation is as weak as Singer appears to have established, then civil disobedience is easily justified, and anarchism rests on far stronger moral grounds than might otherwise have appeared to be the case.[64]

63 Ibid., p. 84.

64 For comprehensive critiques of putative justifications of political obligation, see Carole Pateman, *The Problem of Political Obligation: A Critique of Liberal Theory* (Cambridge: Polity, 1985), which includes a critique of Singer's attempted justification on the basis of 'quasi-consent', and A. J. Simmons, *Moral Principles and Political Obligations* (New Jersey: Princeton University Press, 1979).

7.5 A duty of radical disobedience

Perhaps, though, it is possible to develop an even more powerful and extensive justification of civil disobedience than Singer's. On his approach, it would seem to follow that if one were to participate voluntarily in a genuinely democratic process which constituted a fair compromise between all participants, then one could not, with justification, act disobediently. However, there is an indeterminate class of people who cannot participate in *any* democratic polity we might construct. Yet we can affect that class even to the point of determining its size. At one extreme, it could be as large as the present human population. At the other extreme, it could, conceivably, be infinite in number. I am, of course, referring to those humans who have not yet been born (never mind to future generations of both human and non-human animals). We could ensure that the class is at the small extreme by destroying the planet within a generation. Or, by living sustainably, we could allow that class to be unimaginably large, for it would then comprise generations into the indefinite future. The decisions which we might make democratically could ensure that future generations live well or die horribly in an environmental nightmare. Their lives and their well-being are in our hands. Yet not only do they lack a say in any democratic polity we might devise, *they cannot conceivably have any say in it whatsoever.*

The interests of future generations can only be advocated now by those who are prepared to take their side. If non-human animals appear defenceless and in need of animal liberationists, future generations are even more defenceless. Like non-human animals, they cannot plead their case. But unlike non-human animals, it is *impossible* for future generations even to retaliate against us. To them we are completely invulnerable.[65] If democratic polities were intent on pursuing a course

65 This claim has been challenged by John O'Neill, who argues that future generations *can* harm us – for example, by acting so that the narrative account of our lives ends badly. See John O'Neill, *Ecology, Policy and Politics: Human Well-Being and the Natural World* (London: Routledge, 1993), pp. 27–36. But few seem to be convinced by O'Neill's argument. Perhaps the most obvious way in which future generations might be thought to harm us is by harming our reputations. However, this could not be used to provide a foundation for obligations to future generations by showing that Humean 'circumstances of justice' obtain – in particular, the possibility of mutually inflictable harm. First, harm to our reputations is hardly the end of the world for us, but what we can do to future generations might, literally, be the end of the world for them. In short, there is no genuinely reciprocal relationship here. Second, and more important, what matters to us is our reputation among those who matter to us. If we do not care about future generations, we do not care what they think about us. But if we do care about them, what they think about us will not be our motive for taking them into account. In short, concerning how we treat future generations, our reputation among them does little or no work. Third, and most important, with respect to our reputations, to stop future generations from harming us, all we have to do is stop caring about them. But this is not what an obligation consists in. The whole point about obligations is that they do not disappear the moment we stop caring about those to whom we owe obligations. So, whatever lies at the basis of our obligations to future generations, it surely cannot be dependent upon how much they matter to us. (And these objections seem equally applicable to O'Neill's argument on the basis of narrative accounts.)

of action that would harm the interests of future generations, then disobedience on their behalf might require an even more radical justification than that offered by Singer. This is because, inadvertently, he seems to have established that participants in a genuinely democratic decision-procedure, generating a fair compromise between them, are bound by it.[66] That would have to include those who wished to act on behalf of future generations. Yet it is impossible for future generations to be civilly disobedient now on their own behalf, just as it is impossible for them to participate in our present decision-procedures.

Why is the fact that future generations cannot participate in any democratic polity we might construct morally important? Participating in a democratic procedure could be taken as signifying that one has consented, in accordance with the collective decision, to forgo having some of one's individual interests satisfied.[67] It is *that* apparent consent which could, conceivably, justify the rest of a collective (when carrying out democratically arrived at decisions) acting in a manner that goes against some of the interests of the collective's individual members. But as future generations cannot now participate, it cannot be presumed that they have consented. In fact, it is impossible for us to obtain their consent to our acting against their interests. Hence, it could be argued, we have no justification for acting against their basic interests when it is unnecessary for meeting our own.

But, it might be objected, the fact that future generations cannot participate in our institutions does not lead to constraints on our actions; rather to the converse. Future generations cannot participate because *they do not exist*. Hence, they are not persons. As it is the interests of persons that matter, and as future generations are not at this moment persons, their interests (if, indeed, it can intelligibly be said they have any) do not matter. In fact, as future generations do not exist, then they cannot have interests. Consequently, we cannot act against their interests. In short, we cannot harm future generations.[68]

Certainly, future generations are not, at this moment, persons. They could, however, be regarded as potential persons. Nevertheless, it might then be objected, only persons matter, and potential persons do not now exist as persons. Quite simply, potential persons are not the sort of entity that matters.[69] But, in response, we could distinguish between two kinds of potential person: those that

66 I say 'inadvertently' because Singer's conclusion seems to rule out many of the activities animal liberationists might feel morally obliged to engage in should a genuine democracy arise which lacked a deep concern for the welfare of non-human animals.

67 This could be argued to be the intuition lying behind the social contract tradition.

68 For a convincing challenge to this objection and a defence of both the 'non-concessional view' that future generations have rights now and the 'concessional view' that it is impermissible for us to act now in a manner which will violate the rights which future generations will have, see Robert Elliot, 'The rights of future people', *Journal of Applied Philosophy*, Vol. 6, No. 2 (1989), pp. 159–69.

69 For the most respected argument against 'the potentiality principle', see Michael Tooley, 'Abortion and infanticide' in Peter Singer (ed.), *Applied Ethics* (Oxford: Oxford University Press, 1986).

will, as a matter of fact, be actualized; and those that, as a matter of fact, will never exist – the latter being what Mary Anne Warren terms 'merely potential people'.[70] If we were to destroy the planet in one hundred years from now, those who would have been born after that time had we, instead, chosen to live sustainably, will never exist. But because they would exist if we choose to live sustainably, then they are potential persons. If, as a matter of fact, we do destroy the planet in one hundred years time, they will never exist and, as such, are merely potential persons.

Clearly, merely potential persons cannot possibly be harmed. But it could be argued that potential persons who will be actualized can be. Moreover, regardless of what one thinks about potential persons, it is surely indisputable that a *person* can be harmed after having been actualized. And if we act in a certain way, in the future *real, live persons will be harmed by our actions.* It is this fact which is morally important. Harm rarely occurs at the exact moment that the harmful action is performed. If I pull the trigger of a gun that I am aiming at you, surely I cannot excuse my action by saying that it did not harm you, for you were harmed when the bullet struck you, which was after my action of pulling the trigger (albeit only a fraction of a second later). If I fire a nuclear missile at you which strikes in seven minutes time, surely I cannot use that time-delay to deny with any success all responsibility for the harm that ensues. And if I plant a landmine, which is detonated by a passer-by in one month's time, then for me to claim that my action of planting the mine is not harmful, for it is presently harming no one, surely lacks any cogency. Similarly, if I now leave a bomb lying around timed to explode in one year, surely I cannot excuse myself on the grounds that my action is not harming anyone at this precise moment. Rather, isn't it the case that the action of arming the bomb is morally wrong *now* if someone is likely to be harmed when the bomb explodes next year?

But what if the person who is harmed in a year's time by the explosion has not yet been born? It would not be too controversial to claim that there is little, if any, moral difference between the bomb's harming a two-year-old and its harming an infant of nine months. Surely, the date of birth of the victim is morally insignificant.[71] The fact that the infant was not born when the bomb was planted seems to make no moral difference whatsoever. Yet it is highly probable that some of our

70 See Mary Anne Warren, 'Do potential people have moral rights?' in R. I. Sikora and Brian Barry (eds), *Obligations to Future Generations* (Philadelphia: Temple University Press, 1978).

71 Tooley, however, argues that only those who have the capacity to conceive of themselves as continuing subjects of experiences have a right not to be killed. See Tooley, 'Abortion and infanticide'. This implies that one's age might well be morally significant. It could also be taken to imply that it is morally permissible to act in a way that will lead to the premature deaths of members of future generations, for they do not, at present, possess the requisite conceptual capacity to count in our moral calculations. For a critique of the claim that it is permissible to kill anyone lacking the capacity to conceive of himself for herself as a continuing subject of experiences, see Alan Carter, 'Infanticide and the right to life', *Ratio (new series)*, Vol. 10, No. 1 (April 1997), pp. 1–9.

present actions will, as a matter of fact, harm persons who will exist in the future. And if our present actions lead to the destruction of the life-support systems of this planet, billions of people who do not yet exist are certain to die in horrific conditions. As they do not yet exist, they have, as of yet, not undertaken any actions. In a word, they are wholly innocent. And to harm, needlessly, wholly innocent persons is widely regarded as morally wrong.

However, it might be objected that future generations could turn out not to be innocents. But while they might, in fact, not be innocents at the time they suffered harm, they are certainly innocent at the time some of the actions harmful to them are performed. And surely one cannot justifiably unleash a punishment on someone in advance of a wrong they *might* commit. Moreover, that *none* of them would turn out to be innocent at the time the harm befell them is extremely implausible. Some of them would, at that time, be infants. And it is certainly highly immoral to inflict harm gratuitously on innocents such as young children.[72]

There is, however, an argument put forward by Thomas Schwartz which implies that we cannot possibly harm distant, future generations.[73] If a government were to embark on a long-range environmental protection policy, then different individuals would be born in the distant future than would have been born had that policy not been adopted. If harming someone consists in making him or her worse off than he or she would otherwise have been, then failing to protect the environment would not harm any people in the distant future. They would not be made worse off because, had our government chosen to enforce an environmental protection policy, they would not have existed.

This argument might, conceivably, apply to states, who might well possess the power to determine the existence (or non-existence) of every future person. But does it apply to individuals? If I, individually, were to act in a certain way, then, in the distant future, Rosalind might be born rather than Sebastian. But if my action affects Tania, whose existence is not dependent upon that action, then it appears that I *can* harm Tania. How could I possibly know that there will be no one whose existence is not dependent upon *my*, as opposed to *our collective*, environmentally damaging behaviour? If the existence of Tania has resulted from your environmentally damaging activities rather than mine, my environmentally damaging actions can still harm her.

72 On this point, see Richard Wasserstrom, 'War, nuclear war, and nuclear deterrence: some conceptual and moral issues' in Russell Hardin, John J. Mearsheimer, Gerald Dworkin and Robert E. Goodin (eds), *Nuclear Deterrence and Strategy* (Chicago: Chicago University Press, 1985). For a powerful response (on the basis of not inflicting gratuitous harm) to a number of objections against our having obligations to future generations, see Richard Routley and Val Routley, 'Nuclear energy and obligations to the future', *Inquiry* 21 (1978), pp. 133–79.

73 See Thomas Schwartz, 'Welfare judgments and future generations', *Theory and Decision* 11 (1979), pp. 181–94.

Certainly, an individual would be unable to harm any future person if *every* future person's existence was dependent upon *every* one of his or her otherwise harmful actions. But it is surely absurd to think that any individual has the power through *every* one of his or her environmentally destructive activities to determine the coming into existence of *every* future person. Moreover, a person would only be *unable* to harm any future person if, for every otherwise harmful action which he or she might perform, the existence of every person who would otherwise have been harmed by the action in question was dependent upon *that* particular action.[74] As it is highly implausible that every one of an individual's environmentally damaging actions which will result in, or contribute towards, future suffering are necessarily of that sort,[75] then it seems that each of us is quite capable of harming even the most distant of future people by our present environmentally damaging activities, for each of us can make them worse off than they would otherwise have been.

In short, Schwartz's argument seems to depend upon regarding people as collectivities. We, viewed as a whole, can be considered responsible for the existence of every member of whichever group of people might live in the far, distant future. And that seems to imply that we could not possibly harm them, for were it not for our actions, they would never exist. But the conclusion that none of us is able to harm distant, future generations can be seen to fail the moment environmentally-damaging activities are disaggregated. Hence, it appears that we cannot evade our *individual* responsibilities as easily as Schwartz's argument might at first suggest. Moreover, any environmentally-damaging actions that would, as a matter of fact, determine the existence of future generations are bound to harm nearer generations whose existence would not be dependent upon those actions.

7.5.1 Extending our obligations

But do our obligations to strangers only go as far as demanding that each of us refrains from harming innocents? Singer has presented a powerful argument which appears to demonstrate that we have a further obligation to innocents –

74 This is why I say '*every* one of his or her otherwise harmful actions' and '*every* one of his or her environmentally destructive activities', because even if anyone *were* able to affect the identity of every person in the distant future, it would not follow that he or she could not harm any of them. For example, I could still harm a future person whose identity I determined as long as one of my actions made him or her worse off than he or she would otherwise have been – in other words, as long as that harmful action was not the action which determined his or her identity.

75 For example, imagine that Tania's ancestors, who are our contemporaries, move into a sealed 'biodome', and that, in the far distant future, a minor earthquake causes a breach in its protective skin, letting in the polluted air still remaining from our polluting activities, which proceeds to harm Tania. Clearly, our polluting activities would not have been responsible for Tania's existence, but they would certainly harm her.

namely, to come to their aid.[76] He offers the analogy of an adult passing a shallow pond into which a child has strayed. The child, being small, is drowning. The adult, being tall, could easily save the child, although it would cost him or her a trip to the drycleaners. Clearly, most of us would agree that, if one is the adult in this scenario, one has a moral obligation to wade in and save the child, even though one would get one's clothes wet and muddy.

However, what if I were one of a group of twenty adults passing by the pond? Would that make me only one-twentieth as responsible for saving the child as I would have been had I been the only adult passing by? James Rachels advances an argument which suggests otherwise.[77] Imagine one of the vicious characters the actor Jack Palance has played so well in the movies. Imagine that one such character is watching a child who is sitting next to him slowly starve to death, and he can't even be bothered to pass her the sandwich he is eating. If he invited nineteen of his friends into the room to watch the child die, would he become one-twentieth of the moral monster he would otherwise have been? Similarly, to return to Singer's analogy of the child in the pond, would I reduce my responsibility for saving the drowning child to a fraction of what it was previously by calling a number of my friends over to the side of the shallow pond to watch her drown?[78]

What, though, if there were two drowning children? To transpose another of Rachels' arguments,[79] what if I waded in to save one of them and then left the other to drown, attempting to justify my action on the grounds that one of the friends I summoned over should have saved her? Did I do my bit or, if no one else was prepared to wade in, should I have saved the other child as well? These sorts of examples strongly indicate that each of us is wholly and individually responsible for saving as many innocent persons from harm as we can, irrespective of the indifference displayed by others

But let us now extend Singer's analogy. Suppose, instead, that the child hasn't simply strayed into the pond. Suppose that the child is being drowned by an adult for no other reason than the adult in question simply couldn't care less whether the child lives or dies, or because the child's life is an inconvenience to the adult. Wouldn't one be under as equally strong an obligation in this situation as in the earlier one to wade in and go to the child's assistance? Surely one would. Yet there is strong reason to think, whether we like it or not, that this is the situation we adults are now in. If environmentalists are right, the present generation is acting

76 See Peter Singer, 'Famine affluence and morality', *Philosophy and Public Affairs*, Vol. 1, No. 3 (1972), pp. 229–43.

77 See James Rachels, 'Killing and starving to death' in Jan Narveson (ed.), *Moral Issues* (Toronto: Oxford University Press, 1983), p. 157.

78 Clearly, neither the 'moral mathematics' of helping persons nor of harming them consist of simple division. For a critique of the 'Share-of-the-Total-View', see Derek Parfit, *Reasons and Persons* (Oxford: Clarendon, 1987), pp. 67–70.

79 See Rachels, 'Killing and starving to death', p. 157.

so as to ensure that future children will 'drown', as it were, in a sea of life-threatening pollution. In short, as it appears to be morally incumbent upon us to prevent needless harm befalling innocents, then it appears that it is our duty to interfere in others' actions when by so doing we would prevent such harm. In other words, it seems that if the present generation, through its polluting activities, is harming future generations, then it is our moral responsibility to prevent those among our contemporaries who are responsible from continuing to do so.[80]

But it appears that our moral obligations to future generations extend even further than that. For it is not only widely regarded as immoral to harm innocent people. It is also widely regarded as immoral to put their lives at serious risk. If it is our moral obligation to 'wade in' when in so doing we would prevent harm befalling an innocent, then it is, surely, also our moral obligation to 'wade in' when one person is acting so as to endanger an innocent person's life. So, while the evidence displayed in Chapter 1, above, might not *prove* beyond all doubt that we are acting so as to inflict serious harm upon future generations, it is surely incontrovertible that we are presently acting so as to be running a significant *risk* of so doing – indeed, acting so as to be running a significant risk of causing billions of future people almost unimaginable suffering. But that is surely immoral.[81] All of this suggests, then, that we are morally obliged both to prevent harm befalling future generations and, whether we like it or not, to lessen the *risk* of any harm befalling them. But as there can be no doubt that we *are* running a significant risk of inflicting almost unimaginable suffering on future generations, then *each of us is under a moral obligation* to 'wade in' and change the present situation.

But is it really the case that our generation is, in fact, running a significant risk of causing extensive harm to future people? Well, we have seen that the State-Primacy Theory is not wholly implausible. And we have also seen that, in the modern world, it cashes out, not implausibly, into the environmentally hazardous dynamic depicted in Figure 6.1. But if what environmentalists tell us about environmental tolerances is right, then such an environmentally hazardous dynamic would threaten the life-support systems of our planet. Consequently, in so far as our societies can plausibly be characterized as being entrapped within an

80 It might be objected that this would be to accede to extraordinary moral demands. For a powerful and relentless critique of the shortcomings of ordinary moral thinking, see Shelly Kagan, *The Limits of Morality* (New York: Clarendon, 1991).

81 Even if the risk were far less than that which Chapter 1 suggests, given the billions of future people who could suffer as a result of our actions, then our environmentally damaging activities would seem to be highly immoral. For as Parfit concludes: 'When the stakes are very high, no chance, however small, should be ignored. . . . We can usually ignore a very small chance. But we should not do so when we may affect a very large number of people, or when the chance will be taken a very large number of times. These large numbers roughly cancel out the smallness of the chance.' Parfit, *Reasons and Persons*, p. 75. For an important discussion of how common moral views have become inadequate for dealing with environmental problems in today's world, see ibid., pp. 75–86.

environmentally hazardous dynamic, we are running a very real risk of inflicting appalling suffering on future generations.

In short, there is a real chance that the State-Primacy Theory accurately describes the outcomes of epochal transformations. Thus, there is a very real chance that we are located within an environmentally hazardous dynamic (for, as was argued in the previous chapter, the soundness of the State-Primacy Theory seems to provide a sufficient rather than a necessary condition for the justified belief that we are entrapped within an environmentally hazardous dynamic). And there is a considerable chance that, if we are within such a dynamic, then it would result in the extinction of our own species (never mind the extinction of untold numbers of other sentient life-forms). Hence, we certainly *risk* causing horrendous suffering to billions and billions of innocents. And that is, surely, the very height of immorality.

Now, if we are morally obliged to interfere when someone is harming an innocent, and if we are also obliged to interfere when someone is running a significant risk of harming an innocent, then it seems that we do not distort the situation, and that we lose nothing, by treating the significant risk of harm posed by our possible entrapment within an environmentally hazardous dynamic as if it were a case of harm. More to the point, it can be argued that, irrespective of whether or not we are, indubitably, entrapped within such a dynamic, we should act as if we were so entrapped, and that we should do whatever would be necessary to escape or elude that dynamic. Anything less, would be to renege on our moral obligations to future generations.

What, then, more specifically, is morally required of us? This question can, perhaps, be most easily answered if I first summarize several of the core arguments contained in the previous chapters.

7.5.2 *Eco-reformism, eco-Marxism and eco-authoritarianism revisited*

The interrelationships between the political relations, the political forces, the economic forces and the economic relations described by the State-Primacy Theory can be argued to result, in practice, in an environmentally hazardous dynamic. In order to remain militarily competitive with neighbouring states (and if it fails to do so it might not survive), a state (with specific structures of *political relations*) needs a growing military capability (the development of its *political forces*). That requires ever-more productive technologies (*economic forces*) appropriate to meeting military needs (for example, in present circumstances, nuclear power stations in order to produce plutonium for nuclear weapons). This also involves an ever-expanding surplus to pay for a standing army. In short, there is reason to think that the state's requirements cannot be met without an economic structure (a structure of *economic relations*) appropriate to developing technology and productivity on an ever-increasing scale.

The result today can thus be argued to be an environmentally hazardous dynamic (portrayed in Figure 6.1) which requires a massive consumption of finite resources and which generates a frighteningly high output of pollution. The dynamic also threatens war – and today that could mean nuclear war, conceivably the ultimate environmental catastrophe. It is precisely this dynamic which, it can be argued, is driving our societies to cause so much harm to future generations. And as those who have not yet been born cannot justifiably be thought to deserve such harm, then it is our moral obligation to prevent any such harm from occurring. This means that we have a duty to escape from the environmentally hazardous dynamic if we are presently trapped within it. But more: because of the chance that the above argument is sound, we currently run a *significant risk* of inflicting serious harm upon billions of innocents. Consequently, to reduce that risk – and it is morally incumbent upon us to reduce it – we are morally obliged to act in a manner which, if we were within an environmentally hazardous dynamic, would allow us to escape from it.

How, then, might we act so as to escape from the environmentally hazardous dynamic depicted in Figure 6.1 – a dynamic that can be argued to be driving us towards collective suicide? Reformists, Marxists and right-wing authoritarians each offer different strategies for averting the environmental catastrophe seemingly hurtling towards us.

Eco-reformists seek a gradual transformation of *the political relations*, and they seek it from within the present structure of legal and political institutions. But even eco-reformists propose policies (see Appendix A) which state personnel would most likely find extremely radical. Consequently, the major problem for reformist greens – one which they have tended to ignore – would seem to be this: How can the state apparatus be employed to put such radical policies into effect when its whole complex structure appears to have been developed in order to pursue as effectively as possible the opposite course to that demanded by greens? As Marx writes with respect to the class dictatorship of the proletariat: 'the working class cannot simply lay hold of the ready-made state machinery, and wield it for its own purposes.'[82] This observation that the state cannot be steered in any direction that one likes seems, in important respects, to be even more applicable to radical greens than to Marxist revolutionaries. For at least 'capitalist states' and the 'dictatorship of the proletariat' are thought to share a common interest in greater productivity.

Moreover, if the ostensible means for bringing about a transformation of the political relations is simply electing a greener government which still had to act within a system of competing states, then it would seem to be a wholly inadequate response to the problems that environmentalists claim we face. In most parts of the world, if a genuinely green government operating within this system of militarily competing states tried to leave the dynamic by abandoning the requirement of military competitiveness, it would most likely face a military coup. In other words, any change in the political relations that went against the interests of the

82 Karl Marx, 'The civil war in France' in *Selected Writings*, ed. David McLellan (Oxford: Oxford University Press, 1977), p. 539.

political forces would more likely than not incur military intervention. This threat could be reduced significantly: by safeguarding the interests of the military through continuing to invest in the nation's coercive capacity and thereby remaining militarily competitive. Accordingly, in order to retain power, a green government would most likely find itself having to remain firmly locked within the environmentally hazardous dynamic.

But is it really plausible to insist that the military poses such a threat in a *liberal democratic* society? Well, imagine a green government deciding to transfer all military personnel into socially useful production – which seems to be a requirement of a genuinely green society. Would senior military personnel agree to this quietly? Would they take this lying down, when all their training and years of service make them proficient in only one sphere of employment? The military are surely far too powerful for any government to ride roughshod over their interests. And military coups are not unknown even in Europe. Thus, it is likely that any government would inevitably find itself granting considerable concessions to its armed forces in order to placate them. But this in itself is likely to be sufficient to pose a threat to neighbouring states. Consequently, it can be argued that it is simply not possible to escape from the environmentally hazardous dynamic while a society retains a military apparatus, and that no green government on its own would have sufficient power to abolish it.[83] Most importantly, it seems that present political systems are such that governments only have power while they preserve their repressive apparatuses. That centralized governments should wish to abolish them is, therefore, implausible in the extreme.[84] Reformist approaches – ones that take the present system for granted, and attempt transformations from within it – thus appear doomed to failure. Moreover, eco-reformism only retains its appeal just so long as the environmental threat is regarded as far less menacing than many informed environmentalists adamantly insist it is.

An eco-Marxist might make one of two responses. Regarding the first: Marxists generally believe that capitalist economic relations are the cause of all major social

83 It can be argued that the limitations of governmental power are often overlooked because of a conflation between state power and governmental power. As Miliband writes: 'the treatment of one part of the state – usually the government – as the state itself introduces a major element of confusion in the discussion of the nature and incidence of state *power*; and that confusion can have large political consequences. Thus, if it is believed that the government is in fact the state, it may also be believed that the assumption of governmental power is equivalent to the acquisition of state power. Such a belief, resting as it does on vast assumptions about the nature of state power, is fraught with great risks and disappointments. To understand the nature of state power, it is necessary first of all to distinguish, and then to relate, the various elements which make up the state system.' Ralph Miliband, *The State in Capitalist Society* (London: Quartet, 1973), p. 46. And as he adds: 'the fact that the government does speak in the name of the state and is formally *invested* with state power, does not mean that it effectively *controls* that power.' Ibid., p. 47.

84 As Bakunin asks: 'Has it ever been witnessed in history that a political body . . . committed suicide, or sacrificed the least of its interests and so-called rights for the love of justice and liberty?' Michael Bakunin, *The Political Philosophy of Bakunin: Scientific Anarchism*, ed. G. P. Maximoff (New York: The Free Press, 1964), p. 217.

and political ills,[85] and that replacing capitalist economic relations with communist ones would suffice to solve all of our major problems, including the environmental ones. It is not surprising, then, that most eco-Marxists tend to focus on *the economic relations*. But, from the standpoint of the State-Primacy Theory, focusing almost exclusively on economic relations and seeking transformation there would inevitably fail, for states would simply replace economic relations which were dysfunctional for them with ones that were functional. And there is evidence to support this claim, for this is precisely what Marxist revolutionaries at the head of the Bolshevik state were forced to do! And any 'fair compromise' economic relations, in not being exploitative, would surely fail to extract the surplus required by any state needing to remain militarily competitive.

The alternative response that an eco-Marxist could make is the following: If it is technological development which has explanatory primacy with respect to the outcome of epochal change, then that development might result in a desirable future society. Marx, for example, assumed that the preconditions of post-capitalism would be created within capitalist society.[86] So, perhaps we can rely on some environmentally benign technology being developed that will solve the environmental problems we are creating. But if that technology implies less consumption (which, surely, it would have to in order for it to be environmentally benign), then capitalists do not have an interest in developing or promoting it, for it would reduce their profitability. And if it did not generate the high productivity an expanding military capacity requires (and, surely, if it were genuinely environmentally benign, it would not), then the state wouldn't have an interest in developing or promoting it, either.

In short, the kind of technology which is developed in accordance with the military needs of modern states and that is developed to make profits for industry seems wholly inappropriate to an environmentally sustainable society. For such a society, we would surely need a very different kind of technology, and we cannot expect it simply to arise within the present system.[87]

85 Marx himself subscribes to the view that 'the economical subjection of the man [and woman] of labour to the monopolizer of the means of labour, that is, the sources of all life, lies at the bottom of servitude in all its forms, of all social misery, mental degradation, and political dependence'. Karl Marx, 'Provisional rules of the International' in *The First International and After*, ed. by David Fernbach (Harmondsworth: Penguin, 1974), p. 82. This view was not confined to his later years. A quarter of a century earlier he had claimed that 'the whole of human servitude is involved in the relations of the worker to production, and all relations of servitude are nothing but modifications and consequences of this relation.' Karl Marx, 'Economic and philosophical manuscripts' in *Early Writings*, intro. L. Colletti, trans. R. Livingstone and G. Benton (Harmondsworth: Penguin, 1975), p. 333.

86 For a sustained critique of this assumption, see Carter, *Marx: A Radical Critique*, *passim*.

87 Consider the technology of entertainment: the recent video games revolution has resulted in a privatized form of entertainment whereby individuals, while playing, relate to machines and a virtual reality rather than to other persons. More worrying still, the games themselves seem most suited to training the next generation of soldiers and fighter pilots. They are certainly not cooperative games designed to develop the skills needed for participating democratically in group decisions.

Furthermore, Marxists have traditionally advocated an abundant socialism based upon a highly productive technology. In fact, Marx went so far as to claim that post-capitalism would not be established until capitalism had developed technology as far as it was capable of doing.[88] This would greatly reduce the length of the working day – a precondition, in Marx's view, for real freedom. But G. A. Cohen, for one, at least accepts that 'if the "crisis of resources" is as serious as some say, it is a genuine threat to the realization of forms of communism which depend upon a radically reduced working day, for those forms require astronomically high levels of productive power'.[89]

However, the problem would seem to be even greater than this suggests, for a more serious limitation on technological expansion than finite resources is, surely, the limited capacity which the environment has for acting as a sink for pollution without its life-support systems being seriously compromised. In fact, Marxism appears to be singularly unsuited as an answer to environmental problems, given its faith in massively increased productivity as the essential precondition for socialism. In a word, a more utopian socialism than Marxism is hard to imagine. Thus, it appears that any variant of eco-Marxism which put its faith in technological development – *the economic forces* – would provide no solution, either. Thus, neither of the two eco-Marxist responses seem to provide a solution to the problems we appear to be unloading onto future generations.

What then of a right-wing, eco-authoritarian approach? Eco-authoritarians assume that people will have to be coerced into behaving in an environmentally benign manner. Thus, they place their faith in the power of *the political forces.* But, as the State-Primacy Theory highlights, any emphasis on the political forces and their coercive capacity will pose a threat to neighbouring states, and those states would then, most likely, feel driven to develop their military capacity even further, which the eco-authoritarian state would, in turn, have to respond to if it is to remain secure. (See Figure 6.3.) In other words, replacing the present system with something even more authoritarian would pose such a threat to neighbouring states that not only would they most likely find themselves trapped within an environmentally hazardous dynamic, but any such dynamic would, surely, be given an even greater impetus. Thus, there are strong grounds for thinking that eco-authoritarian responses would accelerate the problem, rather than provide a solution.[90]

88 This claim can be found in Karl Marx, 'Preface to a critique of political economy' in *Selected Writings*, ed. by David McLellan (Oxford: Oxford University Press, 1977), p. 390.

89 G. A. Cohen, *Karl Marx's Theory of History: A Defence* (Oxford: Clarendon, 1978), p. 61.

90 It is interesting that one of the fathers of eco-authoritarianism, Robert Heilbroner, believes that we are trapped within a 'vicious circle', from which 'at present there is no escape', because of threats of war – threats which themselves 'justify' the need for nation states. And it is, of course, nation states which threaten war. See Robert L. Heilbroner, *An Inquiry into the Human Prospect* (London: Calder and Boyars, 1975), p. 46. Yet Heilbroner's recommendation is for '"iron" governments' (ibid., p. 39) to solve environmental crises. As the threat of war appears to have contributed so much to the environmental predicament we now seem to find ourselves in, and as 'iron governments' pose an increased threat, then Heilbroner's ostensible 'solution' would, surely, worsen the problem.

7.5.3 Eco-anarchism

So, armed with the State-Primacy Theory, we can now see more clearly what appear to be the fatal flaws in eco reformism, eco-Marxism and eco-authoritarianism. Each, it seems, would fail to stop us harming future generations. And the reason why none of these responses appears adequate is because *each fails to be genuinely interrelational.* Each focuses upon only one element of what could well be an environmentally hazardous dynamic. Either the focus is on the political relations, the economic relations, the economic forces or the political forces. The problem is, unfortunately, that if we are within an environmentally hazardous dynamic, then it is mutually reinforcing and self-sustaining (at least, possibly, to the point of ecological collapse!). If we are in such a dynamic, and there is ample reason to believe that we are, then the nature of the dynamic is such that changing one element in isolation cannot provide a long-term solution, because the rest of the dynamic will ensure that the transformed element eventually comes back into line. Alternatively, the other elements would simply re-constitute it in a form which is appropriate for serving their purposes. Consequently, every element of this interrelational dynamic would have to be transformed in order to allow long-term sustainability. In other words, *every element of the environmentally hazardous dynamic has to be opposed* if we are to reduce the risk of our societies being driven to inflict major harm on future generations.

This conclusion also bears on the viability of anarchism. The environmentally hazardous dynamic has been identified by the State-Primacy Theory. This theory accords explanatory primacy to the state. If states pose the fundamental problem, and if they are ultimately responsible for accelerated environmental deterioration, then surely, it might be assumed, anarchists would be right to see the answer simply in terms of the abolition of states. But, in fact, an effective *eco*-anarchist response would have to go considerably further than merely demanding the abolition of states if it is to stop an environmentally hazardous dynamic. As we have seen, focusing upon one element in isolation would seem to be the flaw in eco-reformist, eco-Marxist and eco-authoritarian approaches. Anarchists would also fail to provide an effective strategy if all they focused upon was the state. Such an exclusive focus would equally ignore the interrelational nature of the environmentally hazardous dynamic. It would therefore seem that eco-anarchists must, as well as opposing hierarchical political structures, reject the economic relations,[91] the technology and, in general, the coercion characteristic of modern societies.

So, if the environmentally hazardous dynamic of Figure 6.1 broadly depicts our present situation, which many would agree that it does, and if it is as putrid as it seems, how, then, do we stop our societies rolling in it? The answer would appear

91 And this, it would appear, is one very good reason why Nozickian economic libertarianism ought to be rejected. For while it might be critical of certain states, it is uncritical of the kinds of economic relations that seem to be so environmentally destructive.

to be for our communities to move to the environmentally benign interrelationship portrayed in Figure 6.4. Hence, it would seem, the most appropriate social and political form is a decentralized, participatory democracy,[92] utilizing nonviolent methods of social control, which incorporates egalitarian economic relations employing convivial technologies. For only such a society as this appears to be sustainable.

Of course, such an egalitarian, decentralized, participatory democracy would not be a sufficient condition for ending wide-scale pollution or resource depletion. But it does seem to be a necessary condition. A self-sufficient community in economic and political control of its own affairs *might* choose to degrade its environment; but it would not be *compelled* to do so. It would not be forced to over-produce and over-consume, as present societies seem to be, in order to meet the requirements of an economy that is functional for a militarily competitive, hierarchical state.

In short, there are compelling reasons for believing that we are presently ensnared within an environmentally hazardous dynamic resulting from the interrelationships we now occupy, and that this has given rise to global ecological deterioration which threatens our very survival. And only by ending that dynamic will it be possible for our species en masse to escape being impelled towards collective suicide.

Equally, there are compelling reasons for thinking that if we are to escape the environmentally hazardous dynamic, we must move towards egalitarian, decentralized, participatory democracies. Within a community taking such a form, the decisions reached would not be determined by inequalities of power. Therefore, environmental concerns are more likely to be raised and taken into consideration by such a society than by present ones, where those people who most suffer from environmental deterioration have the weakest voice. An egalitarian, decentralized, participatory democracy would also allow those who care passionately about the rest of nature to argue their case on equal terms with everyone else. So, although such a society, striving towards consensus, could, in principle, decide to behave in a manner which was not environmentally

92 It might be wondered whether a decentralized, participatory democracy really does have anything to do with anarchism. Yet probably the most internationally famous eco-anarchist – Murray Bookchin – has, in his numerous writings, advocated municipal democracy. See, for example, Murray Bookchin, *Toward an Ecological Society* (Montreal: Black Rose, 1980). It should also be noted that if we have an obligation not to harm innocents, then participatory democracies would have obligations not to take decisions that would cause harm to future generations. And they would also have an obligation to take steps to avoiding harm befalling present individuals. Hence, constraints would have to be placed on what decisions were legitimate, for a majority might, conceivably, choose to harm some innocent persons within or outside its community. In short, there are good grounds for individuals having rights within or against a participatory democracy.

sustainable, it is far more probable that it would pay proper respect to the environment than any alternative social form would.[93]

7.5.3.1 Freedom and environmentalism

Egalitarian, decentralized, participatory democracies, orientated towards an environmentally sustainable way of living, could also provide the most effective answer to the charge that environmentalists would, inevitably, prove to be enemies of freedom. To see fully how this charge might be answered, and to make explicit how the various components of the argument presented here fit together, allow me to glance back, very briefly, over the terrain we have traversed.

Chapter 1 noted some of the features of the catastrophic threat to human survival which environmentalists claim to have identified, as well as noting a few of the more elementary principles of ecology which have informed their thinking. Chapter 2 argued that the adequacy of the prevailing political approaches appears to be sufficiently in doubt to justify the suspicion that a new political theory is required if that threat is to be addressed effectively. Some of the conceptual groundwork necessary for an alternative political theory was laid in Chapter 3. An interrelationist approach seems most homologous with an ecological perspective. However, having to act within ecologically defined limits is precisely what might be presumed to constitute an unjustifiable restriction on freedom. But what do we mean by this essentially-contested, political concept? The most adequate conception of freedom would seem to be a triadic one. This includes not only the freedom to act but also freedom from certain constraints. When such constraints are imposed by other individuals, they exercise power over us. And the most adequate conception of 'power' would seem to be a 'four-dimensional', counter-factualist one.

Power over others is exercised both politically and economically. How do economic and political power interrelate? Chapter 4 argued that the relations structuring political power stabilize those relations structuring economic power which, on the one hand, are able to finance the political forces and, on the other hand, are conducive to developing those economic forces which the development of the political forces requires. However, this characterization of the complex of interrelationships obtaining between the political and economic relations and forces might appear to be implausible in an era of so-called globalization. Chapter 5 argued, to the contrary, that the theory offered here – the State-Primacy

93 Striving for consensus would seem to require a deliberative or discursive democracy, although not all those who advocate such a democratic programme see consensus as the goal. In recent years, there has been considerable discussion, especially amongst green political theorists influenced by Jürgen Habermas, of the need for a discursive or deliberative democracy. See, for example, John S. Dryzek, *Rational Ecology: Environment and Political Economy* (Oxford: Blackwell, 1987). Also see the contributions by Andrew Dobson, Robyn Eckersley and John Barry in B. Doherty and M. de Geus (eds), *Democracy and Green Political Thought: Sustainability, Rights and Citizenship* (London: Routledge, 1996).

Theory – has no difficulty in explaining global political developments. Indeed, it seems to offer a more comprehensive explanation of them than the most widely supported, alternative theories.

But the theory also enables us to explain the causes of the alarming environmental threat which we now seem to face. As Chapter 6 argued, the State-Primacy Theory reveals that the interrelationships between the political relations, the economic relations, the political forces, the economic forces and the environment would seem to constitute an environmentally hazardous dynamic. And while the State-Primacy Theory exposes this dynamic, the plausibility of the latter is not dependent upon the cogency of that theory. Most importantly, it is this environmentally hazardous dynamic which would appear to be driving us towards our own collective suicide; or, at the very least, the dynamic poses a very significant risk of so doing.

But if green anarcho-communes – organized as egalitarian, decentralized, participatory democracies – offer the only escape route from this dynamic, as the analysis of Chapter 6 suggests, then the charge that environmentalism is inherently authoritarian is surely answered. For, while simultaneously providing the communal resources (both social and economic) needed for individuals to engage in cooperative and autonomous action of their own choosing, a green anarcho-communist society could be expected to minimize the (counterfactually construed) power exercised over individuals, because, in such a society, individuals would be empowered to act creatively without being impeded by any centralized, coercive apparatus and without being subject to exploitative economic relations – both being the major loci of power in modern societies. In other words, whereas environmentalism has often been presumed to be inherently antagonistic to freedom, an environmentally sustainable, anarcho-communist society would, it seems likely, maximize the (triadic) freedom[94] capable of being enjoyed by all generations, while providing the only solution to the environmental threat standing in our path.

Of course, any such maximization of freedom would not include the maximization of all freedoms, such as, say, the freedom to drive one's car whenever one liked irrespective of the consequences.[95] However, while this caveat might appear to be an intolerable restriction on freedom, it could be argued that anyone who insists on such a freedom for himself or herself does not, in fact, genuinely value

94 As the triadic conception of 'freedom' advocated in Section 3.2, above, includes freedom from the potential constraints that might be imposed by a centralized source of power (counterfactually construed), it is therefore, in Joel Feinberg's terms, a 'dispositional liberty' or 'breathing space' conception – which, he claims, is closest to what we ordinarily take 'freedom' to mean. See Joel Feinberg, *Social Philosophy* (New Jersey: Prentice-Hall, 1973), pp. 5–7.

95 At times, in the eyes of Margaret Thatcher, at least, this opportunity for those fortunate enough to own a motor car (which, let us not forget, is a relatively recent invention) appears to have been viewed as if it were the principal human freedom and as if it were a natural right, to boot.

freedom at all. For if our unrestricted polluting activities result in serious harm befalling future generations, then future freedom will, in consequence, be severely curtailed. As with maximizing happiness,[96] the greatest total quantity of freedom which could conceivably be attained is surely not within any single generation, but across time so as to include many, many generations. There would, therefore, be a far greater quantity of freedom enjoyed were human life to be allowed to continue into the indefinite future than if it were to die out within a generation or two because of the collapse of planetary life-support systems.[97] Moreover, how much freedom would be left the last generation alive were they reduced by our profligate actions to a desperate attempt to survive in the midst of ecological collapse?

Arguably, then, the freedom to act so as to compromise ecological integrity is, in the long run, freedom-inhibiting. Hence, the freedom to act so as to destroy the planet and thereby restrict future freedom is, surely, not what anyone who truly valued freedom would demand. The highly selfish activities of the affluent of today are unlikely to be the sorts of things which anyone who genuinely valued freedom would applaud, never mind defend. In a word, anyone who truly valued freedom would surely wish to see freedom enjoyed by future generations, rather than see them fated to suffer horrendous deaths as a result of an environmental catastrophe of our making.

However, all this could easily be argued to have missed the point. For what those who love freedom really value, it might be objected, is their own personal freedom. But there have been many who truly valued freedom for whom this claim would be quite untrue. Under the flag of freedom, many have risked their lives – indeed, freedom is a cause for which many have willingly given their lives. But those who were prepared to sacrifice themselves in the name of freedom could not have been wholly preoccupied with their own personal freedom, for (unless one subscribes to rather strange eschatological views) it is doubtful that one's personal freedom is ever increased by the loss of one's life. Evidently, then, it must have been the freedom of others or the abstract ideal of freedom which many heroic individuals have admirably sought to further. But the demand for this generation to have the freedom to destroy the planet and thereby curtail the freedom of future generations fails to take all others sufficiently into account and hardly constitutes a consistent political ideal.[98] Thus, valuing freedom as a political

96 See Robin Attfield, *The Ethics of Environmental Concern* (Oxford: Blackwell, 1983), p. 128.

97 It goes without saying that, in maximizing the quantity of 'freedom' at different times, the same freedoms would have to be measured if the problem of incommensurability is to be side-stepped. But in the case of future harms, this problem seems to be avoided, for any freedom exercised now which led to the deaths of future people would restrict their enjoyment of *that particular freedom*, whatever it happened to be.

98 In any case, such a demand would surely forfeit freedom's claim to being a *moral* ideal. For example, if universalizability is a necessary condition for any claim to be moral, then the mooted freedom for our generation to destroy the planet, if we so choose, has no moral

ideal, for example, is surely not the same as the selfish demand for the freedom to do whatever one wants irrespective of whether or not it violates the freedom of others. Freedom as a political ideal can be argued to be coherent only when it consists in maximizing the freedom of all. But the freedom of future generations would seem to be no less morally significant than that of our contemporaries.

Consequently, if freedom is to be a convincing political ideal, it appears that it ought to mean maximizing the freedom of all generations. But then, no one who genuinely and consistently valued the freedom of all, including that of future generations, would knowingly and willingly choose to act so as to curtail future freedom by behaving in a manner which contributed to the undermining of ecological integrity. For future persons, and therefore their freedom, depend upon an uncompromised ecosystem. In short, then, we are required to live sustainable lifestyles if all persons (both present and future) are to be maximally free. But only the vision of a green anarcho-communist society seems to hold out any possibility of maximizing freedom by securing its basis into the indefinite future so that it may be enjoyed by an uncountable number of generations to come. Only an anarcho-communist society appears capable of escaping the power of the state and, with it, imprisonment within the environmentally hazardous dynamic in which the state seems to be centrally implicated. In a word, the maximization of our own freedom, along with that of future generations, appears to necessitate green anarcho-communes.

One thing seems clear, then: if the argument advanced here is sound, then a sustainable society is radically different from our own – and considerably more so than either eco-authoritarianism, eco-reformism or even eco-Marxism realizes. Only an eco-anarchist political theory reveals the full extent of the changes that may well have to be made if we are to survive as a species. Some will find the way of life that it advocates attractive. Some will not. The question which the latter must address, therefore, is what else could provide a long-term, workable answer to the problem of human sustainability? From the standpoint of the State-Primacy Theory, it is abundantly clear that nothing could. Only within green anarcho-communist societies could our species survive well into the future.

At first glance, however, many people would assume that suggesting any such alternative system is far too utopian and that it couldn't possibly work – except that, in the view of numerous social anthropologists, societies relevantly similar *have* worked. What is more, they seem to have worked for thousands and thousands of years. The most environmentally benign societies that anthropologists claim to have discovered, which appear to have existed relatively unchanged for far, far longer than any centralized state has been on this Earth, are non-militaristic, decentralized, participatory, egalitarian societies using convivial

---

standing, for it requires a maxim that cannot conceivably be universalized. *Per impossibile*, had a previous generation exercised such a freedom, then the present generation would not have existed, and could not, therefore, have formulated any maxims whatsoever. On the Kantian thesis that morality presumes universalizability, see R. M. Hare, *Freedom and Reason* (Oxford: Oxford University Press, 1965).

technologies (such as the Mbuti,[99] to cite just one example). In other words, the environmentally benign interrelationship depicted in Figure 6.4 appears to have persisted perfectly well for countless years in many non-literate societies. This is not to argue that we should return to the stone age. It is not to argue that we should do without technology; only that, collectively, we ought to develop technologies which are environmentally benign, as well as their political, economic and social prerequisites.

Hence, the big issue, it seems, is not whether the environmentally benign interrelationship would work or not. Rather, it is how we might move from the environmentally hazardous to the environmentally benign. And what all of this means for the individual is the following: One's moral obligation not to cause harm to future people, one's obligation to defend them from being harmed needlessly, and one's obligation to defend them from those who are running a considerable risk of harming them entail that one cannot merely oppose governmental policy. For one cannot, morally, continue to participate in *any* element of a dynamic that is so deadly to innocents. Nor, morally, can one continue to participate in *any* element which, in so far as it forms part of such a dynamic, poses a significant *risk* of causing serious harm to countless billions of innocents. In other words, one must refuse to cooperate not only with the prevailing political relations but also with their political forces, with the predominant economic relations, and with the use and development of their economic forces. In fact, one seems duty bound to go even further. One's obligation to prevent harm to future generations appears to extend to the shutting down of major sources of pollution – by 'ecotage', if need be.[100] I shall term all of this 'radical disobedience'.[101]

99 See Colin Turnbull, *The Forest People* (London: Picador, 1961). Of course, this is not to deny that certain other non-literate peoples have failed to act in an environmentally benign manner.

100 However, as the obligation to engage in 'ecotage' or 'monkeywrenching' has been derived from the obligation to prevent harm to others, then only forms of ecologically-motivated sabotage which did not cause harm to persons would be justified. One famous example of 'ecotage' is tree-spiking, where ceramic spikes are nailed into trees high up their trunks. The result is that, whereas those who cut down the trees with chainsaws are not harmed (because the spikes are inserted above the height at which they work), the blades of the saw-mills are destroyed by the spikes when the logs are sawn into planks of wood. And because of the safety-guards on the blades, no workers are physically harmed. Thus, tree-spiking penalizes logging mills with a rapacious demand for trees – the consequences of such demand being, among other things, the causing of harm through climate change to future generations. Or so environmentalists maintain.

101 It might be thought that Rawls' approach to 'intergenerational justice' could justify radical disobedience on behalf of future generations. Rawls' view is that each generation ought to preserve the benefits of its civilization, maintain its just institutions, and provide posterity with a capital accumulation greater than it inherited from its ancestors. John Passmore construes the latter as requiring of each generation that it ask itself what a society could reasonably expect from its predecessor. 'If it then acts upon the answer at which it arrives, each generation will be better off than its predecessor but no generation will be called upon to make an exceptional sacrifice.' John Passmore, *Man's Responsibility for Nature: Ecological*

However, it might be objected that engaging in any form of morally-motivated disobedience is the height of arrogance, for protesters are fallible, and what makes them more likely to be right than the government? That future generations will need the resources many of us presume they will need is open to doubt. The government might finance research which would free future generations from a reliance on scarce resources. But any suggestion that future generations will be invulnerable to any harm from a polluted environment is highly improbable. And it is clear that, when governments produce nuclear waste without any clear idea of how they will be able to dispose of it safely, then the harms which they are likely to inflict upon future generations are being disregarded. In such cases, protesters *are* more likely to be right than the government, for the government obviously does not care about the harms to future generations it is responsible for. Hence, certain protests in defence of future generations would seem to be unproblematic.

But, more importantly, the analysis offered here in fact side-steps the objection that protesters are fallible. For it provides reason to believe that we are all, including our governments, at present trapped within an environmentally hazardous dynamic, and that this dynamic is *driving* us to harm future generations. Before we could be free to decide on, and then implement, the morally right course of action with respect to future generations, we would need to escape the environmentally hazardous dynamic. In other words, radical disobedience would be the moral precondition for any morally acceptable outcome.[102]

Thus, in conclusion, radical disobedience is not merely permissible,[103] nor (because of an unquestioned assumption that civil disobedience on behalf of others is supererogatory, at best) is it merely commendable. With the aim of

Problems and Western Traditions (London: Duckworth, 1980), p. 87. However, our generation seems to be in the situation of leaving to its successors a planet which has been so harmed that the radical disobedience now apparently required on their behalf would require us to make just such an heroic sacrifice. But, as Passmore argues, given that 'Rawls' theory is based on the concept of justice, fairness, equal shares', then 'it leaves no room for the heroic sacrifice.' Ibid.

102 If we are, indeed, entrapped within the environmentally hazardous dynamic, then it is driving us to harm not only future generations of humans but also future generations of non-human animals, as well as presently existing human and non-human animals. It would also be driving us to compromise the integrity of the ecosphere as a whole. The risk of any of these 'harms' could be employed as a basis for radical disobedience. But given the 'speciesism' of most humans, and rather than rely on any (possibly dubious) argument about our responsibilities to the ecosphere or nature as a whole, I have confined my defence of radical disobedience to what appears to me to be the responsibility easiest to defend: namely, our obligations to other human persons – except in this case, it is to future human persons.

103 Radical disobedience might be thought to be impermissible because of a legal duty to obey the laws of the state. But if we are not prepared to accept as excuses for the most monstrously immoral acts utterances like 'I was only obeying orders', then, surely, we must accept that one can never abdicate one's moral responsibility, no matter what any state might insist one's ostensible legal responsibilities consist in. See Robert Paul Wolff, *In Defense of Anarchism* (New York: Harper and Row, 1976), *passim*.

bringing about environmentally benign societies and terminating any environmentally hazardous dynamic that might obtain, and with the aim of reducing the risk of harm to future generations, our engaging in *radical disobedience is*, quite simply, ***nothing less than the duty of each and every one of us.***

Appendix A
Green policies and core green values

A serious concern for the environment would have to lie right at the very heart of any cogent political theory with a legitimate claim to being 'green'. Moreover, a genuinely green political theory would need to be capable of spawning effective strategies for preserving the ecosystems which our polluting activities appear to threaten. But such a theory is unlikely to be greeted enthusiastically unless something of a 'green ideology' were to become more prevalent.

However, given that the majority of people do have some concern for their own offspring at least, and given that the latter will require the natural environmental to be preserved to some degree, an environmental sensibility could, conceivably, come to be felt universally. And should it eventually dawn on the majority that, rather than continuing to pursue an arrogant Promethean attempt at the complete mastery of nature, humbly living within the bounds of ecological sustainability is probably the precondition for our own continued existence as a species, then environmentalist attitudes might be expected one day to blossom.

But if we are to be certain of surviving the environmental crises that we seem to have precipitated, then we must begin to comprehend how ecosystems (upon which we all depend) can be adversely affected by our actions and how they can be sustained. Only then could the specific political, social, economic and ideological preconditions for both ecological sustainability and for our own continued existence as a species become clearly discernible. Thus, Robert Paehlke is surely right when he observes: 'The basic building blocks of an environmentalist ideology are the twin issues of conservation and pollution. Both rest on an understanding and appreciation of nature and ecology, and both require that one see human society as intertwined with the ecological web of life.'[1] None of the traditional political ideologies seems to have come anywhere near to meeting this requirement, yet its successful accomplishment, many environmentalists would insist, has now become essential for our very survival. Hence, there are reasonable grounds for concluding, as Paehlke does, that '[e]nvironmentalism . . . has the potential to

1 Robert C. Paehlke, *Environmentalism and the Future of Progressive Politics* (New Haven: Yale University Press, 1989), p. 13.

become the first original ideological perspective to develop since the middle of the nineteenth century.'[2]

Even so, considering the complacency which has, until relatively recently, greeted environmental warnings, it is not surprising that only a very short time ago most of the alternatives which have come to be associated with greens were widely considered to be extremely odd, if not downright cranky: vegetarianism, organic gardening, no-growth economics, appropriate technologies, decentralization, communes, workers' cooperatives, participatory democracy, pacifism, and so on. Today, many of these alternatives are being discussed seriously, and those who subscribe to them are no longer just dismissed unquestioningly as cranks – though E. F. Schumacher actually 'enjoyed being called a "crank", since a crank is a small, simple, inexpensive and efficient tool – "and it makes revolutions".'[3] Out of the blue, a number of green proposals seem to have become almost respectable.

This notwithstanding, many people still assume that greens are only concerned with the environment, even though *Die Grünen*, in their famous 1983 election manifesto, proffered a host of policies falling under various rubrics: 'economy and work'; 'foreign policy and peace policy'; 'environment and nature'; and 'individual and society'.[4] At the same time, the Ecology Party (now the British Green Party) presented policies on 'peace', 'work', 'taxing waste rather than work', 'food for the future', 'freedom-privacy-democracy', 'land for the people', 'safe energy', 'a green and pleasant land', 'good health' and 'animal rights'.[5] It is clearly erroneous, therefore, to regard greens or green parties as single-issue groupings when their concerns are so wide-ranging. The environment is not a single issue. Rather, it is all-encompassing. Thus, regarding the environment simply as a single issue could be viewed as committing a category mistake.[6]

Nevertheless, if anything links together green policies, one would expect it to be a concern with ecological sustainability. Thus, as Sandy Irvine and Alec Ponton note, greens 'have spotlighted the direction society must take if it wants a sustainable and satisfying future: partnership with the rest of nature, "soft" technology, "steady-state" economics, human-scale institutions and a population size

2 Ibid., pp. 2–3. It should be noted that Paehlke uses 'ideology' in a non-pejorative sense. (See ibid., p. 5.) Moreover, Paehlke also believes that 'environmentalism can be developed into an ideology as coherent as any of the three classical ideologies of liberalism, conservatism, and socialism.' Ibid., p. 4. However, many environmentalists might be inclined to regard his own attempt at developing environmentalism into a coherent ideology as failing to take into sufficient account the full significance of the present environmental threat.

3 Jonathon Porritt, *Seeing Green: The Politics of Ecology Explained* (Oxford: Blackwell, 1984), p. 16.

4 See *Die Grünen*, *Programme of the German Green Party* (London: Heretic Books, 1983).

5 For a summary, see the Ecology Party, *Politics for Life* (London: The Ecology Party, 1983), p. 26. For the details of these policies, see ibid., pp. 27–33.

6 See Gilbert Ryle, *The Concept of Mind* (Harmondsworth: Penguin, 1963), pp. 17–18.

within the environment's long-term carrying capacity.'[7] As a means of bringing about such 'a sustainable and satisfying future', which involves a 'partnership with the rest of nature', Irvine and Ponton themselves advocate a number of specific policies which have been widely discussed by reformist groupings within the green movement.

First, among the policies which might be implemented in order to bring about a greater use of less environmentally-threatening technologies, Irvine and Ponton propose that priority be accorded 'to many small-scale combined heat and power plants in local communities, and to industrial cogeneration schemes, including heat pumps, in larger enterprises and public buildings.'[8] They also propose that fiscal policy and building regulations 'be progressively revised to discriminate in favour of a low-energy, solar-powered society.'[9] More radical is their insistence that 'energy resources should belong to the public'.[10] Furthermore, Irvine and Ponton propose that the 'framework of subsidies and quotas . . . be altered to encourage a shift to self-sustaining and less damaging forms of organic agriculture.'[11] As they argue in justification of such a policy: 'The right to treat land as private property for whatever purposes its owner decides is incompatible with long-term environmental protection and social justice. Planning controls and penalties should be used to limit environmental degradation.'[12] Clearly, such policies presuppose a very different attitude to private property than has thus far been prevalent in western liberal societies.[13]

Second, among the policies which might be implemented in order to bring about a 'steady-state' economy, Irvine and Ponton propose

> higher rates of value-added tax on resource intensive products and correspondingly lower ones on activities that are labour-intensive, thus encouraging re-use and repair. Discounts for large users, especially of energy,

7 Sandy Irvine and Alec Ponton, *A Green Manifesto: Policies for a Green Future* (London: Optima, 1988), p. 3.
8 Ibid., p. 56.
9 Ibid.
10 Ibid.
11 Ibid., p. 45.
12 Ibid., p. 46. And as they pointedly add: 'Where businessmen shoot grouse, there is a golden opportunity to initiate a recovery of a much richer and more productive ecology than current land ownership and uses permit.' Ibid.
13 However, there is evidence that propertarian values are being restructured to some degree even in the United States: 'Private ownership will never be so sacrosanct again. The myth that a landowner can do what he [or she] pleases regardless of his [or her] neighbour's interests or the broader and longer-term public welfare is rapidly being eroded, even though there is still much resistance to its demise. Increasingly the courts are saying that certain social obligations must be respected when exercising the right to enjoy the use of private property.' Tim O'Riordan, *Environmentalism* (London: Pion, 1981), p. 147. For a discussion of some of the changes that environmental accidents seem to demand of the American legal system, see Richard H. Gaskins, *Environmental Accidents: Personal Injury and Public Responsibility* (Philadelphia: Temple University Press, 1989).

> would be stopped, while subsidies for energy conservation and recycling would be increased. Greens would encourage labour-intensive institutions and technologies rather than those that demand high physical and financial capital. Green economic policy would end measures which penalize the employment of people and encourage mechanization. In general, the burden of taxation would be shifted onto resource use.[14]

But it is clear that such policies would seriously encroach on the ability of major capitalist firms to make profits, and would involve an interference with the free-market that is in stark contrast to the, until very recently, dominant views of the New Right and of those whom they have influenced.

Third, among the policies which might be implemented in order to bring about more 'human-scale institutions', Irvine and Ponton propose, to take one example, that where it is practicable 'medical help and advice . . . be dealt with at community level. . . . The Chinese system of "barefoot doctors" shows that it is possible to demystify medicine and guide the community in health matters.'[15] Their favouring this approach follows from their preference for greater self-help. As they write:

> we start from the assumption that people themselves are best able to judge what satisfies their needs, and that self-help and group initiative, where practicable, are more likely to provide satisfaction than bureaucracies, public or private. While many have gained from the services proffered by caring organizations, bureaucratization and professionalization often frustrate the very purposes these institutions claim to serve.[16]

Moreover, as they also maintain: 'When "service technologies" take over the field of human needs, people themselves tend to be disempowered.'[17] Instead, in their view, 'individuals and groups must be . . . empowered to challenge activities which threaten either themselves or society as a whole.'[18] But this ideal clearly poses a considerable challenge to the vested interests of present bureaucracies and to the faith that many people have in them.

Fourth, Irvine and Ponton suggest several policies which might be implemented in order to contain population growth:

> There could be payments for periods of non-pregnancy and non-birth (a kind of no claims bonus); tax benefits for families with fewer than two chil-

14 Irvine and Ponton, *A Green Manifesto*, p. 30.

15 Ibid., p. 100.

16 Ibid., p. 34. For a discussion of how welfare institutions might be de-bureaucratized, see Michael Walzer, 'Socializing the welfare state' in Amy Gutman (ed.), *Democracy and the Welfare State* (New Jersey: Princeton University Press, 1988).

17 Irvine and Ponton, *A Green Manifesto*, p. 83.

18 Ibid., p. 38.

> dren; sterilization bonuses; withdrawal of maternity and similar benefits after a second child; larger pensions for people with fewer than two children; free, easily available family planning; more funds for research into means of contraception, especially for men; an end to infertility research and treatment; a more realistic approach to abortion; the banning of surrogate motherhood and similar practices; and the promotion of equal opportunities for women in all areas of life.[19]

However, the burden of implementing such policies would most likely fall primarily on the poor and underprivileged. Hence, Irvine and Ponton insist that if such a programme is to be adopted, then 'redistribution of wealth, desirable on many other grounds, becomes even more necessary to ensure that parenting does not become a privilege of the rich.'[20] But it is clear that policies to reduce family size go against many individuals' assumptions about procreative freedom.

All four areas of policy proposed by Irvine and Ponton thus seem to require a radical shift in thinking from that of the status quo. So, as with the policies advocated by other reformist greens, it turns out that there is, in fact, far more to their policy proposals than merely adding a concern for the environment onto what is currently the most widely held set of values. Even reformists within the green movement advocate policies which are extremely radical by conventional standards, while the redistribution envisaged would seem to pose a threat to the affluence enjoyed by many of the most powerful people presently living within capitalist societies.

We have seen that there is far more to being green than merely expressing a concern for the environment. But then, what, precisely, is involved? Jonathon Porritt, formerly Director of Friends of the Earth, and one of the most famous green spokespersons in the UK, lists the following as minimum criteria for being genuinely green:

19 Ibid., p. 23.

20 Ibid. In order to bring about such redistribution, Irvine and Ponton propose a progressive income tax 'on all sources and types of income' combined with a basic income scheme, where citizens would be given 'a basic income sufficient for their essential needs.' Ibid., p. 70. Their favoured scheme would guarantee economic independence for women, and would require a reduced bureaucracy, because everyone would receive the same amount and fewer calculations would be required. A basic income scheme is also proposed as a way of reducing economic growth: 'The dependence of so many full-time jobs on an increasing output of goods and services has caused an addiction to economic growth, regardless of whether we need to produce or can tolerate its destructive effect on society and environment. The basic income scheme would ease that pressure, since people would be able to live in an economy that was no longer demanding more and more land, energy and materials. Resource depletion, pollution and environmental degradation would all be reduced.' Ibid. Such a scheme was a central economic plank in the Ecology Party's 1983 election manifesto and has continued to remain so. See, for example, the Green Party, *Don't Let Your World Turn Grey* (London: The Green Party, 1989). For a critique of such a scheme, see Martin Ryle, *Ecology and Socialism* (London: Radius, 1988), p. 56.

(a) a reverence for the Earth and for all its creatures;
(b) a willingness to share the world's wealth among *all* its peoples;
(c) prosperity to be achieved through sustainable alternatives to the rat race of economic growth;
(d) lasting security to be achieved through non-nuclear defence strategies and considerably reduced arms spending;
(e) a rejection of materialism and the destructive values of industrialism;
(f) a recognition of the rights of future generations in our use of all resources;
(g) an emphasis on socially useful, personally rewarding work, enhanced by human-scale technology;
(h) protection of the environment as a precondition of a healthy society;
(i) an emphasis on personal growth and spiritual development;
(j) respect for the gentler side of human nature;
(k) open, participatory democracy at every level of society;
(l) recognition of the crucial importance of significant reductions in population levels;
(m) harmony between people of every race, colour and creed;
(n) a non-nuclear, low-energy strategy, based on conservation, greater efficiency and renewable sources;
(o) an emphasis on self-reliance and decentralized communities.[21]

On the basis of Porritt's minimum criteria, we must conclude that genuine greens not only have a concern for the environment but also value alongside sustainability: egalitarianism, internationalism, pacifism, participatory democracy, alternative technologies, self-sufficiency and decentralization.[22] However, from a first acquaintance, one would not be unjustified in assuming that this list is purely random. Yet, as I attempt to show in Chapter 6, these values can be linked together coherently – by means of the State-Primacy Theory, which is one reason why greens might feel inclined to accept the theory.

Now, whereas Porritt's minimum criteria are widely accepted within the green movement, it should be noted that very different values, as well as differing theoretical approaches and their corresponding strategies, are evident in such influential green thinkers as Rudolf Bahro, Murray Bookchin, Boris Frankel, André Gorz, William Ophuls, Robert Paehlke, and Martin Ryle, to name but a

21 See Porritt, *Seeing Green*, pp. 10–11. Paehlke presents a very similar list of what he takes to be 'the central value assertions of environmentalism', and which 'have consistently been emphasized in the writings of environmentalists and are implicit in their actions'. See Paehlke, *Environmentalism and the Future of Progressive Politics*, pp. 144–5.

22 *Die Grünen* make it quite clear that they are not solely concerned with ecological problems when they insist: 'Our policy is governed by long-term future considerations, and guided by four basic principles: it is ecological, social, grassroots-democratic and nonviolent.' *Die Grünen*, *Programme of the German Green Party*, p. 7. What they intend by their policy being 'grassroots-democratic' can be gleaned from the following gloss: 'A policy of grassroots democracy means the increased realization of decentralized and direct democracy.' Ibid., p. 8.

few.[23] Combined, their values, approaches and strategies indicate a composite green movement sporting, what seem to be, fundamental inconsistencies. For example, Tim O'Riordan has identified five areas of tension within modern environmentalism:

> (i) [the problem of] short-term selfishness and enlightened longer-term community interest,[24] [the latter seeming to require] the curtailment of individual freedoms in order to ensure greater flexibility of communal choice when managing common property resources . . . ,
> (ii) the protection of national sovereignty while recognizing the existence of global or multinational responsibilities . . . ,
> (iii) guarantees of the rights of racial and other cultural minorities to enjoy diverse lifeways while ensuring that the interests of the majority are not thereby jeopardized . . . ,[25]
> (iv) the protection of options for future generations (including protecting the options of continued existence for certain biotic communities and natural landscapes of intrinsic natural value) while not unreasonably limiting the pleasures of the present generation . . . , and
> (v) the controversies over how much affluence or austerity, what degree of materialism or spirituality, and the extent of redistribution of wealth and social and political opportunity that regularly dominate the growth-nongrowth debate. . . .[26]

And the various different thinkers have leaned towards different sides of these various tensions.

But why does the green movement presently exhibit so many apparent inconsistencies? O'Riordan considers the five tensions he adumbrates to result from 'the divergent evolution of two ideological themes which arose at the birth of the conservation movement':[27] 'the ecocentric mode' and 'the technocentric mode'. The latter can be characterized as faith in 'the application of rational and "value-free" scientific and managerial techniques by a professional elite, who regarded the natural environment as "neutral stuff" from which [hu]man[ity] could profitably shape [its] destiny';[28] whereas the former can be characterized as

23 See, for example, Rudolf Bahro, *Building the Green Movement* (London: Heretic Books, 1986), Murray Bookchin, *Toward an Ecological Society* (Montreal: Black Rose, 1980), Boris Frankel, *The Post-Industrial Utopians* (Cambridge: Polity, 1987), André Gorz, *Ecology as Politics*, trans. P. Vigderman and J. Cloud (London: Pluto, 1980), William Ophuls, *Ecology and the Politics of Scarcity: Prologue to a Political Theory of the Steady State* (San Francisco: W. H. Freeman, 1977), Paehlke, *Environmentalism and the Future of Progressive Politics*, and Ryle, *Ecology and Socialism*.

24 O'Riordan, *Environmentalism*, p. 36.

25 For example, 'when minority cultures are threatened by resource development proposals'. Ibid., p. vii.

26 Ibid.

27 Ibid., p. 1.

28 Ibid.

the belief in a delicately balanced natural order which was disturbed by the entry of human beings. 'Thereafter the "web of life" was broken by a degenerate succession of "disturbed harmonies" leading ultimately to the destruction of [hu]man-[ity] [it]self.'[29] For those partial to the ecocentric mode, their belief is that human beings ought to fit into the natural order, rather than destroy it and themselves along with it.[30]

It could thus be argued that the fundamental inconsistencies which have arisen within the green movement can be attributed to several of those theorists who purport to be green having incorporated a number of technocentric features into their prescriptions. And it could further be argued that a great deal of theoretical chaos has resulted from certain 'greens' retaining too much theoretical baggage left over from earlier and out-dated political ideologies, rather than rigorously discarding any element which is not compatible with an ecocentric perspective or which is not adequate for a cogent green political analysis. In particular, a great deal of the current confusion seems to have arisen because of the technocentricism residing in much of the authoritarian socialist tradition, whereas, even in William Ophuls' view, 'to the extent that the environmental movement shares a common political ideology, it is predominantly anarchist.'[31]

The key question which the major proposals advocated by greens thus gives rise to is this: Are green politics consistent and can they be supported by a theoretical position which is both coherent and cogent? Answering this question has been the burden of this book. And its conclusion is that a coherent green political theory (one based on the State-Primacy Theory) is indeed possible. However, in order to make green thinking consistent, the theory has had to take such a form that it endorses only the more radical of present green strategies, while certain other policies (particularly those proposed by the more conservative and technocentric environmentalists) have had to be rejected as inadequate or inappropriate. What this suggests is that if it is to be coherent, a green political theory (along with the strategies and policies it implies) will be extremely radical, or it will simply fail to be genuinely green.

29 Ibid.

30 As O'Riordan makes clear, modern environmentalism has been influenced in a number of important ways by ecocentrism: first, 'it provides a *natural morality* – a set of rules for [human] behaviour based upon the limits and obligations imposed by natural ecosystems . . . [and it] provides checks to the headlong pursuit of "progress" which, by and large, is the objective of the technocentric mode'. Second, 'it talks of *limits* (blurred perhaps but recognizable) of energy flows or productive capacity, and of the costs of organization and systems maintenance'. Third, 'it talks in ecosystem metaphors of *permanence and stability*, diversity, creativity, homeostasis, and the protection of options'. Fourth, 'it raises questions about *ends and means*, particularly the nature of democracy, participation, communication among groups holding conflicting yet legitimate convictions, the distribution of political power and economic wealth, and the importance of personal responsibility'. And fifth, 'ecocentrism preaches the virtues of *self-reliance and self-sufficiency*.' Ibid., pp. 10–11.

31 Ophuls, *Ecology and the Politics of Scarcity*, p. 235.

Appendix B

Greens and green parties

The constituent elements of a green 'ideology'[1] have a long history, but many of them re-emerged on the political scene in something of an explosion in the late 1960s. The events of May 1968 in France (which, it is widely believed, nearly brought down President de Gaulle's government) brought participatory democracy temporarily to the forefront of the political agenda when striking students attempted to organize themselves by means of direct democracies. In Amsterdam, anarchists, grouped as Provos and Kabouters, initiated novel schemes through the city council, such as the provision of white bicycles (which anyone could take and then, at journey's end, leave available for others to ride). Throughout the western world an 'underground' press grew up. Most of these publications were managed collectively, and they promoted numerous ideas for an alternative way of living. This was a time of optimism – a time when many of the young believed that they could change the world into something far more humane. And many of them set about trying to do just that.

One feature of the prevailing order which many of the young desperately wanted to change was the arms race. The continuing activities of the Campaign for Nuclear Disarmament, heightened by opposition to the war in Vietnam, not only were themselves manifested in non-violent direct action against the military but also were instrumental in leading to a re-birth of interest in pacifism. This grew into a widespread opposition in Europe in the 1980s to any further deployment of nuclear weapons, especially Cruise and Pershing II missiles. And through the formation of women's peace camps in direct response to such mobile nuclear weaponry, many feminists were able to assert their pacifist credentials.

The reaction to the threat of nuclear war has also been used to explain the late 1960s phenomenon of many young people 'dropping out' and forming their own counter-culture.[2] If there is a real possibility of there being no tomorrow, why not just enjoy the here and now, rather than competing in the 'rat race' for a slice of deferred gratification? On the other hand, the phenomenon of the young 'dropping-out' and refusing to participate in the 'rat-race' has also been

1 See Appendix A.

2 See, for example, Jeff Nuttall, *Bomb Culture* (London: Paladin, 1970).

characterized as a rejection of materialistic values.[3] Many experimented with workers' cooperatives or with communes, where community and sharing were viewed as preferable to competitiveness. And in the 1970s, it was not uncommon for people to move from the cities back to the land and to try their hands at self-sufficiency. Many of those who experimented at 'dropping-out' in the 1960s and 1970s are today actively involved in the green movement, and have done much to shape its values.

But, clearly, what has done most to advance the green political perspective is (what many would regard as) the ever-worsening state of the environment. In the 1960s, a small number of path-breaking books on environmental problems were published – for example, by Rachel Carson and by Murray Bookchin (first writing under the pseudonym Lewis Herber).[4] But in the early 1970s, a spate of ecologically concerned publications appeared.[5] These books spawned a small but committed environmental movement. Non-violent direct action in defence of the environment soon followed. While, for many years, there had been several rather tame organizations promoting conservation, suddenly a new breed of more radical campaigning group emerged (such as Greenpeace and Friends of the Earth). But environmentally-motivated, non-violent direct action wasn't confined to the members of these organizations. Several mass actions occurred, with one of the major targets being the expansion of nuclear power. Widely publicized confrontations between opponents of nuclear energy and the authorities took place at Whyl on the German–French border in 1975 and then at Seabrook in the United States in 1977, while numerous smaller confrontations took place elsewhere in Europe.

At first, environmentalists were often denounced as irrational Luddites. But with progressively worsening environmental incidents, such as the poisoning of Lake Minimata in the 1960s, the emission of highly dangerous chemicals in 1976 at Seveso and later at Bhopal, the near meltdown of the nuclear reactor at Three Mile Island in 1979 and, most dramatically, the Chernobyl disaster on 26 April 1986, assurances by the authorities that there were no major environmental problems began to sound more and more hollow, and warnings by ecologists have increasingly been treated with far greater respect.[6]

3 Examples are Charles Reich, *The Greening of America* (Harmondsworth: Penguin, 1972) and Theodore Roszak, *The Making of a Counter Culture* (London: Faber, 1971).

4 Rachel Carson, *Silent Spring* (Boston: Houghton Mifflin, 1962) and Lewis Herber, *Our Synthetic Environment* (New York: Alfred Knopf, 1962).

5 The most famous of these are D. Meadows *et al.*, *The Limits to Growth: A Report for the Club of Rome's Project on the Predicament of Mankind* (London: Earth Island, 1972), Edward Goldsmith *et al.*, *Blueprint for Survival* (Harmondsworth: Penguin, 1972), Barbara Ward and René Dubos, *Only One Earth: The Care and Maintenance of a Small Planet* (Harmondsworth: Penguin, 1972), and Barry Commoner, *The Closing Circle: Nature, Man, Technology* (New York: Alfred Knopf, 1971).

6 As Martin Ryle observed at the end of the 1980s: 'There can be no doubt that "environmental issues" command greater media coverage and evoke more public concern today than they have ever done. Whatever the difficulties, intellectual and practical, of working towards it, an ecological transformation of modern societies is an idea whose time is coming.' Martin Ryle, *Ecology and Socialism* (London: Radius, 1988), p. 60.

The rise of green parties

Apparently as a result of such factors, the sudden growth in support for green parties up to the end of the 1980s was nothing less than astronomical. At the beginning of the 1970s, green parties simply didn't exist. The 'world's first green party'[7] was the United Tasmania Group, which was set up in April 1972 in order to save Lake Peddler, whereas the first genuine national green party was the Values Party, which was founded in New Zealand on 30 May 1972. Interestingly, '[f]or the 1975 national elections the party was able to contest all the constituencies and polled an average of 5.2%, just short of the percentage that gave *Die Grünen* 28 seats in the West German parliament eight years later.'[8] Although *Die Grünen*'s electoral triumph was world news, a comparable vote for the Values Party in New Zealand eight years earlier went unnoticed. Certainly, a lack of proportional representation in New Zealand undermined the significance of the support the Values Party was able to muster.

But the formation of green parties at this time was not confined to Australasia. The first European green party, People, was established as early as February 1973. In 1975, its name was changed to the Ecology Party, and in September 1985 it became the (British) Green Party. However, it was some time before a green party was able to taste electoral success at national level. The first green parties to have representatives elected to a national parliament were the Belgian parties *Agalev* and *Ecolo*. Even after their representatives had succeeded in entering the Belgian parliament in 1981, green parties were still not world news. The most famous breakthrough in parliamentary terms was, of course, the election of 28 members of *Die Grünen* to the German *Bundestag* in March 1983. Their 2 million supporters comprised 5.6 per cent of the national vote. And their entry into parliament, while carrying flowers and branches as symbols of life, and with their colourful clothing contrasting vividly with the sober, dark grey dress of the traditional parties, was headline news throughout the world.

Within a couple of decades of the founding of the first green party, greens had also succeeded in being elected to parliament in Italy, Switzerland, Austria, Finland, Ireland, Luxembourg and Sweden. The Women's Alliance gained representation in the Icelandic parliament; while not describing itself as a 'green' party, it nevertheless showed clear support for green policies. And if one adds to this the two members of the Portuguese parliament who were elected on the Communist Party list and the 'two Green/Anti-Nuclear senators'[9] who acquired seats in the Australian parliament, then one can readily see the explosion of green representation. As Sara Parkin was able to remark at the close of the 1980s: 'By any standards the speed with which green parties have established themselves on the political scene has been phenomenal. . . . We can now say that in less than nine

7 Sara Parkin, *Green Parties: An International Guide* (London: Heretic Books, 1989), p. 280.
8 Ibid., p. 268.
9 Ibid., p. 11.

years greens have been elected to eleven national parliaments around the world.'[10] What is more, 'greens now sit at some level of local government in almost every west European country'.[11] Thus, it has been claimed that we have witnessed the beginnings of 'the most dynamic social and political movement since the birth of socialism',[12] if not 'the fastest growing political movement ever'.[13]

Nevertheless, greens remain in a considerable minority, and the striking absences of representation in western national parliaments are, of course, those countries which lack proportional representation: the United States, France and the United Kingdom – although the UK has an MP who represents both Plaid Cymru (the Welsh nationalist party) and the Green Party. But the absence of parliamentary representation of the green movement in these countries does not mean that the greens lack support. Greens are represented on a number of local councils. Most interestingly, it has been calculated that there are more members of environmental organizations in the UK than there are members of political parties,[14] and that, 'in terms of membership numbers and income', the British environmental movement is 'comparable to the Trade Union movement'.[15] Within the United States, Charlene Spretnak and Fritjof Capra have contacted a number of groups with a combined membership in excess of 2 million who 'are working with means and goals that are consistent with green politics'.[16] And in France, as in the UK, greens have held seats in local government.

But the most striking development was the success of the greens in the elections for the European Parliament in June 1989. One plausible reason for green parties having done badly in the United Kingdom and French national elections (although Antoine Waechter had obtained 1,145,502 votes in the first round of the previous year's French presidential election) is that without a system of proportional representation, a vote for a minor party appears to be a wasted vote. What seems the most pragmatic course of action to take is to vote tactically in order to keep out the most environmentally destructive of the major parties, and that means voting for its main opponent. However, in the European elections, France employs a system of proportional representation. And that enabled *Les Verts* (the French Green Party) to achieve a remarkable breakthrough, polling 10.6 per cent and obtaining representation at Strasbourg for the first time – with nine seats.

10 Ibid.

11 Ibid. Greece is a notable exception.

12 Jonathon Porritt, *Seeing Green: The Politics of Ecology Explained* (Oxford: Blackwell, 1984), p. xiv. And the significance of the emergence of green parties is suggested by the fact that *Miljopartiet*, the Swedish Green Party, 'became the first new party to enter the Swedish parliament for 70 years.' Parkin, *Green Parties*, p. 21.

13 Ibid., p. 23.

14 However, some individuals may well be members of more than one environmental organization, though not many will be members of more than one political party.

15 Sara Parkin, 'I love you green', *Resurgence* 136 (1989), p. 5.

16 Charlene Spretnak and Fritjof Capra, *Green Politics* (London: Paladin, 1985), p. 213.

On the other hand, the United Kingdom retained a first-past-the-post system for the European elections. But this notwithstanding, the Green Party managed to score a colossal 14.9 per cent of the vote, 'taking it in one jump from the lowest to the highest vote for a green party anywhere in Europe'.[17] With 2.3 million votes, it saved its deposit in all 78 seats, and ousted the Social and Liberal Democrats to become the third major political party in the UK at that time. In fact, in the constituency of Sussex West, 25.4 per cent voted Green, while 23 per cent did so in Hereford and Worcester, in the Cotswolds, and in Somerset. 'Overall the party scored more than 20% in 17 constituencies, and over 10% in 67.'[18] Most significantly, the Green Party came second to the Conservatives in six English seats. In that election, throughout Europe, green parties either improved or maintained their position, taking their collective tally of 20 MEPs to 34. Green parties, in virtually no time, became a genuine force in European politics. Since then, however, their futures have fluctuated considerably.

There are also significant green movements in the Third World (as far apart as Brazil and Malaysia), in Canada, in Japan, and in Eastern Europe. As Parkin observes: 'The rapid growth of environmental groups in Central and South America is matched by similar developments in Asia and Africa. Also interesting is the burgeoning of ecological groups in East European countries where governments are faced with some of the worst environmental pollution in the world.'[19] No one can now doubt that support for green policies is both world-wide and an extremely important political phenomenon. What explanation can be given for this support, and what is the green constituency?

The nature of the green movement

It seems evident that much of the core support in the advanced countries for green policies comes from those who are members of what have been termed the 'new social movements', which consist of the 'peace, feminist, ecological, and local-autonomy movements proliferating in the West since the midseventies'.[20] But what is the nature of these 'new social movements'? According to Alberto Melucci:

> The normal situation of today's 'movement' is a network of small groups submerged in everyday life which require a personal involvement in experiencing and practicing cultural innovation. They emerge only on specific issues, as for instance the big mobilizations for peace, for abortion, against nuclear policy, etc. The submerged network, although composed of separate

17 Martin Linton and John Curtice, 'Rising from nowhere to be prime outside contenders', *Guardian*, 20 June 1989.

18 Chris Rose, 'Two million green votes', *Econews*, August/September 1989.

19 Parkin, *Green Parties*, p. 314.

20 Jean L. Cohen, 'Strategy or identity: new theoretical paradigms and contemporary social movements', *Social Research*, Vol. 52, No. 4 (Winter 1985), p. 663.

> small groups, is a system of exchange (persons and information circulate along the network; some agencies, such as local free radios, bookshops, magazines provide a certain unity).[21]

Such networks 'allow multiple membership', the militantism of their members 'is only part-time and short-term', and 'personal involvement and affective solidarity is required as a condition for participation in many of the groups.' What is especially important is that, in Melucci's view, this cannot be regarded as 'a temporary phenomenon but a morphological shift in the structure of collective action'.[22]

These movements have not always been described approvingly. For example, Jean L. Cohen claims that they have 'a self-understanding that abandons revolutionary dreams in favor of the idea of structural reform, along with a defense of civil society that does not seek to abolish the autonomous functioning of political and economic systems – in a phrase, self-limiting radicalism.'[23] Moreover, on the basis of this assessment of 'new social movements' as instances of 'self-limiting radicalism', Cohen also claims that 'we are in an intellectual situation in which revolutionary ideology has moved from Marxism, with its rational theoretical core, to eschatologies that have no discernible relation to the potentials or limits of the social structures to which they are addressed.'[24] However, it could be argued in response that the ecological restrictions which have been identified by ecologists as placing limits on social structures are far more constraining than the economic limits which Marxists claim to have diagnosed.

What, though, is the class composition of these movements? Cohen informs us that the majority of observers are in agreement that 'they come primarily from the "new middle classes," although marginals and members of the "old bourgeoisie" participate.'[25] This has led Klaus Eder to categorize their politics as 'petit bourgeois radicalism'.[26] Nevertheless, 'actors involved in the contemporary movements do not view themselves in terms of a socio-economic class'.[27] But this also makes them very different from the 'Old Left', which explicitly identified with the industrial proletariat. As Claus Offe remarks: 'New middle class politics, in contrast to most working class politics, as well as old middle class politics, is typically a politics *of* a class but not *on behalf of* a class.'[28]

21 Alberto Melucci, 'The symbolic challenge of contemporary movements', *Social Research*, Vol. 52, No. 4 (Winter 1985), p. 800.

22 Ibid.

23 Cohen, 'Strategy or identity', p. 664.

24 Ibid., p. 666.

25 Ibid., p. 667.

26 Klaus Eder, 'The "new social movements": moral crusades, political pressure groups, or social movements?', *Social Research*, Vol. 52, No. 4 (Winter 1985), p. 879.

27 Cohen, 'Strategy or identity', p. 667.

28 Claus Offe, 'New social movements: challenging the boundaries of institutional politics', *Social Research*, Vol. 52, No. 4 (Winter 1985), p. 833. This seems to suggest that members of the 'new social movements' correspond to Mannheim's disinterested 'intelligentsia'. See Karl

This, however, is a rather different view from that of Hans Magnus Enzensberger, who does see the ecology movement as representing middle-class interests. And this is for the reason that green issues were only placed on the political agenda when environmental degradation began to encroach on the lifestyle of the middle class; whereas environmental problems have always been experienced by the proletariat:

> Industrialization made whole towns and areas of the countryside uninhabitable as long as a hundred and fifty years ago. The environmental conditions at places of work, that is to say in the English factories and pits, were – as innumerable documents demonstrate – dangerous to life. There was an infernal noise; the air people breathed was polluted with explosive and poisonous gases as well as with carcinogenous matter and particles which were highly contaminated with bacteria. The smell was unimaginable. In the labour process contagious poisons of all kinds were used. The diet was bad. Food was adulterated. Safety measures were non-existent or were ignored. The overcrowding in the working-class quarters was notorious. The situation over drinking water and drainage was terrifying. There was in general no organized method for disposing of refuse.[29]

Here we have a catalogue of many of the problems that environmentalists are concerned about today, yet

> [i]t occurred to no one to draw pessimistic conclusions about the future of industrialization from these facts. The ecological movement has only come into being since the districts which the bourgeoisie inhabit and their living conditions have been exposed to those environmental burdens that industrialization brings with it. What fills their prophets with terror is not so much ecological decline, which has been present since time immemorial, as its universalization.[30]

And, it might be added, given the 'universalization' of ecological decline, the middle class cannot just turn its back on it, for now it, too, is affected.

Mannheim, *Ideology and Utopia* (London: Routledge and Kegan Paul, 1960), pp. 136–46. And as Robert Paehlke writes: 'Environmentalism is an ideology distinctive . . . in its unwillingness to maximize economic advantages for its own adherents. . . . Environmentalism has minimal appeal by way of personal economic gain; it may be the least economically self-interested of all ideologies.' Robert C. Paehlke, *Environmentalism and the Future of Progressive Politics* (New Haven: Yale University Press, 1989), p. 7.

29 Hans Magnus Enzensberger, 'A critique of political ecology', *New Left Review* 84 (1974), p. 9.

30 Ibid., p. 10. In addition, 'the working class cares little about general environmental problems and is only prepared to take part in campaigns where it is a question of directly improving their working and living conditions. In so far as it can be considered a source of ideology, ecology is a matter that concerns the middle class.' Ibid., p. 10.

However, it can be countered that it is simply not true that the problems posed by the Industrial Revolution failed to give birth to any environmental movement. Romanticism, as David Pepper argues, 'can be seen clearly as a reaction *against* material changes in society – changes in the mode of production which can be regarded as part of the emergence and expansion of industrial capitalism in the 18th century'.[31] Moreover, the members of the Romantic movement

> noticed and hated the way that industrialization made previously beautiful places ugly, and they rejected the vulgarity of those who made money in trade. With the emergence of new social groups, romantics sought their own self-definition in this eschewing of the commodity society. They separated themselves from the vulgar bourgeoisie and working-class proletariat not only by physical means but also by promoting the idea that their own labour – unlike that of capitalism – was not reducible to commodity values. Their labour was intellectual; it was uniquely special.[32]

And Romanticism can certainly be argued to be one of the many 'roots of modern environmentalism'.

Interestingly, there appears to be a structural similarity between the social location of the early Romantics and the 'new social movements': their non-commodified position within society. As Stephen Cotgrove and Andrew Duff discovered in their survey of environmentalists conducted in the late 1970s: 'What is particularly striking is the high proportion of environmentalists in our sample occupying roles in the non-productive service sector: doctors, social workers, teachers, and the creative arts.'[33] This finding gives rise to an important sociological question: Are many environmentalists 'new middle class' because a non-commodified role is the *cause* or because it is the *effect* of their environmental and social awareness? For as Cotgrove and Duff note:

> those who reject the ideology and values of industrial capitalism are likely to choose careers outside the market-place. Moreover, such occupations can offer a substantial degree of personal autonomy for those who have little taste for a subordinate role in the predominantly hierarchical structures of industrial society.[34]

This is a crucial issue for ascertaining the potential constituency of the green movement. If a non-commodified structural location explains one's susceptibility

31 David Pepper, *The Roots of Modern Environmentalism* (London: Routledge, 1989), p. 76.

32 Ibid., pp. 76–7.

33 Stephen Cotgrove and Andrew Duff, 'Environmentalism, middle-class radicalism and politics', *Sociological Review*, Vol. 28, No. 2 (1980), p. 340. More generally, members of 'the radical environmental associations' tend to be 'employed in occupations outside the market sector, where goods and services are sold.' Stephen Cotgrove, *Catastrophe or Cornucopia: The Environment, Politics and the Future* (Chichester: Wiley, 1982), p. 19.

34 Cotgrove and Duff, 'Environmentalism, middle-class radicalism and politics', p. 344.

to green values, then only 'the new middle class' – in particular, those in the caring and educational professions – as well as non-commodified groups such as students and young housewives concerned for the future of their children, would, in general, be likely to remain committed supporters of green policies. If this were the case, for green politics to progress, an alliance with other social groups, such as the working class in general, would be required. That might imply greens having to move towards a far more red-green programme.

If, on the other hand, those who have adopted green values have chosen (and, perhaps because of their education, have been in a position to choose) a non-commodified occupation, and this explains the apparent correlation between members of the environmental movement and 'the new middle class',[35] then it can no longer be assumed that an ecological awareness is bound to be confined to those occupying a certain social location. Consequently, the problem would become not one of amalgamating green and traditional working-class concerns but of getting a clear and coherent green message across to a wider audience than has so far been reached. Whichever strategy is appropriate depends upon the potential constituency of the green movement, and that could only be ascertained by a correct interpretation of the correlation between members of environmental groups and 'the new middle class'.

Now, one explanation which has been forwarded for the rise of the 'new social movements' is the emergence of 'post-materialist values'. This has been attributed to the satisfying of basic needs in the developed countries, which has then given rise to a further demand for the satisfaction of less materialistic ones. Thus, the shift 'from a Materialist emphasis toward a Post-Materialist one' is, according to Ronald Inglehart, the move away 'from giving top priority to physical sustenance and safety, toward heavier emphasis on belonging, self-expression and the quality of life' – a shift he traces 'to the unprecedented levels of economic and physical security that prevailed during the post-war era'.[36] His theory is that a high standard of living in one's early years socializes one into subscribing to post-materialist values, which are then often retained even if the standard of living later declines. Hence, the post-materialist thesis is not falsified by the fact that 'the economic uncertainty of the 1970s did not cause Post-Materialism to disappear – on the contrary, its support seems to have grown in most Western countries.'[37]

However, as Sara Parkin has observed: 'the growth of groups practising a very green sort of politics in Eastern Europe, Latin America and Africa rather knocks the post-materialist thesis on the head'.[38] The Chipko Andalan (tree-hugging movement) in India, for example, is clearly not *post*-materialist. The Indian women who have placed their bodies between trees and those who would fell them are not identifying with nature because they have experienced a high

35 In fact, this is the conclusion that Cotgrove was to draw in *Catastrophe or Cornucopia*, pp. 44–5.

36 Ronald Inglehart, 'Post-Materialism in an environment of insecurity', *The American Political Science Review* 75 (1981), p. 880.

37 Ibid., p. 891.

38 Parkin, *Green Parties*, p. 19.

standard of living and found it insufficiently satisfying. They have never passed through a 'materialist' stage. Consequently, '*post*-materialism' seems far too linear a way of conceptualizing the phenomenon, with its implication of stages of development. Less theoretically-laden and less problematic than 'post-materialism' would be the term 'non-materialism'.

How, then, can we explain satisfactorily the growth of environmental protest if it cannot be completely reduced to a *post*-materialist phenomenon, even were the condition of post-materialism partly to explain its rise? What might explain it is the growing awareness of the preconditions for the survival of one's own social group (as in the case of the Chipko Andalan) or of humanity as a whole. And without doubt, a key period for the expansion of the ecology movement was from the late 1960s up until 1972, the year of the United Nations Conference on the Human Environment held at Stockholm, and of the publication of such influential books as *The Closing Circle*, *The Limits to Growth*, *Only One Earth* and *Blueprint for Survival.* At this time a major concern with (arguably) impending ecological crises was precipitated.

However, it was not long before a systematic campaign was mounted by the defenders of the status quo, as well as by the advocates of economic growth as a means to greater social equality, to discredit the various environmental warnings and denigrate them as hysterical scare-mongering. For a while, this campaign was, by and large, effective. The doom-laden warnings of the early 1970s were widely dismissed as inaccurate or just plain unscientific, and the public interest in the threat human activity posed to the environment waned. It has also been argued that the OPEC-induced oil crisis beginning in late 1973 and the subsequent economic recession turned people's minds to more immediate problems. It was only in the late 1980s, when world-wide environmental threats (such as the possibility of global climate change and the observed depletion of the ozone layer) could no longer be ignored, that a major concern for the environment again burst onto the political agenda.

In Britain, the turning point was Prime Minister Margaret Thatcher's 'green speech', delivered to the Royal Society on 27 September 1988. This proved to be something of a political own-goal, albeit one that probably had to be conceded. As the scientific evidence of global environmental degradation seemed to swell, ecological problems could no longer convincingly be denied. All that the Conservative government could then do was acknowledge the threat in an exercise of political damage-limitation, insisting that it was aware of the problems and that the environment was safe in its hands.[39] But by acknowledging the environmental

39 There is, however, another possible reason for Thatcher's sudden interest in environmental issues. It can be argued that the threat of global warming was cynically used by her to promote Britain's nuclear industry further, thereby increasing the supply of weapons-grade plutonium, while simultaneously reducing the country's dependence on coal-fired power stations and undermining the power of the National Union of Mineworkers (the most powerful British trade union at that time, and a major political actor which had played a key role in bringing down a previous Conservative government).

threat, the government implicitly admitted that at least some of the environmentalist warnings had been right all along.[40] The green movement thus acquired a tacit legitimacy inadvertently conferred upon it by a government forced onto the defensive by evidence of environmental degradation which was difficult to deny or even to ignore. And it soon became clear to many people that the green movement, having focused on these issues for years, had an understanding of the problems and their possible solutions which others glaringly lacked.[41] Hence, rather than simply reduce the growth of the green movement to post-materialism, perhaps we would do better to acknowledge that 'the single largest impetus in the formation of a radical green front has been the failure of the established political parties to do anything about the care and maintenance of the planet.'[42]

This seems to suggest that green politics can be extended beyond a narrow 'new middle class' base to all those who have reason to be concerned by global environmental deterioration – and that would appear to be a very great number of people, indeed. Hence, green politics would seem to have the largest potential constituency of any political movement. However, to jump to such a conclusion would be to ignore two problems. The first is that some social groups may well have a powerful interest in environmental destruction, and would thus not be susceptible to a green approach. The second is that the ecological problems which we appear to face, as well as their solutions, are complex and interrelated – so much so that to be genuinely green seems to require a considerable understanding of environmental and political issues. It is not surprising, therefore, that the core of the older green movement is disproportionately well-educated and literate. Whereas many committed socialists have read very little left-wing political theory, and whereas many on the Right have read very little right-wing political theory, the vast majority of long-standing, committed greens appear to have read a considerable amount of material on environmental problems and on political ecology. And this unusual degree of political literacy seems also to be true of those members of the feminist and peace movements who are not equally concerned with environmental issues.

So, what seems especially significant about long-standing members of the 'new social movements' is not that they tend to be 'new middle class', but that they

40 However, it should be noted that this implicit legitimizing of environmentalists' warnings had been under way for several years. As Cotgrove remarked in 1982: 'The energy crisis and emerging shortages of some essential raw materials are eroding the buoyant optimism of a decade ago and lending an element of credence to what was dismissed as doomsday alarmism.' *Catastrophe or Cornucopia*, p. v.

41 Perhaps not surprisingly, given this history, recent MORI opinion polls have found the public to be now more likely to trust the claims of environmentalists than politicians or even academics. Environmentalism has thus come a long way since the days when it struck the majority of people as cranky.

42 Porritt, *Seeing Green*, p. 25. Cotgrove, similarly, regards 'the combination of influential publications' and 'dramatic events such as the eutrophication of Lake Erie, and the mercury poisoning of Lake Minimata in Japan' as 'what triggered the movement and raised the level of public consciousness'. *Catastrophe or Cornucopia*, p. 8.

have a characteristic which is common amongst 'the new middle class' – namely, that they tend to be highly educated and well read. But so are certain other social groups who do not express a profound concern for the environment. What, then, would make certain sections of 'the new middle class', and not others who are highly educated and well read, especially sympathetic to green values?[43]

One vitally important feature might well be their willingness to question established authority. Offe pinpoints three important processes at work in modern Western societies: 'the simultaneous *broadening*, *deepening*, and increasing *irreversibility* of forms of domination and deprivation',[44] the latter point referring 'to the *structural incapacity* of existing economic and political institutions to perceive and to deal effectively with the global threats, risks, and deprivations they cause.'[45] On the basis of this observation, Offe argues that '[t]he broad constituency of movements as well as their pool of activists are drawn from those social groups which are most likely to be affected by the negative consequences of these processes and/or those who have the easiest cognitive access to the working of these processes and their consequences.'[46] So, those in the caring professions such as social workers, for example, who have to deal with the casualties of modern society, are well placed to perceive its problematic nature.[47]

Now, what most seems to distinguish radical greens from other highly educated groups is that, whereas others in the middle class might be expected to favour statist and technocratic solutions to social problems (for they may well see themselves as the administrators of those ostensible solutions),[48] radical greens exhibit a profound opposition to such ostensible solutions – an opposition which often

43 In his survey of radical environmentalists, nature conservationists, industrialists and the general public, Cotgrove noted that industrialists were also affluent and well-educated, and yet did not share the environmentalists' concerns. Thus: 'A certain level of material security may well constitute a threshold beyond which non-material values surface. But this does not explain why some from secure and well-to-do homes shift their priorities to post-material values and goals, while others as affluent and well-educated pursue careers dedicated to material goals.' Ibid., p. 50.

44 Offe, 'New social movements', p. 845.

45 Ibid., p. 847.

46 Ibid., p. 848.

47 C.f.: 'As teachers, social workers, doctors, research scientists and academics, their roles sensitize them to the limits of self-interest, and indeed, to the needs of the casualties of the market place.' Cotgrove, *Catastrophe or Cornucopia*, p. 72. Thus Cotgrove views 'environmentalists as drawn from a distinct fraction of the middle class, not directly or indirectly involved in the production of wealth, and whose interests therefore diverge from those so involved.' Ibid., pp. 115–16.

48 Hence, it is perhaps not surprising that certain sections of 'the new middle class' – namely, the technical and bureaucratic fractions of the techno-bureaucracy – should frequently hold views which contrast significantly with those held by many members of the 'new social movements'. But not everyone within the 'new social movements' holds a set of views which contrasts radically with the techno-bureaucracy – for example, some remain technocentric rather than ecocentric. Cotgrove, in fact, considers 'the new class' to be 'internally divided between a (technical) intelligentsia and (humanistic) intellectuals.' See *Catastrophe or Cornucopia*, p. 97.

manifests itself in far from conventional political responses. And Offe suspects that

> [t]wo factors may contribute to the direct correlation between levels of education and unconventional forms of political participation. One is that a high level of formal schooling leads to some (perceived) competence to make judgments about complicated and abstract 'systemic' matters in the fields of economic, military, legal, technical, and environmental affairs. The other is that higher education increases the capacity to think (and conceivably even to act) independently, and the preparedness to critically question received interpretations and theories about the world. In other words, educated people would not only be more competent to form their own judgment but also less bound by rigid reliance on the judgment of others.[49]

In Offe's view, then, the members of the 'new social movements' tend to be educated and self-confidently critical. But because they have been made personally aware of the ill-effects of a seemingly failing technocratic system, they lack the faith in technocratic solutions which is shared by the educated in 'old middle class' and other 'new middle class' groupings, who are content for business to go on as usual.[50]

Moreover, in his survey of members of groups such as Friends of the Earth, Cotgrove found that environmentalists tend to have a high degree of autonomy in their work, and therefore seem to be less submissive to established authority.[51] Consequently, such members of 'the new middle class' are often 'attracted to small-scale self-sufficient communities by their promise of personal autonomy, and escape from the restrictions of hierarchical and bureaucratic structures', and are concerned 'to promote the liberation of [hu]man[ity]'.[52] What gives this a profoundly green tinge is the perception that human liberation must be premised upon ecological sustainability.

All of this suggests that the often-heard criticism that environmentalists are inherently conservative and reactionary[53] is largely misplaced. This criticism seems

49 Offe, 'New social movements', pp. 850–1.

50 As Offe writes: 'All major concerns of new social movements converge on the idea that life itself – and the minimum standards of "good life" as defined and sanctioned by modern values – is threatened by the blind dynamics of military, economic, technological, and political rationalization; and that there are no sufficient and sufficiently reliable barriers within dominant political and economic institutions that could prevent them from passing the threshold to disaster.' Ibid., p. 853.

51 '[E]nvironmentalists are also remarkable for the high proportion (46%) in autonomous occupations.' Cotgrove, *Catastrophe or Cornucopia*, p. 48.

52 Ibid., p. 6.

53 For an example of such a simplistic misrepresentation of the ecology movement, see Philip Lowe and Michael Worboys, 'Ecology and the end of ideology', *Antipode*, Vol. 10, No. 2 (August 1978), p. 19, where 'popular ecology' is caricatured as representing 'a deeply conservative response to a perceived crisis of authority in Western society.' Contrast this with

to arise because of a failure to distinguish between two very different groupings who express environmental concern: what Cotgrove dubs 'nature conservationists' and 'radical environmentalists'. The former consist in 'members of conservationist and preservationist societies', and they 'differ little from the general public, except in being better off, and in attaching particular importance to the protection of nature. And there is some justification in labelling them as being preoccupied with "middle class" concerns and promoting middle class interests.'[54] Moreover, nature conservationists 'do not share with the radical environmentalists anti-industrial society attitudes, nor are they post-materialists. Above all they support the dominant social paradigm. In short, they do not wish to change society, nor do they see the protection of the environment as necessitating any such changes.'[55]

Radical environmentalists, on the other hand, 'are different. They want a different kind of society. And they use the environment as a lever to try to bring about the kind of changes they want.'[56] It appears illegitimate, therefore, to tar with the nature conservationist brush those who are more accurately identified as radical environmentalists, for there seems to be a major distinction between them. On the whole, Cotgrove observes, radical environmentalists 'are younger, better educated, left in politics, and more likely to be employed in the non-market sector.'[57] What is more, it appears equally illegitimate to dismiss their political radicalism as a temporary phenomenon associated with their relative youth, for as Cotgrove points out: 'Follow-up studies of student activists have found that they had not matured into taking a more moderate position, but had retained their radical commitment.'[58] If, in general, radical environmentalists are younger than nature conservationists, there is good reason to think that concern for the environment will, over time, become progressively more radical.

Furthermore, if environmental degradation becomes increasingly palpable (and if environmentalists are right about the nature of the environmental threat, then it is certain to), then we could expect green values to become more prevalent. It seems, therefore, that it would be a serious mistake to dismiss without further thought the emergence and growth of the green movement and radical green practice as a passing phenomenon. Rather the green movement could be expected to expand continually were each younger generation to become more environ-

---

what Inglehart observed: 'Despite their relatively privileged social status, Post-Materialists are markedly more favourable to social change than are other value types.' Inglehart, 'Post-Materialism in an environment of insecurity', p. 890. Moreover, Inglehart also found that 'Post-Materialists are far readier to engage in political protest than Materialists.' Ibid., p. 891.

54 Cotgrove, *Catastrophe or Cornucopia*, p. 34.

55 Ibid., p. 34.

56 Ibid., pp. 34–5.

57 Ibid., p. 35.

58 Ibid., pp. 49–50.

mentally aware,[59] as is likely to be the case if ecological problems become ever-more apparent. It is many in the older generations, seemingly set in their ways, who appear incapable of taking on board the radical ecological message.

Now, much of the recent work on the 'new social movements' – including the environmental movement – has been conceptualized in terms deriving from Marx's use of Hegel's distinction between the state and civil society. As Luke Martell writes:

> the main basis on which old and new social movements are often distinguished is that old social movements are seen as being state-oriented and new social movements civil society-oriented. (1) *Location*: old social movements tend to be located in the polity in political parties (Labour and Social Democratic Parties, for instance), whereas the new social movements are autonomous movements outside conventional political institutions. (2) *Aims*: the aims of old social movements are to secure political representation, legislative political reform and rights associated with citizenship in the political community; the new social movements, however, want to defend civil society *against* political power and redefine culture and lifestyle in civil society rather than pursuing legislative change through the state. (3) *Organization*: old social movements adhere to formal and hierarchical modes of internal movement organization whereas the new social movements go for informal or unstructured organization or 'networks' built up from grass-roots participation rather than structures of authority. (4) *Medium of change*: the old social movements are oriented towards political institutions through which change can be achieved. The new social movements go for newer and more innovative forms of direct action and work on redefinitions of meaning and symbolic representation in culture rather than change through the political apparatus.[60]

On the basis of the state/civil society distinction employed in this typology, some sociologists have challenged the claim that the 'new social movements' possess significantly new characteristics. For example, it has been claimed that the traditional social movements displayed very similar features when they were first formed. Later, however, they evolved out of their civil society origins into political entities. Consequently, it has been predicted that today's environmental movement will follow a similar course and will acquire a more mainstream political form.

However, such predictions, as well as claims that the 'new social movements' have a 'self-limiting' or misplaced radicalism in not seeking change within the political level, could be criticized for failing to take into consideration the extent

59 In former West Germany, during the 1980s, over one quarter of first time voters voted green. See Rudolf Bahro, *Building the Green Movement* (London: Heretic, 1986), p. 10.

60 Luke Martell, *Ecology and Society: An Introduction* (Cambridge: Polity, 1994), pp. 112–13.

to which these movements, especially the green movement, are anarchist in their values. Many members of the ecology movement hold beliefs which are considerably more radical and revolutionary than the description 'self-limiting radicalism' implies. Rather than wishing to preserve the autonomy of the political system, the very strong anarchist element within the 'new social movements' wishes to abolish the present political system *tout court.*[61] Consequently, there is reason to think that the 'new social movements' have far more in common with earlier anarchist movements – such as that in Spain prior to 1936 – which never transformed themselves into mainstream political entities. To the extent that the green movement is anarchist, it would be a mistake to expect it to follow the course taken by the traditional social movements.

Similarly, the rejection of state-centred politics neither has to be a limited radicalism nor need it only be a result of having been excluded from political participation or representation. For it is the obvious attitude to take when the state is viewed as the major problem. Those who seek the abolition of the state are neither apolitical nor mildly radical. And many of the strategies adopted by the 'new social movements' are precisely those which anarchists have proposed with the aim of abolishing the state. Consequently, most recent analyses of the 'new social movements' can be argued to miss the point completely either because of the degree to which they under-emphasize the anarchist elements within these movements or because of the social analyst's lack of familiarity with anarchist thought and practice – this unfamiliarity not being uncommon amongst academics, including those who peek into grass-roots activity from the outside.

Moreover, describing the 'new social movements' as 'civil society-oriented' also invites criticism. As the term 'civil society' takes its meaning from Hegel's distinction between the state and the arena of human intercourse for which the state supposedly provides an ethical unity, then *use of the term 'civil society' seems to presume a continuing state.* But many of those who are seeking to abolish the state are working to transform a society which they believe can stand independently of any state, while those who describe them as 'civil society-oriented' appear to be simply taking the continuance of the state for granted. Surely an accurate sociological description of the 'new social movements' would have to be far more sympathetic to a genuine understanding of their *weltanschauung.* Imposing descriptions which take the state for granted upon those who seek to abolish it hardly seems consistent with the pursuit of accuracy.

Radical environmentalists, then, in so far as they subscribe to anarchist values, are discontented with hierarchical and bureaucratic structures, and support human liberation. Thus, they are often in extreme opposition to prevailing social and political institutions. As Offe argues:

61 For one view of the anarchist influence within the 'new social movements', see Murray Bookchin, 'New social movements: the anarchic dimension' in David Goodway (ed.), *For Anarchism: History, Theory, and Practice* (London: Routledge, 1989).

> if institutional mechanisms are seen to be too rigid to recognize and absorb the problems of advanced industrial societies, it would be inconsistent to rely upon these institutions for a solution. The rise of the socio-political movements would thus appear to be the result of a 'provocation' that consists in the more widely and more clearly visible internal contradictions and inconsistencies *within* the value system of modern culture, rather than the result of a clash between the 'dominant' and some 'new' (or, for that matter, romanticist and 'premodern') values.[62]

And it might be posited that many of the members of the 'new social movements' share similar values because so many of them are the critical products of a western higher education.[63] Thus:

> Regarding their implicit moral philosophies, they are rather the *contemporaries* of the societies in which they live and whose institutional embodiments of economic and political rationality they oppose. At any rate, this opposition does not primarily occur between 'old' and 'new' values but between conflicting views concerning the extent to which the different elements *within* the repertory of modern values are satisfied in an equal and balanced way. For instance, personal autonomy is by no means a 'new' value; what is new is the doubt that this value will be furthered as a more or less automatic by-product or covariant of dominant institutions such as property and market mechanisms, democratic mass politics, the nuclear family, or the institutions of mass culture and mass communications. What is at issue is not the values but the mode of implementation of values, and the presupposed links between the satisfaction of different values (e.g., between income and intrinsic satisfaction in work, or the link between control over elites and personal development of judgment and understanding in democratic mass politics). Values such as autonomy, identity, authenticity, but also human rights, peace, and the desirability of balanced physical environments are largely noncontroversial. It is this 'contemporaneous' character of the underlying values of new social movements that leaves their intellectual and political opponents rather defenseless or leads them to misrepresent and often caricature these values as either romanticist (i.e., as politically and/or psychologically regressive) or as luxurious predilections of privileged groups who have lost contact with social 'realities'.[64]

However, there is one respect in which the values of the 'new social movements' can be regarded as 'newer' than Offe admits. The members of the 'new social

62 Offe, 'New social movements', p. 853.

63 Whereas compulsory schooling seems more geared to preserving the status quo, university education – especially in arts or social science subjects – sometimes succeeds in unearthing the originality and powers of critique suppressed by years of state schooling.

64 Ibid., pp. 849–50.

movements' appear to have extended certain contemporary values to new areas. For example, concern in the past had been expressed, by and large, only for citizens and not for slaves. Later it was extended to include all men. The feminist movement has relatively recently extended it to include women. And the animal liberation movement has now extended it to include other animals.[65] Nevertheless, this is not to challenge Offe's assessment that 'the "modern" critique of modernization for which the new middle class element stands is based on universalistic and emancipatory values and ideals'.[66] It is merely to point out that those 'universalistic and emancipatory values and ideals' have been taken in new directions.

But given that the extension of these 'universalistic and emancipatory values and ideals' is only extending into new areas a set of values and ideals which are already widely accepted, then greens do not face the problem of having to convert the mass of the population to some totally alien system of values or ideals. Rather, it seems that the major problem a green *moral* theory faces is that of presenting the universalistic and emancipatory values and ideals it embraces in a form which can be appropriated by a wide social spectrum, instead of being confined to sections within the educated 'new middle class'. In Chapter 7, I attempt to extend in a simple manner one value – the moral weight which most people attach to coming to the aid of a drowning child. And the direction I have attempted to extend it in is forward in time. This, I suggest, is sufficient to justify many of the most important concerns expressed by radical greens.[67]

On the other hand, it seems that the major problem faced by a green *political* theory is to describe the causes of the environmental threat seemingly hurtling towards us, and to identify an effective escape route. Unfortunately, to the extent that the political theory of many greens is anarchist, it is likely to be rejected out of hand by most academic political theorists, who, by and large, simply dismiss anarchism as lacking in any sophistication. Developing the philosophical foundations for a coherent green political theory which is anarchist, yet not without some measure of sophistication or rigour, has been the principal aim of this book.

There is, however, one area of concern which requires less theoretical study for many people to feel compelled to respond. And that is the mistreatment of non-human animals. Inflicting needless suffering on other sentient beings can elicit a profound moral response in many people. It is not surprising, therefore, that many of the less formally-educated, but no less-committed, activists who have

65 See, for example, the extension of utilitarianism to include all sentient creatures in Peter Singer, 'All animals are equal' in Peter Singer (ed.), *Applied Ethics* (Oxford: Oxford University Press, 1986).

66 Offe, 'New social movements', p. 856.

67 Of course, it does not succeed in according intrinsic value to species, for example. But to the degree that a viable and stable ecosystem is likely to require considerable biodiversity, to the degree that we cannot predict which species might be essential for future humans, and to the degree that other species are of aesthetic value to human beings, a concern for future humans seems to imply the preservation of as many species as possible.

now devoted their lives to full-time non-violent direct action in defence of the environment began their protests in the animal liberation movement. In the 1990s, this movement has expanded into a new, full-scale counter-culture in defence of wildlife habitats and against the further encroachments of modern society, with activists living in trees (sometimes for several years) or underground in order to block further road-building or airport expansion, especially when it threatens sensitive habitats. It is within the ranks of those prepared to take direct action that the green movement currently seems to be expanding at its greatest pace.

Whereas the European green parties enjoyed a spectacular rise in the 1980s, their fortunes did not fare so well in the 1990s. For example, after its spectacular capture of 14.9 per cent of the vote in the 1989 European elections, the Green Party in Britain only managed 3.2 per cent in 1994.[68] Greens have done well in local elections, and there have been Greens elected onto parish, district and even county councils. But in national elections, Greens have remained marginalized.[69]

There are a number of factors which might explain the marginalization of the Green Party in Britain. One, of course, is the British electoral system. With a first-past-the-post voting system (where electoral success depends upon obtaining a simple majority), it seems irrational to vote for a party which has no chance of winning, except in order to register one's strength of feeling. But there is little point in doing that if it will merely fall on the deaf ears of a government sitting upon a comfortable majority in Parliament. As there is evidence to suggest that a substantial proportion of voters in Britain vote *against* a party rather than for one (with many of those who vote Conservative doing so to keep the Labour Party out of office and many of those who vote Labour being far less committed to Labour policies than they are to keeping out the Conservatives), few people are likely to vote for the Green Party when such a vote would play no part in keeping out of office a detested party. Changing the political system to proportional representation might allow a green voice in parliament, but there seems to be no compelling reason to think that it would be heard or that it would remain uncompromised. Moreover, the parties which are most likely to support electoral reform are those that are unlikely to obtain a clear majority under the present system. And once a party had gained a clear majority, or once it felt certain that it was about to do so, then it would have less of an interest in making changes to the political system that would result in a reduction in the power enjoyed by those holding office.

Another factor which might explain the marginalization of the British Green

68 See Robert Garner, *Environmental Politics* (Hemel Hempstead: Harvester-Wheatsheaf, 1996), p. 130. For a compelling account of why the May 1989 European elections in Britain were aberrant in nature, see Chris Rootes, 'Environmentalism and political competition: the British Greens in the 1989 elections to the European Parliament', *Politics*, Vol. 11, No. 2 (1991): 39–44.

69 In fact, the Green Party's share of the vote in the seats it contested in national elections between 1979 and 1992 seems to have remained fairly constant, only fluctuating between 1.0 and 1.5 per cent. See Garner, *Environmental Politics*, p. 130.

Party is the claim made by the traditional parties to have become green. But such claims should not be taken at face value when, for a great deal of its finances, the Labour Party is dependent on Trades Unions which often see environmentalism as a middle-class threat to their members' employment, and when the Conservative Party obtains much of its revenue from industrialists. Moreover, the Conservative Party can normally rely on a rural vote. Whereas electoral victories are often thought to depend upon 'floating voters', that assumption takes for granted a party's traditional vote remaining secure. Thus, a Conservative government seeking re-election could not afford to alienate its rural support. One must, therefore, be suspicious of the claims made by a Conservative government about the safety of British agricultural produce (for example, concerning the true extent of BSE infection in cattle) when honesty would obviously go against its interests by ruining the livelihoods of British farmers. On the other hand, a Labour government seeking re-election is unlikely to act in a way that would threaten the jobs of industrial workers. And when a Labour government puts in charge of agriculture its former environment spokesperson, and when that former *environment* spokesperson has continually supported the Sellafield nuclear facility because it provides jobs within his constituency, then the environmental credentials of even a 'new' Labour Party are equally dubious. Clearly, the British parliamentary system cannot be trusted to safeguard the environment.

It is also worth mentioning two possible factors behind the decline in the fortunes of green parties in Europe as a whole. One is the degree to which decentralist and egalitarian principles were abandoned by members of *Die Grünen* once they were first elected to the *Bundestag*. For example, in order to minimize the possibility of power becoming concentrated in the hands of a few party members, elected representatives committed themselves in advance to resigning their posts after a specified period. However, several of those who attained a prominent position reneged on this commitment. Hence, as Tim Hayward observes: 'whilst the German Greens went into parliament with the aim of changing the system, the system also changed them, as one by one the measures designed to ensure grassroots control were dropped.'[70] A second possible factor is the extent of the compromises *Die Grünen* made with the present system, most graphically displayed in the German state of Hesse. There, as a result of forming a coalition with the SPD (the German Social Democratic Party), a green was appointed Minister of the Environment – a green who was soon forced to approve the shipment of nuclear materials through the state. Thus, the exercise of power proved to be as much of an Achilles' heel for greens in Hesse as for Marxists in Eastern Europe. The immediate history of *Die Grünen* following its 1983 election success seems to show full well how difficult it would be for any elected green government to facilitate an effective escape from an environmentally hazardous dynamic such as is depicted in Figure 6.1.

Nevertheless, while the fortunes of *Die Grünen* declined after their first

70 Tim Hayward, *Ecological Thought: An Introduction* (Cambridge: Polity, 1995), p. 193.

electoral success, their popularity has since revived. Of course, we must await with interest their role in the present German government. But it seems very likely that the outcome will be that *Die Grünen* find themselves even more compromised than they did following their experience in Hesse. This certainly seems far more likely than that it will succeed in compelling the SPD into taking a genuinely green stance. But most importantly, to whatever degree *Die Grünen* do succeed in greening the German government, the extent of the environmental threat indicated in Chapter 1 suggests that, as radical environmentalists have always feared with respect to coalitions between green and mainstream parties, any measures undertaken will be all far too little too late. In which case, those who voted green may well come to regard themselves as having been severely let down. If so, they, and those contemplating voting green for the first time, might feel less inclined to vote green in the future.

Thus, as the advance of green political parties at a national level may well have been, and most likely will continue to be, inhibited by their involvement within and reliance upon the present political system, a less reformist political approach seems to be required. In short, *Die Grünen*'s recent electoral success notwithstanding, there is reason to think that the future defence of the planet now lies less in the hands of green parties and more in the actions of the growing numbers of those who are committed to participating in non-violent protest against further environmental devastation.

Appendix C
Deep ecology or social ecology?

Many of those who are currently active in non-violent protests against any further destruction of wildlife habitats are sympathetic to a 'deep ecology' perspective. In the 1980s, however, a fundamental disagreement, which has threatened to split the environmental movement, arose between those who subscribed to the standpoint of deep ecology and those who preferred a different theoretical perspective – namely, that of social ecology. At first, no fundamental differences were perceived between the proponents of each position. However, a considerable antagonism began to form between the two factions. In order to ascertain whether or not these differences are irreconcilable, let me first look at the perspective of deep ecology before I turn to consider social ecology.

Deep ecology

While many of those who, in the past, have shown concern for the environment have done so in a manner which does not seem to challenge prevailing values and ideals, an increasing number of people have felt the need for what they regard as a more radical and penetrating perspective. In a lecture delivered in Bucharest in 1972, the Norwegian philosopher, Arne Naess, attempted to formulate the principles underlying this supposedly 'deeper' perspective. In summary, Naess argued that '[e]cologically responsible policies are concerned only in part with pollution and resource depletion. There are deeper concerns which touch upon principles of diversity, complexity, autonomy, decentralization, symbiosis, egalitarianism, and classlessness.'[1] Whereas, according to Naess, the 'shallow' ecology movement opposes pollution and the depletion of resources in order to further 'the health and affluence of people in the developed countries',[2] the 'deep ecology' movement is not only concerned with pollution and resource depletion but cares about a number of other matters, as well.

In all, Naess spells out seven principles of deep ecology. The first is embracing

1 Arne Naess, 'The shallow and the deep, long-range ecology movement: a summary', *Inquiry* 16 (1973), p. 95.
2 Ibid.

'the relational, total-field image', which implies rejecting 'the [hu]man-in-environment image'. The second is 'biospherical egalitarianism'. Rather than only valuing human life – the hallmark of anthropocentrism – the deep ecologist venerates all other forms of life, too. His or her standpoint is, instead, biocentric. However, given that, in Naess' view, 'any realistic praxis necessitates some killing, exploitation, and suppression',[3] biospherical egalitarianism can only hold 'in principle'. The third is the recognition of the value of diversity and of symbiosis. These are deemed necessary for maximizing survival and coexistence. The fourth is the adoption of an 'anti-class posture'; that is, the deep ecologist values diversity which is non-exploitative, for exploitation inhibits self-realization, according to Naess. The fifth is a concern about pollution and the depletion of resources – a concern which deeper ecologists share with those whom they judge to be shallower. The sixth is the 'complexity-not-complication' principle. Unlike 'complication', Naess regards 'complexity' as evident when a whole is integrated, rather than merely chaotic. The final principle is a concern to maximize local autonomy and decentralization. This is subscribed to because, in Naess' view, the 'vulnerability of a form of life is roughly proportional to the weight of influences from afar, from outside the local region in which that form has obtained an ecological equilibrium'.[4]

Certainly, a number of these principles, around which there has been some convergence within the green movement in recent years, seem to be held by the more radical ecologists. But are all of these principles equally acceptable? It is worth noting that Naess insists that his 'survey does not pretend to be more than one of the possible condensed codifications of these convergences'.[5] Hence, some principles could easily be added, while one or more might be rejected. Principles (3) through (7) do seem to cohere with radical green political thinking in general. What, though, of the first two principles?

The first principle concerns viewing the world in terms of 'the relational, total-field image', while the second consists in biospherical egalitarianism. Subscribing to principle (2) implies the wish to have all life-forms treated equally. But what are the boundaries of a particular life-form? Principle (1), by stressing the total-field image, seems to blur any such boundaries. For example, in an interview in 1982, Naess claimed that a deep ecologist 'will grieve when living beings, including landscapes, are destroyed'.[6] In other words, principle (1) seems to remove what most people would regard as 'natural' boundaries, and the result is that not only individual trees but also whole forests, and even entire landscapes, can be considered to be living entities. But then it is unclear what exactly the 'beings' are which should be treated equally ('even in principle'). For, on this view, a tree is

3 Ibid.
4 Ibid., p. 98.
5 Ibid., p. 99.
6 'Interview with Arne Naess' in Bill Devall and George E. Sessions, *Deep Ecology: Living as if Nature Mattered* (Salt Lake City: Peregrine Smith, 1985), p. 75.

certainly a living being; but so is a forest, and so, too, is a landscape which might contain several forests. One tree would have to be regarded as having the same value as a forest containing a thousand trees,[7] and both would have to be regarded as having the same value as a landscape containing several forests, for each is a 'living being'. Hence,

$$1 = 1000 = 1000(1 + x).$$

Clearly, this would strike many as incoherent; and the incoherence seems to arise from the combination of principles (1) and (2). Hence, if they cannot be combined coherently, then one, at least, must be rejected.

Let me, therefore, examine in a little more detail Naess' principle (1) – the requirement that one embrace 'the relational, total-field image' and reject 'the [hu]man-in-environment image'. According to Naess, deep ecologists, by rejecting 'the [hu]man-in-environment image', see organisms not as discrete, compact entities located in some particular milieu, but as 'knots in the biospherical net or field of intrinsic relations'.[8] One obvious oddity is that this is an *ontological* principle – it concerns the nature of being – whereas Naess claims that 'the significant tenets of the deep ecology movement are clearly and forcefully *normative*'[9] – they concern values. In other words, principle (1) is a very different kind of principle to the others, all of which *are* normative. At first glance, then, it seems rather odd that it is principle (1) which has come to be regarded by many as the core of deep ecology.

Moreover, many philosophers would find it unacceptable simply to assume that an ontological principle – principle (1) – has clear normative implications.[10] Yet this is precisely what some have assumed. Some have argued that the absence of boundaries between entities entails that our own moral considerability must, logically, extend beyond humanity.[11] But any such argument deriving from principle (1) would seem to imply that cutting another person's throat is morally equivalent to lancing a boil on one's arm, and that there is no moral difference between a murderer and his or her victim, because neither is a discrete entity

7 See Richard Sylvan, 'A critique of deep ecology', *Radical Philosophy* 40 (Summer 1985), p. 7.

8 Naess, 'The shallow and the deep, long-range ecology movement', p. 95.

9 Ibid., p. 99.

10 Some might indict any such assumption as a confusion of facts with values, and, certainly, logical positivists and those whom they have influenced would maintain that one cannot legitimately deduce a value-statement from a factual one.

11 Consider Robyn Eckersley, for example, who endorses the use by 'nonanthropocentric ethical theorists' of 'this absence of any rigid, absolute dividing line between humans and nonhumans to point out the logical inconsistency of conventional anthropocentric ethical and political theory that purports to justify the exclusive moral considerability of humans on the basis of our separateness from, say, the rest of the animal world.' Robyn Eckersley, *Environmentalism and Political Theory: Toward an Ecocentric Approach* (London: UCL Press, 1992), p. 50. Eckersley's insertion of 'say' implies that, in her view, it is a mistake to regard oneself as separate from not merely the rest of the *animal* world.

separate from the other – an implication which is clearly absurd. Consequently, this is surely not the kind of argument to base a coherent green political theory upon.

There is a related objection which could be raised against attempting to deduce certain normative implications from principle (1). A not uncommon argument deriving from this principle is that if one understood that one was not distinct from non-humans, then one would be less likely to harm them, for few people want to harm themselves. But as John O'Neill writes:

> the argument provides the wrong kind of grounds for duties to others. While it appears to give an easy route to duties to the 'non-human' world, the duties it provides are too weak. Duties to oneself are in significant ways *less* stringent than duties to others. Thus, while it may be foolish, and perhaps also a dereliction of one's obligations to oneself, to smoke, take no exercise, let one's teeth rot and generally abuse one's body, abuse of the bodies of others is an altogether more serious affair. What is permissible in the former case is impermissible in the latter.[12]

In other words, regarding non-humans as identical to oneself might reduce one's *desire* to harm them, but it seems to weaken one's *moral responsibility* towards them, for, ordinarily, one has a greater moral responsibility to others than to oneself. Most people would agree, for example, that it is far worse to kill another person than it is to commit suicide. Hence, this whole approach might actually attenuate any duty we might otherwise have to save the planet either for its own sake or for the sake of future generations of humans and other sentient beings.

The process of placing principle (1) at the core of deep ecology began in earnest with a number of articles by Bill Devall and George Sessions,[13] and, in particular, with a 1984 article by Warwick Fox. According to Fox, three points characterize the distinction between deep and shallow ecology. First, whereas 'shallow ecology views humans as separate from their environment',[14] deep ecology does not. Instead,

> [f]igure/ground boundaries are replaced by a holistic or gestalt view where, in Devall's words, 'the person is not above or outside of nature . . . [but] . . . is part of a creation on-going.' This 'total-field' conception dissolves not only the notion of humans as separate from their environment but the very notion of the world as composed of discrete, compact, separate 'things'.[15]

12 John O'Neill, *Ecology, Policy and Politics: Human Well-Being and the Natural World* (London: Routledge, 1993), p. 150.

13 These articles form the basis of Devall and Session, *Deep Ecology.*

14 Warwick Fox, 'Deep ecology: a new philosophy of our time?', *The Ecologist*, Vol. 14, Nos 5–6 (1984), p. 194.

15 Ibid.

In a word, the deep ecology movement subscribes to a form of ontological holism (or ontological collectivism). Second, whereas 'shallow ecology accepts by default or positively endorses the dominant metaphysics of mechanistic materialism',[16] deep ecology

> is concerned to criticize mechanistic materialism and to replace it with a better 'code for reading nature'. This code can be generally described as one of 'unity in process'. By this is indicated both the idea that all 'things' are fundamentally (i.e. internally) related and the idea that these interrelationships are in constant flux.[17]

Fox believes that this is more consistent with Eastern spiritual traditions,[18] and there can be no doubt that he finds this aspect especially attractive. Third and finally, whereas 'shallow ecology tends to accept by default or positively endorse the ideology of economic growth which characterizes industrial and developing societies of all political complexions',[19] deep ecology 'is concerned to address existing social, political and economic arrangements and to replace the ideology of economic growth with the ideology of ecological sustainability.'[20] The third point, then, encapsulates the green social, political and economic project.

Thus, Naess' seven principles have come to be replaced by these three points. In fact, as Fox's points (1) and (2) are not normative, he has condensed Naess' normative principles into point (3), while principle (1) forms the basis of Fox's first two points. And it would appear that Fox most cherishes these two points, for, in his opinion, principle (1) represents 'the *central* intuition of deep ecology'.[21] Moreover, as he emphasizes (in response to Naess' reply to his article): 'This attempt to shift the *primary* focus of environmental philosophical concern from ethics to ontology clearly constitutes a fundamental or revolutionary challenge to normal environmental philosophy. It is (and should be) deep ecology's guiding star.'[22]

What seems to have happened, then, is that a predominantly normative position has come to be transformed into a predominantly ontological one. Furthermore, whereas Naess formulated his seven principles of deep ecology in a non-dogmatic fashion, being content to see alternative formulations, Fox appears to have imposed something of a central dogma on deep ecology – the central dogma of a new church, some might fear. And it has not taken very long for some

16 Ibid., pp. 194–5.

17 Ibid., p. 195.

18 Moreover, such a 'conception of the world lends itself more readily to organismic rather than mechanistic metaphors, and thus to panpsychic or pantheistic rather than inert, dead-matter conceptions of the nonhuman world.' Ibid.

19 Ibid.

20 Ibid.

21 Ibid., p. 196.

22 Warwick Fox, 'On guiding stars to deep ecology', *The Ecologist*, Vol. 14, Nos 5–6 (1984), p. 204.

people to suggest that if one does not accept this ontological holism and the spirituality it is supposed to imply,[23] then one is something of an outsider and cannot possibly be sufficiently committed to radical green politics.

Now, at first glance, an inclination towards spiritual matters might seem innocent enough. But there is an ambiguity lurking in the term 'spirituality'. Consider the following passage by Walter and Dorothy Schwarz with which Porritt and Winner preface their discussion of spirituality in *The Coming of the Greens*: 'we have to put back what our dominant industrial-materialistic-scientific world view leaves out. That omitted area is what we mean by the spiritual.' They continue: 'In that sense, the spiritual is not identified with any actual religion, nor confined to religious sentiments; it includes the intuitive, non-measurable, the aesthetic, the caring and the loving.'[24] Most people who are concerned about the environment will have enjoyed the aesthetic experience of gazing at a natural landscape. They will tend to be caring people, and so on. If this is what being spiritually-inclined boils down to, then it is unlikely to prove objectionable to anyone. For one thing, there is no mention of the divine or the supernatural anywhere in this passage.

But when Porritt and Winner come to spell out their own understanding of spirituality, they depict many greens as believing that 'salvation lies in opening our spirit to the presence of the divine in the world, acknowledging joyfully a sense of wonder and humility before the miracle of creation, and *then* going out and taking action to put things right, inspired by that vision.'[25] Now, this *is* something

23 Cf.: 'We feel that deep ecology is spiritual in its very essence. It is a world view that is supported by modern science but is rooted in a perception of reality that goes beyond the scientific framework to a subtle awareness of the oneness of all life, the interdependence of its multiple manifestations, and its cycles of change and transformation. When the concept of human spirit is understood in this sense, as the mode of consciousness in which the individual feels connected to the cosmos as a whole, the full meaning of deep ecology is indeed spiritual.' Charlene Spretnak and Fritjof Capra, *Green Politics* (London: Paladin, 1985), p. 50. Consider also the following: 'a religion-based movement for social change is beginning to flourish that is completely in keeping with Green principles of private ownership [*sic*] and cooperative economics, decentralization, grassroots democracy, non-violence, social responsibility, global awareness – and the spiritual truth of Oneness.' Charlene Spretnak, 'The spiritual dimension of green politics' in ibid., p. 251. John Passmore is not, therefore, without some justification when he writes: 'Science and technology, democracy and free enterprise have always had their enemies; mysticism, primitivism, authoritarianism have always had their adherents. The ecologically-based protest – not only against short-sightedness and greed but, more fundamentally, against those attitudes to nature and society which are used to justify short-sightedness and greed – is . . . fully justified in itself. But it is being deployed as a new and powerful weapon in the old battle between rationality and mysticism.' John Passmore, *Man's Responsibility for Nature: Ecological Problems and Western Traditions* (London: Duckworth, 1980), p. 173. And in his view: 'It is not by abandoning our hard-won tradition of rationality that we shall save ourselves.' John Passmore, 'Attitudes to nature' in R. S. Peters (ed.), *Nature and Conduct* (London: Macmillan, 1975), p. 259.

24 Quoted in Jonathan Porritt and David Winner, *The Coming of the Greens* (London: Fontana, 1988), p. 233.

25 Ibid., p. 253.

that many would view with suspicion. 'Spirituality' is no longer referring to an aesthetic or a caring disposition. It is now, centrally, a belief in a divinity. It is therefore not surprising that, notwithstanding protestations to the contrary, certain long-standing greens have come to feel that their movement has been hijacked by those intent on turning it into a new religion.

The suspicion that only those of a 'spiritual' inclination can really be fully motivated parallels the widespread Christian belief that only the religious can have any real motivation for behaving ethically. But just because one individual acts in a certain way due to his or her religious convictions and would otherwise feel inclined to act differently is no ground for assuming that non-religious people do not have an equally genuine ethical motivation. Their motivation might, instead, come from, for example, a genuine concern for others, rather than from a fear of divine retribution or from 'identifying' with the 'All' and hence not wanting to harm 'Oneself'. Thus, it might be thought unfortunate that, given their understanding of 'spirituality', Porritt and Winner should feel inclined to assert that the 'first thing is to understand that politics and spirituality are *not* separate' and that 'without some understanding of the spiritual dimension, it will always be a rather lifeless, insipid shade of green that we are dealing with'.[26] Religious feelings and an 'identification' with nature can, of course, be a compelling stimulus for environmental action. But they are surely not the only motivations.

It is certainly true that green ideas have attracted many who are religiously inclined. And there is no doubt that their religious convictions have given them great inner strength. But this does not establish that the best way forward for the green movement is to be fundamentally religious or more 'spiritual'. There may well be a limit to the number of people who would be attracted to religious ideas. Everyone else might actually be repelled by them. Having successfully swelled their numbers with others drawn to the 'spiritual' dimension, the religiously-inclined greens might then mutually reinforce each other's convictions, as well as their belief that it is the 'spiritual' message which draws the crowds in. But the green movement, having become saturated with the 'spirituals', might, in consequence, fail to attract anyone else. But with all the greens mutually reinforcing their own religious beliefs, they would be unable to see why they failed to progress any further. And the reason might well be that everyone else thought that a movement which, for example, felt everyone ought to take the idea of Devas at the bottom of the garden seriously was totally out to lunch.

Hence, rather than insisting that green thinking must have a 'spiritual' dimension, perhaps keeping one's religious leanings to oneself, or sharing them only with like-minded others, might prove to be a preferable policy. Proselytizing one's religious beliefs might increase by some small number the size of one's own church. But to do so by saying that subscribing to those religious beliefs is a prerequisite for being green would, in a secular age, be most likely to inhibit the

26 Ibid., p. 240. Also see Jonathan Porritt, *Seeing Green: The Politics of Ecology Explained* (Oxford: Blackwell, 1984), especially pp. 105–6 and pp. 233–4.

acceptance of a green political perspective. There are, without doubt, numerous people in the West today who would be repelled by any movement that gave the strong impression of being quasi-religious, but who might, nevertheless, be receptive to a green political theory which drew the connections between ecological degradation, underdevelopment in the Third World, centralization and capital-intensive technologies – and which omitted all mention of 'spirituality'. In short, putting one's religion before saving the planet could cost us the Earth.

This sort of objection can be extended to Warwick Fox's metaphysics, for his speculative philosophy seems to lead to an unnecessary outlawing of those who, while subscribing to the aspects of green political thought which Fox subsumes under point (3), nevertheless reject ontological holism (or collectivism). As should be clear from the main body of this book, one can formulate a radical green political theory without being an ontological holist. Thus, even if ontological holism were a sufficient condition for holding a green political perspective, it is doubtful that it constitutes a necessary condition.[27] Moreover, were it the case that a green political theory required ontological holism as a necessary condition, then should the metaphysical grounding turn out to be incoherent, it would seriously undermine the political theory resting upon it. Admittedly, one might need to persuade some to change certain of their values. And a 'spiritual' path might accomplish that. But it could also be done by demonstrating that conclusions based upon their present values incorporate factual errors or by showing how the more problematic of their values are inconsistent with other assumptions and values which they hold dear. Surely, one would not need to convince everyone of the need for accepting a dubious and esoteric metaphysics. This said, how cogent is the ontological holism which appears to have become the new dogma for a number of deep ecologists?

A seemingly devastating critique of such ontological holism has come from Richard Sylvan (formerly Richard Routley). As we have seen, Naess' ontological holism, contained in his principle (1), consists in the requirement that one embrace 'the relational, total-field image', which implies the dissolution of any notion that the world comprises discrete or separate 'things'. To which Naess adds that talking about isolable things is to communicate 'at a superficial or

27 Consider the following, which seems to confuse necessary and sufficient conditions: 'But "the recognition of value inherent in all living nature" is an important part of an emerging green spirituality. It stems from the deep ecological awareness that nature and the self are one. And, as Fritjof Capra has pointed out, "this is also the very core of spiritual awareness. Indeed, when the concept of the human spirit is understood as the mode of consciousness in which the individual feels connected to the cosmos as a whole, it becomes clear that ecological awareness is spiritual in its deepest essence, and that the new ecological ethics is grounded in spirituality".' Porritt and Winner, *The Coming of the Greens*, pp. 238–9. That a numinous experience of oneness might be sufficient to lead one to value non-human nature does not entail that any ethics which values non-human nature *must* necessarily be 'grounded in spirituality'. There are many other reasons for valuing non-human nature than having had a mystical experience, say.

preliminary level'.[28] But as Sylvan observes, to talk about isolable things is inevitable, because 'there is no way of communicating everything at once, no communication without selection of components and so abstracting from the whole.'[29] And one can reject the reductionism of individualistic, non-relational approaches without going to the extreme of denying that there are any separate entities. One need only take sufficient cognizance of the relations between separate entities.

Naess' principle (1) also claims that the total-field is one of intrinsic relations, which is what Fox is referring to in his second point about fundamental or internal relations. Naess clarifies his conception of intrinsic relations as follows: 'An intrinsic relation between two things *A* and *B* is such that the relation belongs to the definitions or basic constitutions of *A* and *B*, so that without the relation, *A* and *B* are no longer the same things.'[30] We might think of the concepts 'husband' and 'wife'. Without the relationship of marriage, there couldn't possibly be either husbands or wives. A wife couldn't possibly be a wife without being related to a husband. If *a* is a wife, then she necessarily has a husband. But the claim that all 'things' are connected is not to say that every connection is a necessary one. As Sylvan argues: 'that *a* is wife of *b* does not imply that *a* is necessarily wife of *b*.'[31] For *a* could just as easily have married someone else, instead. But if it is intelligible to say this, and it seems to be, then *a* cannot be *constituted* by her marriage to *b*. 'And so,' Sylvan remarks, 'the constitution theme is false: a wombat is not constituted by the path it took, or the trees it passed, on an evening's foraging.'[32] Hence, Naess' principle (1) appears to be seriously confused.

Nevertheless, ecologists are surely right to reject a narrowly individualistic perspective, for it can be argued that it is partly by failing to observe the vital interrelations between the parts of an ecological whole that humanity has come so perilously close to undermining the very basis of its own continued existence. But that is not to say that ontological individualism must be rejected in favour of ontological holism (or ontological collectivism). For, in Chapter 3, a middle way (namely, interrelationism) was proposed – one that is neither individualist nor holist. Moreover, from an interrelationist standpoint, ontological holists often seem to commit the collectivist fallacy – in other words, confusing relations between parts with pseudo-connections between the parts and the whole which they form.[33] In short, when holists talk about certain sorts of connections between the parts and the whole, they seem to be talking nonsense.

28 Naess, 'The shallow and the deep, long-range ecology movement', p. 95; also quoted in Fox, 'Deep ecology: a new philosophy of our time?', p. 194.

29 Richard Sylvan, 'A critique of deep ecology: Part II', *Radical Philosophy* 41 (Autumn 1985), p. 10.

30 Naess, 'The shallow and the deep, long-range ecology movement', p. 95.

31 Sylvan, 'A critique of deep ecology: Part II', p. 10.

32 Ibid., p. 11.

33 See, for example, the quotation from Spretnak and Capra in note 23, above, for an apparent example of the collectivist fallacy.

Moreover, if it *is* nonsense, it is not innocent nonsense. For rather than such holistic talk showing the interconnectedness of everything, it seems, paradoxically, to turn the whole into something other. For what apart from something other can one be connected to? All talk of 'oneness' notwithstanding, we are invited to view the whole as something separate, something abstract, something mysterious; whereas what is surely required is for us to see how we interrelate with *the rest of the whole*. Rather than view the whole from outside, as it were, surely we need to see ourselves as living beings situated within it, and not see it as some external entity to which we happen to be connected.

Ontological interrelationism, on the other hand, by focusing on the interrelations between the parts, invites each of us to consider how we are related to others, rather than to some mysterious whole. Ecologically, it invites us to see how we are dependent upon other forms of life and how we affect them. Socially and politically, interrelationism invites us to regard ourselves and everyone else as important, rather than to fall on our knees before the collectivity (the social whole). It invites us to ask ourselves how our actions affect others, how others interrelate with each other, and how their actions affect us. It can lead us to reflect both on our autonomy and on our responsibility to others – a responsibility which seems to call out for cooperation, rather than competition. In a word, it can lead to the valuing of a cooperative autonomy where our awareness of the importance of ourselves and others, combined with an awareness of our own autonomous actions and their consequences for others, results in voluntary cooperation. Interrelationism thus illuminates precisely how political is the personal; whereas holism seems to invite us to look at a whole which could very well appear outside of, and thus beyond, our influence.

This tendency of holism to focus on (what might well be) spurious connections between parts and the whole which they form is potentially problematic for political theory. Instead of regarding each part as important, and instead of concentrating on how all the parts interrelate, it is easy, when adopting an 'holistic' approach, to consider the whole as having ultimate importance, and to view the parts as insignificant and dispensable. In fact, this is very much the conclusion which Hegel seems to have reached – and there is a remarkable similarity between the thinking of many deep ecologists and that of Hegel. In political terms, this can easily cash out into the glorification of the state. One manifestation of Hegelian thinking has been Stalinism (through the vehicle of Marx); another has been Fascism (through the vehicle of Gentile). And given the focus on environmental and 'spiritual' matters which Fascism exhibited,[34] this is a tendency against which the environmental movement needs to be on the greatest guard.[35] The safest

34 For one account, see Anna Bramwell, *Ecology in the 20th Century: A History* (New Haven: Yale University Press, 1989).

35 Regarding former West Germany, Spretnak and Capra write: 'The main reason spirituality remains largely unarticulated in the Green party is that Hitler manipulated the pre-Christian Teutonic myths, or sacred stories, to serve the propaganda machine of his National Socialist party.' *Green Politics*, p. 50. Given this appreciation of possible astuteness on the part of

course of action might well be to keep all such holism at arm's length. Thus, greens might do well to think seriously about ditching it as a philosophical presupposition and replacing it with interrelationism.

Interestingly, deep ecology, as originally conceived by Naess, was quite capable of embracing alternative formulations – ones which might well omit the questionable metaphysics. Indeed, he has actively encouraged the formulation of alternative principles.[36] Even more interestingly, in 1984, Naess, along with George Sessions, listed the principles of deep ecology as follows:

1. The well-being and flourishing of human and nonhuman Life on Earth have value in themselves (synonyms: intrinsic value, inherent value). These values are independent of the usefulness of the nonhuman world for human purposes.
2. Richness and diversity of life forms contribute to the realization of these values and are also values in themselves.
3. Humans have no right to reduce this richness and diversity except to satisfy *vital* needs.
4. The flourishing of human life and cultures is compatible with a substantial decrease of the human population. The flourishing of nonhuman life requires such a decrease.
5. Present human interference with the nonhuman world is excessive, and the situation is rapidly worsening.
6. Policies must therefore be changed. These policies affect basic economic, technological, and ideological structures. The resulting state of affairs will be deeply different from the present.
7. The ideological change is mainly that of appreciating *life quality* (dwelling in situations of inherent value) rather than adhering to an increasingly higher standard of living. There will be a profound awareness of the difference between big and great.

German greens, it is most odd that Spretnak and Capra should appear to project so much onto their thinking: 'Unlike the journalists who had previously questioned the Greens, we brought to our interviews an understanding of the holistic political theory informing their work, which provided a basis for our inquiries, scepticism, and enthusiasm.' Ibid., p. xv. As anyone familiar with the methodology of social scientific investigation will realize, this approach seems more than a little flawed. Moreover, it has been observed that their study is 'marked by a persistent anti-Left bias'. Martin Ryle, *Ecology and Socialism* (London: Radius, 1988), p. 119n.

36 See especially his reply to Fox: 'I coined the terms "deep" and "shallow" ecological movements, but my intention was not to monopolize those terms. Instead I welcome some diversity in expression of the basic attitude and intuitions of deep ecology.' Arne Naess, 'Intuition, intrinsic value and deep ecology', *The Ecologist*, Vol. 14, Nos 5–6 (1984), p. 201. And see the far more dogmatic insistence of the primacy of ontology for deep ecology in Fox, 'On guiding stars to deep ecology'.

8. Those who subscribe to the foregoing points have an obligation directly or indirectly to try to influence the necessary changes.[37]

This list, being confined to normative principles, omits Naess' original principle (1) and all mention of ontological holism. Thus, it would seem, a non-metaphysical variety of deep ecology is not impossible.

Why, then, has the deep ecology movement in general come to insist on ontological holism? It would seem, primarily, because the perspective of deep ecology has come more and more to be associated with those of a 'spiritual' persuasion. And their emphasis on the connection between the part and the whole is frequently linked to the often-heard claim by mystics that they have experienced a union with the One.[38] Whereas Naess has always eschewed dogma, it is principally the claim by others (especially by Fox) that ontological holism or (especially by Spretnak and Capra) that 'spirituality' be regarded as the *core* of deep ecology which appears to engender the fundamental incompatibility, and hence potential conflict, between those of a metaphysical persuasion and those who do not share it. Certainly, the attempt to introduce mysticism as an integral part, even the core, of deep ecology (rather than as an optional extra) has profoundly worried a number of radical ecologists.

Now, were the dispute solely of a metaphysical nature, then it would be possible for it to be finessed. For a green political theory which stood above any such metaphysical controversy and that could be accepted irrespective of whichever side of the metaphysical divide one found oneself on might well suffice to side-step any such dispute. Unfortunately, if all political theories require some

37 In Devall and Sessions, *Deep Ecology*, p. 70. This formulation is exclusively normative (apart from a few factual observations which are necessary for deriving certain proposals). There is no claim about *ontology*. Yet Devall and Sessions accept Fox's ontological claim as the central intuition of deep ecology. See ibid., p. 66. This later formulation by Naess is reproduced with an exposition of each point in Arne Naess, 'Basics of deep ecology', *Resurgence* 126 (1988), p. 7.

38 Again, for an example, see the quotation from Spretnak and Capra in note 23, above. Evidently another source of the deep ecologists' fascination with the term 'holism' is holistic medicine. This medical practice insists that 'the whole person' be treated rather than just the symptoms or rather than just the body. But when a practitioner of holistic medicine treats 'a whole person', he or she is usually relating to a whole which is external – it is another person who is to be treated as a whole. (And when a practitioner of holistic medicine treats himself or herself, he or she is not connected to himself or herself as a whole – to say such a thing would be gibberish.) It would surely be illegitimate to extrapolate from the relationship between separate individuals to a relation between oneself and the whole of which one forms a part, for then one would be internal to the whole, not external to it. In a sense, a practitioner of holistic medicine is intelligibly connected to a whole – he or she is 'connected' to another person. But that is because he or she is not a part of that whole. It is surely unintelligible to talk about humanity being connected to the whole of nature of which it forms a part. It is connected to *the rest of that whole* – in other words, to *its complement*. If there is to be any extrapolation from holistic medicine to the care of a whole planet, then it is surely not from a connection between a whole and something else, but from a concern with how everything within a whole of whatever kind interrelates. And that, surely, is the message of ecology.

ontological presuppositions, then finessing this difficulty would be likely to prove far more difficult. However, in so far as deep ecologists make interrelationist claims without always going as far as ontological holism,[39] then an interrelationist perspective would appear to hold out most hope for offering the most comprehensive, or at least the most widely acceptable, underpinning for a green political theory. At worst, interrelationism seems to provide the highest common factor with which to work. Consequently, in presenting a radical green political theory, I have sought to keep to an interrelationist perspective.[40]

However, even if ontological holism and an associated spirituality were not insisted on by certain deep ecologists, there remains another area where disagreement might arise between greens. And that concerns biospherical egalitarianism – the second of the principles Naess originally formulated in 1972. As I have chosen to exclude ontological holism – the first of those principles – from a central role in my attempt at developing a green political theory, then the incoherence which ontological holism appears to generate when combined with biospherical egalitarianism has thereby been avoided. Biospherical egalitarianism could thus be retained. But ought we to keep it just because it no longer appears to be problematic in this regard? Put another way, is it essential that we replace an anthropocentric perspective by a biocentric one?

Biospherical egalitarianism appears to imply that ('in principle') all species should be treated equally. However, at times, all Naess seems to mean by the term is that different species be granted 'the equal right to live and blossom'.[41] But many would still regard even this as an extreme view. And it is improbable that it would acquire universal agreement. Many are unlikely to accord the same value to a life-form which lacks autonomy as they are to a creature that is autonomous,[42]

39 It is worth noting how often ecologists refer to the interrelations between the parts of an ecosystem. Interestingly, the insistence that we attend to the interrelations between the parts of a whole is spread liberally throughout the writings of Spretnak and Capra. Yet they appear to see no distinction between making claims about the interrelations between the parts and making claims about the connections between the parts and the whole which they constitute. I have chosen to use the term 'interrelationism' to refer to the former sort of claim, and to restrict the terms 'holism' and 'collectivism' to the latter variety. This choice of terminology highlights the distinction between these two very different ways of conceptualizing a situation, both of which have previously been lumped together uncritically under the label 'holism'.

40 It must be stressed that my primary intention is not to outlaw ontological holists nor, for that matter, any other variety of metaphysically-inclined green. Rather, it is to present a coherent account of a green political theory which is capable of soliciting support irrespective of any particular ontology or metaphysics. In so far as ontological holists also stress the interrelations between the parts, then they should be able to agree with the conclusions that follow from adopting an interrelationist perspective.

41 Naess, 'The shallow and the deep, long-range ecology movement', p. 96.

42 See, for example, Jonathan Glover, *Causing Death and Saving Lives* (Harmondsworth: Penguin Books, 1977), *passim*.

or to a barely sentient creature as they are to a highly sentient one.[43] And even fewer are likely to accord a virus a 'right to live and blossom' equal to that of any human who might be killed or maimed by it.[44] But even if biospherical egalitarianism were more widely accepted, would it constitute an appropriate watershed principle for dividing deep ecologists from those whom they regard as 'shallow'?

Sylvan thinks not. He argues that the prevalent distinction between 'deep' and 'shallow' environmental positions is both misdescribed and too simplistic. For one thing, in his view, we need to distinguish between more than two positions. First, we need to distinguish between environmentalists and others. In contrast with the dominant western attitude to the environment, where it is usually regarded as being 'there *for* humans to exploit or manage',[45] environmentalists acknowledge 'a certain level of *constraint* with respect to the environmental, the natural environment especially: not anything goes with respect to nature'.[46] Sylvan regards those who are not environmentalists in this sense as not properly ethical, because their lack of constraint with regard to the environment permits its destruction. And to commit such destruction would be to disregard future generations, which, in Sylvan's view, is amoral.

Second, we need to distinguish between different types of environmentalist. And what divides 'shallower' from 'deeper' environmentalists, in Sylvan's view, is 'the sole value assumption', which he puts as follows: 'According to this major assumption, which underlies prevailing Western social theory, humans are the only things of irreducible (or intrinsic) value in the universe, the value of all other things reducing to or answering back to that of humans in one way or another.'[47] This assumption gives rise to what he calls a 'human apartheid', where humanity is considered segregated from nature. 'Deeper' environmental positions reject the sole value assumption, and do not regard humanity as apart from nature but as a

43 Peter Singer has argued powerfully from a utilitarian position that the welfare of non-humans ought to enter into our calculations: 'having accepted the principle of equality as a sound moral basis for relations with others of our own species, we are also committed to accepting it as a sound moral basis for relations with those outside our own species – the nonhuman animals.' Peter Singer, *Practical Ethics* (Cambridge: Cambridge University Press, 1979), p. 48. However, this doesn't mean for Singer that all animals ought to receive equal treatment, for 'there are four possible reasons for holding that a person's life has some distinctive value over and above the life of a merely sentient being: the classical utilitarian concern with the effects of the killing on others; the preference utilitarian concern with the frustration of the victim's desires and plans for the future; the argument that the capacity to have desires about one's future is a necessary condition of a right to life; and respect for autonomy.' Ibid., p. 84. Thus, as John Rodman remarks: 'Of course, there is a pecking order in this moral barnyard.' John Rodman, 'The liberation of nature?', *Inquiry* 20 (1977), p. 93.

44 Murray Bookchin, for one, finds utterly unacceptable David Ehrenfeld's 'Noah Principle' – 'a principle according to which we would be obliged to conserve pathogenic bacteria with the same zealousness that we seek to conserve whales.' Murray Bookchin, 'Social ecology vs. deep ecology', letter in *Resurgence* 127 (1988), p. 46.

45 Sylvan, 'A critique of deep ecology', p. 5.

46 Ibid.

47 Ibid.

part of it. 'Shallower' environmentalists, on the other hand, accept the sole value assumption, and are concerned with environmental issues only in so far as they bear on the quality of human life.

Third, Sylvan argues that we need to draw a distinction within 'deeper' environmentalism, and what distinguishes the 'deep' position from what he calls the 'intermediate position' is 'the greater value assumption', according to which, 'other things being equal, the value of humans is greater than other things; the value of humans surpasses that of all other things in the universe.'[48] The 'intermediate' environmental position, while rejecting the sole value assumption, accepts the greater value assumption, and thus values non-human life, but not as much as it values human beings. The 'deep' environmental position, on the contrary, rejects both the sole value assumption and the greater value assumption.

Now, it is clear that many radical ecologists might very well not be 'deep' ecologists, in this sense. They might be 'intermediate' ecologists – those who, while seeing value in non-human nature, value humanity more. And this difference might cash out in significant disagreements over policy – for example, over whether to preserve wilderness or to turn it into a resource for humans.

But, more interestingly, would 'deep' ecology, in Sylvan's sense, actually imply biospherical egalitarianism? In other words, would a rejection of the greater value assumption entail that all species ought to be granted 'the equal right to live and blossom'? If it did, then biospherical egalitarianism would, indeed, seem to constitute a watershed principle between 'deep' ecologists and the rest. And it is precisely this principle which some followers of Naess have sought to employ in order to separate those who are mainly concerned with issues such as pollution and resource depletion from those of a more radical environmental persuasion.

Sylvan, however, rejects a commitment to biospherical egalitarianism as the criterion for distinguishing 'deep' ecologists from others. For not only is this second of Naess' principles dating from 1972 incompatible with his first, but also it is incompatible with his third – diversity and symbiosis – and with his sixth – 'complexity-not-complication'. As Sylvan points out, a diverse ecosystem, according to the third principle, or a complex organism, according to the sixth principle, must be of more value than a simple one.[49] So, rather than biospherical egalitarianism, what 'is needed, more generally,' in his view, 'is a principle telling against the favouring of one species – humans in particular – over others simply on the basis of species, a principle of *biospecies impartiality*'.[50] This implies 'the avoidance of species chauvinism, that is the avoidance of unfair treatment of items outside the given species'.[51] In other words, according to Sylvan, a more coherent principle for distinguishing between deep and other forms of environmental position would be one of fairness between species, rather than one of equality.

48 Ibid., p. 6.
49 See ibid., p. 7.
50 Ibid., p. 8 (emphasis added).
51 Ibid.

Moreover, one could accept the greater value assumption and, by so doing, reject biospherical egalitarianism, yet still subscribe to the other principles formulated by Naess in 1972. To be precise, the intermediate position, where only the sole value assumption is rejected, seems sufficient to support what Fox regards as the 'key ideas in deep ecology's social, political and economic project',[52] which 'include those of a just and sustainable society, carrying capacity, frugality (or "voluntary simplicity"), dwelling in place, cultural and biological diversity, local autonomy and decentralization, soft energy paths, appropriate technology, reinhabitation, and bioregionalism.'[53] In which case, as the intermediate position could, conceivably, accord with the key values within this social, political and economic project, then biospherical egalitarianism neither distinguishes those who are mainly concerned with pollution and resource depletion from those of a more radical environmental persuasion, nor constitutes a necessary principle of green political theory.[54]

In the main body of this book, I have attempted to present a green political theory which could appeal both to those who adopt a biocentric and to those who prefer a more anthropocentric moral philosophy. Just as the insistence that we all be ontological holists seems, unnecessarily, to exclude those who question such an ontology, the insistence on biospherical egalitarianism could be regarded as unnecessarily excluding those who support exactly the same political principles, but on the basis of a different ethical standpoint. Therefore, in attempting to present a political theory which those who hold a biocentric perspective, on the one hand, and those who prefer an anthropocentric one, on the other, could willingly regard as their own, I have relied neither on the first nor on the second of the principles formulated by Naess in 1972.

I should point out, however, that even if successful, this attempt at presenting a political theory acceptable both to those biocentrically and to those anthropocentrically inclined would not enable radical greens to avoid all substantive disagreements. Even a less extreme perspective than biospherical egalitarianism, such as one favouring biospecies impartiality, might well require actions to preserve species which were of no conceivable use to humanity. And to the extent that such a policy might create difficulties for human populations, it could lead to substantial political differences even between 'deep' and 'intermediate' ecologists, never mind to disagreements with those who are more anthropocentrically

52 Fox, 'Deep ecology: a new philosophy of our time?', p. 195.

53 Ibid. One view commonly held by greens which might seem to be obviously incompatible with the intermediate position is that the human population ought to be reduced because its current size appears to be incompatible with the flourishing of non-human life. But as Naess writes: 'I believe that it's not even good for humans that we are four thousand million.' 'Basics of deep ecology', p. 7. (Of course, the world's population is even larger today.) Moreover, all of the 'key ideas in deep ecology's social, political and economic project' mentioned by Fox could also be interpreted as adding to the quality of human life.

54 It is interesting that biospherical egalitarianism is also absent from Naess' 1984 formulation of the principles of deep ecology.

inclined. In fact, a particular, ecologically-oriented attitude to certain human populations has already given rise to a major dispute between some self-proclaimed deep ecologists and those who prefer to describe themselves as 'social ecologists'.

Social ecology

The central figure in this debate within the environmental movement is Murray Bookchin. As Bookchin is the leading social ecologist, it is worth spelling out how his conception of social ecology differs from deep ecology.

The dispute first erupted when Bookchin addressed the National Gathering of US Greens at Amherst in June 1987. In his speech, Bookchin distinguished social ecology from deep ecology in the following terms:

> The greatest differences that are emerging within the so-called 'ecology movement' of our day are between a vague, formless, often self-contradictory and invertebrate thing called 'deep ecology', and a long-developing, coherent, and socially orientated body of ideas that can best be called 'social ecology'. 'Deep ecology' has parachuted into our midst quite recently from the Sunbelt's bizarre mix of Hollywood and Disneyland, spiced with homilies from Taoism, Buddhism, spiritualism, reborn Christianity, and, in some cases, eco-Fascism, while 'social ecology' draws its inspiration from such outstanding radical decentralist thinkers as Peter Kropotkin, William Morris, and Paul Goodman among many others who have advanced a serious challenge to the present society with its vast hierarchical, sexist, class-ruled, statist apparatus and militaristic history.[55]

Bookchin concluded his denunciation thus: 'Let us face these differences bluntly. "Deep ecology", despite all its social rhetoric, has virtually no real sense that our ecological problems have their ultimate roots in society and in social problems.'[56]

Now, Porritt and Winner clearly think that what Bookchin primarily objects to is the incorporation of spirituality into the ecological approach, and that his major concern is to drum all 'spiritualists' out of the ecology movement. As they write: 'What we find here is an old-fashioned hatred of anything supernatural, anything that seeks to transcend a solidly scientific explanation of life on Earth. [Bookchin] dismisses each and every one of those who believe that there *is* a spiritual dimension as "flaky spiritualists".'[57]

Well, what might a less materialistic view look like? One would assume it might be something like the following:

55 Murray Bookchin, 'Social ecology versus "deep ecology": a challenge for the ecology movement', *The Raven* 3 (1987), p. 221.

56 Ibid.

57 Porritt and Winner, *The Coming of the Greens*, p. 239.

> Ecology . . . advances a broader conception of nature and of humanity's relationship with the natural world. . . . [I]t sees the balance and integrity of the biosphere as an end in itself. Natural diversity is to be cultivated not only because the more diversified the components that make up an ecosystem, the more stable the ecosystem, but diversity is desirable for its own sake, a value to be cherished as part of a spiritized notion of the living universe.[58]

But this passage was actually written by none other than Bookchin. Bookchin did not, in fact, wish to dismiss all ecologists with a predilection for spirituality,[59] as Porritt and Winner presume. It would seem, then, that his ridiculing of the more extravagant of the deep ecologists struck a raw nerve. Porritt and Winner would appear to have reacted defensively to what, one must assume, they considered to be the most threatening part of Bookchin's tirade, whereas his main objection to deep ecology is what in his view is its failure to stress, or even to take seriously, the social causes of ecological crises.[60]

So, what characterizes social ecology is not a rejection of spirituality, but a focus on the social structures which are purported to give rise to the environmental threats we seemingly face. And Bookchin considers this to be of paramount importance, for in his view: 'Either we will go directly to the social roots of the ecological crisis or we will be deceived into an era of totalitarianism'.[61] And he insists that the latter possibility would be not only socially but also ecologically disastrous, because totalitarianism is, in his opinion, incompatible with what is required in order to avoid an environmental disaster. As he argues: 'If we are to survive ecological catastrophe, we must decentralize, restore bioregional forms of production and food cultivation, diversify our technologies, scale them to human dimensions, and establish face-to-face forms of democracy.'[62] But in order to do this, it seems that it would not suffice simply to oppose centralization, bureaucratization and monolithic, dominating technologies. We would also need to root out

58 Murray Bookchin, *Toward an Ecological Society* (Montreal: Black Rose, 1980), p. 59.

59 Though he certainly objects to ecology becoming a religion. See Bookchin, 'Social ecology vs. deep ecology', p. 46.

60 However, Porritt and Winner do mention that social ecology 'emphasizes the role of society' and that some deep ecologists come close to being eco-Fascists. But they nevertheless insist that Bookchin's social/deep ecology polarity is a front for his hatred of spirituality. See Porritt and Winner, *The Coming of the Greens*, pp. 235–41.

61 Bookchin, *Toward an Ecological Society*, p. 39.

62 Ibid., p. 27. If these changes are indeed necessary for avoiding eco-catastrophe, then André Gorz would be wrong to assume that there might be an effective authoritarian answer to environmental problems: 'Ecology, as a purely scientific discipline, does not necessarily imply the rejection of authoritarian, technofascist solutions.' André Gorz, *Ecology as Politics*, trans. P. Vigderman and J. Cloud (London: Pluto Press, 1980), p. 17. Also see Ryle, *Ecology and Socialism*, p. 7, where it is similarly assumed that environmental problems might be solved by authoritarian means. For Bookchin's view of (what he takes to be) the truly radical implications of ecology, see Murray Bookchin, 'Ecology and revolutionary thought' in *Post-Scarcity Anarchism* (London: Wildwood House, 1974).

the causes of these ecologically problematic features, for, according to Bookchin, were we not to do so, they would just re-emerge.

What, then, is the root of our present predicament? In Bookchin's view, the root of all our problems, including ecological ones, is domination. As early as 1965, in his essay 'Ecology and revolutionary thought', he reversed a central claim within neo-Marxist Critical Theory by contending that the 'notion that man must dominate nature emerges directly from the domination of man by man.'[63] And as he later remarks in *Toward an Ecological Society*:

> Indeed, this conception goes back earlier to a time when men began to dominate and exploit women in the patriarchal family. From that point onward, human beings were increasingly regarded as mere resources, as objects instead of subjects. The hierarchies, classes, propertied forms, and statist institutions that emerged with social domination were carried over conceptually into humanity's relationship with nature. Nature too became increasingly regarded as a mere resource, an object, a raw material to be exploited as ruthlessly as slaves on a latifundium.[64]

However, in Bookchin's opinion, 'it was not until organic community relations, feudal or peasant in form, dissolved into market relations that the planet itself was reduced to a resource for exploitation.'[65] This development has reached its apogee with the globalization of capitalism, where in order to survive in the marketplace, every producer is forced to compete with every other, every employer must dominate and exploit his or her employees, and humanity as a whole must dominate and exploit non-human nature[66] – or so the argument goes. As Bookchin puts it: 'Owing to its inherently competitive nature, bourgeois society not only pits humans against each other, it also pits the mass of humanity against the natural world.'[67] This theme of the growth of hierarchy and its ostensible ecological ramifications is most fully developed in Bookchin's major study *The Ecology of Freedom*,[68] which John Clark, for one, regards as 'a major achievement, destined to become a classic of contemporary social thought'.[69]

In short, one of Bookchin's principal claims is that 'the very notion of the

63 Ibid., p. 63.

64 Bookchin, *Toward an Ecological Society*, p. 40.

65 Bookchin, 'Ecology and revolutionary thought', p. 63.

66 See Ted Benton, *Natural Relations: Ecology, Animal Rights and Social Justice* (London: Verso, 1993), for an account of how Marx's theory of alienation could be extended to include non-human animals. For a critique of one aspect of Benton's argument, see Alan Carter, 'Animal rights and social relations', *Res Publica: A Journal of Legal and Social Philosophy*, Vol. 1, No. 2 (1995), pp. 213–20.

67 Bookchin, 'Ecology and revolutionary thought', p. 63.

68 Murray Bookchin, *The Ecology of Freedom: The Emergence and Dissolution of Hierarchy* (Palo Alto: Cheshire Books, 1982).

69 John Clark, *The Anarchist Moment: Reflections on Culture, Nature and Power* (Montreal: Black Rose, 1984), p. 215.

domination of nature by man stems from the very real domination of human by human,'[70] adding that, in his estimation, this constitutes 'a far-reaching reversal of concepts'.[71] Certain Marxists, for example, argue that it is in order to control nature that humans have dominated other humans. Bookchin turns this on its head. However, it should be noted that what he actually claims is that it is the *notion* of the domination of nature by humanity which has arisen from the domination of one human by another. This is a claim about the concept 'domination'. But this is not the same thing as the *actual* domination of nature by humanity. Bookchin argues that pre-literate societies were relatively non-hierarchical. They had no conception of dominating nature. It was only when the elderly began to dominate the young, when men began to dominate women, and, most importantly, when one class began to dominate and exploit another that we came to conceive of dominating and exploiting nature.

Now, it is surely not too implausible to maintain that if humans did not exploit other humans, then they would not employ the term 'exploitation' to describe their relations with the non-human world. Nor is it too implausible to maintain, as Bookchin does, that once hierarchical relationships emerge between people, they are then projected onto the natural world. Bookchin is surely correct to argue that queen bees are not really queens[72] and that lions are not actually kings of the jungle. For one thing, lions are not surrounded by courtiers. Hence, Bookchin makes the important point that it is a mistake to conceive of the relations between and within species in terms of human, hierarchical, social institutions. As he writes:

> ecology recognizes no hierarchy on the level of the ecosystem. There are no 'kings of the beasts' and no 'lowly ants'. These notions are the projections of our social attitudes and relationships on the natural world. Virtually all that lives as part of the floral and faunal variety of an ecosystem plays its coequal role in maintaining the balance and integrity of the whole.[73]

Contrary to the presuppositions of many social Darwinists, ecosystems seem to exhibit a considerable degree of symbiosis between species and mutual aid within them.[74]

70 Bookchin, *The Ecology of Freedom*, p. 1.

71 Ibid.

72 As he writes: 'a "queen" bee is simply an essential part of a reproductive organ we call a beehive, not a link in an institutionalized dynasty.' Murray Bookchin, *The Modern Crisis* (Philadelphia: New Society Publishers, 1986), p. 24.

73 Bookchin, *Toward an Ecological Society*, pp. 59–60. And as he adds: 'No hierarchies were imputed to the natural world, at least not until the human community began to become hierarchical. Thereafter, experience itself became increasingly hierarchical, reflecting the splits that undermined the unity of the early organic human community.' Ibid., p. 269.

74 In the words of William Träger: 'The conflict in nature between different kinds of organisms has been popularly expressed in phrases like the "struggle for existence" and the "survival of the fittest". Yet few people realized that mutual cooperation between organisms – symbiosis – is

However, although it is plausible to claim that if human beings did not exploit other human beings, then they would not employ the term 'exploitation' to describe their relations with the non-human world, that is not to say they would not relate to the natural world in a manner that *we* are inclined to regard as 'exploitative'. For example, a vegetarian could describe pre-literate, egalitarian hunters as 'dominating' non-human nature even if those hunters lacked the concept 'domination'. If the society were to become hierarchical, it might then describe itself as 'dominating nature', having acquired the concept, even though its relationship to non-human nature had not in fact changed at all. So, Bookchin's conceptual reversal does not, it would seem, succeed in establishing that the 'domination of nature' by humans is the product of the domination of human by human.

Nevertheless, it is widely accepted that many pre-literate human societies were in ecological harmony with their surroundings. And it does appear to be the case that non-human nature is relentlessly 'exploited'[75] when producers find themselves in fierce competition with one another in capitalist societies. However, such economic relations may very well be themselves determined (as the State-Primacy Thesis claims), rather than ultimately determining.[76] But this notwithstanding, if capitalist relations force both humans and non-humans to be 'exploited', then Bookchin has good reason to insist that we cannot avoid 'dominating' and 'exploiting' nature unless we transform a social order which involves the domination and exploitation of one human by another. And it seems plausible enough to claim that to do so would require that we no longer regard hierarchy as 'natural'.

Unfortunately, certain assumptions about the natural world do appear to have

just as important, and the "fittest" may be the one that helps another to survive.' Quoted in Bookchin, *The Modern Crisis*, p. 56. For a discussion of intra-species co-operation, see Peter Kropotkin, *Mutual Aid: A Factor of Evolution* (Boston: Extending Horizons Books, n.d.).

75 See, for example, Peter Singer (ed.), *In Defence of Animals* (Oxford: Blackwell, 1985), *passim.*, especially the accounts of factory farming. Also see Peter Singer, *Animal Liberation*, 2nd edition, (London: Pimlico, 1995), Ch. 3.

76 If capitalist economic relations do, indeed, force individuals not only to mistreat other humans but also to mistreat non-human animals (for example, by 'farmers' being forced to keep battery chickens in appalling conditions if their business is to remain profitable), then the State-Primacy Theory, if correct, is an essential theoretical tool for both human liberation movements and for the animal liberation movement. This is because both human and non-human suffering could be expected to continue unabated as long as the state has an interest in stabilizing capitalist economic relations. Furthermore, if capitalist economic relations compel individuals to destroy wildlife habits, even whole rainforests, then the State-Primacy Theory, if correct, is equally an essential theoretical tool for those concerned less with animal welfare and more with species preservation. It is in this regard that the State-Primacy Theory might well provide the necessary political theory not only for those whose concern is anthropocentrically motivated but also for those whose awareness is more biocentric.

underpinned the belief that hierarchy, domination and exploitation are all natural. As Bookchin claims in *The Modern Crisis*:

> We have learned only too well that Hitler's 'blood and soil' naturism, like Stalin's cosmological 'dialectics', can be used as viciously as notions of 'natural law' (with all their Darwinian connotations of 'fitness to survive' and 'natural selection') to collect millions of people in concentration camps, where they are worked to death, incinerated, or both.[77]

However, the science of ecology, in Bookchin's opinion, has far more radical implications than the 'biologism' which has been used to justify social hierarchies. Ecology seems to reveal the tremendous diversity and interdependencies within the natural world. And according to Bookchin, with 'ecology's emphasis on nature's fecundity, on its thrust towards increasing variety, on its limitless capacity to differentiate life-forms and its development of richer, more varied evolutionary pathways that steadily involve ever more complex species, our vision of the natural world begins to change'.[78] Thus he proceeds to argue that from this alternative perception of the natural world – one which is derived from a certain understanding of the nature of ecosystems – an ecological ethics can arise 'which sees the emergence of selfhood, reason, and freedom *from* nature – not in sharp opposition to nature'.[79]

In other words, Bookchin claims that a hierarchical society has given rise to a hierarchical conception of nature, which has then been used to make human hierarchies appear natural. Moreover, in his view, this has given rise to a hierarchical conception of the relationship between humanity and non-human nature – with the former then being conceived as standing in opposition to the latter. So, we think of ourselves as struggling against nature in order to survive, rather than trying to live in harmony within an ecosystem. Yet in order to survive, it is the latter that seems to be what is required of us, and this is what ecology apparently teaches us. We are a part of nature and a part of natural evolution, or so Bookchin insists. Hence, he writes:

> The traditional dualism in human thought that pitted humanity against animality, society against nature, freedom against necessity, mind against body, and, in its most insidious form, man against woman is transcended by due recognition of the continuity between the two, but without a reductionism or 'oneness' that yields, in Hegel's words, 'a night in which all cows are black'.[80]

In a word, we are not identical to the rest of nature. Rather, we have evolved out

77 Bookchin, *The Modern Crisis*, p. 10.
78 Ibid., p. 11.
79 Ibid., p. 12.
80 Ibid.

of it into a highly conscious life-form. And in a very Hegelian manner, Bookchin conceives of humanity as actualizing the potentiality for consciousness which resides in nature.[81]

What Bookchin proceeds to argue is that this conception of evolution overcomes the traditional dualisms which have plagued humanity, while simultaneously indicating the importance of human beings:

> With the use of an evolutionary approach to explain the evolution of humanity out of animality, society out of nature, and mind out of body, we . . . free ourselves from anti-humanism's reductionist dissolution of human uniqueness into a cosmic 'community' in which ants are equatable to people, from the infamous 'life-boat ethic' that denies the need to share the means of life with others who are less privileged, from an overtly National Socialist outlook that validates the authority of self-appointed 'supermen' to dominate 'subhumans', and from a Stalinist reduction of human beings to the raw material of a 'History' governed by the inexorable 'laws' of dialectical materialism.[82]

And it is precisely this hostility to eco-Fascism and its 'life-boat ethic' that appears to lie at the heart of Bookchin's denunciation of deep ecology.

What Bookchin seems most concerned about, then, is the possibility that a certain emphasis on 'Oneness' could lead to the view that human beings are of little significance or worth. Worse, humanity as a whole might even come to be regarded as nothing more than a parasite.[83] In short, it is crucial, in Bookchin's view, that distinctions be drawn and everything not be lumped together or boundaries muddied. For example:

> What is very important to note is that Devall-Sessions [the editors of deep ecology's 'textbook'] invent a fiction called 'humanity' in which people of colour, women, the poor, the exploited, and the [Third] World are dumped

81 Cf.: 'The whole story of the universe is of matter acquiring sensitivity – to the point of awareness, to the point of consciousness, to the point of self-consciousness, to the point of spirituality.' Henryk Skolimowski, *Eco-Philosophy: Designing New Tactics for Living* (Boston: Marion Boyars, 1981), p. 46. However, Skolimowski draws the conclusion that the universe is as it is '[b]ecause we are here!' Ibid., p. 73. From this, he argues for 'an altogether new cosmology' – namely, one 'which is evolution-centered'. Ibid. Skolimowski also ends up with precisely the kind of 'Oneness' that Bookchin so opposes, arguing that '[w]e have to take care of the ecological habitat because it is a part of us and we are a part of it.' Here, Skolimowski continues, ' "we" and "it" are one, and this is a necessity of a symbiotic and holistic attitude'. Ibid., p. 83.

82 Bookchin, *The Modern Crisis*, pp. 12–13.

83 In fact, one deep ecologist has gone so far as to argue in the publication *Earth First!* that radical ecologists 'can see AIDS not as a problem, but a necessary solution. . . . To paraphrase Voltaire: if the AIDS epidemic didn't exist, radical environmentalists would invent one.' Quoted in *The Bulletin of Anarchist Research* 15 (1988), p. 14. And this is because AIDS kills humans without destroying ecosystems.

> into a single category with privileged whites, males, the wealthy, exploiters, and the First World – as though all are conjointly responsible for devastating the planet merely because they belong to the same biological species.[84]

Whereas in Bookchin's view, it is particular social structures which are responsible for the approaching ecological catastrophe that we seem to face. Moreover, in his opinion, it is the very same structures which force people to damage the environment that also lead to so much human suffering. It is not surprising, therefore, that he should feel so outraged by David Foreman, for example, who 'opined in [an] . . . interview that "the worst thing we can do in Ethiopia is to give aid – the best thing would be to just let nature (!) seek its own balance, to let people there just starve . . .".' As Bookchin adds: 'What counts is that Foreman is an enthusiastic promoter of "deep ecology" in the United States.'[85] Moreover, the interview was conducted by Bill Devall, who was quite happy to praise Foreman. And it is also not surprising that Bookchin should feel it necessary to denounce not only such misanthropic views but also the intellectual approach which he considers to underpin it.

It is this seemingly eco-fascist side of certain self-professed deep ecologists that has most led Bookchin to distance himself from the deep ecology movement. In his opinion, deep ecology is problematic, then, primarily because it 'creates a labyrinth that effectively steers away from the *social* roots of the ecological crisis'.[86] Thus, the reason why he is so antagonistic to the metaphysical (not necessarily the spiritual) leanings of some deep ecologists is because their philosophical approach has, in his view, anti-humanist implications and diverts attention away from the social causes of our environmental problems.

However, it might be objected that Bookchin's alternative to an undifferentiated 'Oneness' is not without its own potential problems. We have seen that he wishes to employ 'an evolutionary approach to explain the evolution of humanity out of animality, society out of nature, and mind out of body'.[87] But some might criticize this for having as equally confused a notion of the relationship of parts to wholes as that which appears to be displayed by certain deep ecologists' identification with the 'One'. If *X* arises *out of Y*, then *X* and *Y* must, surely, be separate entities. But then, if humanity were thought to arise out of nature, not only would it be distinguishable from the rest of nature but also it seems that it could not be a *part* of nature. Of course, some might find this conclusion acceptable. Moreover, if humans arise out of 'animality', as Bookchin explicitly claims, this seems to imply equally that they are *not animals*. Again, some might agree that humans are, in some important sense, no longer animal-like. But many environmentalists would be inclined to say that in opposing the 'holistic' approach of

84 Bookchin, 'Social ecology vs. deep ecology', letter in *Resurgence*, p. 46.
85 Ibid.
86 Ibid.
87 Bookchin, *The Modern Crisis*, p. 12.

certain deep ecologists, Bookchin appears to have gone too far in the opposite direction.

This notwithstanding, in order to assess the social ecologists' primary claim – namely, that the causes of ecological crises are social – it would be necessary to examine social and economic structures to see if they do, in fact, induce ecological crises. And an obvious case would appear to be the structural relationships between the First and Third Worlds, for it is in the Third World that ecological crises seem most apparent, and they do appear to be the result of a structure of international exploitation. Nevertheless, this would still fail to establish that the primary claim of social ecology is the fundamental explanation, for social and economic structures which induced ecological crises might in turn be explained by the nature of the prevailing political structures. However, it could still be maintained that the environmental crises seemingly faced by Third World peoples have social and economic causes. And this, it would appear, at least supports social ecology against certain of the views expressed by some self-professed deep ecologists.

But it is worth recalling that the founder of deep ecology, Arne Naess, originally distanced his position from that of the 'shallow ecology movement' because the latter appeared to oppose pollution and the depletion of resources only out of a concern for 'the health and affluence of people in the developed countries'.[88] Thus, if the ill-health and poverty rife in the Third World were no longer to be ignored or dismissed by certain deep ecologists, then it might be possible to unify the environmental movement under one coherent political theory. The theoretical position advanced in this book has sought to meet this challenge by attempting to transcend the divide between deep ecology and social ecology. The theory presented here is neither deep ecology nor social ecology. *It is political ecology.*

In short, this book has attempted to develop a political theory which radical greens can collectively embrace, whether they are deep ecologists, social ecologists or whatever. Certainly, disagreements concerning actual policies would nevertheless still remain between various kinds of greens, primarily because of their *ethical* differences – for example, on the basis of whether they adopt an anthropocentric or a biocentric approach.[89] But it is not unlikely that they all require the same *political* theory. It is *that* political theory which this book has sought to expound.

88 Naess, 'The shallow and the deep, long-range ecology movement', p. 95.

89 For a summary of the basic differences between these approaches, see Paul W. Taylor, *Respect for Nature: A Theory of Environmental Ethics* (New Jersey: Princeton University Press, 1986), pp. 11–13.

Bibliography

Abbey, E., *The Monkey Wrench Gang*, New York, Avon Books, 1976.

Abraham, J., 'Food, development and our inner ecology' in C. Lacey and R. Williams (eds), *Education, Ecology and Development: The Case for an Education Network*, London, The World Wildlife Fund/Kogan Page, 1987.

Achterberg, W., 'Can liberal democracy survive the environmental crisis? Sustainability, liberal neutrality and overlapping consensus' in A. Dobson and P. Lucardie (eds), *The Politics of Nature: Explorations in Green Political Theory*, London, Routledge, 1993.

—— 'Sustainability, community and democracy' in B. Doherty and M. de Geus (eds), *Democracy and Green Political Thought: Sustainability, Rights and Citizenship*, London, Routledge, 1996.

Acton, H. B., *The Illusion of the Epoch*, London, Routledge and Kegan Paul, 1962.

Agassi, J., 'Methodological individualism' in J. O'Neill (ed.), *Modes of Individualism and Collectivism*, London, Heinemann, 1973.

Aiken, W., 'The "carrying capacity" equivocation' in W. Aiken and H. LaFollette (eds), *World Hunger and Morality*, New Jersey, Prentice-Hall, 1996.

Alavi, H., 'The state in post-colonial societies: Pakistan and Bangladesh', in Harry Goulbourne (ed.), *Politics and State in the Third World*, London, Macmillan, 1979.

Alavi, H. and Shanin, T. (eds), *Introduction to the Sociology of 'Developing Societies'*, London, Macmillan, 1982.

Allaby, M. and Bunyard, P., *The Politics of Self-Sufficiency*, Oxford, Oxford University Press, 1980.

Almond, G., 'Introduction: a functional approach' in G. A. Almond and J. S. Coleman (eds), *The Politics of the Developing Areas*, New Jersey, Princeton University Press, 1960.

Althusser, L., 'Ideology and ideological state apparatuses' in *Lenin and Philosophy and Other Essays*, London, New Left Books, 1977.

Althusser, L. and Balibar, É. *Reading Capital*, London, New Left Books, 1977.

Anderson, T. L. and Leal, D. R, 'Free market versus political environmentalism' in M. E. Zimmerman, J. B. Callicott, G. Sessions, K. J. Warren and J. Clark (eds), *Environmental Philosophy: From Animal Rights to Radical Ecology*, New Jersey, Prentice-Hall, 1998.

Arblaster, A., *Democracy*, Milton Keynes, Open University Press, 1987.

Arneson, R. J., 'Equality and equal opportunity for welfare', *Philosophical Studies*, 56, 1989: 77–93.

Arrow, K. J., 'Values and collective decision-making' in P. Laslett and W. G. Runciman (eds), *Philosophy, Politics and Society: Third Series*, Oxford, Blackwell, 1969.

Arthur, J., 'Rights and the duty to bring aid' in W. Aiken and H. LaFollette (eds), *World Hunger and Morality*, New Jersey, Prentice-Hall, 1996.

Atkinson, A., *Principles of Political Ecology*, London, Belhaven, 1991.

Attfield, R., *The Ethics of Environmental Concern*, Oxford, Blackwell, 1983.

—— 'Methods of ecological ethics', *Metaphilosophy*, 14, 3 & 4, July/October, 1983: 195–208.

—— 'Deep ecology and intrinsic value: a reply to Andrew Dobson', *Cogito*, 4, 1, Spring 1990: 61–6.

Attfield, R. and Dell, K. (eds), *Values, Conflict and the Environment*, Aldershot, Avebury, 1996.

Axelrod, R., 'The emergence of cooperation among equals', *The American Political Science Review*, 75, 1981: 306–18.

Bachrach, P., 'Interest, participation, and democratic theory' in J. R. Pennock and J. W. Chapman, *Participation in Politics*, NOMOS 16, New York, Lieber-Atherton, 1975.

Bachrach P. and Baratz, M. S., *Power and Poverty: Theory and Practice*, New York, Oxford University Press, 1970.

Bahro, R., *The Alternative in Eastern Europe*, trans. D. Fernbach, London, New Left Books, 1978.

—— *From Red to Green: Interviews with New Left Review*, trans. G. Fagan and R. Hurst, London, Verso, 1984.

—— *Building the Green Movement*, trans. M. Tyler, London, Heretic, 1986.

Baker, J., *Arguing for Equality*, London, Verso, 1987.

Bakunin, M., *The Political Philosophy of Bakunin: Scientific Anarchism*, ed. G. P. Maximoff, New York, The Free Press, 1964.

—— *God and the State*, New York, Dover, 1970.

—— *Bakunin on Anarchy*, ed. S. Dolgoff, London, George Allen and Unwin, 1973.

Balakrishnan, R. and Narayan, U., 'Combining justice with development: rethinking rights and responsibilities in the context of world hunger and poverty' in W. Aiken and H. LaFollette (eds), *World Hunger and Morality*, New Jersey, Prentice-Hall, 1996.

Baldwin, J. and Brand, S. (eds), *Soft-Tech*, Harmondsworth, Penguin, 1978.

Barclay, H., *People Without Government: An Anthropology of Anarchism*, London, Kahn and Avrill with Cienfuegos Press, 1982.

Barry, B., 'Justice and the common good', *Analysis*, 21, 1960: 86–90.

—— 'The public interest', *Proceedings of the Aristotelian Society*, Suppl. Vol. 38, 1964: 1–18.

—— *Political Argument*, London, Routledge and Kegan Paul, 1965.

—— *The Liberal Theory of Justice: A Critical Examination of the Principal Doctrines in a Theory of Justice by John Rawls*, Oxford, Oxford University Press, 1973.

—— 'Is democracy special' in P. Laslett and J. Fishkin (eds), *Philosophy, Politics and Society: Fifth Series*, Oxford, Blackwell, 1979.

—— 'Justice between generations' in P. M. S., Hacker and J. Raz, *Law, Morality, and Society*, Oxford, Clarendon, 1979.

—— *Theories of Justice*, Hemel Hempstead, Harvester-Wheatsheaf, 1989.

—— *Justice as Impartiality*, Oxford, Clarendon, 1995.

Barry, J., 'The limits of the shallow and the deep: green politics, philosophy, and praxis', *Environmental Politics*, 3, 3, Autumn 1994: 369–94.

Barry, J., 'Sustainability, political judgement and citizenship: connecting green politics and democracy' in B. Doherty and M. de Geus (eds), *Democracy and Green Political Thought: Sustainability, Rights and Citizenship*, London, Routledge, 1996.

Barry, N. P., *An Introduction to Modern Political Theory*, London, Macmillan, 1981.

Bates, R. H., *Essays on the Political Economy of Rural Africa*, Cambridge, Cambridge University Press, 1983.

Bayles, M. D., *Morality and Population Policy*, Alabama, University of Alabama Press, 1980.

Beck, U., *Ecological Politics in an Age of Risk*, Cambridge, Polity, 1995.

Bedau, H. A., 'Civil disobedience and personal responsibility for injustice' in H. A. Bedau (ed.), *Civil Disobedience in Focus*, London, Routledge, 1991.

Benn, S. I., '"Interests" in politics', *Proceedings of the Aristotelian Society*, 60, 1959–60: 123–40.

Benn, S. I. and Peters, R. S., *Social Principles and the Democratic State*, London, George Allen and Unwin, 1959.

Bennett, J., 'Whatever the consequences' in J. Rachels (ed.), *Moral Problems: A Collection of Philosophical Essays*, New York, Harper and Row, 1971.

Benson, J., 'Duty and the beast', *Philosophy*, 53, 1978: 529–49.

Benton, T., 'Humanism = speciesism', *Radical Philosophy*, 50, Autumn 1988: 4–18.

—— 'Animal rights and social relations' in A. Dobson and P. Lucardie (eds), *The Politics of Nature: Explorations in Green Political Theory*, London, Routledge, 1993.

—— *Natural Relations: Ecology, Animal Rights and Social Justice*, London, Verso, 1993.

—— 'Animal rights: an eco-socialist view' in R. Garner (ed.), *Animal Rights: The Changing Debate*, Basingstoke, Macmillan, 1996.

Berki, R. N., *The History of Political Thought*, London, Dent, 1977.

Berkman, A., *What is Anarchist Communism?*, New York, Dover, 1972.

Berlin, I., 'Two concepts of liberty' in A. Quinton (ed.), *Political Philosophy*, Oxford, Oxford University Press, 1967.

—— *Four Essays on Liberty*, Oxford, Oxford University Press, 1969.

Bernstein, H., 'Sociology of underdevelopment vs. sociology of development?' in D. Lehmann (ed.), *Development Theory: Four Critical Essays*, London, Frank Cass, 1979.

Berry, T., 'The viable human' in M. E. Zimmerman, J. B. Callicott, G. Sessions, K. J. Warren and J. Clark (eds), *Environmental Philosophy: From Animal Rights to Radical Ecology*, New Jersey, Prentice-Hall, 1998.

Blackburn, R. (ed.), *Ideology in Social Science*, London, Fontana, 1972.

Blackburn, S., 'Truth, realism, and the regulation of theory' in P. A. French, T. E. Uehling Jr and H. K. Wettstein (eds), *Midwest Studies in Philosophy*, Vol. V, Minneapolis, University of Minnesota Press, 1980.

—— *Spreading the Word: Groundings in the Philosophy of Language*, Oxford, Oxford University Press, 1984.

—— 'Errors and the phenomenology of value' in T. Honderich (ed.), *Morality and Objectivity*, London, Routledge, 1985.

Block, F., 'Beyond relative autonomy: state managers as historical subjects' in R. Miliband and J. Saville (eds), *The Socialist Register 1980*, London, Merlin, 1980.

Bookchin, M., 'The youth culture: an anarcho-communist view' in *Hip Culture: 6 Essays on its Revolutionary Potential*, Times Change Press, 1970.

—— *Post-Scarcity Anarchism*, London, Wildwood House, 1974.

Bookchin, M., 'Radical agriculture' in R. Merrill (ed.), *Radical Agriculture*, New York, Harper and Row, 1976.
—— *Toward an Ecological Society*, Montreal, Black Rose, 1980.
—— *The Ecology of Freedom: The Emergence and Dissolution of Hierarchy*, California, Cheshire Books, 1982.
—— 'Toward a philosophy of nature – the bases for an ecological ethics' in M. Tobias (ed.), *Deep Ecology*, San Diego, Avant Books, 1985.
—— *The Modern Crisis*, Philadelphia, New Society Publishers, 1986.
—— 'Thinking ecologically: a dialectical approach', *Our Generation*, 18, 2, March 1987: 3–40.
—— 'Social ecology versus "deep ecology": a challenge for the ecology movement', *The Raven*, 3, 1987: 219–50.
—— 'Social ecology vs. deep ecology', *Resurgence*, 127, 1988: 46.
—— 'New social movements: the anarchic dimension' in D. Goodway (ed.), *For Anarchism: History, Theory, and Practice*, London, Routledge, 1989.
—— 'Libertarian municipalism: an overview', *Green Perspectives*, 24, 1991: 1–5.
—— 'What is social ecology?' in J. P. Sterba (ed.), *Earth Ethics: Environmental Ethics, Animal Rights, and Practical Applications*, New Jersey, Prentice-Hall, 1995.
Boonin-Vail, D., 'Don't stop thinking about tomorrow: two paradoxes about duties to future generations,' *Philosophy and Public Affairs*, 25, 4, Fall 1996: 267–307.
Bottomore, T. B., *Classes in Modern Society*, London, George Allen and Unwin, 1965.
—— *Elites and Society*, Harmondsworth, Penguin, 1966.
—— *Theories of Modern Capitalism*, London, Unwin Hyman, 1985.
Boulding, K., 'The economics of the coming spaceship Earth' in H. E. Daly (ed.), *Toward a Steady-State Economy*, San Francisco, W. H. Freeman, 1973.
Boyle, G., *Living on the Sun: Harnessing Renewable Energy for an Equitable Society*, London, Calder and Boyars, 1975.
Boyle, G. and Harper, P. (eds), *Radical Technology*, London, Wildwood House, 1976.
Bramwell, A., *Ecology in the 20th Century: A History*, New Haven, Yale University Press, 1989.
Brandt, W. *et al.*, *North–South: A Programme for Survival*, London, Pan, 1980.
Braverman, H., *Labor and Monopoly Capital: The Degradation of Work in the Twentieth Century*, New York, Monthly Review Press, 1974.
Brennan, A., 'The moral standing of natural objects', *Environmental Ethics*, 6, 1, Spring 1984: 35–56.
—— *Thinking about Nature: An Investigation of Nature, Value and Ecology*, London, Routledge, 1988.
—— 'Ecological theory and value in nature' in R. Elliot (ed.), *Environmental Ethics*, Oxford, Oxford University Press, 1995.
Brenner, R., 'The social basis of economic development' in J. Roemer (ed.), *Analytical Marxism*, Cambridge, Cambridge University Press, 1986.
Brewer, A., *Marxist Theories of Imperialism: A Critical Survey*, London, Routledge and Kegan Paul, 1980.
Brinton, M., *The Bolsheviks and Workers' Control 1917–1921: The State and Counter-Revolution*, Detroit, Black and Red, 1975.
Bromley, S., 'Globalization', *Radical Philosophy*, 80, November/December 1996: 2–5.
Brown, A., *Modern Political Philosophy: Theories of the Just Society*, Harmondsworth, Penguin, 1986.

Brown, L. R., 'Facing food insecurity' in L. R. Brown *et al.*, *State of the World 1994*, London, Earthscan, 1994.

Brown, L. R. *et al.*, *State of the World 1996*, London, Earthscan, 1996.

Brundtland, G. H. *et al.*, *Our Common Future*, Oxford, Oxford University Press, 1987.

Buchanan, A., 'Revolutionary motivation and rationality' in M. Cohen, T. Nagel and T. Scanlon (eds), *Marx, Justice and History*, New Jersey, Princeton University Press, 1980.

Budd, M., 'The aesthetic appreciation of nature', *British Journal of Aesthetics*, 36, 3, July 1996: 207–22.

Bunyard, P. and Morgan-Grenville, F. (eds), *The Green Alternative: Guide to Good Living*, London, Methuen, 1987.

Burch, D., 'Appropriate technology for the Third World: why the will is lacking', *The Ecologist*, 12, 1982: 52–66.

Bures, R., 'Ethical dimensions of human attitudes to nature', *Radical Philosophy*, 57, Spring 1991: 10–13.

Burton, R. G., 'A philosopher looks at the population bomb' in W. T. Blackstone (ed.), *Philosophy and Environmental Crisis*, Georgia, University of Georgia Press, 1974.

Cahill, T., 'Cooperatives and anarchism: a contemporary perspective' in D. Goodway (ed.), *For Anarchism: History, Theory, and Practice*, London, Routledge, 1989.

Caldecott, L. and Leland, S. (eds), *Reclaim the Earth: Women Speak out for Life on Earth*, London, The Women's Press, 1983.

Callenbach, E., *Ecotopia*, London, Pluto, 1978.

Callicott, J. B., 'Hume's *is/ought* dichotomy and the relation of ecology to Leopold's land ethic', *Environmental Ethics*, 4, 2, Summer 1982: 163–74.

—— 'Traditional American Indian and Western European attitudes toward nature: an overview', *Environmental Ethics*, 4, 4, Winter 1982: 293–318.

—— 'Intrinsic value, Quantum Theory, and environmental ethics', *Environmental Ethics*, 7, 3, Fall 1985: 357–75.

—— 'The case against moral pluralism', *Environmental Ethics*, 12, 2, Summer 1990: 99–124.

—— 'Animal liberation: a triangular affair' in R. Elliot (ed.), *Environmental Ethics*, Oxford, Oxford University Press, 1995.

—— 'Animal liberation and environmental ethics: back together again' in J. P. Sterba (ed.), *Earth Ethics: Environmental Ethics, Animal Rights, and Practical Applications*, New Jersey, Prentice-Hall, 1995.

—— 'Do deconstructive ecology and sociobiology undermine Leopold's land ethic?', *Environmental Ethics*, 18, 4, Winter 1996: 353–72.

—— 'The conceptual foundations of the land ethic' in M. E. Zimmerman, J. B. Callicott, G. Sessions, K. J. Warren and J. Clark (eds), *Environmental Philosophy: From Animal Rights to Radical Ecology*, New Jersey, Prentice-Hall, 1998.

Campbell, A., *Mondragon 1980*, ICOM, Pamphlet No. 9.

Capra, F., *The Turning Point: Science, Society, and the Rising Culture*, London, Fontana, 1983.

Cardoso, F. H., 'Dependency and development in Latin America', *New Left Review*, 74, 1972: 83–95.

Carlson, A., 'Appreciation and the natural environment', *Journal of Aesthetics and Art Criticism*, 37, 3, Spring 1979: 267–75.

Carlson, A., 'Nature, aesthetic judgment and objectivity', *Journal of Aesthetics and Art Criticism*, 40, 1, Fall 1981: 15–27.

—— 'Nature and positive aesthetics', *Environmental Ethics*, 6, 1, Spring 1984: 5–34.

Carnoy, M., *The State and Political Theory*, New Jersey, Princeton University Press, 1984.

Carroll, J., *Break-Out from the Crystal Palace*, London, Routledge and Kegan Paul, 1974.

Carson, R., *Silent Spring*, Boston, Houghton Mifflin, 1962.

Carter, A., *The Political Theory of Anarchism*, London, Routledge and Kegan Paul, 1971.

Carter, A. B., *Marx: A Radical Critique*, Brighton, Wheatsheaf Books/Boulder, Westview Press, 1988.

—— *The Philosophical Foundations of Property Rights*, Hemel Hempstead, Prentice-Hall/Harvester-Wheatsheaf, 1989.

—— '"Self-exploitation" and workers' cooperatives', *Journal of Applied Philosophy*, 6, 1989: 195–9.

—— 'The right to private property', *Philosophical Books*, 31, 3, July 1990: 129–36.

—— '"Institutional exploitation" and workers' cooperatives', *The Heythrop Journal*, 33, 4, October 1992: 426–33.

—— 'Animal rights and social relations', *Res Publica: A Journal of Legal and Social Philosophy*, 1, 2, 1995: 213–20.

—— 'Infanticide and the right to life', *Ratio (new series)*, 10, 1, April 1997: 1–9.

—— 'The real politics of Karl Marx and Frederick Engels', *Studies in Marxism*, forthcoming.

—— 'Moral theory and global population', *Proceedings of the Aristotelian Society*, forthcoming.

Carter, N., 'Whatever happened to the environment? The British general election of 1992', *Environmental Politics*, 1, 3, 1992: 442–8.

—— 'Worker cooperatives and green political theory' in B. Doherty and M. de Geus (eds), *Democracy and Green Political Thought: Sustainability, Rights and Citizenship*, London, Routledge, 1996.

Casal, P. and Williams, A., 'Rights, equality and procreation', *Analyse and Kritik*, 17, 1995: 93–116.

Caudwell, C., 'A study in bourgeois illusion: liberty' in *The Concept of Freedom*, London, Lawrence and Wishart, 1977.

Chambers, R., *Rural Development: Putting the Last First*, London, Longman, 1983.

Charvet, J., 'The idea of equality as a substantive principle of society', *Political Studies*, 17, 1, 1969: 1–13.

Chomsky, N., 'Notes on anarchism' in *For Reasons of State*, New York, Vintage Books, 1973.

Clapham, C., *Third World Politics*, London, Croom Helm, 1985.

Clark, J., 'What is anarchism?', *Freedom*, 40, 3, 1979: 9–16.

—— *The Anarchist Moment: Reflections on Culture, Nature and Power*, Montreal, Black Rose Books, 1984.

—— 'Marx's inorganic body', *Environmental Ethics*, 11, 3, Fall 1989: 234–58.

—— (ed.), *Renewing the Earth: The Promise of Social Ecology*, London, Green Print, 1990.

Clark, S. R. L., 'Animal wrongs', *Analysis*, 38, 3, June 1978: 147–9.

—— 'The rights of wild things', *Inquiry*, 22, 1979: 171–88.

Clark, S. R. L., 'Gaia and the forms of life' in R. Elliot and A. Gare (eds), *Environmental Philosophy*, Milton Keynes, Open University Press, 1983.

Clarke, R., 'Technology for an alternative society' in R. Clarke (ed.), *Notes for the Future: An Alternative History of the Past Decade*, London, Thames and Hudson, 1975.

Clements, C. D., 'Stasis: the unnatural value' in R. Elliot (ed.), *Environmental Ethics*, Oxford, Oxford University Press, 1995.

Cohen, A. S., *Theories of Revolution: An Introduction*, London, Nelson, 1975.

Cohen, G. A., *Karl Marx's Theory of History: A Defence*, Oxford, Clarendon, 1978.

—— 'Capitalism, freedom and the proletariat' in A. Ryan (ed.), *The Idea of Freedom: Essays in Honour of Isaiah Berlin*, Oxford, Oxford University Press, 1979.

—— 'The labour theory of value and the concept of exploitation' in I. Steedman *et al.*, *The Value Controversy*, London, Verso, 1981.

—— 'Functional explanation, consequence explanation, and Marxism', *Inquiry*, 25, 1982: 27–56.

—— 'Review of Allen W. Wood, *Karl Marx*', *Mind*, 92, July 1983: 440–5.

—— 'Restrictive and inclusive historical materialism', *Irish Philosophical Journal*, 1, 1, Spring 1984: 3–31.

—— 'Are workers forced to sell their labor power', *Philosophy and Public Affairs*, 14, 1, Winter 1985: 99–105

—— 'The structure of proletarian unfreedom' in J. Roemer (ed.), *Analytical Marxism*, Cambridge, Cambridge University Press, 1986.

—— 'Fettering' in *History, Labour and Freedom*, Oxford, Clarendon, 1988.

—— 'On the currency of egalitarian justice', *Ethics*, 99, July 1989: 906–44.

—— 'Incentives, inequality, and community' in S. Darwall (ed.), *Equal Freedom: Selected Tanner Lectures on Human Values*, Ann Arbor, University of Michigan Press, 1995.

Cohen, J. L., 'Strategy or identity: new theoretical paradigms and contemporary social movements', *Social Research*, 52, 4, Winter 1985: 663–716.

Collier, A., 'Value, rationality and the environment', *Radical Philosophy*, 66, Spring 1994: 3–9.

Colwell, T. B., 'Ecology and philosophy' in J. Rachels and F. A. Tillman (eds), *Philosophical Issues: A Contemporary Introduction*, New York, Harper and Row, 1972.

Commoner, B., *The Closing Circle: Nature, Man, and Technology*, New York, Alfred Knopf, 1971.

—— 'Economic growth and environmental quality: how to have both' in J. P. Sterba (ed.), *Earth Ethics: Environmental Ethics, Animal Rights, and Practical Applications*, New Jersey, Prentice-Hall, 1995.

Corcoran, P. E., 'The limits of democratic theory' in G. Duncan (ed.), *Democratic Theory and Practice*, Cambridge, Cambridge University Press, 1983.

Cotgrove, S., 'Environmentalism and utopia', *Sociological Review*, 24, February 1976: 23–42.

—— *Catastrophe or Cornucopia: The Environment, Politics and the Future*, Chichester, Wiley, 1982.

Cotgrove, S. and Duff, A., 'Environmentalism, middle-class radicalism and politics', *Sociological Review*, 28, 2, 1980: 333–51.

Crisp, R., 'Values, reasons and the environment' in R. Attfield and A. Belsey (eds), *Philosophy and the Natural Environment*, Cambridge, Cambridge University Press, 1994.

Crocker, D. A., 'Hunger, capability and development' in W. Aiken and H. LaFollette (eds), *World Hunger and Morality*, New Jersey, Prentice-Hall, 1996.

Crowder, G., *Classical Anarchism: The Political Thought of Godwin, Proudhon, Bakunin and Kropotkin*, Oxford, Clarendon, 1991.

Cullity, G., 'The life-saving analogy' in W. Aiken and H. LaFollette (eds), *World Hunger and Morality*, New Jersey, Prentice-Hall, 1996.

Dahl, R. A., *A Preface to Democratic Theory*, London, University of Chicago Press, 1956.

—— *Who Governs? Democracy and Power in an American City*, New Haven, Yale University Press, 1961.

—— 'Procedural democracy' in P. Laslett and J. Fishkin (eds), *Philosophy, Politics and Society: Fifth Series*, Oxford, Blackwell, 1979.

Daly, H. E., 'The steady-state economy: toward a political economy of biophysical equilibrium and moral growth' in H. E. Daly (ed.), *Toward a Steady-State Economy*, San Francisco, W. H. Freeman, 1973.

—— 'Economics and sustainability: in defense of a steady-state economy' in M. Tobias (ed.), *Deep Ecology*, San Diego, Avant Books, 1985.

Dammann, E., *The Future in Our Hands*, Oxford, Pergamon, 1979.

Daniels, N., 'Equality of what: welfare, resources, or capabilities?', *Philosophy and Phenomenological Research*, 1, Supplement, Fall 1990: 273–96.

Davies, J. C., 'Towards a theory of revolution', *American Sociological Review*, 27, 1962: 5–19.

Davis, D. E., *Ecophilosophy: A Field Guide to the Literature*, California, R. and E. Miles, 1989.

Dearlove, J. and Saunders, P., *Introduction to British Politics: Analyzing a Capitalist Democracy*, Cambridge, Polity, 1984.

de-Shalit, A., 'Is liberalism environment-friendly?' in M. E. Zimmerman, J. B. Callicott, G. Sessions, K. J. Warren and J. Clark (eds), *Environmental Philosophy: From Animal Rights to Radical Ecology*, New Jersey, Prentice-Hall, 1998.

Devall, W. and Sessions, G. (eds), *Deep Ecology: Living as if Nature Mattered*, Salt Lake City, Peregrine Smith, 1985.

Diamond, C., 'Eating meat and eating people', *Philosophy*, 53, 1978: 456–79.

Dickens, P., *Society and Nature: Towards a Green Social Theory*, Hemel Hempstead, Harvester-Wheatsheaf, 1992.

Dickson, D., *Alternative Technology and the Politics of Technical Change*, London, Fontana, 1974.

Dietz, F. J. and Straaten, J. van der, 'Economic theories and the necessary integration of ecological insights' in A. Dobson and P. Lucardie (eds), *The Politics of Nature: Explorations in Green Political Theory*, London, Routledge, 1993.

Dobson, A., *Green Political Thought: An Introduction*, London, Unwin Hyman, 1990.

—— 'Critical theory and green politics' in A. Dobson and P. Lucardie (eds), *The Politics of Nature: Explorations in Green Political Theory*, London, Routledge, 1993.

—— 'Ecologism and the relegitimation of socialism', *Radical Philosophy*, 67, Summer 1994: 13–19.

—— 'Democratizing green theory: preconditions and principles' in B. Doherty and M. de Geus (eds), *Democracy and Green Political Thought: Sustainability, Rights and Citizenship*, London, Routledge, 1996.

Dodds, F. (ed.), *Into the Twenty-First Century: An Agenda for Political Re-alignment*, Basingstoke, Green Print, 1988.

Doherty, B., 'Green parties, nonviolence and political obligation' in B. Doherty and M. de Geus (eds), *Democracy and Green Political Thought: Sustainability, Rights and Citizenship*, London, Routledge, 1996.

Drengson, A. R., 'Shifting paradigms: from the technocratic to the person-planetary', *Environmental Ethics*, 3, 3, Fall 1980: 221–40.

Dryzek, J. S., *Rational Ecology: Environment and Political Economy*, Oxford, Blackwell, 1987.

—— 'Green reason: communicative ethics for the biosphere', *Environmental Ethics*, 12, 3, Fall 1990: 195–210.

—— 'Ecology and discursive democracy: beyond liberal capitalism and the administrative state', *Capitalism, Nature, Socialism*, 3, 2, 1992: 18–42.

—— 'Political and ecological communication', *Environmental Politics*, 4, 4, Winter 1995: 13–30.

Dummett, M., 'The reality of the past' in *Truth and Other Enigmas*, London, Duckworth, 1978.

—— 'Nuclear warfare' in N. Blake and K. Pole (eds), *Objections to Nuclear Defence: Philosophers on Deterrence*, London, Routledge and Kegan Paul, 1984.

Dunleavy, P. and O'Leary, B., *Theories of the State: The Politics of Liberal Democracy*, London, Macmillan, 1987.

Dworkin, R. M., 'Law and civil disobedience' in J. Rachels (ed.), *Moral Problems: A Collection of Philosophical Essays*, New York, Harper and Row, 1971.

—— *Taking Rights Seriously*, London, Duckworth, 1977.

—— 'What is equality? Part 1: equality of welfare', *Philosophy and Public Affairs*, 10, 3, Summer 1981: 185–246.

—— 'What is equality? Part 2: equality of resources', *Philosophy and Public Affairs*, 10, 4, Fall 1981: 283–345.

—— 'Liberalism' in M. J. Sandel (ed.), *Liberalism and its Critics*, Oxford, Blackwell, 1984.

—— 'Rights as trumps' in J. Waldron (ed.), *Theories of Rights*, Oxford, Oxford University Press, 1984.

—— 'Civil disobedience and nuclear protest' in *A Matter of Principle*, Massachusetts, Harvard University Press, 1985.

—— 'Why liberals should care about equality' in *A Matter of Principle*, Massachusetts, Harvard University Press, 1985.

—— 'Liberal community' in S. Avineri and A. de-Shalit (eds), *Communitarianism and Individualism*, Oxford, Oxford University Press, 1992.

—— 'Foundations of liberal equality' in S. Darwall (ed.), *Equal Freedom: Selected Tanner Lectures on Human Values*, Ann Arbor, University of Michigan Press, 1995.

Ecology Party, *Politics for Life*, London, The Ecology Party, 1983.

Eckersley, R., 'Divining evolution: the ecological ethics of Murray Bookchin', *Environmental Ethics*, 11, 2, Summer 1989: 99–116.

—— *Environmentalism and Political Theory: Toward an Ecocentric Approach*, London, UCL Press, 1992.

—— 'Greening liberal democracy: the rights discourse revisited' in B. Doherty and M. de Geus (eds), *Democracy and Green Political Thought: Sustainability, Rights and Citizenship*, London, Routledge, 1996.

Eder, K., 'The "new social movements": moral crusades, political pressure groups, or social movements?', *Social Research*, 52, 4, Winter 1985: 869–90.

Ehrlich, P. R., 'The population explosion: facts and fiction' in H. D. Johnson (ed.), *No Deposit–No Return: Man and His Environment*, Massachusetts, Addison-Wesley, 1970.

Ehrlich, P. R. and Holdren, J. P., 'Population and panaceas: a technological perspective' in J. P. Holdren and P. R. Ehrlich (eds), *Global Ecology: Readings Toward a Rational Strategy for Man*, New York, Harcourt Brace Jovanovich, 1971.

Ekins, P. (ed.), *The Living Economy: A New Economics in the Making*, London, Routledge, 1989.

Elgin, D., *Voluntary Simplicity*, New York, William Morrow, 1981.

Elliot, R., 'Meta-ethics and environmental ethics', *Metaphilosophy*, 16, 2 & 3, April/July 1985: 103–17.

—— 'Environmental degradation, vandalism, and the aesthetic object argument', *Australasian Journal of Philosophy*, 67, 2, June 1989: 191–204.

—— 'The rights of future people', *Journal of Applied Philosophy*, 6, 2, 1989: 159–69.

—— 'Intrinsic value, environmental obligation and naturalness', *The Monist*, 75, 2, April 1992: 138–60.

—— 'Faking nature' in R. E. Goodin (ed.), *The Politics of the Environment*, Aldershot, Edward Elgar, 1994.

Elliott, D., *The Politics of Nuclear Power*, London, Pluto, 1978.

Elliott, D. and Elliott, R., *The Control of Technology*, London, Wykeham Publications, 1976.

Elster, J., 'Sour grapes – utilitarianism and the genesis of wants' in A. Sen and B. Williams (eds), *Utilitarianism and Beyond*, Cambridge, Cambridge University Press, 1982.

—— *Making Sense of Marx*, Cambridge, Cambridge University Press, 1985.

Eltzbacher, P., *Anarchism: Exponents of the Anarchist Philosophy*, New York, Libertarian Book Club, 1960.

Emmanuel, A., 'White-settler colonialism and the myth of investment imperialism', *New Left Review*, 73, 1972: 35–57.

—— 'Myths of development versus myths of underdevelopment', *New Left Review*, 85, 1974: 61–82.

Engels, F., 'On authority' in K. Marx and F. Engels, *Selected Works in Three Volumes*, Vol. 2, Moscow, Progress Publishers, 1969.

—— *Anti-Dühring, Herr Eugen Dühring's Revolution in Science*, Peking, Foreign Languages Press, 1976.

—— *The Condition of the Working Class in England*, Harmondsworth, Penguin, 1987.

—— Letter to T. Cuno, 24 January 1872 in K. Marx and F. Engels, *Collected Works*, Vol. 44, Moscow, Progress Publishers, 1989.

Enzensberger, H. M., 'A critique of political ecology', *New left Review*, 84, 1974: 3–31.

Evans, J., 'Ecofeminism and the politics of the gendered self' in A. Dobson and P. Lucardie (eds), *The Politics of Nature: Explorations in Green Political Theory*, London, Routledge, 1993.

Feinberg, J., 'Justice and personal desert' in *Doing and Deserving: Essays in the Theory of Responsibility*, New Jersey, Princeton University Press, 1970.

—— *Social Philosophy*, New Jersey, Prentice-Hall, 1973.

—— 'The rights of animals and unborn generations' in W. T. Blackstone (ed.), *Philosophy and Environmental Crisis*, Georgia, University of Georgia Press, 1974.

Ferris, J., 'Ecological versus social rationality: can there be green social policies?' in A. Dobson and P. Lucardie (eds), *The Politics of Nature: Explorations in Green Political Theory*, London, Routledge, 1993.

Feyerabend, P., 'How to defend society against science', *Radical Philosophy*, 11, 1975: 3–8.

Finer, S. E., 'State- and nation-building in Europe: the role of the military' in C. Tilly (ed.), *The Formation of National States in Western Europe*, New Jersey, Princeton University Press, 1975.

Foreman, D., 'Earth First!' in J. P. Sterba (ed.), *Earth Ethics: Environmental Ethics, Animal Rights, and Practical Applications*, New Jersey, Prentice-Hall, 1995.

Foster-Carter, A., 'The modes of production controversy', *New Left Review*, 107, 1978: 47–77.

Foucault, M., *Discipline and Punish: The Birth of the Prison*, Harmondsworth, Penguin, 1979.

Fox, W., 'Deep ecology: a new philosophy of our time?', *The Ecologist*, 14, 5–6, 1984: 194–200.

—— 'On guiding stars to deep ecology', *The Ecologist*, 14, 5–6, 1984: 202–5.

—— 'The deep ecology-ecofeminism debate and its parallels' in M. E. Zimmerman, J. B. Callicott, G. Sessions, K. J. Warren and J. Clark (eds), *Environmental Philosophy: From Animal Rights to Radical Ecology*, New Jersey, Prentice-Hall, 1998.

Francione, G. L., 'Animal rights: an incremental approach' in R. Garner (ed.), *Animal Rights: The Changing Debate*, Basingstoke, Macmillan, 1996.

Francis, L. P. and Norman, R., 'Some animals are more equal than others', *Philosophy*, 53, 1978: 507–27.

Frank, A. G., *Capitalism and Underdevelopment in Latin America: Historical Studies of Chile and Brazil*, New York, Monthly Review Press, 1967.

—— 'The development of underdevelopment', *Monthly Review*, 41, 2, June 1989: 37–51.

Frankel, B., *The Post-Industrial Utopians*, Cambridge, Polity, 1987.

Frankena, W. K., *Ethics*, New Jersey, Prentice-Hall, 1963.

—— 'Moral philosophy and world hunger' in W. Aiken and H. LaFollette (eds), *World Hunger and Moral Obligation*, New Jersey, Prentice-Hall, 1977.

—— 'Ethics and the environment' in K. E. Goodpaster and K. M. Sayre, (eds), *Ethics and the Problems of the 21st Century*, London, University of Notre Dame Press, 1979.

Freire, P., *Pedagogy of the Oppressed*, Harmondsworth, Penguin, 1972.

Frey, R. G., 'Animal rights', *Analysis*, 37, 4, June 1977: 186–9.

—— 'Interests and animal rights', *Philosophical Quarterly*, 27, 1977: 254–9.

—— 'Autonomy and the value of animal life', *The Monist*, 70, 1987: 50–63.

—— 'Pain, amelioration, and the choice of tactics' in J. P. Sterba (ed.), *Earth Ethics: Environmental Ethics, Animal Rights, and Practical Applications*, New Jersey, Prentice-Hall, 1995.

Friends of the Earth Europe, *Towards Sustainable Europe: The Study*, London, Friends of the Earth, 1995.

Fromm, E., *The Fear of Freedom*, London, Routledge and Kegan Paul, 1960.

Fromm, E., *To Have or to Be?*, London, Sphere Books, 1979.

Gallie, W. B., 'Essentially contested concepts', *Proceedings of the Aristotelian Society*, 56, 1955–6: 167–98.

Galtung, J., *There Are Alternatives! Four Roads to Peace and Security*, Nottingham, Spokesman, 1984.

Gamble, A., *An Introduction to Modern Social and Political Thought*, London, Macmillan, 1981.

Garner, R., *Environmental Politics*, Hemel Hempstead, Harvester-Wheatsheaf, 1996.

Gaskins, R. H., *Environmental Accidents: Personal Injury and Public Responsibility*, Philadelphia, Temple University Press, 1989.

Gellner, E., 'Explanations in history' in J. O'Neill (ed.), *Modes of Individualism and Collectivism*, London, Heinemann, 1973.

George, S., *How the Other Half Dies: The Real Reasons for World Hunger*, Harmondsworth, Penguin, 1986.

—— 'Several pounds of flesh', *New Internationalist*, 189, November 1988: 18–19.

—— *A Fate Worse than Debt*, Harmondsworth, Penguin, 1990.

Georgescu-Roegen, N., 'The entropy law and the economic problem' in H. E. Daly (ed.), *Toward a Steady-State Economy*, San Francisco, W. H. Freeman, 1973.

Gendin, S., 'The use of animals in science' in J. P. Sterba (ed.), *Earth Ethics: Environmental Ethics, Animal Rights, and Practical Applications*, New Jersey, Prentice-Hall, 1995.

Gershuny, J., *After Industrial Society? The Emerging Self-Service Economy*, London, Macmillan, 1978.

Gewirth, A., 'Starvation and human rights' in K. E. Goodpaster and K. M. Sayre (eds), *Ethics and the Problems of the 21st Century*, London, University of Notre Dame Press, 1979.

Geus, M. de, 'The ecological restructuring of the state' in B. Doherty and M. de Geus (eds), *Democracy and Green Political Thought: Sustainability, Rights and Citizenship*, London, Routledge, 1996.

Geuss, R., 'Freedom as an ideal', *Proceedings of the Aristotelian Society*, Suppl. Vol. 69, 1995: 89–100.

Giddens, A., *New Rules of Sociological Method*, London, Hutchinson, 1976.

—— *A Contemporary Critique of Historical Materialism: Volume I: Power, Property and the State*, London, Macmillan, 1981.

Giddens, A. and Held, D. (eds), *Classes, Power, and Conflict: Classical and Contemporary Debates*, Basingstoke, Macmillan, 1982.

Gilbert, A., *Marx's Politics: Communists and Citizens*, Oxford, Martin Robertson, 1981.

Gilpin, R., *The Political Economy of International Relations*, New Jersey, Princeton University Press, 1987.

Glasser, H., 'Demystifying the critiques of deep ecology' in M. E. Zimmerman, J. B. Callicott, G. Sessions, K. J. Warren and J. Clark (eds), *Environmental Philosophy: From Animal Rights to Radical Ecology*, New Jersey, Prentice-Hall, 1998.

Glover, J., *Causing Death and Saving Lives*, Harmondsworth, Penguin, 1977.

Godlovitch, S., 'Icebreakers: environmentalism and natural aesthetics', *Journal of Applied Philosophy*, 11, 1, 1994: 15–30.

—— 'Things change: so whither sustainability?', *Environmental Ethics*, 20, 3, Fall 1998: 291–304.

Godwin, W., *Enquiry Concerning Political Justice and its Influence on Modern Morals and Happiness*, ed. by Isaac Kramnick, Harmondsworth, Penguin, 1976.

—— *The Anarchist Writings of William Godwin*, ed. with an intro. by P. Marshall, London, Freedom Press, 1986.

Golding, M. P., 'Obligations to future generations', *The Monist*, 56, 1972: 85–99.
Goldsmith, E., 'The way: an ecological world-view', *The Ecologist*, 18, 1988: 160–82.
Goldsmith, E. *et al.*, *A Blueprint for Survival*, Harmondsworth, Penguin, 1972.
Goodin, R. E., 'Ethical principles for environmental protection' in R. Elliot and A. Gare (eds), *Environmental Philosophy*, Milton Keynes, Open University Press, 1983.
—— 'Disarming nuclear apologists', *Inquiry*, 28, 1985: 153–76.
—— 'International ethics and the environmental crisis', *Ethics and International Affairs*, 4, 1990: 91–105.
—— *Green Political Theory*, Cambridge, Polity, 1992.
—— 'Introduction' in (ed.), *The Politics of the Environment*, Aldershot, Edward Elgar, 1994.
Goodman, P., *Compulsory Miseducation*, Harmondsworth, Penguin, 1971.
Goodpaster, K. E., 'On being morally considerable', *The Journal of Philosophy*, 75, 1978: 308–25.
—— 'From egoism to environmentalism' in K. E. Goodpaster and K. M. Sayre (eds), *Ethics and the Problems of the 21st Century*, London, University of Notre Dame Press, 1979.
Goodwin, J. and Skocpol, T., 'Explaining revolutions in the contemporary Third World', *Politics and Society*, 17, 4, 1989: 489–509.
Gore, A., 'A global Marshal Plan' in J. P. Sterba (ed.), *Earth Ethics: Environmental Ethics, Animal Rights, and Practical Applications*, New Jersey, Prentice-Hall, 1995.
Gorz, A., 'Technology, technicians and class struggle' in A. Gorz (ed.), *The Division of Labour: The Labour Process and Class-Struggle in Modern Capitalism*, Brighton, Harvester Press, 1976.
—— *Farewell to the Working Class: An Essay in Post-Industrial Socialism*, trans. M. Sonenscher, London, Pluto, 1982.
—— *Ecology as Politics*, trans. P. Vigderman and J. Cloud, London, Pluto, 1980.
Goulbourne, H. (ed.), *Politics and State in the Third World*, London, Macmillan, 1979.
Govier, T., 'What should we do about future people?', *American Philosophical Quarterly*, 16, 2, 1979: 105–13.
Graham, K. (ed.), *Contemporary Political Philosophy: Radical Studies*, Cambridge, Cambridge University Press, 1982.
—— *The Battle of Democracy: Conflict, Consensus and the Individual*, Brighton, Wheatsheaf Books, 1986.
Grand, J. le, 'Equity versus efficiency: the elusive trade-off', *Ethics*, 100, 3, April 1990: 554–68.
Gray, J., 'Political power, social theory, and essential contestability' in D. Miller and L. Siedentop (eds), *The Nature of Political Theory*, Oxford, Clarendon, 1983.
—— *Liberalism*, Milton Keynes, Open University Press, 1986.
Green Party, *Manifesto for a Sustainable Society*, London, The Green Party, 1988.
—— *Don't Let your World Turn Grey*, London, The Green Party, 1989.
Greenawalt, K., 'Justifying nonviolent disobedience' in H. A. Bedau (ed.), *Civil Disobedience in Focus*, London, Routledge, 1991.
Grundmann, R., *Marxism and Ecology*, Oxford, Clarendon, 1991.
Grünen, Die, *Programme of the German Green Party*, Preface by J. Porritt, London, Heretic Books, 1983.
Guerin, D., *Anarchism: From Theory to Practice*, New York, Monthly Review Press, 1971.

Guha, R., 'Radical American environmentalism and wilderness preservation: a Third World critique', *Environmental Ethics*, 11, 1, Spring 1989: 71–83.

Guin, U. le, *The Dispossessed*, London, Granada, 1975.

Gunn, A. S., 'Why should we care about rare species', *Environmental Ethics*, 2, 1, Spring 1980: 17–37.

Guthrie, R. D., 'Anthropocentrism' in J. P. Sterba (ed.), *Earth Ethics: Environmental Ethics, Animal Rights, and Practical Applications*, New Jersey, Prentice-Hall, 1995.

Gutman, A. (ed.), *Democracy and the Welfare State*, New Jersey, Princeton Universtiy Press, 1988.

—— 'Communitarian critics of liberalism' in S. Avineri and A. de-Shalit (eds), *Communitarianism and Individualism*, Oxford, Oxford University Press, 1992.

Habermas, J., *Towards a Rational Society*, London, Heinemann, 1971.

—— *Legitimation Crisis*, trans. T. McCarthy, London, Heinemann, 1976.

Haksar, V., 'Civil disobedience and non-cooperation' in H. A. Bedau (ed.), *Civil Disobedience in Focus*, London, Routledge, 1991.

Hampton, J., *Hobbes and the Social Contract Tradition*, Cambridge, Cambridge University Press, 1988.

—— *Political Philosophy*, Boulder, Westview, 1997.

Hardin, G., 'The tragedy of the commons' in H. E. Daly (ed.), *Toward a Steady-State Economy*, San Francisco, W. H. Freeman, 1973.

—— 'Living on a lifeboat' in J. Narveson (ed.), *Moral Issues*, Toronto, Oxford University Press, 1983.

—— 'Lifeboat ethics: the case against helping the poor' in W. Aiken and H. LaFollette (eds), *World Hunger and Moral Obligation*, New Jersey, Prentice-Hall, 1977.

Hardin, R., Mearsheimer, J. J., Dworkin, G. and Goodin, R. E. (eds), *Nuclear Deterrence: Ethics and Strategy*, Chicago, University of Chicago Press, 1985.

Harding, N., *Lenin's Political Thought: Theory and Practice in the Socialist Revolution*, London, Macmillan, 1981.

Hare, R. A., *Freedom and Reason*, Oxford, Oxford University Press, 1965.

Hargrove, E., 'Foundations of wildlife protection attitudes', *Inquiry*, 30, 1987: 3–31.

—— 'Ecological sabotage: pranks or terrorism?' in J. P. Sterba (ed.), *Earth Ethics: Environmental Ethics, Animal Rights, and Practical Applications*, New Jersey, Prentice-Hall, 1995.

Harman, G., 'Moral relativism defended', *Philosophical Review*, 84, 1975: 3–22.

—— *The Nature of Morality*, New York, Oxford University Press, 1977.

Harsanyi, J. C., 'Can the maximin principle serve as a basis for morality: a critique of John Rawls' theory', *American Political Science Review*, 69, 1975: 594–606.

—— 'Morality and the theory of rational behaviour' in A. Sen and B. Williams (eds), *Utilitarianism and Beyond*, Cambridge, Cambridge University Press, 1982.

Hart, H. L. A., 'Are there are natural rights?' in A. Quinton (ed.), *Political Philosophy*, Oxford, Oxford University Press, 1967.

Hawken, P., 'A declaration of sustainability' in M. E. Zimmerman, J. B. Callicott, G. Sessions, K. J. Warren and J. Clark (eds), *Environmental Philosophy: From Animal Rights to Radical Ecology*, New Jersey, Prentice-Hall, 1998.

Hayek, F. A., *The Constitution of Liberty*, London, Routledge and Kegan Paul, 1960.

—— 'From *Scientism and the Study of Society*' in J. O'Neill (ed.), *Modes of Individualism and Collectivism*, London, Heinemann, 1973.

Hayward, T., 'Ecosocialism–utopian and scientific', *Radical Philosophy*, 56, Autumn 1990: 2–14.

Hayward, T., 'Ecology and human emancipation', *Radical Philosophy*, 62, Autumn 1992: 3–13.

—— 'The meaning of political ecology', *Radical Philosophy*, 66, Spring 1994: 11–20.

—— *Ecological Thought: An Introduction*, Cambridge, Polity, 1995.

Hegel, G. W. F., *The Philosophy of History*, New York, Dover, 1956.

—— *Philosophy of Right*, trans. T. M. Knox, Oxford, Oxford University Press, 1967.

—— *Hegel's Phenomenology of Spirit*, trans. A. V. Miller, Oxford, Oxford University Press, 1977.

Heilbroner, R. L., *An Inquiry into the Human Prospect*, London, Calder and Boyars, 1975.

Held, D., *Models of Democracy*, Cambridge, Polity, 1987.

Heller, C., 'Toward a radical eco-feminism' in J. Clark (ed.), *Renewing the Earth: The Promise of Social Ecology*, London, Green Print, 1990.

—— 'Take back the earth' in J. P. Sterba (ed.), *Earth Ethics: Environmental Ethics, Animal Rights, and Practical Applications*, New Jersey, Prentice-Hall, 1995.

Henderson H., *Creating Alternative Futures: The End of Economics*, New York, Pedigree Books, 1980.

—— 'Coming of the solar age' in S. Kumar (ed.), *The Schumacher Lectures*, London, Blond and Briggs, 1980.

—— *The Politics of the Solar Age: Alternatives to Economics*, Indianapolis, Knowledge Systems, 1988.

Herber, L., *Our Synthetic Environment*, New York, Alfred Knopf, 1962.

Hill, E. H. Jr, 'Ideals of human excellence and preserving natural environments' in R. E. Goodin (ed.), *The Politics of the Environment*, Aldershot, Edward Elgar, 1994.

Hirsch, F., *Social Limits to Growth*, London, Routledge and Kegan Paul, 1977.

Hobbes, T., *Leviathan*, ed. R. Tuck, Cambridge, Cambridge University Press, 1991.

Holt, J., *How Children Fail*, Harmondsworth, Penguin, 1964.

Honderich, T., *Violence for Equality*, Harmondsworth, Penguin, 1980.

Honoré, A. M., 'Ownership' in A. G. Guest (ed.), *Oxford Essays in Jurisprudence*, London, Oxford University Press, 1961.

Horsburgh, H. J. N., 'Politics of non-violent action', *Inquiry*, 18, 1975: 103–12.

—— 'Reply to Kai Nielsen', *Inquiry*, 24, 1981: 59–73.

Horton, J., *Political Obligation*, Basingstoke, Macmillan, 1992.

Hubbard, F. P., 'Justice, limits to growth, and an equilibrium state', *Philosophy and Public Affairs*, 7, 4, 1977–8: 326–45.

Hubin, D. C., 'Justice and future generations', *Philosophy and Public Affairs*, 6, 1, 1976: 70–83.

Hughes, S., 'The environmental crisis' in F. Dodds (ed.), *Into the Twenty-First Century: An Agenda for Political Re-Alignment*, Basingstoke, Green Print, 1988.

Hume, D., *A Treatise of Human Nature*, ed. A. Selby-Bigge, Oxford, Clarendon, 1951.

Huntington, S. P., *Political Order in Changing Societies*, New Haven, Yale University Press, 1968.

Husami, Z. I., 'Marx on distributive justice', *Philosophy and Public Affairs*, 8, 1, Fall 1978: 42–79.

Icke, D., *It Doesn't Have to Be Like This: Green Politics Explained*, London, Green Print, 1990.

Illich, I., *Deschooling Society*, Harmondsworth, Penguin, 1971.

—— *Tools for Conviviality*, London, Fontana, 1975.

Inglehart, R., 'Post-materialism in an environment of insecurity', *The American Political Science Review*, 75, 1981: 880–900.

Irvine, S. and Ponton, A., *A Green Manifesto: Policies for a Green Future*, London, Optima, 1988.

Iyer, R., *The Moral and Political Thought of Mahatma Gandhi*, New York, Oxford University Press, 1973.

Jackson, R., *Quasi-States: Sovereignty, International Relations and the Third World*, Cambridge, Cambridge University Press, 1990.

Jacobs, M., *The Politics of the Real World: Meeting the New Century*, London, Earthscan, 1996.

Jasay, A. de, *The State*, Oxford, Blackwell, 1985.

Jessop, B., *The Capitalist State*, Oxford, Blackwell, 1984.

Joll, J., *The Anarchists*, London, Methuen, 1979.

Junk, R. C., *The Nuclear State*, London, John Calder, 1979.

Kagan, S., *The Limits of Morality*, New York, Clarendon, 1991.

Kant, I., *Fundamental Principles of the Metaphysic of Morals*, trans. T. K. Abbott, Indianapolis, Bobbs-Merrill, 1949.

—— 'An answer to the question: "What is enlightenment?"' in I. Kant, *Political Writings*, trans. H. B. Nisbet, Cambridge, Cambridge University Press, 1991.

Kavka, G. S., 'Some paradoxes of deterrence', *The Journal of Philosophy*, 75, 6, June 1978: 285–302.

—— 'The futurity problem' in E. Partridge (ed.), *Responsibilities to Future Generations: Environmental Ethics*, Buffalo, Prometheus Books, 1981.

—— 'The paradox of future individuals', *Philosophy and Public Affairs*, 11, 2, Spring 1982: 93–112.

Kavka, G. S. and Warren, V., 'Political representation for future generations' in R. Elliot and A. Gare (eds), *Environmental Philosophy*, Milton Keynes, Open University Press, 1983.

Kealey, D. A., *Revisioning Environmental Ethics*, Albany, State University of New York Press, 1990.

Kenny, A., 'Better dead than red' in N. Blake and K. Pole (eds), *Objections to Nuclear Defence: Philosophers on Deterrence*, London, Routledge and Kegan Paul, 1984.

Kheel, M., 'From heroic to holistic ethics: the ecofeminist challenge' in J. P. Sterba (ed.), *Earth Ethics: Environmental Ethics, Animal Rights, and Practical Applications*, New Jersey, Prentice-Hall, 1995.

King, M. L. Jr, 'Letter from Birmingham City Jail' in H. A. Bedau (ed.), *Civil Disobedience in Focus*, London, Routledge, 1991.

Kitchin, G., *Development and Underdevelopment in Historical Perspective: Populism, Nationalism and Industrialization*, London, Methuen, 1982.

Klosko, G., 'Presumptive benefit, fairness, and political obligation', *Philosophy and Public Affairs*, 16, 3, Summer 1987: 241–59.

—— *The Principle of Fairness and Political Obligation*, Maryland, Rowman and Littlefield, 1992

—— 'Political obligation and the natural duties of justice', *Philosophy and Public Affairs*, 23, 3, Summer 1994: 251–70.

—— 'Fixed content of political obligation', *Political Studies*, 46, 1, March 1998: 53–67.

Kohr, L., 'Appropriate technology' in S. Kumar (ed.), *The Schumacher Lectures*, London, Blond and Briggs, 1980.

Kohr, L., *The Breakdown of Nations*, foreword by I. Illich, London, Routledge and Kegan Paul, 1986.

Krasner, S. D., *Structural Conflict: The Third World against Global Liberalism*, Berkeley, University of California Press, 1985.

Kropotkin, P., *Mutual Aid: A Factor of Evolution*, Boston, Extending Horizons Books, n.d.

—— *The State: Its Historic Role*, London, Freedom Press, 1969.

—— *Kropotkin's Revolutionary Pamphlets*, ed. R. N. Baldwin, New York, Dover, 1970.

—— *Fields, Factories and Workshops Tomorrow*, London, George Allen and Unwin, 1974.

Kuhn, T. S., *The Structure of Scientific Revolutions*, Chicago, Chicago University Press, 1970.

Kukathas, C. and Pettit, P., *Rawls: A Theory of Justice and its Critics*, Cambridge, Polity, 1990.

Kumar, K., *Prophecy and Progress: The Sociology of Industrial and Post-Industrial Society*, Harmondsworth, Penguin, 1978.

Kymlicka, W., *Contemporary Political Philosophy*, Oxford, Clarendon, 1990.

—— 'Liberal individualism and liberal neutrality' in S. Avineri and A. de-Shalit (eds), *Communitarianism and Individualism*, Oxford, Oxford University Press, 1992.

Lacey, C., 'Towards a general framework for a new curriculum and pedagogy: progress towards a socialist education' in C. Lacey and R. Williams (eds), *Education, Ecology and Development: The Case for an Education Network*, London, World Wildlife Fund/Kogan Page, 1987.

Lackey, D. P., 'Missiles and morals: a utilitarian look at nuclear deterrence', *Philosophy and Public Affairs*, 11, 3, Summer 1982: 189–231.

Laclau, E., 'Feudalism and capitalism in Latin America', *New Left Review*, 67, 1971: 19–38.

LaFollette, H. and May, L., 'Suffer the little children' in W. Aiken and H. LaFollette (eds), *World Hunger and Morality*, New Jersey, Prentice-Hall, 1996.

Landauer, G., *For Socialism*, trans. D. J. Parent, St. Louis, Telos Press, 1978.

Lappé, F. M., *Diet for a Small Planet*, New York, Ballantine, 1971.

Lappé, F. M. and Collins, J., *Food First*, London, Abacus, 1982.

Leahy, M., 'Brute equivocation' in M. Leahy and D. Cohn-Sherbok (eds), *The Liberation Debate: Rights at Issue*, London, Routledge, 1996.

Lee, D. C., 'On the Marxian view of the relationship between man and nature', *Environmental Ethics*, 2, 1, Spring 1980: 3–16.

—— 'Toward a Marxian ecological ethic: a response to two critics', *Environmental Ethics*, 4, 4, Winter 1982: 339–43.

Lee, K., *Social Philosophy and Ecological Scarcity*, London, Routledge, 1989.

—— 'To de-industrialize – is it so irrational?' in A. Dobson and P. Lucardie (eds), *The Politics of Nature: Explorations in Green Political Theory*, London, Routledge, 1993.

Lenin, V. I., *The Immediate Tasks of the Soviet Government*, Moscow, Progress Publishers, 1970.

—— *The State and Revolution*, Peking, Foreign Languages Press, 1973.

—— *Imperialism, the Highest Stage of Capitalism: A Popular Outline*, Peking, Foreign Languages Press, 1975.

Lenin, V. I., *Left-Wing Communism, An Infantile Disorder*, Peking, Foreign Languages Press, 1975.

—— *What Is to Be Done?*, Peking, Foreign Languages Press, 1975.

Lenin, V. I., *One Step Forward, Two Steps Back: The Crisis in Our Party*, Peking, Foreign Languages Press, 1976.

Leopold, A., 'The land ethic' in *A Sand County Almanac*, San Francisco, Sierra Club/Ballantine, 1970.

Leys, C., 'Capital accumulation, class formation and dependency – the significance of the Kenyan case' in R. Miliband and J. Saville (eds), *The Socialist Register 1978*, London, Merlin, 1978.

—— 'Samuel Huntington and the end of classical modernization theory' in H. Alavi and T. Shanin (eds), *Introduction to the Sociology of 'Developing Societies'*, London, Macmillan, 1982.

Linton, M. and Curtice, J., 'Rising from nowhere to be prime outside contenders', *Guardian*, 20 June 1989.

Linzey, A., 'For animal rights' in M. Leahy and D. Cohn-Sherbok (eds), *The Liberation Debate: Rights at Issue*, London, Routledge, 1996.

Lively, J., *Democracy*, Oxford, Blackwell, 1975.

Locke, J., *Two Treatises of Government*, London, Dent, 1924.

Lovins, A. B., *Soft Energy Paths*, New York, Harper and Row, 1979.

Lowe, P. and Worboys, M., 'Ecology and the end of ideology', *Antipode*, 10, 2, August 1978: 12–21.

Lucardie, P., 'Why would egocentrists become ecocentrists? On individualism and holism in green political theory' in A. Dobson and P. Lucardie (eds), *The Politics of Nature: Explorations in Green Political Theory*, London, Routledge, 1993.

Lucas, J. R., 'Against equality', *Philosophy*, 40, 1965: 296–307.

—— 'Because you are a woman', *Philosophy*, 48, 1973: 161–71.

—— 'Against equality again' in W. Letwin (ed.), *Against Equality: Readings on Economic and Social Policy*, London, Macmillan, 1983.

Lukács, G., *History and Class Consciousness*, London, Merlin, 1971.

Lukes, S. M., *Individualism*, Oxford, Blackwell, 1973.

—— *Power: A Radical View*, London, Macmillan, 1974.

—— 'Socialism and equality' in *Essays in Social Theory*, London, Macmillan, 1977.

MacCallum, G. C. Jr., 'Negative and positive freedom' in P. Laslett, W. G. Runciman and Q. Skinner (eds), *Philosophy, Politics and Society: Fourth Series*, Oxford, Blackwell, 1972.

McCloskey, H. J., 'Rights', *Philosophical Quarterly*, 15, 59, April 1965: 115–27.

—— 'Ecological ethics and its justification: a critical appraisal' in D. S. Mannison, M. A. McRobbie and R. Routley (eds), *Environmental Philosophy*, Canberra, Australian National University, 1980.

MacIntyre, A., *After Virtue: A Study in Moral Theory*, London, Duckworth, 1981.

McLaren, D., *Soils and Sustainability*, London, Friends of the Earth, 1994.

McLaren, D., Bullock, S. and Yousuf, N., *Tomorrow's World: Britain's Share in a Sustainable Future*, London, Friends of the Earth/Earthscan, 1998.

McLellan, D., *Karl Marx: His Life and Thought*, St. Albans, Granada, 1973.

McMahan, J., 'Problems of population theory', *Ethics*, 92, 1, October 1981: 96–127.

McMichael, P., Petras, J. and Rhodes, R., 'Imperialism and the contradictions of development', *New Left Review*, 85, 1974: 83–104.

Macpherson, C. B., *The Life and Times of Liberal Democracy*, Oxford, Oxford University Press, 1977.

Madeley, J., 'Does economic development feed people', *The Ecologist*, 15, 1985: 36–41.

Malatesta, E., *Anarchy*, London, Freedom Press, 1974.

Mandelbaum, M., 'Societal laws' in J. O'Neill (ed.), *Modes of Individualism and Collectivism*, London, Heinemann, 1973.

Manes, C., 'Ecotage' in M. E. Zimmerman, J. B. Callicott, G. Sessions, K. J. Warren and J. Clark (eds), *Environmental Philosophy: From Animal Rights to Radical Ecology*, New Jersey, Prentice-Hall, 1998.

Mann, M., 'The global future of the nation-state', revised version of a paper presented at the conference on 'The Direction of Contemporary Capitalism', University of Sussex, 26–28 April 1996.

Mannheim, K., *Ideology and Utopia*, London, Routledge and Kegan Paul, 1960.

Manor, J., 'Politics and the neo-liberals' in C. Colclough and J. Manor (eds), *States or Markets? Neo-liberalism and the Development Policy Debate*, Oxford, Clarendon, 1991.

—— 'Introduction' in J. Manor (ed.), *Rethinking Third World Politics*, London, Longman, 1991.

Mansbridge, J. J., *Beyond Adversary Democracy*, Chicago, University of Chicago Press, 1983.

Marcuse, H., *One-Dimensional Man*, London, Sphere, 1972.

Marglin, S. A., 'What do bosses do? The origins and functions of hierarchy in capitalist production' in A. Gorz (ed.), *The Division of Labour: The Labour Process and Class-Struggle in Modern Capitalism*, Brighton, Harvester Press, 1976.

Marshall, P., 'Human nature and anarchism' in D. Goodway (ed.), *For Anarchism: History, Theory, and Practice*, London, Routledge, 1989.

—— *Nature's Web: An Exploration of Ecological Thinking*, London, Simon and Schuster, 1992.

—— *Demanding the Impossible: A History of Anarchism*, London, Fontana, 1993.

Martell, L., *Ecology and Society: An Introduction*, Cambridge, Polity, 1994.

Martin, M., 'Ecosabotage and civil disobedience', *Environmental Ethics*, 12, 4, Winter 1990: 291–310.

Marx, K., 'The nationalization of the land' in K. Marx and F. Engels, *Selected Works in Three Volumes*, Vol. 2, Moscow, Progress Publishers, 1969.

—— *The First International and After*, Harmondsworth, Penguin, 1974.

—— *Early Writings*, intro. L. Colletti, trans. R. Livingstone and G. Benton, Harmondsworth, Penguin, 1975.

—— *Capital*, Vol. I, trans. B. Fowkes, Harmondsworth, Penguin, 1976.

—— 'The results of the immediate process of production', appended to *Capital*, Vol. I, trans. B. Fowkes, Harmondsworth, Penguin, 1976.

—— *Selected Writings*, ed. D. McLellan, Oxford, Oxford University Press, 1977.

—— *The Poverty of Philosophy*, Peking, Foreign Languages Press, 1978.

—— *Capital*, Vol. III, trans. D. Fernbach, Harmondsworth, Penguin, 1981.

Marx, K. and Engels, F., *Selected Works in One Volume*, London, Lawrence and Wishart, 1970.

—— *Collected Works*, Vol. 44, Moscow, Progress, 1989.

Mathews, F., 'Value in nature and meaning in life' in R. Elliot (ed.), *Environmental Ethics*, Oxford, Oxford University Press, 1995.

Meadows, D. H., Meadows, D. L., Randers, J. and Behrens, W. W., *The Limits to Growth: A Report for the Club of Rome's Project on the Predicament of Mankind*, London, Earth Island, 1972.

Measor, N., 'Games theory and the nuclear arms race' in P. Singer (ed.), *Applied Ethics*, Oxford, Oxford University Press, 1986.

Mellor, M., *Breaking the Boundaries: Towards a Feminist Green Socialism*, London, Virago, 1992.

—— 'Green politics: ecofeminist, ecofeminine or ecomasculine?', *Environmental Politics*, 1, 2, 1992: 229–51.

Melotti, U., *Marx and the Third World*, trans. P. Ransford, London, Macmillan, 1977.

Melucci, A., 'The symbolic challenge of contemporary movements', *Social Research*, 52, 4, Winter 1985: 789–816.

Melville, K., *Communes in the Counter-Culture*, New York, Morrow Quill, 1979.

Merrill, R., 'Toward a self-sustaining agriculture' in R. Merrill (ed.), *Radical Agriculture*, New York, Harper and Row, 1976.

Middleton, J. and Tait, D. (eds), *Tribes Without Rulers: Studies in African Segmentary Systems*, London, Routledge and Kegan Paul, 1970.

Midgley, M., 'Duties concerning islands' in R. Elliot and A. Gare (eds), *Environmental Philosophy*, Milton Keynes, Open University Press, 1983.

—— 'The mixed community' in J. P. Sterba (ed.), *Earth Ethics: Environmental Ethics, Animal Rights, and Practical Applications*, New Jersey, Prentice-Hall, 1995.

Miliband, R., *The State in Capitalist Society*, London, Quartet, 1973.

—— *Marxism and Politics*, Oxford, Oxford University Press, 1977.

Mill, J. S., *Utilitarianism, On Liberty and Essay on Bentham*, ed. M. Warnock, London, Fontana, 1962.

Miller, D., *Social Justice*, Oxford, Oxford University Press, 1979.

—— 'The competitive model of democracy' in G. Duncan (ed.), *Democratic Theory and Practice*, Cambridge, Cambridge University Press, 1983.

—— *Anarchism*, London, Dent, 1984.

Miller, P., 'Value as richness', *Environmental Ethics*, 4, 2, Summer 1982: 101–14.

Mishan, E. J., 'The postwar literature on externalities: an interpretative essay' in R. E. Goodin (ed.), *The Politics of the Environment*, Aldershot, Edward Elgar, 1994.

Montagu, A., *Learning Non-Aggression*, Oxford, Oxford University Press, 1978.

Moore, G. E., 'The conception of intrinsic value' in J. Rachels (ed.), *Ethical Theory 1: The Question of Objectivity*, Oxford, Oxford University Press, 1998.

Morreall, J., 'The justifiability of violent civil disobedience' in H. A. Bedau (ed.), *Civil Disobedience in Focus*, London, Routledge, 1991.

Morris, W., *News from Nowhere*, London, Routledge and Kegan Paul, 1970.

Mortimore, G. W., 'An ideal of equality', *Mind*, 77, 1968: 222–42.

Mulhall, S. and Swift, A., *Liberals and Communitarians*, 2nd ed., Oxford, Blackwell, 1992.

Murray, R., 'The internationalization of capital and the nation state', *New Left Review*, 67, 1971: 84–109.

Myers, N. (ed.), *The Gaia Atlas of Planet Management*, London, Pan, 1985.

Naess, A., 'The shallow and the deep, long-range ecology movement: a summary', *Inquiry*, 16, 1973: 95–100.

—— 'A defence of the deep ecology movement', *Environmental Ethics*, 6, 3, Fall 1984: 265–70.

—— 'Intuition, intrinsic value and deep ecology', *The Ecologist*, 14, 5–6, 1984: 201–3.

Naess, A., 'Identification as a source of deep ecological attitudes' in M. Tobias (ed.), *Deep Ecology*, San Diego, Avant Books, 1985.

—— 'Basics of deep ecology', *Resurgence*, 126, 1988: 4–7.

—— 'The deep ecological movement: some philosophical aspects' in M. E. Zimmerman, J. B. Callicott, G. Sessions, K. J. Warren and J. Clark (eds), *Environmental Philosophy: From Animal Rights to Radical Ecology*, New Jersey, Prentice-Hall, 1998.

Nagel, E., *The Structure of Science: Problems in the Logic of Scientific Explanation*, London, Routledge and Kegan Paul, 1961.

Nagel, T., *The Possibility of Altruism*, New Jersey, Princeton University Press, 1970.

—— 'Poverty and food: why charity is not enough' in P. G. Brown and H. Shue (eds), *Food Policy: The Responsibility of the United States in the Life and Death Choices*, New York, The Free Press, 1977.

—— 'Equality' in *Mortal Questions*, Cambridge, Cambridge University Press, 1979.

—— 'The limits of objectivity' in S. M. McMurrin, *The Tanner Lectures on Human Values*, Vol. I, Salt Lake City, University of Utah Press, 1980.

—— 'The fragmentation of value' in J. Rachels (ed.), *Ethical Theory 2: Theories About How We Should Live*, Oxford, Oxford University Press, 1998.

Narveson, J., 'Utilitarianism and new generations', *Mind*, 76, 1967: 62–72.

—— 'Moral problems of population', *The Monist*, 57, 1973: 62–86.

—— 'Pacifism: a philosophical analysis' in J. Rachels (ed.), *Moral Problems: A Collection of Philosophical Essays*, New York, Harper and Row, 1971.

—— 'Morality and starvation' in W. Aiken and H. LaFollette (eds), *World Hunger and Moral Obligation*, New Jersey, Prentice-Hall, 1977.

Nell [O'Neill], O., 'Lifeboat Earth', *Philosophy and Public Affairs*, 4, 3, 1975: 271–97.

Nickel, J. W., 'A human rights approach to world hunger' in W. Aiken and H. LaFollette (eds), *World Hunger and Morality*, New Jersey, Prentice-Hall, 1996.

Nielsen, K., 'On justifying violence', *Inquiry*, 24, 1981: 21–57.

Norman, R., *Free and Equal*, Oxford, Oxford University Press, 1987.

Norton, B., 'Environmental ethics and nonhuman rights', *Environmental Ethics*, 4, 1, Spring 1982: 17–36.

—— 'Environmental problems and future generations', *Environmental Ethics*, 4, 4, Winter 1982: 319–37.

—— 'Environmental ethics and weak anthropocentrism', *Environmental Ethics*, 6, 2, Summer 1984: 139–48.

Nozick, R., 'Coercion' in P. Laslett, W. G. Runciman and Q. Skinner (eds), *Philosophy, Politics and Society: Fourth Series*, Oxford, Blackwell, 1972.

—— *Anarchy, State and Utopia*, New York, Basic Books, 1974.

Nuttall, J., *Bomb Culture*, London, Paladin, 1970.

Oakeshott, M., 'Political education' in P. Laslett (ed.), *Philosophy, Politics and Society: First Series*, Oxford, Blackwell, 1967.

O'Connor, J., 'Socialism and Ecology' in M. E. Zimmerman, J. B. Callicott, G. Sessions, K. J. Warren and J. Clark (eds), *Environmental Philosophy: From Animal Rights to Radical Ecology*, New Jersey, Prentice-Hall, 1998.

Odum, E. P., *Ecology and our Endangered Life-Support Systems*, Massachusetts, Sinauer, 1989.

Offe, C., *Contradictions of the Welfare State*, ed. J. Keane, London, Hutchinson, 1984.

Offe, C., 'New social movements: challenging the boundaries of institutional politics', *Social Research*, 52, 4, Winter 1985: 817–68.

O'Neill, J. (ed.), *Modes of Individualism and Collectivism*, London, Heinemann, 1973.

O'Neill, J. F., 'The varieties of intrinsic value', *The Monist*, 75, 2, April 1992: 119–37.

—— *Ecology, Policy and Politics: Human Well-Being and the Natural World*, London, Routledge, 1993.

—— 'Humanism and nature', *Radical Philosophy*, 66, Spring 1994: 21–9.

O'Neill, O., 'How do we know when opportunities are equal?' in J. English (ed.), *Sex Equality*, New Jersey, Prentice-Hall, 1977.

—— *Faces of Hunger: An Essay on Poverty, Justice and Development*, London, Allen and Unwin, 1986.

—— 'Ending world hunger' in W. Aiken and H. LaFollette (eds), *World Hunger and Morality*, New Jersey, Prentice-Hall, 1996.

—— 'Consistency in action' in J. Rachels (ed.), *Ethical Theory 2: Theories About How We Should Live*, Oxford, Oxford University Press, 1998.

Ophuls, W., *Ecology and the Politics of Scarcity: Prologue to a Political Theory of the Steady State*, San Francisco, W. H. Freeman, 1977.

Oppenheimer, F., *The State*, trans. J. Gitterman, Montreal, Black Rose, 1975.

O'Riordan, T., *Environmentalism*, London, Pion, 1981.

Osmond, J. and Graham, A., *Alternatives: New Approaches to Health, Education, Energy, the Family and the Aquarian Age*, Wellingborough, Thorsons, 1984.

Ostergaard, G., 'Indian anarchism: the curious case of Vinoba Bhave, anarchist "Saint of the Government"' in D. Goodway (ed.), *For Anarchism: History, Theory, and Practice*, London, Routledge, 1989.

Paehlke, R. C., 'Democracy, bureaucracy, and environmentalism', *Environmental Ethics*, 10, 4, Winter 1988: 291–308.

—— *Environmentalism and the Future of Progressive Politics*, New Haven, Yale University Press, 1989.

Page, T., 'The conservation criterion' in R. E. Goodin (ed.), *The Politics of the Environment*, Aldershot, Edward Elgar, 1994.

Panitch, L., 'Globalization and the state' in R. Miliband and L. Panitch (eds), *Socialist Register 1994: Between Globalism and Nationalism*, London, Merlin, 1994.

Parfit, D., 'On doing the best for our children' in M. D. Bayles (ed.), *Ethics and Population*, Massachusetts, Schenkman, 1976.

—— 'Future generations: further problems', *Philosophy and Public Affairs*, 11, 2, Spring 1981: 111–72.

—— 'Overpopulation and the quality of life' in P. Singer (ed.), *Applied Ethics*, Oxford, Oxford University Press, 1986.

—— *Reasons and Persons*, Oxford, Clarendon, 1987.

—— 'Acts and outcomes: a response to Boonin-Vail', *Philosophy and Public Affairs*, 25, 4, Fall 1996: 308–17.

—— 'Later selves and moral principles' in J. Rachels (ed.), *Ethical Theory 2: Theories About How We Should Live*, Oxford, Oxford University Press, 1998.

Parkin, F., *Marxism and Class Theory: A Bourgeois Critique*, London, Tavistock, 1981.

Parkin, S., *Green Parties: An International Guide*, London, Heretic Books, 1989.

—— 'I love you green', *Resurgence*, 136, 1989: 4–5.

Passmore, J., 'Attitudes to nature' in R. S. Peters (ed.), *Nature and Conduct*, London, Macmillan, 1975.

Passmore, J., *Man's Responsibility for Nature: Ecological Problems and Western Traditions*, London, Duckworth, 1980.

Pateman, C., *Participation and Democratic Theory*, Cambridge, Cambridge University Press, 1970.

—— *The Problem of Political Obligation: A Critique of Liberal Theory*, Cambridge, Polity, 1985.

Patterson, A. and Theobald, K. S., 'Local Agenda 21, Compulsory Competitive Tendering and local environmental practices', *Local Environment*, 1, 1, February 1996: 7–19.

Pearce, D., Markandya, A. and Barbier, E. B., *Blueprint for a Green Economy*, London, Earthscan, 1989.

Pepper, D., *The Roots of Modern Environmentalism*, London, Routledge, 1989.

—— 'The basis of a radical curriculum in environmental education' in C. Lacey and R. Williams (eds), *Education, Ecology and Development: The Case for an Education Network*, London, World Wildlife Fund/Kogan Page, 1987.

—— *Eco-Socialism: From Deep Ecology to Social Justice*, London, Routledge, 1993.

—— *Modern Environmentalism: An Introduction*, London, Routledge, 1996.

Pettit, P., *Judging Justice: An Introduction to Contemporary Political Philosophy*, London, Routledge, 1980.

Phillips Griffiths, A., 'How can one person represent another?', *Proceedings of the Aristotelian Society*, Suppl. Vol. 34, 1960: 185–208.

Plamenatz, J., *Man and Society*, 2 Vols, London, Longman, 1963.

—— *German Marxism and Russian Communism*, London, Greenwood, 1975.

Plant, R., *Modern Political Thought*, Oxford, Blackwell, 1991.

Plumwood [Routley], V., 'Ecofeminism: an overview and discussion of positions and arguments', *Australasian Journal of Philosophy*, Supplement to Vol. 64, June 1986: 120–38.

—— 'Women, humanity and nature', *Radical Philosophy*, 48, Spring 1988: 16–24.

—— 'Nature, self and gender: feminism, environmental philosophy, and the critique of rationalism' in R. Elliot (ed.), *Environmental Ethics*, Oxford, Oxford University Press, 1995.

Pogge, T., *Realizing Rawls*, New York, Cornell University Press, 1989.

—— 'An egalitarian law of peoples', *Philosophy and Public Affairs*, 23, 3, Summer 1994: 195–224.

Polsby, N. W., *Community, Power and Political Theory*, New Haven, Yale University Press, 1963.

Popper, K. R., *Conjectures and Refutations: The Growth of Scientific Knowledge*, London, Routledge and Kegan Paul, 1972.

Porritt, J., *Seeing Green: The Politics of Ecology Explained*, Oxford, Blackwell, 1984.

Porritt, J. and Winner, D., *The Coming of the Greens*, London, Fontana, 1988.

Poulantzas, N., *Political Power and Social Classes*, London, New Left Books, 1973.

—— *Fascism and Dictatorship: The Third International and the Problem of Fascism*, London, Verso, 1974.

—— *Classes in Contemporary Capitalism*, London, Verso, 1978.

Pratt, B. and Boyden, J. (eds), *The Field Directors' Handbook: An Oxfam Manual for Development Workers*, Oxford, Oxford University Press, 1985.

Proudhon, P.-J., *What is Property? An Inquiry into the Principle of Right and of Government*, New York, Dover, 1970.

Prout, C., *Market Socialism in Yugoslavia*, Oxford, Oxford University Press, 1985.

Quarrie, J. (ed.), *Earth Summit 1992: The United Nations Conference on Environment and Development*, intro. by Boutros Boutros-Ghali, London, Regency, 1992.
Quinton, A. (ed.), *Political Philosophy*, Oxford, Oxford University Press, 1967.
Rachels, J., 'Killing and starving to death' in J. Narveson (ed.), *Moral Issues*, Toronto, Oxford University Press, 1983.
—— (ed.), *Ethical Theory 1: The Question of Objectivity*, Oxford, Oxford University Press, 1998.
—— (ed.), *Ethical Theory 2: Theories About How We Should Live*, Oxford, Oxford University Press, 1998.
Rainbow, S. L., 'Why did New Zealand and Tasmania spawn the world's first green parties?', *Environmental Politics*, 1, 3, 1992: 321–46.
Rawls, J., 'Outline of a decision procedure for ethics', *Philosophical Review*, 60, 1951: 177–97.
—— 'Justice as fairness' in P. Laslett and W. G. Runciman, *Philosophy, Politics and Society: Second Series*, Oxford, Basil Blackwell, 1962.
—— 'Constitutional liberty and the concept of justice' in C. J. Friedrich and J. W. Chapman (eds), *NOMOS VI: Justice*, New York, Atherton Press, 1963.
—— 'Legal obligation and the duty of fair play' in S. Hook (ed.), *Law and Philosophy*, New York, New York University Press, 1964.
—— 'Two concepts of rules' in P. Foot (ed.), *Theories of Ethics*, Oxford, Oxford University Press, 1967.
—— 'Distributive justice' in P. Laslett and W. G. Runciman (eds), *Philosophy, Politics and Society: Third Series*, Oxford, Blackwell, 1969.
—— 'The sense of justice' in J. Feinberg (ed.), *Moral Concepts*, Oxford, Oxford University Press, 1969.
—— *A Theory of Justice*, Massachusetts, Harvard University Press, 1971.
—— 'The justification of civil disobedience' in J. Rachels (ed.), *Moral Problems: A Collection of Philosophical Essays*, New York, Harper and Row, 1971.
—— 'Fairness to goodness', *Philosophical Review*, 84, 1975: 536–54.
—— 'The basic structure as subject' in A. I. Goldman and J. Kim (eds), *Values and Morals: Essays in Honor of William Frankena, Charles Stevenson, and Richard Brandt*, Dordrecht, D. Reidel, 1978.
—— 'A well-ordered society' in P. Laslett and J. Fishkin (eds), *Philosophy, Politics and Society: Fifth Series*, Oxford, Blackwell, 1979.
—— 'Kantian constructivism in moral theory', *The Journal of Philosophy*, 77, 9, September 1980: 515–72.
—— 'Social unity and primary goods' in A. Sen and B. Williams (eds), *Utilitarianism and Beyond*, Cambridge, Cambridge University Press, 1982.
—— 'The priority of right and ideas of the good', *Philosophy and Public Affairs*, 17, 4, Fall 1988: 251–76.
—— 'Justice as fairness: political not metaphysical' in S. Avineri and A. de-Shalit (eds), *Communitarianism and Individualism*, Oxford, Oxford University Press, 1992.
—— 'The law of peoples' in S. Shute and S. Hurley (eds), *On Human Rights: The Oxford Amnesty Lectures 1993*, New York, Basic Books, 1993.
—— *Political Liberalism*, New York, Columbia University Press, 1996.
Ray, D. L., 'Acid rain' in J. P. Sterba (ed.), *Earth Ethics: Environmental Ethics, Animal Rights, and Practical Applications*, New Jersey, Prentice-Hall, 1995.
Raz, J., *The Morality of Freedom*, Oxford, Clarendon, 1988.

Raz, J., 'Civil disobedience' in H. A. Bedau (ed.), *Civil Disobedience in Focus*, London, Routledge, 1991.

Redclift, M., *Development and the Environmental Crisis: Red or Green Alternatives?*, London, Methuen, 1984.

—— 'Learning from the environmental crisis in the South' in C. Lacey and R. Williams (eds), *Education, Ecology and Development: The Case for an Education Network*, London, World Wildlife Fund/Kogan Page, 1987.

—— *Sustainable Development: Exploring the Contradictions*, London, Routledge and Kegan Paul, 1987.

Rees, J., *Equality*, London, Macmillan, 1971.

Regan, D. H., 'Duties of preservation' in R. E. Goodin (ed.), *The Politics of the Environment*, Aldershot, Edward Elgar, 1994.

Regan, T., 'Animal rights, human wrongs', *Environmental Ethics*, 2, 2, Summer 1980: 99–120.

—— 'The nature and possibility of an environmental ethic', *Environmental Ethics*, 3, 1, Spring 1981: 19–34.

—— 'The case for animal rights' in P. Singer (ed.), *In Defence of Animals*, Oxford, Blackwell, 1985.

—— 'Does environmental ethics rest on a mistake?', *The Monist*, 75, 2, April 1992: 161–82.

Reich, C., *The Greening of America*, Harmondsworth, Penguin, 1972.

Reville, R., 'The ghost at the feast', *Science*, 186, 4146, 15 November 1974: 589.

Ritter, A., *Anarchism: A Theoretical Analysis*, Cambridge, Cambridge University Press, 1980.

Roberts, M., 'Analytical Marxism – an ex-paradigm? The odyssey of G. A. Cohen', *Radical Philosophy*, 82, March/April 1997: 17–28.

Robertson, J., *The Sane Alternative: A Choice of Futures*, Oxfordshire, James Robertson, 1983.

Rodman, J., 'The liberation of nature?', *Inquiry*, 20, 1977: 83–145.

Roemer, J., *A General Theory of Exploitation and Class*, Massachusetts, Harvard University Press, 1982.

—— 'New directions in the Marxian theory of exploitation and class', in John Roemer (ed.), *Analytical Marxism* (Cambridge: Cambridge University Press), 1986.

Rollin, B. E., 'Environmental ethics and international justice' in J. P. Sterba (ed.), *Earth Ethics: Environmental Ethics, Animal Rights, and Practical Applications*, New Jersey, Prentice-Hall, 1995.

Rolston III, H. 'Is there an ecological ethic?', *Ethics*, 85, 1974–5: 93–109.

—— 'Are values in nature subjective or objective?' in R. Elliot and A. Gare (eds), *Environmental Philosophy*, Milton Keynes, Open University Press, 1983.

—— 'Values gone wild', *Inquiry*, 26, 1983: 181–207.

—— 'Duties to endangered species' in R. Elliot (ed.), *Environmental Ethics*, Oxford, Oxford University Press, 1995.

—— 'Feeding people versus saving nature' in W. Aiken and H. LaFollette (eds), *World Hunger and Morality*, New Jersey, Prentice-Hall, 1996.

—— 'Challenges in environmental ethics' in M. E. Zimmerman, J. B. Callicott, G. Sessions, K. J. Warren and J. Clark (eds), *Environmental Philosophy: From Animal Rights to Radical Ecology*, New Jersey, Prentice-Hall, 1998.

Rootes, C. A., 'Environmentalism and political competition: the British Greens in the 1989 elections to the European Parliament', *Politics*, 11, 2, 1991: 39–44.

Rootes, C. A., 'The British Green Party: from marginality to triumph to marginality', paper presented at the Joint Sessions of the European Consortium for Political Research, University of Essex, March 1991.

—— 'The new politics and the new social movements in Britain', paper presented at the Political Studies Association Annual Conference, University of Lancaster, 1991.

Rose, C., 'Two million green votes', *Econews*, August/September 1989.

Rosen, F., 'Basic needs and justice', *Mind*, 86, 1977: 88–94.

Rosenberg, A., *Philosophy of Social Science*, Oxford, Clarendon, 1988.

Roszak, T., *The Making of a Counter Culture*, London, Faber, 1971.

—— *Person/Planet: The Creative Disintegration of Industrial Society*, London, Paladin, 1981.

Rousseau, J. J., *Du Contrat Social ou Principles du Droit Politique*, intro. by C. E. Vaughan, Manchester, The University Press, 1918.

Routley [Sylvan], R., 'Is there a need for a new, an environmental, ethic?', *Proceeding of the XV World Congress of Philosophy*, Vol. 1, Sofia, 1973: 205–10.

—— 'Roles and limits of paradigms in environmental thought and action' in R. Elliot and A. Gare (eds), *Environmental Philosophy*, Milton Keynes, Open University Press, 1983.

—— 'On the alleged inconsistency, moral insensitivity and fanaticism of pacifism', *Inquiry*, 27, 1984: 117–48.

Routley [Sylvan], R. and Routley [Plumwood], V., 'Nuclear energy and obligations to the future', *Inquiry*, 21, 1978: 133–79.

—— 'Against the inevitability of human chauvinism' in K. E. Goodpaster and K. M. Sayre (eds), *Ethics and the Problems of the 21st Century*, London, University of Notre Dame Press, 1979.

—— 'Social theories, self management, and environmental problems' in D. S. Mannison, M. A. McRobbie and R. Routley (eds), *Environmental Philosophy*, Canberra, Australian National University, 1980.

Routley [Plumwood], V., 'Critical notice of John Passmore, *Man's Responsibility for Nature*', *Australasian Journal of Philosophy*, 53, 2, August 1975: 171–85.

—— 'On Karl Marx as an environmental hero', *Environmental Ethics*, 3, 3, Fall 1981: 237–44.

Rowbotham, S., Segal, L. and Wainwright, H., *Beyond the Fragments: Feminism and the Making of Socialism*, London, Merlin, 1979.

Roxborough, I., *Theories of Development*, London, Macmillan, 1979.

Ryan, A., *The Philosophy of the Social Sciences*, London, Macmillan, 1970.

Ryle, G., *The Concept of Mind*, Harmondsworth, Penguin, 1963.

Ryle, M., *The Politics of Nuclear Disarmament*, London, Pluto, 1981.

—— *Ecology and Socialism*, London, Radius, 1988.

Sabine, G. H. and Thorson, T. L., *A History of Political Theory*, Illinois, Dryden, 1973.

Sagoff, M., 'On preserving the natural environment' in R. E. Goodin (ed.), *The Politics of the Environment*, Aldershot, Edward Elgar, 1994.

—— 'Animal liberation and environmental ethics: bad marriage, quick divorce' in J. P. Sterba (ed.), *Earth Ethics: Environmental Ethics, Animal Rights, and Practical Applications*, New Jersey, Prentice-Hall, 1995.

—— 'Can environmentalists be liberals?' in R. Elliot (ed.), *Environmental Ethics*, Oxford, Oxford University Press, 1995.

Sahlins, M., *Stone Age Economics*, London, Tavistock Publications, 1974.

Sale, K., *Human Scale*, London, Secker and Warburg, 1980.

—— *Dwellers in the Land: The Bioregional Vision*, San Francisco, Sierra Book Club, 1985.

—— 'Bioregionalism – a new way to treat the land' in R. E. Goodin (ed.), *The Politics of the Environment*, Aldershot, Edward Elgar, 1994.

Salleh, A. K., 'Deeper than deep ecology: the eco-feminist connection', *Environmental Ethics*, 6, 4, Winter 1984: 339–45.

—— 'Working with nature: reciprocity or control?' in M. E. Zimmerman, J. B. Callicott, G. Sessions, K. J. Warren and J. Clark (eds), *Environmental Philosophy: From Animal Rights to Radical Ecology*, New Jersey, Prentice-Hall, 1998.

Sandbach, F., 'Ecology and the "limits to growth" debate', *Antipode*, 10, 2, August 1978: 22–32.

Sandel, M., 'The procedural republic and the unencumbered self' in S. Avineri and A. de-Shalit (eds), *Communitarianism and Individualism*, Oxford, Oxford University Press, 1992.

Santos, T. Dos, 'The crisis of development theory and the problem of dependence in Latin America' in H. Bernstein (ed.), *Underdevelopment and Development: The Third World Today*, Harmondsworth, Penguin, 1976.

Saward, M., 'Green democracy?' in A. Dobson and P. Lucardie (eds), *The Politics of Nature: Explorations in Green Political Theory*, London, Routledge, 1993.

—— 'Must democrats be environmentalists?' in B. Doherty and M. de Geus (eds), *Democracy and Green Political Thought: Sustainability, Rights and Citizenship*, London, Routledge, 1996.

Saul, J. S., *The State and Revolution in Eastern Africa*, London, Heinemann, 1979.

—— 'The state in post-colonial societies: Tanzania' in R. Miliband and J. Saville (eds), *The Socialist Register 1974*, London, Merlin, 1974.

Scanlon, T. M., 'Preference and urgency', *The Journal of Philosophy*, 72, 19, 1975: 655–69.

—— 'A theory of freedom and expression' in R. M. Dworkin (ed.), *The Philosophy of Law*, Oxford, Oxford University Press, 1977.

—— 'The significance of choice' in S. Darwall (ed.), *Equal Freedom: Selected Tanner Lectures on Human Values*, Ann Arbor, University of Michigan Press, 1995.

—— 'Contractualism and utilitarianism' in J. Rachels (ed.), *Ethical Theory 1: The Question of Objectivity*, Oxford, Oxford University Press, 1998.

Schecter, D., *Radical Theories: Paths Beyond Marxism and Social Democracy*, Manchester, Manchester University Press, 1994.

Scheffler, S., 'The appeal of political liberalism', *Ethics*, 105, 1, October 1994: 4–22.

Schell, J., *The Fate of the Earth*, London, Picador, 1982.

Schelling, T. C., 'Prices as regulatory instruments' in R. E. Goodin (ed.), *The Politics of the Environment*, Aldershot, Edward Elgar, 1994.

Schmitt, R., 'What classes are: Bolshevism, democracy and class theory', *Praxis International*, 2, 4, 1983: 389–407.

Schram, S. R., *The Political Thought of Mao Tse-tung*, Harmondsworth, Penguin, 1969.

Schumacher, E. F., *Small is Beautiful: A Study of Economics as if People Mattered*, London, Abacus, 1974.

Schumpeter, J., *Capitalism, Socialism and Democracy*, London, George Allen and Unwin, 1987.

Schwartz, T., 'Welfare judgments and future generations', *Theory and Decision*, 11, 1979: 181–94.

Schwarzmantel, J., *Structures of Power*, Brighton, Wheatsheaf Books, 1987.

Scott, K. J., 'Methodological and epistemological individualism' in J. O'Neill (ed.), *Modes of Individualism and Collectivism*, London, Heinemann, 1973.

Sears, P. B., 'The steady state: physical law and moral choice' in P. Shepard and D. McKinley (eds), *The Subversive Science: Essays Toward an Ecology of Man*, Boston, Houghton Mifflin, 1969.

Sen, A. K., 'Rational fools: a critique of the behavioral foundations of economic theory', *Philosophy and Public Affairs*, 6, 4, 1977: 317–44.

—— 'Equality of what?' in *Choice, Welfare and Measurement*, Oxford, Blackwell, 1982.

—— 'Goods and people' in W. Aiken and H. LaFollette (eds), *World Hunger and Morality*, New Jersey, Prentice-Hall, 1996.

Sen, G., *The Military Origins of Industrialization and International Trade Rivalry*, London, Frances Pinter, 1984.

Sennett, R., *The Uses of Disorder: Personal Identity and City Life*, New York, Vintage, 1970.

Sessions, G., 'Ecological consciousness and paradigm change' in M. Tobias (ed.), *Deep Ecology*, San Diego, Avant, 1985.

—— 'Ecocentrism, wilderness, and global ecosystem protection' in M. E. Zimmerman, J. B. Callicott, G. Sessions, K. J. Warren and J. Clark (eds), *Environmental Philosophy: From Animal Rights to Radical Ecology*, New Jersey, Prentice-Hall, 1998.

Seymour, J. and Girardet, H., *Far from Paradise: The Story of Human Impact on the Environment*, Basingstoke, Green Print, 1988.

Shanin, T., 'Class, state, and revolution: substitutes and realities' in H. Alavi and T. Shanin (eds), *Introduction to the Sociology of 'Developing Societies'*, London, Macmillan, 1982.

Sharp, G., *The Politics of Nonviolent Action*, 3 vols, Massachusetts, Porter Sargent, 1973.

Shatz, M. S. (ed.), *The Essential Works of Anarchism*, New York, Bantam, 1971.

Shiva, V., *Staying Alive: Women, Ecology and Development*, London, Zed Books, 1988.

Shue, H., 'Solidarity among strangers and the right to food' in W. Aiken and H. LaFollette (eds), *World Hunger and Morality*, New Jersey, Prentice-Hall, 1996.

Siedentop, L., 'Two liberal traditions' in A. Ryan (ed.), *The Idea of Freedom: Essays in Honour of Isaiah Berlin*, Oxford, Oxford University Press, 1979.

Sikora, R. I. and Barry, B. (eds), *Obligations to Future Generations*, Philadelphia, Temple University Press, 1978.

Simmons, A. J., *Moral Principles and Political Obligations*, New Jersey, Princeton University Press, 1979.

—— 'The anarchist position: a reply to Klosko and Senor', *Philosophy and Public Affairs*, 16, 3, Summer 1987: 269–79.

Singer, P., 'Famine, affluence, and morality', *Philosophy and Public Affairs*, 1, 3, 1972: 229–43.

—— 'Altruism and commerce: a defense of Titmuss against Arrow', *Philosophy and Public Affairs*, 2, 3, 1973: 312–20.

—— *Democracy and Disobedience*, Oxford, Clarendon, 1973.

—— 'Reconsidering the famine relief argument' in P. G. Brown and H. Shue (eds),

Food Policy: The Responsibility of the United States in the Life and Death Choices, New York, The Free Press, 1977.

Singer, P., 'Rights and the market' in J. Arthur and W. H. Shaw (eds), *Justice and Economic Distribution*, New Jersey, Prentice-Hall, 1978.

—— *Practical Ethics*, Cambridge, Cambridge University Press, 1979.

—— (ed.), *In Defence of Animals*, Oxford, Blackwell, 1985.

—— (ed.), *Applied Ethics*, Oxford, Oxford University Press, 1986.

—— *Animal Liberation*, 2nd ed., London, Pimlico, 1995.

—— 'Animal liberation' in R. Garner (ed.), *Animal Rights: The Changing Debate*, Basingstoke, Macmillan, 1996.

Skocpol, T., *States and Social Revolutions: A Comparative Analysis of France, Russia and China*, Cambridge, Cambridge University Press, 1979.

Skolimowski, H., *Eco-Philosophy: Designing New Tactics for Living*, Boston, Marion Boyars, 1981.

Slote, M. A., 'The morality of wealth' in W. Aiken and H. LaFollette (eds), *World Hunger and Moral Obligation*, New Jersey, Prentice-Hall, 1977.

Smart, B., 'Defining civil disobedience' in H. A. Bedau (ed.), *Civil Disobedience in Focus*, London, Routledge, 1991.

Smart, J. J. C., 'Extreme and restricted utilitarianism' in P. Foot (ed.), *Theories of Ethics*, Oxford, Oxford University Press, 1967.

Smart, J. J. C. and Williams, B., *Utilitarianism: For and Against*, Cambridge, Cambridge University Press, 1973.

Smith, M. P., *The Libertarians and Education*, London, George Allen and Unwin, 1983.

—— 'Kropotkin and technical education, an anarchist voice' in D. Goodway (ed.), *For Anarchism: History, Theory, and Practice*, London, Routledge, 1989.

Smith, S. A., *Red Petrograd: Revolution in the Factories 1917–1918*, Cambridge, Cambridge University Press, 1983.

Snyder, G., 'The place, the region, and the commons' in M. E. Zimmerman, J. B. Callicott, G. Sessions, K. J. Warren and J. Clark (eds), *Environmental Philosophy: From Animal Rights to Radical Ecology*, New Jersey, Prentice-Hall, 1998.

Sober, E., 'Philosophical problems for environmentalists' in R. Elliot (ed.), *Environmental Ethics*, Oxford, Oxford University Press, 1995.

Sorell, T., *Hobbes*, London, Routledge, 1986.

Spretnak, C. and Capra, F., *Green Politics*, London, Paladin, 1985.

Sprigge, T. L. S., 'Professor Narveson's utilitarianism', *Inquiry*, 11, 1968: 332–48.

—— 'Non-human rights: an idealist perspective', *Inquiry*, 27, 1984: 439–61.

—— 'Some recent positions in environmental ethics examined', *Inquiry*, 34, 1991: 107–28.

Spring, J., *A Primer of Libertarian Education*, Montreal, Black Rose, 1975.

Stammers, N., 'Human rights and power', *Political Studies*, 41, 1, 1993: 70–82.

Sterba, J. P., 'Abortion, distant peoples, and future generations', *The Journal of Philosophy*, 77, 7, 1980: 424–40.

—— 'Reconciling anthropocentric and nonanthropocentric environmental ethics' in J. P. Sterba. (ed.), *Earth Ethics: Environmental Ethics, Animal Rights, and Practical Applications*, New Jersey, Prentice-Hall, 1995.

—— 'Global justice' in W. Aiken and H. LaFollette (eds), *World Hunger and Morality*, New Jersey, Prentice-Hall, 1996.

Stone, C. D., 'Moral pluralism and the course of environmental ethics', *Environmental Ethics*, 10, 2, Summer 1988: 139–54.

—— 'Should trees have standing? – Toward legal rights for natural objects' in R. E. Goodin (ed.), *The Politics of the Environment*, Aldershot, Edward Elgar, 1994.

Storing, H. J., 'The case against civil disobedience' in H. A. Bedau (ed.), *Civil Disobedience in Focus*, London, Routledge, 1991.

Strang, C., 'What if everyone did that?' in J. J. Thomson and G. Dworkin (eds), *Ethics*, New York, Harper and Row, 1968.

Strawson, P., *Freedom and Resentment and Other Essays*, London, Methuen, 1974.

Suchting, W., *Marx: An Introduction*, Brighton, Wheatsheaf Books, 1983.

Switzer, J. V., 'Climatic change: challenges and options' in J. P. Sterba (ed.), *Earth Ethics: Environmental Ethics, Animal Rights, and Practical Applications*, New Jersey, Prentice-Hall, 1995.

Sylvan [Routley], R., 'A critique of deep ecology', *Radical Philosophy*, 40, Summer 1985: 2–12.

—— 'A critique of deep ecology: part II', *Radical Philosophy*, 41, Autumn 1985: 10–22.

Tawney, R. H., *Equality*, intro. by R. M. Titmuss, London, George Allen and Unwin, 1964.

—— 'Property and creative work' in C. B. Macpherson (ed.), *Property: Mainstream and Critical Positions*, Oxford, Blackwell, 1978.

Taylor, C., 'Neutrality in political science' in P. Laslett and W. G. Runciman (eds), *Philosophy, Politics and Society: Third Series*, Oxford, Blackwell, 1969.

—— 'What's wrong with negative liberty?' in A. Ryan (ed.), *The Idea of Freedom: Essays in Honour of Isaiah Berlin*, Oxford, Oxford University Press, 1979.

—— 'The diversity of goods' in A. Sen and B. Williams (eds), *Utilitarianism and Beyond*, Cambridge, Cambridge University Press, 1982.

—— 'Atomism' in S. Avineri and A. de-Shalit (eds), *Communitarianism and Individualism*, Oxford, Oxford University Press, 1992.

Taylor, M., *Anarchy and Cooperation*, London, John Wiley, 1976.

—— *Community, Anarchy and Liberty*, Cambridge, Cambridge University Press, 1982.

—— *The Possibility of Cooperation*, Cambridge, Cambridge University Press, 1987.

—— 'Rationality and revolutionary collective action' in Michael Taylor (ed.), *Rationality and Revolution*, Cambridge, Cambridge University Press, 1988.

—— 'Structure, culture and action in the explanation of social change', *Politics and Society*, 17, 2, 1989: 115–62.

Taylor, P. W., 'In defense of biocentrism', *Environmental Ethics*, 5, 3, Fall 1983: 237–43.

—— *Respect for Nature: A Theory of Environmental Ethics*, New Jersey, Princeton University Press, 1986.

—— 'The ethics of respect for nature' in J. P. Sterba (ed.), *Earth Ethics: Environmental Ethics, Animal Rights, and Practical Applications*, New Jersey, Prentice-Hall, 1995.

Temkin, L. S., 'Inequality', *Philosophy and Public Affairs*, 15, 2, Spring 1986: 99–121.

Thero, D. P., 'Rawls and environmental ethics: a critical examination of the literature', *Environmental Ethics*, 17, 1, Spring 1995: 93–106.

Thomas, C., 'Alternative technology: a feminist technology?' in L. Caldicott and

S. Leland (eds), *Reclaim the Earth: Women Speak out for Life on Earth*, London, The Women's Press, 1983.

Thomas, P., *Karl Marx and the Anarchists*, London, Routledge, 1980.

Thompson, E. P., 'Notes on exterminism: the last stage of civilization', *New Left Review*, 121, May–June 1980: 3–31.

Thompson, J. L., 'Preservation of wilderness and the good life' in R. Elliot and A. Gare (eds), *Environmental Philosophy*, Milton Keynes, Open University Press, 1983.

—— 'A refutation of environmental ethics', *Environmental Ethics*, 12, 2, Summer 1990: 147–60.

—— 'Aesthetics and the value of nature', *Environmental Ethics*, 17, 3, Fall 1995: 291–305.

Thoreau, H. D., *Walden and Other Writings*, ed. J. W. Krutch, New York, Bantam, 1962.

Thornley, J., *Workers' Cooperatives: Jobs and Dreams*, London, Heinemann, 1982.

Timberlake, L., *Only One Earth: Living for the Future*, London, BBC Books/ Earthscan, 1987.

Titmuss, R. M., *The Gift Relationship: From Human Blood to Social Policy*, London, George Allen and Unwin, 1970.

Todaro, M. P., *Economic Development in the Third World*, 3rd ed., New York, Longman, 1985.

Tokar, B., *The Green Alternative: Creating an Ecological Future*, California, R. and E. Miles, 1987.

Tolstoy, L., 'What is to be done?' in I. Horrowitz (ed.), *The Anarchists*, New York, Dell, 1964.

—— *On Civil Disobedience and Non-Violence*, New York, Signet, 1968.

Tooley, M., 'Abortion and infanticide' in P. Singer (ed.), *Applied Ethics*, Oxford, Oxford University Press, 1986.

Tourraine, A., *The Post-Industrial Society*, trans. L. F. X. Mayhew, London, Wildwood House, 1974.

—— 'An introduction to the study of social movements', *Social Research*, 52, 4, Winter 1985: 749–87.

Trainer, F. E., *Developed to Death*, London, Green Print, 1989.

Trammell, R. L., 'Saving life and taking life', *The Journal of Philosophy*, 72, 1975: 131–37.

Trebilcot, J., 'Sex roles: the argument from nature' in J. English (ed.), *Sex Equality*, New Jersey, Prentice-Hall, 1977.

Tribe, L. H., 'Ways not to think about plastic trees: new foundations for environmental law' in R. E. Goodin (ed.), *The Politics of the Environment*, Aldershot, Edward Elgar, 1994.

Trotsky, L., *The Revolution Betrayed*, New York, Pathfinder, 1972.

Tuck, R., *Hobbes*, Oxford, Oxford University Press, 1989.

Tucker, R. C., 'Marx and distributive justice' in C. J. Friedrich and J. W. Chapman (eds), *NOMOS VI: Justice*, New York, Atherton Press, 1963.

Turnbull, C. M., *The Forest People*, London, Picador, 1976.

Unger, P. K., *Living High and Letting Die: Our Illusion of Innocence*, Oxford, Oxford University Press, 1996.

Vaughan, C. E., Introduction to J.-J. Rousseau *Principes du Droit Politique*, Manchester, The University Press, 1918.

Vincent, A., 'The character of ecology', *Environmental Politics*, 2, 2, 1993: 248–76.

—— *Modern Political Ideologies*, Oxford, Blackwell, 1995.

Voisey, H., Beuermann, C., Sverdrup, L. A. and O'Riordan, T., 'The political significance of Local Agenda 21: the early stages of some European experience', *Local Environment*, 1, 1, February 1996: 33–50.

Waldron, J., 'Theoretical foundations of liberalism', *Philosophical Quarterly*, 37, 147, April 1987: 127–50.

—— *The Right to Private Property*, Oxford, Clarendon, 1988.

Walker, K. J., 'The environmental crisis: a critique of neo-Hobbesian responses' in R. E. Goodin (ed.), *The Politics of the Environment*, Aldershot, Edward Elgar, 1994.

Waller, M. and Millard, F., 'Environmental politics in Eastern Europe', *Environmental Politics*, 1, 2, 1992: 159–85.

Wallerstein, I., *The Modern World-System: Capitalist Agriculture and the Origins of the European World-Economy in the Sixteenth Century*, New York, Academic Press, 1974.

Walzer, M., *Spheres of Justice*, New York, Basic Books, 1983.

Ward, B. and Dubos, R., *Only One Earth: The Care and Maintenance of a Small Planet*, Harmondsworth, Penguin, 1972.

Ward, C., *Utopia*, Harmondsworth, Penguin, 1974.

—— *Anarchy in Action*, London, Freedom Press, 1982.

Waring, M., *If Women Counted: A New Feminist Economics*, London, Macmillan, 1989.

Warren, B., 'Imperialism and capitalist industrialization', *New Left Review*, 81, 1973: 3–44.

—— *Imperialism: Pioneer of Capitalism*, ed. J. Sender, London, New Left Books, 1980.

Warren, K. J., 'Feminism and ecology: making connections', *Environmental Ethics*, 6, 1, Spring 1987: 3–20.

—— 'The power and promise of ecological feminism' in J. P. Sterba (ed.), *Earth Ethics: Environmental Ethics, Animal Rights, and Practical Applications*, New Jersey, Prentice-Hall, 1995.

Warren, M. A., 'Do potential people have moral rights?' in R. I. Sikora and B. Barry (eds), *Obligations to Future Generations*, Philadelphia, Temple University Press, 1978.

—— 'The rights of the nonhuman world' in J. P. Sterba (ed.), *Earth Ethics: Environmental Ethics, Animal Rights, and Practical Applications*, New Jersey, Prentice-Hall, 1995.

Wasserstrom, R. A., 'Racism and sexism' in *Philosophy and Social Issues: Five Studies*, Notre Dame, University of Notre Dame Press, 1980.

—— 'War, nuclear war, and nuclear deterrence: some conceptual and moral issues' in R. Hardin, J. J. Mearsheimer, G. Dworkin and R. E. Goodin (eds), *Nuclear Deterrence and Strategy*, Chicago, Chicago University Press, 1985.

Watkins, J. W. N., 'Historical explanation in the social sciences' in J. O'Neill (ed.), *Modes of Individualism and Collectivism*, London, Heinemann, 1973.

—— *Hobbes's System of Ideas*, London, Hutchinson, 1973.

—— 'Ideal types and historical explanation' in A. Ryan (ed.), *The Philosophy of Social Explanation*, Oxford, Oxford University Press, 1973.

—— 'Methodological individualism: a reply' in J. O'Neill (ed.), *Modes of Individualism and Collectivism*, London, Heinemann, 1973.

Watson, M. and Sharpe, D., 'Green beliefs and religion' in A. Dobson and P. Lucardie (eds), *The Politics of Nature: Explorations in Green Political Theory*, London, Routledge, 1993.

Watson, P., 'Tora! Tora! Tora!' in J. P. Sterba (ed.), *Earth Ethics: Environmental Ethics, Animal Rights, and Practical Applications*, New Jersey, Prentice-Hall, 1995.

Weber, M., *From Max Weber: Essays in Sociology*, ed. H. H. Gerth and C. W. Mills, London, Routledge and Kegan Paul, 1970.

Wenar, L., '*Political Liberalism*: an internal critique', *Ethics*, 106, 1, October 1995: 32–62.

West, D., 'Power and formation: new foundations for a radical concept of power', *Inquiry*, 30, 1–2, 1987: 137–54.

—— *An Introduction to Continental Philosophy*, Cambridge, Polity, 1996.

Weston, J. (ed.), *Red and Green: The Politics of the Environment*, London, Pluto, 1986.

White, G., 'Revolutionary socialist development in the Third World: an overview' in G. White, R. Murray and C. White (eds), *Revolutionary Socialist Development in the Third World*, Brighton, Wheatsheaf Books, 1983.

White, L., 'The historical roots of our ecological crisis' in P. Shepard and D. McKinley (eds), *The Subversive Science: Essays Toward an Ecology of Man*, Boston, Houghton Mifflin, 1969.

Wilkins, B., 'Debt and underdevelopment: the case for cancelling Third World debts' in R. Attfield and B. Wilkins (eds), *International Justice and the Third World: Studies in the Philosophy of Development*, London, Routledge, 1992.

Williams, B. A. O., 'The idea of equality' in P. Laslett and W. G. Runciman (eds), *Philosophy, Politics and Society: Second Series*, Oxford, Basil Blackwell, 1962.

—— *Morality*, Cambridge, Cambridge University Press, 1972.

—— 'Egoism and altruism' in *Problems of the Self*, Cambridge, Cambridge University Press, 1973.

—— *Moral Luck*, Cambridge, Cambridge University Press, 1981.

—— *Ethics and the Limits of Philosophy*, London, Fontana, 1985.

—— 'Ethics and the fabric of the world' in J. Rachels (ed.), *Ethical Theory 1: The Question of Objectivity*, Oxford, Oxford University Press, 1998.

—— 'Persons, character, and morality' in J. Rachels (ed.), *Ethical Theory 2: Theories About How We Should Live*, Oxford, Oxford University Press, 1998.

Williams, M. B., 'Discounting versus maximum sustainable yield' in R. Elliot (ed.), *Environmental Ethics*, Oxford, Oxford University Press, 1995.

Williams, R., 'The politics of nuclear disarmament', *New Left Review*, 124, November/December 1980: 25–42.

Winch, P., *The Idea of a Social Science and its Relations to Philosophy*, London, Routledge and Kegan Paul, 1963.

Winckler, S., 'Stopgap measures' in J. P. Sterba (ed.), *Earth Ethics: Environmental Ethics, Animal Rights, and Practical Applications*, New Jersey, Prentice-Hall, 1995.

Wissenburg, M., 'The idea of nature and the nature of distributive justice' in A. Dobson and P. Lucardie (eds), *The Politics of Nature: Explorations in Green Political Theory*, London, Routledge, 1993.

Wittgenstein, L., *Philosophical Investigations*, trans. G. E. M. Anscombe, Oxford, Blackwell, 1974.

Wolf, S., 'Moral saints', *Journal of Philosophy*, 79, 8, August 1982: 419–39.

Wolff, J., 'What is the problem of political obligation?', *Proceedings of the Aristotelian Society*, 91, 1990/1: 153–69.

—— *Robert Nozick: Property, Justice and the Minimal State*, Oxford, Polity, 1991.

—— 'Playthings of alien forces: Karl Marx and the rejection of the market economy', *Cogito*, 6, 1, 1992: 35–41.

—— 'Political obligation, fairness and independence', *Ratio*, 8, 1, 1995: 87–99.

—— *An Introduction to Political Philosophy*, Oxford, Oxford University Press, 1996.

—— 'Anarchism and skepticism' in J. T. Sanders and J. Narveson (eds), *For and Against the State: New Philosophical Readings*, Maryland, Rowman and Littlefield, 1996.

Wolff, R. P., *The Poverty of Liberalism*, Boston, Beacon Press, 1968.

—— *In Defense of Anarchism*, New York, Harper and Row, 1976.

Wolin, S. S., *Politics and Vision: Continuity and Innovation in Western Political Thought*, Boston, Little, Brown and Co., 1966.

Wollheim, R., 'How can one person represent another?', *Proceedings of the Aristotelian Society*, Suppl. Vol. 34, 1960: 209–24.

—— 'A paradox in the theory of democracy' in P. Laslett and W. G. Runciman (eds), *Philosophy, Politics and Society: Second Series*, Oxford, Blackwell, 1962.

Wood, A., 'The Marxian critique of justice', *Philosophy and Public Affairs*, 1, 3, Spring 1972: 3–41.

—— 'Marx on right and justice: a reply to Husami', *Philosophy and Public Affairs*, 8, 3, Spring 1979: 106–34.

Woodcock, G., *Anarchism*, Harmondsworth, Penguin, 1975.

—— (ed.), *The Anarchist Reader*, London, Fontana, 1977.

World Development Movement, *Piggy Banks*, London, WDM, 1991.

Wright, E. O, *Class, Crisis and the State*, London, New Left Books, 1978.

Xiaorong Li, 'Making sense of the right to food' in W. Aiken and H. LaFollette (eds), *World Hunger and Morality*, New Jersey, Prentice-Hall, 1996.

Yearley, S., *The Green Case: A Sociology of Environmental Issues, Arguments and Politics*, London, Routledge, 1992.

Young, S. C., 'The different dimensions of green politics', *Environmental Politics*, 1, 1, 1992: 9–44.

Zimmerman, M. E., 'Feminism, deep ecology, and environmental ethics,' *Environmental Ethics*, 9, 1, Spring 1987:21–44.

Index